The Truth, The Way, The Life,
An Elementary Treatise on Theology

B. H. ROBERTS, c. 1930. (courtesy Marriott Library, University Of Utah)

This book ["The Truth, The Way, The Life"] from my judgment of it is the most important work that I have yet contributed to the Church, the six-volumed Comprehensive History of the Church *not omitted.*

—B. H. ROBERTS TO HEBER J. GRANT,
9 February 1931

The Truth, The Way, The Life, An Elementary Treatise on Theology:

THE MASTERWORK OF B. H. ROBERTS

Edited by

STAN LARSON

Forewords by

THOM D. ROBERTS
and
LEONARD J. ARRINGTON

Introductions by

STERLING M. MCMURRIN
and
ERICH ROBERT PAUL

SMITH RESEARCH ASSOCIATES SAN FRANCISCO 1994

To

Hugh B. Brown

and

Edwin B. Firmage

who preserved Roberts's manuscript

Cover design by Ron Stucki

❧

The Truth, The Way, The Life was
composed, printed, and bound in the United States
and was printed on acid free paper.

98 97 96 95 6 5 4 3 2

❧

Library of Congress Cataloging-in-Publication Data
The Truth, the way, the life : an elementary treatise on theology:
the masterwork of B. H. Roberts / edited by Stan Larson;
forewords by Thom D. Roberts and Leonard J. Arrington;
introductions by Sterling M. McMurrin and Erich Robert Paul.
p. cm.
Includes bibliographical references and index.
ISBN: 1-56085-074-4, cloth
ISBN: 1-56085-077-9, paper
1. Church of Jesus Christ of Latter-Day Saints–Doctrines.
2. Mormon Church–Doctrines. 3. Roberts, B. H.
(Brigham Henry), 1857 - 1933. I. Larson, Stan.
BX8635.2.T78 1994
230'.9332–dc20 94-14856
CIP

TABLE OF CONTENTS

The Truth, The Way, The Life

PART I. THE TRUTH

PART II. THE WAY

PART III. THE LIFE

FOREWORD

Thom D. Roberts

As a great grandson of B. H. Roberts, I am pleased to see and be able to read this publication of "The Truth, The Way, The Life."

My father, Brigham E. Roberts, inherited and had many papers and documents written by and about B. H. Roberts, including numerous letters; two drafts of his autobiography; two political scrapbooks covering B. H.'s congressional case in 1898-99; a scrapbook on polygamy, politics, and other subjects; "startling points of resemblance and suggestive contact" (between the Book of Mormon and *View of the Hebrews*); "A Parallel" (between the Book of Mormon and *View of the Hebrews*); "Book of Mormon Difficulties: A Study"; "A Book of Mormon Study"; along with other items. However, a complete copy of "The Truth, The Way, The Life" was not among them.

It was my father's desire and intent that these items be studied and published and negotiations were underway when he passed away in 1978. In 1981 my mother, Virginia D. Roberts, my brother, William D. Roberts, and I gave all these documents to the Marriott Library at the University of Utah. At that time I kept the original (but allowed the library to make a photocopy) of a prized possession—an 1825 edition of Ethan Smith's *View of the Hebrews; or the Tribes of Israel in America*, with marginal notes and annotations by B. H. In 1991 my mother and I donated the book to the library.

Growing up, I never had access to or read a complete version of "The Truth, The Way, The Life." I want to extend my thanks and appreciation to Edwin B. Firmage for his donation of a complete copy of the manuscript to the Marriott Library, for without his actions this publication (and my reading of it) would not be possible. The members of my family—and I feel I speak for all B. H.'s descendents—are glad to see this work *finally* in print.

After various discussions it was decided that half of the royalties normally going to the editor and essayists of this volume would be donated to the B. H. Roberts Society (on behalf of the descendants of B. H.'s first wife, Sarah Louisa Smith, of whom I am one) and the B. H. Roberts Family Organization (representing the descendants from Roberts's second wife, Celia Dibble).

FOREWORD

Leonard J. Arrington

There is still considerable interest in the life and thought of B. H. Roberts. He was born in Warrington, England, in 1857, crossed the plains to Utah in 1866, worked in mining camps from 1871 to 1874, was briefly disfellowshipped in 1874, attended the University of Deseret (now the University of Utah) in 1877-78, published his first book, *The Gospel*, in 1888, became an LDS general authority as one of the First Seven Presidents of Seventies in 1888, was imprisoned for polygamy in 1889, was elected to (but not seated in) the U.S. House of Representatives in 1899, published *The Mormon Doctrine of Deity* (which is still in print) in 1903, served as president of the Eastern States Mission from 1922 to 1927, became the senior president of the First Quorum of Seventies in 1924, and died in Salt Lake City in 1933. His eventful life makes quite a story, and one can learn more about it by reading his biographies[1] or Roberts's own autobiography.[2]

B. H. Roberts considered "The Truth, The Way, The Life" to be the most important work he had written. While people may differ with him on that judgment, this ambitious treatise deserves to be published. True, many of the ideas discussed by Roberts are now outdated, many have radically changed, and many new concepts have arisen in the sixty-six years since this work was written—but still this effort shows a great mind grappling with great issues.

B. H. Roberts was a prolific writer, publishing during his lifetime thirty-five books, scores of pamphlets, and over three hundred articles. I hope the present work may lead to a new surge in reading Roberts's books and articles—for many of his pieces for periodicals were never compiled into book form.

A quarter-century ago I conducted a survey and reported those considered to be the greatest intellectuals in Mormon history, with B. H. Roberts being at the top of the list.[3] His stature has not diminished. In fact the results of another survey

---

1. See Robert H. Malan, *B. H. Roberts: A Biography* (Salt Lake City: Deseret Book Co., 1966). A more thorough treatment is Truman G. Madsen, *Defender of the Faith: The B. H. Roberts Story* (Salt Lake City: Bookcraft, 1980).

2. B. H. Roberts, *The Autobiography of B. H. Roberts*, ed. Gary James Bergera (Salt Lake City: Signature Books, 1990).

3. Leonard J. Arrington, "The Intellectual Tradition of the Latter-day Saints," *Dialogue:*

have recently been published, and Roberts is still not only at the top of the list, but has an even stronger lead.[4]

B. H. Roberts has already had a considerable impact on Mormonism, and I am glad that his long-unavailable text of "The Truth, The Way, The Life" is now being published.

A Journal of Mormon Thought 4 (Spring 1969): 13-26.

4. Stan Larson, "Intellectuals in Mormonism: An Update," *Dialogue: A Journal of Mormon Thought* 26 (Fall 1993): 187-89.

INTRODUCTION
The Mormon Theology of B. H. Roberts

Sterling M. McMurrin

In 1969 and again in 1993 Brigham H. Roberts by vote of qualified LDS scholars was named the "most eminent intellectual in Mormon history." This high estimate was based on his many years of writing as both historian and theologian. Roberts was not a major historian or a theologian of the first order. But within the limits of the intellectual life of the Mormon people, he was pre-eminent as both historian and theologian. His knowledge of Occidental intellectual history influenced his treatment of theological issues, and his theological interests deepened his historical consciousness as well as determined the focus of much of his historical writing. And Roberts's sensitivity to the philosophical implications of theological ideas and his comprehensive grasp of historical events—coupled with a rich vision of world history and a strong interest in the scientific description of the universe—gave his work a quality that for many years captured the interest and admiration of a large segment of the Mormon people.

Roberts considered his large work "The Truth, The Way, The Life" (hereafter TWL) to be the crowning achievement of his long and celebrated career as a theologian, rating it in importance even higher than his massive six-volume *Comprehensive History*. It is a summary of his theological work, setting forth in considerable detail, and often with extensive commentaries, his understanding of the basic doctrines of the LDS church.

Although there is an extensive mining of some of the more basic doctrines, as, for instance, the eternity of intelligences and the meaning of the Atonement, this study does not add materially to the expositions and arguments already found in Roberts's earlier writings.[1]

---

1. For Roberts's treatment of LDS theology and philosophy in his earlier writings, see *Joseph Smith, The Prophet-Teacher: A Discourse* (Salt Lake City: Deseret News, 1908); *The Mormon Doctrine of Deity; The Roberts-[Cyrill] Van Der Donckt Discussion, to Which Is Added a Discourse, Jesus Christ, The Revelation of God* (Salt Lake City: Deseret News, 1903); *The Gospel: An Exposition of Its First Principles; and Man's Relationship to Deity*, 3d ed. (Salt Lake City: Deseret News, 1901); *The Seventy's Course in Theology*, vol. 1 (1907, 1908), and vol. 2

Roberts was fully committed to the principle of reasonableness in religion and theology, and one of his great virtues as a church leader and writer was his determined effort to raise the intellectual level of his readers and introduce them to the powers of reasoning and the importance of factual evidence. Like much of his earlier writing, especially *The Seventy's Course in Theology*, TWL is replete with materials quoted from what he regarded as the best authoritative sources in science, history, and theology. He wanted his readers, the rank and file of the church, to have some acquaintance with high-level scholarship and up-to-date knowledge. Some of the authorities whom he quotes with approval have stood the test of time and are recognized today. Others have become somewhat antiquated and have been superseded by more recent scientists and scholars.

The strong commitment to the importance of science for the understanding of religion (as well as the intrinsic value of scientific knowledge) that has commonly characterized Roberts's thought, as expressed in both his addresses and publications, is much in evidence in this work. He is at great pains almost to force his more conservative readers to break away from the traditional orthodox view of the six-day creation and the orthodox limited conception of the age of the earth to get them to think in larger terms of both the temporal and spatial extent of the universe. Here he devotes extensive space to cosmological speculation, quoting from recognized authorities in physics, astronomy, and geology. But, of course, the sciences have moved a long way since Roberts was writing seven decades ago—he died in 1933—and his figures are sometimes far out of line with today's estimates. But while numerous factual discrepancies discount the current value of Roberts's work, in principle his commendable interest in expanding his readers' perspective is unaffected. Considering what is now going on in the physical and biological sciences, Roberts would be in authors' heaven if he were writing today. He liked nothing more than to argue that Mormon theology and the most modern science are compatible, and he struggled mightily to demonstrate the truth of this judgment. But it was sometimes like attempting to square the circle.

Roberts wisely attempted to inform his readers of historical developments in religion and philosophy that were pertinent to an understanding and appreciation of Mormon thought. Here, as in the sciences, he depended heavily on a variety of authors whom he quoted extensively, hoping to impart some knowledge, for instance, of such schools of thought as Platonism, Epicureanism, and Stoicism, as well as the major Oriental religions. But when it came to Mormonism, he was on

---

(1910, 1911, 1912), reprint ed. (Dallas: S. K. Taylor Publishing Co., 1976); *A Comprehensive History of the Church of Jesus Christ of Latter-day Saints, Century I* (Salt Lake City: Church of Jesus Christ of Latter-day Saints, 1930), vol. 2, chap. 63.

his own firm ground, justifiably confident that no one knew more about it than he did.

Roberts's strength as a church theologian was his talent for discerning the distinctive characteristics of the teachings of Joseph Smith which mark the defection of Mormonism from mainstream Christian doctrine and his grasp of the theological implications of those unorthodox ideas. His treatment of them in TWL generally conforms to his earlier work, but here there are usually more exacting analyses and more extensive commentaries.

The crucial idea that more than anything else determines the character of Mormon theology is the nonabsolutistic or finitistic conception of God. It is here that the theology so radically undercuts the chief foundation of Christian orthodoxy, both Catholic and Protestant—the divine absolutism inherited from the Hebraic concept of God as creator and lawgiver, joined with the Platonic absolutism in the theory of ultimate reality.

Absolutism is contrasted with relativism. Whatever is absolute is unrelated and unconditioned. An absolute moral principle would in effect say, for instance, "killing is evil"—not "killing is evil under certain conditions," but "killing is evil under any and all conditions." In thoroughgoing absolutistic metaphysics, as in the pre-Socratic Greek philosopher Parmenides or the seventeenth-century philosopher Spinoza or the twentieth-century British philosopher F. H. Bradley, *the* Absolute is the totality of reality. The Absolute includes whatever exists: space, time, and all relations. Everything is internal to the Absolute. The Absolute is not related to anything external to itself. Traditional Christian theism is absolutistic in the sense that original being is God, who is not in time or space, and everything that exists is God's creation, created from nothing. God is related to the world, but it is a world created by his absolute power and knowledge. Only God has *necessary* existence; that is, he could not *not*-exist. Everything else that exists is *contingent*, contingent upon God's powers; that is, it *could* not-exist.

The idea of an *ex nihilo* creation guarantees God's absoluteness. As the total creator of the world, of everything that is, God, in the orthodox tradition, is unrelated and unconditioned. Only the traditional omnis can describe the absolute God—omnipotence, omniscience, omnipresence, omnibenevolence, and all the rest.

Roberts's attack on divine absolutism centered on his argument that the biblical account of the Creation does not justify the doctrine of *ex nihilo* creation. He quite rightly argued that the Genesis statement does not mean that God created from nothing, and he insisted on the so-called "eternity" of the world, that it had no beginning and will have no end—a position held by Plato and the Greek philosophers generally and which was basic in the teachings of Joseph Smith. If

God is not totally the creator, he is conditioned by whatever is real and uncreated, and it can be argued that the divine power is not absolute.

Roberts's critique of absolutism is somewhat restrained and is directed primarily to the idea of God's omnipotence and omniscience. God, he argued, is limited in power by an environment which he did not create, an environment of matter and intelligences, and his knowledge of the future is not absolute, because the free will of those intelligences which are co-eternal with him means that the future is not totally determined. But in some other characteristics God is absolute, as in his infinite mercy and justice. There are no limitations on the moral qualities of divinity.

In keeping with the dominant tradition in Mormon thought, Roberts describes God as a temporal rather than an eternal being—that is, God is within the context of time, with a past, present, and future, rather than a timeless being for which there is no past or future. This doctrine of divine temporality, which is entirely consonant with the biblical conception of God, contradicts the Hellenic theory of the timelessness of ultimate reality—an idea which dominated Platonic metaphysics and became the basic description of God in Christian theology.

A very important corollary of the acceptance of divine temporality is the basic doctrine that God is in process—that God is not a timeless, static being, but is in a dynamic world of movement and development. The Hebrew Bible is the prime exhibit of a scripture that describes God as a creative power in human history. But the melding of Jewish Christianity with Greek metaphysics resulted in theological dogmas that removed God from the ongoing processes of the world. Nothing is more important in Mormon theology than the doctrine that God is a temporal, dynamic being, and more effectively than any other LDS author, Roberts drove that point home in his theological writings. To place God within the context of time gives purpose to moral endeavor and meaning to human history.

Another major departure of LDS theology from mainstream orthodoxy is the rejection of the traditional doctrine of the Trinity. The trinitarian doctrine was set forth by the Council of Nicaea, affirming the numerical identity in substance of the Father and the Son and the unity of the Godhead. Roberts never failed to insist on tritheism, that the Father, Son, and Holy Ghost are three numerically distinct personages. He argued that the unity or oneness of the Godhead consists of a unity of purpose, will, and action. The Nicene Creed, which issued from the Council of Nicaea convoked in 325 A.D. by the Emperor Constantine and is the primary theological symbol for both Catholicism and Protestantism, resulted from a dispute over the question of the divinity of Christ.

The Creed was designed to protect the monotheism inherited from the Jewish biblical religion as the foundation of Christian theology while providing for the full divinity of Christ and the Holy Spirit as well as God the Father. It employed an Aristotelian conception of substance to account for the three persons of the Godhead being a numerically single entity in their essential being. This concept of the Trinity is regarded in the Catholic church as a mystery—something that is to be believed on the authority of the Bible or the church, even though it cannot be understood by natural reason. Roberts insisted that the separate reality of each person of the Godhead is clearly evidenced in scripture and that the traditional trinitarianism is meaningless.

Perhaps more radical even than its tritheism is Mormon theology's frank affirmation of a plurality of gods, a doctrine that abandons the dominant and defining characteristic of Occidental theology, its monotheism. Although here and there LDS theologians have attempted to soften this heresy by a variety of subtle arguments, Roberts exploits it quite fully by tying it to his descriptions of an infinite universe which has plenty of room and plenty of time for any number of deities and their worlds.

And, of course, to complete the theological heresy, Roberts strongly defended the divine anthropomorphism which was basic in the teachings of Joseph Smith. Roberts insisted on taking literally the anthropomorphisms that are obvious in the Bible, and he supported the doctrine as well by reference to the Book of Mormon, Pearl of Great Price, and modern revelation.

Correlative to the concept of God in theology is the doctrine of the human soul. Here, again, Mormon theology is radically opposed to the traditional Christian belief, both Catholic and Protestant. In contrast to the established doctrine that God creates the soul or spirit either at the time of birth or sometime from conception to birth, LDS theology follows the dictum of Joseph Smith that the spirit exists prior to its earthly life, and its essential nature, the intelligence, is uncreated, eternally existing alongside God. More than any other Mormon theologian, Roberts sensed the great importance of the philosophical and theological implications of this principle, and he did more than any other writer to exploit its meaning. In particular, he advanced and developed the idea that the uncreated intelligence is free, that freedom is central to its meaning and nature, and that this freedom is a condition on the very power of God.

In the orthodox Christian tradition, where it is held that God creates both the body and soul *ex nihilo*, from nothing, the freedom of the will, free agency, is not always considered essential to the nature of the individual person. St. Augustine, the most influential of all Christian theologians, held that in the Fall, man, who was created with freedom to do good or evil, lost his freedom to do good; and both Luther and Calvin, the chief fountainheads of Protestant theology, insisted that due to the Fall, man is by nature corrupt and without free will to do good. In contrast, Roberts interpreted Joseph Smith's conception of the uncreated intelligence as meaning that the very nature of the individual person lies in the fact of the freedom of the will. Nothing can destroy it.

The LDS denial of original sin is basic to its theological distance from orthodox Christianity. No Mormon theologian has appreciated this more than did Roberts, and none has done more to identify the implications of this rejection of a doctrine so fundamental to the traditional religion and morality. According to Catholicism, in the Fall, Adam and his descendants lost the supernatural gift of sanctifying grace that assured salvation; but since it was a loss of something supernatural rather than natural, human reason and human freedom were not destroyed. There remained, therefore, the possibility of at least partial merit for salvation. But in the teachings of strict Lutheranism and Calvinism, the Fall resulted in the corruption of human nature and a loss of freedom that destroyed the possibility of merit for salvation. Salvation can come only as a free gift–by the grace of God only. Roberts made much of the fact that since in Mormon theology the Fall was actually in accordance with God's ultimate purpose, what has been called a "fall upward" or the "paradox of the fortunate fall" entailed no loss of free will or of the possibility of some merit for salvation.

The denial of original sin eliminated the negative conception of humanity from LDS theology, encouraging the development of a positive philosophy of human possibility and human endeavor. Roberts made the most of this elimination of the blight of sin as an original condition of the human person, and in his theology and philosophy he celebrated the moral and intellectual achievements of both the individual and society.

Of fundamental importance in Christian thought is God's gift of the possibility of salvation that completes the theological picture, a relationship of God and humankind that centers on the problem of the Fall and Atonement. The meaning of Christ in Christian theology has always meant more than simply the idea of a Messiah. Christ's death and resurrection are interpreted as an atonement, a reconciliation of humanity and God that overcomes the alienation and estrangement from God that resulted from the fall of Adam. The effect of the Fall, in the main tradition, was to bring physical death and the spiritual death of alienation and original sin into the world. Christ took upon himself the sins of the world, suffered death for those sins, and by his resurrection made possible the resurrection of humankind to eternal life.

Mormonism accepts the traditional doctrine that Christ's resurrection overcame both physical and spiritual death, but since it rejects the belief in original sin, it does not have that element in its theology as a factor in explaining the meaning of the Atonement and the justification for Christ's vicarious suffering. In TWL Roberts devoted a great deal of space to the Atonement, and here and in his other writings he produced the most acceptable explanation to be found in LDS literature.

He based his analysis of the doctrine on the reconciliation of divine justice with divine mercy in a manner set forth in Alma in the Book of Mormon. It is an interpretation of the Atonement not unlike that of St. Anselm in the tenth century, whose *Cur Deus Homo* has been the classic work on the problem of why God became man—that God took upon himself the satisfaction of justice to clear the way for the saving gift of mercy.

Having abandoned belief in original sin, the human condition of sinfulness resulting from Adam's sin, it has been necessary for the Mormon theologians to provide some meaning for spiritual death that will explain the necessity for an atonement through the crucifixion and resurrection of Christ, an atonement that makes possible redemption through the resurrection of the body and the reconciliation of the human soul and God. Roberts's treatment of this problem in several chapters in TWL includes an extensive argument for the necessity of divine vicarious suffering to atone for human sin and is a detailed exposition of the meaning of spiritual death in terms of estrangement from God.

Roberts's concern for the problem of evil and suffering, the most difficult and persistent issue faced by theistic philosophy, indicates his recognition of the strength of the Mormon heresy of finitism as opposed to theological absolutism. More effectively than any other accepted church writer, he returned again and again to the theodicy that describes the divine power as conditioned by the uncreated matter and law of the natural world and the free will of uncreated intelligences.

The problem of theodicy in theism is how to reconcile the absolute power and absolute goodness of God with the facts of moral evil and the suffering caused by such natural events as floods, earthquakes, and disease. One of the angles of this triangle has to go.

Of course, moral evil, the evil perpetrated by human beings, is commonly explained in terms of the freedom of the will, the free moral agency with which humanity is endowed. Roberts agrees with this explanation. But free will has been denied by some Christian theologians, and even where it is accepted, there remains the question of why an omnipotent God would create or permit freedom that results in evil. The devil is portrayed in much Christian theology, including conservative Mormonism, as a factor in the cause of moral evil. But this fails as an explanation in the face of traditional divine omnipotence, because the problem remains of why God does not eliminate the devil now, rather than waiting for the millennium, which is always coming but never gets here.

There are instances in the Old Testament where God is described as the author of moral evil, and in strict Calvinism, which has taken its doctrine of the absolute sovereignty of the divine will from the Old Testament, this idea is something of a constant threat—as in the doctrine sometimes espoused that God not only predestines some to heaven and salvation, but others to hell and damnation. In many ways, especially in its strong commitment to the moral law, Mormonism has Calvinistic characteristics, but, as Roberts has effectively argued, Mormon thought denies predestination and divine election and insists on the primacy of the freedom of the will in every discussion of its philosophy and theology.

In keeping with the well-established position in Mormon philosophy, Roberts held that moral evil and suffering are positive realities which cannot be discounted by the arguments of those who see them as factors essential to the harmonious structure of the world—a view that converts morality to art, ethics to aesthetics. Or explains them as negative, privative factors, the absence rather than the presence of something, as darkness is the absence of light, a not-uncommon technique of handling the problem of theodicy that was inherited by early Christianity from Roman Neoplatonism.

The suffering caused by natural events, sometimes called natural evil, is a persistent problem for traditional absolutistic theology because it refuses to abandon the omnipotence of God. But for Mormonism, the material universe and natural law are not totally under the control of an omnipotent God, a principle that Roberts never failed to invoke when faced with the problems of theodicy. In primitive religions natural calamities are often explained as the consequence of immoral human behavior, but cultured religion is unable to accept such an explanation.

It is a source of strength in B. H. Roberts's exposition and analysis of LDS doctrine that he made the freedom of the will a central element in both theology and philosophy, going so far as to describe the uncreated intelligences that figure prominently in Joseph Smith's theology as having, if not actually being, free will. But, unfortunately, while celebrating free will in his extensive writings, Roberts made no contribution to the solution of the large problem occasioned by the concept of free will: how to reconcile freedom with what is commonly regarded as basic to the structure of the world, the universality of causal law—that every event is the result of a prior cause.

Nothing is more characteristic of the Mormon conception of reality than its materialism, the belief that whatever is real is material, that although the body and spirit are distinguishable, they are both material (spirit being a form of refined matter). Although this extreme materialism was a violent departure from the traditional Christian metaphysics, which described the spirit or soul as immaterial substance, the Mormon materialism seemed to LDS writers to be compatible with the strong materialistic trend in nineteenth-century science and philosophy. Roberts was fully committed to materialism as the foundation of Mormon philosophy, and while he made no contribution to materialistic theory or to the solution of the crucial question of the relation of mind or spirit to the material body, he made, as always, a serious effort to call attention to what he regarded as scientific support for the LDS doctrine.

Though in describing the modern world's high achievements in technology Roberts refers to such things as Lindbergh's flight to Paris and the wonders of zeppelins, he lived during a most important era of profound scientific development. Born two years before the publication of Darwin's *Origin of Species*, Roberts was later to give much attention to the problem of evolution, and he reached maturity when the very foundations of classical Newtonian physics were being revolutionized by relativity theory and quantum mechanics. When he died in 1933, science and technology were approaching the threshold of such spectacular breakthroughs in knowledge and practical affairs that even with his expansive interests and rich imagination, Roberts could not have begun to anticipate the kind of world we live in today—a world in which even children are at home with highly sophisticated electronics, instant communication, space travel, genetic manipulation, and remarkably advanced medicine. He would have found great satisfaction in today's astronomy, which seems to support his speculations in cosmology, and he would have been delighted that responsible persons and agencies have been active in exploring the possibility of intelligent life on other planets, something for which he argued in support of the position advocated by Joseph Smith. How he would have reveled in the Hubble space telescope!

In his copious use of materials drawn from the scientific writings of his day, Roberts seems to have had two very important motives: to inform his readers of current scientific thought in matters which he considered important for theology, especially in the area of what might be called cosmology, and to drive home in others his conviction that in principle science and religion are not in conflict, and that some understanding of science is essential to rational religion. Although he accepted the claims of revelation in Mormonism, insisting that the knowledge of the existence of God, for instance, is primarily grounded in revelation, he was an avowed enemy of irrationalism in religion. He held that theology must be amenable to reason, that revelation must have rational support, and that it is perilous to religion to oppose or even neglect the findings of science.

While Roberts certainly called on important scientists of his own era in seeking support for Mormon thought, like so many other theologians, he often neglected to feature those scientists and scientific works that told the other side of the story. It is unfortunate for today's readers of his "masterwork" that the science he called upon for support is now outdated. One of his main interests in his opposition to the six-day creation of Genesis, for instance, was convincing his readers of the great age of the earth, that the best scientific estimates were in the neighborhood of a billion and a half or two billion years. This was a most worthy purpose, to break down the slavish dependence on the Creation story that is so common among the faithful. But now, with far better techniques for estimating age, the earth is presumed to be more in the neighborhood of 4.5 billion years old.

The discovery of new galaxies, however, does not affect Roberts's idea of the extent of space, because he defended the view of Joseph Smith and others that space and time are infinite—nothing can be added. He may have been unaware of the theory in relativity physics that the universe may be finite. But whatever views might prevail in science, for Roberts, as indicated earlier, there was room enough to accommodate the multiple deities and their worlds that Joseph Smith's theology called for.

Although Roberts gave attention to developments in science that seemed to him to relate to Mormon theology, he was ill-equipped to face the intricate technicalities of the scientific theories which interested him. While, because it conformed to the pronouncements of early Mormon philosophy, LDS writers had for decades played on the nineteenth-century idea in physics that matter is indestructible, in his late years Roberts encountered the shift to the theory that matter is convertible to energy. This was not a crucial problem for him, but at least it confirmed the principle that while theology should have full respect for science, if it ties itself to specific scientific theory it may lose in the long run. But neither Roberts nor any other Mormon theologian who enjoys the respect of the church has faced the crucial problem of what spirit as refined matter can be like when in twentieth-century physics even gross matter is considered to be a collection of electrical events rather than space-filling stuff.

In TWL Roberts pursues one of his favorite themes, lauding Joseph Smith's definition of truth that "truth is knowledge of things as they are, and as they were, and as they are to come" (D&C 93:24). Actually, this conception of truth was not as original with the prophet as Roberts supposed, and although it has the virtue of stressing that the world and all that is in it is in process, rather than static and frozen, it is seriously flawed as a definition of truth. Even in Roberts's analysis, it confuses the meaning of truth with what it is that is true: it confuses truth with knowledge. Roberts gives no evidence of having seriously examined the common conceptions of the nature of truth—in particular, the correspondence and coherence concepts—and he treats the entire matter with more rhetoric than logic. Truth is a property of propositions. Propositions, if they are cognitively meaningful, are either true or false. Knowledge of whether they are true or false is a different matter.

In the final chapter of TWL Roberts writes eloquently about the marriage covenant, which exists for *companionship* and *procreation*, and he strikes out at the evils of the decade in which he was writing, the 1920s: easy divorce, out-of-wedlock sex, "companionate marriage," and associated lapses in moral behavior that were destroying, he said, the very foundations of the social order. An appendage to the chapter gives an idealized description of plural marriage as practiced for half a century in the LDS church, described by Roberts as a divine institution willed by God, a "holy sacrament" with the inspiring motive of "race culture," to "give to succeeding generations a superior fatherhood and motherhood." There is here no mention of marriage for companionship—only procreation "in the name of a divinely ordered species of eugenics."

Those who are acquainted with B. H. Roberts's high level of sophistication as a historian, his sagacity as a philosopher, his profound insights as a theologian, his commitment to the worth of scientific knowledge, and his quite extensive competence in intellectual history, may well be somewhat shocked and disappointed to discover that in this "masterwork" of his mature years he is bound and prescribed by an almost abject biblical literalism that betrays his intellectual accomplishments. He takes great pains to discount the six-day creation in Genesis and argues effectively for the great age of the earth, but he fails miserably to distinguish myth and legend from factual history in the Old Testament. The early Genesis stories which he might have seen as cultural myth are for him true narratives of historical persons and historical events. Adam and Eve were in fact in the garden, the flood in Noah's day actually covered the earth, and on and on. It was because of this biblical literalism which he attempted to square with the great age of the earth that he came into collision with other church authorities and was prevented from having his work published by the church. The fanciful and nonsensical pre-Adamite theory that resulted from his attempt to square the reality of a historical Adam with a scientific description of the earth's history was the crux of the problem.

It is probably fair to say that, considering the great weight of his intellectual leadership of the church, in this work, Roberts might have done much to liberate the LDS people from the burden of biblical literalism that so often is an impediment to their religious thought and sentiment. He has instead put his imprimatur on an outworn and obsolete and damaging mode of interpretation and understanding.

In an address published in the *Improvement Era* in 1911 entitled "Higher Criticism and the Book of Mormon," Roberts wrote, "The Book of Mormon must submit to every test, literary criticism with the rest. Indeed, it must submit to every analysis and examination. It must submit to historical tests, to the tests of archeological research and also to the higher criticism."[2] In his essays on the Book of Mormon, published in 1985 under the editorship of Brigham D. Madsen, Roberts followed his own admonition as a higher critic, which led him to quite negative conclusions on the Book of Mormon.[3] But even though competent biblical

2. B. H. Roberts, "Higher Criticism and the Book of Mormon," *Improvement Era* 14 (June 1911): 667.

3. B. H. Roberts, *Studies of the Book of Mormon*, ed. Brigham D. Madsen (Urbana:

studies were burgeoning all over the place during Roberts's career as a writer, with the works of celebrated historians, theologians, and archaeologists on both Testaments appearing in profusion, Roberts's TWL totally ignored them. It is as if he had been entirely innocent of what was happening during his own time in the scholarly world of religious studies. While reveling in the work of the physical sciences, he apparently ignored the scholarly work being done on the Bible—at great loss to his church. At least he failed to bring that work to the attention of his readers, and apparently it had little or no impact on his "masterwork." It should be said, of course, that Roberts's generous employment of the LDS scriptures, especially the books of Moses and Abraham in the Pearl of Great Price, had the effect of locking him into biblical literalism. In this he was faithful to conservative Mormon orthodoxy.

Finally, a word about Roberts's pre-Adamites. By the turn of the century, the great hassle over organic evolution had largely shifted from Europe to America. There were scientists and religionists on both sides of the argument—some insisting that evolution is evidence of divine creativeness, others arguing that evolution is not compatible with religious belief. Roberts, who could not resist a battle, entered the fray on the side of evolution. His somewhat acrimonious dispute with Apostle Joseph Fielding Smith, in the 1920s, over evolution and the age of the earth was a major intellectual event in the church's history. He did not win the battle, but he did not lose it, since the church did not announce an official decision either for or against evolution. Generally, of course, evolution has won the day, but the question of whether the process of evolution is by Darwinian natural selection is still an issue among the most competent scientists.

Believing that Adam was a real historical person, the progenitor, with Eve, of the human race, Roberts had the problem of what to do about the great age of the earth and evolution. Refusing to accept the documentary thesis on the composition of Genesis, which he barely mentions in passing, he was confused by the two accounts of the Creation. He hit upon a simple solution: the evolutionary process, whatever it was, took place before Adam, and a grand catastrophe wiped things out. Then Adam was transplanted, full-blown, from another planet, and things were started all over again—but the process of evolution was in the past. This was a piece of pious nonsense which, fortunately, did not convince the president of the church and other ecclesiastical colleagues. Roberts had worked on his pre-Adamite theory, a view that some other church leaders had espoused, as early as his 1889 essay "Man's Relationship to Deity," published with *The Gospel* in 1893. His view on evolution was of development within the several species that had been special creations by God. Roberts did not embrace

---

University of Illinois Press, 1985; reprint, Salt Lake City: Signature Books, 1992).

the Darwinian origin of species by natural selection. Moreover, he entertained the rather strange notion that the scientific theory of evolution resulted from absurdities on human origins perpetrated by the orthodox theologians in their reading of Genesis, especially the six-day *ex nihilo* creation.

For far too many years, the name of Brigham H. Roberts has been in eclipse in the LDS church. The publication of "The Truth, The Way, The Life" should help to bring that important name to the full attention of a generation that is seriously inquiring into the nature and meaning of Mormonism.

INTRODUCTION
B. H. Roberts on Mormonism and Science[1]

Erich Robert Paul

While the central theme of B. H. Roberts's summa theologica, "The Truth, The Way, The Life" (hereafter TWL), focuses on Jesus Christ, this treatise explores the nature of humankind and the cosmos standing in relation to God as both creator and savior. In it Roberts deals extensively with science and its relationship to religion. Although the treatise itself is not strikingly innovative in particulars, the depth and forcefulness with which Roberts argued for his version of a Mormon theology coupled with modern scientific and secular learning mark it as a unique contribution to Mormon religious and intellectual thinking.

In some respects Roberts's views represent the culmination of ideas on natural law and science as expressed most authoritatively in the writings of apostle-scientists James E. Talmage, John A. Widtsoe, and Joseph F. Merrill, and in the views of Mormon scholars Frederick J. Pack and Nels L. Nelson.[2] On the scientific side, Roberts extensively treated issues dealing with astronomy, cosmology, the antiquity of humankind, and evolution, because these sciences deal most directly with theological issues—the origin and nature of humans and the universe.

SCIENTIFIC THINKING

Although he treated the secular literature broadly, Roberts recognized the need to read his sources discriminately, "not accepting either all the premises laid down,

1. The University of Illinois Press has granted permission to use some material on B. H. Roberts's science from my *Science, Religion, and Mormon Cosmology* (Urbana: University of Illinois Press, 1992), 148-55.

2. For a discussion of these apostle-scientists, see Paul, *Science, Religion, and Mormon Cosmology*, 146-168. On the ideas of Pack and Nelson, see especially Frederick J. Pack, *Science and Belief in God* (Salt Lake City: Deseret News Press, 1924) and Nels L. Nelson, *Scientific Aspects of Mormonism* (New York: Dutton, 1904).

or the conclusions reached." In the third chapter of TWL Roberts briefly commented on the nature of time, space, matter, and force—what he calls the "building stones of knowledge": "I shall not attempt any discussion of the 'reality' of them at all: shall only deal with such definitions and treatment of them as will make clear what may be presented as the general sum of man's partial knowledge of the solar and sidereal systems that make up the universe in which he lives."[3]

While Roberts's discussion of these ideas is mostly definitional and not critical, he clearly recognized some significant issues and, in fact, was relatively current in his thinking. For example, noting the nineteenth-century views on the indestructibility and nonconvertability of both matter and energy (force), Roberts, under the subheading "Twentieth Century Advancement in Physics," noted:

> It has occurred to me that some of our more recent writers and students may take exception to the matter as here set forth. . . . Some of our present day professors hold that the principle of the "indestructibility of matter" has proven to be "definitely invalid"; and it is now sometimes held that a definite portion of matter has entirely disappeared as a distinct, separate entity of any system, *energy taking its place.* That is, matter changes into radiant energy, and vice-versa.[4]

Citing Robert A. Millikan, dean of early twentieth-century American physics, and Albert Einstein as his sources, Roberts concluded that "matter has not been dissolved into 'nothing.'. . . There has been no break in the continuity; something has existed all the while, and the old truth on the conservation of matter and force has not in reality been changed, but emphasized." Noting that according to Mormon scripture "all spirit is matter" (D&C 131:7) and that "there are many worlds that have passed away" (Moses 1:35, 38), Roberts emphasized that the "making and unmaking" of worlds conforms well to this doctrine of the changeability (but not destructibility) of matter-energy.[5]

Roberts emphasized that "order" or the "reign of law" is a *sine qua non* for understanding the nature of the universe.[6] This was not simply a basic premise of

3. TWL, final draft, known as Ms III, chap. 3, p. 1.

4. TWL, Ms III, chap. 3, p. 11.

5. TWL, Ms III, chap. 3, pp. 11-15. See Robert Kargon, *The Rise of Robert Millikan: Portrait of a Life in American Science* (Ithaca: Cornell University Press, 1982).

6. Additional sources cited include John William Draper, *History of the Conflict between Religion and Science*, 6th ed. (New York: D. Appleton and Co., 1875); Andrew D. White, *A History of the Warfare of Science with Theology in Christendom*, 2 vols. (New York: D. Appleton and Co., 1896); John Fiske, *Studies in Religion, Being the Destiny of Man, The Idea of God, Through Nature to God, Life Everlasting* in *The Miscellaneous Writings of John Fiske, with Many Portraits of Illustrious Philosophers, Scientists, and Other Men of Note* (Boston: Houghton, Mifflin and Co., 1902), vol. 9; and the German evolutionist, Ernst Haeckel, *The*

science, but, in Roberts's view, a rare insight into the actual operations of the universe. Despite Roberts's earlier caveat about our inability to know finality, on at least this issue, Roberts argued, science had penetrated to the core of physical reality. Roberts understood that even though scientists were compelled to hold this assertion as a fundamental premise for the doing of science, it is still a statement of belief and therefore metaphysical. But Roberts's religious commitments furnished the added assurance that *this* issue indeed is ontologically grounded.

If law and order are supreme in the physical universe, what, pondered Roberts, is the causative agent of the material universe? Assuming the nondestructibility of matter-energy, Roberts argued that "the universe itself is uncaused since it always existed, and is all that is, including all forces whatsoever, as also all intelligences, or mind–it is 'the sum of existence.'"[7] Similarly, it was not because scientists had somehow demonstrated this assertion but rather, argued Roberts, because Joseph Smith had revealed that (1) because all spirit is matter and spirit is indestructible, matter too must be without beginning, and (2) there never was a time when something material (spirit, etc.) did not exist. Therefore, Roberts also rejected the Aristotelian notion of a "first cause," suggesting contrariwise the idea of an "eternal cause." Furthermore, "this 'first cause' idea involves us in the whole argument of the designer of the universe, a designer that at once is outside of and transcends the universe."[8] Rejecting this traditional Christian view of God and carrying this heresy into his theology, Roberts claimed God is both "in time" and "historical" and, therefore, must be existentially conditioned. Ultimately the purpose of his argument is to convince us that science and Mormonism are reasonably compatible–that, exercising proper caution, we can rely on the statements of science to cast additional, but secondary, light on the statements of "revealed" religion.

ASTRONOMY, COSMOLOGY, AND THE NATURE OF THE UNIVERSE

In the early chapters Roberts discussed contemporary views of the nature of the solar system and the sidereal system (Milky Way in contemporary parlance).

Riddle of the Universe at the Close of the Nineteenth Century, trans. Joseph McCabe (New York: Harper and Bros., 1900).

7. TWL, Ms III, chap. 7, p. 4. By contemporary standards, Roberts's statement is not unproblematic, because present-day twentieth-century astrophysics now asserts that the universe began *originally* in a "big-bang," prior to which there was simply *nothing* (at least we can never know of anything prior to this singular event). For some intriguing religious implications of this view, see Robert Jastrow, *God and the Astronomers* (New York: Warner Books, 1978), and Keith E. Norman, "Mormon Cosmology: Can It Survive the Big Bang?" *Sunstone* 10, no. 9 (1986): 19-23.

8. TWL, Ms III, chap. 7, p. 5.

Roberts was certainly current in his discussion. For example, during the 1920s a major conceptual revolution in astronomy and cosmology had occurred, subsequently dubbed the "second astronomical revolution," in which American astronomers Harlow Shapley and Edwin Hubble were among the principal theorists. They showed that (1) the sun and its solar system are not centrally located in the sidereal system (Shapley); (2) the Milky Way system is about ten times larger than the stellar system previously propounded (Shapley); (3) there exist external clusterings or galaxies of stars (Hubble); and (4) the universe is expanding (Hubble). Although this new cosmology of the universe has been subsequently modified in important ways, it has received increasing assent from the astronomical community since 1930.[9]

On this point, Roberts was representing the cutting edge of modern astronomical research. But the concern that was foremost in Roberts's mind dealt with the *meaning* of the cosmos. Now that astronomers had demonstrated the extent of the physical universe, what, asked Roberts rhetorically, was the meaning of it all? In a major address before the American Association for the Advancement of Science in 1925, Forest R. Moulton, professor of astronomy at the University of Chicago, noted the most recent discoveries of the larger dimensions of the Milky Way (Shapley) and the existence of exterior galaxies (Hubble) and suggested that "it is not improbable–it is in fact probable–that a majority of [stars] have planets circulating about them, as our earth revolves about the sun. It may be that a fraction of [stars], perhaps in all hundreds of millions, are in a condition comparable to that of the earth, and that they support life!"[10]

Roberts's discussion throughout the TWL is thoroughly saturated with scientific evidence in support of his premise that science and theology properly conceived are mutually supportive. In his enthusiasm, however, he was not always careful nor sufficiently critical of his sources. On the issue of planetary formation, absolutely essential for his understanding of Mormon cosmology, Roberts confused two radically conflicting scientific views–one of which supports the Mormon idea

---

9. The Copernican revolution of the sixteenth century has been designated as the first astronomical revolution. On the emergence of the "new" astronomy of the 1920s, see Richard Berendzen, Richard Hart, and Daniel Seeley, *Man Discovers the Galaxies* (New York: Science History Publications, 1976); Robert Smith, *The Expanding Universe: Astronomy's "Great Debate" 1900-1931* (New York: Cambridge University Press, 1982); and Erich Robert Paul, *The Milky Way Galaxy and Statistical Cosmology, 1890-1924* (Cambridge, Eng.: Cambridge University Press, 1993). Shapley's estimates for the size of the Milky Way system were later reduced by a factor of two-thirds (to 100,000 light years diameter) to conform to additional empirical evidence.

10. Forest R. Moulton, quoted in TWL, Ms III, chap. 5, p. 5.

of "worlds without number" while the other does not. The first view, known as the nebular hypothesis, proposed that the formation of stars and planets had resulted from the rotation, contraction, and condensation of the primeval solar material and gases.[11] Promoted most forcefully by the French cosmologist Pierre Simon de Laplace, the nebular hypothesis became the prevailing theory of planetary formation during the nineteenth century. In chapter 31 Roberts correctly noted that this was the generally accepted scientific view. He then went on to equate this view with its scientific competitor, the planetesimal hypothesis, which argued that planets and satellites were formed as a result of a close encounter of the sun with another star. Under this view, as our ancestral sun (or any star, for that matter) was approached by an intruder star, planets and satellites began to form from the accretion of parts of other pre-existent materials torn away from the sun and the star themselves.[12] Because the planetesimal hypothesis seemed to be vaguely similar to the ideas of Joseph Smith–to wit, that planets were organized from pre-existent materials–Roberts, James E. Talmage, and other Mormon intellectuals favored the latter over the nebular hypothesis.[13]

Unfortunately, the planetesimal hypothesis requires extremely close cosmic encounters that are both empirically nonexistent and theoretically nearly impossible. Thus if the hypothesis were true, the likelihood of numerous stars possessing "worlds without number" would, despite Moulton's assertion to the contrary, be infinitesimal. Still on the authority of Moulton and the British cosmologist, Sir James Jeans, Roberts assented to the planetesimal hypothesis.[14]

Although Roberts confused the nebular hypothesis with the planetesimal hypothesis, he not only digested Moulton's cosmological point, but went on to note Moulton's argument in support of a fundamental premise of science that suggested a deeper meaning to the universe:

> The impressive thing to the astronomers is not the magnitude of the galaxy, nor the long periods of time during which stars exist, nor the tremendous forces of nature; but the most impressive thing is that all this vast universe which we have been able to explore is found to be orderly. The orderliness of the universe is the foundation on

11. On the nebular hypothesis, see Ronald L. Numbers, *Creation by Natural Law: Laplace's Nebular Hypothesis in American Thought* (Seattle: University of Washington Press, 1977).

12. On the history of the planetesimal hypothesis, see Stephen G. Brush, "A Geologist among Astronomers: The Rise and Fall of the Chamberlin-Moulton Cosmology," *Journal for the History of Astronomy* 9 (Feb.-June 1978): 1-41, 77-104.

13. On Joseph Smith's views on this matter, as well as those of Orson Pratt and James E. Talmage, see Paul, *Science, Religion, and Mormon Cosmology*, 156-57.

14. TWL, Ms III, chap. 31, p. 4.

which science is built. It is the thing that enables us to understand the present, to look back over the past, and to penetrate the remote future.[15]

Having completed his discussion of some basic scientific and methodological concepts, as well as having introduced various views of science on the nature and origin of the physical universe, Roberts commenced an examination of the one scientific issue that is central to Mormonism's unique theology, to wit, the plurality of worlds.

> We have ascertained from . . . various authorities upon astronomy that it is possible and even probable that the suns which make up our galaxy—our universe—have circulating about them groups of opaque worlds, even as our sun has nine such worlds moving about him in their respective orbits. But is it true that each of these suns of the sidereal system, or even a considerable number of them, has a like group of planets to which it is the center of gravitation, and from which these planets receive light and warmth and vital force, resulting in life such as we know it on our own earth?[16]

Though Roberts was definitely committed to a plurality of worlds, he realized the speculative nature of the *scientific* question whether in fact there exist worlds without number: "The answer must necessarily be that this is not definitely known, and hence scientists in astronomy speak with caution, and only say that it may possibly be so. It may even be probable. But science can speak with no positive assurance on this subject, because really scientists do not know."[17] Using already familiar philosophical arguments, Roberts asserted that (1) by analogy to the sun's system, stars must be centers of solar systems whose planets must contain sentient, intelligent life; (2) it would be a waste of stellar energy if the sun supported the only inhabited planet in the cosmos; and (3) if there were no other inhabited planets, then what possible purpose would the universe serve? For instance, continued Roberts, the earth would be utterly without purpose if not created and made for humans; everything in and on the earth would ultimately be wasted and have no meaning, if not for humankind. These arguments—by analogy, of plenitude and of teleology—are, in Roberts's view, compelling.

Roberts did not stop with asserting the simple view of a plurality of worlds. Tacitly accepting the nineteenth-century belief in the inevitable progress of human-

---

15. TWL, Ms III, chap. 6, p. 3.

16. TWL, Ms III, chap. 10, pp. 1-2. The reference to "*nine* such worlds" refers to the fact that the ninth planet, Pluto, was discovered in 1930. In Roberts's original 1928 manuscript only eight planets were mentioned; the correction to "nine" was subsequently added by Roberts.

17. TWL, Ms III, chap. 10, p. 2.

kind, he felt inclined to suggest certain personal and civilizational characteristics that extraterrestrials must possess:

> And there may have been developed also higher and mightier intelligences than any that have been developed on our earth. If such intelligences do exist, in other worlds, may we not enter upon the same line of reasoning from what we know, apply the principle we have been following to the social and sympathetic and moral qualities as connected with these higher intelligences? This we know in respect of the inhabitants of our own world, that higher intellectual life and higher states of civilization produce exalted moral feelings, resulting in higher states of righteousness and love of truth and sympathy for fellow men, leading to desire for the uplift of those less highly developed, and thus is produced among our own earth-people a desire to restrain the strong and vicious by laws . . . and to uplift and better the conditions of the lowly and undeveloped.[18]

Again, by analogy to human conditions, Roberts argued for altruistic and progressive conditions for extraterrestrials. Although Roberts served as a chaplain during World War I, apparently his experiences and reflections were still not sufficient to embitter him on the question of the human condition. It would perhaps take another world war to convince him that intelligent life, at least of the variety we are all familiar with, is capable of inflicting incalculable suffering and tragedy.[19]

Roberts also provided scriptural support for his view of universal, ennobled intelligent life. Noting that Enoch spoke of worlds without number, Roberts quoted the scriptures to reveal a pluralism of life: "I [God] also created [worlds] for mine own purpose. . . . Adam, which is many" (Moses 1:33-34). "From the last statement," wrote Roberts, "it appears that Adam is a generic name, that there are many Adams carrying the significance perhaps of being first placed on the creations of God."[20] But the heavens, Enoch mentioned, are many, and they are numbered only unto God (Moses 1:35). These worlds are peopled by beings which, in the parlance of the Book of Abraham and the Doctrine and Covenants, are described as "intelligences," and which, in Roberts's view, are necessary vis-à-vis contingent beings. In the scope of astronomical understanding, these intelligences refer to "other and older world systems." "Be it remembered here," Roberts wrote, "that these kingdoms and the inhabitants thereof are the kingdoms of the space depths in the universe, all the worlds, and the world systems, and by the word of God they have their inhabitants."[21]

---

18. TWL, Ms III, chap. 10, p. 9.

19. On Mormonism's retreat from a full-fledged positive scientism during the time that Roberts was active, see Paul, *Science, Religion, and Mormon Cosmology*, 162-64.

20. TWL, Ms III, chap. 10, p. 12.

21. TWL, Ms III, chap. 10, p. 15. Roberts quoted the relevant sections of Abr. 3 and

THE ANTIQUITY OF THE EARTH, THE ORIGIN OF HUMANKIND, AND EVOLUTIONARY DEVELOPMENTALISM

Roberts's exploration of gospel principles and the best of modern secular learning was in a long tradition, dating to Orson Pratt in the 1850s, of discussing science and Mormonism within the same context. Ultimately, Roberts's manuscript was an attempt to construct a coherent view of God and humankind within the whole cosmic context of human existence. As a result, scientifically, Roberts's chapters on cosmology and the universe would have been incomplete without a discussion of human origins within Mormonism's larger vision of human experience.

As Roberts made clear, the sciences of astronomy and cosmology (1) have provided compelling arguments that the universe is teeming with life and (2) have offered overwhelming evidence that the solar system is of ancient origin. Consequently, for Roberts the scientific evidence for the existence of plants, animals, and various human groups having existed on the planet earth during its remote history is equally overwhelming. The problem for Roberts, therefore, was to reconcile the paleontological and geological evidence while addressing the scriptural interpretation that Adam was the first man in the earth and that only following the events surrounding the Garden of Eden and the Fall did death enter into the world. Roberts affirmed the scriptural view that Adam was the first man of the *human* race. But he also believed there was overwhelming scientific evidence that there had existed life including humanoid forms who had lived upon the earth prior to the Adamic Dispensation.[22]

Arguing by analogy to the days of Noah when, with the exception of Noah's family and the inhabitants of the ark, all life had been destroyed, Roberts argued that "may it not be that some such condition as this which we have supposed in the case of Noah, really happened in regard to the 'beginning' of things with Adam?"[23] Therefore, the "lone and dreary" world spoken of in Genesis was scriptural evidence to Roberts that the earth had been cleansed of all pre-Adamic life by some cataclysmic event that left only the paleontological remains found by modern science: "Previous to the advent of Adam upon the earth, some destructive cataclysm, a universal glacial period or an excessive heat period left the earth empty

---

4, and D&C 76:37-39, 45.

22. David N. Livingstone, *The Preadamite Theory and the Marriage of Science and Religion* (Transactions of the American Philosophical Society, vol. 82, pt. 3) (Philadelphia: American Philosophical Society, 1992). Also see Hugh Nibley, "Before Adam," in *Old Testament and Related Studies: The Collected Works of Hugh Nibley*, eds. John W. Welch, Gary P. Gillum, and Don E. Norton (Salt Lake City: Deseret Book Co., 1986), 1:82-83.

23. TWL, Ms III, chap. 30, p. 7.

and desolate, and it became the mission of Adam to 'replenish' the earth with inhabitants."[24]

As would occur later in the days of Noah, the world was replenished from the Adamic stock. Consequently, Adam, while the first man of the human race, was not the first "man" to have existed on the earth.

Roberts's initial discussion of pre-Adamites was introduced in chapter 30 of TWL entirely within the context of a traditional Mormon exegesis of the creation process described in Genesis and the Mormon scriptures. In chapter 31, Roberts provided scientific evidence of pre-Adamites by drawing on the sciences of geology, paleontology, and anthropology. After reviewing briefly the evidence for various human remains of ancient origin, including those for Java Man, Heidelberg Man, Neanderthal Man, Piltdown Man,[25] Cro-Magnon Man, and Peking Man, Roberts marshalled the support of one authority after another from Charles Lyell, the most influential geologist of the nineteenth century, to James Jeans, one of the most highly respected cosmologists of the early twentieth century. As additional support Roberts cited at some length (as he did throughout TWL) the views of two highly influential American intellectuals, Andrew D. White and John W. Draper, who, during the last decades of the nineteenth century, had published books dealing with the alleged incompatibility of science and religion.[26]

Although Roberts's discussion of pre-Adamites was not original—indeed it has a history that dates to the seventeenth century—his advocacy, with one exception, of the pre-Adamite theory within Mormonism was novel. In marshalling ecclesiastical support of the pre-Adamite theory, Roberts, citing Orson Hyde as one of the "original Apostles of the New Dispensation," noted that Hyde had advanced the pre-Adamite theory in a general conference address in 1854:

> The world was peopled before the days of Adam as much so as it was before the days of Noah. It was said that Noah became the father of a new world, but it was the same old world still, and will continue to be, though it may pass through many changes. When God said go forth and "replenish" the earth, it was to replenish the inhabitants of the human species and make it as it was before.[27]

Not only did this provide Roberts with prior apostolic support, but, suggested

---

24. TWL, Ms III, chap. 30, p. 7. This interpretation on pre-Adamites is again given in TWL, Ms III, chap. 31, p. 10.

25. Roberts did note some evidential problems with Piltdown Man, which in 1953 was shown to be a fraud.

26. Draper, *Conflict between Religion and Science*, and White, *Warfare of Science with Theology*.

27. Quoted in TWL, Ms III, chap. 31, pp. 11-12, from Orson Hyde, "The Marriage Relations," *Journal of Discourses* 2 (1855): 79.

Roberts, Brigham Young explicitly concurred with Hyde's comments at the conclusion of the latter's discourse.[28] Young's comment, however, was typical of the support President Young provided all speakers whenever he spoke at church conferences. In this case, Young's remarks endorsed the general theme of Hyde's sermon on marriage, and not Hyde's introductory remarks on pre-Adamites.

Although it was principally his pre-Adamic theory that some authorities found objectionable,[29] in chapter 24 Roberts adopted a scientifically acceptable view of evolution. Affirming the antiquity of the earth from scientific sources and using the language of Genesis, to wit, "in the beginning God created the heavens and the earth," Roberts promoted the scriptural interpretation that suggested that the word "beginning" was sufficiently pliable to support the modern idea of scientific evolution. Quoting the social evolutionist Herbert Spencer and the philosopher Will Durant, Roberts argued, in the sense of not explicitly rejecting the conventional view, that evolution is an integration of simpler, indefinite, and incoherent substances into material forms with definite, well-organized, and increasingly coherent complexity. In chapter 25 Roberts advanced a somewhat ambiguous view for the "transmutation" of species. As with his earlier discussion of astronomy and cosmology and his later exploration of evidences for early humans, Roberts was impressed with the scientific support for Darwinian speciation. But as with his interpretation of pre-Adamites within a scriptural context, he remained theological committed to the scriptural injunction that all living creatures reproduce only "after their own kind."

Unable to reconcile evolutionary theory with scripture under the traditional, literal biblical interpretation equating "kind" with "species," Roberts found himself in a dilemma. In his attempt to reconcile creation with evolution, Roberts, deliberately blurring the meaning of the word "kind," promoted a "developmental view":

> And from a few other forms of life transported to the earth, there could be development of varied kinds of life yet adhering closely to the great law of creation, so constantly repeated—"each after his kind." Not necessarily rigidly limited to stereotyped individual forms, but developing the kinds from the subdivisions of vegetable and animal kingdoms into various species through development from primeval forms.[30]

The precise meaning which Roberts had in mind of this and other passages

---

28. Brigham Young, "Marriage Relations of Bishops and Deacons," *Journal of Discourses* 2 (1855): 90.

29. For a discussion of the reaction to Roberts's view on human origins as developed in TWL by certain LDS general authorities and the theological controversy it engendered, see the editor's Introduction, in this volume.

30. TWL, Ms III, chap. 25, pp. 10-11.

in TWL relating to speciation and "development" is not entirely clear. The logic of this statement could easily compel outright support of scientific evolution without the necessity of tempering one's view theologically. But by doing so Roberts would completely undercut the basic premise of TWL that science and religion properly understood are complementary and not inherently combative.

SCIENCE AND RELIGION IN TWL

Perhaps more so than any other place in TWL, Roberts came closest to his ultimate dilemma in the discussion of evolution: to wit, while engaging science in a highly supportive manner, Roberts was attempting to reconcile two ontologically different systems of thought. Still, Roberts understood fully that the overwhelmingly prevailing *opinion* held that science and religion were fundamentally incompatible. Draper and White argued that science and religion/theology were fundamentally at odds—and essentially always had been. Despite the title of his book, *The History of the Conflict between Religion and Science*, Draper focused on the Roman Catholic church as the arch villain of enlightenment. The Vatican's persecution of scientists, argued Draper, was calculated, deliberate, and designed to smash any ideas, particularly scientific and certain philosophic, that differed with the received view of the church. Draper's study is parochial, however, and his language is emotionally charged and designed to cause anger among its readership inclined toward Catholicism. By contrast, Draper argued that Protestants, with their emphasis on private scriptural interpretation, provided a receptive climate for the emergence of modern science in the sixteenth and seventeenth centuries. Whereas Catholic authoritarianism constantly thwarted science, Protestant pluralism mitigated any tendency toward undue control. Although sharing Draper's anathema for theology, White's study was more broadly conceived. White argued, in his *History of the Warfare of Science with Theology*, that theology, not religion, had become dogmatic and that this dogmatism regarded the Bible as a scientific text—a mistake that caused an essential conflict between science and religion. The words *conflict* and *warfare* were intentionally used to emphasize a military siege between science and religion, with science clearly on the side of enlightenment, and religion, or at least theology, as the culprit.[31] In citing both Draper and White uncritically and extensively

31. At the time of their publication, Draper received twenty-seven critical reviews, including one Mormon review, while of White's twenty-eight reviews, the eleven that were religious in tone included eight from Protestants, two from Catholics, and one from a Mormon source. See Donald Fleming, *John William Draper and the Religion of Science* (New York: Octagon Press, 1972), and David C. Lindberg and Ronald L. Numbers, "Beyond War and Peace: A Reappraisal of the Encounter between Christianity and Science," *Church History* 55 (1986): 338-54, which reappraises White's warfare thesis in light of a reassessment

throughout TWL, Roberts was tacitly accepting the warfare thesis and thus intellectually promoting a potentially dangerous interpretation.

Although many scholars took note of the ideas of Draper and White and used them profitably at times, both Draper and White wrote, at least partially, for public consumption—and much of the public including Mormons were influenced. They took great interest in Draper and White, and throughout much of the Mormon press it is clear that they basically agreed with them. Whereas Draper and White, in the Mormon view, were dealing with uninspired science and apostate religion, they both argued that there is no conflict between true science and true religion.[32] This point was not lost on the Mormon mind, and Roberts along with virtually every Mormon writer argued that there would simply be no conflict between true (divine) science and revealed religion (Mormonism).

Roberts was an extremely positive advocate for a full-fledged scientism, the view that true science could provide in large measure a complementary understanding of both the moral and physical universe. His use of science to substantiate not only his understanding of Mormonism but also his vision of a moral life was reasonably certain. He tried to remain current in matters scientific and, in large measure, succeeded. He was willing to defend science as a legitimate means epistemologically for acquiring knowledge. Although his enthusiasm for science at times could be explosive, he also recognized, with the sensitivity of the philosopher, the importance of being constructively critical of the scientific enterprise. Altogether his caution was tempered with a genuine respect for science. In the end, Roberts succeeded in weaving the two forms of human understanding—religion and science—into a richly colored fabric.

But Roberts also recognized something more. A less critical mind would likely conclude that, epistemologically, science could easily be used as the foundation for the various claims of religion, thus reducing religion to an irrelevancy. In his chapter entitled "From What We Know to Faith: The Possibility of Revelation," Roberts rhetorically asked, "What is the meaning of the universe?" Listing around twenty-five statements and questions concerned with the "meaning of life," Roberts finally concluded that "in all that we have contemplated in our review of what humans know, we have found nothing that brings a solution to these inquiries." Citing Tom Paine's *Age of Reason*, Roberts argued that reason alone (here represented by Paine) is utterly inadequate in answering ultimate questions. Under the heading "Testimony of the Works of Nature Inadequate," Roberts argued:

---

of the relationship of science and religion.

32. All of the twenty-seven critical reviews of Draper, including the LDS review, agreed with him that there would be no conflict between true science and true religion.

> The universe itself conveys no information on these matters. "Turn not to that inverted bowl men call the sky," for answer to these questions; for the worlds of the universe are impotent to answer. I know how forceful in testimony the heavens and the glory of them can be in supplementing a certain positive message. . . . The heavens and the glory of them, however, are and can be only auxiliary witnesses to the principal message that shall impart the knowledge we seek. Until that knowledge comes, however, appeal to the creation is vain in hope of finding anything conclusive upon the questions that are here presented.[33]

Revelation only in the final analysis, concluded Roberts, could provide such knowledge.[34]

33. TWL, Ms III, chap. 11, pp. 2-3.
34. TWL, Ms III, chap. 12.

EDITOR'S INTRODUCTION

B. H. Roberts is best known for his publications on LDS history, such as his six-volume *Comprehensive History of the Church* and his editing of the seven-volume *History of the Church*. However, he also wrote significant articles and books discussing and defending Mormon doctrine. Roberts wanted to summarize and consolidate all his theological writings into a unified whole; his desire was also to reconcile the scientific knowledge of his day with the scriptures.

Assessments of his completed manuscript of "The Truth, The Way, The Life" (hereafter TWL) are generally positive. Davis Bitton, former assistant LDS church historian, said that TWL "is the single most ambitious and in some ways the most important theological treatise ever written by a Latter-day Saint. . . . [It] can be appreciated as one of the finest productions of a Mormon pen."[1] Erich Robert Paul, a Mormon historian of science, wrote that Roberts's project "blended a lifetime of views on religion, philosophy, Mormonism, and science into a sort of systematic theology."[2] Truman G. Madsen, one of Roberts's biographers, said that TWL is "a kind of historical workbook of science and Mormon theology, showing one mind grappling, after solid homework in world thought, with a driving concern to 'pull things together.'"[3] Richard Sherlock, a Mormon philosopher, wrote that Roberts "undertook nothing less than a comprehensive, coherent account of the whole cosmic context of human existence—from the intelligence of God, through the organization of the universe, the creation of man and the development of life on earth, to the role of Christ."[4] And finally LDS apostle

1. Davis Bitton, "The Truth, The Way, The Life: B. H. Roberts' Unpublished Masterwork," 2, typed manuscript, in the David J. Buerger Collection, Ms 622, Bx 10, Fd 7, Manuscripts Division, Marriott Library, University of Utah, Salt Lake City (hereafter Buerger).

2. Erich Robert Paul, *Science, Religion, and Mormon Cosmology* (Urbana: University of Illinois Press, 1992), 149.

3. Truman G. Madsen, *Defender of the Faith: The B. H. Roberts Story* (Salt Lake City: Bookcraft, 1980), 345.

4. Richard Sherlock, "'We Can See No Advantage to a Continuation of the Discussion': The Roberts/Smith/Talmage Affair," *Dialogue: A Journal of Mormon Thought* 13 (Fall 1980): 63; reprinted in Richard Sherlock and Jeffrey E. Keller, "The B. H. Roberts/Joseph Fielding Smith/James E. Talmage Affair," *The Search for Harmony: Essays*

George Albert Smith told a colleague that TWL "will be the most comprehensive treatise of the Gospel that has yet been published."[5]

The central theme throughout TWL is the life and mission of Jesus the Christ, and it was for this reason that Roberts chose to title the work based on Jesus' declaration: "I am the way, the truth, and the life: no man cometh unto the Father, but by me" (John 14:6). Roberts conceived of using this scripture as the title while listening to the Mormon hymn which contains the line "O Thou by Whom We Come to God, the Life, the Truth, the Way!"[6] Even so, Roberts chose not to follow the exact order and placed truth in first position. TWL summarized and synthesized the distinctive doctrines of Mormonism into three sections: (1) the *truth* about the world and the importance of revelation, (2) the *way* to salvation and eternal life for humanity, and (3) the *life* of Christ and the Christian character.

Within TWL there is a dated reference to the time period when Roberts was writing it. In chapter 46, entitled "Departure from 'The Way,'" Roberts discussed the apostasy from original Christianity and in the footnote to his own writings on the topic points out that *Outlines of Ecclesiastical History* "is now (1924) in its fourth edition." This was during Roberts's five-year presidency of the Eastern States Mission. The wording was later rephrased with the manuscript stating that this volume "is in its fourth edition (1924)." This provides a terminus of no later than 1927—at least for this particular section of TWL—since a fifth edition of *Outlines of Ecclesiastical History* appeared in late 1927.

During his tenure as president of the Eastern States Mission, Roberts did some sporadic work on the TWL. Though he was released in April 1927, he took a six-month vacation (with the approval of church president Heber J. Grant) to stay in New York City and dictate a draft of TWL to his former mission secretary, Elsie Cook, who observed in Roberts a "new resolve and concentration."[7] Evidently, much of TWL was dictated during this period.

---

on Science and Mormonism, eds. Gene A. Sessions and Craig J. Oberg (Salt Lake City: Signature Books, 1993).

5. George Albert Smith to John A. Widtsoe, 26 Feb. 1929, in George Albert Smith Collection, Manuscript 36, Manuscripts Division, Marriott Library (hereafter Smith).

6. "Prayer Is the Soul's Sincere Desire," in *Hymns of the Church of Jesus Christ of Latter-day Saints* (Salt Lake City: Church of Jesus Christ of Latter-day Saints, 1985), no. 145. Truman G. Madsen, "B. H. Roberts: The Book of Mormon and the Atonement," in *The Book of Mormon: First Nephi, The Doctrinal Foundation*, eds. Monte S. Nyman and Charles D. Tate, Jr. (Provo, Ut: Religious Studies Center, Brigham Young University, 1988), 313, found this information when reading the notebooks in Roberts's now-restricted collection at LDS Archives, Historical Department, Church of Jesus Christ of Latter-day Saints, Salt Lake City.

7. Madsen, *Defender*, 338.

When Roberts returned to Salt Lake City in October 1927, he continued revising and rewriting the manuscript throughout the next year. In September 1928 Roberts submitted the manuscript of TWL to the Council of Twelve Apostles for approval to publish it as a course of study for the Seventies, and perhaps for all the Melchizedek priesthood of the church.[8] Having already checked with the Deseret News Press, Roberts figured that the book could be printed and ready to distribute by mid-November 1928 and he hoped "to incorporate within its pages a full harvest of all that I have thought, and felt, and written through the nearly fifty years of my ministry, that is, on the theme of the title."[9]

At the time Roberts submitted TWL to the Twelve in September 1928 there were only 53 chapters in the manuscript. Later he added chapter 54 on the ethic of the last dispensation and many new section headings within the chapters. He also assembled as an appendix to the manuscript a one-page analysis of each chapter, which summarized the headings in the text with an indication of the associated scriptural references. Then in 1929 he wrote chapter 55 on eternal marriage (based on an article published the previous year),[10] inserted a paragraph (filling one typewritten page) in chapter 47 on the same subject, and later added to the end of chapter 55 a seven-page explanation of Mormon polygamy. Finally, he distributed the appendix containing all the chapter analyses to the beginning of the respective chapters.

Roberts continued to revise the text and add material to the TWL after it was submitted to the Twelve for approval in September 1928. Roberts added to chapter 4 a page from an article published in September 1930 concerning the discovery of the planet Pluto, which was discovered earlier that year, though it had been predicted in 1905 due to certain irregularities in the motion of Uranus and Neptune.[11] At about the same time he updated the statement in chapter 10 concerning the number of planets in our solar system from "eight" to "nine." In conjunction with Roberts's presentation to the Quorum of the Twelve Apostles in January 1931, he deleted two sections ("A Catholic Comment" and "The Author's

---

8. Truman G. Madsen, "The Meaning of Christ—The Truth, The Way, The Life: An Analysis of B. H. Roberts' Unpublished Masterwork," *Brigham Young University Studies* 15 (Spring 1975): 259, incorrectly states that it was for an MIA, instead of a priesthood, study course.

9. B. H. Roberts to Rudger Clawson, 17 Sept. 1928, in Ernest Strack Collection, Manuscript A 296, Library, Utah State Historical Society, Salt Lake City (hereafter Strack).

10. B. H. Roberts, "Complete Marriage—Righteousness; Mutilated Marriage—Sin," *Improvement Era* 31 (Jan. 1928): 181-92.

11. "The Latest News from Pluto," *The Literary Digest* 106 (6 Sept. 1930): 18.

Comment") in chapter 31 of TWL–these have accordingly been relegated to an editorial footnote.

The final arrangement of the TWL chapters resembles the five-volume series known as *The Seventy's Course in Theology*, with an initial analysis summarizing the major topics and a list of scriptural and other references.

THE CONTROVERSY

On 3 October 1928 Rudger Clawson, president of the Quorum of the Twelve Apostles, named George Albert Smith, David O. McKay, Joseph Fielding Smith, Stephen L. Richards, and Melvin J. Ballard as a reading committee to determine if Roberts's manuscript was suitable as a church study manual.[12] The committee met often to read and discuss the manuscript of TWL. In mid-January 1929 Joseph Fielding Smith noted in his diary that the reading committee "met with some difficulties in theories advanced by the author." In a meeting with Roberts on 26 March 1929 the committee discussed the parts they found objectionable, "trying to agree on some points of difference."[13] Roberts realized the possibility that his manuscript might never be published, but he refused to "change it [even] if it has to sleep."[14] In September 1929 Roberts wrote to a former missionary that he expected that as soon as TWL was published it "would 'catch like wildfire' among the youth" of the church.[15]

In October 1929 George Albert Smith, chair of the reading committee, submitted a report of the committee's conclusions to Rudger Clawson.[16] First, he offered praise that the manuscript "is very worthy treating subjects dealing with the mission of Jesus Christ and gospel principles, which it would be well for all members of the Church to understand." Then he stated that committee members found "some objectionable doctrines advanced, which are of a speculative nature and appear to be out of harmony with the revelations of the Lord and the fundamental teachings of the Church," attaching a list of specific items in the chapters that needed revision.[17]

---

12. Rudger Clawson to Elders George Albert Smith, David O. McKay, Joseph Fielding Smith, Stephen L. Richards, and Melvin J. Ballard, 3 Oct. 1928, in Strack.

13. Joseph Fielding Smith Journal, 15 Jan. and 26 Mar. 1929, according to typescript in Buerger, Bx 10, Fd 8.

14. B. H. Roberts to Heber J. Grant, May 1929, cited by Madsen, *Defender*, 344.

15. B. H. Roberts to Elizabeth Skolfield Hinckley, 8 Sept. 1929, cited by Madsen, *Defender*, 341.

16. Madsen, "Meaning," 259, incorrectly states that David O. McKay chaired the committee.

17. George Albert Smith to Rudger Clawson, 10 Oct. 1929, with a one-page "List of

Early in May 1930 the review committee submitted another report about Roberts's manuscript. The committee stated their concern about the inevitable importance placed by church members on books written by general authorities, especially when the church is the publisher:

> It is the duty of the general authorities of the Church to safeguard and protect the membership of the Church from the introduction of controversial subjects and false doctrines, which tend to create factions and otherwise disturb the faith of the Latter-day Saints. There is so much of vital importance revealed and which we can present with clear and convincing presentation and which the world does not possess, that we, the committee, see no reason for the introduction of questions which are speculative, to say the least. More especially so when such teachings appear to be in conflict with the revelations of the Lord.[18]

The committee's second report was re-written. Then on 15 May 1930 the Council of Twelve Apostles as a body wrote a letter to Heber J. Grant and his counselors, noting that "Roberts declined to make the changes or modifications suggested by the Twelve."[19] Accompanying this letter was a list of "Doctrinal Points Questioned by the Committee." This final list omitted seven problems that had been included in the initial committee report seven months earlier. One of these is enlightening, since the committee had questioned "the superiority of the Prophet [Jospeh Smith]'s definition" of truth.[20] Roberts had quoted Smith's 1833 statement that "truth is knowledge of things as they are, and as they were, and as they are to come," and added that this explanation "ought to be the completest definition of

---

Points on Doctrine in Question by the Committee in Relation to B. H. Robert[s]'s Ms," in B. H. Roberts Correspondence, Manuscript SC 1922, Special Collections and Manuscripts, Lee Library, Brigham Young University, Provo, Utah (hereafter Roberts Correspondence at BYU).

18. Report of Committee to the Council of the Twelve, early May 1930, in Buerger, Bx 10, Fd 8. However, Sherlock, "'We Can See No Advantage to a Continuation of the Discussion,' 67, 77, reprinted in Sherlock and Keller, "The B. H. Roberts/Joseph Fielding Smith/James E. Talmage Affair," *Search for Harmony*, 94, 111, cites these same words as being "Council of the Twelve to Heber J. Grant, May 15, 1930, Clawson Papers." The words of the quotation in the text are not at issue, since both sources agree verbatim, but determining which person or committee said them and when they were written can only be resolved by examining the restricted Clawson and Roberts collections at LDS Church Archives.

19. Council of the Twelve to Heber J. Grant, 15 May 1930, in Buerger, Bx 29, Fd 4.

20. "List of Points on Doctrine in Question by the Committee in Relation to B. H. Robert[s]'s Ms," attached to George Albert Smith to Rudger Clawson, 10 Oct. 1929, in Roberts Correspondence at BYU.

truth extant among men."[21] Later the committee decided not to oppose a revelation of Joseph Smith, which had been incorporated into LDS scripture as D&C 93:24. Accordingly, this objection to TWL was dropped.

The official list of doctrinal problems in TWL given in the May 1930 report of the twelve apostles reiterated the rest of the October 1929 objections but added a narrative explanation to most of them. These objections provide a barometer, showing the areas considered sensitive at the time. A representative sampling (from the serious to the trivial) can be covered in the following seven questions[22]:

1. Did pre-Adamite races of human beings exist on this earth before Adam and Eve? This is the most controversial idea in TWL. Apostle Orson Hyde in a general conference talk in October 1854 said: "The world was peopled before the days of Adam, . . . When God said, Go forth and replenish the earth, it was to replenish the inhabitants of the human species, and make it as it was before."[23] Roberts argued that church president Brigham Young approved of Hyde's doctrine (although Young's remarks probably endorsed Hyde's sermon on marriage in general, not Hyde's notion of pre-Adamites).[24] The methodology pursued by Roberts was to accept "the truths of science no less than the truths of revelation."[25] In an effort to reconcile the biblical account about Adam with the paleontological record about the age of humankind, Roberts postulated that there were pre-Adamite races on the earth long before Adam.[26] The review committee objected to his hypothesis, saying that "it is speculation leading to endless controversy." They also admitted "that one of the brethren (Orson Hyde) in an early day advocated this teaching; however, we feel that the brethren of the general authorities cannot be too careful, and should not present as doctrine that which is not sustained in the

---

21. TWL, final draft, known as Ms III, chap. 1, p. 6.

22. The complete texts of the October 1929 "List of Points on Doctrine in Question by the Committee in Relation to B. H. Robert[s]'s Ms," the early May 1930 Report of Committee to the Council of the Twelve with a listing of objections, and the final 15 May 1930 "Doctrinal Points Questioned by the Committee Which Read Manuscript of Elder B. H. Roberts, Entitled The Truth, The Way, The Life" are printed in the appendix at the end of this volume.

23. Orson Hyde, "The Marriage Relations," *Journal of Discourses* 2 (1855): 79. Hyde interprets the King James Version "replenish" at Genesis 1:28 to mean "re-fill," but the Hebrew word means to "fill." Joseph Fielding Smith, *Answers to Gospel Questions* (Salt Lake City: Deseret Book Co., 1957), 1:208, correctly points out the Hebrew meaning.

24. Brigham Young, "Marriage Relations of Bishops and Deacons," *Journal of Discourses* 2 (1855): 90.

25. Karl C. Sandberg, "Modes of Belief: David Whitmer, B. H. Roberts, Werner Heisenberg," *Sunstone* 12 (Sept. 1988): 13.

26. TWL, Ms III, chap. 31, p. 1.

standards of the Church." Roberts's handwritten responses were that he had "not so presented" this teaching and that Orson Hyde's teaching "was approved also by Pres. Young."

2. Was life on the earth destroyed and made desolate before the time of Adam? Roberts pointed out the two creation accounts in the first two chapters of Genesis. The first, which begins with chaotic matter, discusses a natural development, and culminates in the creation of man, is found in Genesis 1:1–2:3a. The second, which begins with the creation of man, the placing of him in the garden, and the creation of animal life, birds, and fish, is found in Genesis 2:3b-25. In the second creation account Roberts offered the interpretation that "man seems to get his earth-heritage in a barren state, as if some besom [broom] of destruction had swept the earth; and it must be newly fitted up as a proper abode for him from desert barrenness to a fruitful habitat."[27] Roberts speculated that "previous to the advent of Adam upon the earth, some destructive cataclysm, a universal glacial period, or an excessive heat period left the earth empty and desolate."[28] The pre-Adamites and other life on earth were destroyed due to this overwhelming cataclysm before the time of Adam, leaving the earth in a "desolate" state.[29] The committee responded that "the place of man in the order of creation is questioned."

3. Did Adam come to this earth as a translated being? Roberts, using Brigham Young's controversial Adam-God discourse of 9 April 1852, asserted that Adam came to this earth from some other world. Roberts, however, did not accept Young's view that Adam was God, that he had "a celestial body" when he came to the earth, and that he became mortal through eating the forbidden fruit.[30] Roberts's position was that Adam was a "translated" being.[31] The committee said "the doctrine that Adam came here a 'translated' being from some other world is not accepted as a doctrine of the Church." They also added that the fall of Adam "brought death into the world."

4. How is an intelligence different from a begotten spirit? Actually, Joseph Smith used the terms "intelligence," "spirit," "soul," and "mind" synonymously. In the early Nauvoo, Illinois, period he taught that "the Spirit of Man is not a

---

27. TWL, Ms III, chap. 30, pp. 6-7.

28. TWL, Ms III, chap. 30, p. 7.

29. TWL, Ms III, chap. 32, p. 3.

30. Brigham Young taught this in his 9 April 1852 discourse, entitled "Self-Government–Mysteries–Recreation and Amusements Not in Themselves Sinful–Tithing–Adam, Our Father and Our God," *Journal of Discourses* 1 (1854): 46-53. For Young's controversial Adam-God Doctrine, see David J. Buerger, "The Adam-God Doctrine," *Dialogue: A Journal of Mormon Thought* 15 (Spring 1982): 14-58.

31. TWL, Ms III, chap. 32, p. 3.

created being; it existed from Eternity & will exist to eternity,"[32] "I believe that the *soul* is eternal; and had no beginning; it can have no end,"[33] and "the spirit or the intelligence of men are self-Existent principles before the foundation [of] this Earth."[34] On 7 April 1844 during the King Follett discourse, which some consider to be his finest doctrinal sermon, Smith said: "The soul–the immortal spirit–the mind of man. Where did it come from? All doctors of divinity say that God created it in the beginning, but it is not so. The very idea lessens the character of man, in my estimation. . . . Man existed in spirit; the mind of man–the intelligent part–is as immortal as, and is coequal with, God Himself. . . . I take my ring from my finger and liken it unto the mind of man–the immortal spirit–because it has no beginning or end."[35] Since in Smith's view the human spirit existed from eternity, there was no need to describe a point when a spiritual birth or creation occurred.

One of the current distinctive doctrines of Mormonism is the belief that all human spirits are the offspring of God through a spiritual birth process. Consequently, a philosophical dilemma exists for Mormon theologians. One scholar explains that "harmonizing Joseph Smith's teaching that spirits have no beginning with the contemporary Mormon belief that spirits come into existence through a spirit birth" has produced two solutions.[36] The first explains that uncreated intelligence is combined with a spiritual body begotten from heavenly parents to produce a conscious spirit person. In this way the human spirit is eternal in the sense that the elements are eternal. The other explanation is that the conscious mind or intelligence always existed, but the next major stage in progress is the union of the individual intelligence with a spirit body, which is created through procreation. This difference of interpretation still persists today.[37]

---

32. Andrew F. Ehat and Lyndon W. Cook, eds. *The Words of Joseph Smith* (Provo, UT: Religious Studies Center, Brigham Young University, 1980), 9.

33. Ibid., 33; emphasis in original.

34. Ibid., 68; spelling has been corrected.

35. See the editor's "The King Follett Discourse: A Newly Amalgamated Text," *Brigham Young University Studies* 18 (Winter 1978): 203-204.

36. Van Hale, "The Origin of the Human Spirit in Early Mormon Thought," in Gary James Bergera, ed., *Line upon Line: Essays on Mormon Doctrine* (Salt Lake City: Signature Books, 1989), 122.

37. Dennis J. Packard, "Intelligence," in *Encyclopedia of Mormonism*, ed. Daniel H. Ludlow (New York: Macmillan Publishing Co., 1992), 2:692, says that "some LDS leaders have interpreted this to mean that intelligent beings–called intelligences–existed before and after they were given spirit bodies in the premortal existence. Others have interpreted it to mean that intelligent beings were organized as spirits out of eternal intelligent matter, that they did not exist as individuals before they were organized as spirit beings in the premortal existence."

Roberts argued that "man is spirit (intelligence within a spirit body) and this spirit is native to the 'light of truth.'"[38] The committee objected that his use of the terms intelligence and spirit is confusing, saying that an intelligence was an unorganized, unbegotten, uncreated "eternal entity" and that only after intelligences become begotten spirits could they rebel. Roberts wrote in response that this objection was "of no substance or importance" and that there was a "misapprehension here," since intelligence was "that which perceives truth." However, in response to (and in accordance with) the committee's suggestion Roberts revised his text of TWL by adding the three words in italics: "Some intelligences as spirits will rebel against the order of things in the universe as did Lucifer and his following."[39] Accordingly, Roberts was not stubbornly defending every word of TWL, as is sometimes stated.

5. When does the pre-existent spirit enter the body? Answers in Mormon doctrinal discussion have been varied—from conception, to quickening, to birth.[40] Roberts discussed the doctrine of "infusionism" as propounded by Origen in the third century, which states that the pre-existent human soul is infused into the physical body at conception or at birth.[41] Since there exists no official LDS statement on this issue, the committee "questioned the advisability of stating any given time when the spirit unites with the body." Actually, Roberts did not here state whether this union of body and spirit occurs at conception or at birth, but five chapters later he expresses an opinion in favor of birth based on the pre-existent Christ's statement to Nephi that the next day he would be born (3 Ne. 1:12-13).

6. Does God's omniscience mean that he increases in knowledge? In the 1850s Brigham Young and Orson Pratt argued over this question. Pratt had written in 1853 that "the Father and the Son do not progress in knowledge and wisdom, because they already know all things past, present, and to come."[42] Young countered in 1854 that "there never will be a time to all Eternity when all the Gods of Eternity will scease [*sic*] advancing in power knowledge experience & Glory."[43]

38. TWL, Ms III, chap. 27, p. 8.

39. TWL, Ms III, chap. 27, p. 5.

40. Jeffrey E. Keller, "When Does the Spirit Enter the Body?" *Sunstone* 10 (Mar. 1985): 42-44.

41. TWL, Ms III, chap. 21, p. 9.

42. Gary James Bergera, "The Orson Pratt-Brigham Young Controversies: Conflict within the Quorums, 1853 to 1868," *Dialogue: A Journal of Mormon Thought* 13 (Summer 1980): 11, quoting *The Seer* 1 (Aug. 1853): 117.

43. Scott G. Kenney, ed., *Wilford Woodruff's Journal: 1833-1898 Typescript* (Midvale, UT: Signature Books, 1983), 4:288, at 17 Sept. 1854. Woodruff also records Young's 17 February 1856 statement that "the Gods & all intelligent Beings would never scease [*sic*] to learn except it was the Sons of perdition they would continue to decrease untill [*sic*] they

In conjunction with the principle of eternal progression, Roberts asserted that God's omniscience is limited, since he still progresses in knowledge. Roberts offered a revised definition of omniscience, saying that it is not the case "that God is Omniscient up to the point that further progress in knowledge is impossible to him; but that all the knowledge that is, all that exists, God knows; all that shall be he will know."[44] The committee objected that this doctrine was "limiting God" and would "cause needless controversy" among church members. The committee added that God's "progress is because of his knowledge and that he is the author of law." Roberts's handwritten response was "Meaningless."

7. Does the Church of Christ change? Lastly, Roberts described the organized structure of the LDS church in the early 1830s as the "humble first forms of the Church."[45] The committee questioned this phraseology since "the thought may be conveyed that the forms of the Church had been changed, rather than developed." Roberts wrote in the margin that this objection was "Nonsense!"[46]

On 22 May 1930 Roberts told Heber J. Grant that he was "determined not to make any change" in the manuscript to TWL. Grant felt "very sorry to think that Brother Roberts is determined to put in the book some things that I think are problematical and cannot be demonstrated."[47]

A month before the committee's report was submitted, Joseph Fielding Smith, a member of the reading committee, publicly criticized Roberts's ideas in an April 1930 discourse, even though he did not mention Roberts by name. Smith proclaimed:

> Even in the Church there are a scattered few who are now advocating and contending that this earth was peopled with a race—perhaps many races—long before the days of Adam. These men desire, of course, to square the teachings in the Bible with the teachings of modern science and philosophy in regard to the age of the earth and life upon it. If you hear any one talking this way, you may answer them by saying that the doctrine of "pre-Adamites" is not a doctrine of the Church, and is not advocated nor countenanced in the Church. There is no warrant in the scripture, not an authentic word, to sustain it. . . . *There was no death in the earth before the fall of Adam.* I do not

---

became dissolved back into their native Element & lost their Identity" (ibid., 402).

44. TWL, Ms III, chap. 42, p. 9.

45. TWL, Ms III, chap. 47, p. 13.

46. "Doctrinal Points Questioned by the Committee Which Read the Manuscript of Elder B. H. Roberts, Entitled The Truth, The Way, The Life," with marginal handwritten notes by B. H. Roberts, attached to Rudger Clawson to Heber J. Grant, 15 May 1930, in Buerger, Bx 29, Fd 4.

47. Heber J. Grant Diary, 22 May 1930, according to typescript in Buerger, Bx 10, Fd 8.

> care what the scientists say in regard to dinosaurs and other creatures upon the earth millions of years ago that lived and died and fought and struggled for existence. . . . *All life in the sea, the air, on the earth, was without death. Animals were not dying. Things were not changing as we find them changing in this mortal existence, for mortality had not come.*[48]

Smith thus emphatically denied that death existed before the fall of Adam and stated that the existence of "pre-Adamites" was not church doctrine.

Roberts, furious over the publication of Smith's discourse, considered it "a veiled attack" on his TWL.[49] On 15 December 1930 Roberts demanded a chance to present his position to President Heber J. Grant, telling him that:

> If Elder Smith is merely putting forth his own opinions I call in question his competency to utter such dogmatism either as a scholar or as an Apostle. I am sure he is not competent to speak in such manner from general learning or special research work on the subject; nor as an Apostle, as in that case he would be in conflict with the plain implication at least of the scriptures, both ancient and modern, and with the teaching of a more experienced and learned and earlier Apostle [Orson Hyde] than himself.[50]

The apostles were indignant at Roberts's strong words and wrote to Grant that they regarded Roberts's language "as very offensive on the part of Elder Roberts, who fails to show the deference due from one brother to another brother of higher rank in the Priesthood."[51] On 30 December 1930 Rudger Clawson asked Roberts for more details on his objections. The next day Roberts basically reiterated to Clawson the 15 December letter.

The apostles agreed to listen to both opponents. In preparation for this meeting Roberts almost quadrupled the size of chapter 31, which discussed the antiquity of humankind on the earth.[52] On 7 January 1931 Roberts read to the

---

48. Joseph Fielding Smith, "Faith Leads to a Fullness of Truth and Righteousness," *Utah Genealogical and Historical Magazine* 21 (Oct. 1930): 147-48, emphasis in original.

49. Wesley P. Lloyd Diary, 7 Aug. 1933, Accession 1338, Manuscripts Division, Marriott Library. Roberts was not the only one disturbed by Smith's discourse. Geologist Sterling B. Talmage, son of James E. Talmage, wrote (with guidance from his father) a twelve-page open letter to Joseph Fielding Smith, detailing his objections. See the Sterling B. Talmage Collection, Accession 724, Manuscripts Division, Marriott Library (hereafter S. B. Talmage).

50. B. H. Roberts to Heber J. Grant, 15 Dec. 1930, in Scott G. Kenney Collection, Ms 587, Bx 4, Fd 19, Manuscripts Division, Marriott Library. Roberts was referring to Apostle Orson Hyde.

51. Rudger Clawson to Heber J. Grant, 21 Jan. 1931.

52. Originally as submitted in September 1928 chapter 31 contained only nine pages.

assembled Quorum of Twelve Apostles his fifty-page paper on the "Antiquity of Man," which argued for pre-Adamites and documented his objections to the discourse of Joseph Fielding Smith. Roberts accepted the chronology for Adam as about 6,000 to 8,000 years ago; he never questioned the literalness of the story of Adam in the book of Genesis nor did he try to interpret it symbolically. But since he also accepted the scientific dating of the geological record, he was forced to postulate the existence of pre-Adamites, a cataclysm before the advent of Adam, and the Adamic dispensation as a new beginning for the earth. Roberts said:

> You Brethren will have observed also perhaps that I have not followed any pin-picking method of argument in dealing with the excerpts from Elder Smith's discourse presented here, but rather have depended upon great, sweeping, cumulative, and to me overwhelming evidences of man's ancient existence in the earth. . . . But they [the scriptures] may be reconciled with the facts of death upon the earth in ages previous to Adam—as the discoveries of men undoubtedly prove—if Adam's advent is understood as describing the introduction of a special dispensation on the earth to accomplish some particular purpose of God in the development of man such as bringing him into special spiritual relationship with him, and men into special relationship with one another.[53]

One week later Heber J. Grant and Anthony W. Ivins of the First Presidency met with James E. Talmage, who was both an apostle and a geologist, and asked for his opinion concerning the antiquity of humanity. Then on 21 January 1931 Joseph Fielding Smith read his paper to the Twelve, with Roberts in attendance.[54] Smith stated that the Devil or Satan is actively "giving revelation and poisoning the minds of men" and then asserted his position that "the doctrine of organic evolution which pervades the modern-day sciences, proclaiming the edict that man

---

In an effort to present the most up-to-date information Roberts added twenty-five pages to the text, with the latest newspaper report being mid-December 1930, just three weeks before his presentation to the apostles.

53. B. H. Roberts, presentation to the Quorum of Twelve Apostles, partial typescript, 7 Jan. 1931, in Buerger, Bx 10, Fd 7.

54. The delivery of the paper occurred on 21 January 1931, but the paper itself was finished and dated on 14 January 1931, being written after and in response to Roberts's presentation on 7 January 1931. Consequently, Richard Sherlock, "A Turbulent Spectrum: Mormon Reactions to the Darwinist Legacy," *Journal of Mormon History* 5 (1978): 33 (reprinted in *Search for Harmony*, 67), being misled by the date at the beginning of the paper, incorrectly assumed that Joseph Fielding Smith presented his paper to the assembled apostles on 14 January. He corrected this error in his more detailed study, "We Can See No Advantage," 68, 78; reprinted in Sherlock and Keller, "B. H. Roberts . . . Affair," in *Search for Harmony*, 95, 111.

has evolved from lower forms of life through the Java skull and last, if not least, the 'Peking man,' who lived millions of years ago, is as false as their author who reigns in hell!"

Smith also pointed out that Roberts's teaching on pre-Adamites "has caused indignation, some resentment, and a great deal of serious concern" among church members.[55] However, there was no discussion among the apostles at either meeting concerning the merits of either position. The next day Rudger Clawson reported at the apostles' regular Thursday council meeting in the temple concerning the presentations by Roberts and Smith, and Smith expressed pride that Clawson's summary was "favorable to me."[56]

After President Grant read the papers by Smith and Roberts, he said: "I feel that sermons such as Brother Joseph [Fielding Smith] preached and criticisms such as Brother Roberts makes of the sermon are the finest kind of things to let alone entirely. I think no good can be accomplished by dealing in mysteries, and that is what I feel in my heart of hearts these brethren are both doing."[57] Roberts expressed his own feelings during this period: "I have been passing through the severest mental and spiritual strain of my life during the past two months—Doctrinal questions before the Twelve and the First Presidency in connection with my book *The Truth, The Way, The Life*, respecting which there seems to be little prospect of settlement."[58]

Quietly James E. Talmage wrote to his son, Sterling Talmage, also a geologist, and asked him to ascertain the reputation of George McCready Price, whose book entitled *The New Geology* was being used by Joseph Fielding Smith against Roberts. Sterling wrote back that "neither the book nor its author has any standing whatever among American geologists," and the only school using Price's book as a geology textbook was the fundamentalist Wheaton College.[59] This information was useful to Talmage, who attempted to preserve "ostensible neutrality or official non-cognizance of some thing."[60]

---

55. Joseph Fielding Smith, Statement to Rudger Clawson, 14 Jan. 1931.

56. Joseph Fielding Smith Journal, 22 Jan. 1931, according to typescript in Buerger, Bx 10, Fd 8.

57. Heber J. Grant Diary, 25 Jan. 1931, in Thomas G. Alexander, "'To Maintain Harmony': Adjusting to External and Internal Stress, 1890-1930," *Dialogue: A Journal of Mormon Thought* 15 (Winter 1982): 58n37.

58. B. H. Roberts, Letter, Jan. 1931, in Madsen, *Defender*, 344, but the letter should be dated as 3 Mar. 1931.

59. Sterling B. Talmage to James E. Talmage, 9 Feb. 1931, in Ronald L. Numbers, *The Creationists* (New York: Alfred A. Knopf, 1992), 311.

60. Sterling B. Talmage to James E. Talmage, 29 June 1931, in S. B. Talmage.

Since no discussion had occurred during the two presentations, Roberts asked Grant for a chance to respond to Smith's presentation. Roberts asserted to Grant that Smith's views were weaker than "a house of cards," but that it was due to "such pabulum" uttered by Elder Smith that the publication of TWL was being suspended.[61] Two weeks later the First Presidency met with Roberts for two hours to discuss the problem.

The Twelve could not resolve the opposing positions and transferred the problem to the First Presidency for resolution. The First Presidency concluded not to make a decision on this issue, and a seven-page statement, probably written by Anthony W. Ivins, was distributed on 5 April 1931 to all general authorities.[62] In this document, which did not favor one side or the other, the First Presidency said:

> The statement made by Elder Smith that the existence of pre-Adamites is not a doctrine of the Church is true. It is just as true that the statement: "There were not pre-Adamites upon the earth" is not a doctrine of the Church. Neither side of the controversy has been accepted as a doctrine at all. Both parties make the scripture and the statements of men who have been prominent in the affairs of the Church the basis of their contention; neither has produced definite proof in support of his views. . . . We can see no advantage to be gained by a continuation of the discussion to which reference is here made, but on the contrary are certain that it would lead to confusion, division, and misunderstanding if carried further.[63]

Two days later the First Presidency reaffirmed in a meeting with general authorities that the church had no position on this controversial matter. George Albert Smith stated that the brethren sustained the First Presidency's decision that "we know nothing about such a people" as the pre-Adamites.[64] Apostle George F. Richards recorded that "the subject of pre-Adamites [was] not to be discussed in public by the brethren," whether speaking for or against the pre-Adamite theory.[65] Apostle James E. Talmage felt that the First Presidency had made a wise decision and added that "this is one of the many things upon which we cannot preach with assurance, and dogmatic assertions on either side are likely to do harm rather than good."[66]

---

61. B. H. Roberts to Heber J. Grant, 9 Feb. 1931, in 5 Apr. 1931 letter of the First Presidency to General Authorities, in Roberts Correspondence at BYU.

62. Heber J. Grant Diary, 30 Mar. 1931, according to typescript and handwritten note in Buerger, Bx 10, Fd 8.

63. First Presidency to Council of the Twelve, First Council of Seventy, and Presiding Bishopric, 5 Apr. 1931, in Roberts Correspondence at BYU; photocopy of pp. 5-7 in Strack.

64. George Albert Smith Diary, 7 Apr. 1931, in Smith, Bx 67, Bk 10.

65. George F. Richards Diary, 7 Apr. 1931, according to typescript in Strack.

66. James E. Talmage Diary, 7 Apr. 1931, Manuscript 229, Special Collections and

Rudger Clawson wrote to the reading committee, asking them to again request Roberts to remove from TWL all references to pre-Adamites and the other matters found objectionable. Suspecting that their efforts might not be fruitful, Clawson also told the committee that they should make clear to Roberts that the church would not publish TWL or use it as a textbook in priesthood quorums unless he complied with this request. Clawson closed by saying that he hoped Roberts would realize that the wisest policy to follow would be to make recommended changes, so that "an excellent work may not go unpublished and be lost to the Church."[67]

Roberts was not willing to make the suggested alterations. Later that month wrote that the "addition of scientific evidences added to this chapter was prepared for a special paper for the Twelve" on 7 January 1931, and he wanted this additional material included in chapter 31.[68]

On 9 August 1931 James E. Talmage delivered a discourse at the Salt Lake tabernacle entitled "The Earth and Man," which delineated a middle-of-the-road position "between elders Smith and Roberts by denying Elder Smith's attacks on the scientific method and recognizing the speculative nature of Roberts's position."[69] In contrast to Smith's publicly stated view, Talmage clearly declared that life and death occurred before the fall of Adam:

> The oldest, that is to say the earliest, rocks thus far identified in land masses reveal the fossilized remains of once living organisms, plant and animal. The coal strata, upon which the world of industry so largely depends, are essentially but highly compressed and chemically changed vegetable substance. The whole series of chalk deposits and many of our deep-sea limestones contain the skeletal remains of animals. These lived and died, age after age, while the earth was yet unfit for human habitation.[70]

Manuscripts, Lee Library, Brigham Young University (hereafter abbreviated to Talmage at BYU).

67. Rudger Clawson to George Albert Smith, 10 Apr. 1931, in Strack.

68. Note of B. H. Roberts, 29 Apr. 1929, inserted before chapter 31 of TWL, in B. H. Roberts Collection, Manuscript 106, Bx 17, Fd 4, Manuscript Division, Marriott Library (hereafter Roberts at UU).

69. Thomas G. Alexander, *Mormonism in Transition: A History of the Latter-day Saints, 1890-1930* (Urbana: University of Illinois Press, 1986), 288.

70. James E. Talmage, *The Earth and Man: Address Delivered in the Tabernacle, Salt lake City, Utah, Sunday, August 9, 1931* (Salt Lake City: Church of Jesus Christ of Latter-day Saints, 1931), 4. Talmage himself had earlier examined the altar of stones at Spring Hill, Missouri, which Joseph Smith identified as Adam's altar, and found fossilized animals in the stones. Consequently, he concluded that "if those stones be part of the first altar, Adam built it of stones containing corpses, and therefore death must have prevailed in the earth before Adam's time" (James E. Talmage to Sterling B. Talmage, 21 May 1931, cited by Jeffrey E. Keller, "Discussion Continued: The Sequel to the Roberts/Smith/Talmage Affair,"

Talmage asserted that the scientific record and the biblical account will eventually coincide, since they are different approaches to the same truth: "The Creator has made record in the rocks for man to decipher; but He has also spoken directly regarding the main stages of progress by which the earth has been brought to be what it is. The accounts can not be fundamentally opposed; one can not contradict the other; though man's interpretation of either may be seriously at fault."[71] He also discussed the hypothesis of pre-Adamic races but pointed out that there is no settled consensus concerning it:

> Geologists and anthropologists say that if the beginning of Adamic history dates back but 6000 years or less, there must have been races of human sort upon earth long before that time—without denying, however, that Adamic history may be correct, if it be regarded solely as the history of the Adamic race. This view postulates, by application of [James D.] Dana's affirmation already quoted: "that the intervention of a power above Nature" brought about the placing of, let me say, Adam upon earth. It is but fair to say that no reconciliation of these opposing conceptions has been effected to the satisfaction of both parties.[72]

Initially there was strong opposition by some apostles to having Talmage's discourse published, since they worried that church members might wonder: "If there was life and death and a race of men before the fall of Adam, then there must have been two Adams and two falls, also two fathers of the human family, all of which would lead to utter confusion."[73] The advice of Apostle John A. Widtsoe, who was presiding over the church's European Mission, was sought, and he recommended that Talmage's discourse be published. Later Widtsoe discovered that fellow apostle Joseph Fielding Smith "felt personally betrayed and humiliated by this response."[74] After at least four meetings on this matter the First Presidency

---

Dialogue: A Journal of Mormon Thought 15 [Spring 1982]: 83; reprinted in Sherlock and Keller, "The B. H. Roberts/Joseph Fielding Smith/James E. Talmage Affair," *Search for Harmony*, 99).

71. Ibid., 5.

72. Ibid., 11, emphasis in original. Evidence now available in the form of letters between Talmage and his geologist son, Sterling B. Talmage, indicate that Apostle Talmage personally believed in the existence of pre-Adamites. See Keller, "Discussion Continued," 82-83, reprinted in Sherlock and Keller, "B. H. Roberts . . . Affair," in *Search for Harmony*, 93-115.

73. "Report of President Clawson made at the regular weekly meeting of the First Presidency and the Council of the Twelve, October 1," two-page typescript, dated 20 Nov. 1931, in Roberts Correspondence at BYU.

74. Duane E. Jeffery, "'We Don't Know': A Survey of Mormon Responses to Evolutionary Biology," in *Science and Religion: Toward a More Useful Dialogue*, eds. Wilford

"authorized its publication" in November 1931, both in the church section of the *Deseret News* and as a separate pamphlet.[75] Talmage admitted that Joseph Fielding Smith was well aware that "my address was in some important respects opposed to his published remarks."[76] This is confirmed by a copy of Talmage's pamphlet, upon which Joseph Fielding Smith wrote the words "False doctrine."[77]

In March 1932 Roberts gave Talmage one chapter of TWL, which he read and returned three days later.[78] From Roberts's comment that he had added more evidence on the antiquity of humankind, this chapter can be identified as the controversial chapter 31, "An Adamic Dispensation."

During a discourse delivered at the April 1932 general conference Stephen L Richards, a member of the TWL reading committee, preached that fanaticism and bigotry among members were "the deadliest enemies of religion in the past" and asked LDS members to have more "sympathy and tolerance" for others. Richards continued:

> No man's standing in the LDS church should be affected by his belief in the beginning of man's life or the beginning of the universe. He [Richards] held that it is the privilege of members to differ on this and other subjects and still be good Latter-day Saints. He added, however, that no one with a real affection for the church will urge views on these points which will tend to undermine the faith of the young in their religion.[79]

M. Hess, Raymond T. Matheny, and Donlu D. Thayer (Geneva, IL: Paladin House, 1979), 2:24.

75. Heber J. Grant Diary, 7 Nov. 1931, according to typescript in Strack.

76. James E. Talmage Diary, 21 Nov. 1931, in Talmage at BYU.

77. Thomas G. Truitt identified the handwriting of Joseph Fielding Smith on a copy of *The Earth and Man*, a photocopy of which is in Strack.

78. B. H. Roberts to James E. Talmage, 18 Mar. 1932, and James E. Talmage to B. H. Roberts, 21 Mar. 1932, in Roberts at UU, Bx 18, Fd 1.

79. "Leader Attacks Dogma, Bigotry as Enemies of Faith," *The Salt Lake Tribune*, 10 Apr. 1932, 12. This particular conference talk by Richards has a unique history. That same afternoon the First Presidency and twelve apostles met to discuss "the question of allowing the address delivered by Elder Stephen L. Richards" to be published. Richards had also suggested that church members have tolerance towards those who violate the Word of Wisdom, and the Brethren were concerned "whether the effect of this address will be that of leading to the thought that the Church is lowering its standards" (Talmage Diary, 9 Apr. 1932). As a result of Richards's liberal attitude about the Word of Wisdom and probably also his statement that "some changes in the ordinances, forms, and methods of the church had been made in recent years and that these changes had disturbed some of the members" (quoted from the *Tribune*), his entire discourse was omitted from the published conference report without comment. This was done in spite of the statement on the title page of *One-hundred and Second Annual Conference of the Church of Jesus Christ of Latter-day Saints*

In March 1933 Roberts wrote in *The Improvement Era* that "truth, whether revealed of God or discovered by research of man, must be harmonious" and that the LDS church is not bound to the outdated theory of "the limited time of duration for the existence of the world."[80] Near the end of his life he expressed the desire that members of the church "would carefully and thoroughly examine every [gospel] principle advanced to them and not only intellectually assent to it as a grand system of truth, but also become imbued with its spirit and feel and enjoy its powers."[81]

As early as 1929 when the reading committee began objecting to various statements in TWL, Roberts warned them that he might publish the book "on his own responsibility," without church approval.[82] By August 1933 he had decided to follow this course and planned to publish TWL "under his own direction without Church backing" and the only thing standing in his way was raising enough money to finance publication.[83] He no longer feared ecclesiastical retribution, which might cause him to lose his position in the First Council of the Seventy or in the church. Roberts died the next month before he was able to raise the funds necessary to publish TWL.[84] Roberts family members tell the story that the day he died, Joseph Fielding Smith went into Roberts's office and took his manuscripts of TWL.[85]

Even though neither Joseph Fielding Smith nor Roberts obtained church approval to publish their respective views when the matter was decided in April 1931, Smith outlived Roberts and those sympathetic to his position. James E.

(Salt Lake City: Church of Jesus Christ of Latter-day Saints, 1932) that it contains "a Full Report of All the Discourses." Forty-seven years later this discourse was finally published in *Sunstone*; see Stephen L. Richards, "Bringing Humanity to the Gospel," *Sunstone* 4 (May-June 1979), 43-46.

80. B. H. Roberts, "What College Did to My Religion," *Improvement Era* 36 (Mar. 1933): 262.

81. "Foreword," *Discourses of B. H. Roberts* [ed. Elsie Cook] (Salt Lake City: Deseret Book Co., 1948), [7].

82. George Albert Smith to Rudger Clawson, 10 Oct. 1929, in Roberts Correspondence at BYU.

83. Lloyd Diary, 7 Aug. 1933.

84. Unlike President Joseph F. Smith, who died in 1918 with an estate worth $421,783 and a net worth of $415,180, Roberts was not wealthy and at his death his net worth was only $348. See D. Michael Quinn, "The Mormon Hierarchy, 1832-1932: An American Elite," Ph.D. diss., Yale University, 1976, 141, 149-50, 154.

85. Richard Hollingshaus to Duane E. Jeffery, 23 Nov. 1975, located in Duane E. Jeffery Collection, Accession 1372, Manuscripts Division, Marriott Library (hereafter Jeffery).

Talmage had also died in 1933, and by the end of 1952 John A. Widtsoe and Joseph F. Merrill—two others who were both apostles and scientists—died. Then in 1953 Smith began giving public discourses on the origin of humanity, using a literalistic interpretation of scripture and deriding the theories of scientists. He also made minor revisions updating his own book-length manuscript, asked Mormon scientist Melvin Cook to offer suggested improvements,[86] and in April 1954 published it as *Man: His Origin and Destiny.*

In this volume Smith quoted various LDS leaders, but the professionally trained scientists among the apostles (Talmage, Widtsoe, and Merrill) were not even mentioned. Smith stated the following about pre-Adamites, again without mentioning B. H. Roberts: "There is no Redeemer other than Jesus Christ for this earth and since Adam could not have brought death on pre-Adamite life, such life could not obtain the blessings of the resurrection. Yet the Lord has declared that through the atonement all things partaking of the fall will be redeemed. So there were no pre-Adamites."[87]

Pointing out that the Piltdown Man was discovered in 1953 to be a forgery, Smith announced with great delight:

> The advocates of this pernicious theory [organic evolution] go to the most ridiculous lengths and resort to the most absurd conclusions based on imaginary discoveries and fables. They are possessed with imaginary minds and when the facts fail them, as the facts always do, they can create species and groups and supply missing parts which in their imaginations disappeared millions of years ago. . . . In all of these "finds" the wish has been father to the thought, so overly anxious have these "discoverers" been to find some connecting links between man and the lower animals that would give evidence of a common origin. These "missing links" have not been forthcoming and the plotters have been forced to resort to fraud and deception to bolster up their futile attempts to prove a Satan-inspired cause, the real purpose being to destroy faith in God.[88]

Duane E. Jeffery, professor of zoology at Brigham Young University, states concerning *Man: His Origin and Destiny:*

> The work marks a milestone. For the first time in Mormon history, and capping a full half-century of publication of Mormon books on science and religion, Mormonism had a book that was openly antagonistic to much of science. The long-standing concern of past Church presidents was quickly realized: the book was hailed by many

86. Melvin A. Cook to Joseph Fielding Smith, 4 Mar. 1954, in Melvin A. Cook Collection, Accession 1148, Manuscripts Division, Marriott Library.

87. Joseph Fielding Smith, *Man: His Origin and Destiny* (Salt Lake City: Deseret Book Co., 1954), 279.

88. Ibid., 157.

as an authoritative Church statement that immediately locked Mormonism into direct confrontation with science, and sparked a wave of religious fundamentalism that shows little sign of abatement.[89]

Henry Eyring, dean of the University of Utah graduate school and an eminent LDS scientist, responded to Smith's book by saying that "the consensus of opinion among the foremost earth scientists places the beginning of life on this earth back at about one billion years and the earth itself as two or three times that old."[90]

In late June 1954 Joseph Fielding Smith, quoting numerous times from his recently-published book, told Mormon seminary and institute of religion teachers at Brigham Young University that "the hypothesis of organic evolution is one of the most cunningly devised among the fables" made by men.[91] A little over a week later J. Reuben Clark, Jr., second counselor in the First Presidency, delivered to the same audience his speech on when the teachings of church leaders are scripture, explaining that "when any man, except the President of the Church, undertakes to proclaim one unsettled doctrine, as among two or more doctrines in dispute, as the settled doctrine of the Church, we may know that he is not 'moved upon by the Holy Ghost,' unless he is acting under the authority of the President."[92] Clark's speech amounts to a response to, and rebuke of, Smith's remarks nine days earlier.

Joseph Fielding Smith died in July 1972 and his *Man: His Origin and Destiny* was reprinted for the last time the next year; it had gone through seven printings and more than 31,000 copies were published.

After Harold B. Lee succeeded Smith as church president, there were renewed negotiations to publish the TWL. Truman G. Madsen, a professor of philosophy and religion at BYU, during a lecture to his school's philosophy colloquium in October 1973 announced that President Lee wanted TWL to be published and

89. Duane E. Jeffery, "Seers, Savants and Evolution: The Uncomfortable Interface," *Dialogue: A Journal of Mormon Thought* 8 (1973): 65-66; reprinted in Sessions and Oberg, *Search for Harmony*, 176.

90. Henry Eyring to Adam S. Bennion, 16 Dec. 1954, Henry Eyring Collection, Manuscript 477, Box 22, Fd 5, Manuscripts Division, Marriott Library. Eyring referred to the geological record as "the Creator's revelations written in the rocks" and went on to say: "The world is filled with radioactive clocks, . . . The radioactive clocks, together with the orderly way many sediments containing fossils are laid down, prove that the earth is billions of years old. In my judgement anyone who denies this orderly deposition of sediments with their built in radioactive clocks places himself in a scientifically untenable position."

91. Joseph Fielding Smith, "Discusses Organic Evolution Opposed to Divine Revelation," Church News Section, *Deseret News*, 24 July 1954, 4.

92. J. Reuben Clark, Jr., "When Are Church Leader's [*sic*] Words Entitled to Claim of Scripture," Church News Section, *Deseret News*, 31 July 1954, 11.

that it would be published in 1974.[93] Lee's unexpected death in December 1973 scuttled these plans.

In 1973 Duane E. Jeffery wrote an article on organic evolution and was allowed to mention Roberts's manuscript in a footnote since Madsen had been officially commissioned to write on it.[94] The next year Davis Bitton, who as assistant church historian had access to the manuscripts of TWL in LDS Church Archives, wrote a still-unpublished paper on Roberts's "masterwork."[95] In 1975 Madsen analyzed the role of Jesus Christ in TWL and included short quotations from numerous chapters.[96] He then devoted a chapter on TWL in his 1980 biography of B. H. Roberts.[97] That same year Richard Sherlock published an article surveying the controversy between Roberts and Smith on evolution and pre-Adamites.[98]

By mid-1981 photocopies of a group of TWL chapters—chapters 24-26, 30-32, 37, and the appendage to 55—had begun circulating among LDS researchers. From these newly-surfaced chapters of TWL, chapter 26 was published in *The Seventh East Press*, an unofficial BYU student newspaper, in December 1981.[99] Continuing his interest in TWL, Truman Madsen published an article in 1988 on Roberts's analysis of the doctrine of the Atonement in the Book of Mormon.[100]

---

93. Truman G. Madsen, Philosophy Colloquium, Brigham Young University, Provo, 18 Oct. 1973, notes taken by Duane E. Jeffery, in Buerger, Bx 10, Fd 5.

94. Jeffery, "Seers, Savants and Evolution," 75n86; reprinted in Session and Oberg, *Search for Harmony*, 186n54. See Duane E. Jeffery to Richard Hollingshaus, 25 Nov. 1975, located in Jeffery.

95. Bitton, "The Truth," in Buerger, Bx 10, Fd 7.

96. Madsen, "Meaning," 259-92.

97. Madsen, *Defender*, 338-45.

98. Sherlock, "We Can See No Advantage," 63-78; reprinted in Sherlock and Keller, "B. H. Roberts . . . Affair," in Sessions and Oberg, *Search for Harmony*, 93-115. Sherlock read TWL at LDS Archives in the early 1970s and was told that the manuscript would be open to researchers after Madsen's study appeared (see Richard Sherlock to Everett L. Cooley, 25 Jan. 1981, in Everett L. Cooley Collection, Accession 73, Manuscripts Division, Marriott Library). Since Madsen's article was published in 1975, Sherlock erroneously stated in note 2 of his 1980 *Dialogue* article that TWL "has recently been made available to researchers by the First Presidency." Sherlock's assumption was wrong because the promise of publication had not been fulfilled.

99. B. H. Roberts, "The Truth, The Way, The Life: An Elementary Treatise on Theology [chapter 26]," *Seventh East Press* 1 (1 Dec. 1981): 6-7, 12. Page 16 of the eighteen-page chapter was accidentally placed between pages 6 and 7, resulting in the misplacement of two paragraphs of Roberts's text.

100. Truman G. Madsen, "B. H. Roberts: The Book of Mormon and the Atonement," in *The Book of Mormon: First Nephi, The Doctrinal Foundation*, eds. Monte S. Nyman and

As of 1985 twenty-three chapters were still missing in the TWL text available outside LDS Archives. This material included places where words were illegible. In addition, entire pages were missing and poor photocopies made it unclear whether Roberts intended the material as part of the text or as a footnote. In spite of these problems Brian H. Stuy in 1984 published the available chapters as "excerpts" from Roberts's TWL.[101]

In January 1992 Edwin B. Firmage donated to the University of Utah Marriott Library his personal copy of Roberts's typed manuscript of TWL. It contains the entire fifty-five chapters.[102] Previously the library's B. H. Roberts Collection was missing the following chapters: 4-5, 11-19, 22-23, 29, 36, 38, 46-48, 50-53; as well as pages 3-4 of the introduction and pages 13 and 15 of chapter 3. These 330 missing pages amounted to 42 percent of the entire manuscript.

The provenance of the Firmage manuscript of "The Truth, The Way, The Life," which is used in the present edition, is as follows. Firmage received the manuscript from his maternal grandfather, Hugh B. Brown, in the late 1960s. Brown had admired Roberts, and they often traveled together and spoke from the same pulpit. Brown reminisced that Roberts "became my ideal so far as public speaking was concerned and contributed much to my own knowledge of the gospel and to my own methods of presenting it."[103] In the mid-1960s Brown became concerned that "Joseph Fielding Smith, long a fierce rival of Roberts and opponent to publication of the [TWL] manuscript, might destroy this document upon becoming President of the Church."[104] Brown was then first counselor to President David O. McKay and essentially acting president of the church due to the declining health of McKay, who was *non compos mentis* from mid-1965 until his death in January 1970. Brown, on his own authority as a member of the First Presidency, made a copy of Roberts's manuscript of TWL and gave it to his grandson, Edwin B. Firmage, with instructions that it be preserved.

When Firmage donated the manuscript of "The Truth, The Way, The Life" to the Marriott Library on 16 January 1992, he stated that he was not claiming

---

Charles D. Tate, Jr. (Provo, UT: Religious Studies Center, Brigham Young University, 1988), 297-314.

101. B. H. Roberts, *Excerpts from The Truth, The Way, The Life: An Elementary Treatise on Theology* [ed. Brian H. Stuy] (Provo, UT: B. H. S[tuy]., [1984]).

102. Actually, the manuscript of TWL donated by Firmage was missing page 10 of chapter 3, but a photocopy of this page was supplied by an individual living in Salt Lake City.

103. Hugh B. Brown, *An Abundant Life: The Memoirs of Hugh B. Brown*, ed. Edwin B. Firmage (Salt Lake City: Signature Books, 1988), 17.

104. Edwin B. Firmage to Stan Larson, 31 Jan. 1992.

copyright to TWL or that he necessarily wanted or did not want TWL to be published.[105] After receiving his gift, I informed Firmage that I intended to edit TWL for publication.

Because the LDS church has restricted its B. H. Roberts Collection (Manuscript 1278), Roberts's papers there cannot be examined. This includes the following three "drafts" of TWL: (a) Draft #1 (hereafter Ms I), an early typed draft with handwritten additions probably done in New York in 1927; (b) Draft #2 (hereafter Ms II), a clean typescript incorporating suggested additions from Ms I, with additional handwritten corrections; and (c) Draft #3 (hereafter Ms III), a carbon copy of the clean typescript of Ms II, with typed additions of the handwritten corrections in Ms II, and further handwritten corrections, as well as material dated from 1929, 1930 and 1931. The manuscript at the Marriott Library is a copy of the most important of the three drafts—Ms III.[106]

EDITORIAL APPROACH

My rationale in the present volume has been to provide an accurate and complete text of TWL, using mainly the latest of the three manuscripts. However, to present the final wording intended by Roberts, this edition is necessarily an eclectic text, because unintentional errors in the manuscript have been corrected (with the reading of the manuscript given in the notes). I do not suggest which are Roberts's stronger points and which are weaker—determining the validity of Roberts's arguments is reserved for the reader. The following are the major guidelines used in producing this edition.

The underlining in the text of TWL, which is here printed as italics, has been retained. If needed for consistency or better readability, periods, commas, apostrophes, colons, semicolons, quotation marks, question marks, capitals, hyphens, and dashes have been deleted, changed, or silently introduced into the text. Spelling errors have been changed. The ampersand (&) has been expanded to "and," except in the abbreviation "D&C." Sometimes paragraphing has been modified. The use of asterisks (* * *) by Roberts to indicate the omission of short or long segments in

105. This donation was added as part of the 1992 addendum to the Edwin B. Firmage Collection, Accession 1074, Boxes 44-45, and placed in the Manuscripts Division, Marriott Library.

106. Having access to Ms I and Ms II (which only contains chapters 29-55) would answer some technical questions and show more of the development of Roberts's ideas, but Ms III is the most important since it indicates Roberts latest intentions, including notes up to April 1931. It would have been even more valuable to examine in the Roberts Collection at LDS Archives his notebooks on TWL and the annotations in his personal copies of the various works he quoted from.

a quotation has been altered to the current style of using an ellipsis of three periods. There were a few instances where verbs were changed to either a singular or plural form to provide grammatical agreement with the subject, or where nouns used as adjectives have been changed to their adjectival forms. The insertion of *sic* has been made in a few instances to indicate that the wording is exactly as given.

Words unintentionally repeated in the original and other inadvertent and typographical errors have been silently corrected. Sometimes an internal quotation within a paragraph has been set apart as an indented block quotation, requiring minimal rearrangement of the introductory wording. Unexpectedly, it was often found that what appeared in the typed Ms III to be Roberts's wording was in fact a verbatim quotation by Roberts from another source—accordingly such sections were indented as block quotations, with the identifying bibliographic reference added. However, Roberts also extensively quotes from his own previously-published articles and books (especially the five volumes of *The Seventy's Course in Theology*), but such quotations are not set off as block quotations.

To distinguish clearly between Roberts's comments and my own, parentheses in the text and square brackets in quotations enclose Roberts's comments, while carets surround my editorial additions in both the text and quotations. Footnotes by me are placed at the bottom of the page among the footnotes by Roberts, but are enclosed by carets and have "—*Ed.*" at the end. The printed text represents the latest form intended by Roberts, incorporating his interlinear or marginal revisions.

Sometimes the printed text follows the wording in the quoted source, but the incorrect text of TWL may also be given in the footnote as "Ms III." In many places where the earlier text of TWL has some interest, the original reading of the third draft of TWL (indicated by the term "Ms III*") is cited in the careted footnotes, with enough context given to understand what was changed. This provides a glimpse into Roberts's wording in Ms III before his own correction. The "Ms III*" readings fall into two categories: (1) the original text of Ms III before being *revised* or (2) the original text of Ms III before being *deleted*. Sometimes it is helpful to know what words were *added* to the original text of Ms III—these later additions are indicated in the footnotes by the term "Ms III^{c}," and show how the "Ms III*" developed into the printed text. There are two instances where it is necessary to distinguish not between an original and a revised reading of Ms III, but a revised text made *in response to* the reading committee report of May 1930. These cases are indicated by "Ms III^{2}" and are located in chapters 16 and 27. Again it must be emphasized that the manuscript readings of Ms III cited in the careted footnotes are only a selection of the manuscript changes—I have chosen those instances that reveal alterations or refinements in Roberts's thinking.

There are a few instances of accidental doubling in "Ms III*," which suggest that Roberts was reading from an earlier draft of TWL and unintentionally his eye skipped *up* one line, resulting in a doubling of the text (see an example in chapter 34). On the other hand, there are cases of unintentional omission in "Ms III*," in which his eye skipped *down* one line (see examples in chapters 9, 11, 12, 33, 35, 43, 44, 49, and 50). This supports the view that TWL went through at least one earlier revision.

There are several indications that Roberts dictated the text to his secretary, Elsie Cook. For example, in chapter 1 during a quotation from John W. Draper the error "science" is typed instead of the correct "sense," in chapter 8 in a quote from Herbert Spencer the heraldic term "naissant" is typed for the correct "nascent," in chapter 9 in a quote from John Stuart Mill the homophone "reigns" is typed instead of the correct "reins," in chapter 19 the misspelling "Syphians" is typed for the correct "Scythians," in chapter 31 "the *most* Mousterian epoch" is found, probably because Roberts re-pronounced the term "Mousterian" as he was reading from a newspaper account, in chapter 42 quoting Acts 17:27 the error "happily" appears instead of "haply" (meaning, "perchance"), in chapter 46 quoting 2 Timothy 2:18 the spelling "passed" is used for "past," in chapter 47 error "event" is typed instead of the correct "advent," in chapter 48 the homophone "adherence" occurs for "adherents," and likewise, in chapter 51 the homophone "straight" appears for "strait." All of these *sound* very much alike.

The concurrence of both types of errors mentioned in the two previous paragraphs indicates that Roberts, reading from an earlier draft of TWL, dictated the text to Cook. Roberts in performing his task occasionally misread the text, and Cook, likewise, at times misheard the dictated text.

In quotations from the scriptures Roberts introduced quotation marks to show the words spoken by an individual. Roberts applied this valuable device sporadically, so I have introduced them more consistently. Likewise, Roberts often capitalized second- and third-person pronouns referring to God, so I have made this a consistent practice. The scriptural references, which Roberts usually gives as footnotes, have been standardized in the form "John 14:6" and placed in parentheses in the text at the end of the quotation. The standard LDS abbreviations for scriptural references have been used. Minor errors in the references have been silently corrected. If Roberts does not supply the reference for a scriptural quotation, this has been silently added at the end of the quotation within the usual parentheses. The editorial addition of "cf." within these parentheses and before the scriptural citation indicates that there is some variation in Roberts's quotation from the King James Version text of the Bible or the other LDS scriptures.

The titles to books, which Roberts generally enclosed by quotation marks or typed in full capitals, have been converted to italics and cited in accordance with modern bibliographic style, often with additional information on full name of author, complete title, publication place, publisher, and year. These improvements have been made in both the footnotes and the "References" column of the synopses at the beginning of each chapter, but not in the text proper of TWL. Two examples of this bibliographic expansion will show how the references have been modified: (1) in chapter 38 Roberts's reference to "Biblical Theological and Ecclesiastical Enc. by McClintoc & Strong" has been changed to "John M'Clintock and James Strong, 'Melchizedek,' *Cyclopædia of Biblical, Theological, and Ecclesiastical Literature*"; and (2) in chapter 42 Roberts's reference to "Nelsons's 'Bible Treasury'" has been corrected to "William Wright, ed., *The Illustrated Bible Treasury* (New York: Thomas Nelson and Sons, 1896)." If the bibliographic reference is wholly my work, it is enclosed within carets.

The purpose of my footnotes is to cite the variant manuscript readings of Roberts's Ms III, but the footnotes also update some of the scientific information which has changed in the last six decades, refer to modern scholarly studies on the topic at hand, and point out textual problems in scriptural passages. If readers are interested in seeing Roberts's manuscript just as he last left it, they can examine it in the Manuscripts Division of the Marriott Library at the University of Utah.

I believe the present publication fulfills B. H. Roberts's intention by printing the complete text of his Ms III of TWL. Nothing has been left out, including valuable material that Roberts indicated should be added to chapter 31. Truman G. Madsen argues that if Roberts were "alive today, he would likely be anxious that the book remain unpublished. He had, in fact, begun to feel that way before his death."[107] Wesley P. Lloyd's diary provides contemporary evidence against Madsen's position, since it records Roberts's decision in 1933 to publish TWL "without Church backing."[108]

The first public announcement of this edition of TWL was given on 6 February 1992 in Salt Lake City at a meeting of the B. H. Roberts Society. The following year in May I sent letters to descendants of B. H. Roberts, asking their permission to publish TWL, since copyright to TWL resides in Roberts's heirs. Roberts's descendants from his wife, Sarah Louisa Smith, and his polygamous wife, Celia Dibble, gave their approval. (There were no children by his post-Manifesto wife, Margaret Curtis Shipp.) Two months later I attended the B. H. Roberts Family Reunion, where I explained to descendants the current project. The next month at the annual Sunstone Symposium in Salt Lake City I presented a paper on "The Controversy concerning B. H. Roberts's Unpublished Manuscript 'The Truth, The Way, The Life,'" reviewing Roberts's difficulties with church leaders.

In September 1993 I met with John W. Welch, editor of *Brigham Young University Studies* which is producing a separate edition of TWL, about collaborating

107. Madsen, *Defender*, 345.

108. Lloyd Diary, 7 Aug. 1933.

with him. Welch decided against any joint effort. Two months later he announced publicly that the TWL manuscript at the LDS Church Archives had been "newly released."[109] After reading about this "release" of TWL, I went to the archives but found that their Roberts Collection was still closed. I then decided to make a minor request of LDS Archives: to examine just one page of the manuscript. The Firmage manuscript lacks the footnotes at the bottom of the fifth page of chapter 1, since the bottom third of the page had been covered by a handwritten note attached by Roberts himself. In January 1994 LDS Archives granted me permission to examine this one page of Ms III of TWL in their Roberts Collection. I discovered that under the pinned-on note was a previously unknown footnote by Roberts, which is now printed as the twelfth note of chapter 1. The cooperation of LDS Archives in this matter is gratefully acknowledged.

B. H. Roberts would be flattered with the recent revival of interest in his work. Though it is sixty-one years after his death, his long-cherished desire to publish "The Truth, The Way, The Life" is now fulfilled. The volume stands as a testament to his insight into LDS gospel principles and to his courage in stating his opinion in spite of ecclesiastical pressure from higher church authorities.

---

109. John W. Welch, "B. H. Roberts Affirms Book of Mormon Antiquity in Newly Released Manuscript," *Insights: An Ancient Window*, no. 6 (Nov. 1993): 2.

ACKNOWLEDGMENTS

Edwin B. Firmage's donation to the University of Utah Marriott Library of his copy of Roberts's "The Truth, The Way, The Life" ensured preservation of Roberts's masterwork in its entirety.

Gregory C. Thompson of Special Collections, Marriott Library, University of Utah, allowed the Firmage copy to be used as the base text for this edition and offered encouragement and advice throughout the project. Nancy V. Young, of the Manuscripts Division, allowed me to examine materials kept in the division safe. Walter Jones of the Western Americana Division provided me with a secure place to keep the working copy of the manuscript. Madelyn D. Garrett of the Rare Books Division retrieved many rare books, cited by Roberts. Linda L. Burns of the Interlibrary Loan Department acquired numerous volumes not available in Utah.

Larry W. Draper supplied many entries for the bibliography of selected publications by B. H. Roberts.

Paul M. Tinker provided important information at a critical time during the publication process.

Staff members of the Harold B. Lee Library at Brigham Young University, the library of the Utah State Historical Society, and the archives of the Church of Jesus Christ of Latter-day Saints, were also very helpful.

Special thanks to Leonard J. Arrington, Sterling M. McMurrin, Erich Robert Paul, and Thom D. Roberts for their contributions.

The accuracy of this volume has been improved by the corrections offered by Brian H. Stuy, but I am fully responsible for any errors.

THE TRUTH, THE WAY, THE LIFE
An Elementary Treatise on Theology

By

ELDER B. H. ROBERTS

Senior President of the First Council of the Seventy

Author of
New Witnesses for God (3 vols.)
Outlines of Ecclesiastical History
Mormon Doctrine of Deity
Defense of the Faith and the Saints (2 vols.)
Comprehensive History of the Church, Century I (6 vols.)
Etc., Etc., Etc.

In One Volume
and
Three Parts

Religion, to be effective, must appeal to the understanding as well as to the emotions of man.

PART I
THE TRUTH

"I am . . . the Truth."

THE CHRIST TO ST. THOMAS, JOHN 14:6

"Truth's a gem that loves the deep."

THE BASIS OF RESEARCH

Say first of God above and man below,
How can we reason but from what we know?

ALEXANDER POPE, "AN ESSAY ON MAN"

INTRODUCTION[1]

The Right of Man to Know the Meaning of Life

All men know that they must die. And it is important that we should understand the reasons and causes of our exposure to the vicissitudes of life and of death, and the designs and purposes of God in our coming into the world, our sufferings here, and our departure hence. What is the object of our coming into existence, then dying and falling away, to be here no more? It is but reasonable to suppose that God would reveal something in reference to the matter, and it is a subject we ought to study more than any other. We ought to study it day and night, for the world is ignorant in reference to their true condition and relation. If we have any claim on our Heavenly Father for anything, it is for knowledge on this important subject (Joseph Smith, *History of the Church, Period I: History of Joseph Smith, the Prophet by Himself*, ed. B. H. Roberts, 6:50).

It is not only a privilege but a duty for the saints to seek unto the Lord their God for wisdom and understanding, to be in possession of the Spirit that fills the heavens, until their eyes are anointed and opened to see the world as it really is . . . to look through the "why's" and "wherefore's" of the existence of man, like looking through a piece of glass perfectly transparent, and understand the design of the Creator[2] of this beautiful creation (Brigham Young).[3]

This treatise is to be a search for THE TRUTH, as it relates to the universe and to man; a consideration of THE WAY, as it relates to the attainment of those ends which may be learned as to the purpose of man's earth-existence; and the

1. EDITOR'S NOTE: In the text of TWL the parenthetical comments by B. H. Roberts are enclosed by parentheses. In quotations included in the text, explanations by the author of the quote are enclosed by parentheses ( ) and comments concerning the quote inserted by Roberts are enclosed by square brackets [ ]. Throughout the text, quotations, and footnotes of TWL the additions by the editor are enclosed by carets < >.

2. <The printed text in the *Journal of Discourses* has "understand the design of the Great Maker"—*Ed.*>

3. <The handwritten Ms III[c] adds "Discourse of Brigham Young, June 13, 1852 Des. News, vol. iv, no. 6," but the quotation is from Brigham Young's discourse delivered on 8 May 1853, entitled "President B. Young's Journey South—Indian Difficulties—Walker—Watching and Prayer—Thieves and Their Deserts—Eastern Intelligence—Financial State of the Church—Gaining Knowledge," *Journal of Discourses* 1 (1854): 111—*Ed.*>

contemplation of THE LIFE, that will result from the knowledge of the Truth and the Way.

It is to be a new study of an old theme: "The Whence," "The Why," and "The Whither" of human existence. It intends to find out whether or not there is any purpose in human life; any scheme of things in the universe; and if ordinary men may cognize them and follow them. Is there a TRUTH, a WAY, a LIFE, that can be made to appeal to reason as well as to faith? Can it be made to satisfy the understanding as well as the longings of the human heart? Will it lead to something more than a "pleasing hope," a "fond desire," a mere "longing after immortality"? Or shall we accept the last statement and what is described as the most characteristic sentences of Professor William James, the American philosopher and psychologist, which he left written upon his desk at his death, namely:

> There is no conclusion. What has concluded, that we might conclude in regard to it? There are no fortunes to be told, and there is no advice to be given. Farewell![4]

To find all this out is the task we set before us; and when we contemplate the largeness of the theme, the height and the depth of it, and recall how many world-geniuses have wrecked their thought upon it, we marvel at the audacity that dares to attempt so much!

Yet there is great need that someone should seek to bring forth to the clear understanding of men the Truth, the Way, and the Life, for there is great confusion existing among men on these matters of such high import.

If the author of this proposed treatise were depending upon his own learning, or on any way of wisdom in himself to justify the investigation of these high themes, then he would not only shrink from the task, but would abandon it altogether, as being inadequate to such an undertaking. But the author believes himself to be living in what, in the parlance of his faith, is called the "Dispensation of the Fullness of Times," in which a great volume of Truth has been revealed in addition to, but in harmony with, the Truth revealed in former dispensations. In fact, in this "Dispensation of the Fullness of Times" all Truth of former dispensations and the whole volume of it, is being merged into a unity. The veil of mystery is being rent to reveal the things of God in their completeness and it is upon the basis of this more-fully-revealed knowledge that the author ventures to speak, rather than from any learning or intellectual excellence in himself.

The method of approach to the heart of the general theme is through the apparently paradoxical mental process of assuming that:

---

4. <This statement by James was actually published one month before his death as the final words to his last-written essay, "A Pluralistic Mystic," *The Hibbert Journal* 8 (July 1910): 739-59–*Ed.*>

I know in order that I may believe;
I believe in order that I may know.

In other words, the author is seeking a basis for faith in the revealed things of God by examination of the things we know. Nor in this does he recognize any inconsistency in seeking for belief in revealed Truth from a basis of knowledge. "Faith is . . . the evidence of things not seen" (Heb. 11:1), says St. Paul; and "evidence" must be the things known that lead to belief, which is "faith" in its simplest forms. Speaking of belief in God, Paul asks, "How shall they believe in him of whom they have not heard, and how shall they hear without a preacher?" (Rom. 10:14)—one sent to teach them. "So, then, faith cometh by hearing" (Rom. 10:17)—by hearing the evidence on which faith in its simplest form necessarily rests, from which evidence faith struggles into existence and develops into robust life that shall enable it at last to attain to the sublime power of accepting and enduring as seeing that which is invisible. But one must find some basis of knowledge, some ground of evidence from which he may believe; from which ground of faith he may arise to the higher knowledge of things as they are.

One other working principle will frequently recur in the treatise—"how can we reason but from what we know?"[5] Accepting the implication of the question as true, knowledge again becomes imperative, and hence our opening division of the treatise, what is Truth and how much do we know of it? And what foundation does it lay for that faith which leads to the realization of the deeper and higher truths of life, and its purposes, and of God?

The answer to these[6] questions we trust will be found in the text of the discussion which follows.

It has been suggested that this work could be used to advantage as a textbook on theology, and to make it available for such use each chapter has been constructed in a manner and given such relation to the developing theme that it may be so utilized. Also, a Lesson Analysis has been made for each chapter with collected References so that the textbook idea may be easily put into effect. These Lesson Analyses with accompanying References are printed as addenda at the end of the volume.[7]

---

5. <Alexander Pope, "An Essay on Man," in Pat Rogers, ed., *Alexander Pope* (Oxford: Oxford University Press, 1993), 270-309—*Ed.*>

6. <Ms III[c] adds "se" to make "these"—*Ed.*>

7. <As stated here, Roberts's original idea was to have all the lesson analyses gathered at the end of TWL. However, he later decided to disperse these analyses to the beginning of each individual chapter. Since the manuscript of TWL represents this later decision, this format is followed in the present edition—*Ed.*>

CHAPTER I

Dissertation on Truth

SCRIPTURE READING LESSON*

Analysis #

I. Pilate's Question: What Is Truth?
   Answer of Jesus: Silence!
   Former Answer: "I Am . . . the Truth and the Life."

II. Despair of the Ancients over Truth.
   Doubt of the Moderns.
   Definition of Truth.

III. Inspired Definition—Joseph Smith:
   (a) Relative Truth
   (b) Absolute Truth
   (c) "The Sum of Existence"—Complete Truth.

IV. The World's Best Hope: Progress in the Knowledge of the Truth.

V. Workers in the Field of Truth.

VI. Ode to Truth.

References

John 18:33-38; 14:6.

Robert Jamieson, A. R. Fausset, and David Brown, A *Commentary: Critical, Practical, and Explanatory of the Old and New Testaments*, 4 vols. (New York: Funk and Wagnalls, 1888); also John R. Dummelow, ed., *A Commentary on the Holy Bible by Various Writers, Complete in One Volume* (New York: The Macmillan Co., 1922); John 18; Herbert Spencer, *First Principles*, A System of Synthetic Philosophy, no. 1. (New York: D. Appleton, 1896), 141; John Fiske, *Outlines of Cosmic Philosophy*, 1:102-103.

D&C 93.

Jacob 4:13.

Sacred Hymns and Spiritual Songs for the Church of Jesus Christ of Latter-day Saints, 24th ed. (Salt Lake City: The Deseret News Co., 1905), 71-72.

*The selection of these scripture lessons should be assigned to class members in advance; in making selection special reference should be made to suitableness to the lesson subject. For the present lesson and as a sample selection St. John 18:33-38 is proposed.

#The subdivisions of the lesson analysis may be used as lesson assignments.

CHAPTER I

Dissertation on Truth

Taking up the terms of our title in the order in which I have placed them, we come to the first member, the TRUTH. Logical order of procedure requires that we say something of Truth at the very beginning of our treatise.

"What is Truth?" inquired Pontius Pilate of Jesus of Nazareth when the latter had just told him that it was his mission in life to bear witness unto the Truth (John 18:37-38). Jesus was silent. On a previous occasion he had said, "I am . . . the Truth and the Way"[1] (cf. John 14:6).

"Thou stirrest the question of questions," says a standard commentary on the Bible, when dealing with this passage, "which the thoughtful of every age has asked, but never man yet answered."[2]

Another writer of note, also a modern—1875—commenting upon the question Pilate asked the Christ, remarks: "Often and vainly has that demand been made <before>—often and vainly has it been made since. No one has yet given a satisfactory answer." Then by way of historical illustration of this assertion, our author goes on to say:

> When, at the dawn of science in Greece, the ancient religion was disappearing like a mist at sunrise, the pious and thoughtful men of that country were drawn into a condition of intellectual despair:
>
> Anaxagoras plaintively exclaims, "Nothing can be known, nothing can be learned, nothing can be certain, sense is limited,[3] intellect is weak, life is short."
>
> Xenophanes tells us that it is impossible for us to be certain, even when we utter the truth.
>
> Parmenides declares that the very constitution of man prevents him from ascertaining absolute truth.

---

1. <Ms III^c adds the typewritten "Jesus was silent. On a previous occasion he had said, 'I am * * * The Truth and The Way'"—*Ed.*>

2. Robert Jamieson, A. R. Fausset, and David Brown, *A Commentary: Critical, Practical, and Explanatory of the Old and New Testaments*, 4 vols. (New York: Funk and Wagnalls, 1888), comment on St. John 18:37-38.

3. <Ms III "science is limited," but Draper's text has "sense"—*Ed.*>

> Empedocles affirms that all philosophical and religious systems must be unreliable, because we have no criterion by which to test them.
>
> Democritus asserts that even things that are true can not impart certainty to us; that the final result of human inquiry is the discovery that man is incapable of absolute knowledge; that, even if the truth be in his possession, he can not be certain of it.
>
> Pyrrho bids us reflect on the necessity of suspending our judgment of things, since we have no criterion of truth. So deep a distrust did he impart to his followers that they were in the habit of saying, "We assert nothing; <no,> not even that we assert nothing."
>
> Epicurus taught his disciples that truth can never be determined by reason.
>
> Arcesilaus, denying both intellectual and sensuous knowledge, publicly avowed that he knew nothing—not even his own ignorance!
>
> The general conclusion to which Greek philosophy came was this—that, in view of the contradiction of the evidence of the senses, we can not distinguish the true from the false, and such is the imperfection of reason, that we can not affirm the correctness of any philosophical deduction.[4]

This rather settles the matter so far as the antique world is concerned; and the remark of the same writer with reference to time since the Christ that "no one had, as yet [i.e., to the time of his writing, 1875], given a satisfactory answer" to Pilate's question, "What is Truth?" would seem to settle the matter equally as well for the modern world. However, it is only proper that we should consider some of the attempted modern definitions of Truth. The one which appears to be most simple, and yet most comprehensive, is that to be found in the *Webster Dictionary* for 1927, and especially under the numeral "4" of this noted work, viz.:

> Truth is . . . conformity to fact or reality; exact accordance with that which is, or has been, or shall be. . . . "The character [i.e., characteristic] of truth is the capability of enduring the test of universal experience and coming unchanged out of every possible form of fair discussion" (Sir J<ohn> Herschel).[5]

---

4. John William Draper, *History of the Conflict between Religion and Science*, 6th ed. (New York: D. Appleton and Co., 1875), 201-202. <Ms III[*] "any philosopher's deduction," but Ms III[c] "any philosophical deduction" brings TWL into agreement with Draper's text—*Ed.*>

5. This definition of truth is not found in Mr. <Noah> Webster's first edition of his *A Compendious Dictionary of the English Language* (n. p.: Sidney's Press, 1806), but is found in *An American Dictionary of the English Language*, the two-volumed edition of 1828 published by S. Converse, New York, and in all subsequent editions. <See *Webster's New International Dictionary of the English Language*, eds. W. T. Harris and F. Sturges Allen (Springfield, Massachusetts: G. and C. Merriam Co., 1927), 2209—*Ed.*>

Mr. Herbert Spencer, author of the *Synthetic Philosophy* and one of the first intellects of the English race, gives as a definition of Truth the following:

> Debarred as we are from everything beyond the relative, truth, raised to its highest form, can be for us nothing more than perfect agreement, throughout the whole range of our experience, between those representations of things which we distinguish as ideal and those presentations of things[6] which we distinguish as real.[7]

John Fiske, the interpreter of Spencer's *Synthetic Philosophy*, defines absolute Truth in these terms: "Truth . . . [is] the correspondence between the subjective order of our conceptions, and the objective order of the relations among things;" but he insists that for this absolute Truth "we can have no criterion." "We can have no criterion of absolute truth, or of truth that is not correlated with the conditions of our intelligence."[8] With David Hume and others he accepts the theory that uniformity of experience is a sufficient criterion for contingent truth, but not of universal or absolute Truth.[9]

With the Hindus "Truth is that which is." This <is> the significance of their word for truth according to Max Müller;[10] and for simplicity and comprehensiveness, comes more near to exactness[11] than the more labored definitions of the Western world. And yet, in reality, comes short of being complete since it takes no account of that "which has been" or that "which shall be"—the becoming—the continual birth of Truth.

Quite unnoticed by the writers of the modern world, however, a book was published in 1830 purporting to be the revealment of an inspired scripture abridged from larger authoritative writings had among the ancient peoples of America, in which one of their inspired teachers is represented as saying:

> He that prophesieth, let him prophesy to the understanding of men; for the Spirit speaketh the truth and lieth not. Wherefore, it speaketh of things as they really are;

---

6. <Ms III "those perfections of things"—*Ed.*>

7. Herbert Spencer, *First Principles*, A System of Synthetic Philosophy, no. 1. (New York: D. Appleton, 1896), 139. In passing it might be asked if the reader can suppose the Christ making an answer to Pilate like Spencer's?

8. John Fiske, *Outlines of Cosmic Philosophy*, in *The Miscellaneous Writings of John Fiske, with Many Portraits of Illustrious Philosophers, Scientists, and Other Men of Note* (Boston: Houghton, Mifflin and Co., 1902), 1:102-103.

9. Ibid., 71-72, cf. 105.

10. F. Max Müller, *India: What Can It Teach Us?* (New York: Longmans, Green, 1910), lecture ii, 102-103.

11. <Ms III "comes more nearly exactness"—*Ed.*>

> and of things as they really will be; wherefore, these things are manifested unto us plainly, for the salvation of our souls (Jacob 4:13).

Again, in 1833, but unknown to Mr. John W. Draper, who in 1875 declared that no satisfactory definition of Truth had yet been written; and before either Mr. Spencer or Mr. Fiske had written their definitions of Truth, there had another voice spoken upon this subject which claimed for itself a divine authority to speak upon this and kindred questions, and this is what it said of truth: "TRUTH IS KNOWLEDGE OF THINGS AS THEY ARE, AND AS THEY WERE, AND AS THEY ARE TO COME" (D&C 93:24).[12]

Our Prophet also taught that "Intelligence is the light of Truth"; or the power by which truth is cognized and absorbed; and which he holds forth as eternal, uncreated and uncreatable; therefore, eternal as truth itself–a parallel existence with Truth: Intelligence–Truth! The Existence–Truth; and the Light which discerns it–Intelligence.[13]

If this is spoken with a divine sanction, under inspiration of God, then it ought to be the completest definition of Truth extant among men.[14] I hold it to be so. It deals with Truth under several aspects: relative truth; absolute Truth; and Truth in the "becoming" or unfolding; and Truth in the sum.

---

12. It might be thought that the definition of truth above taken from the Doctrine and Covenants is suspiciously near to the definition given by Noah Webster in the edition of his dictionary of 1828, and in subsequent editions, and therefore in common use throughout the United States five years before the date of the revelation of May 6, 1833, from which the definition of truth in the text is taken. Webster's definition of truth is: "*Exact accordance with that which is, or has been, or shall be.*" While Joseph Smith's definition is: "*Truth is knowledge of things as they are, and as they were, and as they are to come.*" The uniqueness of Joseph Smith's definition, however, consists in regarding truth as the *knowledge* of things as they are, and as they were, and as they are to come (i.e., as they shall be). All which is worked out in the discussion of the text and lifts, as I trust will be seen, the definition of the revelation far beyond the definition of the dictionary. <The photocopy of TWL in the Edwin B. Firmage Collection at the Marriott Library does not contain this note, because it was covered by Roberts's slip of paper which contains the next paragraph in the body of the text–*Ed.*>

13. <This paragraph is actually a Ms III^{c}, which Roberts wrote on a 3 3/4" x 7 3/4" slip of paper and pinned to TWL, covering up two footnoted scriptural references and a note; the words "and absorbed" are an even later pencilled addition to this slip of paper–*Ed.*>

14. <The October 1929 report of the review committee, headed by George Albert Smith, questioned "the superiority of the Prophet's definition" of truth, though this objection was dropped in the May 1930 report (see "List of Points on Doctrine in Question by the Committee in Relation to B. H. Roberts's Ms," attached to George Albert Smith to Rudger Clawson, 10 Oct. 1929, in B. H. Roberts Correspondence, Manuscript SC 1922, Archives and Manuscripts, Lee Library, Brigham Young University, Provo, Utah)–*Ed.*>

It may be objected to this definition of Truth, that it is defective in that it appears to make Truth dependent upon knowledge. "Truth is *knowledge* of things as they are." The answer to this objection would be that at this point the definition deals with relative truth only. "Truth can only be relative to us," says S. Baring-Gould, "because we are relative creatures, with only a relative perception and judgment. We appreciate that which is true to ourselves—not that which is universally true."[15] In other words, to each individual, knowledge of things as they are and as they were, and as they are to become, will be to him the truth and the fullness thereof, though not necessarily all the Truth that is. This will be each man's truth, or relative truth.

There is Truth, however, beyond relative truth, and independent of any individual's knowledge of it. To illustrate: America existed though all Europe was without knowledge of it for ages; until Columbus discovered it, in fact. The power of steam always existed, but men did not know it until modern times. So also with the mysterious force called electricity, it always existed; but not until recent years did men know it as a force that could be utilized. And so as to many other forces and truths in God's universe that are now existing and have always existed, but man as yet has no knowledge of them. This means merely that the storehouse of Truth is not yet exhausted by man's discoveries. There are more truths in heaven and earth than are yet cognized by man, or dreamed of in human philosophies. It may be, however, that running parallel with those existences and their relations, as yet unknown by man, there may exist intelligences that cognize such existences and such relations. To recur to one item in the illustration above, America existed though all Europe was without knowledge of it until discovered by Columbus; but America had inhabitants, intelligences of her own that knew of the existence of these Western Continents, which were their habitat. And so it might be if one could be transported to Mars. There is much we do not know about Mars. Has it an atmosphere and oceans, for instance? Has it continents and mountain ranges and rivers? Is it inhabited? If so, are the inhabitants of it highly intellectual? If so, what is the present status of their civilization? All these questions relative to life on Mars may yet be answered affirmatively, but our Earth inhabitants as yet do not humanly know of them; but the intelligent inhabitants on Mars (if there be such) would know of these things and a thousand more that are unknown to us.[16] And

15. <Sabine Baring-Gould, *The Origin and Development of Religious Belief* (London: Rivingtons, 1869-1870), 2:41—*Ed.*>

16. <See Michael J. Crowe, *The Extraterrestrial Life Debate, 1750-1900: The Idea of a Plurality of Worlds from Kant to Lowell* (Cambridge: Cambridge University Press, 1986), and Van Hale, "Mormons and Moonmen: A Look at Nineteenth Century Beliefs about the Moon—Its Flora, Its Fauna, Its Folks," *Sunstone* 7 (Sept.-Oct. 1982): 12-17—*Ed.*>

so in like manner as to the most distant planets and planetary systems. Everywhere things exist <that> may be paralleled by existing intelligences that cognize them; and so in the last analysis of the matter, wheresoever there are existences there may be intelligences[17] to cognize them, perhaps control them, dominate them, and through them work out a sovereign will.

All this as to relative truth. This definition under consideration, however, also deals with universal or absolute Truth. When you say that Truth is that which is, that which has been, and that which is to be in future, you circumscribe all there is or can be of Truth. You make it "the sum of existence." You will include the past, present, and future of all existences—their "sum;" and this is Truth: the "sum" of existences[18]—past, present, and yet to be.

It may be said that the absolute Truth as here set forth is beyond the grasp of the finite mind. That is conceded, but because finite mind can not comprehend the sum of existences,[19] the absolute Truth, it does not follow that the definition is at fault, or that it can be displaced by one meaning more or less. Reflection upon the definition here presented will develop the fact that it is a self-evident proposition, it may not be proven by any other thing; but the statement itself is its own proof. The proof is in the fact.

One other reflection on this definition. Note the words: "Knowledge of things . . . as they are to come." This presents a view of Truth seldom, if ever, made. With it is given the idea of movement. Truth is not a stagnant pool, but a living fountain; not a Dead Sea, without tides or currents. On the contrary, it is an ocean, immeasurably great, vast, co-extensive with the universe itself. It is the universe, bright-heaving, boundless, endless, and sublime! Moving in majestic currents, uplifted by cosmic tides in ceaseless ebb and flow, variant but orderly; taking on new forms from ever-changing combinations, new adjustments, new relations—multiplying itself in ten thousand times ten thousand ways, ever reflecting the Intelligence of the Infinite, and declaring alike in its whispers and its thunders the hived wisdom of the ages!

Truth, then, is that which is, which has been, which shall be; it is the sum of existence; and knowledge of so much of all this as each individual intelligence possesses is *his* truth, his measure of himself and of the universe.

Some years ago the question was submitted to the writer for a special article in the Christmas issue of a leading western publication, "What is the World's Best Hope" for a given year?

I confess to an ambition at the time to give an answer that would be worthy

---

17. <Ms III^{c} adds "there may be intelligences"—*Ed.*>

18. <Ms III* "the 'sum' of existence"—*Ed.*>

19. <Ms III* "the sum of existence"—*Ed.*>

not only as the "World's Best Hope" for the specified year, but for all years; all ages and for all time, since the answer was to relate to the whole world. As I thought upon the nature of my answer, the world seemed to rise above the horizon of my consciousness. All the continents and islands; all the seas and oceans–the world's highways between the great divisions of the land; all the nations were before me, all the tribes and the races of men, with all their hopes and fears and varied interests, ranging from barbarism to civilization; all their ambitions, great and small, together with all their plots and counter-plots, race pride and national pride; all their activities in trade and commerce; all their plans for peace and their preparations for war; all the fierce struggle for existence, both among savage men and civilized. Also, all their philosophies and all their religions; their relations to time and eternity, their hopes of immortality and eternal life–all this arose before me and was to be considered when making my answer.

In fixing upon the answer that would be the "World's Best Hope"–the world thus conceived–it stood as follows: "THE WORLD'S BEST HOPE IS THE WORLD'S CONTINUED PROGRESS IN KNOWLEDGE OF THE TRUTH." That answer was adequate, I shall venture to say as the "World's Best Hope" for any given year, or any series of years, or for any age or series of ages.

Necessarily the answer so given demanded a definition of Truth, and then the definition of Truth was given substantially as in the foregoing pages of this chapter: Truth is that which is, and all that is, or has been, or shall be–Truth, the sum of existence![20]

Then, as now, this brings us face to face with the infinite; for Truth thus conceived is infinite; unlimited; and since progress in the infinite must necessarily be without limits, there is no end to the progress of intelligences in that infinite, the Truth. Man–oh, blessed thought!–may ever be learning and coming to a knowledge of Truth that is infinite. As Truth is infinite, one may not look for finality in respect of progress in that which is infinite. Each goal attained in the Truth will be but a new starting point; an end that but marks a new beginning; while the ultimate of Truth will always be like the horizon one pursues over the ocean–ever receding as one approaches it. One may conceive of the existence of the infinite, but may never hope to encompass it; and hence eternal progress for intelligences which possess innate power to cognize Truth.

WORKERS IN THE FIELD OF TRUTH[21]

But now this continued progress in Truth–in knowledge of the Truth–what

20. <Ms III* "Truth is the sum of existence"–*Ed.*>
21. <Ms III[c] adds "Workers In The Field of Truth"–*Ed.*>

a work it is! And how many are active in it! Some are seeking it by the perusal of the printed tomes of past ages, in the musty manuscripts of old libraries and monasteries. Some of this class are even now pushing back the horizon of recorded knowledge into ages before books were known, and are removing mountains from buried cities to get at the libraries of inscribed clay tablets, the hieroglyphic-covered stone monuments, and engraved plates of bronze and gold. Such is the branch of knowledge men call history and archaeology. They are seekers after Truth, after knowledge of things as they have been. Others are reading the story of the earth's formation in its various strata. They are studying the flora and fauna of bygone ages, seeking to determine the life-forms that once abounded in the earth. Others listen to every tremor of the earth and watch the rise of mountain chains, the slowly sinking shores in other parts; and note the ever-changing contour of oceans and continents. By their patient observation they seek to learn the forces that have been operating in past ages, and that have fashioned the earth to its present form and excellence.

Others are in the laboratories to deal with substance and its elements. These elements they group and analyze, pursuing substance beyond the realm of the senses, down to the mystic borderline where matter seems to shade off into energy, and energy drifts back into what is recognized as matter, until the bewildered students of substance are wondering if in the last analysis of things it will not be found that matter and energy are really one—spirit?

Still others make a study of the heavens. They turn their telescopes upon the fixed stars and measure their wonderful distances from the earth and from each other. They resolve star mist and nebulae into congeries of worlds undreamed of by men of former times. Nay, more; by the aid of photography, which man by his skill has converted into the "wonderful eye of science," he photographs and brings within the realm of his knowledge distant universes, if one may be allowed so to speak—universes that no human eye has ever seen, even aided by the most powerful telescopes; and thus to some purpose indeed he makes "the heavens declare the glory of God; and the firmament to show his handiwork; where day unto day uttereth speech, and night unto night showeth knowledge" (cf. Ps. 19:1-2). Surely "there is no speech nor language where their voice is not heard, and their line has gone out through all the earth, and their words to the end of the world" (Ps. 19:3-4).

Coming back from the contemplation of the heavens to things within our own world, we find some men pursuing Truth in the practical affairs of life, seeking to determine the right relationship of individuals to each other; also the relationship of the individual to society, and society to the individual. Others are seeking to determine the just principles on which the products of man's industry shall be distributed. Others seek to determine the just laws of trade and commerce, and the right attitude of nations toward each other. Still others are seeking Truth by utilizing what, in general terms, we call natural forces, and applying them to industrial and commercial activities. To locomotion on land and sea; to the production of light and heat and mechanical power; thus increasing the supply of the world's necessities, conveniences, comforts, luxuries, and adding to its progress in material ways, until it would seem that millennium conditions dreamed of by saints, sang of by poets, and predicted by prophets, would not only be realized but surpass all the excellence of anticipation, even of inspired anticipation.

Standing in the midst of all the varied seekers after Truth is he who seeks it by faith and prayer, by appeals to God; by the pursuit of it through holy thinking and righteous living; by faithful vigils of the night and words and deeds of charity through the day; who now and then pauses in the solitude of mountain tops, or of desert plains, or silent cloister, or in the crowded streets; and fancies—nay, hears the whisper of the still small voice, which tells him that good angels and God labor with him, confirming his work by giving him assurance that his faith is not vain, and that his spiritually-touched mind really sees God and angels as his co-laborers, and not mere phantoms, creations of the subjective mind. These are, par excellence, seekers after Truth, since they seek the Truth at the very source of it, by communion with and service for God. These are your prophets—world teachers in the ways and in the things of God. Seekers after Truth and teachers of it, with whose services the world may not dispense without sustaining great loss.[22]

Such is the great and varied host of seekers after Truth, and as we contemplate them from the departing days of passing years, we shout to them with all our voice, and say, Success to you! The world's best hope for all time is your continued progress! Seek on, and let each one bring to the service of man that which he shall find of the Truth, confident that the world's progress, the advancement of civilization, man's best welfare, and God's greatest glory will be in exact proportion to your success. Legends, venerable for their age, you may destroy; myths, though beautiful, you may discredit; creeds, formulated on misconceptions of Truth, may crumble at your touch; half-truths, dear to some, you may rend from men's belief. With all these there may go much to which the world has become attached, and your work at times may seem iconoclastic; but in the end all will be well, nothing will perish but that which is false and evil. Truth alone will ultimately survive and endure; and truth, as one of our own poets has said, "Though the heavens depart and the earth's fountains burst, Truth, the sum of existence, will weather the worst."

I say again, the World's Best Hope for all ages to come is the continued progress of man in the knowledge of the Truth—man's progress in "the knowledge of things as they are, and as they have been, and as they are to come."

---

22. <Truman G. Madsen, *Defender of the Faith: The B. H. Roberts Story* (Salt Lake City: Bookcraft, 1980), 340, identifies this paragraph as autobiographical—*Ed.*>

All this concerns our present undertaking, the discussion, of the Truth, the Way, and the Life; and since our accepted definition of Truth is knowledge of that which is, the next logical step in the development of our theme must be, What does man know? And that will be the subject of a few succeeding chapters. However, in closing this opening chapter on Truth, I shall do so by quoting an Ode to Truth, inspired by the definition of Truth given in Joseph Smith's revelation of May 6, 1833, and quoted in the text.

TRUTH

O, say, what is truth? 'Tis the fairest gem
    That the riches of worlds can produce;
And priceless the value of truth will be when
    The proud monarch's costliest diadem

Is counted but dross and refuse.
    Yes, say, what is truth? 'Tis the brightest prize
To which mortals or Gods can aspire;
    Go search in the depths where it glittering lies

Or ascend in pursuit to the loftiest skies;
    'Tis an aim for the noblest desire.
The sceptre may fall from the despot's grasp,
    When with winds of stern justice he copes

But the pillar of truth will endure to the last,
    And its firm-rooted bulwarks outstand the rude blast
And the wreck of the fell tyrant's hopes.
    Then say, what is truth? 'Tis the last and the first,

For the limits of time it steps o'er;
    Though the heavens depart and the earth's fountains burst,
Truth, *the sum of existence*, will weather the worst,
    Eternal, unchanged, evermore.[23]

---

23. The author is John Jaques (1827-1900), member of the LDS Church and Assistant Church Historian; *Sacred Hymns and Spiritual Songs for the Church of Jesus Christ of Latter-day Saints*, 24th ed. (Salt Lake City: The Deseret News Co., 1905), 71-72.

CHAPTER II

Of Knowledge: What Man Knows

SCRIPTURE LESSON READING*

Analysis

I. Consciousness of Self and Other Selfs.

II. Knowledge of External Things.

III. Knowledge of Mind Qualities.

IV. Conscious of Power To Form Judgments.

V. Conscious of Power To Will and To Do—Free Agency.

VI. Free Agency More Than a Choice of Alternatives.

VII. Free Agency Is Practical Life.

References

Any standard work on psychology, especially William James' work, *Psychology* (New York: Henry Holt and Co., 1892), abridged edition for schools, and especially his chapters on "The Self" (chap. 12), and on "Will" (chap. 26) should be read, not with the view of accepting all Mr. James' premises or his conclusions (especially in his chapter on "Will"), but to become familiar with the subject and its treatment.

A much finer treatment on "The Will" and Free Moral Agency will be found in François P. G. Guizot, *The History of Civilization, from the Fall of the Roman Empire to the French Revolution*, trans. William Hazlitt (New York: D. Appleton and Co., 1867), vol. 2, lecture 5.

A summary of Guizot's treatment will be found in the *Seventy's Course in Theology, 2nd Year*, lesson 2.

See on VI and VII, William H. Mallock, *The Reconstruction of Religious Belief* (New York and London: Harper and Bros., 1905), bk. ii, chap. 4.

*To the class instructor: The scripture lesson reading should be assigned a week in advance of the lesson treatment that a selection suitable to the theme of the lesson may be obtained, and the reading practiced. As this chapter is rather difficult the writer suggests Ezek. 18, as the reading lesson.

CHAPTER II

Of Knowledge: What Man Knows

CONSCIOUSNESS OF SELF AND OTHER SELFS[1]

First, as to existences: man knows himself as existing. He is a self-conscious entity. He knows himself as existing by many manifestations. He knows himself as seeing, hearing, tasting, smelling; as feeling—meaning by that only the sense of touch. But most of all in these manifestations through which man attains self-consciousness, he knows himself as thinking: "I think, therefore I am." This of a long time now has been the most acceptable formula for expressing self-consciousness—assurance of self-existence. One thinks, and one acts: therefore one is.

And not only is one conscious of one's self, but he is also conscious of other selfs, of other men, such as he himself is, in the main; with the same kind of qualities which he himself possesses, including this self-consciousness arrived at through the exercise of the same faculties and learned by the same series of manifestations. And while he notes these resemblances to his fellows, he notes also the differences as to himself and them—in height and form and weight; the differences also in race and speech; likewise the varying mental qualities. He knows himself as inferior in some things to his fellows; superior in others. And so all in all he is as able to differentiate himself from others, as he is also to identify himself in common sameness with them.

KNOWLEDGE OF ETERNAL THINGS[2]

One's knowledge is not limited to this consciousness of self and other selfs: the likeness and the difference between himself and other selfs. He is conscious of the existence of a large external world. He knows of the existence of earth: land, water, and air. He knows the earth is divided into islands and continents, seas and oceans, rivers and bays. He knows of the existence of the town or hamlet or countryside where he was born. In time he knows by visitation the capital of his county, of his state, of his country. He knows, at least by report, of the great centers

---

1. <Ms III^c adds "Consciousness of Self And Other Self"—*Ed.*>
2. <Ms III^c adds "Knowledge of Eternal Things"—*Ed.*>

of world population. He has verified so many things reported to him that he has confidence quite generally in what is reported to him, and seems supported by the consensus of opinion of others who have experienced them. By this act of belief he incorporates in his workable knowledge very many things that he does not know by actual personal contact or experience. Indeed, the larger volume of his knowledge is of this kind—knowledge that seeps into his consciousness by faith in the reports of others.

Man knows many objects by form, texture, and quality. He knows objects as round, or square, or cubical; as hard or soft; as solid or liquid or gaseous. He knows objects as living or dead; as useful or useless (relatively). He knows objects by position, as horizontal or perpendicular or parallel. He knows them as transient or relatively permanent; and can rise to the conception that the mountains, in the light of eternity, are as transient as the clouds. He knows heights and depths, and is conscious even of the great space depths. He knows something of sun, moon, and the planets; something also of the stars. The list drawn out of what man knows grows voluminous; though, of course, in comparison with that which lies beyond his ken, what he knows is insignificant.

KNOWLEDGE OF MIND QUALITIES[3]

Nor is man's knowledge confined to material things. He is conscious of qualities, even of intellectual and moral qualities. He is conscious of thought mysteries. He has a mind capable through the imagination of creating worlds and peopling them with creatures of his mind, that may become realities to his thought. He has power to call up states of existence, and postulate conditions in which his mind-creations shall live.

Man knows himself as competent to form normal judgments and realizes self-responsibility for his actions. In the first place, he is capable of forming comparisons between moral states and conditions. He can pass before his mind varied states that enter into common, human experiences. He may observe that those whose conduct is characterized by industry, frugality, honesty, temperance, physical skill in doing things, accompanied by steadiness and regularity of deportment, are prosperous, contented, and happy, as happiness goes in this world. While on the other hand, he may observe that those who are indolent, extravagant, dishonest, intemperate, given to knavery, unskilled in useful employments—these are unprosperous, destitute, discontented, untrusted, unloved, without self-respect or the respect of others.

---

3. <Ms III^c adds "Knowledge of Mind Qualities"—*Ed.*>

THE POWER TO FORM JUDGMENT[4]

Reviewing these two states in which he may find mortals, man is conscious of being able to pass judgment upon these two classes of persons; and seeing that the industrious, the skilled in the knowledge of honorable employments, and possessed of the positive virtues noted above, live in more desirable states or conditions than those do who are unskilled in useful employments, who are dishonest, intemperate and generally reprobate, he forms his judgment that the former state is more to be desired than the latter. The same holds good in other respects: conformity to laws which time and experience approve as just, is better than violation or resistance to such laws. Honorable conduct is superior to chicane; and living in harmony with what has been generalized as virtuous, is better than living under a system generalized as vicious.

MAN'S FREE AGENCY[5]

So passing things in review and pronouncing judgment upon them as good or evil, better or worse, man becomes conscious of a very wonderful power that he recognizes as existing within himself—the consciousness of Will; the power of self-determination; the power to choose which of two or more courses he will take. He can do as he wills to do. While there may be persuasive influences drawing him to the one side or the other, yet he is conscious of the power within himself to determine what his action shall be. He recognizes the truth avowed by the English poet, "It is in our Wills that we are thus or thus." This is not to assert man's power to do impossible things. Especially impossible physical things, such as lifting himself over a mountain into an adjoining valley; or creating two mountains without a valley between; or be bodily present in two places at one and the same moment of time; or at any time be himself and somebody else. None of these things has been in mind in the foregoing remarks on the existence and the powers in man's will. I have had in mind rather the fact of free moral agency, man's power to recognize good and evil, by their effects in human life; and his power to choose between them; to choose which he will follow.

I am not unmindful of the fact that there is much that modifies the free action of man's will. There is the influence of public opinion upon one brought face to face with the necessity of acting in some given case: "What will people say if I take the step I really desire to take?" may "give him pause"; and persuading himself that

4. <Ms III^{c} adds "The Power to Form Judgment"—*Ed.*>

5. <Ms III^{c} adds "Man's Free Agency"—*Ed.*>

"a decent respect for the opinions[6] of mankind," may require him to act in a manner different from the promptings of his own desire or judgment. He may find his power to will and to do modified by this consideration. The opinions of an inner circle of his friends may act upon his freedom in the same way. The effect upon his immediate material fortune, or his social advantage or that of his friends, may deter or urge his action one way or the other and thus modify the action of his will. He will find the influence of his education, home influence, community tradition, national or racial prejudices–all these may rise to modify his judgment and bias his determination. He may be a weakling, lacking the courage to formulate a determination, or the boldness to proclaim it, or the firmness to persevere in it. Such men there be. But after full allowance is made for all these factors that may arise to confuse clear conceptions and to persuade to one side or the other of a given action, after all is said and done, there remains the fact that man does have within him, considering all the factors, the power to form a resolution, of which he looks upon himself as the author, which arises because he wishes it, and which would not arise unless he desired it to arise. In fact bade it arise, and perhaps will order a course contrary to all the influences of environment, or the prejudice of education, or the urging of personal friends. Here the fact of agency is shown. It resides complete in the resolution which man makes after deliberation; it is the resolution which is the proper act of man, which subsists by him alone; a simple fact independent of all the facts which precede or surround it.

So much, in brief, for what we know; our self-consciousness and consciousness of other selfs; our knowledge of external things; and our knowledge of our mind powers. Our purpose has been to indicate the fact of, and the scope of all this, not to exhaust it by enumeration or by thorough analysis.

FREE AGENCY MORE THAN A CHOICE BETWEEN ALTERNATIVES

> When most people talk of believing in moral freedom, they mean by freedom a power which exhausts itself in acts of choice between a series of alternative courses; but, important though such choice as a function of freedom is, the root idea of freedom lies deeper still. It consists in the idea, not that a man is, as a personality, the first and the sole cause of his choice between alternative courses, but that he is, in a true, even if in a qualified sense, the first cause of what he does, or feels, or is, whether this involves an act of choice, or consists of an unimpeded impulse. Freedom of choice between alternatives is the consequence of this primary faculty. It is the form in which the faculty is most noticeably manifested; but it is not the primary faculty of personal freedom itself. That this faculty of the self-origination of impulse is really what we mean by freedom, and what we mean by personality also, is shown by the only supposition

---

6. <Ms III* "for the opinion"–*Ed.*>

> which is open to us, if we reject this. If a man is not in any degree—be this ever so limited—the first cause or originator of his own actions or impulses, he must be the mere transmitter or quotient of forces external to his conscious self, like a man pushed against another by the pressure of a crowd behind him. In other words, he would have no true self—no true personality at all.[7]

FREE AGENCY IN PRACTICAL LIFE, LITERATURE, HISTORY

In his work on *The Reconstruction of Religious Belief*, W. H. Mallock devotes a chapter to "Mental Civilization and the Belief in Human Freedom,"[8] the tenor of which assumes that in the practical affairs of life, in literature and in history, we proceed upon the assumption that man is a free agent and can determine, within certain limits at least, both his physical and moral conduct; and argues that without this power, the life of man would be meaningless. In the matter of love he decides with Shakespeare's Iago that "it is in ourselves that we are thus or thus. Our bodies are the gardens to which our wills are the gardeners." That this is true he holds to be "attested not only by the private experiences of most civilized men, but also by all the great poetry in which the passion of love is dealt with. Such poetry is, in Shakespeare's words, a mirror held up to nature; and it is only recognized as 'great' because it reflects faithfully."[9] In the matter of heroism in the face of physical danger, he holds that the same story repeats itself.

> A man who for some great end undergoes prolonged peril, and deliberately wills to die for the sake of that end, if necessary, is no doubt valued, . . . [because such] conduct . . . originates in the man's conscious self, which he has deliberately chosen, when he might just as well have chosen its opposite and which is not imposed on him by conditions, whether within his organism or outside it.[10]

The virtue which arises from forgiveness of sin exists in consequence of recognition of this force we call agency in man. Our author says:

> Forgiveness is an act which, in the absence of a belief in freedom [free agency], not only would lose its meaning, but could not take place at all. To forgive an injury implies that, bad as the offence may have been, the man who committed it was better than his own act, and was for this reason not constrained to commit it; and while it is only the assumption of the better potential self in him that makes him a subject to whom moral blame is applicable, it is only for the sake of this self that

---

7. William H. Mallock, *The Reconstruction of Religious Belief* (New York and London: Harper and Bros., 1905), 75-76.

8. Ibid., bk ii, chap. 4.

9. Ibid., 78.

10. Ibid., 79-80.

forgiveness can abstain from blaming. The believer in freedom says to the offending party, "I forgive you for the offense of not having done your best." The determinist [one who believes that man has not the power of free will] says, "I neither forgive nor blame you; for although you have done your worst, your worst was your best also."[11]

Of the great characters of literature, Mr. Mallock also says:

> They interest us as born to freedom, and not naturally slaves, and they pass before us like kings in a Roman triumph. Once let us suppose these characters to be mere puppets of heredity and circumstance, and they and the works that deal with them lose all intelligible content, and we find ourselves confused and wearied with the fury of an idiot's tale.[12]

Historical characters are placed in the same category. All praise or blame only has meaning as we regard these historical characters as free moral agents:

> All this praising and blaming is based on the assumption that the person praised or blamed is the originator of his own actions, and not a mere transmitter of forces. . . . Man's significance for men [in the whole category of human experiences] resides primarily in what he makes of himself, not in what he has been made by an organism derived from his parents, and the various external stimuli to which it has automatically responded.[13]

---

11. Ibid., 80.
12. Ibid., 81.
13. Ibid., 83-84.

CHAPTER III

Of Knowledge: Definitions: Time, Space, Matter, Force, Mind

SCRIPTURE LESSON READING

Analysis

Building Stones of Knowledge

I. Duration-Time; That in Which Things and Events Come To Pass.

II. Space; Expanse; Local and Unlimited; That Which Holds Things.

III. Matter; Eternity of; the Stuff Things Are Made of.

IV. Force; an Active Element in Things.

V. Mind; Intelligent, Purposeful Force—the Master Power of the Universe.

*References**

Herbert Spencer, *First Principles* (New York: D. Appleton, 1896), chap. 3.

John Stuart Mill, *Three Essays on Religion* (New York: H. Holt, 1884), especially the division of the essay on "Utility of Religion" (latter part); also essay on "Theism," especially division on "Argument for a First Cause."

J. Arthur Thomson, *The Outline of Science: A Plain Story Simply Told*, 4 vols. (New York and London: G. P. Putnam's Sons, 1922), 1:9-63.

Francis W. Rolt-Wheeler, ed., *The Science-History of the Universe*, 10 vols., (New York: The Current Literature Publishing Co., 1909), vol. 3, *Physics*, chap. 1, "Analysis of Matter," chap. 2, "Properties of Matter."

John Fiske, *Outlines of Cosmic Philosophy*, vol. i, chaps. 1-4, 6; also *Studies in Religion*, vol. 9, section on "Mystery of Evil," both in *The Miscellaneous Writings of John Fiske, with Many Portraits of Illustrious Philosophers, Scientists, and Other Men of Note* (Boston and New York: Houghton, Mifflin and Co., 1902).

*All the works given in the column of "References" should be read with discrimination; not accepting either all the premises laid down or the conclusions reached. They are given merely as sources through which the student may pursue his thought-investigations, not for unquestioning acceptance.

CHAPTER III

Of Knowledge: Definitions: Time, Space, Matter, Force, Mind

So far in treating of our knowledge it has been of earth-bound knowledge that we have spoken, limited to things we know of earth and earth-life; and even within these limits it has narrowed to the indication merely of a very few things. Our proposed objective in this book, however, will require a broader view of man's knowledge. We must consider in outline at least what he knows of the solar system, of the things that exist beyond the earth and earth-life.

BUILDING STONES OF KNOWLEDGE[1]

To make this survey will require that we deal in a limited way with some definitions as to time, and space, and matter, and force, as necessary elements to our survey in outline of man's knowledge of the universe. Of course, I am proposing no deep, metaphysical inquiry into the nature of these building stones of knowledge—time, space, matter, and force. I shall not attempt any discussion of the "reality" of them at all—shall only deal with such definitions and treatment of them as will make clear what may be presented as the general sum of man's partial knowledge of the solar and sidereal systems that make up the universe in which he lives.

DURATION-TIME

First, then, as to a workable definition of time.[2] Time is said to be that part of duration in which events happen; and in which events are distinguished with reference to concurrence of before and after; beginning and end; relation with reference to concurrence or succession. Also, it is that within which change is effected. Also, the express relation of change to continuity.

---

1. <Ms III[c] adds "Building Stones of Knowledge"—*Ed.*>

2. <Ms III[*] "First then as to a workable definition of time. I. DURATION-TIME"—*Ed.*>

What is considered as absolute time—"time in itself"—is conceived as flowing at a constant rate, unaffected by the speed or slowness of the motion of material things. This flowing aspect of time—as indeed as to all its aspects—will be more clearly realized when it is considered with reference to its divisions of present, past, and future; for time is conceived as so divided. The present really consists of but one moment, the "instant" that enters into past time ere one can name it as forming the present;[3] even as it stands as the present moment, another moment from the future side of the present crowds it into past time, and this proceeds in constant succession. It is only by arbitrary arrangement that one may construct a present longer than this fleeting moment, and that is by stipulating your present as the present hour, or day, or month, or year, or century. Then the present holds as you have arbitrarily named it.

Time has another division that should be mentioned. It may be conceived as limited or unlimited. This division is usually expressed as time and eternity. "Time" in this use means a limited period of duration; and eternity means time without limitation—endless duration. To still more firmly grasp in consciousness this illusive thing called "time," let us consider it both in this limited and unlimited phase. Limited time is that part of duration which stands between two events, such as the time of the birth of the Christ, and the birth of George Washington; or the founding of Rome or the beginning of the New World Republic—the United States of America.

In considering limitless time—time without beginning or end—let us take this present moment, or hour, or year, or century. First, use the hour for our unit of measurement. Let us draw a perpendicular line, and let it stand for the present hour, then on the right side of this perpendicular line representing the present hour draw other lines, several of them, and let them represent hour-periods of future time. Then, on the left of the line standing for the present hour, draw several other perpendicular lines to represent the past. And now, what was before this present hour? Another hour. And what before that? Another hour. And what before that? Still another hour, and yet another, and another—on to infinity. Turn now to the other side of the present hour. What preceded this present hour into the past? The hour next beyond it in the past. And what preceded the second hour that went into the past? The third hour beyond it that went into the past, and the fourth hour, and the fifth that went beyond it into the past. And so on without limit.

Starting in either direction from the present, into the past or into hours yet to come from the future, you could never reach either beginning or end of them. They

3. <Ms III^{c} adds "as forming the present"—*Ed.*>

Duration Plate

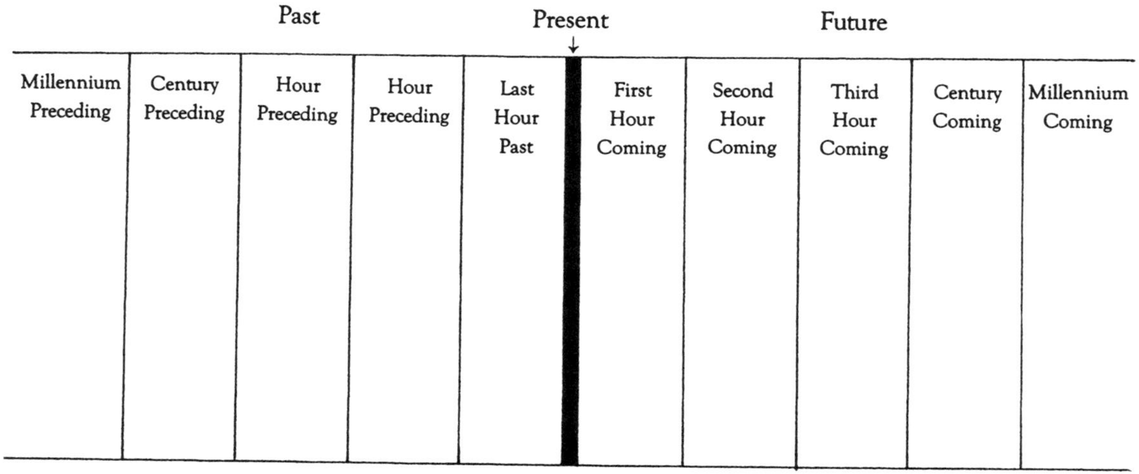

Past					Present ↓			Future	
Millennium Preceding	Century Preceding	Hour Preceding	Hour Preceding	Last Hour Past	First Hour Coming	Second Hour Coming	Third Hour Coming	Century Coming	Millennium Coming

Illustration 1

would stretch out to infinity. Time is without limits, it extends to eternity. This will readily appear, if instead of using the hour as the unit we use the same spaces marked off, calling them centuries, or a million years, or periods that stand for billions ofyears,[4] you would get the same results. What preceded the present period of a million years? That period of a million years which is now gone to make up part of the limitless past; and what stands waiting to come in when the present period of a million years shall have passed? Just such another period stands waiting to take the place of the present such period. It is impossible to postulate to consciousness the contrary, viz., that duration, future, or past has limitations.

This brings us to what in philosophy is held to be "a necessary truth." "Necessary truths," says <William> Whewell, quoted with approval in *Webster's International Dictionary*, under the definition of truth, "are those in which we not only learn that the proposition is true, but see that it must be true; in which the negation of the truth is not only false, but impossible; in which we cannot even by an effort of imagination or a supposition conceive the reverse of that which is asserted." When the mind reaches that state of consciousness it rests as having arrived at a point beyond which it cannot go—it has reached a necessary truth.

Time, then, is that in which things happen, a broad stream of duration[5] in which endless changes go on. It has no beginning! It can have no end; it will always be; it is eternity—infinite after its kind.[6]

SPACE[7]

Space is said to be that which is characterized by dimensions in boundless expanse and of indefinite divisibility; and also the boundless expanse itself. Space has to do with dimensions, position, and direction; continuous extension in all directions in which objects may exist and change their position. It is that in which matter or substances may be said to exist. Like its parallel existence, duration, it is without beginning or end—limitless. As in the case of duration, so with space, it can be demonstrated to be boundless. In this effort of illustration, we will not use the "moment," but a "point" mathematically defined (and in that sense we here use it)—a point is that which is conceived to have position merely, but no parts or dimensions. It is really the negative of extension. It is a position to which an imaginary line may lead, or a position from which imaginary lines may radiate in all directions.

---

4. <Ms III* "for millions or billions"—*Ed.*>
5. <Ms III* "a boundless ocean of duration"—*Ed.*>
6. <Ms III^{c} adds "infinite after its kind"—*Ed.*>
7. <Ms III^{c} adds "SPACE"—*Ed.*>

We will suppose a point before us as a starting place from which extension shall begin through a series of enlarging circles, and our measuring unit shall be a thousand miles separating the lines. Having started from the line which circles our point, we come to the line next to it, and have passed over a thousand miles of extension[8] to the next line; and what is beyond this second line? Another thousand miles of space to the next line. And what beyond that third line? Still another thousand miles of extension. And beyond that? Still another thousand miles. Still other stretches of space of like distance, and so on to infinity, without being able to postulate a line or point beyond which there would not be further extension. We could never reach a point or a line beyond which there would be no "beyond." And the mind is again forced to the conclusion of the existence of another necessary truth. The opposite of this[9] limitless expanse can not be conceived. We may not postulate a point or line of which there is not a "beyond."

And now this by way of illustration. Astronomers tell us that between our earth and the sun there are about 93,000,000 miles of space. What is beyond the sun in a straight line from us? Space. 93,000,000 miles of it? Yes, and if 93,000,000 miles be multiplied by 93,000,000 miles the space in a direct line from us beyond the sun would not begin to be measured! At this point a mile seems so paltry a unit of measurement. Let us take a ray of light from the sun as our unit of measure. Scientists tell us that in one tick of a pendulum of a clock a ray of light would pass eight times around the circumference of the earth, 186,000 miles! From Alpha Centauri, the brightest star in the constellation of Centaur, and the nearest to the earth, it would take a ray of "light about three and a half <4.4> years to reach us. It has also been estimated that it would take light over 16 <8.8> years to reach us from Sirius, about 18 <26> years to reach us from Vega, . . . and over forty <652>[10] years [to reach us] from the Polar star."[11]

So much space then lies between us and the Polar star. What space lies in a direct line from us beyond the Polar star? As much more space as that between our earth and the Polar star. And if the distance between us and some other star of the universe were so distant as to require a billion years for a ray of light to reach us

---

8. <Ms III[*] "of space"—*Ed.*>

9. <Ms III[c] adds "of this"—*Ed.*>

10. <According to Valerie Illingworth, ed., *Facts on File Dictionary of Astronomy*, 2d ed. (New York and Oxford: Facts On File Publications, 1985), 288, Polaris, the current pole star, is at a distance of 200 parsecs or 652 light-years—*Ed.*>

11. Joseph A. Gillet and William J. Rolfe, *Astronomy for the Use of Schools and Academies* (New York: American Book Co. 1882), 364-65. <For an account of modern astronomy, see David Morrison and Sidney C. Wolff, *Frontiers of Astronomy* (Philadelphia: Saunders College Publishing, 1990)—*Ed.*>

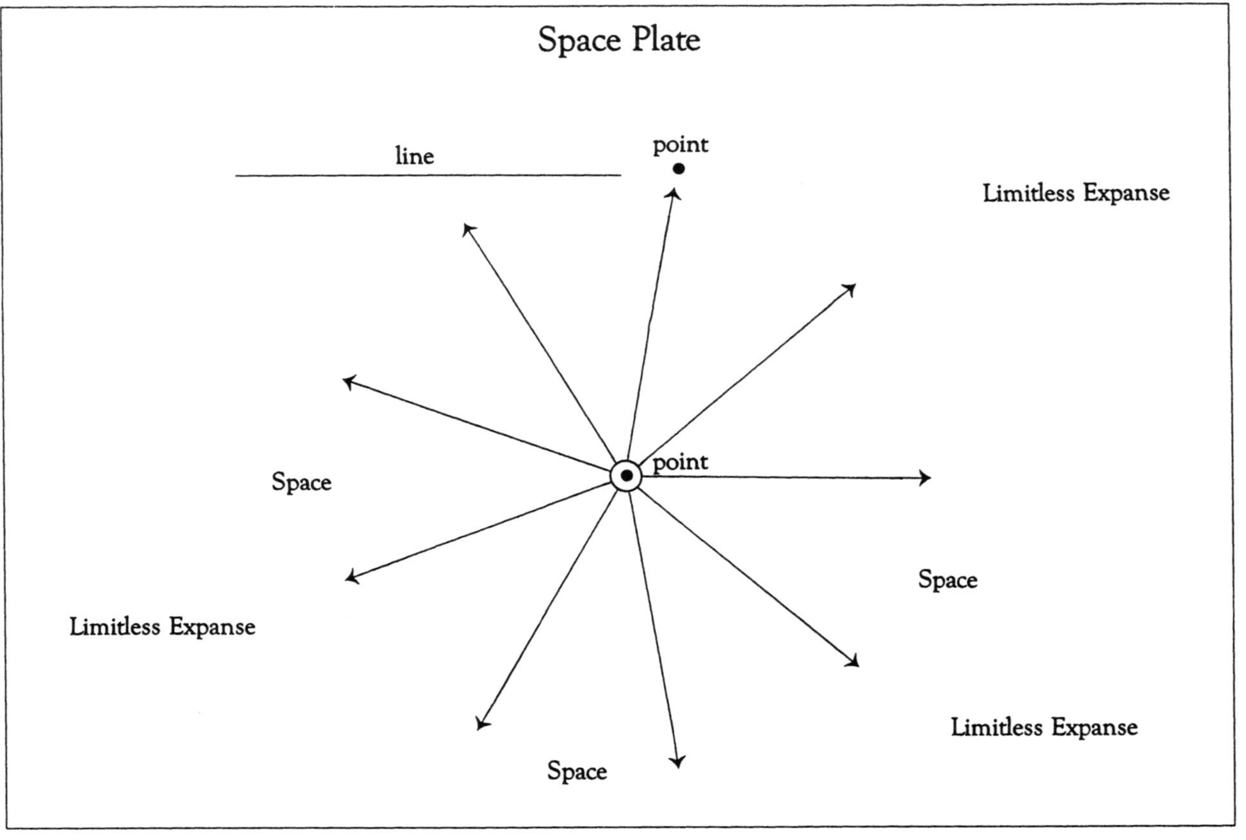

Illustration 2

from it, the space in a direct line beyond would be just as great as between our earth and the supposed distant star: and so on, and on, without limit!

Space, then, is boundless. It is without a center; it is without circumference! The contrary is inconceivable. We again arrive at a necessary truth. And space is infinite after its kind.

MATTER[12]

Matter is usually defined as that of which any physical object is composed; material, "the stuff that things are made of." In physics it is said to be that which occupies space, that which is conceived to constitute the body of the outward or physical universe; and, with energy, to form the basis of objective phenomena. The ultimate nature of matter is considered to be unknown, and the physicist can only describe certain of its properties and speculate as to its structure. The occupancy of space implies extension and impenetrability. The study of bodies under the action of forces has led to the conception of mass as a universal attribute of matter.

The general forms in which matter exists are solids, liquids, and gases. The chief thing that concerns us in the reference that we shall make to matter is its eternity and its limitless extension; its indestructibility and the necessary corollary of that quality, its un-creatability. Experiments have demonstrated the fact that the form of matter can be changed, but it can never be annihilated, equally certain is it that it can not be created in the sense that from nothing matter can be produced. On the point of the nature of "matter in itself" being unknown, Prof. R. K. Duncan says:

> What matter is, in itself and by itself is quite hopeless of answer, and concerns only metaphysicians. The *ding an sich* is forever outside the province of science. If all men stopped to quarrel over the <inner> inwardness of things, progress, of course, would cease. Science is naïve; she takes things as they come and rests content with <some> such practical definition[13] as will serve to differentiate matter from all other forms of non-matter.[14] This may be done, strictly provisionally in this place,[15] by defining matter as that which occupies space and possesses weight. Using these two properties, it is readily possible to sift out matter from all the heterogeneous phenomena, that present themselves to the sense and that, in this place, is what we want. Thus, wood, water, copper, oil, and air are forms of matter, for they evidently possess weight and fill space. But light, heat, electricity, and magnetism we cannot consider to fill so

12. <Ms III[c] adds "MATTER"—*Ed.*>
13. <Ms III "with such practical definitions"—*Ed.*>
14. <Ms III "forms of unknown matter"—*Ed.*>
15. <Ms III "strictly professionally in this place"—*Ed.*>

> many quarts or weigh so many pounds. They are, therefore, forms of non-matter [light, heat, electricity are properties of matter]. In like manner, such things as grace, mercy, justice, and truth, while they are existing entities as much as matter, are unquestionably non-matter.[16]

Grace, mercy, justice, and truth are qualities or attributes of mind, or spirit, which may be matter, but of a finer quality than that which is cognized by the senses.

As to what is called the "conservation of mass," meaning by that the maintenance of the sum total of matter, the author of *The New Knowledge* says:

> This law, known as the law of conservation of mass, states that no particle of matter, however small, may be created or destroyed. All the king's horses and all the king's men cannot destroy a pin's head. We may smash the pin's head, dissolve it in acids, burn it in the electric furnace, employ, in a word, every annihilating agency, and yet that pin's head persists in being. Again, it is as uncreatable as it is indestructible. In other words, we cannot create something out of nothing. The material must be furnished for every existent article. The sum of matter in the universe is *x* pounds—and, while it may be carried through myriad forms, when all is said and done, it is just *x* pounds.[17]

<John W. Draper says:>

> Chemistry . . . has disposed of the idea of the destruction and creation of matter. It accepts without hesitation the doctrine of the imperishability of substance; for though the aspect of a thing may change through decompositions and recombinations, in which its constituent parts are concerned, every atom continues to exist and may be recovered by suitable processes, though the entire thing may have seemingly disappeared.[18]

"The annihilation of matter," says Herbert Spencer, "is unthinkable, for the same reason that the creation of matter is unthinkable."[19]

This indestructibility of matter and its uncreatability—not an atom of it capable of being created from nothing; and each atom impossible of annihilation, together with its limitless extension throughout space and equally throughout duration,

---

16. Robert K. Duncan, *The New Knowledge: A Popular Account of the New Physics and the New Chemistry in Their Relation to the New Theory of Matter* (New York: A. S. Barnes and Co., 1905), 2.

17. Ibid., 3.

18. John William Draper, *History of the Intellectual Development of Europe* (New York: Harper and Brothers, 1876), 2:375.

19. Herbert Spencer, *First Principles* (New York: D. Appleton, 1896), 177-78.

brings to us the generalization of scientific thought best expressed in Haeckel's Law of Substance, viz.:

THE LAW OF SUBSTANCE[20]

> 1. Through all eternity the infinite universe has been, and is, subject to the law of substance. . . .
>
> 2. The extent of the universe is infinite and unbounded: it is empty in no part, but everywhere filled with substance.
>
> 3. The duration of the world [i.e., universe] is equally infinite and unbounded; it has no beginning and no end: it is eternity.
>
> 4. Substance is everywhere and always in uninterrupted movement and transformation: nowhere is there perfect repose and rigidity; yet the infinite quantity of matter and of eternally changing force remains constant.[21]

FORCE: PERSISTENCE OF FORCE[22]

To this statement in respect of the uncreatability and indestructibility of matter there must be added its necessary corollary, the conservation of, or the persistence in undiminished entirety the sum of force or energy throughout the universe. Force, as it concerns physics, is recognized as an active element in things;[23] that which is in all natural phenomena, and is continually passing from one portion of matter to another.

Force is manifested in various forms, as mechanical, electrical, thermal, chemical, and changes[24] under suitable conditions from one form into another.[25] As matter may not be created nor destroyed, so with force. The conservation of force rests upon the fundamental proposition that the quantity of force in the universe is invariable, but though its quantity can never be increased or diminished, the forms under which it expresses itself may be transmuted into each other, and while this idea may not "be as universally accepted as the indestructibility of matter, yet so numerous and so cogent are the arguments adduced in its behalf that it stands in an imposing way as altogether true."

---

20. <Ms III^{c} adds "The Law of Substance"—*Ed.*>

21. Ernst Haeckel, *The Riddle of the Universe at the Close of the Nineteenth Century*, trans. Joseph McCabe (New York and London: Harper and Bros., 1900), 242.

22. <Ms III* "PERSISTENCE OF FORCE, OR ENERGY"—*Ed.*>

23. <Ms III* "active element in things; that which acts, in contra-distinction to that which is acted upon"—*Ed.*>

24. <Ms III* "mechanical, electrical, thermal, chemical, energies and changes"—*Ed.*>

25. <Ms III* "from any one form into another"—*Ed.*>

John W. Draper, author of *The Intellectual Development of Europe* and of *The Conflict between Religion and Science*, says:

> It was in India that men first recognized the fact that force is indestructible and eternal. This implies <ideas> more or less distinctly, that which we now term its "correlation and conservation." Considerations connected with the stability of the universe gave strength to this view, since it is clear that, were there either an increase or a diminution, the order of the world must cease. The definite and invariable amount of energy in the universe must, therefore, be accepted as a scientific fact. The changes we witness are in its distribution [not in its creation and annihilation].[26]

As stated in the law of substance given above, "the infinite quantity of matter and of eternally changing force remains constant."

TWENTIETH CENTURY ADVANCEMENT IN PHYSICS

Since writing the above which pertains chiefly to the indestructibility of matter and the conservation of force, it has occurred to me that some of our more recent writers and students may take exception to the matter as here set forth, regarding the writers quoted as far behind the recent knowledge of those who have taken the field since such writers as I have referred to above passed on, say some quarter of a century ago. Some of our present-day professors hold that the principle of the "indestructibility of matter" has proven to be "definitely invalid"; and it is now sometimes held that "a definite portion of matter has entirely disappeared as a distinct, separate entity of any system, *energy taking its place.*" That is, matter changes into radiant energy and vice versa. "The change of a small amount of matter giving enormous quantities of energy."

In other words the new knowledge largely sustained by <Albert> Einstein and Dr. Millikan, the latter in his book on *Evolution in Science and Religion*, the "Terry Lectures for 1927"—Lecture I, "Evolution of Twentieth Century Physics." The sum of the matter amounts to this: the atom is found to be not the ultimate unit of material elements, indestructible and impenetrable as hitherto held to have been; but on the contrary, is a complex thing made up of a number of electrons, containing particles of positive and negative electricity capable of manifesting immense energy. It is held that atoms once regarded as the ultimate factors of matter may now be broken up and changed into something else, viz., into radiant[27] energy. Thus, it is held that the indestructibility of matter is proven to be "definitely

26. John William Draper, *History of the Conflict between Religion and Science*, 6th ed. (New York: D. Appleton and Co., 1875), 126.

27. <Ms III[c] adds "radiant"—*Ed.*>

invalid." But not so fast! Let it be noted that the definite amount of matter has not been annihilated, but merely changed to something else, namely into "energy"—"radiant energy"; a small amount of matter giving off "enormous quantities of energy." Be it so. And note again that our twentieth-century physicists (and we speak respectfully of them, of course) say that, "beginning in 1901 the mass of an electron was shown by direct experiment to grow measurably larger and larger as its speed is pushed closer and closer to the speed of light" (186,000 miles per second). And elsewhere in the lecture Dr. Millikan says that in accordance with Dr. Einstein's equation on the matter "is it not more than probable that the process is also going on somewhere in the opposite sense, <and> that radiant energy is condensing back into mass, that new worlds are thus continually forming as old ones are disappearing?"[28]

Certainly; and that is the very truth one ought to say. But why say, as Dr. Millikan does say, that "matter may be annihilated"? Only to follow it immediately with "radiant energy appearing in its place"? The whole truth is that matter has been changed to radiant energy, and radiant energy, by motion approaching the speed of light, has been brought back to mass; that is, to matter. Matter has not been dissolved into "nothing"—into "non-existence," and "nothing" by motion has not been brought into "something." There has been no break in the continuity; something has existed all the while, and the old truth on the conservation of matter and force has not in reality been changed, but emphasized. For what have we here but the cube of ice placed on the stove where for a moment it sputters in water and steam and gases, then disappears to be seen no more? But even household chemistry teaches one that the steam and gases that have disappeared might have been condensed to steam again, the steam condensed to water, the water frozen into ice, and the original cube of ice restored. It seems no more than this has been done to the atom of Dr. Millikan's treatise. Matter has not been absolutely destroyed; nor has it been recreated absolutely from nothing. The continuity of existence has not been broken at any point. All that has happened is that a forward step has been taken towards that truth announced by that inspired Prophet of the New Dispensation, when he said, "All spirit is matter; but it is more fine or pure, and can only be discerned by purer eyes. We cannot see it; but when our bodies are purified, we shall see that it is all matter" (D&C 131:7-8). This in May 1843.

Or further, the reader may be[29] enlightened by the loftier passage from the writings of Moses, as found in a passage from a fragment of his ancient writings

---

28. Robert Andrews Millikan, *Evolution in Science and Religion* (New Haven, Connecticut: Yale University Press, 1927), 15-17.

29. <Ms III[c] adds "the reader may be"—*Ed.*>

also brought to light by Joseph Smith in June 1830, and published in the Pearl of Great Price (chapter 1), where he says:

> Behold, there are many worlds that have passed away by the word of my power; and there are many that now stand, and innumerable are they unto man; but all things are numbered unto me, for they are mine, and I know them. . . . And as one earth shall pass away, and the heavens thereof, so shall another come; and there is no end to my works, neither to my words (Moses 1:35, 38).

This somewhat antedates Dr. Millikan's remark (1927), that Lord Kelvin (an astronomer of the 19th century–antiquated according to Dr. Millikan) would be shocked[30] "if he should hear the modern astronomers talking about the stars radiating away their mass<es> through the mere act of giving off light and heat! And yet this is now orthodox astronomy." And again: "If they do so in accordance with the Einstein equation, then is it not more than probable that the process is also going on somewhere in the opposite sense and that radiant energy is condensing back into mass, that new worlds are thus continually forming as old ones are disappearing?" "These," he adds, "are merely the current speculations of modern physics, based, however, upon the now fairly definite discovery that conservation of matter in its nineteenth century sense is invalid."[31]

The Prophet's remarks through the Book of Moses–we repeat–somewhat antedate Dr. Millikan's and Dr. Einstein's notion concerning the making and unmaking of worlds, but we can scarcely see that there has been[32] any serious or real[33] disturbance of the "old" 19th century doctrine of the conservation of mass and of energy or force. We shall let that doctrine stand, therefore, as we have placed it in the text of preceding paragraphs. "The elements are eternal"–when you get to them.[34]

MIND: INTELLIGENT FORCE

Mind is to be here spoken of only in its relations to matter and force. Its proper and fuller treatment in the general scheme of things will be found in chapter 9 of this division of our general theme (part I). But mind deserves mention here

---

30. <Ms III[c] adds "would be shocked"–*Ed.*>

31. Millikan, *Evolution*, 17-18.

32. <Ms III "see that here has been"–*Ed.*>

33. <Ms III[c] adds "or real"–*Ed.*>

34. <For a comparison of Mormon cosmology with Einstein's relativity and quantum physics, see Keith E. Norman, "Mormon Cosmology: Can It Survive the Big Bang?" *Sunstone* 10, no. 9 (1986): 19-23–*Ed.*>

in connection with force and matter, because of its relationship to them as a factor in causation, and in the sustaining, and the directing of creation; the one thing which may provide the purposeful element in the universe, and constitute the eternal cause, if not of the universe, at least of the cosmos, the orderly status and procession of things.

We sometimes speak of "blind force." This is when we regard it in its mechanical, electrical, thermal, or chemical manifestations; in gravitation as attracting and repelling power produced by masses of matter and relative distances. But there is a force operating in the universe that is not blind, and that is not mechanical or chemical merely; and this force, or energy, is mind. It is intelligent, and manifests purpose, and gives evidence of possessing powers of causation, of origination. All these manifestations are seen in man, in mind as manifested in man. He can regard himself as the nearest approach to a *vera causa*—true cause—than is immediately met with elsewhere in human experience. Man has learned that he can originate many things. He can take a great variety of materials scattered about, gather them together, and from them build a house according to a plan which his mind originated, and he becomes the cause of the house. By his mind the purpose and plan was conceived, and his hands by assembling and using the material, according to plan, caused the house. His mind also from the large field of its knowledge and experience, can build sciences, found governments, formulate systems of philosophy—create many things; they proceed from his mind, hence product of mind operating as an intelligent force. Often this mind in man makes use of other kinds of force, mechanical forces, electrical forces, thermal forces, chemical forces; and uses matter, things we call material, at will.

Man has learned to regard the succession of phenomenon as effects, and can largely attribute to each some cause. When he comes to that cause, however, he finds it to be the effect of an antecedent cause, and so on, back and back seemingly to infinity. But the mind can not rest in an endless chain of cause-effects, he feels that somewhere there must either be a first cause, or an eternal one,[35] in any event a real one; and when it is found will it not be of the nature of that power which in man wells up as mind, with its true power of origination, but of course transcending the human mind in majesty, and power, and glory; a universal mind, proceeding from all harmonized, divine intelligences, the very "spirit of God," everywhere present and present with power—the eternal cause and sustaining power of the cosmos, whose glory is Intelligence, the master power of the universe.

---

35. First or eternal cause is discussed in chapters ___ <7 and 24>, all to the point of "eternal cause" being the truth of the matter.

CHAPTER IV

Of Knowledge: The Solar System

SCRIPTURE READING LESSON

Analysis

The Solar System:

I. The Sun: Self-Luminous Center of the System.

II. Mercury: The Planet Moving nearest the Sun.

III. Venus: The Second Planet from the Sun.

IV. Earth: Third Planet from the Sun.

V. Mars: The Fourth Planet from the Sun; and Much Like the Earth.

VI. Jupiter: The Giant Planet of the System.

VII. Saturn: The Planet Beautiful of the System.

VIII. Uranus: The Seventh Planet from the Sun.

IX. Neptune: The Eighth Planet from the Sun; Distance from It, 2,791,000,000 Miles!

References

Any standard work on astronomy.

Simon Newcomb, *Popular Astronomy: School Edition* (New York: Harper and Brothers, 1883), comprehensive and within reasonable compass with fine illustrations.

Joseph A. Gillet and William J. Rolfe, *Astronomy for the Use of Schools and Academies* (New York: American Book Co. 1882), designed for academies and high schools; a more primary work than Newcomb's, but with superior colored illustrations of high value.

David P. Todd, *A New Astronomy* (New York: American Book Co., 1926), issued from Amherst College, especially valuable for its experimental demonstrations of astronomical subjects.

J. Arthur Thomson, "The Romance of the Heavens," *The Outline of Science: A Plain Story Simply Told* (New York and London: G. P. Putnam's Sons, 1922), 1:7-51.

Theodore E. R. Phillips and William H. Steavenson, *Splendour of the Heavens: A Popular Authoritative Astronomy*, 2 vols., (New York: Robert M. McBride and Co., 1925), profusely and splendidly illustrated work.

CHAPTER IV

Of Knowledge: The Solar System

With these definitions determined as far as it is necessary to our purpose, we may now proceed with the investigation of man's knowledge of the universe, beginning with his knowledge of the solar system, that is, the sun and the group of worlds held in balance by it and their mutually attracting and repelling forces.[1]

THE SUN[2]

The sun is the most conspicuous object to the knowledge of man external to the earth, and with it he forms an early acquaintanceship–it becomes a childhood consciousness. Its brightness, together with its welcome glow of warmth, make it a conspicuous object of knowledge. The regularity of its "rising," reaching high noon, and slowly declining to its "setting;" all this not only makes the sun a conspicuous and wonderful object of knowledge, but constantly renews it for us, until one may say truly that it is the most conspicuous object of knowledge external to the earth. Its wonderfulness grows upon us the more we become acquainted with it. From our present knowledge, developed through long years of observation by man, the sun is regarded as an immense spherical mass of substance aflame, with a diameter approximately 888,000 <864,000> miles; while the earth, which we regard as so large, has a diameter approximately of only 8,000 miles! The circumference of the sun would be its diameter multiplied by three–that is, 2,664,000 <2,714,000> miles; while the earth, to us so large, is but 24,000 miles in circumference! So large is the sun that its mass is said to be equal to 750 times the mass of all the planets and their satellites (moons) of the solar system. How large such a mass is will better appear after what is to be said of these planets is set down.

The sun, as already stated, is the center of a group of planets or worlds held by attracting and repelling forces in regular movement about the sun in orbits

---

1. <For a modern survey of the sun and planets, see J. Kelly Beatty and Andrew Chaikin, *The New Solar System*, 3d ed. (Cambridge, Eng.: Cambridge University Press, 1990; Cambridge, MA: Sky Publishing Corp., 1990)–*Ed.*>

2. <Ms III[c] adds "THE SUN"–*Ed.*>

determined by the operation of these forces. These planets so far as we now know are eight <with Pluto, nine> in number; but moving between the orbits of two of them are what are called the asteroids, apparently a swarm of fragments of a world or worlds broken into bits. Little is known of the nature of them, but they move in a fixed course between the orbits of two of the planets, Mars and Jupiter.[3]

MERCURY[4]

The first of the planets of the solar system, first in nearness to the sun, is Mercury. Its mean distance from the sun in moving around its orbit is 36,000,000 miles; its diameter is 3,030 miles; its sidereal period, the time required to move in its orbit around the sun, is 87.96 days. The axial revolution of Mercury–the revolutions upon its axis, which determines the length of its days–is uncertain.[5] Mercury has no satellites.

VENUS[6]

The second planet of the solar system is Venus. Its mean distance from the sun in moving around its orbit is 67,000,000 miles; its mean diameter is 7,700 <7520> miles; its sidereal period is 224 days; the axial revolution is uncertain;[7] it has no satellites.

EARTH[8]

The third planet of the system is the Earth. Its mean distance from the sun is 93,000,000 miles; its mean diameter is approximately 8000 miles; its sidereal period <is> 365 days; its axial revolution practically 24 hours; it has one satellite.

MARS[9]

The fourth planet is Mars. Its mean distance[10] from the sun is 141,000,000

---

3. <For a modern study of asteroids, see Charles T. Kowal, *Asteroids: Their Nature and Utilization* (Chichester, Eng.: Ellis Horwood Limited, 1988)–*Ed.*>
4. <Ms III^{c} adds "MERCURY"–*Ed.*>
5. <Its rotation period is 58.6 days–*Ed.*>
6. <Ms III^{c} adds "VENUS"–*Ed.*>
7. <Its rotation period is 243 days–*Ed.*>
8. <Ms III^{c} adds "EARTH"–*Ed.*>
9. <Ms III^{c} adds "MARS"–*Ed.*>
10. <Ms III* "Its mean distance of miles"–*Ed.*>

miles <142,000,000>; its mean diameter is 4,230 miles; its sidereal period <is> approximately 687 days;[11] its axial revolution is 24 hours, plus; it has two satellites.

JUPITER[12]

The fifth planet is Jupiter. Its mean distance from the sun is 463,000,000 <483,000,000> miles; its mean diameter approximately 87,000 miles; its sidereal period <is> 4,332 days, plus; its axial revolution approximately 9½ hours; it has five satellites.[13]

Jupiter is known as the "giant planet" of the system, and here we have an opportunity for comparison with the Earth, which will give us opportunity to form some notion of the great masses of the separate planets, and the greatness of the planetary system. Our Earth, for example, is but 93,000,000 miles from the sun, and that we think of as an enormous distance; but how insignificant it is in the comparison with the distance of Jupiter from the sun, which is 463,000,000 <483,000,000> miles! Our Earth, which we think of as so large, has a diameter of only 8,000 miles; while Jupiter's diameter is 87,000 miles! Our Earth requires only 365 days, plus, to make the complete circuit around the sun, but it requires Jupiter about 4,432 <4332> days to circle the sun! This comparison will suggest to the reader-student the making of other comparisons with the remaining planets of the system, and with the same amazing result of a constantly growing consciousness of the immensity of these respective planets, the distances that separate them from each other, and their immense distances from the sun.

SATURN[14]

The sixth planet of the solar system is Saturn. Its distance from the sun is nearly double the mean distance of Jupiter from the sun, being 886,000,000 miles; its mean diameter, though less than Jupiter's, is still 71,000 <74,900> miles; its sidereal period is 10,759 days,[15] plus; its axial revolution is 10 hours, plus. Saturn has eight satellites,[16] which distinguishes it, in addition to the well-known and

---

11. <Ms III "6,807" is a typographical error for the correct "687"; someone was aware of the problem because Ms III^{c} adds a "check" mark below the number–*Ed.*>

12. <Ms III^{c} adds "JUPITER"–*Ed.*>

13. <With the three satellites discovered by Voyager in 1979, the known satellites of Jupiter rose to sixteen–*Ed.*>

14. <Ms III^{c} adds "SATURN"–*Ed.*>

15. <Ms III "10,756 days" has been corrected to "10,759 days," since Roberts at the end of the chapter correctly lists Saturn's sidereal period as 10,759.22–*Ed.*>

16. <With the two satellites discovered by Voyager in 1985, the known satellites of

beautiful bands of seeming light which circle the planet, giving it the distinction of "the most beautiful world of the planetary system," while its eight moons, circling it in regular order, make it appear almost as a miniature solar system by itself.

URANUS[17]

The seventh planet of the system is Uranus. Its mean distance is more than double the distance of Saturn from the sun, being 1,781,000,000 <1,784,000,000>; its mean diameter is 31,900 miles; its sidereal period 30,686 days, plus; its axial revolution is uncertain;[18] it has four satellites.[19]

NEPTUNE[20]

The eighth planet is Neptune. Its mean distance from the sun is 2,791,000,000 <2,793,000,000> miles; its diameter is 34,800 <30,770> miles; its sidereal period is 60,181 days,[21] plus; its axial revolution is uncertain;[22] so far as discovered, it has but one satellite.[23]

In order that the above information may be more clearly visualized, I place it in tabulated form at the close of this chapter.[24]

Saturn rose to nineteen; see David Reidy and Ken Wallace, *The Solar System: A Practical Guide* (North Sydney, Australia: Allen and Unwin, 1991), 161–*Ed.*>

17. <Ms III^c adds "URANUS"–*Ed.*>

18. <Its rotation period has been estimated from 16 to 18 hours–*Ed.*>

19. <With the nine satellites discovered by Voyager in 1986, the known satellites of Uranus rose to fifteen–*Ed.*>

20. <Ms III^c adds "NEPTUNE"–*Ed.*>

21. <Ms III* "hours" is an error; on the photocopy of TWL in the Edwin B. Firmage Collection, Marriott Library, a non-BHR hand has written above the word "hours" the correction "days?" in a blue pen (presumably written by Hugh B. Brown or Edwin B. Firmage)–*Ed.*>

22. <Its rotation period has been estimated from 15 to 19 hours–*Ed.*>

23. <With the six satellites discovered by Voyager in 1989, the known satellites of Neptune rose to eight–*Ed.*>

24. <The existence of another planet in our solar system had been predicted in 1905 due to certain irregularities in the motion of Uranus and Neptune. At the Lowell Observatory, Flagstaff, Arizona, twenty-three-year-old Clyde William Tombaugh, the only American to discover a major planet, discovered in February 1930 a new planet, which would be named Pluto. It was officially announced the following month. See William Graves Hoyt, *Planets X and Pluto* (Tucson, AZ: University of Arizona Press, 1980), and A. J. Whyte, *The Planet Pluto* (Oxford, Eng.: Pergamon Press, 1980). Roberts added to the end of chapter 4 an article entitled "The Latest News from Pluto," *The Literary Digest* 106 (6 Sept. 1930),

THE SOLAR SYSTEM TO BE A BASIS OF FUTURE COMPARISON[25]

All these particulars respecting the solar system are set down here, not with the idea that something new or special is being given out about the solar system, for the writer very well knows that all this is but the commonest knowledge of the grade and the high schools; but this common knowledge is here set out for the purpose of bringing home to the readers and the students of this book the consciousness of the immensity of that scale on which the solar system is drawn, that it may become a sort of measuring wand by which, through comparisons, we may form some judgments of the still greater immensities to be considered when dealing with the sidereal or star system of the universe; and all this consideration of the greatness and the extent of the solar system, and the still greater vastness of the sidereal system, in order that the student may appreciate somewhat the greatness of the theme upon which we are entering, the search for the heart of all this, the master secret[26] of it all; its soul! God!

SOLAR SYSTEM
<See text for corrections—*Ed.*>

Names of the Planets	Mean Distance from the Sun in Millions of Miles	Mean Diameter in Miles	Sidereal Periods in Days–Around Orbits.	Axial Revolution in Hours.	Number of Satellites.
1. MERCURY	36.0	3,030	87.96	uncertain	0
2. VENUS	67.2	7,700	224.70	uncertain	0
3. EARTH	92.9	7,918	365.25	23.56	1
4. MARS	141.5	4,230	686.95	24.37	2
ASTEROIDS					
5. JUPITER	463.0	86,500	4332.580	9.55	5
6. SATURN	886.0	71,000	10,759.22	10.14	8
7. URANUS	1,781.0	31,900	30,686.82	uncertain	4
8. NEPTUNE	2,791.0	34,800	60,181.11	uncertain	1
<9.> <PLUTO>	<3,674>	<1395>	<90,800>	<153>	<1>

THE SUN Mean diameter in miles 888,000. The mass of the sun is 750 times that of all the planets and moons of the solar system added together.

18, which discussed the recent discovery of the planet Pluto—*Ed.*>

25. <Ms III[c] adds "The Solar System to Be A Basis of Future Comparison"—*Ed.*>

26. <Ms III[*] "the Master Secret"—*Ed.*>

CHAPTER V
Of Knowledge: Sidereal System

SCRIPTURE READING LESSON

Analysis

I. The Stars: Number of, to the Naked Eye.
II. Difference between Planets and Stars.
III. Number of the "Fixed Stars."
IV. Our Galaxy—Distances within.
V. Multiplicity of Galaxies.
VI. A Universe of "Magnificent Distances."

References

All the works on astronomy cited under "References" in the Lesson Analysis of Chapter 4; and also in addition, Richard A. Proctor, *Other Worlds Than Ours: The Plurality of Worlds Studied under the Light of Recent Scientific Researches* (New York: J. A. Hill and Co., 1904) and Garrett P. Serviss, *Astronomy with the Naked Eye: A New Geography of the Heavens, with Descriptions and Charts of Constellations, Stars, and Planets* (New York and London: Harper and Bros., 1908).

Abraham 3 and cuts, with Joseph Smith's partial translation.

CHAPTER V

Of Knowledge: Sidereal System

The sidereal system, meaning by that the star system, sometimes called the stellar universe, comprises all the stars and the nebula<e> outside our own solar system. This stellar universe includes not only the stars which are visible to the naked eye (about 5,000 only are so visible), but hundreds of thousands or millions besides, which are so distant that their existence is known only as they are revealed by the most powerful telescope and the most sensitive photographic plates.

DIFFERENCE BETWEEN PLANETS AND STARS[1]

As an evidence that these stars are not similar in constitution to the planets of our solar system, which shine only by the reflected light from the sun, astronomers point to the remoteness of these stars of the stellar universe. Neptune, they say (the planet of our system most distant from our sun, be it remembered),[2] is too faint for the naked eye to see its light. Yet it is only 2,791,000,000 <2,793,000,000> miles—nearly three billions of miles—from the sun; but the nearest fixed star from our earth (Alpha Centauri,[3] meaning the star of the first magnitude of the constellation of the Centaur) is nine hundred times more distant![4] Hence the conclusion that, if Neptune on the frontier of our system may not be seen by the naked eye, while Alpha Centauri, nine hundred times farther away may

---

1. <Ms III[c] adds "Difference Between Planets and Stars"—*Ed.*>

2. <Roberts's statement was true in 1928 when he submitted TWL to the apostles for approval, but Pluto was discovered in 1930—*Ed.*>

3. <Alpha Centauri to the naked eye appears as a single star, but it is part of a three-star system. The nearest of these three stars, Proxima Centauri, is 4.3 light years away, while Alpha Centauri and the third star are 4.4 light years away. See Valerie Illingworth, ed., *Facts on File Dictionary of Astronomy*, 2d ed. (New York: Facts On File Publications, 1985), 9, 57, 298—*Ed.*>

4. <The relative distances are much greater, since Alpha Centauri is over nine thousand times farther; David P. Todd, A *New Astronomy* (New York: American Book Co., 1926), 421, says that "the nearest fixed star is about 9000 times more distant," so Roberts appears to have misread 9,000 as 900—*Ed.*>

be so seen, then the difference as to these two objects of our night sky must arise from some difference in their constitution. "The very brightness of the lucid stars," leads observers to suspect that these stars of the sidereal system "must be self-luminous like [our own] sun; and when their light is analyzed with the spectroscope, the theory that they are suns is actually demonstrated."[5] This leads to the formula that "The sun is a star; the stars are suns." Our sun looks big as compared with the other suns or stars of the stellar universe only "because of its comparative nearness to us. The universe is a stupendous collection of millions of stars or suns."[6]

THE NUMBER OF THE "FIXED STARS"[7]

No one, of course, knows how many of these fixed stars exist in the sidereal system. Astronomers have variously estimated them from thirty, fifty, to one hundred millions, but the later estimates by authorities go far beyond these figures, even into the billions. John W. Draper, author of *The Intellectual Development of Europe*, says:

> Man, when he looks upon the countless multitude of stars, when he reflects that all he sees is only a small portion of those which exist, yet each is [or may be] a light and life-giving sun to multitudes of opaque and therefore invisible worlds–when he considers the enormous size of these various bodies and their immeasurable distance from one another, may form an estimate of the scale on which the world [universe] is constructed.[8]

Again, Prof. Samuel Kinns, Ph.D., F.R.A.S., says:

> These distant suns are many of them much larger than our <Sun.> Sirius, the beautiful Dog Star [in the constellation Canis Major] is so far as can be judged by its amount of light, nearly three thousand times larger, and, therefore, its system of dependent worlds must be so much more important than those which form our solar system. Its planets many say exceed ours in size and revolve at far greater distances; for such a sun would throw its light and heat very much beyond a distance equal to that of our Neptune.[9]

---

5. Todd, *New Astronomy*, 421-22.

6. J. Arthur Thomson, *The Outline of Science: A Plain Story Simply Told* (New York and London: G. P. Putnam's Sons, 1922), 1:12.

7. <Ms III[c] adds "The Number of the 'Fixed Stars'"–*Ed.*>

8. John William Draper, *History of the Intellectual Development of Europe* (New York: Harper and Brothers, 1876), 2:279.

9. Samuel Kinns, *Moses and Geology; or, Harmony of the Bible with Science*, 2d ed. (London: Cassell and Co., 1895), 238.

"OUR" GALAXY[10]

Prof. Newcomb, in all this branch of science always a standard authority, says of these fixed stars:

> Turning our attention from this solar system to the thousands of fixed stars which stud the heavens, the first thing to be considered is their enormous distance asunder, compared with the dimensions of the solar system, though the latter are themselves inconceivably great. To give an idea of the relative distances, suppose a voyager through the celestial spaces could travel from the sun to the outermost planet of our system in twenty-four hours. So enormous would be his velocity, that it would carry him across the Atlantic Ocean, from New York to Liverpool, in less than one-tenth of a second of the clock. Starting from the sun with this velocity, he would cross the orbits of the inner planets in rapid succession and the outer ones more slowly, until, at the end of a single day, he would reach the confines of our system, crossing the orbit of Neptune. But though he passed eight planets the first day, he would pass none the next, for he would have to journey eighteen or twenty years, without diminution of speed, before he would reach the nearest star, and would then have to continue his journey as far again before he could reach another. All the planets of our system would have vanished in the distance, in the course of the first three days, and the sun would be but an insignificant star in the firmament. The conclusion is that our sun is one of an enormous number of self-luminous bodies, scattered at such distances that years would be required to traverse the space between them, even when the voyager went at the rate we have supposed.[11]

MULTIPLICITY OF GALAXY–UNIVERSES[12]

A still more recent statement of these wonderful things concerning the extent of the universe, the number of the fixed stars, and the distance apart of these innumerable suns, is made by Professor Frank <Forest> R. Moulton of the University of Chicago, in an address before the American Association for the Advancement of Science, on the evening of December 31, 1926 <1925>. He said of our stellar galaxy, which he called the largest organism "whose evolution has ever been considered":

> Our galaxy consists of at least one billion suns, each one like our own, averaging a million times the volume of the earth. These suns occupy a disk-like or watch-shaped region in space whose thickness is the distance light travels in about 30,000 years, and

10. <Ms III^c adds "'Our' Galaxy"—*Ed.*>

11. Simon Newcomb, *Popular Astronomy: School Edition* (New York: Harper and Brothers, 1883), 104.

12. <Ms III^c adds "Multiplicity of Galaxies-Universes"—*Ed.*>

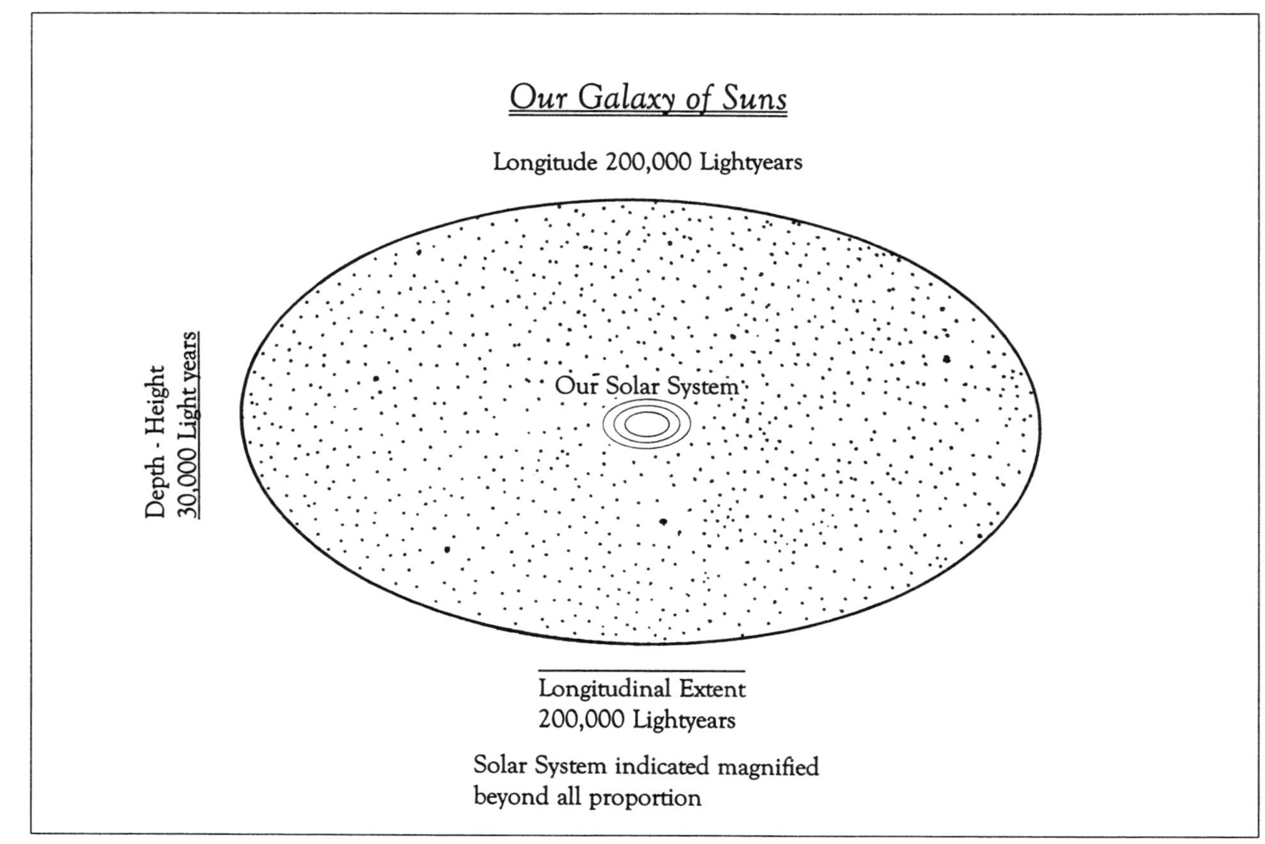

Illustration 3

> light travels 186,000 miles per second! The longer diameter of the galaxy is about 200,000 light years.
>
> The stars of this galaxy move around among one another something like bees in a swarm. This does not mean that they dart quickly from one side to the other, for although our sun is moving at the rate of four hundred million miles a year, the distance between the stars are so vast that its relations to other suns have not changed appreciatively in historic time.

Of course, these distances are beyond human comprehension or realization; but we can know, and do know, on the report of those competent to speak with authority, that these immense numbers, representing the distances which separate the stars from each other, are facts, and being facts, they almost overwhelm one by their immensity.

UNIVERSE OF "MAGNIFICENT DISTANCES"[13]

Prof. Moulton, continuing his lecture, showed a photograph which was taken with light that had been on its way a million years, then continued his remarks:

> Until recently many astronomers thought there was only vacant space beyond our galaxy, but now it is known that there are exterior galaxies similar to our own in size and shape and the number of suns. Only about a year ago Dr. Edwin P. Hubble at Wilson Observatory determined the distance of an exterior galaxy which had heretofore been called the Andromeda Nebula, and found it to be a million light years. About half of the thousand million stars [suns] in our own galaxy are in size and constitution and temperature essentially similar to our own sun. It is not improbable—it is in fact probable—that a majority of them have planets circulating about them, as our earth revolves about the sun. It may be that a fraction of them, perhaps in all hundreds of millions, are in a condition comparable to that of the earth, and that they support life!

One might continue to multiply authoritative statements concerning the vastness of the universe and the wonderfulness of it, but my only purpose in calling attention to all this is merely to impress the mind of the reader with the greatness of these existing stellar universes, to make it the basis of reasoning to be followed later on. What is here set down, being of unquestioned authority, may be sufficient to my purpose, to be developed in future chapters.

---

13. <Ms III^c adds "Universe of 'Magnificent Distances'"—*Ed.*>

CHAPTER VI

Creation: The Reign of Law

SCRIPTURE READING LESSON

Analysis

I. What Is Creation?

II. The Reign of Law.

III. Order—the Evidence of a Reign of Law.

IV. Authorities on a Reign of Law.

V. Reign of Law in the Spiritual World.

VI. The Intrusion of "Miracles."

VII. Destructive Forces under Law.

VIII. Modern Revelation on the Universe and a Reign of Law—Joseph Smith.

References

All the works referred to in the text of this chapter. With a view, of course, of a wider reading of them than the quoted passages herein.

D&C 88:36-47.

Also, Moses and Abraham. I especially commend Henry Drummond's *Natural Law in the Spiritual World* (New York: James Pott and Co., 1893) for a reading.

CHAPTER VI
Creation: The Reign of Law

WHAT IS CREATION?

The next question that logically rises to meet our inquiry is: How came all these galaxy-universes, solar systems, and planets and their satellites into existence? By chance? By creative decree of harmonized Intelligences—God? Or by self-evolution from forces within the chaotic elements—automatic creation?

The universe coming into existence by chance may be dismissed at once, not only as altogether unlikely but positively unbelievable—the one fact of order in the universe rendering it so; and with that observation that division of the inquiry may be closed ere it is opened.

Committed as we already are in these pages to the existence of limitless space and eternal duration, to the eternal existence of matter and energy, and mind or spirit, it follows that "creation" can only consist of certain events or changes in, and within, these eternal existences. That creation is not a bringing forth of something from nothing, but a transmutation of one form of substance into another form. As for example, water is caused, or "created," by a union of hydrogen and oxygen—both gaseous substances—in certain definite proportions. These gases are changed in their nature by being united in the proportion of two volumes of hydrogen to one volume of oxygen; and changed from gases to liquid. But the water is not created or caused from nothing, but from these two pre-existing gases; and whatever should effect the bringing together of these two gases in this proportion, would be the "cause" or "creator" of water; the gases themselves, however, being "con-causes" since the water could not exist but for them, hence they enter into the causation of the water.

Creation, therefore, with those who accept the eternal existence—and, therefore, the co-eternal existence—of matter, force, and mind, can only regard "creation" as events or changes wrought in an eternal universe. "Creation" thus conceived, while it would never mean "create" in the sense of bringing into existence force or matter or mind (spirit), yet it might be conceived of as bringing into new relations matter and force; and bring into existence new combinations, which would really bring into being new things or new conditions. Even "mind" or "spirit" might be brought into such relationships with matter as to be an indwelling force in varied life-forms, influencing the trend of things in the universe tremendously, bringing about awe-inspiring results, changing the whole aspect of a universe, giving it a development worthy <of> the highest order of intelligence, and imparting to it a definite object of achievement.

It is not in this chapter, however, that we have designed to discuss at length the nature of the universe, and the subject of creation. That theme is reserved for a later chapter; here we merely bring the subject to the reader's attention to preserve the natural sequence of thought-development. Hence, so much of passing surface comment on the existence of the wonderful universe and how it may have been wrought to be, as it now is.

THE REIGN OF LAW

A subject more pertinent at this stage of our unfolding theme is the control or governance of the universe—this immensity—this eternal thing! Thoughtful minds are ready to say and do say that the impressive thing about the universe is not really its immensity or its eternity, but the fact of order within it, a thing which seems to be of its essence, or a quality of it. Professor Frank C. <Forest R.> Moulton, of the University of Chicago, whose lecture before the American Association for the Promotion <Advancement> of Science (December 31, 1925), we have already quoted on the extent and greatness of the universe, has this to say also on the "orderliness" of the universe:

> The impressive thing to the astronomers is not the magnitude of the [our] galaxy, nor the long periods of time during which stars exist, nor the tremendous forces of nature; but the most impressive thing [to him] is that all this vast universe, which we have been able to explore, is found to be orderly. The orderliness of the universe is the foundation on which science is built. It is the thing that enables us to understand the present, to look back over the past, and to penetrate the remote future. This discovery more than compensates us for the relatively unimportant position that man occupies physically.

ORDER—THE EVIDENCE OF A REIGN OF LAW[1]

John W. Draper says:

> The orderly movement of the heavens could not fail in all ages to make a deep impression on thoughtful observers—the rising and setting of the sun; the increasing or diminishing light of the day; the waxing and waning of the moon; the return of the seasons in their proper course<s>; the measured march of the wandering planets in

1. <Ms III^{c} adds "Order The Evidence of a Reign of Law"—*Ed.*>

the sky—what are all these and a thousand such, but manifestations of an orderly and unchanging procession of events? The faith of early observers in this interpretation may perhaps have been shaken by the occurrence of such phenomenon as an eclipse, a sudden and mysterious breach of the ordinary course of <natural> events; but it would be resumed in tenfold strength as soon as the discovery was made that eclipses themselves recur and may be predicted.

Astronomical predictions of all kinds depend upon the admission of this fact—that there never has been and never will be any intervention in the operation of natural laws. The scientific philosopher affirms that the condition of the world at any given moment is the direct result of its condition in the preceding moment, and the direct cause of its condition in the subsequent moment.[2]

AUTHORITIES ON THE REIGN OF LAW[3]

In the remainder of the chapter above quoted, Draper traces the struggle between the idea of government by special providence and government by "unvarying law," until the latter triumphs in modern thought and science.

To the same purpose Andrew D. White, once professor of history at Cornell University and president of the university for twenty-five years, published his great work, *A History of the Warfare of Science with Theology*.[4] The title of a few of the chapters will show the drift of the thought: "From Creation to Evolution," "From 'Signs and Wonders' to Law in Heaven," "From Genesis to Geology," "From Magic to Chemistry and Physics," "From Miracles to Medicine," and so following.

John Fiske of Harvard, in his *Studies in Religion*, says:

> We have so far spelled out the history of creation as to see that all has been done in strict accordance with law. . . . So beautiful is all this orderly coherence, so satisfying to some of our intellectual needs, that many minds are inclined to doubt, if anything more can be said of the universe than that it is a Reign of Law, an endless aggregate of coexistences and sequences.[5]

This last suggestion of Fiske's, however, is a thought against which the reader should brace his mind, for the universe, however completely under a reign of law,

---

2. John William Draper, *History of the Conflict between Religion and Science*, 6th ed. (New York: D. Appleton and Co., 1875), 229-30.

3. <Ms III^{c} adds "Authorities on the Reign of Law"—*Ed.*>

4. Andrew D. White, *A History of the Warfare of Science with Theology*, 2 vols. (New York: D. Appleton and Co., 1903).

5. John Fiske, *Studies in Religion*, in *The Miscellaneous Writings of John Fiske, with Many Portraits of Illustrious Philosophers, Scientists, and Other Men of Note* (Boston and New York: Houghton, Mifflin and Co., 1902), 9:337-38.

is something more than law, and the "reign" of it, even if there is added Fiske's qualifying words of "an endless aggregate of coexistences and sequences." For a reign of law observed in the universe suggests something more of which the reign of law is but a part and not the whole;[6] namely, Mind, Intelligence. The reign of law should rather be conceived as the means through which Intelligence is working to the achievement of some high purpose.

REIGN OF LAW IN THE SPIRITUAL WORLD[7]

Henry Drummond in 1893[8] published his *Natural Law in the Spiritual World* with a view, as the title suggests, of bringing the phenomena of the spirit-world into harmony with the modern scientific conceptions that obtain respecting the natural world. His self-imposed task was to "demonstrate the naturalness of the supernatural"—that the natural and the spiritual world are one. Drummond's conception was a noble one and resulted in the production of a very notable and convincing book, though meeting in some quarters with the impatience that attaches to works of its class, viz., the class that attempts to work out harmony between science and religion, or between the natural and the spiritual world.[9]

The idea of law itself implies the possibility of disorder, which must result from infraction of law, that is, a departure from or violation of law. But "that which is governed by law," it may be reasonably supposed, will be preserved by law, "and perfected and sanctified by the same" (D&C 88:34).

---

6. <Ms III[*] "the reign of law is but the effect"—*Ed.*>

7. <Ms III[c] adds the typewritten "Reign of Law In The Spiritual," and then follows with the handwritten "Word," doubtless intending the word "World"—*Ed.*>

8. <The first edition was published about 1884—*Ed.*>

9. Thus, Andrew D. White in his *A History of the Warfare of Science with Theology in Christendom* (New York: D. Appleton and Co., 1896), 1:218, speaking of the phases of theological attack upon science, represents the third and the last as "an attempt" at compromise—"compromise by means of far-fetched reconciliations of textual statements with ascertained fact." That Drummond himself was aware that these "attempts at compromise" of the "conflict" between science and religion, or the "natural and spiritual world," is evident from his preface, where he says: "No class of works is received with more suspicion, I had almost said derision, than those which deal with Science and Religion. Science is tired of reconciliations between two things which never should have been contrasted. Religion is offended by the patronage of an ally which it professes not to need; and the critics have rightly discovered that, in most cases where Science is either pitted against Religion or fused with it, there is some fatal misconception to begin with as to the scope and province of either" (Henry Drummond, *Natural Law in the Spiritual World* [New York: James Pott and Co., 1893], v).

THE INTRUSION OF MIRACLES

In all this about the reign of law the question may arise as to the intrusion of "miracles" into the scheme of things. If the universe is governed by law, does the universal reign of law permit of "miracles," or acts of special providence, which are usually of a nature that they apparently interfere with existing law? For a miracle is regarded as something that happens in violation of law, or by the supervening of it. A miracle is defined as "an event or effect contrary to the established constitution and course of things, or a diversion from the known laws of nature." Renan, the great French writer, defines a miracle to be not simply the inexplicable, "it is a formal derogation from recognized laws in the name of a particular desire." "It is not, therefore, in the name of this or that philosophy," he continues, "but in the name of constant experience that we banish miracles from history. We do not say the miracle is impossible. We say there has been hitherto no miracle performed."[10]

MIRACLE MERGED UNDER LAW[11]

This resolving of miracles into events or effects contrary to the established constitution and course of things, or a deviation from the known laws of nature, is a wrong viewpoint. What is especially faulty in this definition of miracles is that they are held to be outside of or contrary to the laws of nature. Let us examine this. Two hundred years ago the only motive powers known to ocean navigators were wind and the ocean currents. Suppose at that time the old mariners had seen one of our modern ocean steamers running against both ocean currents and the wind; and, withal, making better speed in spite of both wind and tide than the old-time sailing vessel could with both wind and tide in its favor. What would have been the effect of such a sight on the mind of the old-time sailor?[12] "It's a miracle!" he would have exclaimed; that is, it would have been to him "an effect contrary to the constitution and course of things," "a derogation from recognized law." But would such a thing, to us who know something of the force of steam, be contrary to the laws of nature? No, it is simply the employment of a force in nature of which the old-time mariner was ignorant; and while it would have been a "miracle" to him, to us it is merely the application of a comparatively new discovered force of nature, and it is now so common that we cease to look upon it with wonder.

---

10. Ernest Renan, *The Life of Jesus*, trans. Charles E. Wilbour (New York: G. W. Dillingham, 1888), 43-45.

11. <Ms III^{c} adds "Miracle Merged Under Law"—*Ed.*>

12. <Ms III "the minds of the old-time sailor," but the text has been changed to the singular "mind" in order to agree with the immediately-following "sailor"—*Ed.*>

So with many things that people now in ignorance call "miracles": the healing of the sick, restoring the blind to sight, making the lame to walk, through the exercise of faith; and the resurrection of the dead—all these instead of being in derogation from recognized law,[13] may yet turn out to be simply the application of laws of which we are as yet in ignorance. As urged by George Rawlinson, "miraculous interpositions on fitting occasions may be as much a regular, fixed, and established rule of . . . government as the working ordinarily by what are called natural laws." In other words, what men in their ignorance call miracles, are doubtless the results of application of higher laws or forces of nature not yet learned by men, and miracles are to be viewed not as happenings contrary "to the established constitution and course of things," under a universal reign of law, but as part of the not-yet-understood application of law to things and conditions that seem to produce effects that are in derogation of the ordinary course of the natural order of things. From this viewpoint the integrity of a universal reign of law is not incompatible with what may be regarded as Mind interposition, or acts of Providence.

DESTRUCTIVE FORCES UNDER LAW

When a reign of law is conceived as governing in the physical world, then the conception must include the destructive or disintegrating forces, as operating under law as well as the constructive or integrating forces; else the reign of law would not be universal. On the subject of destructive forces being operative in the universe Ernst Haeckel has the following vivid passage in his *Riddle of the Universe:*

> While new cosmic bodies arise and develop out of rotating masses of nebula in some parts of the universe, in other parts old, extinct, frigid suns come into collision and are once more reduced by the heat generated to the condition of nebulae. . . .
>
> While minute and then larger bodies are being formed by this pyknotic [condensing] process in one part of space, and the intermediate ether[14] increases its strain, the opposite process—the destruction of cosmic bodies by collision—is taking place in another quarter. The immense quantity of heat which is generated in this mechanical process of the collision of swiftly moving bodies represents the new kinetic energy which effects the movement of the resultant nebulae and the construction of new rotating bodies. The eternal drama begins afresh.[15]

---

13. <Ms III* "from organized law"—*Ed.*>

14. <For the theory of the ether, see Edmund T. Whittaker, *A History of the Theories of Aether and Electricity*, 2 vols. ([Los Angeles:] Tomash Publishers, 1987; [New York:] American Institute of Physics, 1987)—*Ed.*>

15. Ernst Haeckel, *The Riddle of the Universe at the Close of the Nineteenth Century*, trans. Joseph McCabe (New York and London: Harper and Bros., 1900), 240, 243.

<Waldemar Kaempffert says:>

> It is clear that the building of suns and the building of worlds is a process . . . in which the original matter must undergo transformation. The process may be continuous and may extend through infinite time. The collision of suns [which could result no otherwise than in destruction of their world-system] may have produced nebulæ <and these nebulæ> in turn may gradually develop themselves into suns again. It seems reasonably certain that nebulæ are the stuff from which the stars are made.[16]

This[17] is not the place for the discussion of the application of this reign of law idea to morals, or to the realm of the things of the spirit, or of mind; that will come later; but we may so far premise as to say that when we reach those realms of discussion we shall find the spiritual and ethical world as universally under the dominion of the reign of law as the physical universe.

JOSEPH SMITH ON THE UNIVERSE AND THE REIGN OF LAW[18]

It is my general policy in the thought-development of my theme to hold in reserve the introduction of the teachings of Joseph Smith with reference to the subject matter of these introductory chapters, but just here, what Joseph Smith said in part on this subject of the extent of the universe and the reign of law in that universe,[19] is so pertinent, and precedes in time of utterance the best and highest scientific pronouncements upon these matters, that I can not withhold from quoting a few brief passages from his revelations, noting the date at which they were set forth:

> There are many kingdoms [meaning by that worlds and systems of worlds-galaxies-universes, and all that in them is]; for there is no space in the which there is no kingdom; and there is no kingdom in which there is no space, either a greater or a lesser kingdom (D&C 88:37).

This is a statement which represents the universe as being quite as extensive and as all comprehending as does Haeckel's "Law of Substance" (quoted in full, chap. 3), though couched in different phrase from that used by the German

---

16. Waldemar Kaempffert, *Astronomy*, vol. 1 of *Science-History of the Universe*, ed. Francis W. Rolt-Wheeler (New York: The Current Literature Publishing Co., 1909), 318. <In the ellipsis Roberts deleted Kaempffert's words "of evolution"—*Ed.*>

17. <Ms III* "The Spiritual World Under A Reign of Law. This"—*Ed.*>

18. <Ms III^c adds "Joseph Smith On The Universe And the Reign of Law"—*Ed.*>

19. <Ms III^c adds "and the reign of law in that universe"—*Ed.*>

scientist, who states as follows: "The extent of the universe is infinite and unbounded; it is empty in no part, but everywhere filled with substance."[20]

Again the revelation:[21]

> And unto every kingdom is given a law; and unto every law there are certain bounds and conditions. All beings who abide not in those conditions are not justified. For intelligence cleaveth unto intelligence; wisdom receiveth wisdom; truth embraces truth; virtue loveth virtue; light cleaveth unto light. . . . [A law has been given] unto all things, by which they move in their times and seasons; and their courses are fixed, even the courses of the heavens and the earth, which comprehend the earth and all the planets. And they give light to each other in their times and in their seasons, in their minutes, and in their hours, in their days, in their weeks, in their months, in their years (D&C 88:38-40, 42-44).

In these terms is the reign of law proclaimed by Joseph Smith and I know of no more emphatic pronouncement upon this subject than the above quotation; and the unique thing about it is that it is set forth as a revelation from God, given in December 1832; Haeckel's *Riddle of the Universe* was published <in German> in 1899!

One further item in the Prophet's[22] statement is particularly significant; namely, the passage: "unto every law there are certain bounds also and conditions." Implying that even law itself is subject to or limited by law. A bold conception this, especially when it is found in a writing formulated a century ago, before men began to voice such conceptions. This same idea of law itself having limits and bounds, or law itself being subject to law, Henry Drummond, one of the recognized thinkers of the nineteenth century, also expressed, but following Joseph Smith by more than half a century. He said: "One of the most striking generalizations of recent times is that even laws have their law[s]."[23] John Fiske also says: "In order to be always sure that we are generalizing correctly, we must make the generalizing process itself a subject of generalization," which is but a recognition of Drummond's idea that "laws have their law[s]" and Joseph Smith's, "to every law there are certain bounds also and conditions."

---

20. <Ernst Haeckel, *The Riddle of the Universe at the Close of the Nineteenth Century*, trans. Joseph McCabe (New York: Harper and Bros., 1900), 242—*Ed.*>

21. <Ms III^{c} adds "the revelation"—*Ed.*>

22. <Ms III^{c} adds "Prophet's"—*Ed.*>

23. Drummond, *Natural Law*, 37. <Drummond's wording is "of recent science is that even Laws have their Law"—*Ed.*>

CHAPTER VII

Nature of the Universe: Eternal or Transient? Caused or Uncaused?

SCRIPTURE READING LESSON

Analysis

I. Universe Conceived as Eternal.

II. Immensity of Universe Suggests Eternity of It.

III. The Nature of Force.

IV. Causation: "First" or "Eternal" Cause?

V. Eternal Cause the More Rational.

VI. First Cause and "Design."

VII. Elements of Cause.

VIII. Dominance of Man in the World:

(a) Over the Animal Kingdom;

(b) Over Vegetable and All Plant Life;

(c) Over the Mineral Kingdom;

(d) Dominion in Social and Civil Life.

IX. From What We Know: Man as *vera causa*

References

John Stuart Mill, *Three Essays on Religion* (New York: H. Holt, 1884), chapter on "Argument for a First Cause," 142-54.

See enlightening comment on Mill by John Fiske, *Studies in Religion*, in *The Miscellaneous Writings of John Fiske, with Many Portraits of Illustrious Philosophers, Scientists, and Other Men of Note* (Boston and New York: Houghton, Mifflin and Co., 1902), 9:81, 126-27, 177-80, 235-38.*

Francis W. Rolt-Wheeler, ed., *Science-History of the Universe* (New York: The Current Literature Publishing Co., 1909), vol. 10 *Philosophy*, especially chaps. 2 and 3.*

*It must be understood always, that the works cited in the column of "References" are by no means accepted by the writer as conclusive authorities (except as to citations to the scriptures); or that he agrees with the conclusions of the authors quoted, or that his text in the chapter agrees with them. His text is an independent treatise, often opposite in its conclusions from the works referred to, though here and there supported by them. The works cited in the reference column are given to encourage a wide reading on the general theme.

CHAPTER VII

Nature of the Universe: Eternal or Transient? Caused or Uncaused?

THE UNIVERSE CONCEIVED AS ETERNAL

The next step in the development of our theme will be to consider briefly the nature of this universe we have contemplated. What is it by nature? Eternal or transient? Has it had a beginning in time and must it come to an end? Or is it eternal, without beginning and without end? Authorities may be martialed on both these views, the eternity of the universe and the universe transient. Some claiming on this head to speak from the result of human investigation, human science, and human philosophy; and others giving interpretation of revelations as the ground of their belief. The fact, however, of an eternal or a transient universe may not be satisfactorily settled by quotations of authorities, and so it is for us to search it out as best we may both by consideration of reasoning from what we know, as also (ultimately) from interpretation of revelation.

The conception of the eternity of the universe may be said to run parallel with certain other eternal things that we have considered; namely, space, duration, and the "conservation of mass," meaning by the last the indestructibility of matter, and its twin-truth, the uncreatability of it. Here we have eternal things to deal with, and we have already in a previous chapter traced them to the point where the conception of their eternity becomes a necessary truth, because the contrary—the bounding of space, the limiting of duration, the destruction and creatability of matter are inconceivable. It may be that the eternity of the universe can be treated in the same manner.

IMMENSITY OF THE UNIVERSE SUGGESTS ETERNITY OF IT[1]

From the extent of the universe, already traced in these chapters, the immensity of it, even of the cosmos—if it is shown that <that> immensity of it is also

1. <Ms III[c] adds "Immensity of the Universe Suggests Eternity of it"—*Ed.*>

limitless[2]–goes far towards establishing the inconceivability of its beginning in time or ending in time; but the extent of it, we may be sure, as suggested by that which is revealed to us by telescope, supplemented by the eye of science–meaning the photographic eye of science–it is still greater than that to our thought; and thought itself becomes lost, and intelligence a bit confused in trying to grasp the limitlessness of it;[3] and the time, and the place, and the manner of its beginning may not be conceived. Equally true is it that the end of it may not be conceived; but the realization of its eternity may be apprehended when we are reminded that there must be room in infinite space for all matter, organized and unorganized; cosmos and chaos. Room for the endless multiplication of worlds and solar systems of worlds and galaxies, which may be termed local universes–if the paradoxical expression may be pardoned–*ad infinitum*. Room for the working out of changes that affect the development of all that is, from lower forms of existences to higher forms, and all those endless changes necessary to this development–there is room for all this in boundless space; and time for it in endless duration; and material for it in the existence of exhaustless and enduring matter. An eternal universe, in fact, seems to match these other three eternal things and conditions–space and time and matter; and while, as I have said, the existence of an eternal universe is difficult to hold in consciousness, it is not as difficult as it is to form a conception of its having a beginning or of reaching an end. Nay, indeed, beginning and end seem inconceivable and, hence, impossible; and again we arrive at the establishment of a necessary truth because the opposite is unthinkable. Also, the parallel eternities of space, time, and matter seem to require an eternal universe as a necessary concomitant of the whole realm of thought and fact.

THE NATURE OF FORCE

Another thing to be considered in our progressive thought is that of force in the universe, which may be considered the power by which things move, which compells, so far as human knowledge knows, the changes that take place in all parts of the known universe. What is this force? Mechanical or intelligent; the effect of mind upon matter, or is it the blind, mechanical power of "dead matter," such as the force called gravitation is supposed to be, existing and depending upon masses of matter, and their relative distances from each other for the manifestation of force in attraction or in repulsion?

---

2. <Ms III[c] adds "if it is shown that immensity of it is also limitless"–*Ed.*>
3. <Ms III[*] "the immensity of it"–*Ed.*>

CAUSATION: "FIRST" OR "ETERNAL" CAUSE?[4]

With these remarks on the eternity of the universe, arises naturally the question of the causation or the "cause" of things, or of events, which are but changes within the universe. The idea of a "first cause" is necessarily eliminated by the conception of the eternity of the universe. "First Cause" implies a time when there was no cause; when there was absolute inaction, or absence of causation; but as the universe is eternal and includes in that eternal existence the existence of force and mind as well as of matter, there can be no "first" but there may be <an> "eternal cause";[5] and that cause eternally present is the cause of events or changes in the eternal universe. The universe itself is uncaused, since it has always existed, and is all that is, including all forces whatsoever,[6] as also all intelligence or mind–it is[7] "the sum of existence!"

ETERNAL CAUSE MORE RATIONAL[8]

The operation of an eternal cause constantly present and acting in an eternal universe, is more rational than the conception of a "first cause," followed by secondary causes. For that "first" presents a mental problem more difficult to account for than an eternal universe in which is operating eternal causation, and that "causation" when regarded as eternal leads up to the conception of the dominance of mind over matter as completely as when the universe and its phenomena are accounted for by the conception of a "first cause," and all that follows it. For if we could trace all things up to the "first cause," we would be brought face to face with that which would challenge our question–Whence is this?–this first cause?

OF DESIGN IN THE UNIVERSE[9]

This "first cause" idea involves us in the whole argument of the designer of the universe, a designer that at once is outside of and transcends the universe; and of which idea the "watch" illustration of Dean Paley's *Natural Theology* is usually depended upon to establish; and which briefly is as follows:

A watch is found and learning the complexity of its structure, and finding the

---

4. <Ms III^{c} adds "'First' Or 'Eternal' Cause?"–*Ed.*>
5. <Ms III* "no 'first cause' but 'eternal cause'"–*Ed.*>
6. <Ms III* "all forces of whatsoever origin"–*Ed.*>
7. <Ms III^{c} adds "it is"–*Ed.*>
8. <Ms III^{c} adds "Eternal Cause More Rational"–*Ed.*>
9. <Ms III* of section heading "'First' or 'Eternal' Cause"–*Ed.*>

adjustments of its parts to be such that it is a measure of passing time, the finder concludes it must have had a designer, it bears so many evidences of that fact. So man beholds the universe; he finds so many evidences of design in it that he arrives at the conclusion that it, too, must have had a designer, a "cause." The application of the illustration to the universe will be obvious. To all which some deist makes answer: the watch finder analyzes the watch, notes the adjustment of the parts to the whole, and the end it serves—the measurement of time—and is satisfied that it had a designer, and goes in search of him. He finds that the designer, the "cause" of the watch, to be a man; but the watchmaker, the man, is more wonderful by far than the watch, the thing he created; and the question is—who caused or designed the watchmaker? For if the watch by being so wonderful, and its parts so adjusted as to achieve a certain, useful end, then surely the watch designer, more wonderful than the watch, must be accounted for by causation back of him. And doubtless if the designer of, or the creator of, the man could be found, he would yet be more wonderful than the man, and clamor more loudly than the man for an accounting for; and so on *ad infinitum.*[10]

This brings home to the consciousness the inadequacy of this argument for a first cause; and also suggests that the mind can not rest in an endless chain of cause-effects; that it can come to rest only in the conception of an "eternal cause" rather than a "first cause." This <is> "a necessary truth" because the mind can not rationally conceive and hold how it could be otherwise.

ELEMENTS OF CAUSE

"Cause" is defined as the power or efficient agent producing anything or an event. "In a comprehensive sense" the "cause" has to do with "all the circumstances [powers, occasions, actions, and conditions] necessary for an event, and necessarily followed by it—the entire antecedent of an event." Causes may be regarded, and are regarded, as efficient, material, formal, and final; efficient cause is the power or agency producing anything or an event, the power to produce completely; material cause is the material out of which, by the efficient causes, anything is made; formal cause is the pattern, place, or form, according to which anything is produced by the operation of efficient causes; final cause is that eternal power within the eternal and uncaused universe, but existing nevertheless,[11] which is the source of all power producing change, motion, and life. "It," mind or intelligence, is that which acts

10. William Paley, *Natural Theology; or, Evidences of the Existence and Attributes of the Deity, Collected from the Appearances of Nature* (New York: Sheldon and Co., 1854), American ed., chap. 1.

11. <Ms III* "uncaused universe, uncreated, but existing nevertheless"—*Ed.*>

as eternal cause and produces change and development. The human mind may not rest in an endless chain of cause-effects, as before stated; but it can rest in the thought of the universe being eternal, in having neither beginning nor end, in time, or space, or substance; because the mind can not conceive the beginning of the universe or the "first cause" of it. But the mind can rest in the conception of an eternal universe as being all that is, the "sum of existence," including all mind, all intelligence—the light by which truth is discerned, as well as all matter; which is to say, including that which acts—force, mind—as well as that which is acted upon—matter. With mind or intelligence recognized as the eternal power and the eternal cause whence proceeds the ever-changing development within and throughout the universe—this relieves the mind of the perplexities of a "first cause," and at the same time does no violence to the requirements of the mind for the presence and operation of efficient, material, formal, and final causation in the universe.

So far as human experiences are concerned, it is quite evident from what we know from those experiences that force, and ultimately mind, dominates matter. In our modern experiences this dominance of mind over matter is being emphasized.

THE DOMINANCE OF MAN IN THE WORLD[12]

(a) Over the Animal Kingdom

It is represented in some revelations[13] that when God had created man he gave him dominion over all the earth, with a commandment to subdue it, and have dominion over all that was upon it (Gen. 1). And responding to this commandment whether resulting from revelation or from powers inherent in man by nature, he has been carrying out such a decree, and with ever-increasing success he is holding and developing his dominion. He has mastered the animal kingdom in air, sea, and earth. Though physically inferior in brute strength to many of earth's creatures, in all three realms named, he has subdued them to his will, compelled them to receive his mastery, and by the force of mind has created those instrumentalities which make him superior to them even in physical destructive powers, where that becomes necessary to assert his mastery. Many of these creatures he has compelled to be his servants, to carry himself and his belongings with all their speed from place to place; to aid him in his toil of cultivating the earth, and in all his labor. The skins of the animal kingdom yield him clothing, and their flesh, in part, supply his food.

---

12. <Ms III[c] adds "The Dominance of Man in the World"—*Ed.*>

13. <Ms III[*] "in some alleged revelations"—*Ed.*>

(b) Over Plant Life[14]

In like manner he has taken possession and bent to his using the product of the plant life of the earth. The wild variety of fruits he has improved by cultivation and has created infinite variety to please his taste and provide the variations in diet essential to his health. The grains and other plant life have received similar treatment, man multiplies and so largely controls their production that in the matter of necessary food products the race may feel fairly secure; and famines and the possibility of their recurrence are constantly growing less frequent.

From plant life as well as from animal life man takes that which clothes his body. The cotton-plant whose bursting bowls whitening in the autumn sun of southern lands, as well as wool from countless thousands of sheep, and the shining thread of the silk worm, combined to give apparel in modern days more glorious than clothed the limbs of a voluptuous Solomon in all his glory.

(c) Over the Mineral Kingdom[15]

Man has broken into the coal reserves of the earth's bowels and brought them forth to release the sunshine of past ages stored in them to give him light, to warm his dwellings, and drive his machinery; he has tapped the oil lakes of the earth's interior, and released the stored energy found in oil to drive his trains, his ships, his automobiles, and his airplanes. From the silver seams of the mountains and the gold-laden sands of river beds and the ancient quartz-sites, and the gem-laden gravels of great depths—all these he has gathered, and converted into ornaments to beautify his dwellings and his person. Sad to say, also, he has combined chemical substances in such manner as to create explosive forces employed in his destructive wars. He has made conquest over distances by bringing all parts of the world into instant means of communication. He has gradually lessened the inconvenience of distance by rapid means of transportation through express trains, automobiles, his palatial steam-driven ocean vessels, and now the more rapid means of transportation through the air by zeppelins and airplanes. In a word, in the realm of physical mastery, man has been gaining great victories of late.

(d) Dominion in Social and Civil Life[16]

Also in the social and the civil spheres as represented by municipal, national, and international life, man has made great gains. In the realm of knowledge, also, he has made advancement—almost miraculously; at least far beyond all progress in

---

14. <Ms III^c adds "(b) Over Plant Life"—*Ed.*>
15. <Ms III^c adds "(c) Over The Mineral Kingdom"—*Ed.*>
16. <Ms III^c adds "(d) Dominion In Social and Civil Life"—*Ed.*>

former ages. Although perhaps less noticeably, man has also made advancement in moral and spiritual things. His social relations are characterized by more kindness than in the past. He is more humane in caring for the unfortunate, than in the past. A truer sense of justice for those occupying the lowly stations in life are improved. There are juster laws operating in human relations than in past times. A wider enjoyment of civil and political rights than heretofore; a wider distribution of material comforts. The race is better housed and fed and clothed than in ages gone by.[17] More have access to the enjoyment of luxuries than ever before, and the trend of all things human is in the direction of the betterment of human lives, both individually and in society at large. There is a note of optimism in human life that prophesies wider and greater and deeper and more permanent welfare for the children of men, and for the nations, for civilization. Man is evidently fulfilling what is represented in revelation to be the decree of God that man should have dominion over the earth and subdue it.

In man's experiences, intelligence, or mind, is in creasingly dominating matter. It leads to the conception that everywhere it must be so. It is so in this world of ours. We know it to be so. And reasoning from what we know, it must be so in other worlds—in all worlds. Has it not always been true? Will it not always be true, that mind, whatever may be conceded to mechanical forces—such as gravitation and chemical reactions—mind will always dominate matter and manipulate eternally-existing force in such manner as to achieve its purpose? Great weight will yet attach to the utterance of an ancient American prophet, viz., that phenomena, when traced to their last analysis, rest upon two things; viz.: "That which acts, and that which is acted upon" (2 Ne. 2:13-14) and that from this fact proceeds all that is; from which action and reaction proceed creations and re-creations within the universe, arising from ever-changing processes, culminating in development in boundless space, and endless time, and indestructible, inexhaustible matter.

FROM WHAT WE KNOW: MAN AS VERA CAUSA

Let us again resort to reasoning from what we know. Undoubtedly man finds in himself a principle of causality in the light of which he interprets the external world. In fact, man finds within himself the nearest approach to a *vera causa*—a true or real cause. How does this power of causation proceed with and through him? He is in the world with all that environs him—a world of things and forces are about him. He conceives the notion of building a house. If he builds it, he will be the efficient cause of its existence; but his power of causation of which he is self-conscious, as resident within himself, he finds to be subject to his will. He may

17. <Ms III* "than in times past"—*Ed.*>

or may not conclude to build the house–it will be just as he chooses. But he concludes to build it, to suit his convenience and to meet his felt needs. He did not have to create out of nothing the things of which he made the house, they already existed; all that he had to do was to effect certain changes in materials about him, assemble them in a certain order and the house is completed. The builder caused its existence. In all this procedure the mind of the man that was operating as a power of causation, was operating somewhat as a mind anywhere might act where like conditions obtained–as eternal mind might be found acting or causing. The man was acting as the intelligent factor in causation.

Instead of one man building a house we may think of a large group of men building, or causing to come into existence, a city. To do this, however, the men must be united–that is, their minds must be united as one mind, and when many minds are perfectly united in agreement, they can be as effective in that unity as if there was but one mind. They are one mind, though made up of many individual minds. They form a community mind and may be spoken of as "one." So the minds or intelligences of the universe may be spoken of, when harmonized as the universal mind, or simply mind, or intelligence. The group of men we have supposed, caused their city as the one man caused his house to come into existence. The group of men, no more than the one man, had <not> to create out of nothing the materials for their city; they as minds united were already existent and were there. All they had to do was to come to agreement of purpose to effect changes in materials already existing, assemble them in a given manner, by the manipulation of forces already existent, and the city was caused or builded.

In all this procedure the minds of these men united were operating as a power of causation, and operating as minds united anywhere might act, where like conditions obtain; and these conditions obtain in an eternal universe, that comprehends all things, and is the "sum of existence"–all mind or minds; all intelligence or intelligences, with all forces mechanical or chemical existent, as also all matter and conceivable substance in boundless space in endless time, the mass of it constant, so that it can not be created nor annihilated, nothing added to it and not possible to be diminished by so much as a single atom, but subject to infinite changes; and with force or energy equally as conserved as matter, and equally impossible for the amount of it to be increased or diminished, but capable of being infinitely transmuted from one thing to another–all this, with eternal mind as eternal power of causation in all its phases present–change and development, what we call creation and progress, may go on as it has eternally been going on, without beginning and without end; secure in its eternity, which is to say secure in its existence–and under the guidance of all intelligence–all the intelligence there is–we may be assured that the universe is secure, and progress within it also secure. The universe will not die. It will not sink into chaos. It has been and will be eternal.

CHAPTER VIII
Intelligence or Mind and Minds

SCRIPTURE READING LESSON

Analysis

I. The Nature of Intelligence—the Sense in Which Used.

II. Mind Powers:

(a) Generalization.

(b) Imagination, Example, Flight of

(c) Power to Form New Combinations.

(d) To Deliberate; to Will.

III. Eternity of Intelligences.

IV. "The Mysterious Something."

V. Summary of Mind-Element in the Universe.

References

William James, *Psychology* (New York: Henry Holt and Co., 1892), especially chap. 12, "The Self."

Sir Oliver Lodge, *Science and Immortality* (New York: Moffat, Yard, and Co., 1908).

William Poland, Professor of Philosophy in St. Louis University, *The Truth of Thought or Material Logic: A Short Treatise on the Initial Philosophy, the Groundwork Necessary for the Consistent Pursuit of Knowledge* (New York: Silver, Burdett and Co., 1896).

D&C 93.

Joseph Smith, *The King Follett Discourse; The Being and Kind of Being God Is; The Immortality of the Intelligence of Man,* delivered at Nauvoo in April 1844, annotated by B. H. Roberts (Salt Lake City: Magazine Printing Co., 1926), pamphlet.

François P. G. Guizot, *The History of Civilization, from the Fall of the Roman Empire to the French Revolution,* 4 vols., trans. William Hazlitt (New York: D. Appleton and Co., 1867), vol. 2, lecture 5, 115-25.*

*Of all the treatis<es> on the subject of the "Will" it has been my lot to read, I have found nothing that excels this treatise by Guizot. A summary of it will be found in my *Outlines of Ecclesiastical History* (Salt Lake City: George Q. Cannon and Sons, 1893), part II, section ii.

CHAPTER VIII

Intelligence or Mind and Minds

THE NATURE OF INTELLIGENCE

This chapter has especially to do with the mind-element of the universe; for we shall hold here that there is a distinction between mind and matter, as there is a difference between that which acts and that which is acted upon; as there is a difference between the thinking essence or substance and that which has or manifests mechanical force merely, and which for the manifestation of that force is dependent upon its mass and its relative distance from other masses—gravitation; as[1] also there is a difference between intelligence viewed as "the light of truth"—the power by which truth is discerned—and substances capable merely of manifesting chemical force dependent upon union in certain combinations and proportions with other substances. Moreover, we shall hold that there is a difference in mind stuff as there are differences in matter; distinction between the intelligence of man and the instinct of brutes. As this work is concerned chiefly with man, it is of man's mind, or man as[2] an intelligence, that we shall here speak of him, and of his relationships to other intelligences of this and of other worlds.

The sense in which the term "intelligence" is to be used in this discussion is that of a mind, or an intelligent entity. Milton makes such use of the term as the latter when he represents Adam as saying to the angel Raphael, who has given him a lesson on human limitations:

> How fully hast thou satisfied me, pure
> Intelligence of heaven, angel serene![3]

And so Tennyson:

---

1. <Ms III[*] "masses—gravitation; or upon combination or separation of substances as"—*Ed.*>

2. <Ms III[c] adds "as"—*Ed.*>

3. John Milton, *Paradise Lost*, ed. Roy Flannagan (New York: Macmillan Publishing Co., 1993), bk 8, l. 181, 438.

The great Intelligences fair,
That range above our mortal state.[4]

Also, the Being whom men call God is referred to as the "Supreme Intelligence." It is in this sense, then, that I use the term "intelligence"–a being that is intelligent, capable of apprehending facts or ideas; possessed also of power to think, to will, and to act. In other words, the term "intelligence" is descriptive of the thing to which it is applied. Intelligence (mind), or intelligences (minds), thus conceived, are conscious beings. Conscious of self and of the not-self; of the "me" and the "not me." "Intelligence is that which sees itself (as), or is, at once, both subject and object." It knows itself as thinking, that is, as a subject; thinking of itself, it knows itself as an object of thought–of its own thought. And it knows itself as distinct from a vast universe of things which are not itself; itself the while remaining constant as a distinct individuality amid the great universe of things not self. Fiske calls consciousness "the soul's fundamental fact" and "the most fundamental of facts."[5] It may be defined as the power by which intelligence knows its own acts and states. It is an awareness of mind–it is mind in awareness. By reason of awareness–consciousness–an intelligence when dwelling in a body–as we best know it, as man–knows itself as seeing, hearing, smelling, tasting, touching; also as searching and finding; as inquiring and answering; as active or at rest; as loving or hating; as contented or restless; as advancing or receding; as gaining or losing; and so following, in all the activities in which intelligences, as men, engage.

POWER OF GENERALIZATION

By another power or faculty, intelligence (mind) "can perceive, as connected with the things that sense perceives, something that cannot be taken in by sense perception." That is to say, intelligence can generalize. "Sense can get at the individual, concrete thing only: 'this triangle,' 'this orange,' 'that triangle,' 'those oranges,' etc." By the consideration of the individual, concrete object, however, "the mind can form an idea, a concept, a general notion–'triangle,' 'orange'–which does not specify this or that individual [object], but fits to any individual 'triangle' or 'orange' . . . past, present, or future, and even the possible oranges that never

---

4. Alfred Lord Tennyson, *In Memoriam*, in Susan Shatto and Marion Shaw, eds. (Oxford: Clarendon Press, 1982), stanza 85, 100.

5. John Fiske, *Studies in Religion*, in *The Miscellaneous Writings of John Fiske, with Many Portraits of Illustrious Philosophers, Scientists, and Other Men of Note* (Boston and New York: Houghton, Mifflin and Co., 1902), 9:244-45.

shall be grown."[6] In other words, intelligence can rise from consideration of the particular to the general.

Again, there are *a priori* principles, which the mind can perceive to be incontrovertible and of universal application, by mere reflection upon the signification of the principles and without going into the applications.[7] Such, for example, as that one and one make two, that two and one make three. To continue the illustration above, borrowed from the late Professor William James, for some time Professor of Psychology in Harvard University:

> It is either a principle or a definition that one and one make two; that two and one make three, . . . that white differs less from gray than it does from black; that when the cause begins to act the effect also commences. Such propositions hold of all possible "ones," of all conceivable "whites," and "grays," and "causes." The objects here are mental objects. Their relations are perceptually obvious[8] at a glance, and no sense-verification is necessary. Moreover, once true, always true, of those same mental objects. Truth here has an "eternal" character. If you can find a concrete thing anywhere that is "one" or "white" or "gray" or an "effect," then your principles will everlastingly apply to it. It is but a case of ascertaining the kind, and then applying the law of its kind to the particular object. You are sure to get truth, if you can <but> name the kind rightly, for your mental relations hold good of everything of that kind without exception.[9]

IMAGINATION

By a mind-power known as imagination, or imaginative memory, intelligence, as known to us through men, can hold before consciousness, in picture, what has been perceived by an outward sense, and this even when the outward sense has been shut off from the outward world of matter. I once saw an orange tree with a number of ripe oranges scattered through its branches, but on other branches of the same tree, and at the same time, were orange blossoms. What the outward senses then perceived, when I was standing before the tree, has been shut off; but at will I can call before the vision of my mind and hold in consciousness the picture of that tree with its mixture of ripe fruit and fruit blossoms. This power of imagination is also constructive. Intelligences (men) can put before themselves in

---

6. William Poland, Professor of Rational Philosophy, St. Louis University, *The Truth of Thought or Material Logic: A Short Treatise on the Initial Philosophy, the Groundwork Necessary for the Consistent Pursuit of Knowledge* (New York: Silver, Burdett and Co., 1896), 41.

7. Ibid.

8. <Ms III "Their relations are perpetually obvious"–*Ed.*>

9. William James, *Pragmatism: A New Name for Some Old Ways of Thinking: Popular Lectures on Philosophy* (New York: Longmans, Green, and Co., 1908), 209-10.

mental picture, combinations which are fashioned from the varied stores of memory.

> Sensations, once experienced, modify the nervous organism, so that copies of them arise again in the mind after the original outward stimulus is gone. No mental copy, however, can arise in the mind, of any kind of sensation which has never been directly excited from without.
>
> The blind may dream of sights, the deaf of sounds, for years after they have lost their vision or hearing; but the man born deaf can never be made to imagine what sound is like, nor can the man born blind ever have a mental vision. In <John> Locke's words, . . . "The mind can frame unto itself no one, new, simple idea." The originals of them all must have been given from without. Fantasy, or imagination, are the names given to the faculty of reproducing copies of originals once felt.[10] The imagination is called "reproductive" when the copies are literal; "productive" when elements from different originals are recombined so as to make new wholes.[11]

EXAMPLE, FLIGHT OF IMAGINATION

As I have elsewhere said:

> I am this moment sitting at my desk and am enclosed by the four walls of my room—limited as to my personal presence to this spot. But by the mere act of my will, I find I have the power to project myself in thought to any part of the world.[12] Instantly I can be in the crowded streets of the world's metropolis—[London]. I walk through its well-remembered thoroughfares, I hear the rush and roar of its busy multitudes, the rumble of vehicles, the huckster's cries, the cabman's calls,[13] sharp exclamations and quick retorts in the jostling throngs; the beggar's piping cry, the sailor's song, fragments of conversation, broken strains of music, the blare of trumpets, the neighing of horses, ear-piercing whistles, ringing of bells, shouts, responses, rushing trains and all that mingled din and soul-stirring roar that rises in clamor above the great town's traffic.
>
> At will, I leave all this and stand alone on mountain tops in Syria, India, or overlooking old Nile's valley, wrapped in the awful grandeur of solemn silence. Here I may bid fallen empires rise and pass into grand procession before my mental vision and [make them] live again [in my thought] their little lives; fight once more their battles; begin again each petty struggle for place, for power, for control of the world's affairs; revive their customs; live again their loves and hates, and preach once more their religions and their philosophies—all this the mind may do, and that as easily and as

---

10. <Ms III[*] "of originals once left"—*Ed.*>

11. William James, *Psychology* (New York: Henry Holt and Co., 1892), 302.

12. <Ms III[c] adds the handwritten "I have visited," which is then deleted—*Ed.*>

13. <Ms III "the cabmen's calls," but Roberts's text in *The Mormon Doctrine of Deity* has "the cabman's calls"—*Ed.*>

quickly as in thought it may leave this room, cross the street to a neighbor's home, and there take note of the familiar objects within his habitation.[14]

POWER OF FORMING NEW MENTAL[15] COMBINATIONS

"The mind [intelligence] can combine various general principles, or individual facts and principles;[16] and in the combination and comparison of them, it can perceive other facts and principles."[17] In other words, intelligence is capable of reasoning; of building up conclusions from the data of its knowledge. It has the power of deliberation and of judgment; by which it may determine that this state or condition is better than another state or condition. That this, tending to good, should be encouraged; and that, tending to evil, should be discouraged; or, if possible, destroyed; and at least controlled.

POWER OF DELIBERATION:[18] THE WILL

Intelligence, as embodied in man, is also conscious of the power, within certain limitations, to will, and to perform what is willed; to rise up, to sit down; to raise an arm, to let it fall; to walk, to run, to stand; to go to Paris, to Berlin, or to Egypt; to write a book, to build a house, to found a hospital; to control largely his actions, physical and moral; he can be sober or drunken; chaste or a libertine; benevolent or selfish; honest or a rogue. Having deliberated upon this and that and having formed a judgment that one thing is better than another, or that one condition is better than another, he has power to choose between them and can determine to give his aid to this and withhold it from that. So that volition, within certain limitations, at least, seems also to be a quality of intelligence. It is, of course, possible to conceive of intelligence and its necessarily attendant consciousness, existing without volition; but intelligence so conceived is shorn of glory, since under such conditions it can make no certain use of its powers. Its very thinking, since it must end in thinking, in the case here supposed—would be valueless; its consciousness would be distressing. If active at all, its actions would be without purpose, and as chaotic as its thinking would be; unless it could be thought of as both thinking

---

14. B. H. Roberts, *The Mormon Doctrine of Deity; The Roberts-[Cyrill] Van Der Donckt Discussion, to Which Is Added a Discourse, Jesus Christ, The Revelation of God* (Salt Lake City: The Deseret News, 1903), 132.

15. <Ms III^{c} adds "Mental"—*Ed.*>

16. <Ms III "general principles of individual facts and principles," but Poland's text has "or individual facts"—*Ed.*>

17. Poland, *Truth of Thought*, 41.

18. <Ms III^{c} adds "Power of Deliberation"—*Ed.*>

and acting as directed by an intelligent, purposeful will external to itself; which would still leave the intelligence a mere automaton, without dignity or moral quality, or even intellectual value.

I, therefore, conclude that while it is possible to conceive of intelligence, with its necessarily attendant consciousness, as without volition, still, so far as we are acquainted with intelligence, as manifested through men, volition—sometimes named soul-freedom, the spirit's freedom, or free agency—is a quality that within certain limitations, attends upon intelligences, and may be an inherent quality of intelligence, a necessary attribute of its essence, as much so as is consciousness itself.

ETERNITY OF INTELLIGENCES

At this point the question arises as to the nature of intelligence (mind-element in the universe) with reference to its origin or its[19] eternity. Is it eternal, or had it a beginning? Is it a product, or an eternal thing? Already in discussing matter and force it has been shown that these are eternal, capable of infinite changes; in form, as to the first, and capable of infinite transitions and transmutations as to the second. If we may say this of force in the realm of mechanical and chemical energy, which seems to be the holding together, the balancing force in the universe, what shall be said when we come to the more wonderful force of mind, which may originate action and make it purposeful and guide it to the attainment of worthwhile ends? What shall we say of it—this mind-force, this force of forces, this intelligence? May we trace its lightening to an origin, or must we assign it a place in the category of eternal things, as in the case of space, time, matter, and mechanical and chemical energy, as a necessary[20] concomitant of them in the workings of an eternal universe and as part of it? Shall we not say, are we not compelled to say, by the very nature of the thing itself that mind—intelligence—never was "created or made, neither indeed can be" (D&C 93:29), it is eternal? John Fiske says of force, in an ultimate analysis of it, that:

> It is the belief that force, as manifested to our consciousness, can neither arise out of nothing nor lapse into nothing; can neither be created nor annihilated. And the negation of this belief is unthinkable; since to think it would be to perform the impossible task of establishing in thought an equation between something and nothing.[21]

---

19. <Ms III^c adds "origin or its"—*Ed.*>

20. <Ms III^c adds "necessary"—*Ed.*>

21. John Fiske, *Outlines of Cosmic Philosophy*, in *The Miscellaneous Writings of John Fiske, with Many Portraits of Illustrious Philosophers, Scientists, and Other Men of Note* (Boston

If this may be said of mechanical and chemical force, can it not with equal truth be said of the more wonderful force which we call mind, and which in the argument for the eternity of mind-force would be as strong as for the eternity of other kinds of force?

Mr. Herbert Spencer says of causation:

> We are no more able to form a circumscribed idea of cause than of space or time; and we are consequently obliged to think of the cause which transcends the limits of our thought as positive, though indefinite. Just in the same manner that on conceiving any bounded space, there arises a nascent consciousness[22] of space outside the bounds.[23]

That is to say, the idea of cause being eternal is forced upon our consciousness in the same manner that the eternity of space and matter is. If this can be said for the eternity of cause, must not as much be said of the eternity of mind so inescapably associated with purposeful causation—the causation that has produced the cosmos at least?

THE MYSTERIOUS VITAL SOMETHING[24]

Sir Oliver Lodge when arguing for the reality and eternity of that "mysterious, vital something," which builds up from earth elements an oak, an eagle, or a man, closes his argument with the question: "Is it something which is really nothing, and soon shall it be manifestly nothing?" He answers:

> Not so, nor is it so with intellect and consciousness and will, nor with memory and love and adoration, nor <all> the manifold activities which at present strangely interact with matter and appeal to our bodily senses and terrestrial knowledge. They [meaning human minds] are not nothing, nor shall they ever vanish into nothingness or cease to be. They did not arise with us; they never did spring into being; they are as eternal as the Godhead itself, and in the eternal Being they shall endure for ever.[25]

---

and New York: Houghton, Mifflin and Co., 1902), 1:218.

22. <Ms III "a naissant consciousness," but Spencer's text has "a nascent consciousness"—*Ed.*>

23. Herbert Spencer, *First Principles* (New York: D. Appleton, 1896), 93.

24. <Ms III[c] adds "The Mysterious Vital Something"—*Ed.*>

25. Sir Oliver Lodge, *Science and Immortality* (New York: Moffat, Yard, and Co., 1908), 160. Add note from King Follett Sermon. <These last six words are Roberts's handwritten addition in Ms III[c] and indicate his intent to insert one of his own notes from *The King Follett Discourse; The Being and Kind of Being God Is; The Immortality of the Intelligence of Man*, annotated by B. H. Roberts (Salt Lake City: Magazine Printing Co., 1926)—*Ed.*>

SUMMARY[26]

We have found, then, in this review of Intelligence, or the mind-element of the universe:

1. That intelligences are so-called because intelligence is their chief characteristic;

2. That consciousness is a necessary quality of intelligence;

3. That intelligences are both self-conscious and conscious of an external universe not self;

4. That intelligences have the power to generalize—to rise from the contemplation of the particular to the general; from the individual to the universal;

5. That intelligences can perceive the existence of certain *a priori* principles that are incontrovertible—necessary truths, which form a basis of knowledge and of ratiocination—deducing conclusions from premises.

6. That intelligences, as known through men, possess a power of imagination or imaginative memory, by which they hold pictures of sense perceptions before the mind, and may form from them new combinations of thought and consciousness;

7. That intelligences have power to deliberate, to form judgments, and to will;

8. That intelligences have volition, that have relation with[27] physical, mental, and moral conditions[28]—within certain limitation—a power both to will and to do; in other words, they are free, moral agents.

9. That intelligences are eternal—are among the uncreated things—and the indestructible things.

It should be understood that these brief remarks respecting intelligence and intelligences are in no sense a treatise, even brief and cursory, on psychology; they are made merely to indicate some of the chief qualities that are inseparably connected with intelligence and intelligences, so that when the words are used in this writing, some definite idea may be had as to what is meant.

---

26. <Ms III^c adds "Summary"—*Ed.*>

27. <Ms III^c adds "that have relation with"—*Ed.*>

28. <Ms III^c adds "conditions"—*Ed.*>

CHAPTER IX

Nature of the Universe: Monistic or Pluralistic?

SCRIPTURE READING LESSON

Analysis

I. Systems:

(a) Monism;

(b) Dualism;

(c) Pluralism.

II. The Theological View.

III. Intelligence Pluralistic.

IV. Highest Spiritual Manifestation in Union with Matter.

V. The Many as One.

VI. An Optimistic Universe.

References

William James, A *Pluralistic Universe: Hibbert Lectures at Manchester College on the Present Situation in Philosophy* (New York: Longmans, Green and Co., 1909).

D&C 29, 76, 84, 88, 93, 121.

Joseph Smith, *The King Follett Discourse; The Being and Kind of Being God Is; The Immortality of the Intelligence of Man*, delivered April 1844, annotated by B. H. Roberts (Salt Lake City: Magazine Printing Co., 1926), pamphlet.

CHAPTER IX

Nature of the Universe: Monistic or Pluralistic?

The next step in the development of our knowledge of the universe brings us to the question as to whether it is monistic or pluralistic. Monism is described to be the doctrine which refers all phenomena to a single, ultimate constituent or agent, and is used in contradistinction to dualism, or pluralism, of which more later.

SYSTEMS

(a) Monism

The doctrine of monism has been held in three generic forms: first, matter and its phenomena are explained as modifications of mind, resulting in what is known as idealistic monism; second, mind is explained by and "resolved into matter"—this is known as materialistic monism; third, matter, mind, and their phenomena are held to be manifestations or modifications of some one substance, an "unknown something," which is capable of an objective and subjective aspect.[1]

(b) Dualism

Dualism stands for two-foldness, a system which is founded on a double principle or two-fold distinction. A conception of the universe, arising from the existence of the two original elements—spirit and matter[2]—with action and reaction of these, resulting in the phenomena of the universe.

With the details of these systems of thought and the hair-splitting refinements as to whether matter shades off into spirit, or spirit rises by imperceptible manifestations into matter-phenomena, and merges into tangibility—we need not concern ourselves overmuch.[3] I realize that our new knowledge is constantly producing what is almost new revelation on the constitution of matter, and that the very dust is shown to have "complexity and activity heretofore unimagined,"

---

1. *Webster's International Dictionary.*
2. <Ms III* "the two original elements, and spirit, and matter"—*Ed.*>
3. <Ms III* "tangibility need not concern us overmuch"—*Ed.*>

and that such phrases as "dead matter" and "inert matter" are passing out of use so far as possessing any significance is concerned. The new theory of the atom is said to amount almost to a new conception of the universe itself. The atom is no longer the indivisible particle it was once thought to be; it is now said to be known that there is an "atom" within an "atom." That which scientists thought was elementary and final a generation ago can now be divided and broken up; that instead of the atom being the unit of substance, it is found to be almost a world in itself, with action and reaction within its small compass that is quite amazing.[4]

All the new knowledge, however, respecting the atom and all that comes of it, including resolving it into electrons, leaves us with the fact that it has within it something which "acts" and something which is "acted upon"; a seemingly necessary positive and negative substance in action and reaction out of which things proceed an atom, an aggregation of atoms, a world, or a universe of worlds.

We may leave these systems of philosophy that try to account for the starting point of things, with the conviction that we may be assured that the positive which acts, and the negative which is acted upon, are both eternal things; and may they not be the ultimate factors–spirit and matter–acting and reacting upon each other by which the universe is up-builded and sustained?

(c) Pluralism

Turning from these considerations of monism and dualism, we may conduct our inquiries as to the nature of the universe along other and broader lines. Is this universe monistic or pluralistic? It seems almost useless to ask the question in view of what has already been set forth. We have already before us a number of things, eternal things, that go to the making of the universe; and these many things proclaim the pluralistic character of it–time, space, matter, force, or energy; and causation, and mind, or intelligence. All these <are> eternal by the nature of them; self-existent, without beginning and without end, and so many of them, that if number in things constituted plurality, then here we have plurality–a pluralistic universe.

THE THEOLOGICAL VIEW

The phase of this matter, however, which concerns us chiefly is with reference to mind and intelligence outside of our own world. The old and generally accepted idea about our world, supposed to rest upon the authority of revelation, was that

4. See J. Arthur Thomson, ed., "Introduction," *The Outline of Science: A Plain Story Simply Told* (New York and London: G. P. Putnam's Sons, 1922), 4-5. <Here Roberts inserts the following handwritten note of Ms III[c]: "add an atom from Man & his universe"–*Ed.*>

the world was created out of nothing by a supreme Intelligence, and within recent times.[5] That the chief characteristic of this Intelligence was one-ness, that He transcended the universe, and acted from the outside of it in its creation; that sun, moon, and stars were created for the earth, the sun to be its light by day, and the moon and stars especially created to break up somewhat the otherwise utter darkness of the night; that the earth alone was the one world in which this Intelligence (God) was concerned; and whatever other beings existed were angels and spirits ministering for God, and to the benefit of the human race.

It is scarcely necessary to say that this view does not fit the universe as we have reviewed it here in the light of the knowledge we now have in respect of the extent and the vastness of the universe, and including as it does, thought of the great likelihood of the thousands of millions of suns being circled by groups of inhabited planets, numberless as the sands upon the seashore.

INTELLIGENCE PLURALISTIC

The structure of the universe as we have learned it, and now know it to be, leads inevitably to the conclusion that the universe, as to the intelligence which apparently stands dominant therein, is pluralistic. That is to say, many intelligences are bound together in at least a workable and perhaps a perfect unity; and this unity of many intelligences bound together in agreement may be and is sufficient to give the sense of one-ness to all that is. John Stuart Mill, in his "Essay on Theism," in speaking of the evident unity in nature which suggests that nature is governed by mind which is one, goes on to say that "no one kind of event can be absolutely preordained or governed by any Being but one who holds in his hands the reins[6] of all nature, not of some department only." Then he gives a splendid alternative to this by saying: "At least if a plurality be supposed, it is necessary to assume so complete a concert of action and unity of will among them, that the difference is for most purposes immaterial between such a theory and the absolute unity of the Godhead."[7] This alternative presents the ground of the reconciliation between the unity of the universe and the existence of many intelligences which undoubtedly enter into and compose that unity.

---

5. <Most modern scholars admit that *ex nihilo* creation is not a biblical doctrine; see Bernhard W. Anderson, "Creation," in *The Interpreter's Dictionary of the Bible*, ed. George A. Buttrick (New York: Abingdon Press, 1962), 1:728—*Ed.*>

6. <Ms III "holds in his hands the reigns," but Mill's text has "reins"—*Ed.*>

7. John Stuart Mill, "Essay on Theism," in *Three Essays on Religion* (New York: H. Holt, 1884), 132-33.

HIGHEST SPIRITUAL MANIFESTATION IN UNION WITH MATTER

Again we may resort to our method of finding truth by reasoning from what we know, confining our thought for the moment to our own Earth. We know that the highest manifestation[8] of the thing we call Intelligence is found in man; is found, therefore, in union with material elements; for man, the intelligence, the spirit of him, is in union with matter; the spirit *and* the body, the latter a definite amount of matter united with a spirit, constitute the being we know as man. And in this union both spirit and matter attain the highest and most desirable manifestation in this our mortal life. Man is an intelligence; but he is an intelligent entity, an individual, separate and distinct from every other individual man; and as there are many such separate intelligences, we may say for our world that, as to intelligence (mind), also as to many other things, it is a pluralistic world. That being true as to our world, may it not be equally true of all the inhabited planets of our own solar system?[9] And of all the solar systems of the universe?[10]

THE MANY AS ONE[11]

Let us start from another viewpoint. The attainment of the highest wisdom, the mightiest achievements of intelligences on our earth, is not attained by the individual man acting alone, but rather by action of the individual in union with his fellows.[12] By choosing the most highly-developed intelligences of the commu-

---

8. <Ms III* "that the best manifestation"—*Ed.*>

9. <George Laub recorded in his diary that Hyrum Smith, Joseph Smith's brother, preached a sermon in 1843 in Nauvoo, Illinois, in which he stated that "The Sun & Moon is inhabited & the Stars" (Eugene England, ed., "George Laub's Nauvoo Journal," *Brigham Young University Studies* 18 [Winter 1978]: 177). Oliver B. Huntington received a patriarchal blessing on 7 December 1836 from his father William Huntington, in which he was promised that "thou shalt have power with God even to translate thyself to Heaven, & preach to the inhabitants of the moon or planets, if it shall be expedient" (Van Hale, "Mormons and Moonmen: A Look at Nineteenth Century Beliefs about the Moon—Its Flora, Its Fauna, Its Folks," *Sunstone* 7 (Sept.-Oct. 1982): 14—*Ed.*>

10. <For nineteenth-century speculations on life elsewhere in the universe, see Michael J. Crowe, *The Extraterrestrial Life Debate, 1750-1900: The Idea of a Plurality of Worlds from Kant to Lowell* (Cambridge: Cambridge University Press, 1986)—*Ed.*>

11. <Ms III^{c} adds "The Many as One"—*Ed.*>

12. <Ms III* "is not attained by the individual in union with his fellows," but due to an error in skipping from "the individual" to "the individual," the words "man acting alone, but rather by action of the individual" from the earlier draft were accidentally omitted and these are reinserted above the line—*Ed.*>

nity as representatives, and bringing them together in councils of various kinds, parliaments, congresses, cabinets, courts, and other national assemblies—from these, nations and the world finally get expressed the wisest and, therefore, the best judgments as to what ought to obtain as public policies and provide for the best securities for the freedom of men and the welfare of nations. From the deliberations of such bodies rise the wisest and best systems of governments and laws. Though the personal studies and investigations of individual scientists and philosophers may carry them far in unearthing knowledge of things, and understanding the relation of forces, they may establish science, and as flaming torch-bearers these individuals may lead the way, and blaze the trails over which the crowd may follow. Yet that wisdom expressed in laws for individual, community, national, and even international relationships—all that comes from men taking counsel with his fellow men, and unitedly devising and working out the things that ordain and establish the order of society which concerns individual and community welfare, and provides the best securities for liberty; and through these establish man's greatest happiness, and the highest development of that thing which we think of as world civilization—it is the wisdom massed from united intelligences.

This is what we know from human experience in the development of human wisdom, as applied to the practical things of life, the welfare of humanity; and it is vouched for by all history. And now, reasoning from what we know of conditions respecting all these things as to our own world, we ask the question: May not this be the status of things in other worlds? Only, of course, in the older planets and planetary systems—the greater and the more highly-developed worlds, inhabited by superior intelligences—the means employed would be more perfect, and the results correspondingly more satisfactory, in that there would be established in those older worlds higher states of civilization, and there would be undoubtedly individuals of higher intelligence with corresponding increase of power and influence. To attempt to say to what heights of development and glory intelligences may have attained to in these older, and more advanced worlds, of course, would be merely speculation; but it is not inconceivable, that as the heavens are higher than the earth, so are these developments in more advanced worlds[13] higher than our developments; so are their ways above our ways; and their thoughts above our thoughts.

What infinite opportunity for development in such a universe as we are here contemplating! When viewed from the standpoint of the existence of these thousands of millions of suns, surrounded by much greater and more glorious planetary systems than our own solar system, and inhabited by intelligences superior to those that we know as the human race—what may not come of such a

13. <Ms III[c] adds "in more advanced worlds"—*Ed.*>

universe and of our world as part of it? For to intelligence[14] there is no end of progress; however great its present attainment, there is still a beyond to higher glory, greater majesty, increase of excellence. There are no ultimates to progress for intelligences, there is always becoming, but no end. This constitutes the joy of existence—this possibility of eternal progress!

AN OPTIMISTIC UNIVERSE

All this makes the universe[15] an optimistic universe, where hope eternally reigns, where achievements but furnish wings for still higher achievements. It makes possible the contemplation of a universe filled with the brotherhood of divine Intelligences, presided over by graded councils of prayer and authority, rising one above another in designated spheres and authority, and yet all operating in harmonious relations, knowing that no power or authority can in reality, or ought to, be exercised over intelligences by their fellow intelligences, but by persuasion, by long suffering, by gentleness and meekness, and by love unfeigned; by kindness and pure knowledge, which shall greatly enlarge the soul without hypocrisy and without guile. Reproving with sharpness at times, as may be necessary for correction and understanding of things as they are, but followed by such manifestations of love and good will that even the "reproof" shall be seen to be but love in stern guise, for the government of our contemplated universe is to be and can not be otherwise than a moral government; a government that rests upon knowledge, persuasion, and love (D&C 121:41-43).

---

14. <Ms III* "For to intelligences"—*Ed.*>
15. <Ms III* "It makes the universe"—*Ed.*>

CHAPTER X

Of Knowledge: To the Point of Moral Certainty

SCRIPTURE READING LESSON

Analysis

Great Questions Proposed:

I. Are the "Fixed Stars" Centers of Solar Systems?

II. Is There Life on Other Worlds Than Our Own?

III. Is Life on Other Worlds Climaxed with the Equivalent of Human Life?

IV. Is the Earth and All Things in It Made for Man?

V. What Is the Trend of Authority on the Inhabitancy of Other Worlds?

VI. Are There Worlds and World-Systems Older Than Our Own?

VII. What of the Altruism of Other World Inhabitants?

VIII. The Voice of Revelation on the Habitancy of Other Worlds.

References

All the authorities quoted in the text of this chapter.

B. H. Roberts, *New Witnesses for God* (Salt Lake City: The Deseret News, 1911), 1:439-41.

Moses 1:30-42.

Abraham (a fragment), chaps. 3-5.

D&C 88:37-39, 42-61 (the revelation given December 1832); also, D&C 130:4-8.

CHAPTER X

Of Knowledge: To the Point of Moral Certainty

Say first of God above and man below,
how can we reason but from what we know?
POPE'S "ESSAY ON MAN"[1]

GREAT QUESTIONS PROPOSED[2]

The field of our knowledge is now sketched out before us. Knowledge of ourselves, of other selves; in a limited way also knowledge of things of the earth, air, and sea; knowledge of the sun and moon; knowledge of the solar system, as to the number of planets at least, something of their size and their distance from the sun and from each other. Something we know in outline of the sidereal system. Its extent, its immensity, and its orderliness—the most striking thing about it, as we have seen,[3] from the quoted comments of Prof. <Forest> Moulton, is its orderliness. And now we have reached the point where something else must be learned, something else we need to know in order to attain our purpose in this writing, but which can only be known with approximate certainty, and only to be found out by the process of ratiocination, from that which we most definitely know to what we may know only approximately, and yet know, as I think, up to the point of moral certainty. Let us put the process of reasoning from what we know to the probability of what is not absolutely known to the test.

We have ascertained from our quotations from various authorities upon astronomy that it is possible and even probable that the suns which make up our

---

1. <Alexander Pope, "An Essay on Man," in Pat Rogers, ed., *Alexander Pope* (Oxford: Oxford University Press, 1993)—*Ed.*>

2. <Ms III* has "Great Questions" before the quotation from Pope, and Ms III^c adds "Proposed" and moves the section heading to its present position—*Ed.*>

3. <In this case the text follows Ms III* "as we have seen," instead of the later Ms III^c "as we shall see in the chapter following this," because the quotation from Forest R. Moulton on the universe's orderliness precedes in chapter 6 rather than follows in chapter 11. Perhaps Roberts intended at one point to rearrange the placement of the Moulton quote, but this was never done—*Ed.*>

galaxy—our universe—have circling about them groups of opaque worlds, even as our sun has nine[4] such worlds moving about him in their respective orbits. But it is true that each of these suns of the sidereal system, or even a considerable number of them, has a like group of planets to which it is the center of gravitation, and from which these planets receive light and warmth and vital force, resulting in life such as we know it on our own earth? The answer must necessarily be that this is not definitely known, and hence scientists in astronomy speak with caution, and only say that it may possibly be so. It may even be probable. But science can speak with no positive assurance on this subject, because really scientists do not know.[5]

ARE THE "FIXED STARS" CENTERS OF SOLAR SYSTEMS?[6]

The distance, as we have seen, lying between our earth and its sun and the nearest fixed star is so great that if there are planets moving about Alpha Centauri, then the borrowed light in which they shine is so dim, and the planets themselves so small that they are lost to vision by us who are inhabiting the earth, even though we use our mightiest telescopes[7] in our efforts to discover them. We are thus barred by these immense distances, and the but-faintly-illuminated opaque worlds, that we have no real knowledge as to their existence. But this we do know, namely, that our own sun, in constitution like the other suns of the stellar universe, has a group of opaque planets moving about him in great regularity and order; and reasoning from this knowledge it would seem at least not improbable that a similar condition obtains with reference to other suns so like ours[8] in every other way. Also, the thought obtrudes itself into the mind, why should it be thought that our sun, much smaller and therefore less powerful than other and mightier suns, is the only one around which groups of opaque planets revolve? And when we think of the great galaxy making up the stellar universe,[9] we are naturally led to the reflection: what a waste of energy there must be in the existence of these suns of the universe, if only one out of the hundreds of millions of them is to have an attendant group of worlds!

---

4. <Ms III* "eight," but the handwritten Ms III^{c} updates to "nine" and must therefore be dated no earlier than late 1930, when Roberts became aware of the discovery of Pluto—*Ed.*>

5. <Ms III^{c} adds "really they do not know"—*Ed.*>

6. <Ms III^{c} adds "Are The 'Fixed Stars' Centers of Solar Systems?"—*Ed.*>

7. <Ms III^{c} adds an "s" to make "telescopes"—*Ed.*>

8. <Ms III* "him," i.e., our sun—*Ed.*>

9. <Ms III* "stellar universe as being so immense"—*Ed.*>

IS THERE LIFE ON OTHER WORLDS THAN OUR OWN?[10]

There remains also still another, and even we may say a more important question, which I shall confine for the moment to the planets of our own solar system, viz.: Is there life upon these planets—vegetable, and animal, and human?[11] To that question man must answer that he does not know. But this he knows, that his own earth sustains life—vegetable and animal and human. And reasoning from what he knows as to conditions upon his own earth, it would at least seem that similar conditions might obtain upon other planets of his world-system; if not, then again the thought, what a waste of energy, for without life upon these worlds how vain is their existence! And we might well ask to what purpose do they exist, if they are without life? Or, even if they bring forth life, vegetable and animal life, and not human life, or something akin to it, the same question would be pertinent. Nothing can be clearer than that our own earth would become meaningless, if human life were not here. Human life is unquestionably the crowning fact and glory of our earth, and such sentient and intelligent life as humans possess, or some intelligent life forms superior to humans, would alone[12] seem to justify the existence of these worlds.

IS LIFE IN OTHER WORLDS CLIMAXED WITH THE EQUIVALENT OF HUMAN LIFE?[13]

What good purpose would be served by such worlds—the worlds of all the universe, unless, as in the case of our own earth, the life upon them—if such exists—is not climaxed by sentient and intelligent life, such as we know on our earth, or something equivalent or superior to it? Or some form of life which, through some sort of development, might be capable of becoming equal to or superior to human life?

IS THE EARTH AND ALL THINGS IN IT MADE FOR MAN?

Nothing can be clearer to intelligence than that our earth, however rich it might

---

10. <Ms III^{c} adds "Is There Life On Other Worlds Than Our Own?"—*Ed.*>

11. <See Michael J. Crowe, *The Extraterrestrial Life Debate, 1750-1900: The Idea of a Plurality of Worlds from Kant to Lowell* (Cambridge: Cambridge University Press, 1986), and Van Hale, "Mormons and Moonmen: A Look at Nineteenth Century Beliefs about the Moon—Its Flora, Its Fauna, Its Folks," *Sunstone* 7 (Sept.-Oct. 1982): 12-17—*Ed.*>

12. <Ms III^{c} adds "alone"—*Ed.*>

13. <Ms III^{c} adds "Is Life In Other Worlds Climaxed With The Equivalent of Human Life?"—*Ed.*>

be in vegetable and animal life, would be without purpose worthwhile with human life absent from it. To become thoroughly aware of the truth of this statement it is only necessary to suppose the human race, with all it has produced, banished from the earth. Let all things else remain: the earth's place in the solar system and its form; let the islands and the continents be as they are now; also the seas, the majestic mountain ranges, the imperial valleys, the extensive plains; let these be clothed with the richest verdure, with the most fragrant flowers in profusion, with shrubbery and forests abounding; let all this be bathed in the glory of the sunlight. Let all forms of animal life abound in all the seas and the rivers, and in the air and on the earth, in the mountains and the plains, and in the woods; let the birds fly through the air and fill the silence with their songs; let the seasons follow each other in their regular course, refreshing spring and glowing summer; let the grains and the fruits come to ripeness in autumn; let the forests put forth the glory of their foliage in the springtide and in summer, and then in the autumn fall to enrich the soil whence they grew,[14] only to be followed by more foliage the next summer, which shall fall upon the ground in the succeeding autumn, and rot and enrich the soil in which it grew! Let the moon come out and look upon the scene of the earth in its glory night after night, age after age. Let the stars from their immense distances look down upon it night after night, and age after age, and see all these things save only man on the earth; and with him absent, what would all this earth with its wealth of beauty and glory, with its vegetable and animal life, mean?

What would it matter that enormous coal fields underlie the earth's surface with their vast stored-up energy drawn from the sunlight of past ages? There would be no man on the earth to let loose that energy for useful production—man is not here! What would it matter that other parts of the earth's interior hold vast oil reservoirs, another kind of stored-up energy? It would be there with no purpose with man absent from the earth. What matter the stores of iron, of granite, and marble, of clay for bricks? Man the builder is not in the earth, and with the builder absent all these would be unused and worthless. What avails the store of faultless Venetian marble, with man the sculptor not here to fashion it into all but living, breathing statuary? What does it matter that there are pigments of endless variety in the earth? Man, the artist, is not here to blend them on the canvas into a landscape of dreamy beauty, or paint a portrait true to life of the great, and thus perpetuate the memory of noble persons and great deeds?

What boots it if the everlasting hills are seamed with silver, or that the quartz strata, or the river sands, hold the precious gold stores? Man is not here to fashion them into objects of beauty or utility. What matters the existence of precious stones

---

14. <Ms III* "whence it grew"—*Ed.*>

deep buried in the selected places of the earth, or hidden in the "midnight caves of ocean"[15]—no queens or princesses or other women of grace and beauty are on earth for whom they will be fitting adornments for enhancement or comeliness; there is no beauty—woman absent—that they can fittingly adorn!

Who of all the creatures inhabiting the earth—man absent—would appreciate the earth and the things associated with it? Who would love dawn or passing evening? Who would contemplate that "inverted bowl we call the sky,"[16] with all its star-glory? Who would love the flowers or the song of birds? Who would uplift the face to think of God? Man is the only erect and upward-looking being in earth-life. Who would desire immortality or long for higher things than just bare existence, brutish life? Contemplate the earth with man absent from it—how stale, flat, unprofitable, and meaningless it all would be! And as it would be with our earth and the group of planets of which it is but one—so would it be with all these billions of suns with their attendant group of planets, if tenantless by intelligent beings who would be equal to, if not superior to, human earth inhabitants! If tenantless by such beings, or at least beings capable of rising to such excellence, and to higher stages of development—they might as well sink into the oblivion of non-existence, as to be, and not to be the habitat of intelligent, progressive beings—intelligences!

WHAT IS THE TREND OF AUTHORITY ON THE INHABITANCY OF OTHER WORLDS?[17]

So impressive is the likelihood of the inhabitancy of other worlds than our own, however, that, as we have already seen in the excerpts from the lecture of Professor <Forest> Moulton, quoted in chapters 5 and 6,[18] that he holds that about half of the billion stars of our galaxy, being in size and constitution and temperature essentially similar to our own sun—he holds that "it is not improbable—it is in fact probable—that a majority of them have planets circling about

15. <Thomas Gray, "Elegy Written in a Country Church Yard," in *The Complete Poems of Thomas Gray: English, Latin and Greek*, ed. Herbert W. Starr and John R. Hendrickson (Oxford: Clarendon Press, 1966), 39, reads: "Full many a gem of purest ray serene, the dark unfathom'd caves of ocean bear"—*Ed.*>

16. <Edward FitzGerald, trans., *Rubáiyát of Omar Khayyám*, ed. Louis Untermeyer (New York: Random House, 1947), stanza 72—*Ed.*>

17. <Ms III* "The Inhabitancy of Other Worlds," and then Ms III[c] adds "What Is The Trend of Authority On" and the question mark at the end—*Ed.*>

18. <Ms III* "in chapter V"—*Ed.*>

them[19] as our earth revolves about the sun." "It may be," he continues, "that a fraction of them, perhaps in all hundreds of millions, are in a condition comparable to that of the earth, and that they support life!"

Some years ago the celebrated English astronomer Sir Robert Ball, in the American press (September 30, 1894) in dealing with the subject "Possibility of Life on Other Worlds," and reviewing the subject[20] at that time and the state of the question from a scientific standpoint, said: "No reasonable person will, I think, doubt that the tendency of modern research has been in favor of the supposition that there may be life on some of the other globes."[21] Later, however, Sir Robert Ball grew bolder and in a subsequent statement to the above said:

> Granting the, to us, impossible hypothesis that the final cause of the universe is "accident," the fortuitous concourse of self-existent atoms, still the "accident" which produced thinking beings upon this little and inferior world [of ours], must have frequently repeated itself; while if, as we hold, there is a sentient Creator, it is difficult to believe, without a revelation to that effect, that he has wasted such glorious creative powers upon mere masses of insensible matter. God can not love gases. The probability, at least, is that there are millions of worlds (for after all what the sensitized paper sees must be an infinitesimal fraction of the whole) occupied by sentient beings.

Still later, August 27, 1910, the Associated Press announced that in a lecture before the Popular Educational Society, known also as the "Materialistic Association," Professor T<homas> J. J. See is represented as saying, that in the completion of his researches in "Cosmic Evolution," to which he had devoted ten years, his conviction was[22] "that the planets revolving about the fixed stars are inhabited by some kind of intelligent beings." He also cited an address delivered at Philadelphia in 1897 by Professor <Simon> Newcomb, in which similar views were held, and said that the proof is much more complete now—1910—the time of Professor See's declaration—than at that time—1897. "Life flourishing on the earth and believed to exist in Mars and Venus," continued Professor See, "is but a drop in the Pacific Ocean as compared to that flourishing on the thousands of billions of habitable worlds now definitely proved to revolve about the fixed stars with the habitability of these extensive worlds."

Sustained by such authority, I think we may proceed in future discussions of

---

19. <Ms III* "planets circulating about them"—*Ed.*>

20. <Ms III* "and renewing the subject"—*Ed.*>

21. <Robert S. Ball, "Possibility of Life on Other Worlds: Recent Discoveries Bear Out Old Arguments That Other Planets May Be Inhabited," *McClure's Magazine* 5 (July 1895): 156—*Ed.*>

22. <Ms III* "ten years, stated as his conviction"—*Ed.*>

this great theme—the habitancy of other worlds than our own—upon the assumption that this inhabitancy may be fairly well assured. It should also be observed that this line of reasoning, limited in the foregoing to the planets of the solar system, can be just as consistently applied to the sidereal universe and the attendant group of planets that may be circling their suns, only it is with increasing emphasis that we are forced to the thought of wastefulness by misuse of matter and energy, if the millions of suns have no attendant worlds and the worlds no sentient, intelligent life upon them.

ARE THERE WORLDS AND WORLD-SYSTEMS OLDER THAN OUR OWN?[23]

Again, we question in order to form the basis of more reasoning. Are any of the suns of the sidereal system and their supposed attendant systems of worlds older than our own sun and its system of worlds? Again, we can not speak with positive knowledge, but we do know that things in our own earth are younger and older than other things, and it is not unreasonable to conclude from the knowledge that this fact imparts to us, that some of these greater suns of the universe and their probable group of planets may be many millions of years older than our own.

Again, referring to our earth experience. We know that age sometimes affects, and favorably, development; that there is cumulative knowledge and cumulative experience which results in higher excellencies, and reasoning from this truth, in larger and more desirable developments both as to individuals and states of civilization. Reasoning[24] from what we know, may it not be that in some of the older suns of our galaxy and their attendant worlds, there may be superior conditions existing in such worlds because of the longer time element which has led to larger knowledge and to deeper wisdom, resulting in more exalted states of intellectual life and of civilization, than those which are known to us on our earth? And there may have been developed[25] also higher and mightier intelligences than any that have been developed on our earth.[26] If such higher intelligences do exist in other worlds, may[27] we not enter upon the same line of reasoning[28] from what

---

23. <Ms III* of section heading "The Age of Worlds"—*Ed.*>

24. <Ms III^{c} adds "Reasoning"—*Ed.*>

25. <Ms III^{c} adds "there has been developed"—*Ed.*>

26. <Ms III* "on our own earth"—*Ed.*>

27. <Ms III* "in other worlds, and higher states of civilization, may"—*Ed.*>

28. <Ms III* "line of questioning and reasoning," then Ms III^{c} marks out "questioning" and adds a handwritten "reasoning"; then later this revision and the following "and" are deleted—*Ed.*>

we know, <and> apply the principle we have been following to the social[29] and sympathetic and moral qualities as connected with these higher intelligences?

This we know in respect of the inhabitants of our own world, that higher intellectual life and higher states of civilization produce exalted moral feelings, resulting in higher states of righteousness and love of truth and sympathy for fellow men, leading to desire for the uplift of those less highly developed, and thus is produced among our own earth-people a desire to restrain the strong and vicious by laws and group agencies under forms of governments, and to uplift and better the conditions of the lowly and undeveloped peoples. This is manifested in the missionary work that Christian people, especially, undertake in uplifting the undeveloped peoples of our world. Large sums of money and noble lives are devoted to, and sometimes sacrificed in, the reclamation of what are called the heathen tribes and races of our earth's population. Are such qualities as these characteristic of the highly developed intelligences of other worlds? And may they be moved by sympathy arising from the love of kindred inhabitants of other worlds to seek a similar uplifting, perhaps even redemption, of other world inhabitants they esteem less fortunate than themselves, less highly developed yet capable of improvement? And may it not be that their highly developed knowledge of the means of transition through space have led[30] to interplanetary visitations[31] that they may carry on large missionary and social service work[32] throughout all this vast universe we have been contemplating?

WHAT OF THE ALTRUISM OF OTHER WORLD INHABITANTS?[33]

Do these higher intelligences of the stellar universe and planetary systems have so developed in themselves the quality of love that it makes it possible to think of them as being willing to sacrifice themselves—to empty themselves in sacrifice to bring to pass the welfare of others whom they may esteem to be[34] the undeveloped intelligences of the universe? And may they not be capable of giving the last full measure of sacrifice to bring to pass the higher development of the "lowly" when no other means of uplift can be serviceable? Is the great truth operative among

---

29. <Ms III* "apply what we have been following in relation to the social"—*Ed.*>

30. <Ms III* "the transitions through space lead"—*Ed.*>

31. <Ms III* "interplanetary, inter-world system communication and visitation"—*Ed.*>

32. <Ms III* "they may be able to carry on large interplanetary, inter-world system missionary and social service work"—*Ed.*>

33. <Ms III* "Altruism of Other World Inhabitants," and then Ms III[c] adds "What Of The" and the question mark at the end—*Ed.*>

34. <Ms III[c] adds "to be"—*Ed.*>

these untold millions of Intelligences that greater love hath no Intelligence for another than this, that he would give his life in the service of kindred Intelligences when no other means of helpfulness is possible? Is it possible that there exist throughout all these worlds conceived of in this chapter–is it possible that there are races of Intelligences kindred to our own, and are they bound together by mutual ties of sympathy and interests, born of love, and begetting a sense of universal brotherhood? And may there be, when the way is found, some psychic means, and perhaps some physical means, of interplanetary and inter-solar-system method of communication among all these worlds and world-systems, by which they may impart–in the case of some of these worlds–knowledge of their needs; and in the case of other worlds of higher development, ability to dispatch the helpfulness necessary to achieve the uplift desired?

Again, the questions asked with reference to these high things must be answered with the statement that we do not know, with absolute knowledge of human origin–by man's wisdom–that these worlds are inhabited by such Intelligences. But this we know, viz., that our own earth is peopled with sentient intelligences, who, whatever may be their limitations and shortcomings, are nevertheless capable of attaining unto, and have attained unto, very high things in intellectual, moral, and spiritual life, and deep sympathies born of love, which lead them to restrain the vicious by wholesome community laws, and raise the lowly by deeds of kindly helpfulness; and reasoning from that knowledge, it is not difficult to rise to the conception that other worlds and world-systems do sustain multifarious life forms, including beings akin to our human race, and that in some cases they may be far advanced beyond our earth inhabitants in physical perfections (perhaps have learned how to become immortal!), in moral virtues, and in spiritual exaltations; and reasoning from what we know, from our own earth and its inhabitants, such existing populations for the universe of worlds seem not outside the realms of likelihood. And if it be not so!–then again that reflection: what a waste of force and matter in the existence of all these worlds and world-systems, if they are tenantless by intelligences! To what purpose do they exist? To think of such a universe as we have contemplated in these pages as tenantless by sentient Intelligences, except for the inhabitancy of our earth, violates all reason, and makes hesitancy in affirming a positive conclusion about it insufferable pedantry.

<THE VOICE OF REVELATION ON THE HABITANCY OF OTHER WORLDS>[35]

Here I can not refrain from adding the voice of revelation, the "more sure

35. <This section heading has been added, based on its presence in the synopsis to

word of prophecy" (2 Pet. 1:19) to these tentative admissions of scientists, their more or less weak "probabilities," "possibilities," and their tentative "perhapses" in relation to the habitancy of other worlds and world-systems than our own. The Prophet of the New Dispensation brought forth and developed more or less this "sure word of prophecy" upon the subject in the Mosaic fragment–Book of Moses–chapter 1. It is written as part of the vision of Moses there described, that "he beheld many lands; and each land was called earth, and there were inhabitants on the face thereof" (Moses 1:29). Then Moses is represented as saying, as he talked with his Lord face to face:

> Tell me, I pray Thee, why these things are so, and by what Thou madest them? . . . And the Lord God said unto Moses: "For mine own purpose have I made these things. Here is wisdom and it remaineth in me. . . . And worlds without number have I created; and I also created them for mine own purpose; and by the Son I created them, which is mine Only Begotten. And the first man of all men have I called Adam, which is many" (Moses 1:30-31, 33-34).

From the last statement it appears that Adam is a generic name, that there are many Adams carrying the significance perhaps of being first placed on the creations of God. "And the Lord God spake unto Moses, saying, 'The heavens, they are many, and they cannot be numbered unto man; but they are numbered unto me, for they are mine'" (Moses 1:37).

The whole Mosaic[36] fragment seems to take for granted the habitancy by sentient, intelligent beings of the same race with men and divine beings.

The Abrahamic fragment–Book of Abraham–seems even more explicit with reference to the habitancy of other worlds. Here the Lord reveals to Abraham, by Urim and Thummim, the great creations of the space depths:

> I saw the stars, that they were very great, and that one of them was nearest unto the throne of God; and there were many great ones which were near unto it; and the Lord said unto me, "These are the governing ones" (Abr. 3:2-3).

As he proceeds with the description of these creations, it seems always taken for granted that they were inhabited. Addressing Abraham the Lord says of these creations:

> I dwell in the midst of them all; I now, therefore, have come down unto thee to deliver unto thee the works which my hands have made, wherein my wisdom excelleth them all, for I rule in the heavens above, and in the earth beneath, in all wisdom and prudence, over all the intelligences thine eyes have seen from the beginning (Abr. 3:21).

---

this chapter–*Ed.*>

36. <Ms III[c] adds "Mosaic"–*Ed.*>

Then follows the description of the pre-existent intelligences and spirits which the Lord revealed to Abraham.

In chapter 4 of this fragment comes the account of the creation of the earth, and throughout that chapter the various acts of creation are represented as the accomplishment of "the Gods," the title always used in the plural. The chapter opens as follows:

> Then the Lord said, "Let us go down." And they went down at the beginning and they, that is the Gods, organized and formed the heavens and the earth. . . . And the Spirit of the Gods was brooding upon the face of the waters. And they (the Gods) said, "Let there be light," and there was light (Abr. 4:1-3).

And so on throughout all the creative acts. And the same plural is used in the fifth chapter. And what were these creative Intelligences designated as "the Gods," but the higher Intelligences of other and older world-systems engaging in the creation of this earth to which our revelations for the most part[37] are limited.

In the revelation received by the Prophet in behalf of the church in December 1832, and called by him, because of its gracious spirit, the Olive Leaf, and wonderful for the enlightening power of it, there he directly teaches, by this revelation from God, the habitancy of other worlds. For instance, in paragraphs 37-39 of the revelation he says:

> There are many kingdoms; for there is no space in the which there is no kingdom; and there is no kingdom in which there is no space, either a greater or a lesser kingdom. And to every kingdom is given a law; . . . all beings who abide not in those conditions are not justified (D&C 88:37-39).

The intimation being that this infinity of kingdoms is inhabited by intelligences. In verse 45 our Prophet says:

> The earth rolls upon her wings, and the sun giveth his light by day, and the moon giveth her light by night, and the stars also give their light, as they roll upon their wings in their glory in the midst of the power of God. Unto what shall I liken these kingdoms, that ye may understand? . . . Behold, I will liken these kingdoms unto a man having a field, and he sent forth his servants into the field to dig in the field. And he said unto the first, "Go ye and labor in the field, and the first hour I will come unto you, and ye shall behold the joy of my countenance." And he said unto the second, "Go ye also into the field, and in the second hour I will visit you with the joy of my countenance." And also unto the third, saying, "I will visit you." And unto the fourth, and so on unto the twelfth. And the Lord of the field went unto the first in the first hour, and tarried with him all that hour, and he was made glad with the light of the countenance of his

37. <Ms III[c] adds "for the most part"—*Ed.*>

> Lord. And then he withdrew from the first that he might visit the second also, and the third, and the fourth, and so on unto the twelfth. And thus they all received the light of the countenance of their Lord, every man in his hour, and in his time, and in his season; . . . every man in his own order, until his hour was finished, even according as his lord had commanded him, that his lord might be glorified in him and he in his lord, that they all might be glorified. Therefore, unto this parable I will liken all these kingdoms *and the inhabitants thereof*—every kingdom in its hour, and in its time, and in its season, even according to the decree which God hath made (D&C 88:45-46, 51-58, 60-61).

Be it remembered here that these kingdoms and the inhabitants thereof are the kingdoms of the space depths in the universe, all the worlds, and the world-systems, and by the word of God they have their inhabitants.

CHAPTER XI

From What We Know to Faith: The Possibility of Revelation

SCRIPTURE READING LESSON

Analysis

I. Review of Previous Chapters.

II. What Is the Meaning of the Universe.

III. Inadequacy of the Testimony of the Works of Nature.

IV. Yearning for the Light.

V. Of Tradition in General.

VI. The Hebrew Tradition.

VII. The God of Tradition.

VIII. Sources of Tradition:

(a) From Fear;

(b) From Gratitude.

IX. Tradition as Broken Fragments of Revelation.

X. Written Tradition.

References

Previous works on Science and Philosophy cited.

Theological works of Thomas Paine.

The "Six Lectures on Faith," published in the Book of Doctrine and Covenants, all editions previous to the edition of 1921.

Ps. 78.

Deut. 4, esp. verses 9-49.

Flavius Josephus, *The Works of Flavius Josephus: Antiquities of the Jews*, William Whiston's translation (Baltimore: Armstrong and Berry, 1837), bks. i and ii; also bk. xii, chap. 10.

B. H. Roberts, *The Gospel: An Exposition of Its First Principles; and Man's Relationship to Deity*, 3d ed. (Salt Lake City: The Deseret News, 1901), chap. 9.

CHAPTER XI
From What We Know to Faith: The Possibility of Revelation

REVIEW[1]

We have now before us in outline the general groundplan of what we know. First, that which we may say we know definitely, from contact with it in our experiences in one form or another; and second, what we may be said to know only up to the point of moral certainty, obtained by reasoning from what we know to that which may be possible; thence to that which may be probable; thence to that which is of moral certainty, for the reason that it must be reality because of its conformity to reason, and because the contrary is inconceivable.

This has led us[2] to the consideration of things that deal with self-consciousness and other consciousness; to things cognized through the senses, knowledge of things of life and of the earth; and then to knowledge of things external to the earth, things of the solar system; thence to such knowledge of things as we have out in the space depths of the sidereal system; its immensity, the almost inconceivable distances that separate the suns and the probability of their inhabitancy by sentient intelligences.

WHAT IS THE MEANING OF THE UNIVERSE?

And now the question: Is what we know to be true of this vast field we have contemplated entirely satisfactory? What does it all teach us in relation to the important, fundamental things that man ought to know? What is the significance and meaning of constantly changing forms of and in matter, and yet the conservation of its mass? Is there some mighty purpose under all this great universe we have contemplated, or is it without purpose? Is there in existence some "far off event" to which all the world-systems are moving? What mean all the activities within this universe?[3] Is there some stupendous plan being worked out worthy and commen-

---

1. <Ms III[c] adds "Review"—*Ed.*>
2. <Ms III[*] "This review has led us"—*Ed.*>
3. <Ms III[*] "Is there in existence some 'far off event' to which all the world-systems

surate with all this immensity of space and time and substance and force? What is the mystery of man's life and death—of all life and death? And whither are all things tending? Is man's life through a union of spirit and body by some process or other to be made immortal? Or is the union of body and spirit to be permanently broken by death? If such is to be his end—the spirit and body eternally separated, the body resolved to dust, the spirit to oblivion or at least to an unknown end—then what was the purpose of man coming into existence as spirit and body united? In all that we have contemplated in our review of what man knows, we have found nothing that brings a solution to these inquiries; and yet without this knowledge life is a riddle that man knows not what to make of. To what source shall he turn for this necessary knowledge that will solve these vital, human problems?

TESTIMONY OF THE WORKS OF NATURE INADEQUATE

The universe itself conveys no information on these matters. "Turn not to that inverted bowl men call the sky"[4] for answer to these questions; for the worlds of the universe are impotent to answer. I know how forceful in testimony the heavens and the glory of them can be in supplementing a certain positive message, did we but possess such a message. The heavens and the glory of them, however, are and can be only auxiliary witnesses to the principle message that shall impart the knowledge we seek. Until that knowledge comes, however, appeal to the creation is vain in hope of finding anything conclusive upon the questions that are here presented. The Psalmist may say, as he beautifully does say:

> The Heavens declare the glory of God, and the firmament showeth His handywork. Day unto day uttereth speech, and night unto night showeth knowledge. There is no speech, nor language where their voice is not heard. Their line is gone out through all the earth, and their words to the end of the world (Ps. 19:1-4).

But what do the heavens and the glory of them say upon the questions already submitted to the reader in this chapter?

We are mindful also of what Paul says: "The invisible things of Him [i.e. of God] from the creation of the world are clearly seen, being understood by the things that are made, even His eternal power and Godhead" (Rom. 1:20). But what do

---

are moving?" but due to acciddentally skipping from one "?" to another "?" the words "What mean all the activities within this universe?" from the earlier draft were omitted and these are reinserted above the line—*Ed.*>

4. <Edward FitzGerald, trans., *Rubáiyát of Omar Khayyám*, ed. Louis Untermeyer (New York: Random House, 1947), stanza 72—*Ed.*>

"the things that are made" say of God's "eternal power and Godhead"? What do they say upon the important questions submitted to the reader in this chapter?

If men of such classic mold as David and Paul fail to bring definite answers from the heavens and the glory of them upon the questions herein submitted, then it is vain to hope that men of lesser mold would be successful in a like attempt. Not that such have not tried, however; they have tried, but unfortunately they sought to make definite statement of what the message from the "structure of the universe" conveyed, which only resulted in showing how weak and inadequate the message was conceived to be. In illustration I quote from one of the best attempts in this kind, and the author of which is the best known of deists and credited with possession of the keenest mind, and was of unusual literary ability.

Thomas Paine said:

> The wonderful structure of the Universe, and everything that we behold in the system of the creation prove to us, far better than books can do, the existence of God and at the same time proclaim his attributes. It is by exercise of our reason that we are enabled to contemplate God in his works, and imitate him in his ways. When we see his care and kindness extended over all his creatures, it teaches us our duty towards each other, while it calls forth our gratitude to him.

Again he remarks:

> The Almighty Lecturer [Deity], by displaying the principles of science in the structure of the universe, has invited man to study and to imitation. It is as if He had said to the inhabitants of this globe that we call ours, I have made an earth for man to dwell upon, and I have rendered the starry heavens visible, to teach him science and the arts. He can now provide for his own comfort, and learn from my munificence to all, to be kind to each other.[5]

YEARNING FOR THE LIGHT

May not what is here set forth as conveying a message from the "structure of the universe" be regarded as far-fetched? And on the important questions submitted in this chapter, what does that message definitely say? Nothing. Lame and impotent must be the verdict respecting these messages supposed to come from "the heavens and the glory of them" and from the "structure of the universe." When measured by their value as answers to the questions put forth in this chapter, they fail to satisfy the inquiring mind. And what is more, and necessary to be connected with what we have here said upon this appeal to the universe for knowledge, and its

---

5. Thomas Paine, *The Age of Reason: Being an Investigation of True and Fabulous Theology* (Chicago: Belfords, Clarke and Co., 1879), 32-33.

failure to give an adequate answer—the mental powers of man, so far as developed, give no ground of hope that he will ever have the ability, more than he has it now, to formulate an answer from "the things that are made" to the questions we have submitted.

What, then, is left? To what source shall man turn for help to aid him in rending the veil of mystery that surrounds him and the vast universe? Do we really stand "between two barren peaks" crying in vain, "Whence, Why, and Whither?"[6] And is there no voice answering from the silence on either side to instruct the mind and quiet the spirit of restless man in his search for a solution of these mysteries? Has none of the higher intelligences we have supposed to be inhabiting the distant and older worlds found it in his heart to send some friendly message of hope and assurance by enkindling knowledge as to why all is that is, and as it is? A message that would solve the mystery, break the spell of ignorance, and clear the vision? Is not that or something akin to that the only hope for solution to all these inquiries? And may it not be true that something like that has happened? May it not be that the traditions of our race, held in varied forms, about a down-bending in some way or other of some higher intelligence imparting knowledge about the world and the purpose of its existence, and something about man's origin and destiny? And may this not be what that same tradition calls revelation?

OF TRADITION

Surely what we have observed about the universe and the probability of millions of other worlds than our own being inhabited by great Intelligences—greater than those of our world—would tend to the conception of the possibility of their sending forth a revelation as we have supposed.[7] And not only to the possibility of it, but to the probability of it, since they are as likely to possess the altruistic spirit as well as their[8] high mental endowments. Shall we not, then, give attention to the tradition of mankind? May there not be substance in it? Shall we be justified in our search after truth, if we neglect this possible source of knowledge? Is tradition to be despised because it bears the name "tradition"? Sometimes

---

6. Ingersoll's oration at the grave of his brother. <Robert G. Ingersoll, "A Tribute to Ebon C. Ingersoll," in *The Works of Robert G. Ingersoll* (New York: The Dresden Publishing Co., C. P. Farrell, 1901), 12:390; Ingersoll's words are "Life is a narrow vale between the cold and barren peaks of two eternities. We strive in vain to look beyond the heights. We cry aloud, and the only answer is the echo of our wailing cry"—*Ed.*>

7. <Ms III[*] "the conception of the possibility of such a thing"—*Ed.*>

8. <Ms III[c] adds "well as their"—*Ed.*>

tradition may carry on its broad stream—unworthy things—mere myths and childish fables, I know; but may we not use discrimination as to other things not fables and rightly divide the word of truth from the error in this as in other things.

Tradition, of course, comes out of the dim past; but we are not compelled to begin with its beginning. It is possible to go upstream as well as down. Let us in our first view at least consider tradition and the force of it by going upstream rather than down. Take this notion that comes from tradition about the existence of Deity.[9] How came it to us? This present generation learned it from the last generation. And whence did they get it? From the generation that preceded their own; and they of a previous generation; and so on, back and back, into the time ages of antiquity. The tradition of Deity[10] is so old that "the memory of man runneth not to the contrary."[11] We may not be able to trace it quite to its source, but it is something transmitted from a great antiquity down to the present day.

THE HEBREW TRADITION

The Hebrew race felt especially called upon to keep alive this tradition of God, and of creation, and all that goes with it, which they had received from their ancestors even before they were separated from the main Semitic race in the valley of the Euphrates. This, together with the traditions which grew out of the alleged "oral law" through their great prophet Moses, which God is said to have delivered to Moses by word of mouth, this they committed to tradition which in time came to be regarded as well nigh at par with their "scripture" or the "Sacred Books."[12]

One of the ancient Hebrew prophets, in a very ecstacy of enthusiasm for tradition says:

> Give ear, oh my people, to my law. Incline your ears to the words of my mouth. I will open my mouth in a parable. I will utter dark sayings of old which we have heard and known and our fathers have told us. We will not hide them from the children, showing to the generation to come the praises of the Lord, and His strength, and His wonderful works that he hath done. For He established a testimony in Jacob and

---

9. <Ms III* "the existence of a Deity"—*Ed.*>

10. <Ms III* "The tradition of a Deity"—*Ed.*>

11. <William Blackstone, *Commentaries on the Laws of England*, ed. William Carey Jones (San Francisco: Bancroft-Whitney Co., 1916), bk. i, introd., sect. 3, 1:113—*Ed.*>

12. See article by Prof. Archibald Henry Sayce, in William Wright, ed., *The Illustrated Bible Treasury* (New York: Thomas Nelson and Sons, 1896), 27-42. Also Alexander Cruden's article on "Tradition" in *A Complete Concordance to the Holy Scriptures of the Old and New Testaments* (Hartford, Connecticut: S. S. Scranton and Co., 1899).

appointed a law in Israel, which he commanded our fathers that they should make them known to our children; that the generation to come might know them, even the children which should be born; who should arise and declare them to their children, that they might set their hope in God and not forget the works of God, but keep His commandments (Ps. 78:1-7).

Another prophet said of the knowledge that the Hebrews had received concerning God:

> Take heed to thyself and keep thy soul diligently; lest thou forget the things which thine eyes have seen, and lest they depart from thy heart all the days of thy life; but teach them thy sons and thy sons' sons (Deut. 4:9).

THE GOD OF TRADITION

The traditions respecting God, in the higher forms of them, represent Him usually as the creator and preserver of all things. And this is found among nearly all nations and races of men. Even among some of the undeveloped peoples of the earth traces of tradition in this phase of it are to be found; as well as in the traditions of the Hebrew race. It is found in all the mythologies of the ancient world, as well among Greeks and Romans as among the Hebrews. Also in the mythologies—which are but varied forms of tradition—of India, China, Egypt, and the American Indians; all these, in one form or another, carry this phase of the tradition of God as the origin of all things and the directing force of all movement.

SOURCES OF TRADITION[13]

Following this stream of tradition[14] upward must finally bring us to its source. For however far distant the head of it may be, it must disclose a beginning.

From Fear[15]

There are only two sources whence it could start. One would be that the god-idea came to man out of his experiences with the elements, destructive and benign, with which he was forced into contact; and out of which contact primitive man created his god-idea. Those who regard this as the source of the god-idea of the human race, stress man's experiences with the destructive forces of the world rather than with the benign forces. Primitive man heard the thunder and trembled; he saw the flash of lightning and hid in terror; the earth beneath him shook and he was sick

---

13. <Ms III* of section heading "Origin of Traditions"—*Ed.*>
14. <Ms III* "this stream of traditions"—*Ed.*>
15. <Ms III[c] adds "From Fear"—*Ed.*>

with[16] dread; fierce tempests uprooted the forest and destroyed his rude dwellings; desolating sickness visited the tribe and swept half of it to death; famine stalked through the land and took its toll. Reasoning from introspection of his own nature and finding that when he was angry with a rival in the struggle for food—which meant struggle for existence—or in fierce contests for desirable mates and for other earth-possessions, he was moved by bitter hatred and he sought to destroy those with whom he was angry. Hence, when he found himself assailed by destructive forces, he reasoned that whatever or whoever invoked these destructive forces against him were angry with him, and hence he sought to appease their wrath. Thus came the conception of angry gods, who must be propitiated and generally with sacrifices, sometimes human sacrifices, as affording the most precious of offerings.[17]

From Gratitude[18]

There is, however, a kindlier side to this notion of the origin of the god-idea arising from man's experiences. Man is capable of the emotion of gratitude as well as of fear. He takes note of what makes for his prosperity, for his health, for his peace, and for the plenty which ministers to his comfort, as well as of calamitous events. He is grateful for the sunshine which warms the earth; for the gentle rains which with the sunshine accelerate life and make the earth fruitful. He rejoices at the plentifulness of the wildlife on which he feeds; for the food supplies in ocean, and river, and forests, and plain. Hence, primitive[19] man's gratitude to whatever powers there be that produce this abundance on which he feeds; that clothes him, and makes him prosperous. He is aware that all this comes not from himself, but seems to be the result of the beneficence of the powers that stand back of all these manifestations of goodwill towards men; and so out of a sense of gratitude man makes acknowledgment through offerings that he believes must be pleasing to the powers that so bless him. Hence, came to man conceptions of benign deities who must be worshipped.

TRADITION AS BROKEN FRAGMENTS OF REVELATION[20]

It may be conceded that tradition of the god-idea comes from both these

---

16. <Ms III^c adds "with"—*Ed.*>

17. <Ms III^c adds "s" to make plural "offerings"—*Ed.*>

18. <Ms III* of section heading "Influence of Gratitude on the God Idea"—*Ed.*>

19. <Ms III^c adds "primitive"—*Ed.*>

20. <This section heading is an interlinear addition. Originally the heading "Tradition Fragment from Revelation" of Ms III* was located at the beginning of the next paragraph—*Ed.*>

sources—fear and gratitude; for we still have among the undeveloped tribes of men those who entertain the first idea of God—he is a being to be feared for his wrath, which must be appeased. There are large masses of the world's population that have not received the enlightenment that would surely come from revelation; and hence, they are still in that less-than-half-enlightened state where men grope about in great uncertainty with reference to knowledge of God. In some cases, however, it would not be unreasonable to suppose that the partial enlightenment such men possess comes from the broken fragments of previously known revelation among their ancestors, or contact with those who have been so enlightened. That tradition, which has its source—even though indirectly—from revelation, is of much firmer texture than that which has its commencement in the experiences of the race in contact only with the forces of nature, benign and malignant; and of which their god-idea is but the interpretation.

That part of the stream of tradition which has its source in revelation, according to the Hebrew scriptures, represents man in association with God in the early morning of the world, manifested in the most intimate relations by tangible presence and conversation, man even naming the animal creation as they were presented to him by the Creator—"and whatsoever Adam called every living creature, that was the name thereof" (Gen. 2:19). Then came the fall of man, which separated him from this familiar association with God. But in the wreck that seems to have followed this seeming disaster, one thing was preserved, viz., man's knowledge of God. That knowledge which man had of God in Eden, he brought with him into the "outer world," into which he was banished.

According to the Hebrew scripture account of the ante-diluvian patriarchs, this tradition about God had opportunity to become well grounded. These patriarchs each lived to attain to a great age, so that they were contemporaneous with each other for several hundreds of years; and not only brought the Eden-acquired knowledge of God into a post-Eden world, but brought it also from the ante-diluvian world to the post-diluvian era.

WRITTEN TRADITION

It may be thought that in the last paragraph dealing with tradition of the Hebrews—really found in their "scriptures"—we have been appealing to revelation, to the Bible, instead of tradition, as men commonly understand tradition, viz., something handed down from age to age by oral communication without the aid of written memorials. But the Bible may be regarded in more than one aspect. Commonly it is held to be a volume of inspired writings, revelations indeed; but also, without inconsistency, it may be regarded as a body of traditions crystallized into writings, and it may not be contradicted that traditions may be written as well as other things. It is in this sense that I have at this point considered it, viz., as a record of the Hebrew traditions.

This tradition concerning the existence of God or of Gods, speaking now with reference to tradition in general, and without reference to any particular people, or special conceptions of what kind of beings the gods may be—this general tradition is so old that it[21] may not be thrust aside as unworthy to have influence upon the great task upon which we are engaged—viz., our search for the knowledge of God. This human-race tradition of God rises to the character of a universal or truly catholic tradition; it has been practically believed, we may say, "always, everywhere, and by everybody." It is worthy of respectful consideration, and such it is to receive in these pages.

The other remaining source for the knowledge of God is revelation; but that is a theme so large that it will require a chapter by itself for the consideration of it.

---

21. <Ms III* "tradition is so old that 'the memory of man runneth not to the contrary' and it." The eliminated clause already occurs at the end of the section "Of Tradition" above—*Ed.*>

CHAPTER XII
Seekers after God: Revelation

SCRIPTURE READING LESSON

Analysis

I. The Impetus of Tradition to Seekers after God.

II. The Possibility of Revelation.

III. The Problem of Interplanetary Communication.

IV. Achieved Fact of Revelation.

V. The Function of Revelation.

VI. Visualization with Spoken Revelation.

VII. Actual Visitation of Intelligences from One World to Another.

VIII. Interplanetary Transportation Considered.

IX. Man's Achievements in Earth Transportation.

X. The Argument Based upon Man's Achievements.

XI. Unity of Testimony for God.

(a) Tradition;

(b) Works of Nature;

(c) Revelation.

References

It is difficult to give references for the subject matter of this chapter, so much of it is based on the current magazines and news periodicals of recent years; and I have found little in books to guide me in the thoughts presented in this chapter.

Except in closing division—the unity of testimony for God, in tradition, works of nature, revelation—this comes largely from the six "Lectures on Faith," published in the Doctrine and Covenants in all editions preceding the edition of 1921.

CHAPTER XII

Seekers after God: Revelation

IMPETUS GIVEN TO SEARCH FOR GOD BY TRADITION

One result, growing out of this god-idea of the traditions, is of first-rate importance, viz.: it has been an inspiration to certain great souls to seek after God. Men who have not been contented with the intimations to be derived from the works of nature nor with just the fragmentary and somewhat confused outgivings of the traditions of men; but, inspired by the works of nature and those traditions, they have boldly attempted to ascertain the fact of God for themselves. If there be a Deity, transcendent of or immanent in the universe, they have said, Why not find him? Or if the universe itself—nature—be Deity, may not this be found out by searching? Hence, came "Seekers after God." In the book of Job is found the pregnant question: "Canst thou by searching find out God? Canst thou find out the Almighty unto perfection?" (Job 11:7). In this question there is a doubt disclosed, but the significance of that passes when it is observed that the question is asked by Zophar, false friend of Job, and not noted for the depth of his understanding. An affirmative answer is given as the word of the Lord to Israel, and surely by one of the "Seekers after God" more capable to speak upon the subject than Zophar: "Ye shall seek me and find me," God is represented as saying, through Jeremiah, the prophet, "when ye shall search for me with all your heart" (Jer. 29:13). Here not only the possibility of finding God is declared, but also the prime condition essential to the achievement is given—"when ye shall search for me with all your heart."

IS REVELATION POSSIBLE?

The question of the possibility of revelation may be raised: i.e.,[1] the ability of the higher intelligences of other worlds to communicate knowledge to man. But this can only be entertained for a moment. We have in previous chapters held forth the very great likelihood of the worlds and world-systems that we have contemplated being inhabited by intelligences, and some of them most likely of superior

1. <Ms III[c] adds "(i.e.)"—*Ed.*>

intelligence to the inhabitants of our earth; the probability of which is far above any reasonable doubt, and notwithstanding the immense distances that separate them from our earth, yet distance may not affect the assurance that inter-world communication of intelligences is possible; for distance has little to do with thought—or things of the spirit.

At this point we are able to apply again our method of reasoning from what we know to that which is possible, yea, even probable up to the point of moral certainty. And this is what we know from human experiences on the subject of marvelous means of communication.

THE QUESTION OF COMMUNICATION

It is within the recollection of men yet living when the only means of communication between places distant from each other was by means of letters transmitted at best by the speed of the stage coach or equestrian mail carriers. This was followed by the invention and adoption of the electric telegraph devices, and soon the land became a network of telegraphic lines to establish the facilities of rapid means of communication. Not even the wide-spreading ocean was to bar islands and continents from this new method of transmission of messages from land to land. Cables were laid upon the ocean bed linking together the most distant continents, and bringing them well nigh within the possibility of instant communication one with another. This was followed later by the invention of the telephone, by which means the human voice was made to be heard, first at short distances,[2] then at longer distances, until at the present time through this means of communication it is made possible for the human voice to be heard across the oceans and over the greatest extent of land distances. Nor is this method of communication any longer dependant upon the stretching of wires over the land and under the oceans; but by means of radio inventions the human voice is marvelously broadcasted to all lands and over the seas.

All this makes the argument possible from what we know, viz.: if man with his limited development in this matter of communicating intelligence from land to land among his fellows, can achieve so much, what may it not be possible for higher intelligences of older and more advanced worlds to have accomplished in the matter of inter-world communication by superior methods created by their intelligence; until distance, however great, renders no obstruction to the communication of higher intelligences with each other, and with the inhabitants of our world. Indeed, may not the development in this kind upon our own earth have been the result of suggestion, and through the inspiration supplied by some means of communication

---

2. <Ms III* "at short distances from each other"—*Ed.*>

from mind to mind by interplanetary communications? At any rate, in the presence of means recently developed in improved methods of communication, so wonderful that to men of two generations ago they would have appeared miraculous, any doubt concerning the possibility of communication between the intelligences of other worlds or world-systems with our own, must disappear.

THE ACHIEVED FACT OF REVELATION

Moreover, and again adopting our process of reasoning from what we know, we have found among men, and especially among men of most highly developed intellectual and moral and spiritual nature, a desire for the improvement of less developed and barbarous peoples, an impulse to help the lowly and the unfortunate by giving themselves and their fortunes to the uplifting of their fellow men, and the betterment of conditions of all, and especially to enlighten by education the ignorant. This being true of men of this class, may it not be true, and increasingly true of intelligences of other worlds, and especially of those of the higher intellectual types of older and more-developed worlds? If this reasoning from what we know is sound, will not all objections to the possibility of inter-world communication of intelligences have been set aside, and may we not conclude that revelation is not only possible, but very probable; and may it not be true that some of the "Seekers after God" of our own world in their search for God, may really have found Him, and brought back a message from the inner fact of things?

It is quite evident, of course, that all "Seekers after God" have not found Him; and even among those who have, it is quite equally evident that they have not found Him in anything like equal measure; for it must be admitted that there are great differences in the messages they have reported to their fellows.[3] In some instances their messages are not very clear, or coherent; and not always in agreement with each other. This, however, not because of any defectiveness in the source of knowledge, but from the unequal ability of those who are entrusted to interpret rightly their contact with the higher sources of intelligence. The fault is with the medium of interpretation rather than with the source or the reality of their inspiration. The great thing in the whole matter is, however, the achieved fact of revelation. Once the contact <is> made, the union established between earth intelligences and the higher intelligences of other worlds, that contact may be

---

3. <Ms III* "it is quite equally evident that they have reported to their fellows," but due to accidentally skipping from "they have" to "they have" the words "they have not found him in anything like equal measure; for it must be admitted that there are great differences in the messages" from the earlier draft were omitted and these are reinserted above the line—*Ed.*>

trusted to lead to the development of a constantly increasing clearness of the message to be imparted, until earth inhabitants will be instructed by knowledge imparted from higher sources of intelligence than their own minds for their guidance; but undoubtedly in such fashion, and in such progressive degrees, as not to be overwhelmed with knowledge that might hinder rather than accelerate the true development of powers from within by the intelligences receiving these administrations. For development of intelligences—which may be called education—results not so much from acquiring a mere knowledge of things, as from the development within of the mind-powers to seek and find things each for himself.

THE FUNCTION OF REVELATION

The function of higher intelligences, through revelation, would be to encourage and inspire by contact, here and there, the efforts to self-development of those whom they would assist. Men have learned that what we humans call education is not mere "cramming" with knowledge of facts, but the development in those who are taught of the power to think for themselves, and to think straight and right. That power established in the mind, the student will find the facts for himself, absorb them in his own mind, and learn the application of them for himself. Undoubtedly the higher intelligences of other worlds with which our world in some way may be in physical connection, and in moral and spiritual union and sympathy—they[4] wishing our development—will minister their helpfulness to us in some such spirit as this; and the fact that they would so proceed doubtless accounts for the limited and rather infrequent dispensations of revelations to our earth. Those revelations are undoubtedly intended to be progressive and ministered in such fashion as to lead to human development from within, and also are administered in such manner as not to interfere with the free agency of man, and not to break into or destroy the purposes of man's earth-life. The present order of things as to revelation and other things, has been devised in the wisdom of higher intelligences to impart to man a self-culture and development that has been planned in the highest wisdom. Planned in the wisdom of those who have more extensive knowledge than we can fathom by our partial vision of things.

VISUALIZATION WITH SPOKEN REVELATION

There remains to be accounted for some manifestations of an occult power of the mind of man in the matter of communication between intelligences. Telepathy, or the power of one mind to be in such sympathetic affections, feelings, or emotions

---

4. <Ms III^{c} adds "they"—*Ed.*>

with another as to make thought transference possible between them is now accepted by men of science as a reality.[5]

In addition to being almost in instant communication with all parts of the world by wireless telegraphy <and> the telephone, the daily press is in use of the process by which fairly accurate photographs[6] are sent from great distances by means of picture telegraphic instruments; and already the television instrument that shall make it possible when using the telephone to also visualize the one with whom the conversation is being had, is an assured accomplishment for the near future. The recently-developed ability of man through tele-autography to actually affix signatures to a document from great distances—one such case being reported in the current press as taking place between London and New York in July 1927. With such powers of communication of thought by telepathy; of vision by the use of the instrument of television; and by obtaining signatures even overseas by tele-autography, the recorded instances in Holy Writ and other true records of man's experience—the recorded instances of receiving revelation from higher intelligences—from God, may not be regarded as so miraculous or so impossible as some would have us believe.

ACTUAL VISITATION OF INTELLIGENCES OF OTHER WORLDS TO OUR OWN

Up to this point we have considered only the matter of mind[7] communication of knowledge by the higher intelligences of other worlds to the inhabitants of our earth. The question, however, of actual visitation of the higher intelligent personages to our earth is of equal importance. The visitation of angels, the alleged descent to and appearance of God to man, the levitation and ascent of those who have lived upon the earth into heaven, there to dwell with God—the possibility of all this must be considered. And this actual visitation of divine personages to our earth involves the whole thought of overcoming the immense distances which separate us from other worlds. It involves the question of interplanetary visitation of the inhabitants of the universe. Do there exist means of transportation, and may there be palpable, actual intermingling of mutually intelligent inhabitants of world-systems? If so, knowledge of that fact would do away with much of the mystery attendant upon reported visitation of angels and spirits, and even of what are regarded as more tangible, physical personages.

---

5. <For a modern study of telepathy, see Leea Virtanen, *"That must have been ESP!": An Examination of Psychic Experiences* (Bloomington: Indiana University, 1990)—*Ed.*>

6. <Ms III "photographs fairly accurate"—*Ed.*>

7. <Ms III[c] adds "mind"—*Ed.*>

INTERPLANETARY TRANSPORTATION

As in the case of establishing the possibility and likelihood of the interplanetary communication of knowledge by means of revelation, by process akin to thought-transference, let us work out this same problem of interplanetary visitation of personages[8] and doubtless also of things.

Reasoning again from what we know out of the experiences of men in this matter of transportation, we know that transportation is a thing in which there has been marked advancement of late years in our world. Within the memory of men now living time can be recalled when the means of traveling from one place to another was either by horse-drawn vehicles or by equestrian riding. It was not until in the second and third decade of the nineteenth century that the power of steam for wheel-drawn vehicles over rails was adopted, and then was commenced that rapid construction of railways which soon made the continents networks of them, uniting all parts of civilized lands. Overland travel was so established by this means that it gave easy, comfortable, and rapid transit from one place to another and the disadvantage of separation by distance was greatly lessened.

It was in 1807 that Robert Fulton launched the *Clermont* on the Hudson River, the first application of the power of steam to water vessels.[9] Previous to this oceans and seas were traversed only by the power of wind- and ocean-current-propelled boats; but now steam-driven vessels are in the "seven seas" and all their connections, so that rapid and secure means of transportation has been secured, and the oceans, once the dread of all those who went down to the sea in ships, have lost their terror, and are now merely the convenient highways between the continents. The voyage between Europe and America, which once was a matter of many weeks and attended with great danger, is now reduced to a matter of less than six days; and in greater comfort and security than attends upon traveling on the land.[10]

Also, there has come into existence the self-propelled automobile, capable of moving with equal speed of the lightning express trains, rendering travel swift and safe on the ordinary roads of the country without the use of rails, until rapid and safe means of travel in all lands is provided.

MAN'S ACHIEVEMENTS IN EARTH TRANSPORTATION[11]

Within the last twenty-five years man has made rapid progress in his conquest

---

8. <Ms III* "interplanetary transportation of personages"—*Ed.*>

9. <Ms III* "steam vessels to water vessels"—*Ed.*>

10. <In Ms III^c Roberts adds "question on acct of Doc & Cov. sec 61!" which speaks of the destroyer riding on the waters—*Ed.*>

11. <Ms III^c adds "Man's Achievements in Earth Transportation," which was

of the air, in which, both in speed and sustained flight, he surpasses the eagle or the sea gull[12] in their flight. Two methods have been employed in attaining man's conquest of the air. First, the device was by the inflation of huge canvas bags by hydrogen gas, which made the balloons lighter than air and hence capable of rising from the earth to great heights. In these men were wholly at the mercy of the upper air currents to which they rose, as they had no means by which they might steer their course. A notable event in this kind of air aviation took place about 150 years ago, when Vincent Blanchard and John Jeffries (the latter an American) on January 7, 1785, crossed the English Channel from Dover to Calais in a balloon. Their achievement, however, is set down as a piece of sheer luck, as the aeronauts had no control of their craft, they merely drifted across the channel. Development in that line of aviation, however, has gone on until now we have the dirigible lighter-than-air German zeppelin—largely a world-war development—capable of being fully controlled as to its direction and of such sustaining power that in October 1924 the ZR-3, a German zeppelin, now the American airship Los Angeles, crossed the Atlantic, flying from Friedrichshafen, Germany, to Lakehurst Naval Air Station in New Jersey, a distance of 5,066 miles, in 81 hours and 17 minutes; and when she landed, still had unused fuel that would have been sufficient to have taken her as far westward as Chicago. On this voyage the airship was in constant communication with the world over which she flew by means of radio instruments.[13] It was a somewhat similar flight that was made across the Atlantic by the R-34, English dirigible airship, under command of Major <George> H. Scott of the Royal Air Force, starting from East Fortune, Scotland, on July 2, 1919, and landing at Mineola, Long Island, on July 6th, with nearly her last gallon of fuel spent. She made the flight, a distance of 3,130 miles, in 108 hours, 12 minutes; but returned to Pulham, England, in 74 hours, 56 minutes; showing, it is claimed, that crossing from America to Europe presents fewer difficulties than a journey from Europe to America. It was in a similar airship that the Norwegian explorer, <Roald> Amundsen, accompanied by <Lincoln> Ellsworth and <Umberto> Nobile, engineers, flew over the North Pole of our world on May 12, 1926.

FLIGHT WITH HEAVIER-THAN-AIR MACHINES

The development of the other branch of air conquest—by use of heavier-than-air means of transportation—has been even more wonderfully developed than the

---

originally placed at the beginning of the previous paragraph and then moved to its present location—*Ed.*>

12. <Ms III* "or the sea gulls"—*Ed.*>

13. <Ms III* "by means of radio communication"—*Ed.*>

lighter-than-air mode of transportation. It is <in 1927> only twenty-five years ago that the Wright brothers, Wilbur and Orville, of America, constructed their glide planes, which with the aid of wind and favorable declivity of a hill from which to start, they could make but a few feet of distance; but that accomplishment convinced them that they could build a heavier-than-air device capable of carrying not only a passenger, but a motor, and thus become automotively independent of wind and air currents, and able to direct an airplane under whatever difficulties might be presented. This same year, 1902, witnessed the triumph of their conception. They succeeded in constructing an engine, placed it in the airplane device and the plane on a monorail track, and heading straight into the teeth of a favorable wind the machine with its driver rose in the air and made 105 feet for the first flight of a heavier-than-air machine for flying. This under guidance of Wilbur Wright, who in the toss of a coin with his brother for first privilege of trying the airplane, won. The next day, in the second flight, with Orville Wright now at the throttle, the distance of 120 feet was made. The triumph of such a machine that is heavier than air was seen seven years later[14] in such achievements as carrying Louis Bleriot across the English Channel (July 1909); in the flight of United States Navy planes starting from Trespasse, Newfoundland, and flying across the Atlantic to the Azores, in 15 hours and 13 minutes, covering over 1,250 miles. This on the 11th of May, 1919; and from the Azores to London, by way of Lisbon, covering a total of 2,472 miles in 26 hours and 51 minutes of actual flying time.

Thence rose the ambition among the airmen to make a non-stop trans-Atlantic flight. This dream was first realized with Captain John Alcock and Lieutenant Arthur W. Brown, officers in the British Royal Air Force, who started from St. Johns, Newfoundland, and landed in a bog in Ireland, after a flight of 16 hours, 12 minutes, making a distance of 1,960 miles at an average speed of 120 miles an hour. United States heavier-than-air planes circled the globe in 1924. The starting point was Seattle, Washington, and the journey, covering 26,103 miles, was made in 175 days, crossing the Atlantic in two jumps, from Iceland to Greenland, and from Greenland to Labrador. Also in these air journeys with heavier-than-air machines is to be noted Commander Richard E. Byrd's journey to the North Pole, May 9, 1926, in which he flew to the pole and back to his place of starting, a distance of 1600 miles, in 15 hours and 50 minutes. Charles A. Lindbergh's air voyage over the Atlantic Ocean—of such notable fame—may not be left unnoticed. The triumphant journey was made in a monoplane from New York to Paris in 33 hours, 30 minutes, starting May 20, 1927, and covering a distance of 3,610 miles in one continuous flight. A few days later Clarence D. Chamberlin, carrying a

---

14. <Ms III "nine years later," which is corrected to "seven"—*Ed.*>

passenger, Charles A. Levin, performed a similar feat, flying from New York to Eisleben, distance of 3,905 miles in 43 hours.

In addition to these flights made for setting records of achievement in the mastery of the air, there has been established regular air transportation service in many parts of the civilized world, for the transportation both of mail and passengers, and air travel and transportation of mails is becoming a commonplace method of such transportation service. So secure is this method of traveling that in the two years of German civil aviation just past (1926-1927), during which time 55,185 passengers were carried, and 3,073,171 miles flown, there were only two fatalities, or approximately one fatality for each million and a half miles[15] of travel. This promises that air travel in the near future will be as safe as travel by ocean steamer, railway express trains, or by the automobile.

THE ARGUMENT BASED ON MAN'S ACHIEVEMENTS

The argument built upon this development of man's mastery of distance, intercontinental travel by means of ocean liners, airplanes, and zeppelins is this: that if man in his as-yet-limited mental development can accomplish so much in mastering earth and ocean and air in the matter of communication and transportation, who shall formulate any dictum as to the impossibility of his attaining to interplanetary communication and transportation? And much less assert the inability, or impossibility, of the more highly developed intelligences of other worlds to master distance and carry on both interplanetary communications and transportation, both for themselves and for things; and is it unreasonable to believe that they are even now masters of interplanetary communication and transportation, as man is master over intercontinental communication and transportation on this our earth?

We have before us now in bare outline the probability of there being substance in the traditions of men about God; and the possibility, and even probability, of revelation. As to this last, if we but place proper emphasis on the fact already suggested in a previous chapter, that the intelligences of other worlds may reasonably be supposed to possess altruistic sentiments entertained towards intelligences of other worlds, perhaps less advanced in knowledge and experience than themselves, perhaps less fortunate than they are—yet capable of advancement to better things—then it would be easy to conceive of their possessing a most earnest desire to communicate that knowledge, and administer that helpfulness which would come of such communication of knowledge from them to the intelligences of undeveloped, or but partially developed, worlds.

---

15. <Ms III^{c} adds "miles"—*Ed.*>

THE UNITY OF TESTIMONY

The three sources of knowledge of God I have somewhat reviewed in chapter 11 and in this chapter—works of nature, tradition, and revelation—these combined may be a very strong evidence for the existence of God and all that goes with God-in-the-Universe conception. Without here allowing ourselves to be diverted into the too extensive field of thought and investigation as to the truthfulness of revelation, and the supporting power which would come to such a revelation from tradition, and works of nature, let us consider for a moment at least, how these lines of evidence work out into a very fine unity of testimony.

Commencing with the course followed so far in this work, let us consider the first, the works of nature, as constituting our present major line of evidence as to the existence of, and the dominance of, mind in the universe. The presence of self-existing matter in eternal duration and space, with force or energy also present, together with the orderliness of all this universe of suns, planets, and planetary systems, which[16] we have found to bear witness to the existence of a reign of law, with mind dominant over matter, matter chaotic, and matter organized into a cosmos—all this proclaims mind[17] as the eternal cause functioning in the universe, constructing and maintaining the order of things, being the directing power towards whatever ends may be designed as the purpose of the unfolding creation. So far the works of nature throughout the universe, and the orderliness of it, suggest the presence and the operation of a mighty intelligence, which doubtless is supreme. This, at present, shall be our major line; and now turning to tradition as a contributing line of evidence to this main idea proclaimed by the works of nature, we see that the evidence of tradition supports the testimony of nature, and undoubtedly the somewhat variant and confused testimony of tradition does have a supplementary and strengthening influence upon the testimony of the works of nature to the existence and operation of that kind, of which the works of nature bear evidence; and which all through the ages tradition has been trying to tell us about.

Below this our major line of evidence, for the moment, we may consider the other line of contributing evidence, viz., revelation—what the prophets and seers have reported of their findings in their search for God. Thus is fashioned a three-fold cord of evidence, which—we are assured—"is not quickly broken" (Eccl. 4:12).

I give below a simple form, the lines represented by this presentation of the above idea:

---

16. <Ms III[c] adds "which"—*Ed.*>
17. <Ms III[*] "all which proclaims mind"—*Ed.*>

I. The Works of Nature

Line of Revelation, contributing to evidence from Works of Nature.

Line of the Works of Nature for the Evidence of God.

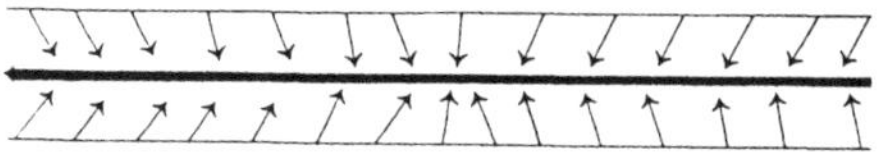

Line of Tradition, contributing to evidence from Works of Nature.

Second, we take tradition as the main line to be considered and major on that for the moment, and then following the same treatment as we did when the works of nature was the major line, we find tradition supported both by the line of revelation and also by the line of the works of nature.[18]

II. Tradition

Line of Revelation, contributing to Tradition

Line of Tradition.

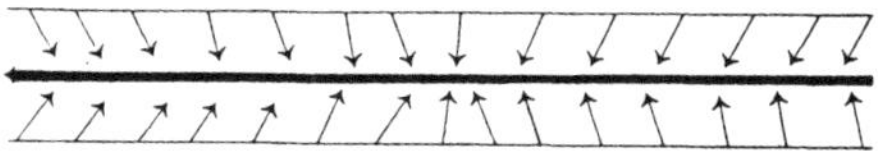

Line of Works of Nature, contributing to Tradition

Then third, and with increasing effect, and presenting the thought also in the true relation in which the different lines of evidence for God's existence ought to stand—and not only for His being, but the kind of being He is—we make revelation our major line, and draw it strong as being at once the most powerful and definite means through which man may know God. Then tradition becomes a supplementary line of evidence, supporting revelation and on the other side, the works of nature become a contributing and important line of evidence for the being and for the glory of God.[19]

---

18. <Ms III* "the works of nature. I give a simple illustration of the presentation of the above idea:"—*Ed.*>

19. <Ms III* "the glory of God. Here follows a simple illustation of the third idea:"—*Ed.*>

III. *Revelation*

If the comparison of these lines in any one of the illustrations given makes out a strong case by accumulation of the three evidences for the existence of God—revelation, tradition, and the works of nature—then the conception of them, arising from the placing of emphasis upon each of the respective lines, in turn—making the others for the time being supplementary—undoubtedly will result in still further increasing the testimony, making sure our inherited knowledge for the existence of God.

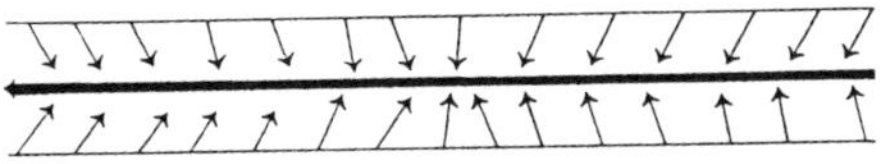

CHAPTER XIII

A Review of Ancient Religions I

SCRIPTURE READING LESSON

Analysis

I. Babylonian-Assyrian Religion.

II. Spiritual Elements.

III. Astrological Phase.

IV. Conceptions of God; Names and Trinities.

V. Belief in a Future Life.

VI. Ethics.

VII. The Egyptian Religion: Origin of the Egyptians.

VIII. Esoteric and Exoteric Forms.

IX. Nature of the Gods.

X. Survival of the Dead.

XI. Morals of the Egyptians: Disparagement <Disparity> between Precepts of Religion and Morals in Life.

XII. Religion of the Medes and Persians.

XIII. The Phoenician Religion.

XIV. Carthaginian Religion

References

All the works cited in the footnotes of this lesson. Some of these may be out of print, and may be only obtainable in the public libraries.

I especially recommend James Freeman Clarke, *Ten Great Religions*, 2 vols. (Boston: Houghton, Mifflin and Co., 1899).

F. Max Müller, *Chips from a German Workshop*, 5 vols. (New York: Charles Scribner's Sons, 1891).

And for a work of a more recent date: Lewis Browne, *This Believing World: A Simple Account of the Great Religions of Mankind* (New York: The MacMillan Co., 1926).

CHAPTER XIII

A Review of Ancient Religions I

Having established the possibility of revelation and even the likelihood of its being a verity, the next step in our inquiry is to find out what is reported by the "Seekers after God," who claim to have made contact with the infinite and brought back a message from "the inner fact of things." To make this inquiry we shall find it most convenient, owing to the limits prescribed for this work, to report the respective messages as they have been accepted by great masses of humanity, and what is the net result of such reporting by the "seers" upon the faith of their followers. In thus proceeding we shall be relieved of considering each one of the many teachers of mankind, and at the same time the status of those large groups will in a way interpret to us the effect of such teaching, religious and philosophical, as they have received.[1]

BABYLONIAN-ASSYRIAN RELIGION[2]

Commencing with the most ancient groups, we start with the races inhabiting the valley of the Euphrates and the Tigris rivers. These constituted the Babylonian and Assyrian empires and peoples. The religion of these people reflected, of course, their views of the deities reported to them by their prophets—their "inspired" teachers, who ventured to instruct them upon supposedly divine things, including the existence of, and the nature of, whatever gods they conceived to exist. Their religion in the main consisted of a combination of the Shamanistic beliefs, that is, a belief that each force of nature had its spirit, good or bad. It is declared on the part of some historians that the peoples accepting Shamanism generally believed in a supreme being, but that the government of the world was in the hands of a

1. <For modern studies of comparative religion, see H. Byron Earhart, ed., *Religious Traditions of the World: A Journey through Africa, Mesoamerica, North America, Judaism, Christianity, Islam, Hinduism, Buddhism, China, and Japan* (San Francisco: Harper San Francisco, 1993), and Roger Eastman, ed., *The Ways of Religion: An Introduction to the Major Traditions*, 2d ed. (New York: Oxford University Press, 1993)—*Ed.*>

2. <Ms III* has "Babylonian-Assyrian Religion" at the beginning of the previous paragraph, but Ms III^{c} moved the heading to its present location—*Ed.*>

number of secondary gods, both benevolent and malevolent toward man, and that it was absolutely necessary to propitiate them by magic, rites, and spells. This claim, however, is denied by others of equal authority as historians. Myers, for instance, in his *General History*, says that:

> In the earliest period made known to us by the native records, we find the pantheon to embrace many local deities . . . , but at no period do we find a Supreme God. The most prominent feature from first to last of the popular religion was the belief in spirits, particularly in wicked spirits, and the practice of magic rites and incantations to avert the malign[ant] influence of these demons.[3]

SPIRITUAL ELEMENTS[4]

A second important feature of the religion was what is known as astrology, or the foretelling of events by the aspect of the stars. This side of the religious system was most elaborately and ingeniously developed until the fame of the Chaldean astrologers[5] was spread throughout the ancient world.

This historian, however, admits that:

> Alongside of these low beliefs and superstitious practices, there existed . . . higher and purer elements. This is . . . illustrated by the so-called penitential psalms, some of them dating from the second millennium B.C., which breathe a spirit like that which pervades the penitential psalms of the Old Testament.

In confirmation of this statement Myers quotes one of these psalms, translated by <Morris> Jastrow.

> O, my god, who art angry with me, accept my prayer. . . .
> May my sins be forgiven, my transgressions be wiped out. . . .
> (May) flowing waters of the stream wash me clean!
> Let me be pure, like the sheen of gold.[6]

"The cuneiform writings on the tablets," says James Freeman Clarke, author of *Ten Great Religions*, "show us that the Assyrians also prayed." On an unpublished tablet in the British Museum is the prayer of an Assyrian king, the date 650 B.C.:

> May the look of pity that shines in thine eternal face dispel my griefs.
> May I never feel the anger and wrath of the God.

---

3. Philip Van Ness Myers, *A General History for Colleges and High Schools*, rev. ed. (Boston: Ginn and Co., 1904), 38.

4. <Ms III[c] adds "Spiritual Elements"—*Ed.*>

5. <Ms III "Chaldean astrology," but Myers's text has "Chaldean astrologers"—*Ed.*>

6. Myers, *General History*, 38.

May my omissions and my sins
be wiped out.
May I find reconciliation with Him,
for I am the servant of his power,
the adorer of the great gods.
May thy powerful face come to my help;
May it shine like heaven,
and bless me with happiness and abundance of riches.
May it bring forth in abundance, like the earth,
happiness and every sort of good.[7]

Dobbins, in his *World's Worship,* says that the Babylonians having a conception both of a supreme being and unity in that being:

> When we penetrate beneath the surface which gross polytheism has acquired from popular superstition, and revert to its original and higher conceptions, we shall find the whole based on the idea of the unity of the deity, the last relic of the primitive revelation, disfigured indeed, and all but lost in the monstrous idea of pantheism, confounding the creature with the creator; and transforming the deity into a world-god,[8] whose manifestations are to be found in all the phenomena of nature. Beneath this supreme and sole god, this great ALL, in whom all things are lost and absorbed, are ranked in an order of emanation corresponding to their importance, a whole race of secondary deities, who are emanations from His very substance, who are mere personifications of His attributes and manifestations. The difference between the various pagan religions is chiefly marked by the differences between these secondary divine beings.[9]

THE ASTROLOGICAL PHASE

Commenting upon the astrological phase of the Babylonian-Assyrian religion, especially that part of it devoted to astronomy, Dobbins saw in the astral and especially in the planetary system, a manifestation of the divine being:

> They considered the stars as His true external manifestation, and in their religious

---

7. James Freeman Clarke, *Ten Great Religions* (Boston: Houghton, Mifflin and Co., 1899), 2:234.

8. <Dobbins's text has "into a god-world"—*Ed.*>

9. <Frank S. Dobbins, *Story of the World's Worship: A Complete, Graphic, and Comparative History of the Many Strange Beliefs, Superstitious Practices, Domestic Peculiarities, Sacred Writings, Systems of Philosophy, Legends and Traditions, Customs and Habits of Mankind throughout the World, Ancient and Modern* (Chicago: The Dominion Co., 1901), 126—*Ed.*>

system made them the visible evidence of the subordinate divine emanations from the substance of the infinite being, whom they identified with the world, his work.[10]

CONCEPTIONS OF GOD: NAMES AND TRINITIES[11]

On the part of those who hold that the Babylonian-Assyrians had the conception of a supreme deity, from whom all other deities were derived, was given the name of Ilu, which signified God, par excellence. Dobbins writes:

> Their idea of him was too comprehensive, too vast, to have any determined external form; or, consequently, to receive in general the adoration of the people. . . . In Chaldea it does not seem that any temple was ever specially dedicated to him, but at Nineveh, and generally throughout Assyria, he seems to have received the peculiarly[12] national name of Asshur. . . . The inscriptions designate him as "Master of all, chief of the gods."[13]

There is also traced in the religion of these early people a shadowy triad, or trinity, or a series of such trinities.

> Below Ilu, the universal and mysterious source of all, was placed a triad, composed of his three first external and visible manifestations, and occupying the summit of the hierarchy of gods in popular worship. [The names of this triad are] Anu, . . . the lord of darkness; Bel,[14] the demiurgus, [the wonder worker,] the organizer of the world; [and] Ao, called also Bin, . . . the "divine son,"[15] par excellence, the divine light, the intelligence, penetrating truth, and vivifying the universe.[16] These three divine person[age]s [were] esteemed as equal in power and con-substantial, [that is, of the same substance,] were not held as of the same degree of emanation, but were regarded as having, on the contrary, issued the one from the other, [and were variously represented in semi-human and animal forms].[17]
>
> A second triad is produced with personages no longer vague and indeterminate in character, like those of the first, but with a clearly-defined[18] sidereal aspect, each representing a known celestial body and especially those in which the Chaldeo-Assyri-

---

10. Ibid., 127.
11. <Ms III^{c} adds "*Conceptions of God, Names And Trinities*"—*Ed.*>
12. <Ms III "peculiar," but Dobbins's text has "peculiarly"—*Ed.*>
13. Dobbins, *World's Worship*, 127. <The wording and capitalization in Dobbins is "Master or Chief of the Gods"—*Ed.*>
14. <Ms III "Bell"—*Ed.*>
15. <Dobbins's text has "the divine 'Son'"—*Ed.*>
16. <Dobbins's text has "penetrating, directing and vivifying the universe"—*Ed.*>
17. <Dobbins, *World's Worship*, 128—*Ed.*>
18. <Ms III "clearly divided," but Dobbins's text has "clearly-defined"—*Ed.*>

ans saw the most striking astrological manifestations[19] of the deity. These were Shamash, the sun; Sin, the moon god, and a new form of Ao, or Bin, inferior to the first, representing him as god of the atmosphere or firmament. Thus, [says Dobbins,] did they industriously multiply deities and representations of them.[20]

BELIEF IN A FUTURE LIFE

The general belief respecting another life by those accepting these Shamanistic beliefs, appears to be that the condition of man in the future existence will be poorer and more rigid than in the present; hence, death is regarded with great dread.

One of the most interesting things connected with the Babylonian-Assyrian religion is that more than any other ancient religion it interlocks with the Bible narrative, and apparently had connection with some primitive religion, that may have had revelation as its source. Lewis Browne, in his *This*[21] *Believing World* (MacMillan Co., 1926), ascribes to the Semites (descendnts of Shem of the Bible), whom Browne describes as having–"for reasons that cannot . . . be made out"–"a peculiar genius for religion."[22] He ascribes to them the origin of the Babylonian-Assyrian religion.

ETHICS OF THE BABYLONIANS

Browne says:

> Ethically the Babylonians were little more than grown-up children. Fear still had hold of them and kept them slaves. Even though they were rich and powerful, even though they were the lords of the green earth and thought themselves the masters of the starry skies, still they remained cravens in their hearts. Beneath all their bluster they were timorous and worried. They were afraid.[23]

THE EGYPTIAN RELIGION

Of equal importance to the Babylonian-Assyrian race were the inhabitants of the Nile valley, the Egyptians. It may be said to be the consensus of opinion of those who have dealt with the history of these ancient people that, though living in Africa, they are not an African people, that is, they were not an indigenous race. The Egyp-

---

19. <Dobbins's text has "most striking external manifestations"–*Ed.*>

20. Condensed from Dobbins, *World's Worship*, 128-29.

21. <Ms III[c] adds "This"–*Ed.*>

22. <Lewis Browne, *This Believing World: A Simple Account of the Great Religions of Mankind* (New York: The MacMillan Co., 1926), 66–*Ed.*>

23. Ibid., 75.

tian language, it is held, "while of a peculiar type has analogies which connect it both with the Semitic and with the Indo-European forms of speech, more especially with the former. We must regard the Egyptians, therefore, as an Asiatic people," immigrants into the valley of the Nile, which they entered from the east.[24]

The theory that the Egyptians immigrated from the south (Ethiopia) down the Nile is discussed by historians, but generally discredited. Josephus, when speaking of one of the ancient Egyptian kings, Sethosis, says, upon the authority of Manetho, that Sethosis was called "Egyptus" and that the country also was called from his name, Egypt.[25]

According to Herodotus, writing in the 5th century B.C., the Egyptians were a very religous people—"religious to excess, far beyond any other race of men." Religion so "permeated the whole being of the people," and their "writing so full of sacred symbols and of allusions to <the> mythology, that it was scarcely possible to employ it on any subject which lay outside of their religion." He also says that the subject is "one of great complexity and considerable obscurity."

ESOTERIC AND EXOTERIC FORMS OF THE FAITH

It appears, however, that the Egyptian religion, like most other religions of antiquity, had two phases or aspects:

> One, in which it was presented to the general public . . . ; the other in which it was presented to the minds of the intelligent, the learned. . . . To the former it was a polytheism of a multitudinous, and in many respects of a gross, character; to the latter it was a system combining strict monotheism with a metaphysical, speculative philosophy on the two great subjects—the nature of God[s] and the destiny of man, in which the effort was made to exhaust those deep and unfathomable mysteries.[26]

---

24. George Rawlinson, *History of Ancient Egypt* (London: Longmans, Green, and Co., 1881), 1:97. <Egyptian is no longer considered to have any connection to Indo-European. See Philip Baldi, *An Introduction to the Indo-European Languages* (Carbondale: Southern Illinois University Press, 1983—*Ed.*>

25. See Flavius Josephus, *The Works of Flavius Josephus: Against Apion*, William Whiston's translation (Baltimore: Armstrong and Berry, 1837), bk. i, p. 584. In the Book of Abraham, translated by Joseph Smith, the prophet of the New Dispensation, gives the information that the king reigning over Egypt at the time of Abraham's sojourn in that land, was a descendant of Ham, son of Noah. Ham had married a wife of a race with whom the sons of Noah were forbidden to intermarry—the descendants of Cain—and thus through Ham and Egyptus, that race was perpetuated after the flood. This Egyptus, however, seems to have been of an enterprising character. It was she who discovered the Nile valley and brought her descendants there to inhabit it (see Abr. 1).

26. Rawlinson, *History of Ancient Egypt*, 1:313.

It is held by some that even in the Egyptian religion formulated for the masses, it was understood that "the idea of a single, self-existent deity" was conceived, the evidence of which "is to be found not unfrequently in the hymns and prayers of the ritual." In the esoteric religion of the Egyptians:

> The primary doctrine . . . was the real, essential unity of the divine nature. The sacred texts taught that there was a single being, "the sole producer of all things both in heaven and earth, himself not produced of any"—"the only true [and] living God, self-originated"—"who exists from the beginning"—"who has made all things, but has not himself been made."[27] This being seems never to have been represented by any material, even [in] symbolical form. It is thought that he had no name, or if he had, that it must have been unlawful either to pronounce or write it. He was a pure spirit, perfect in every respect—all wise, almighty, supremely good.
>
> The gods of the <popular> mythology were understood, in the esoteric religion, to be either personified attributes of the deities[28] or parts of the nature which he had created, considered as informed and inspired by him. Num, sometimes called Kneph, represented the creative mind; Phthah, the creative hand, or act of creating; Maut represented matter; Ra, the sun; Khons, the moon; Seb, the earth; Khem, the generative power in nature; Nut, the upper hemisphere[29] of heaven; Athor, the lower world or under hemisphere; Thoth personified the divine wisdom; Ammon, perhaps, the divine mysterious<ness> or incomprehensibility; Osiris (according to some), the divine goodness. It is difficult in many cases to fix on the exact quality, act, or part of nature intended, but the principle admits of no doubt.
>
> No educated Egyptian priest certainly, probably no educated layman, conceived of the popular gods as real, separate, and distinct beings.[30] All knew that there was but one God and understood that when worship was offered . . . [to the several gods] the one God was worshipped under some one of his forms or in some one of his aspects.[31]

As for example:

> Ra was not a sun deity with a distinct and separate existence, but the supreme

---

27. <Ms III* "has not made himself been made"—*Ed.*>

28. <Rawlinson's text has "personified attributes of the Deity"—*Ed.*>

29. <Ms III "atmosphere," but Rawlinson's text has "hemisphere"—*Ed.*>

30. <Rawlinson's text has "the popular gods as really separate and distinct beings"—*Ed.*>

31. Rawlinson, *History of Ancient Egypt*, 1:314-15. <For modern studies of Egyptian Gods, see Clive Barrett, *The Egyptian Gods and Goddesses: The Mythology and Beliefs of Ancient Egypt* (London: Aquarian Press, 1992), and Jane B. Sellers, *The Death of Gods in Ancient Egypt: An Essay on Egyptian Religion and the Frame of Time* (London: Penguin Books, 1992)—*Ed.*>

God acting in the sun, making his light to shine on the earth, warming, cheering, and blessing it.[32]

Burder says:

> To exhibit in symbol form the Egyptian ideas of their gods was the very essence of the Egyptian Religion. This [he holds,] brought about the grossest of superstitious worship. To set forth in symbol the attributes, quality, and nature of their gods, the priests chose to use animals; the bull, cow, ram, cat, crocodile, ape, etc. . . . were all emblems of the gods. . . . But let it be remembered, that the Egyptians never worshipped images or idols, they worshipped living representations of the gods, and not liveless images of stone or metal. Their sculptures were never made for worship; they chose animals that corresponded as nearly as possible to the ideas of the nature of the gods.[33] . . . Popularly these animals were regarded as gods, and were really worshipped; by the priests they were regarded simply as the representatives of the gods.[34]

SURVIVAL OF THE DEAD[35]

The Egyptians believed in the survival of the spirit of man after death, and ultimately that the spirit would rejoin the body it had inhabited in life in a resurrection from the dead.[36]

---

32. Ibid., 1:315-16.

33. <Ms III[c] adds "nature of the"; Burder's text has "as nearly as possible to their ideas of the gods"–*Ed.*>

34. William A. Burder, *A History of All Religions, with Accounts of the Ceremonies and Customs, or the Forms of Worship, Practised by the Several Nations of the Known World, from the Earliest Records to the year 1872* (Philadelphia: William W. Harding, 1872), 507-508.

35. <Ms III has this heading before the previous sentence, in the middle of the quotation from Burder–*Ed.*>

36. After telling the drama of the life and resurrection of Osiris, the author of *This Believing World*, Lewis Browne, says: "Osiris came to life again! He was miraculously resurrected from the dead and taken up to heaven and there in heaven, so the myth declared, he lived on eternally! . . . The Egyptians reasoned that if it was the fate of God Osiris <to be resurrected after death>, then a way could be found to make it the fate of man, too. Of course! All one had to do was to be buried properly. If only a man's soul were committed safely into the hands of Osiris, and his body embalmed and preserved in a tomb, then some day of a surety the two would get together again, and the man would walk the earth as of yore. At least, so it came to be believed in Egypt as long as 4000 years ago" (Browne, *This Believing World*, 83-85).

DISPARAGEMENT BETWEEN PRINCIPLE AND PRACTICE[37]

One thing respecting the Egyptian religion remains mysteriously dark, viz., the disparagement <disparity> between the very exalted moral doctrines of the religion and the immorality of those who followed it. Rawlinson remarks:

> In morals the Egyptian combined an extraordinary degree of theoretic perfection with an exceedingly lax and imperfect practice. It has been said that "the forty-two laws of the Egyptian religion contained in the 125th chapter of the 'Book of the Dead' fall short in nothing of the teachings of Christianity," and [it is even] conjectured that Moses, in compiling his code of laws [for Israel], did but "translate into Hebrew the religious precepts which he found in the sacred books" of the people among whom he had been brought up.[38]

"Such expressions are no doubt exaggerated," remarks our historian, "but they convey what must be allowed to be a fact, viz., that there is a very close agreement between the moral law of the Egyptians and the precepts of the Decalogue."[39] Yet notwithstanding this profound knowledge of high moral truth, the practice of the people was rather below than above the common level.

> The Egyptian women were notoriously of loose character, and whether as we meet with them in history or as they are depicted in Egyptian romance, appear as immodest and licentious. The men practiced[40] impurity openly and boasted of it in their writings. They were industrious, cheerful, nay, even gay, under hardships, and not wanting in family affection; but they were cruel, vindictive, treacherous, avaricious, prone to superstition, and profoundly servile.[41]

And yet the high praise for the moral law as given above is borne out by answers that the spirit of man must make before Osiris in the judgment hall, where the decisive sentence is pronounced, either admitting the candidate to happiness or excluding him forever. He must show that his knowledge of life is great enough to give him the right to be admitted to share the lot of glorified spirits. Before each of the forty-two judges who question him in turn, he must be able to tell the name of each judge and what it means. Among other things he is obliged to give an account of his whole life, in which he must be able to say that he has not blasphemed, has not stolen, nor smitten men privily; that he

---

37. <Ms III^c adds "Disparagement Between Principle and Practice"—*Ed.*>

38. Rawlinson, *History of Ancient Egypt,* 1:104. <Rawlinson is quoting Heinrich Brugsch, *Histoire d'Egypte,* 17—*Ed.*>

39. Ibid., 1:104.

40. <Ms III^c adds "d" to make "practiced"; Rawlinson's text has "practiced"—*Ed.*>

41. Rawlinson, *History of Ancient Egypt,* 1:104-105.

has not treated any person with cruelty, nor started up trouble; that he has not been idle nor intoxicated; and has not practiced any shameful crime, nor must he when before the judges confine himself merely to denying any ill conduct, he must speak of the good he has done in his lifetime; that he has made proper offerings to the gods, given food to the hungry, drink to the thirsty, and clothes to the naked.

> If in all sincerity [he could report affirmatively upon all these heads], then the soul was straightway gathered into the fold of Osiris. But if it could not, if it was found wanting when weighed in the heavenly balances, then it was cast into a hell, to be rent to shreds by the "Devouress." For only the righteous souls, only the guiltless, were thought to be deserving of life everlasting![42]

All which makes one wonder why the disparagement <disparity> between the high demand of religious principles and the[43] Egyptian low state of righteous living.

AN EXPLANATION[44]

Some in the explanation of this disparagement <disparity> between the high morality of the religion of the Egyptians and the low state of morals in their lives, say that it arises from this circumstance, viz., that the religion itself was derived from contact with the true religion of the ante-diluvian patriarchs of the Bible, but being left in the hands of a people who soon fell away from righteous principles to the practice of gross sensualism, the divergence between moral theory and moral practice soon set in and drifted wider and wider apart until we have the result observed and commented upon by the authorities above quoted. This observation may apply also to nearly all the ancient religions of the world subsequent to the flood.

RELIGION OF THE MEDES AND PERSIANS

The religion of the Medes and Persians is accorded so great an antiquity, that it is supposed to have been taught by one of the grandsons of Noah, who planted colonies on the plateau of Persia soon after the confusion of languages.

> In Persia the first idolaters were called Sabians, who adored the rising sun with the profoundest veneration. To that luminous sphere[45] they consecrated a most

---

42. Browne, *This Believing World*, 86-87.
43. <Ms III[c] adds "the"—*Ed.*>
44. <Ms III[*] of section heading "Immorality of the Egyptians"—*Ed.*>
45. <Ms III[*] "To that planet," and Burder's text also has "To that planet"—*Ed.*>

magnificent chariot, to be drawn by horses of the greatest beauty and magnitude on every solemn festival. . . . In consequence of the veneration they paid to the sun, they worshipped fire and invoked it in all their sacrifices. In their marches they carried it before their kings, and none but the priests were permitted to touch it, because they made the people believe that it came down from heaven. . . .

Persian adoration, however, was not confined to the sun. They worshipped the water, and the earth, and the winds, as so many deities. Human sacrifices were offered by them; and they burnt their children in fiery furnaces, appropriated to their idols. Both Medes and Persians at first worshipped two gods; namely, Arimanius <Ahriman>, the god of evil; and Oromasdes <Ahura Mazda>, the giver of all good. By some it was believed that the good god was from eternity and the evil one created; but they all agreed that they would continue to the end of time and that the good god would overcome the evil one. They considered darkness as the symbol of the evil god and the light as the image of the good one. They held Arimanius, the evil god, in such detestation, that they always wrote his name backward. Some ancient writers have given us a very odd account of the origin of this god Arimanius. . . . Oromasdes, they say, considering that he was alone, said to himself, "If I have no one to oppose me, where then is all my glory?" This single reflection of his created Arimanius, who, by his everlasting opposition to the divine will, contributed against inclination to the glory of Oromasdes.[46]

James Freeman Clarke, commenting upon the religion of the Persians, follows Herodotus in his description of the religion of the Persians and agrees that they had:

No temples, no altars, no idol worship of any kind. The Supreme Being is worshipped by one symbol, Fire, which is pure and purifies all things. The prayers are for purity, the libation the juice of a plant. Ormazd <Ahura Mazda> has created everything good and all his creatures are pure. Listen to the priest chanting his litany thus:

"I invoke and celebrate Ahura Mazda, brilliant, greatest, best. All-perfect, all-powerful, all-wise, all-beautiful, only source of knowledge and happiness. He has created us, he has formed us, he sustains us. He belongs to those who think good; to those who think evil he does not belong. He belongs to those who speak good; to those who speak evil he does not belong. He belongs to those who do good; to those who do evil he does not belong."

This is the religion of the great race who founded the Persian Empire. To these worshippers life did not seem to be a gay festival, as to the Greeks, nor a single step on the long pathway of the soul's transmigration, as to the Egyptians; but a field of battle between mighty powers of good and evil, where Ormazd and Ahriman[47] meet

46. Burder, *History of All Religions*, 623-24.
47. <Ms III "Ahriaman"—*Ed.*>

in daily conflict and where the servant of God is to maintain a perpetual battle against the powers of darkness by cherishing good thoughts, good words, and good actions.[48]

THE PHOENICIANS

As near neighbors to the Persians the Phoenicians and their religion deserve mention. Myers claims:

> The Phoenicians were of [the] Semitic race [and that] their ancestors lived in the neighborhood of the Persian Gulf. From their seats in that region they migrated westward, like the ancestors of the Hebrews, and reached the Mediterranean before the light of history had fallen upon its shores.[49]

The Phoenicians had somewhat the same religious notions as the Babylonians and worshipped some of the same gods, Baal, for instance.[50]

> Baal was the supreme male divinity of the Phoenician and Canaanitish[51] nations; Ashtoreth was their female divinity. The name Baal means Lord. He was the Sun God. The name is generally used in connection with other names, Baal-Gad, that is, Baal the fortune-bringer; Baal-Berith, or covenant-making Baal; Baal-Zebub, the fly-god. The people of Israel worshipped Baal [for some time] up to the [seership] time of Samuel, at whose rebuke they forsook this iniquity for nearly 100 years. The practice was introduced again at the time of Solomon and continued until the days of the captivity, [early in the sixth century B.C.].[52]

THE CARTHAGINIANS[53]

Saturn, under the name of Moloch, was the god most honored by the Carthaginians, a colony of the Phoenicians.

> This idol was the deity to whom they offered up human sacrifices, and from this proceeds the fable of Saturn having devoured his own children. Princes and great men, under particular calamities, used to offer up their most beloved children to this idol. Private persons imitated the conduct of their princes, and thus in time the practice became general; so general that they carried their infatuation so far, that those who had

---

48. Clarke, *Ten Great Religions*, 2:11-12. See also Myers, *General History*, 63.

49. <Myers, *General History*, 54–*Ed.*>

50. George Crabb, *New Pantheon; or, Mythology of All Nations* (London: James Blackwood and Co., 1878), chap. 55.

51. <Ms III "Cananitish"–*Ed.*>

52. See Dobbins, *World's Worship*, 142.

53. <Ms III^{c} adds "The Carthegenians"; in each instance the spelling "Carthegenians" is corrected to "Cathaginians"–*Ed.*>

> no children of their own purchased those of the poor, that they might not be deprived of the benefits of such a sacrifice! . . . This horrid custom prevailed among the Phœnicians, the Tyrians, and the Carthaginians; and from them the Israelites borrowed it, although expressly contrary to the order of God.[54]

---

54. Burder, *History of All Religions*, 613; 2 Kings, chaps. 16, 21. <For a modern study of child sacrifice among the Carthaginians, see Shelby Brown, *Late Carthaginian Child Sacrifice and Sacrificial Monuments in Their Mediterranean Context* (Sheffield, Eng.: Sheffield Academic Press, 1991)–*Ed.*>

CHAPTER XIV

A Review of Ancient Religions II

SCRIPTURE READING LESSON

Analysis

I. Religion of the Greeks and the Romans.

II. Ontology of the Greek and Roman Religions.

III. The Sects of the Greek and Roman Cultus:

(a) The Stoics;

(b) The Epicureans;

(c) The Academicians.

IV. The Religions of Northern Europe.

V. The Mohammedan Religion.

(a) The Creed of Islam;

(b) The Acceptance of Other Prophets Than Mohammed.

References

All the works cited in the text and footnotes of the chapter.

I recommend especially for the religion of the Greeks and the Romans *Cicero's Tusculan Disputations; also Treatises on the Nature of the Gods and on the Commonwealth,* translated for the Harvard <Harper's> Classics by C. D. Yonge (New York: Harper, 1894), "The Nature of the Gods," 209-355.

George Crabb, *New Pantheon; or, Mythology of All Nations* (London: James Blackwood and Co., 1878).

James Freeman Clarke, *Ten Great Religions,* 2 vols. (Boston: Houghton, Mifflin and Co., 1899), parts.

The Koran; or, Alcoran of Mohammed, translation by George Sale (London: William Tegg, 1850).

Thomas Carlyle, "Heroes and Hero Worship," lecture ii, Mohammed, in *On Heroes, Hero-Worship, and the Heroic in History* (Chicago: A. C. McClurg and Co., 1892).

Lewis Browne, *This Believing World: A Simple Account of the Great Religions of Mankind* (New York: The MacMillan Co., 1926).

CHAPTER XIV
A Review of Ancient Religions II

RELIGION OF THE GREEKS AND THE ROMANS

The religion of the Greeks and Romans may be treated under one head, since the Romans largely derived their religion from the Greeks, and the Greek religion in turn was greatly influenced by contact with the Egyptians. Many of the Greek philosophers—teachers of religion to their countrymen—travelled into Egypt, where they gathered all the notions then current concerning the gods, the transmigration of souls, a future state of existence, and other points, which they modeled into a system that was afterwards enriched and adorned by all the charms of embellishments that poetry and art could furnish. Thomas Dew in his *Digest of Laws, Customs, Manners, and Institutions of Ancient and Modern Nations,* says on this matter of Greek religion being derived in great measure from the Egyptians: "Still a large portion [i.e., of the Greek religion] was of Greek origin, and that, even though taken from Egypt became Grecian in character."[1]

The Greek and Roman deities are distinguished into three classes, namely the superior gods, the inferior gods, and the demi-gods. The superior gods, otherwise called the Dii Majorum Gentium, that is, gods of the superior house or families, answering to the patricians or the nobility of Rome, were so named because they were believed to be immanently employed in the government of the world. They were also styled the "select gods," of whom twelve were admitted into the council of justice (the supreme court), and on that account denominated "consentes." The images of those twelve gods were first in the forum of Rome, six of them being males and six females. These twelve gods were supposed to preside over the twelve months, to each of them was allotted a month.

The inferior gods comprehended what Ovid called the celestial populace, answering to the plebians among the Romans, who had no place in heaven. These were called the "Penates-Lares"—rural deities. The third class, or demi-gods, was composed of such as derived their origin from a god or goddess and a mortal; or

---

1. <Thomas Dew, *A Digest of the Laws, Customs, Manners, and Institutions of the Ancient and Modern Nations* (New York: D. Appleton and Co., 1893), 54—*Ed.*>

such as by their valor and exploits had raised themselves to the rank of immortals. Some mention a fourth class, called novensiles; they were the least of all that were reckoned among the gods. They were the deities by whose help and means, according to Cicero, men are advanced to heaven and obtain a place among the gods![2]

ONTOLOGY OF THE GREEK AND ROMAN RELIGIONS

By both Greek and Roman account of origins, chaos (void space) was first, then came into being "broad-breasted earth," the gloomy Tartarus, and Love. Chaos produced Erebus and Night, and this last bore to Erebus Day and Ether.

According to the history of the early tribes who settled in Italy, the Etruscans, the following is the account of the creation: God created the universe in six thousand years and appointed the same period of time to be the extent of its duration. In the first part of the thousand years God created the heavens and the earth; in the second, the visible firmament; in the third, the sea and all the waters that are in the earth; in the fourth, the sun, moon, and stars; in the fifth, every living soul of birds, reptiles, and quadrupeds which have their abode either on the land, in the air, or in the water; and in the sixth, man alone.[3] The close adherence of this order of creation with Genesis would naturally lead to the conclusion that this notion of creation was derived from that Hebrew source.[4]

THE SECTS OF THE GREEK AND ROMAN CULTUS

The religion of both the Greeks and the Romans gave rise to a multitude of deities, mostly identical in character, but under different names, and by both Greeks and Romans were worshipped but indifferently, a tone of insincerity running through the whole cultus. The followers of religion and philosophy—for the two were closely blended by these ancient peoples—were mainly grouped into three sects or schools: the Stoics, Epicureans, and the Academicians. All three schools existed before the opening of the Christian Era.

THE STOICS

Zeno was the founder of the Stoics. He lived in the third century B.C. and

---

2. George Crabb, *New Pantheon; or, Mythology of All Nations* (London: James Blackwood and Co., 1878), 6-7. <For modern surveys of Greek and Roman religion, see Walter Burkert, *Greek Religion* (Cambridge, MA: Harvard University Press, 1985), and Margaret Lyttelton, *The Romans: Their Gods and Their Beliefs* (London: Orbis, 1984)—*Ed.*>

3. Crabb, *New Pantheon; or, Mythology*, chap. 2.

4. <Ms III* "this notion of creation was derived from Genesis"—*Ed.*>

taught at Athens in a public porch (*stoa*, in Greek) from which came the name applied to his followers.

> The Stoics inculcated virtue for its own sake. They believed—and it would be difficult to frame a better [human] creed—that "man's chief business . . . is to do his duty." They schooled themselves to bear with composure any lot that destiny might appoint. Any sign of emotion on account of calamity was considered unmanly. Thus, a certain Stoic, when told of the sudden death of his son, is said merely to have remarked, "Well, I never imagined that I had given life to an immortal."[5]

The Stoics believed (1) that there were gods; (2) they undertook to define their character and nature; (3) they held that the universe is governed by them; (4) that they exercise a superintendency over human affairs. The evidence for the existence of the gods they saw primarily in the universe itself. "What can be so plain and evident," they argued, "when we behold the heavens and contemplate the celestial bodies, as the existence of some supreme, divine intelligence, by which these things are governed?"

Of the nature of the deity, they held two things: first of all, that he is an animated though impersonal being; second, that there is nothing in all nature superior to him. "I do not see," says one versed in their doctrines, "what can be more consistent with this idea and preconception than to attribute a mind and divinity to the world, the most excellent of all things."[6]

THE EPICUREANS

The school of the Epicureans was founded by Epicurus (341-270 B.C.).

> [He] taught [somewhat] in opposition to the Stoics that pleasure is the highest good. He recommended virtue, indeed, but only as a means for the attainment of pleasure; while the Stoics made virtue an end in itself. In other words, Epicurus said,[7] "Be virtuous, because virtue will bring you the greatest amount of happiness." Zeno said, "Be virtuous, because you ought to be."
>
> Epicurus had many followers in Greece, and his doctrines were eagerly embraced by many of the Romans during the later corrupt period of the Empire. Many of these disciples[8] carried the doctrines of their master to an excess, . . . Allowing full indulgence

---

5. <Philip Van Ness Myers, *General History for Colleges and High Schools*, rev. ed. (Boston: Ginn and Co., 1904), 185-86—*Ed.*>

6. <For modern surveys of Stoicism, see John M. Rist, *Stoic Philosophy* (Cambridge: Cambridge University Press, 1969), and A. A. Long, *Hellenistic Philosophy: Stoics, Epicureans, Sceptics*, 2d ed. (Berkeley: University of California Press, 1986)—*Ed.*>

7. <Ms III "says," but Myers's text has "said"—*Ed.*>

8. <Ms III "his disciples," but Myers's text, and Roberts's quotation of it in *The*

to their appetites, for the whole philosophy was expressed in the proverb, "Let us eat and drink, for tomorrow we die."[9]

The Epicureans held that gods existed, they accepted the fact from the constant and universal opinion of mankind, independent of education, wisdom, or law. It must be necessary, so they said, that this knowledge is implanted in our minds, or rather, is innate in us. Their doctrine was that the opinion respecting which there is a general agreement in universal nature, must necessarily be true; therefore, it must be allowed that there are gods. Of the form of the gods they held that because the human body is more excellent than that of other animals, both in beauty and for convenience, therefore, the gods are in human form. Yet these forms of the gods were not "body, but something like body"; nor do they contain blood, but something like blood; nor are they to be considered as bodies of any solidity; nor is the nature or the power of the gods to be discerned by the senses, but by the mind. They held that the universe arose from chance, and the gods neither did nor could extend their providential care to human affairs. The duty to worship the gods was based upon the fact of their superiority to man.[10]

THE ACADEMICIANS

The Academicians can scarcely be regarded as a school of religion or[11] philosophy, though they refer their origin to Plato.[12] Their name stands for a method of thought rather than for a system of truth. They had no philosophy but rather speculated about philosophy. They advocated nothing; they were the agnostics of their time—that is, they were people "who did not know," and like our modern agnostics, had a strong suspicion that nobody else knew. They represented merely the negative

---

Seventy's Course in Theology: Third Year, The Doctrine of Deity (Salt Lake City: The Caxton Press, 1910), 82, have "these disciples"—*Ed.*>

9. In these remarks on both these schools, I follow Myers, *General History*, 184-86.

10. See *Cicero's Tusculan Disputations; also Treatises on the Nature of the Gods and on the Commonwealth*, trans. Charles D. Yonge (New York: Harper, 1894), "The Nature of the Gods," 266-68. I commend to those who would have from first-hand information on the religion of the Greeks and the Romans, these disputations. <For Epicurus and his school, see John M. Rist, *Epicurus: An Introduction* (Cambridge: Cambridge University Press, 1972), and Richard W. Hibler, *Happiness through Tranquility: The School of Epicurus* (Lanham, MD: University Press of America, 1984)—*Ed.*>

11. <Ms III^c adds "religion or"—*Ed.*>

12. See William Smith, *History of Greece from the Earliest Times to the Roman Conquest with Supplementary Chapters on the History of Literature and Art*, rev. George W. Greene (New York: Harper and Brothers, 1871), 596.

attitude of mind of their times, but numbered in their following some of the most considerable[13] men of Rome, Cicero being among the number. The Academy is said to have exactly corresponded to the moral and political needs of Rome in the days of Cicero,[14] which means that most men in the empire at that period were in a state of doubt in respect of God and of all human relationship to him.

THE RELIGIONS OF NORTHERN EUROPE

Turning from the south of Europe to the northern regions among the Scandinavian and Germanic tribes, there was held a shadowy, and not-well-understood belief in the existence of an all-pervading influence or spirit; a supreme being to whom the people of those lands gave the name of "Alfader," meaning the father of all; yet, strange to say, they paid him no divine honors, gave him no worship, but contented themselves in worshipping inferior deities, their old war heroes in the main, whom they had apotheosized; and who represented the national quality of the people of northern Europe at that time. To this "Alfader" they attributed infinite power, knowledge, and wisdom, and forbade any representation of this being under a corporeal form, and enjoined the celebration of his worship in consecrated woods. Under the "Alfader" they recognized a number of inferior divinities, who were supposed to govern the world and preside over the celestial bodies. The doctrine of a future state formed an important part of the mythology of these people, but as to the state of the soul after the death of the body there was a diversity of beliefs. Their fundamental maxims were to serve the deity with sacrifice and praise, to do no wrong to others, to be brave and intrepid. That they worshipped the sun and moon may be inferred from two days in the week being sacred to them, "Sonndag" and "Mondag," that is, Sunday and Monday. The heaven of these northern tribes was in the highest regions of the earth and consisted of two abodes, namely, Valhalla, or Hall of Odin, where warriors only were admitted; and a higher abode called Gimle, where the good and virtuous in general were to be admitted. They also had two abodes for the wicked, namely, Nifleheim or Evilhome, and Nastrond, the shore of the dead.[15]

---

13. <Ms III^{c} adds "considerable"—*Ed.*>

14. See "Academy," *The Encyclopædia Britannica: A Dictionary of Arts, Sciences, Literature and General Information*, 11th ed. (Cambridge and New York: Cambridge University Press, 1910-1911), 1:105-106.

15. See Crabb, *New Pantheon; or, Mythology*, 165-67; also William A. Burder, *A History of All Religions, with Accounts of the Ceremonies and Customs, or the Forms of Worship, Practised by the Several Nations of the Known World, from the Earliest Records to the year 1872* (Philadelphia: William W. Harding, 1872), 525-26; Frank S. Dobbins, *Story of the World's*

THE MOHAMMEDAN RELIGION

Mohammed, the son of Abdallah and Amina, was born in Mecca, 569 A.D. It was not until he was forty years of age, however, that he began delivering his message to the world, and this after a long period of communing with his own heart in the silence of the mountains, himself silent, open to the still small voices, which he claimed to hear, and the visitation of supernatural appearances, the voices often "accosting him as the Prophet of God, even the stones and trees joined in the whispering," until he suspected himself as becoming insane. Then a happy interpretation by his wife, Cadijah, of these mysterious voices and appearances, declaring them to be good spirits and angels, threw a note of optimism into his gloomy meditations and the career of the prophet began. Since those days to the present, it is estimated that "9,000,000,000 of human beings have acknowledged him to be a prophet of God."[16]

THE CREED OF ISLAM

> There is no God but God, the living, the self-subsisting; he hath sent down unto thee the book of the Korân with truth, confirming that which was revealed before it; for he had formerly sent down the law, and the gospel, a direction to men; and he had also sent down the distinction between good and evil. Verily, those who believe not the signs of God shall suffer a grievous punishment; for God is mighty, able to revenge. Surely nothing is hidden from God, of that which is on earth, or in heaven; it is he who formeth you in the wombs, as he pleaseth; there is no God but he, the mighty, the wise. . . . It is God who hath created you, and hath provided food for you; hereafter will he cause you to die; and after that will he raise you again to life. Is there any of your false gods, who is able to do the least of these things? . . . It is God who sendeth the winds, and raiseth the clouds, and spreadeth the same in the heaven, as he pleaseth; and afterwards disperseth the same; and thou mayest see the rain issuing from the midst thereof; and when he poureth the same down on such of his servants as he pleaseth, behold, they are filled with joy. . . . It is God who created you in weakness, and after weakness hath given you strength; and after strength, he will again reduce

---

Worship (Chicago: The Dominion Co., 1901), 88; John William Draper, *History of the Intellectual Development of Europe* (New York: Harper and Brothers, 1876), 1:240. <For surveys of northern Europe religions, see H. R. Ellis Davidson, *Myths and Symbols in Pagan Europe: Early Scandinavian and Celtic Religions* (Syracuse, NY: Syracuse University Press, 1988) and *Scandinavian Mythology*, rev. ed. (New York: Peter Bedrick Books, 1986)—*Ed.*>

16. Draper, *Intellectual Development*, 1:330-31. <Roberts has paraphrased most of this paragraph from Draper. The latest information lists the total number of Muslims as 971 million. For a modern survey of Islam, see Gerhard Endress, *An Introduction to Islam*, trans. Carole Hillenbrand (New York: Columbia University Press, 1988)—*Ed.*>

you to weakness and grey hairs; he createth that which he pleaseth; and he is the wise, the powerful.[17]

Gibbon[18] comments:

> The creed of Mohammed is free from suspicion and ambiguity, and the Koran is a glorious testimony to the unity of God. The prophet of Mecca rejected the worship of idols and men, of stars and planets, on the rational principle[s] that whatever rises must set, and whatever is born must die, that whatever is corruptible must decay and perish. In the author of the universe his rational enthusiasm confessed and adored an infinite and eternal being, without form or place, without issue or similitude, present to our most secret thoughts, existing by the necessity of his own nature, and deriving from himself all moral and intellectual perfection. These sublime truths, thus announced in the language of the prophet, are firmly held by his disciples and defined with metaphysical precision by the interpreters of the Koran.[19]

THE ACCEPTANCE OF OTHER PROPHETS THAN MOHAMMED[20]

Mohammed allowed of inspiration in other teachers than himself, who had preceded him; from Adam to his own time there had been hundreds of inspired men. <Edward Gibbon says:>

> The authority and station of Adam, Noah, Abraham, Moses, Christ, and Mohammed rise in just gradation above each other; but whosoever hates or rejects any one of the prophets is numbered with the infidels.[21]

For the author of Christianity, the Mohammedans are taught by the Prophet to maintain a high and mysterious reverence. Verily, Christ-Jesus, son of Mary, is the apostle of God, and his word, which he conveyed unto Mary and the spirit proceeding from him honorable in this world, and in the world to come, and one of those who approached near to the presence of God.

These elements of truth in the doctrine of Mohammed together with his zeal

---

17. Al Koran, chaps. 3 and 30. As announced in the Koran, the syllable "al" in single quotations in the word "Al" Koran, sometimes written Al Coran, is the Arabic article signifying "the," and ought to be omitted when the English article is prefixed, hence "the Koran" of the text. See George Sale, trans., *The Koran; or, Alcoran of Mohammed* (London: William Tegg, 1850), 40.

18. <Ms III inexplicably has "Claybourn"—*Ed.*>

19. Edward Gibbon, *The History of the Decline and Fall of the Roman Empire*, ed. John B. Bury (London: Methuen and Co., 1909-1914), chap. 50, 5:361-62.

20. <Ms III^c adds "The Acceptance of Other Prophets Than Mohammed"—*Ed.*>

21. <Gibbon, *Decline and Fall*, 5:363—*Ed.*>

against idolatry in all its forms, constituted the strength of that faith which at one time menaced even Christian Europe with a seemingly all-conquering front. It had a mighty strength in it, this faith of the Arabian Prophet. "*Allah Akbar*—God is great!" And then also the other part of the faith, which so influenced the lives of so many of God's children: "Submit the will to God!" Carlyle best stresses this for Islam: "Our whole strength lies in resigned submission to Him, whatsoever He do to us. For this world and for the other! The thing He sends to us, were it death and worse than death, shall be good, shall be best. We resign ourselves to God."[22]

---

22. Thomas Carlyle, *On Heroes, Hero-Worship, and the Heroic in History* (Chicago: A. C. McClurg and Co., 1892), lecture ii, Mohammed.

CHAPTER XV

A Review of Ancient Religions III

SCRIPTURE READING LESSON

Analysis

I. The Religions of India
 (a) The Vedas;
 (b) Brahmanism;
 (c) Hindu Triads;
 (d) Buddhism.

II. Nirvana: Is It, or Is It Not, Annihilation?

III. The Morality of Buddhism.

IV. Religions of China
 (a) Buddhism;
 (b) Confucianism;
 (c) Taoism.

V. Spiritual Touches: Reflection on Ancient Religions.

References

All the works cited in the quotations and footnotes of this chapter.

The articles on the various religious cults in *The Encyclopædia Britannica* will be standard presentations of the old faiths.

F. Max Müller's works, *Chips from a German Workshop*, 5 vols. (New York: Charles Scribner's Sons, 1891) and *Lectures on the Science of Religion; with a Paper on Buddhist Nihilism, and a Translation of the Dhammapada or "Path of Virtue"* (New York: Charles Scribner's Sons, [1893]) give acceptable treatment of the religions considered herein.

Matthew <i.e., Edwin> Arnold's *Light of Asia* (London: John Lane the Bodley Head Ltd., 1926) is a sympathetic treatment of Buddhism.

James Freeman Clarke, *Ten Great Religions*, 2 vols., is standard on all these themes.

See also Lewis Browne, *This Believing World: A Simple Account of the Great Religions of Mankind* (New York: The MacMillan Co., 1926).

CHAPTER XV

A Review of Ancient Religions III

THE RELIGIONS OF INDIA

We next turn to the religions of Asia and consider first the ancient faiths of India.

(a) The Vedas

The knowledge of the Hindu faiths is to be derived from the Vedas, which means "knowing" or "knowledge." This name is given by the Brahmans, the priests of the cultus, "not to one work, but to the whole body of their . . . ancient sacred literature," comprising more than a hundred books, grouped into four classes. The Greek equivalent of Vedas is "I know," and in the English "wise" or "wisdom."[1]

The Vedas are based upon the conception of "a universal Spirit pervading all things." God they held to be a unity; and according to the teachings of the Vedas:

> There is . . . but one Deity, the Supreme Spirit, the Lord of the universe, whose work is the universe. The God above all gods, who created the earth, the heavens, and the water. The world was considered an emanation of God, and therefore a part of him; it is kept in a visible state by his energy and would instantly disappear, if that energy were for a moment withdrawn. Even as it is, it is undergoing unceasing changes, every thing being in a transitory state. . . . In these perpetual movements the present can scarcely be said to have any existence, for as the past is ending, the future has begun. In such a never-ceasing career, all material things are "flowing" and their forms continually changing, and returning through revolving cycles to similar states. For this reason it is thought we may regard our earth, and the various celestial bodies, as having had a moment of birth, as having a time of continuance, in which they are passing onward to an inevitable destruction, and that after the lapse of countless ages a similar progress will be renewed and a similar series of events will occur again and again.[2]

---

1. F. Max Müller, *Chips from a German Workshop* (New York: Charles Scribner's Sons, 1891), 1:8.

2. John William Draper, *History of the Intellectual Development of Europe* (New York: Harper and Brothers, 1876), 1:58-59. <For a modern survey of the Vedas, see Wilhelm Halbfass, *Tradition and Reflection: Explorations in Indian Thought* (Albany: State University

(b) Brahmanism

The Hindu religion may be summed up in the word Pantheism. "God is one, because he is All." The Vedas in speaking of the relation of nature to God make use of the expression that he is the material as well as the cause of the universe; "the clay, as well as the potter." Draper continues:

> They convey the idea that while there is a pervading spirit existing everywhere of the same nature as the soul of man, though differing from it infinitely in degree, visible nature is essentially and inseparably connected therewith; that as in man the body is perpetually undergoing changes, perpetually decaying and being renewed, or, in the case of the whole human species, nations come into existence and pass away, yet still there continues to exist what may be termed the universal human mind–so for ever associated and for ever connected are the material and the spiritual. And under this aspect we must contemplate the Supreme Being, not merely as a presiding intellect, but as illustrated by the parallel case of man, whose mental principle shows no tokens except through its connection with the body; and so matter, <or nature,> or the visible universe, is to be looked upon as the corporeal manifestation of God.[3]

It should be observed, however, that pantheism has two general aspects. First, the pantheism that sinks all nature into one substance and one essence, and then concludes that the one substance or essence is God. This undoubtedly is the view of the old Hindu faiths, sometimes referred to as "purest monism." That is, the one substance theory; and is regarded by some philosophers as the purest theism. The existence of one God truly, since as stated above by Draper, "God is one, because he is all." Second, the other form of pantheism expands the one substance into all the varieties of objects that we see in nature and regards those various parts expanded into nature as gods. This leads to the grossest kind of idolatry, as it did in Egypt–at least among the common people of that country. Under this form of pantheism men have worshipped various objects in nature, the sun, moon, stars; in fact anything and everything that boded forth to their minds some quality or power or attribute of the deity. This is the pantheism of Egypt as contrasted with the pantheism of India.

(c) Hindu Triads[4]

In some of the Vedic hymns some find a conception of a trinity of deities.

---

of New York Press, 1991)–*Ed.*>

3. Draper, *Intellectual Development of Europe*, 1:58-60. <For a modern survey of Brahmanism, see Stephanie W. Jamison, *The Ravenous Hyenas and the Wounded Sun: Myth and Ritual in Ancient India* (Ithaca, NY: Cornell University Press, 1991)–*Ed.*>

4. <Ms III^{c} adds "C. Hindoo Tri-ads" (with the spelling indicated)–*Ed.*>

The matter is somewhat confused because of frequent changes in the names of the triad, but resolves itself to at least this: Agni, god of fire, becomes Brahma; Surya, the sun-god, becomes Vishnu; and Indra, the atmosphere-god, becomes Siva. These constitute what is called the "trimurti," and are generally said to represent one god, as creator, preserver, and destroyer. A verse in their honor stands as follows:

> In those three persons the one god was shown.
> Each first in place, each last–not one alone;
> Of Siva, Vishnu, Brahma, each may be
> First, second, third, among the blessed three.[5]

Not much importance, however, is to be attached to these triads; there seems to be several of them, and the significance is chiefly fanciful.

(d) Buddhism

From India came Buddhism, established by Siddhartha, or Gautama, who assumed the title Buddha, meaning "the enlightened." He was born between 562-552 B.C. He is said to have passed his youth in opulence, was married, had a son, who later became a member of his cult. At the age of 29 Gautama left parents, wife, and son for the spiritual struggle of a recluse. After seven years he believed himself possessed of perfect truth and assumed the title of "Buddha." He passed through a long period of doubt as to whether to keep for himself the knowledge he had won or share it with others. Love of others is said to have triumphed and he began to preach, first at Benares. He did not array himself against the old religion of India. His doctrines are said to be rather the outgrowth of Brahmanical schools. His special concern was to produce salvation from sorrow, which he saw to be inseparably connected with individual desire and life; and hence the main object of his teaching was to rid men of desire and induce a state of mind of perfect rest and peace, which is difficult to distinguish from a state of mental coma, a quiescence of all the senses. This <is> the "Nirvana" of Buddhism generalized. There are those, however, who insist–from its many forms and interpretations of the faith in many lands–upon interpreting nirvana to be annihilation–nihilism pure and simple.[6] It

---

5. Frank S. Dobbins, *Story of the World's Worship: A Complete, Graphic, and Comparative History of the Many Strange Beliefs, Superstitious Practices, Domestic Peculiarities, Sacred Writings, Systems of Philosophy, Legends and Traditions, Customs and Habits of Mankind throughout the World, Ancient and Modern* (Chicago: The Dominion Co., 1901), 216.

6. The subject is discussed at length by F. Max Müller in his *Chips from a German Workshop*, vol. 1, chap. xi. Cf. Frank S. Dobbins, *Story of the World's Worship*, 517, and also

is difficult to believe that any one would hold to the "hopeless despairing doctrine of annihilation," since that would be to believe that non-existence is to be preferred to existence, even an existence which might give more happiness than sorrow. Edwin Arnold[7] in his *Light of Asia* represents Gautama as saying:

> If any teach Nirvâna is to cease,
> Say unto such, they lie.
> If any teach Nirvâna is to live,
> Say unto such they err; not knowing this
> Nor what light shines beyond their broken lamps,
> Nor lifeless, timeless, bliss.[8]

Speaking of one who has entered the state of Nirvana, Arnold further represents the teaching of Gautama to be:

> No need hath such to live as ye name life;
> That which began in him when he began,
> Is finished: he hath wrought the purpose through
> Of what did make him man.
> Never shall yearnings torture him, nor sins
> Stain him, nor ache of earthly joys and woes
> Invade his safe eternal peace; nor deaths
> Nor lives recur. He goes
> Unto Nirvâna. He is one with life,
> Yet lives not. He is blest, ceasing to be.
> Om, Mani Padme, Om! The dewdrop slips
> Into the shining sea![9]

NIRVANA: IS IT ANNIHILATION?[10]

To the refinement of metaphysical minds this may not spell annihilation even

---

Lewis Browne, *This Believing World*, 134-50.

7. <Ms III "Matthew Arnold," which is corrected to "Edwin Arnold"—*Ed.*>

8. <Sir Edwin Arnold, *Light of Asia* (London: John Lane the Bodley Head Ltd., 1926), 173—*Ed.*>

9. <Arnold, *Light of Asia*, 165-66. For a modern survey of Buddhism, see Richard H. Robinson, *The Buddhist Religion: A Historical Introduction*, 3d ed. (Belmont, CA: Wadsworth Publishing Co., 1982)—*Ed.*>

10. <Ms III[c] adds "Nirvana: Is It Annihilation?"—*Ed.*>

to the individual soul, since that soul may be held to be "one with life," though he "lives not"; and though the "dew drop slips into the shining sea," and that particular dew drop shall not again recur, yet the sea remains, and "the dew drop" remains with it. This may not be annihilation for the "dew drop," yet for all practical purposes it is so close akin to it, that it is not worthwhile to dispute about the difference.

As a religion Buddhism is inadequate to all human needs; it rises from mystery and ends in silence. It is a bridge suspended in midair; one end seemingly lodged on shrouded mists, and the other lost in darkness. A bridge, the existence of which is a misfortune, since it serves no purpose. Worse it is than a bridge of sighs; for under the best phases of Buddhist teaching, it is a bridge of torture that leads to no assured advantage to those who traverse its painful distance, and the best that can be hoped for is to escape from it: "he is blest, ceasing to be!"

Of the understanding of things, the universe, the sympathetic versified presentation by Edwin Arnold[11] represents the thought to be:

> . . . Measure not with words
> Th' immeasurable; nor sink the string of thought
> Into the fathomless. Who asks doth err,
> Who answers, errs. Say naught!
>
> Pray not! The darkness will not brighten!
> Ask naught from the silence, for it cannot speak![12]

Gautama set forth four alleged "noble thoughts" on which his doctrine rests: (1) existence of suffering; (2) cessation of pain is possible through (and only through) the suppression of desire—the desire for existence with the rest; (3) the way to this is "the knowledge and observance of the good law of Buddha," which may be said to be a highly moral law with self-suppression as its objective; and (4) the attainment of Nirvana—the ending of conscious existence.

THE MORALITY OF BUDDHISM[13]

Whatever may be said of these alleged "four great truths" and the whole Buddhist system, as a religion, in effect, Buddhism writes down the universe and conscious personal existence, itself, as a failure. And yet its following is estimated

---

11. <Ms III "Matthew Arnold," which is corrected to "Edwin Arnold"—*Ed.*>
12. <Arnold, *Light of Asia*, 158-59—*Ed.*>
13. <Ms III^c adds "The Morality of Buddhism"—*Ed.*>

to be from three hundred fifty to five hundred millions of human beings![14] It has the most numerous following of any of the religions. While disappointing as a religion, however, Buddhism stands high as a system of morals, and it is this, doubtless, which commends it to its numerous following. Buddhism as a religion and as a political fact, was a reaction from Brahmanism, though it retained much of that more primitive form of faith and worship.

Max Müller says:

> The morality which it [Buddhism] teaches is not a morality of expediency and rewards. Virtue is not enjoined because it necessarily leads to happiness. No; virtue is to be practiced, but happiness is to be shunned, and the only reward for virtue is that it subdues the passions, and thus prepared the human mind for that knowledge which is to end in complete annihilation. There are ten commandments which Buddha imposes on his disciples. They are:
>
> 1. Not to kill.
> 2. Not to steal.
> 3. Not to commit adultery.
> 4. Not to lie.
> 5. Not to get intoxicated.
> 6. To abstain from unseasonable meals.
> 7. To abstain from public spectacles.
> 8. To abstain from expensive dresses.
> 9. Not to have a large bed.
> 10. Not to receive silver or gold.[15]

These precepts were enjoined[16] upon all; those who specifically entered the religious life as teachers, their duties were more severe, and their lives of self-denial even more rigid than these moral precepts imply.

The philosophy which presented such a moral code to its devotees, think what you will of it as a religion, is entitled to the respect of mankind.

RELIGIONS OF CHINA

China has a population—all divisions—of 400,800,000[17] and three general systems of religion. These are Buddhism, Confucianism, and Taoism. The state tolerates all three and a Chinaman may be at the same time an adherent of all three of the national religions. The mass of the Chinese people accept the three and see

---

14. <The latest information lists the total number of Buddhists as 315 million—*Ed.*>
15. Müller, *Chips from a German Workshop*, 244.
16. <Ms III* "These duties were enjoined"—*Ed.*>
17. <The latest information lists the population of China as 1,169,600,000—*Ed.*>

no inconsistency in so doing. It is somewhat as if Americans and Englishmen were at the same time Protestants, Romanists, and Sceptics. The Chinese support the priests of all these religions, worship in all their temples, and believe in the gods of all.

(a) Buddhism

Of Buddhism we have already sufficiently spoken. That faith early penetrated China; one missionary is mentioned in the Chinese annals as early as 217 B.C. It was not, however, until the year 66 A.D. that Buddhism was officially recognized by the government as a third state religion in China.

(b) Confucianism

The most influential teacher of the Chinese, however, is Confucius, 551-478 B.C. He was not a "prophet" in the sense that he presented himself as a teacher sent of God; in fact, he laid no claims to a supernatural knowledge of God or of the hereafter. He said nothing of an infinite spirit, and but little of a future life. His cardinal precepts were obedience to parents and superiors, and reverence for the ancients and imitation of their virtues. He himself walked in the old paths, and added the force of example to that of precept. On one occasion he was asked how the "spirits could be served?" To which he made answer, "If we are not able to serve man, how can we serve the spirits?" On another occasion he said to his followers, "Respect the gods and keep them at a distance." He gave the Chinese the golden rule, stated in the negative way, however, as follows: "What you don't want others to do to yourself, do not do to others." The influence of Confucius has been greater than that of any other teacher so far as mass of followers is concerned, excepting Christ and Buddha. The influence, however, can scarcely be accredited to a religion, but to the force of merely human moral precepts. Confucianism speaks to moral nature, it discourses on virtue and vice, and the duty of compliance with the law, and the dictates of conscience. Its worship rests on this basis: the religious veneration paid to ancestors—for that is the worship of the system—is founded on the duty of filial piety, the moral sense of the Chinese is said to be offended if they are called on to resign this custom.[18]

(c) Taoism

Taoism is accounted materialistic, and yet it approaches more nearly to religious concepts than the doctrines of Confucius; its notion of the soul is of something physical, "a purer form of matter." The soul is supposed to gain

---

18. <For a modern survey of Confucianism, see Rodney L. Taylor, *The Way of Heaven: An Introduction to the Confucian Religious Life* (Leiden: E. J. Brill, 1986)—*Ed.*>

immortality by a physical discipline, a sort of chemical process, which transmutes it into a more ethereal essence and prepares it for being transferred to the regions of immortality. The gods of Taoism are also very much what might be expected of a system which has such notions as these of the soul. It looks upon the stars as divine, it deifies hermits, and physicians, magicians, and seekers after the philosophers' stone, and the plant of immortality. Max Müller in his *Science of Religion* sums up the character of the religions of China proper in the following paragraph. He describes the religion as:

> A<n ancient> colorless and unpoetical religion; a religion we might almost venture to call monosyllabic, consisting of the worship of a host of single spirits, representing the sky, the sun, storms and lightning, the mountains and rivers; one standing by the side of the other without any mutual attraction, without any higher principle to hold them together. In addition to this, we likewise meet in China with the worship of ancestral spirits, the spirits of the departed, who are supposed to retain some cognizance of human affairs, and to possess peculiar powers which they exercise for good or evil. This double worship of human and natural spirits constitutes the old and popular religion of China, and it has lived on to the present day, at least in the lower ranks of society, though there towers above it a more elevated range of half-religious and half-philosophical faith, a belief in two higher powers, which in the language of philosophy may mean "Form and Matter," in the language of ethics, "Good and Evil," but which in the original language of religion and mythology are represented as "Heaven and Earth."
>
> It is true that we know the ancient popular religion of China from the works of Confucius only, or from even more modern sources. But though Confucius is called the founder of a new religion, he was really but the new preacher of an old religion. He was emphatically a transmitter, not a maker. He says himself: "I only hand on; I cannot create new things. I believe in the ancients, and therefore I love them."[19]

SPIRITUAL TOUCHES[20]

Such was the ancient religion of China and such, to a very large extent, is the religion of China today. And one can not find in it as a religion, whatever may be accorded to its moral qualities, much that commands our respect; and yet now and then, there arises from the Chinese classics, a touch of spirit conception that would

---

19. F. Max Müller, *Lectures on the Science of Religion; with a Paper on Buddhist Nihilism, and a Translation of the Dhammapada or "Path of Virtue"* (New York: Charles Scribner's Sons, [1893]), 61-62. <For a modern survey of Taoism, see Livia Kohn, *Taoist Mystical Philosophy: The Scripture of Western Ascension* (Albany: State University of New York Press, 1991)–*Ed.*>

20. <Ms III[c] adds "Spiritual Touches"–*Ed.*>

lead one to think that this great body of people had not been left without some streakings of the morning light of a high spirituality. For instance, a Chinese writer of the thirteenth century—1279 A.D., in fact—Wan Tien Hsiang, had opposed Kublai Khan, the Tartar conqueror. Hsiang was imprisoned by the Tartar conqueror for three years, and in his prison he wrote as follows:

> In all that is or ever was,
> Or ever yet will be,
> There "Is" what shapes the sun and stars,
> And makes the land and sea.
>
> In man "It's" spirit; but unnamed
> In earth and sea and air,
> Below us and above, around—
> Behold, "It's" everywhere.
>
> And though in harmony and peace
> "It's" not perceived by men,
> When storm and stress the nations shake,
> We all can see "It" then.
> . . . O "It" pervades
> The sky, sun, land, and sea;
> From all eternity has been
> And ne'er can cease to be.

A fine recognition of God as universal spirit among those whom Christians call heathens.

This completes our brief review of the world's chief religions outside of those which may be more especially considered as directly the result of revelation—meaning the Hebrew and Christian faiths. Of course, our review could only be cursory, and yet some such review is necessary to the completeness of our theme, and in order to get before the reader the reports of those who have been "seekers after God." It perhaps will have occurred to the reader that at bottom all these religions have much in common, that certain characteristics tend to unite their several cults into one source of origin and to point to one objective unity. One could easily conceive of them as but the broken rays of light from some noble sun of truth of an antiquity greater than these systems, if such they may be called. They seem, however, to be as detached stones that have broken off and rolled away from some ancient wall, in which they once found orderly place. In other words they are fragments from the primitive revelation given to the ancient patriarchs of ante-diluvian days and early post-diluvian days, of which the Bible speaks. This <is> the source of those truths, spiritual and moral, found in these religions, and which constitutes such truth, and beauty, and virtue as they possess—and this is not inconsiderable—since it certainly may not be thought to be the purpose of an Intelligence dominant in the universe to permit the light of truth to enter into total eclipse with any part of the human race. More consistent is it with right reason—which is but intelligence in action—to accept the light-giving and inspiring thought of the ancient American scripture—the Book of Mormon—where it says:

> Behold, the Lord doth grant unto all nations of their own nation and tongue to teach his word; yea, in wisdom, all that he seeth fit that they should have (Alma 29:8).

And, of course, that which "he seeth fit they should have" is that measure of the truth suited to their capacity and their development. This, we shall hope, will grow more apparent as the general theme unfolds.

CHAPTER XVI

A Review of Ancient Religions IV—The Hebrew Religion I

SCRIPTURE READING LESSON

Analysis

I. The Hebrew Scriptures.

II. Integrity of the Hebrew Scriptures.

III. Testimony of the New Testament to the Integrity of the Old.

IV. The Revealed Religion of the Hebrews.

V. Developments Following Creation Events.

VI. Enter Death.

VII. The Hope of Deliverance.

VIII. The Call and Mission of Abraham and of Israel.

IX. The Effective Testimony of Israel.

References

Though now out of print, suggest that when it can be obtained the use of the *Seventy's Course in Theology: First Year, Outline History of the Seventy and A Survey of the Books of Holy Scripture* (Salt Lake City: The Deseret News, 1907), part ii, "A Study of the Hebrew Scriptures—The Old Testament," 22-73.

The respective books of the Old Testament referred to in the text.

Horatio B. Hackett and Ezra Abbot, eds., *Dr. William Smith's Dictionary of the Bible, Comprising Its Antiquities, Biography, Geography, and Natural History*, 4 vols. (Boston: Houghton, Mifflin and Co., 1894).

John Kitto, *A Cyclopædia of Biblical Literature*, 2 vols. (New York: Mark H. Newman, 1845), under appropriate subject titles.

CHAPTER XVI

A Review of Ancient Religions IV—The Hebrew Religion I

THE HEBREW REVELATION

In this review of the ancient religions, I have purposely reserved consideration of the Hebrew religion to the last, because that religion, more than any other, must be accorded higher claims upon direct revelation for its origin, and will, therefore, bring us more closely to grips with the question of revealed religion.

THE HEBREW SCRIPTURE

The record of the alleged Hebrew revelation is to be found in what is commonly known as the Old Testament, comprising, according to Josephus (writing near the beginning of the Christian Era), twenty-two sacred books. In our Protestant version of the Old Testament they are distributed into thirty-nine books; the difference arises from a slightly altered grouping of the several books from that followed by Josephus.[1]

I think Josephus is the most reliable authority that may be followed on the origin of the sacred literature of the Hebrews, and, therefore, quote him somewhat at length on the subject. After granting superiority for excellence of composition and eloquence to the writings of the Greeks, Josephus claims the honor of accuracy and integrity for the Hebrew writings, and details with what care the Hebrew writers of sacred things were chosen.

---

1. What are generally known as the Minor Prophets, twelve in number is connected as one book in the grouping by Josephus; the Book of Ruth is coupled with the Book of Judges; Ezra with Nehemiah, Lamentations with Jeremiah, while the two books each of Samuel, Kings, and Chronicles are counted but one book each, making a reduction of seventeen in number from the authorized Protestant version, which plus the twenty-two books counted by Josephus would complete the thirty-nine books of our authorized King James Version of the Old Testament. <For a study of the biblical canon, see Frederick F. Bruce, *The Canon of Scripture* (Downers Grove, IL: InterVarsity Press, 1988)—*Ed.*>

JOSEPHUS ON THE INTEGRITY OF THE HEBREW SCRIPTURES[2]

He then proceeds to say:

> Everyone is not permitted of his own accord to be a writer, nor is there any disagreement in what is written; they being only prophets that have written the original and earliest accounts of things, as they learned them of God himself by inspiration; and others have written what hath happened in their own time, and that in a very distinct manner also: for we have not an innumerable multitude of books among us, disagreeing from and contradicting one another (as the Greeks have), but only twenty-two books, which contain the records of all the past times, which are justly believed to be divine. And of them, five belong to Moses, which contain his laws and the traditions of the origin of mankind until his death. This interval of time was little short of three thousand years; but as to the time from the death of Moses [1451 B.C.—<James> Ussher] till the reign of Artaxerxes,[3] king of Persia, who reigned after Xerxes [these two kings—father and son—reigned from 485 B.C. to 424 B.C.]; the prophets who were after Moses wrote down what was done in their times in thirteen books. The remaining four books contain hymns to God and precepts for the conduct of human life. It is true, our history hath been written since Artaxerxes very particularly but hath not been esteemed of the like authority with the former by our forefathers, because there hath not been an exact succession of prophets since that time; and how firmly we have given credit to these books of our own nation is evident by what we do; for during so many ages as have already passed no one hath been so bold as either to add anything to them, to take anything from them, or to make any change in them; but it is become natural to all Jews, immediately and from their very birth, to esteem these books to contain divine doctrines and to persist in them, and if occasion be, willingly to die for them. For it is no new thing for our captives, many of them in number and frequently in time, to be seen to endure racks and deaths of all kinds upon the theaters, that they may not be obliged to say one word against our laws and the records that contain them.[4]

I may add that comparatively recent discoveries by George Smith, Professor <Archibald Henry> Sayce, and others of more recent times, showing that in the ancient religions of Chaldea and Babylonia there were elaborate narratives of the creation which in most prominent features may have been the source of the creation

---

2. <Ms III^{c} adds "Josephus On The Integrity of the Hebrew Scriptures," though it is inserted after the introductory "He then proceeds to say"—*Ed.*>

3. <Ms III* "the Artaxerxes," but Ms III^{c} appears to have deleted the definite article—*Ed.*>

4. Flavius Josephus, *The Works of Flavius Josephus: Against Apion*, trans. William Whiston (Baltimore: Armstrong and Berry, 1837), bk. i, 582-83.

statements in the Old Testament, do[5] not disparage the account here given by Josephus of the origin of the Hebrew literature. There can be no doubt but that the accounts of the creation and other ancient events found in both Assyrian and Egyptian sources are earlier than those written by Moses; and that their account of ancient events are somewhat similar in import; but because of these facts, it is not necessary to disclaim either the Mosaic authorship of the five books of the Bible accredited to that prophet, or doubt the inspiration of those accounts given by Moses; and yet on many minds this has been the result to some extent of these discoveries.[6] The truth is, that the outstanding facts of the creation, the fall of man, the flood, etc., have been known by the human race from the earliest historical times, from the days of Adam, in fact. They were matters of common knowledge by tradition among the ante-diluvian patriarchs, and through the family of Noah were preserved to the families and races of men subsequent to the flood. The variously distorted creation stories and other ancient events possessed by nearly all people. But all this did not prevent the Lord from revealing the creation history to Moses, together with subsequent events; nor does this new knowledge require us to doubt the inspiration which rested upon him and that enabled him to weave into splendid, coherent form the fragmentary truth among the ancient Egyptian, Babylonian, and other peoples.

TESTIMONY OF THE NEW TESTAMENT TO THE INTEGRITY OF THE OLD[7]

It should also be noted that in addition to the testimony of Josephus, the writers of the New Testament give emphatic testimony to the authenticity and divine authority of the Old Testament, since these writers so frequently quoted it as a work of divine authority. A group of commentators on the New and Old Testament say:

> Indeed, the references are so numerous and the testimonies so distinctly borne of the existence of the Mosaic books throughout the <whole> history of the Jewish nation and the unity of character, design, and style pervading these books is so clearly perceptible, notwithstanding the rationalistic assertion<s> of their forming a series of separate and unconnected fragments, that it may with all safety be said, there is immensely stronger and more varied evidence in proof of their being the authorship

---

5. <Ms III^c adds "do"—*Ed.*>

6. <Ms III* "yet this has been the result to some extent of these discoveries on many minds"—*Ed.*>

7. <Ms III^c adds "Testimony Of the New Testament To The Integrity of the Old"—*Ed.*>

> of Moses, than any of the Greek or Roman classics being the production<s> of the authors whose names they bear.[8]

One thing more should be borne in mind with reference to this whole volume of ancient Hebrew scripture, the Old Testament, and that is whatever the subdivisions may be—history, legislation, poetry, prophecy, biography, or proverbs—it is alleged to have been written under the inspiration of God. That does not mean that human elements are not to be found in it, but rather that a divine spirit is present in the midst of human elements, giving forth light and truth and wisdom such as is to be found in no merely human production. There is a divine spirit always present in these scripture narratives, prophecy, and poetry, that makes the whole to contain a revelation of God, and an account of his methods of doing things among men. All of which gives those writings an authority that does not pertain to the ordinary writings of men.

THE REVEALED RELIGION OF THE HEBREWS

The message of these scriptures to the world on the great themes that have occupied thus far our attention, the source or origin of things, the nature of the world, and man's place in it, are now to be considered. God is referred to as the Creator of the world and all that is in it. The story of the creation as given by Moses is the most magnificent account known among men. Listen to its opening statement:

> In the beginning God created the heaven and the earth. And the earth was without form and void; and darkness was upon the face of the deep. And the Spirit of God moved upon the face of the waters. And God said, "Let there be light." And there was light. And God saw the light, that it was good; and God divided the light from the darkness. And God called the light Day and the darkness He called Night. And the evening and the morning were the first day (Gen. 1:1-5).

Then follow the successive acts of the creation, the waters were divided and gathered together and called seas; the dry land appeared and was called earth; and God said, "Let the earth bring forth grass and the herb yielding seed, and the fruit tree yielding fruit, after his kind" (Gen. 1:11). The seas also were made to bring forth life "abundantly"; and the fowls of the air also were to multiply, each after his kind.

> And God made the beasts of the earth, after their kind, and cattle after their kind,

8. Robert Jamieson, A. R. Fausset, and David Brown, *A Commentary: Critical, Practical, and Explanatory of the Old and New Testaments* (New York: Funk and Wagnalls, 1888), 1:5.

and every thing that creepeth upon the earth after its kind, and God saw that it was good (cf. Gen. 1:25).

Thus the earth was made ready for the coming of man, but when that point was reached in creation by the Divine Intelligence, or Intelligences[9]—for there appears to have been more than one person in the work of creation—then something special seems to have happened, for God said:

> "Let us make man in our image, after our likeness; and let him have dominion over the fish of the sea, and over the fowl in the air, <and> over the cattle, and over all the earth." . . . So God created man in His own image, in the image of God created He him, male and female created He them. And God blessed them, and God said unto them, "Be fruitful and multiply and replenish the earth and subdue it." . . . And God saw every thing that He had made, and behold, it was very good (Gen. 1:26-28, 31).

This story of creation, the origin of the various forms of life upon the earth, and finally crowned with the advent of man upon it, his commission to have dominion over the earth, and subdue it—all this, at once so simple, yet sublime, involves us in none of the speculations, and hair-splitting definitions of "being" and "becoming"; and of "matter," of "space," and of "spirit." It simply shows us God at work in the midst of things, of which in the proper place we shall have more to say, and upon it much will depend for the right unfolding of the great theme we have undertaken. But for the present this will be sufficient on this point of origins—this accounting for the commencement of things according to revelations.[10]

DEVELOPMENTS FOLLOWING CREATION[11]

Following this commencement came the development of events that have made the history of man in the earth. It seems that man was created "sufficient to stand," yet "free to fall"—if he so willed it; and the opportunity was afforded in the economy of the Creator to test this man's power of free, moral agency. The

9. <That Roberts's term "Divine Intelligences" implies the Mormon doctrine of a plurality of Gods is supported by his 1895 statement "there has been and there now exists an endless line of Gods, stretching back into the eternities, that had no beginning and will have no end," in which sixteen years later the word "Gods" was changed to "Divine Intelligences—Deities"; see B. H. Roberts, *A New Witness for God* (Salt Lake City: George Q. Cannon and Sons, 1895), 466, and compare his *New Witnesses for God* (Salt Lake City: The Deseret News, 1911), 1:461—*Ed.*>

10. <Ms III[*] "the commencement of things as revelations"—*Ed.*>

11. <Ms III[c] adds "Developments Following Creation"—*Ed.*>

commandment was given concerning a certain fruit, which seemed to have in it in some way the elements of death.[12] Of all the fruit of God's garden man was at liberty to partake save only this one—the fruit of the tree of "the knowledge of good and evil." "In the day thou eatest thereof," ran the divine commandment, "thou shalt surely die." That is to say,[13] it might not be eaten without certain consequences following the partaking of it.

The story is well known, and we need not dwell upon the details of it. The tempter came, contradicting the decree of the Almighty. "Thou shalt not surely die" was the tempter's assurance. "Eat and ye shall be as Gods, knowing good and evil!" The law was broken and man learned that God's word was true. Death ensued and has reigned in the earth from then until now. Separation from God, a spiritual death; and later separation of man's spirit from his body, resulting in physical death.

ENTER DEATH[14]

Man, I say, learned God's decree was true, death entered the world, but it was not intended that a lasting victory should be granted unto death. Even when announcing the sentence upon man, in consequence of his transgression of the commandment, the word of hope was whispered to his heart. Pronouncing the curse upon the tempter who had induced man to break the law, God said of the "seed of the woman," that while his heel should be bruised by the tempter, the tempter's head should be bruised by the seed of the woman (Gen. 3:15).

THE HOPE OF DELIVERANCE[15]

The time came when the unfolding of this hope of deliverance through the promised seed of the woman, took the form of a more direct prediction of the advent of God into man's earth-life. One of the inspired prophets declared that a

---

12. <Ms III[*] "the elements of life and death." The revision of Ms III[2] "the elements of death" was made by Roberts in response to the committee report of May 1930, which questioned that "the Tree of the Knowledge of Good and Evil had in it the seeds of life and death" ("Doctrinal Points Questioned by the Committee Which Read the Manuscript of Elder B. H. Roberts, Entitled The Truth, The Way, The Life," attached to Rudger Clawson, Letter to Heber J. Grant, [15 May 1930], in David J. Buerger Collection, Manuscript 622, Bx 10, Fd 8, Manuscripts Division, Marriott Library, University of Utah, Salt Lake City)—*Ed.*>

13. <Ms III[c] adds "to say"—*Ed.*>

14. <Ms III[*] of section heading "God's Decree Found True"—*Ed.*>

15. <Ms III[c] adds "The Hope of Deliverance"—*Ed.*>

virgin would "conceive and bear a son, and shall call his name Immanuel," which by interpretation means God with us, or God with man (see Isa. 7:14; cf. Matt. 1:23).

In another prophecy the message ran:

> Unto us a child is born, unto us a son is given; and the government shall be upon his shoulder, and his name shall be called Wonderful, Counsellor, the Mighty God, the Everlasting Father, the Prince of Peace (Isa. 9:6).

And, of course, what he is "called" that he will be—the "Mighty God," the "Everlasting Father," "Immanuel"—God among men!

Again, the advent of God among men is prophetically proclaimed, including the promise of a resurrection from the dead of all the hosts of Israel, and impliedly of all men—by Isaiah. To comfort Israel, at a period when Israel was painfully conscious of failure to establish the things of God hoped for—then Isaiah took the account of their afflictions before God. "We have not wrought any deliverance in the earth," was Isaiah's complaint. "Neither have the inhabitants of the world fallen" (Isa. 26:18). Then God, to give comfort to this prophet and to his people, said—and gave it to his prophet as a message to Israel:

> Thy dead men shall live, together with my dead body shall they arise; awake and sing, ye that dwell in dust; for thy dew is as the dew of herbs, and the earth shall cast out the dead (Isa. 26:19).

This has in it the same ring of assurance as that found in the Book of Job, included in Hebrew literature, who said, when his fortunes were at their lowest:

> I know that my Redeemer liveth, and that he shall stand at the latter day upon the earth; and though after my skin, worms destroy this body, yet in my flesh shall I see God, whom I shall see for myself and mine eyes shall behold him and not another, though my reins be consumed within me (cf. Job 19:25-27).[16]

This conviction of a resurrection from physical death (which is in part a redemption from the consequences of the broken law in Eden, viz., redemption from physical death), implanted in the heart of Israel, inspired the prophet Daniel to say:

> And many of them that sleep in the dust of the earth shall awake, some to everlasting life, and some to shame and everlasting contempt (Dan. 12:2).

---

16. <Instead of the Christian concept of a "Redeemer," the Hebrew *gōʾēl* means "arbiter" or "avenger." See Edwin M. Good, *In Turns of Tempest: A Reading of Job with a Translation* (Stanford, CA: Stanford University Press, 1990), 257-59—*Ed.*>

THE CALL AND MISSION OF ABRAHAM AND ISRAEL[17]

Going back now to the early period of the Hebrew literature, we have in Genesis the story of the patriarchs to the time of the flood, the destruction of the world by that cataclysm, and the subsequent story of mankind to the selection of a special family, the family of Abraham, a family through whose "seed" all the nations of the earth were to be blessed. This is a promise frequently iterated in the sacred records.[18] This family was finally to be developed into a chosen people with a mission, the mission of being God's witnesses in the earth. A people, who, whatever might be their fortunes—prosperous or disastrous, obedient or disobedient—they should, nevertheless, be a witness for God and for the truth of this body of sacred literature (the Old Testament) among all people. God made a covenant with the Hebrews before the death of their prophet Moses, the consequences of which were set forth in great plainness; on the one hand, for good; on the other hand, for evil. This was the covenant, the Lord said:

> And it shall come to pass, if thou shalt hearken diligently unto the voice of the Lord thy God, to observe and to do all His commandments, which I command thee this day, the Lord thy God will set thee on high above all nations of the earth. And all these blessings shall come on thee, if thou wilt hearken unto the voice of the Lord thy God (Deut. 28:1-2).

Then follows an enumeration of blessings that should come upon Israel for their obedience; and truly that blessing includes everything that national well-being could hope to enjoy. No blessing or power that would make for prosperity, or honor, or glory, or power for good <is left out>. The enumeration rears a monument to national aspiration, prosperity, and perpetuation that would satisfy the highest righteous ambition of the patriot and the statesman (Deut. 28:3-14).

Per contra, the terms of the covenant were:

> But it shall come to pass, if thou wilt not hearken unto the voice of the Lord thy God, to observe to do all His commandments and His statutes, which I command thee this day, that all these curses shall come upon thee and overtake thee. . . . And they shall be upon thee for a sign and for a wonder, and upon thy seed forever (Deut. 28:15, 46).

Then follows an enumeration of curses that would follow disobedience. These

---

17. <Ms III^{c} adds "The Call and Mission of Abraham and Israel"—*Ed.*>

18. Genesis 18:19—"I know him," [Abraham, said the Lord], "that he will command his children and his household after him, and they shall keep the way of the Lord, to do justice and judgment; that the Lord may bring upon Abraham that which he hath spoken of him." See also Genesis 22.

are[19] the most awful and calamitous that could possibly befall a people or nation. Every disaster that could come within human experience is therein enumerated. But I must ask the reader to turn to the original document for a perusal of them, as the document is too long to quote at length, and nothing but completeness can reveal how terrible it all is (Deut. 28:16-68).

THE EFFECTIVE TESTIMONY OF ISRAEL[20]

I say nothing more terrible than this prophecy of disaster may be found in human literature, and that is true. But there is the more terrible truth that Israel, having been disobedient, has reaped the full harvest that grew from his sowing of the dragon's teeth of disobedience, and every calamity mentioned in the conditional prophecy has overtaken Israel, and especially the Jewish tribe of Israel. Whether Israel would or not, having accepted the role or witness given him of God, and accepted by him, he could not, and has not escaped producing that evidence in his national and racial history. It was ordained that it should be so. For obedience, prosperity, and God's upholding power; for disobedience, calamity the like of which has overtaken no other people. Bishop Lightfoot was right when he said:

> You may question, if you will, every single prophecy in the Old Testament, but the whole history of the Jews is one continuous prophecy, more distinct and articulate than all; you may deny, if you will, each successive miracle which is recorded therein, but again the history of the Jews is from first to last one stupendous miracle, more wonderful and convincing than all.[21]

Such <is> the evidence that God has given for the truth of this great revelation contained in the Hebrew Old Testament. This line of thought will be resumed when in addition to what is here set down, we shall take up what is properly supplemental to the Hebrew Old Testament account of this revelation, namely, the advent of the Christ among the Jews and the fulfillment of his mission in redeeming man from the fall through the resurrection from the dead and the re-establishment of man's union with God, thus bringing to pass, ultimately, the complete healing of that wound which brought death into the world and "all our woe," and the alienation of man from God. Meantime there are yet two other things in regard to the revelation of God to the world through the Hebrew scriptures that are of the utmost importance; and each has to do with the nature of the Deity revealed.

---

19. <Ms III^c adds "are"—*Ed.*>
20. <Ms III^c adds "The Effective Testimony of Israel"—*Ed.*>
21. Bishop <Joseph> Lightfoot, *Quarterly Review*, April 18, 1888.

CHAPTER XVII

A Review of Ancient Religions IV—The Hebrew Religion II

SCRIPTURE READING LESSON

Analysis

I. The Interpretation of "Elohim."

II. Christian Scholars' Interpretation of "Elohim."

III. Bible Use of Plural Form—Gods.

IV. The Conviction of Reason on Plurality of Presiding Intelligences—Gods.

V. "And the Spirit of God"—Deity Viewed as Unity.

VI. The Form of God.

References

All works of reference cited under Lesson 16. Also, King Follett Sermon, published in *Millennial Star* 23 (April-May 1861): 245-48, 262-64, 279-80. The sermon was delivered April 7, 1844. The sermon *The King Follett Discourse; The Being and Kind of Being God Is; The Immortality of the Intelligence of Man*, annotated by B. H. Roberts, now printed by Magazine Printing Co., Salt Lake City, 1926.

Also, a discourse of Joseph Smith, delivered on June 16, 1844, on the "Plurality of Gods," and published in *History of the Church of Jesus Christ of Latter-day Saints, Period I: History of Joseph Smith, the Prophet by Himself*, 6:473-79.

B. H. Roberts, *The Mormon Doctrine of Deity; The Roberts–[Cyrill] Van Der Donckt Discussion, to Which Is Added a Discourse, Jesus Christ, The Revelation of God* (Salt Lake City: The Deseret News, 1903).

CHAPTER XVII
A Review of Ancient Religions IV—The Hebrew Religion II

The two things referred to in the closing lines of the preceding chapter, as having to do with the nature of the Deity revealed in the Hebrew scriptures, are, first, Deity[1]—plural or singular; and the second has to do with the "form" of God. Here we take up the first.

THE INTERPRETATION OF "ELOHIM"

The Hebrew word "Elohim" used in Genesis is plural; and if literally translated the passage in the creation story would read: "In the beginning Elohim [the Gods] created the heavens and the earth. . . . And the Spirit of Elohim [the Spirit of the Gods] moved upon the face of the waters; and Elohim [the Gods] said, Let there be light, and there was light" (Gen. 1:1-3). And so following throughout the story of creation. It is quite generally conceded by scholars that Elohim is of plural form—of which the singular is Eloah—and represents more than one. A variety of devices has been employed to explain away this use of the plural form of the noun in the first chapter of Genesis, and to make it conform to "the one only God" idea. Some Jews, in explanation of it and in defense of their belief in "one only God," hold that there are several Hebrew words that have a plural form, but are singular in meaning, of which "Elohim" is one. They quote as proof of this the word "maim," meaning water; "shamaim," meaning heaven; "panim," meaning the face or surface of a person or thing. A Christian Jewish scholar, the Rev. H. Highton, M.A., and Fellow of Queen's College, Oxford, says:

> But, if we examine these words we shall find that though apparently they may have a singular meaning, yet in reality they have a plural and collective one; thus, for instance, "maim," water, means a collection of waters, forming one collective whole; and thus again, "shamaim," heaven, is also in reality, as well as in form, of the plural number, meaning what we call in a general way in English, "the

1. <Ms III[c] adds "Deity"—*Ed.*>

heavens," comprehending all the various regions which are included under that title.[2]

Other Jewish scholars content themselves in accounting for this inconvenient plural in the opening chapter of Genesis by saying that in the Hebrew, Elohim (the Gods) better represents the idea of strong, the mighty, than the singular form would, and for this reason it was used; a view accepted by many Christians. Dr. Elliott, Prof. of Hebrew in Lafayette College, Easton, Pa., says: "The name Elohim is the generic name of God, and being plural in form is probably a plural of excellence and majesty."[3]

Rabbi Jehuda Hallevi (twelfth century) "found in the usage of [the plural] 'Elohim' a protest against idolaters,[4] who call each personified power . . . 'Eloah,' and all collectively 'Elohim.' He interpreted it as the most general name of the Deity, distinguishing Him as manifested in the exhibition of His power, without reference to His personality, or moral qualities, or any special relations which He bears to man."[5]

<Heinrich A. C.> Hävernick derives the word "Elohim" from a Hebrew record now lost, "Coluit," and "thinks that the plural is used merely to indicate the abundance and super-richness contained in the Divine Being."[6]

CHRISTIAN SCHOLARS' INTERPRETATION OF "ELOHIM"[7]

A number of Christian scholars attempt to account for the plural "Elohim" by saying that it "foreshadows the doctrine of the Christian Trinity!" That is, it recognizes the existence of the three persons in one God. "It is expressive of omnipotent power; and by its use here [Gen. 1:1] in the plural form, is obscurely taught at the opening of the Bible, a doctrine clearly referred to in other parts of

---

2. <H. Highton, "God a Unity and Plurality," *The Voice of Israel*, Feb. 1844—*Ed.*>

3. Charles Elliott, A *Vindication of Mosaic Authorship of Pentateuch* (Cincinnati, Ohio: Walden and Stowe, 1884), 65. <Ernest Klein, A *Comprehensive Etymological Dictionary of the Hebrew Language for Readers of English* (New York: Macmillan Publishing Co., 1987), 29, considers the plural form "Elohim" to be a plural of majesty—*Ed.*>

4. <Ms III "a process against idolaters"—*Ed.*>

5. William A. Wright, "Jehovah," in Horatio B. Hackett and Ezra Abbot, eds., *Dr. William Smith's Dictionary of the Bible, Comprising Its Antiquities, Biography, Geography, and Natural History* (Boston: Houghton, Mifflin and Co., 1894), 2:1242.

6. E. Michelson, "God," in John Kitto, ed., A *Cyclopædia of Biblical Literature* (New York: Mark H. Newman, 1845), 1:777. <Michelson's wording is that Elohim is derived "from an ancient Hebrew root, now lost, *'lh* coluit"—*Ed.*>

7. <Ms III[c] adds "Christian Scholars' Interpretation of 'Elohim'"—*Ed.*>

it, *viz.*, [namely,] though God is one, there is a plurality of persons in the Godhead—Father, Son, and Holy Spirit, who were engaged in the creative work."[8]

This view was maintained at length by Rev. H. Highton in the Christian Jewish periodical, *The Voice of Israel*. "But[9] Calvin, Mercer, Dresigius, Ballarmine," says Dr. Hackett of the Theological Institution of Newton, Mass., editor of *Smith's Bible Dictionary*, "have given the weight of their authority against an explanation so fanciful and arbitrary." Others explain the use of the plural "we" or "us" by saying that in the first chapter of Genesis Moses represents God as speaking of himself in that manner in imitation of the custom of kings, who speak of themselves as "we" instead of the singular "I." In other words, it is "the royal" "we" or "us." This theory, however, is answered, as pointed out by Rev. H. Highton, by the fact that the use of what is called the "royal plural" is a modern, not an ancient custom, and refers to the usage of the kings of the Bible, which discloses the fact that they always spoke of themselves as "I" or "me."

BIBLE USE OF PLURAL FORM—"GODS"[10]

Throughout, these several suggestions take on a sort of confession and avoidance of a rather stern fact, namely, that a plurality of divine persons were engaged in the creation, according to the use of the word "Elohim" in the Hebrew scriptures. In addition to the use of the plural form "Elohim" (the Gods), however, there is the further fact that when Elohim contemplated the creation of man, "Elohim said, 'Let us make man in *our* image, after *our* likeness'" (Gen. 1:26). Nor is that the whole of the story. In other parts of the Old Testament writings occur other pluralistic expressions which indicate the existence of a plurality of deities, though, doubtless, harmonized intelligences all, so that really but one mind, a community mind, enters into the plan of creation and of the government of the world.

Some of these expressions referred to are as follows:

"The Lord your God is God of Gods, and Lord of Lords" (Deut. 10:17). That is from Moses.

"The Lord God of Gods, He knoweth, and Israel He shall know" (Josh. 22:22). That is from Joshua.

---

8. Robert Jamieson, A. R. Fausset, and David Brown, *A Commentary: Critical, Practical, and Explanatory of the Old and New Testaments* (New York: Funk and Wagnalls, 1888), on Genesis 1:1-2.

9. <Ms III* "Before quoting"—*Ed.*>

10. <Ms III^c adds "Bible Use of Plural Form—'Gods'"—*Ed.*>

"O give thanks unto the God of Gods, . . . O give thanks unto the Lord of Lords" (Ps. 136:2-3). That is from David.

"And shall speak marvelous things against the God of Gods" (Dan. 11:36). That is from Daniel.

"God standeth in the congregation of the mighty; He judgeth among the Gods. . . . I have said, 'Ye are Gods; and all of you are children of the most High'" (Ps. 82:1, 6). That is from David again.

Were such expressions taken from the lips of pagan kings, or false prophets who are sometimes represented as speaking in the scriptures, we might question the force of such quotations as representing a multiplicity of divine Intelligences—Gods. But coming, as they do, from recognized prophets and servants of God, who may deny the force of the testimony they give to the truth that is here contended for, namely, a multiplicity of divine Intelligences, harmonized into a community mind, and which through taking counsel in knowledge and wisdom, control and direct the affairs of the universes in perfect harmony?

THE CONVICTION OF REASON ON PLURALITY OF PRESIDING INTELLIGENCES—GODS[11]

Far stronger, however, as affecting this question of a multiplicity of divine ruling Intelligences in the universe—far stronger than all the pluralistic references in the scriptures concerning the Elohim (the Gods) will be the consciousness of that truth that must rise in the mind of man as he contemplates the vastness of the universe, and the great number of suns, extending into thousands of millions, some of them—and likely most of them—peopled by sentient and intelligent inhabitants. Also, further that[12] many of these inhabitants without doubt <are> superior Intelligences to those we have known in our earth; Intelligences who have subdued the worlds given to them as habitations, and which they have carried into immensely higher states of social order and excellence than we know, and whose affairs are governed by councils of Intelligences, rising in gradations of power and authority over worlds or world-groups, and these groups gathered into immense empires of orderly worlds, all governed by harmonized Intelligences who have partaken of the one God-Nature. These governing Intelligences are incarnations of that Nature, of all the qualities or attributes of it, for in them, and in each of them, "dwells all the fullness of the Godhead bodily" (Col. 2:9). These, gathered into assemblies and into councils, constitute David's congregation of the "Mighty

11. <Ms III^{c} adds "The Conviction of Reason on Plurality of Presiding Intelligences—Gods"—*Ed.*>

12. <Ms III^{c} adds "Also further that"—*Ed.*>

Ones"—the Gods of eternity and of the universe. Not distraught and divided and confused, but harmonized into One-ness that makes our universe, though pluralistic in its nature, yet also uni-verse: a Uni-verse where system obtains, where orderly government controls, where all things exist under "reign of law."

"AND THE SPIRIT OF GOD"—DEITY VIEWED AS UNITY[13]

Proceeding forth from these divine and harmonized Intelligences—the Gods, as rays of light vibrate from our sun and from all the thousands of millions of suns of the universe to give us cosmic light and cosmic power, so from the presence of these divine Intelligences proceeds the Spirit of the Gods, "to fill the immensity of space"; becoming God Omniscient, God Omnipotent, and God Omnipresent in the world; everywhere present, and everywhere present with knowledge, and everywhere present with power; with power to act, power to be self-moving, power to move other things than self; creative power in fact; upholding power; intelligence-inspiring power; vital force—a mighty Ocean of Being, extending God everywhere; holding within its Ocean of Being all that is—a Spirit proceeding from, and yet ever united to its source[14]—the Divine, Harmonized Intelligences of the Universe! All this is told in the first unmarred verses of Genesis:

> In the beginning
> *The Gods created the heavens and the earth;*
> And the earth was without form and void;
> And darkness was on the face of the deep.
> *And the Spirit of the Gods moved upon the face of the waters.*
> And the Gods said, "Let there be light." And there was light. . . .
> And the Gods said, "Let us make man in our image,
> After our likeness" (cf. Gen. 1:1-3,26).

In other words, as in each of the great created classes of animals we are repeatedly told, they were created, and were to reproduce each "after his kind"; so man was produced, after his kind: he, the offspring of God.

> These are the generations of the heavens and of the earth, when they were created, in the day [i.e., in the period] that the Lord God made the earth and the heavens (Gen. 2:4).

---

13. <Ms III[c] adds "'And The Spirit of God'—Deity Viewed As Unity"—*Ed.*>
14. <Ms III[*] "yet ever returning to its source"—*Ed.*>

It is not difficult, with this large vision of the universe and its innumerable Intelligences before us as set forth in previous chapters—it is not difficult, I say, to understand how that in the creation of our little earth in the universe, a plurality of Divine Personages were united in directing its organization, and decreeing the lines of its development, and these Intelligences were the incarnation of all that is known as Deity, each one of them;[15] and doubtless were the Intelligences known as the Father, Son, and Holy Spirit. We can understand now that "as pertaining to us," there is indeed but these—one Godhead! And in being loyal to this Godhead, incarnated in that Trinity, or Divine Council; and in each One of that Trinity God and the fullness of God, even as such "fullness of Godhead bodily," was said to have dwelt in Jesus Christ (Col. 2:9). And in being loyal to Them—the Father, Son, and Holy Ghost—we shall be loyal to all that is or can be included in that greatest of all generalization—God!

THE FORM OF GOD[16]

The second matter we promised to consider here, and having to do with the form of God, is a question much debated through the ages; and pertinent here to our unfolding Truth. That, too, is determined in the Hebrew scriptures, the "Let us make man in our image, after our likeness. . . . So God created man in His own image, in the image of God created He him" (Gen. 1:26-27). It must follow, as clearly as the night the day, if God created man in His own image, then God also is in the image or form[17] of man. I know there has accumulated a lot of theological rubbish about this scripture meaning man being created in the "moral image" of God—meaning consciousness, intelligence, and will; and limiting what should be a full-length portrait of Deity—including mind qualities and also physical form—to this so-called "moral image." This limitation is the work of the theologians, an assumption purely without authority of the revelation itself (Gen. 1:26-27).

When the same terms are used in another chapter of Genesis, we have no difficulty in understanding the significance of them; viz., "And Adam lived 130 years and begat a son in his own likeness, after his image, and called his name Seth" (Gen. 5:3). The unstrained meaning of which is that[18] Seth was like unto his father; and in like manner the creation of man "in the image and likeness of God" should be understood.

All through the revelation contained in the Old Testament this truth is iterated

---

15. <Ms III^c adds "each one of them"—*Ed.*>
16. <Ms III^c adds "The Form of God"—*Ed.*>
17. <Ms III^c adds "or form"—*Ed.*>
18. <Ms III^c adds "that"—*Ed.*>

and reiterated. It occurs in nearly all the passages in which God as a person is unveiled. It was so in the visitation of Divine Beings to Abraham in the plains of Mamre, when the three "men" came into his tent, one of whom is always spoken of as "the Lord" (Gen. 18:1-15), who conversed with Abraham in the most familiar terms, and even partook of the patriarch's food!

Jacob's contact with a divine personage is equally vividly described, and with all evidence of physical contact. Jacob sought to learn the name of his visitor, but it was not revealed. Nevertheless, he blessed Jacob, and Jacob called the name of the place of his experience, Peniel, "for," he said, "I have seen God face to face, and my life is preserved!" (Gen. 32:30).

There surely was physical manifestation of God unto Israel both in Mt. Sinai and later to a special company made up of Moses and his inner council, and "seventy of the Elders of Israel," for it is recorded:

> Then went up Moses, and Aaron, Nadab, and Abihu, and Seventy of the Elders of Israel; and they saw the God of Israel; and there was under His feet as it were <a paved work of a sapphire stone, and as it were>[19] the body of heaven in his clearness! And upon the nobles of the children of Israel He laid not His hand; also they saw God and did eat and drink (Ex. 24:9-11).

And this in the presence of the Lord.

Summing up the experiences of Israel at Sinai, and the giving of the law, Moses reminds Israel in his recital of those events that:

> The Lord spoke unto all your assembly in the mount out of the midst of the fire, of the cloud, and of the thick darkness, with a great voice, and He added no more. And He [the Lord] wrote them [his commandments] upon two tables[20] of stone, and delivered them unto me (Deut. 5:22).

He said again:

> The Lord talked with you face to face . . . out of the midst of the fire (Deut. 5:4).[21]

What shall I say more? Joshua, during the siege of Jericho, beheld a personage in the form of a man with drawn sword in hand, and asked him, "Art thou for us, or for our adversaries?" "Nay," said the personage, "but as captain of the host of the Lord am I now come." And Joshua paid him divine honors by an act of worship:

---

19. <Ms III accidentally omits the words "a paved work of a sapphire stone, and as it were"—*Ed.*>

20. <Ms III* "in two tables"—*Ed.*>

21. <In Ms III Roberts cites these last two scriptural quotations as coming from Ex. 4 and Ex. 5, respectively—*Ed.*>

> And Joshua fell on his face to the earth and did worship. . . . And the captain of the Lord's host said unto him, "Joshua, loose thy shoe from off thy foot; for the place whereon thou standest is holy." And Joshua did so (cf. Josh. 5:13-15).

Isaiah, prophet par excellence, also "saw . . . the Lord . . . upon a throne, high and lifted up." And in his ecstasy, and yet in humility, he cried out, "Woe is me! for I am undone, because I am a man of unclean lips, . . . for mine eyes have seen the King, the Lord of hosts" (Isa. 6:1, 5).

There are visions of other prophets and seers in Israel to the same effect. The revelations of the Old Testament are full of this anthropomorphism, but the climax of its demonstration must be necessarily reserved for a later chapter, when dealing with the supplemental phase of the Hebrew revelation found in the New Testament, and in the mission of Messiah of the Old Testament revealed in Christ Jesus of the New Testament.

CHAPTER XVIII

The Mission Given to Israel

SCRIPTURE READING LESSON

Analysis

I. Items of Israel's Mission.

II. Israel Not Always Faithful to His Mission.

III. Greek Translation of the Hebrew Scriptures.

IV. Philo of Alexandria; His Mischievous Interpretations.

V. Philo's False Doctrines of God.

VI. Earth Advent of Messiah.

VII. Preparation for the Revelation of God.

VIII. Witness of the Shepherds.

IX. Witness of the Magi.

X. The Message of the Son of God.

XI. The Mission of the Son of God.

References

All the citations of scriptures and their contexts cited in this chapter.

Flavius Josephus, *The Works of Flavius Josephus: Antiquities of the Jews*, trans. William Whiston (Baltimore: Armstrong and Berry, 1837), here and there.

Alfred Edersheim, *The Life and Times of Jesus the Messiah*, 2 vols., 8th ed. (New York: Longmans, Green, and Co., 1898).

Horatio B. Hackett and Ezra Abbot, eds., *Dr. William Smith's Dictionary of the Bible, Comprising Its Antiquities, Biography, Geography, and Natural History*, 4 vols. (Boston: Houghton, Mifflin and Co., 1894), under appropriate titles.

Also, encyclopedias under appropriate headings, such as "Hebrews," "Israel," "Philo," "Jews," etc.

Also, *The Jewish Encyclopedia: A Descriptive Record of the History, Religion, Literature, and Customs of the Jewish People from the Earliest Times to the Present Day*, 12 vols., ed. Isidore Singer (New York: Funk and Wagnalls Co., 1901), under appropriate headings.

CHAPTER XVIII

The Mission Given to Israel

ENUMERATION OF MISSION ITEMS[1]

This was the mission given to Israel by his revealed religion: to testify to the reality of God; that He is Creator of the heavens and of the earth, and all things that in them are; that He is the Eternal Cause of events within the universe.

To testify to the unity of God, but a unity arising from harmonized personal Intelligences: each the incarnation of the One God Nature. And yet such a unity as will warrant the prophet's ringing message, "Hear, O Israel, the Lord . . . God is one Lord" (Deut. 6:4). For Israel and for this world[2] there is no other.

To testify of the definite form of God—of all Divine Intelligences, who are but incarnations of the One God Nature; that man was made in the very image and likeness of God; and that man possesses this form of God, as well as the moral qualities, mind, or intelligence, and a will.

To testify that men are "the children of the Most High." That a redemption was promised through a Messiah, that was to come, and who would "save that which was lost" (Luke 19:10) through disobedience to law: that the original innocence[3] of man might be regained; and redemption from physical death would be secured through resurrection from the dead.

This <was> the mission given unto Israel. This <was> the means through which the seed of Abraham would be a blessing unto all nations of the earth; because through his seed these several things would be made known to the world, and through his seed would the Messiah come to earth.

ISRAEL NOT ALWAYS FAITHFUL TO HIS MISSION

It must be confessed that Israel was not wholly true to this high mission. There

---

1. <Ms III[c] adds "Enumeration of Mission Items," which was originally placed after "This was the mission given to Israel by his revealed religion" and then moved to its present location—*Ed.*>

2. <Ms III[*] "For them and this world"—*Ed.*>

3. <Ms III[c] adds "innocence," followed by a question mark, above Ms III[*] "righteousness," which itself is not crossed out—*Ed.*>

is throughout, after his deliverance from Egypt, a tendency to play fast and loose with this mission. He was not sufficiently faithful to warrant God giving to him a complete victory over the land of Palestine, which had been promised as an heritage to him. Remnants of old tribes remained in the land to plague Israel; and it was not until the reigns of David and Solomon that the Israelites won entire possession of the land, and when they so possessed it, it was but for a short period. With the close of Solomon's reign came the revolt of the ten tribes against Rehoboam,[4] resulting in the establishment of the Northern Kingdom, which in 722 B.C. was overthrown by the Assyrians. The Northern Kingdom <was> destroyed, its population carried into Assyria, and from there led away, and finally lost among the northern peoples of Europe; and ever since they have been spoken of as "the lost tribes."

Judah and half of the tribe of Benjamin which remained with him continued 135 years longer and then that kingdom was also overthrown, and the king and the people carried away captive to Babylon, where they remained until delivered under Cyrus; but not again to become an established sovereign and independent people. They became victims first to one of the neighboring kingdoms, and then to another; and finally came under the jurisdiction of all-conquering Rome. Such <was> their political condition at the time of the coming of their Messiah.

This <is> the outline merely of the melancholy history of Israel. During the early centuries of their existence in Palestine, including the reign of the Judges, there was all the while an inclination to follow after the false gods of the lands which they took possession of; and the chief messages and preachments of their prophets were against this infidelity and sacrilege of the chosen people. Then just at the time when the great climax of their revelation was about to be reached in the advent of their Messiah, they were in the lowest state of their apostasy from God and neglect of the high mission given to them.

THE GREEK TRANSLATION OF THE HEBREW SCRIPTURES[5]

The fact of this apostasy[6] is noted by many historians and scholars. Among them Alfred Edersheim, the author of a two-volume work[7] on *The Life and Times of Jesus, the Messiah.* He holds as a preliminary to the turning away of Israel from this high mission, and as contributing to it, the Greek translation of the Hebrew scripture usually called the Septuagint or the "LXX." This latter name is given to

---

4. <Ms III[*] "Reaboam"—*Ed.*>
5. <Ms III[c] adds "s" to make "Scriptures"—*Ed.*>
6. <Ms III[c] adds "of this apostasy"—*Ed.*>
7. <Ms III[*] "a splendid two-volume work"—*Ed.*>

the version because of the tradition that the translation was accomplished by seventy Elders of the Jews. The most generally accepted theory concerning it, however, is that it was a work accomplished at various times between 280-150 B.C. The Books of Moses were translated as early as the time of Ptolemy Philadelphus, 284-246 B.C. The Prophets and Psalms were translated somewhat later. After mentioning "clerical mistakes" in the work, "misreadings" and "making allowance for errors of translation, ignorance, and haste" in the performance of the work, Edersheim says:

> The distinctly Grecian elements, however, are at present of chief interest to us. They consist of allusions to Greek mythological terms and adaptations of Greek philosophical ideas. However few, even one well authenticated instance would lead us to suspect others, and in general give to the version the character of Jewish Hellenizing. In the same class we reckon what constitutes the prominent characteristic of the LXX version, which for want of better terms, we would designate as rationalistic and apologetic. Difficulties, or what seemed such, are removed by the most bold methods and by free handling of the text; it need scarcely be said, often very unsatisfactory, and more especially a strenuous effort is made to banish all anthropomorphisms, as inconsistent with their ideas of the Deity.[8]

It was this version of the Hebrew scripture that became really the people's Old Testament to that large Jewish world through which Christianity was afterwards to address itself to mankind. Edersheim says:

> It was part of the case that this translation should be regarded by the Hellenists [Greeks] as inspired like the original. Otherwise it would have been impossible to make final appeal to the very words of the Greek; still less, to find in them a mystical and allegorical meaning.[9]

This translation of the Hebrew scripture laid the foundation for a superstructure of false philosophy, and there was not wanting builders who were anxious to place a pagan structure upon it. About the middle of the second century B.C., one Aristobulus, a Greek Jew of Alexandria, sought to so explain the Hebrew scriptures as "to bring the Peripatetic Philosophy [the philosophy of Aristotle, Greek philosopher who flourished in the fourth century B.C.] out of the law of Moses and out of the other prophets." Following is a sample, according to Edersheim, of his allegorizing:

> Thus, when we read that God "stood," it meant the stable order of the world

8. Alfred Edersheim, *The Life and Times of Jesus the Messiah*, 8th ed. (New York: Longmans, Green, and Co., 1898), 1:27-28.

9. Ibid., 1:29.

[stood]; that He "created the world in six days," the orderly succession of time; "rest of the sabbath," the preservation of what was created.

And in such manner could the whole system of Aristotle be found in the Bible. But how was this to be accounted for? Of course, the Bible had not learned of Aristotle, but he and <all the> other philosophers had learned from the Bible. Thus, according to Aristobulus, Pythagoras, Plato, and all the other sages had really learned from Moses, and the broken rays found in their writings were united in all their glory in the "Torah," [meaning the Pentateuch, or the five Books of Moses, "the Law"].[10]

PHILO OF ALEXANDRIA: HIS MISCHIEVOUS INTERPRETATIONS

Following Aristobulus in the same kind of philosophy was Philo, the learned Jew of Alexandria, born about the year 20 B.C. He was supposed to be a descendant of Aaron and belonged to one of the wealthiest and most influential families among the merchants of Egypt. He is said to have united a large share of Greek learning with Jewish enthusiasm. According to him the Greek sages had learned their philosophy from Moses, in whom alone was all truth to be found. Edersheim says:

> Not indeed in the letter, but under the letter, of Holy Scripture. If in Numbers 23:19 we read "God is not a man" and in Deuteronomy 1:31 that the Lord was "as a man," did it not imply on the one hand the revelation of absolute truth by God, and on the other accommodation to those who were weak? Here, then, was the principle of a two-fold interpretation of the word of God—the literal and the allegorical. . . . To begin with the former: the literal sense must be wholly set aside, when it implies anything unworthy of the Deity—anything unmeaning, impossible, or contrary to reason. Manifestly this canon, if strictly applied, would do away not only with all anthropomorphisms, but cut the knot wherever difficulties seem insuperable. Again, Philo would find an allegorical, along with the literal, interpretation indicated in the reduplication of a word, and in seemingly superfluous words, particles, or expressions. These could, of course, only bear such a meaning on Philo's assumption of the actual inspiration of the LXX [Septuagint] version [of the Bible].[11]

It is not necessary to enter into further details[12] as to Philo's method except to note what another has said in relation to the results growing out of that method. This "other" (in the *Encyclopædia Britannica*) says:

> So far as we can judge . . . his [Philo's] aim was to put upon the sacred text a

10. Ibid., 1:36.
11. Ibid., 1:41.
12. <Ms III* "to enter the further details"—*Ed.*>

sense which would appeal <even> to Greek readers, and in particular to get rid of all anthropomorphic utterances about God.[13]

PHILO'S FALSE DOCTRINE ABOUT GOD[14]

> [Philo's] doctrine . . . starts from the idea that God is <a> "Being," absolutely bare of [all] quality. All quality in finite beings has limitation, and no limitation can be predicated of God, who is eternal, unchangeable, simple substance, free, self-sufficient, better than the good and the beautiful. To predicate any quality of God would be to reduce Him to the sphere of finite existence. Of Him we can only say *that* He is, not *what* He is, and such purely negative predications as to His being appear to Philo . . . the only way of securing His [God's] absolute elevation above the world [that is, above and outside of the material universe]. . . . A consistent application of Philo's abstract conception of God would exclude the possibility of any active relation of God to the world, and therefore of religion; for a Being absolutely without quality and movement cannot be conceived as actively concerned with the multiplicity of individual things. And so, in fact, Philo does teach that the absolute perfection, purity, and loftiness of God would be violated by direct contact with imperfect, impure, and finite things.[15]

Of which it will be sufficient to say that such is not the God of Abraham, Isaac, and Jacob, nor of Moses, nor of the prophets of Israel, nor of the Bible, or any part of it.

In all Philo's wresting of the Jewish scriptures one sees only too plainly the efforts to harmonize Jewish theology with Greek philosophy—an effort to be rid of the plain anthropomorphism of the Hebrew scriptures, for the incomprehensible "being" of Greek metaphysics. And thus the Jews, the people who had been chosen witnesses for God to the world, appeared to have grown weary of the mission given to them, tired were they of standing in a position where their hands seem to be raised against all men, and all men's hands raised against them, because of this message of theirs. They had lost the spirit that had supported their fathers, and hence were searching out these cowardly compromises by which harmony could be shown to exist between the philosophy of the Gentiles and the revelation of God to their fathers.

This ends our survey of the ancient religions, including this Hebrew religion

---

13. <Emil Schürer and Charles Bigg, "Philo," *The Encyclopædia Britannica: A Dictionary of Arts, Sciences, Literature and General Information*, 11th ed. (Cambridge: Cambridge University Press, 1910-11), 21:409. Roberts's quotation is actually about an earlier Jewish philosopher, Philometor, who lived in the mid-second century B.C.—*Ed.*>

14. <Ms III[c] adds "Philo's False Doctrine about God"—*Ed.*>

15. Prof. Emil Schürer, of University of Giessen, <and Charles Bigg,> "Philo," *Encyclopædia Britannica*, 21:410.

which more emphatically than any of the others is founded upon direct revelation from God; and as to that, we must have seen that the people to whom the positive and direct revelation of God was given, often appeared to be unfaithful to the trust imposed in them, and from the beginning gave evidence of an inclination to follow after other gods—the gods of the heathen; and in the last phases of their national existence, philosophized themselves out of the robust religion contained in their scriptures to accept the attenuated, hair-splitting metaphysics of the subtle Greek mind; substituting these speculations for the revelations of God, until we shall presently see, when the supreme moment had arrived for the complete manifestation of God in the flesh, their minds were prepared to reject him and to cry blasphemy when he proclaimed himself God, "The Son of God," and "God manifested in the flesh" (1 Tim. 3:16).

EARTH ADVENT OF MESSIAH[16]

It was in the midst of these conditions as to the affairs of Israel, that the promised Messiah of the chosen people was born in Bethlehem of Judea, two thousand years ago. The greater part of Israel (ten tribes) more than seven centuries before[17] had been carried captive into Assyria; thence led away and dispersed among the peoples of northern Europe. The tribes of Judah and Benjamin after captivity and varied national experiences, arising chiefly in being subjected to one or another of the neighboring kingdoms, were now in complete subjection to Rome, shorn of national glory, in a state of apostasy against God; and indifferent to their mission as God's witness to the world.

PREPARATION FOR THE REVELATION OF GOD: BETROTHAL OF MARY[18]

The betrothal of Mary of Nazareth, in preparation of the birth of the "only begotten Son of God" in the flesh,[19] was conducted by the angel Gabriel, the account of which is given in St. Luke's Gospel in the most delicate terms. The angel said to Mary, after his gentle "all hail" to her:

> Blessed art thou among women, . . . for thou hast found favor with God; and behold, thou shalt conceive . . . and bring forth a Son and shall call his name Jesus. He shall be great, and shall be called the Son of the Highest. . . . The Holy Ghost shall

16. <Ms III^c adds "Earth Advent of Messiah"—*Ed.*>
17. <Ms III "more than a century before," which is corrected to "seven centuries"—*Ed.*>
18. <Ms III^c adds "Betrothal of Mary"—*Ed.*>
19. <Ms III^c adds "in the flesh"—*Ed.*>

> come upon thee, and the power of the Highest shall overshadow thee: therefore also that Holy Thing which shall be born of thee shall be called the Son of God (Luke 2:28, 30-32, 35).

And, of course, He will be what He is called—"The Son of God"!

WITNESS OF THE SHEPHERDS

At his birth in the humble quarters of the stable at Bethlehem, God sent His angels to bear witness of the fact of it to the shepherds who were watching their flocks in the fields by night. "The angel of the Lord came to them, and assured them of good tidings—Christ, the Lord, was born." Then came other angels with their song of "glory to God in the highest, and on earth peace, good will to men" (Luke 2:14).

Later the shepherds found the babe in the manger, as they were told they would; and they made known the great message which had been revealed to them—Christ the Lord had been born in the city of David—Bethlehem!

THE WITNESS OF THE MAGI

From afar came other witnesses and of a different class. These were learned men from the East, who had seen his star which they followed and had come to worship him. They, as befit their station, called at Herod's palace in Jerusalem, and desired to know where "he that was born King of the Jews" was to be found. The palace could give them no information, so they followed the "star" until it stood where the young child was, and there, where the humble shepherds had first found him, the wise men also found him, and paid him royal, if not divine honors, with their "gifts of gold, frankincense, and myrrh" (Matt. 2:11).[20] Warned in a dream not to return to the palace to disclose what they had learned, the birth of him who is destined to be King of the Jews, and of all the earth, they departed to their far-off homes which some traditions place respectively in Persia, India, and Egypt.

Thus began the life of God's Son in the earth. Childhood was spent in Egypt, until the passing of those who in their jealous hate sought his life. His youth was spent in the humble village of Nazareth, until the beginning of his formal ministry, which opened when he was about thirty years of age; a ministry in which was proclaimed the full message and mission of God's Son.

---

20. <There are significant differences between Matthew's "house" at Matt. 2:11 and Luke's reference to an inn and "manger" at Luke 2:7-16; see Alan Hugh McNeile, *The Gospel according to St. Matthew: The Greek Text with Introduction, Notes, and Indices* (London: Macmillan and Co., 1915), 17—*Ed.*>

THE MESSAGE OF THE SON OF GOD

That the "Word" which was in the beginning with God "and which was God" was now made flesh and dwelt with men and was "the only begotten of the Father in the flesh" (John 1:1-2, 14).

That Jesus of Nazareth was and is the Son of God (John 10:36).

That Jesus and the Father are one, by being alike in nature and power and knowledge and wisdom and glory—one (i.e., alike) in all things (John 10:30; 17:21-23).

That Jesus was God manifested in the flesh—i.e., revealed in the flesh (Matt. 3:17; cf. 1 Tim. 3:16).

That Jesus is the Savior of men and that he is the Redeemer of the world; that no other name under heaven is given whereby men may be saved (John 3:14-19; Acts 4:12; Matt. 3:17; Acts 2:22-43).

That men through him must be born again of the water and of the spirit, in order for entrance into the kingdom of heaven (John 3:1-11).

That Jesus is the resurrection and the life, and that through him all men will be raised from the dead in their order; "for as in Adam all die, so in Christ shall all be made alive" (1 Cor. 15:1-26; Matt. 27:50-53 et sq.; Mark 16:1-20; Luke 24:1-53; John 20:1—21:25; Acts 1:1-11).

THE MISSION OF THE SON OF GOD

(Of course, the message above overlaps in places the mission, since they are so closely allied.)

To bear witness to the Truth (John 3:11; 18:37).

To "teach all things" and witness the Truth that Jesus was the Son of God.

Woman: "I know that Messias cometh, which is called Christ; when he is come, he will tell us all things."

Jesus: "I that speak to thee am He" (John 4:25-26).

Jesus (to one whom he had healed): "Dost thou believe on the Son of God?"

The Man: "Who is he, Lord, that I may believe?"

Jesus: "Thou hast both seen him, and it is he that talketh with thee!"

The Man: "Lord, I believe. And he worshipped him" (John 9:35-38).

"To preach good tidings unto the meek; . . . to bind up the broken-hearted; . . . to proclaim the acceptable year of the Lord, and the day of vengeance of our God" (Isa. 61:1-2).

"To comfort all who mourn" (Isa. 61:2).

Messengers from John the Baptist: "Art thou he that should come, or do we look for another?"

Jesus: "Go and shew John again those things which ye do hear and see: the blind receive their sight, and the lame walk, the lepers are cleansed, and the deaf hear, the dead are raised up, and the poor have the gospel preached to them. And blessed is he, whosoever shall not be offended in me" (Matt. 11:3-6).

"To proclaim liberty to the captives and the opening of the prison to them that are bound" (Isa. 61:1). "Christ also hath once suffered for sins, the just for the unjust, that he might bring us to God, being put to death in the flesh but quickened by the Spirit; by which also he went and preached to the spirits in prison; which sometime were disobedient when once the longsuffering of God waited in the days of Noah" (1 Pet. 3:18-20). "For for this cause was the gospel preached also to them that are dead, that they might be judged according to men in the flesh, but live according to God in the spirit" (1 Pet. 4:6).

To be a Light to the Gentiles, as well as to Israel, and a universal savior.

Prophecy as to the Messiah—the Christ: "It is a light thing that thou shouldest be my servant to raise up the tribes of Jacob, and to restore the preserved of Israel; I will also give thee for a light to the Gentiles, that thou mayest be my salvation unto the end of the earth" (Isa. 49:6; cf. John 11:52).

Jesus: "Father, glorify Thy name."

Voice: "I have both[21] glorified it, and will glorify it again." (The people heard the voice. Some thought it thundered and others said an angel spake to him.)

Jesus: "This voice came not because of me, but for your sakes. Now is the judgment of this world; now shall the prince of this world be cast out. And I, if I be lifted up from the earth [i.e., upon the cross], will draw all men unto me" (John 12:28-32).

This in outline <is> the message and the mission of the Christ, which message and mission is testified of in the collection of books known as the New Testament; and which, when united with the prophetic message of the Old Testament, makes up the whole mission of Israel to the world.[22]

At this stage in the development of our theme, we shall concern ourselves next with developing the fact of the true Deity of the Christ, as that truth is set forth in

---

21. <Ms III[c] adds "both"—*Ed.*>

22. <At the bottom of the page of the manuscript the following handwritten Ms III[c] appears: "Add—'other sheep I have'—Christ mission to western continents. St Jno. 10 ch."—*Ed.*>

both the Old and in the New Testament, leaving the other phases of the message and mission of the Christ to be dealt with under the middle title of our three-fold theme—THE TRUTH, THE WAY, THE LIFE.

CHAPTER XIX
The Revelation of God in Jesus Christ

SCRIPTURE READING LESSON

Analysis

I. The Coming of God through Incarnation Promised.

II. The Christ Proclaimed To Be God.

III. Jesus Proclaims Himself To Be God, and in the Form of God.

IV. Jesus Is To Be Worshipped, Hence God.

V. Jesus Christ Is the Creator, Hence God.

VI. Jesus Christ Is Equal with God the Father, Hence God.

VII. God Revealed to the World in the Person of Jesus Christ.

References

The twenty-three citations of scripture and other authorities referred to, and the contexts of the scriptures cited in this chapter.

Also, 3 Ne. 11, the appearance of the risen Christ to the Nephites; also, Ether 3, appearance of the pre-existent Christ to the brother of Jared.

Joseph Smith's First Vision, Pearl of Great Price, Writings of Joseph Smith <JS-H>.

B. H. Roberts, *The Mormon Doctrine of Deity; The Roberts-Van Der Donckt Discussion, to Which Is Added a Discourse, Jesus Christ, The Revelation of God* (Salt Lake City: The Deseret News, 1903), here and there.

Joseph Smith, *King Follett Discourse; The Being and Kind of Being God Is; The Immortality of the Intelligence of Man*, annotated by B. H. Roberts (Salt Lake City: Magazine Printing Co., 1926), pamphlet.

CHAPTER XIX

The Revelation of God in Jesus Christ

THE COMING OF GOD THROUGH INCARNATION PROMISED

Prophetically in the Old Testament, the coming of God into the world is proclaimed. In previous pages we have noted that a "Virgin would conceive and bear a Son" and call his name "Immanuel," the interpretation of which is "God with us"–that is, God with men (Isa. 7:14; Matt. 1:23).

Again, "a child" under special circumstances is to be "born" in Israel, and "the government" is to be upon his shoulder, and his name shall be called "Wonderful," "Counselor," "the Mighty God," "the Everlasting Father," "the Prince of Peace" (Isa. 9:6).

The Prophet Isaiah in giving comforting words to Israel, said: "Your dead men shall live; together with my dead body shall they arise, . . . and the earth shall cast out the dead" (Isa. 26:19). This was Jehovah (the pre-existent spirit of the Christ) speaking to Isaiah, and is a plain prophecy that Jehovah, the spiritual personage and Deity who manifested himself to the ancients–and especially to Moses–shall have a "body," shall "die," and shall be raised from the dead. All which, of course, the reader will recognize the Christ did, according to the New Testament seven hundred years after Isaiah's time. Hence, it is proper to proclaim this "child," this "Son that was given"–Jesus of Nazareth–to be "the Mighty God," the "Everlasting Father," "God with us," and "God manifested in the flesh."

THE CHRIST PROCLAIMED TO BE GOD

Turn we now to the New Testament, and first to that sublime poem of St. John's preface to his gospel, which, like the book of Genesis, carries us back to the "beginning" "when God created"–not the universe, but our earth and its heavens.

> In the beginning was the Word and the Word was with God, and the Word was God. The same was in the beginning with God, . . . And the Word was made flesh and dwelt among us, and we beheld his glory, the glory as of the only begotten of the Father, full of grace and truth. . . . For the law was given by Moses, but grace and truth came by Jesus Christ (John 1:12, 14, 17).

There can be no question but direct reference is here made to the Lord Jesus

Christ as being the "Word," and the "Word," or Jesus, being with the Father in the beginning "when" he created our heaven and our earth; and the "Word," or Jesus Christ, also being God. So then the "Word" as used here by John is one of the titles of Jesus in his pre-existent estate as a spirit. Called the "Word," because by "Word" we give forth expression, and since Jesus Christ was to be an expression or revelation of God, he was called so to be the brightness of His (the Father's) glory and the express image of His (the Father's) person (Heb. 1:3).

JESUS DECLARES HIMSELF TO BE GOD AND IN THE FORM OF GOD

> Let this mind be in you, which was also in the Lord Jesus: who, being in the form of God, thought it not robbery to be equal with God; but made himself of no reputation and took upon himself the form of a servant, and was made in the likeness of men (cf. Philip. 2:5-7).

Jesus was crucified on the charge that he was an imposter, that he, though plainly to the Jews being a man, said that God was his Father, making himself equal with God. Jesus had said to a helpless cripple on this occasion[1]—a cripple of thirty-eight years standing, "Rise, take up thy bed and walk" (John 5:8), and the man arose, healed. This healing attracted the attention of the Jews, and because this act of mercy was done on the sabbath day they were scandalized greatly and sought to kill the Christ, but Jesus answered rather independently, "my Father worketh hitherto and I work" (John 5:17). On which they sought the more to kill him because from their viewpoint he had not only broken the sabbath in healing the cripple, but had now blasphemed by saying that God was his Father, making himself equal with God. Further he answered: "Verily, verily, I say unto you, the Son can do nothing of himself, but what he seeth the Father do; for what things soever He doeth, these also doeth the Son likewise" (John 5:19).[2]

Again, this Son of God offended the Jews by saying: "The works that I do in my Father's name, they bear witness of me. . . . I and my Father are one" (John 10:25, 30). On this declaration the Jews took up stones to stone him. Then Jesus said unto them: "Many good works have I showed you from my Father, for which of these works do ye stone me?" The Jews answered him, saying: "For a good work we stone thee not, but for blasphemy, and because that thou, being a man, makest thyself God" (John 10:33). Did Jesus deny that he was God to these infuriated

---

1. <Ms III[c] adds "on this occasion"—*Ed.*>

2. The whole chapter should be read as it manifests the close relations and sympathetic cooperation between this God's Son, the Christ, and that Father who begot him into this earth-life, to be the revelation of God to the world.

Jews? What an opportunity to correct their misconception, if misconception it was! But Jesus did not deny their charge, on the contrary he confirmed it by a quotation from the Old Testament:

> "Is it not written in your law, 'I said, ye are Gods'? If he called them Gods, unto whom the word of God came, and the scripture cannot be broken [i.e., denied], say ye of him, whom the Father hath sanctified and sent into the world, 'Thou blasphemest,' because I said, I am the Son of God? If I do not the works of my Father, believe me not. But if I do, though ye believe not me, believe the works; that ye may know and believe that the Father is in me, and I in Him." Therefore, the Jews sought again to take him, but he escaped out of their midst (cf. John 10:34-39).

Again, when accused before Pilate who declared he could "find no fault in him," the Jews answered: "We have a law, and by our law he ought to die, because he made himself the Son of God." When before the Sanhedrin of the Jews, the High Priest in the court said directly to Jesus: "I adjure thee by the living God, that thou tell us whether thou be the Christ, the Son of God." Jesus answered him, "Thou hast said." And further on, "Hereafter shall ye see the Son of man sitting at the right hand of power,[3] and coming in the clouds of heaven" (Matt. 26:63-64).

Once the Christ himself turned questioner of the Jews, and said to them, "What think ye of Christ"—having reference, of course, to the Anointed One, the Messiah of the Old Testament—and of whom there was lively expectation that this Messiah would manifest himself unto Israel; and the question of Jesus referred to that Anointed One, then yet to be revealed—so:

> "What think ye of Christ? Whose Son is He?" And they say unto him, "The Son of David." He saith unto them: "How then doth David in spirit call him Lord, saying, 'The Lord said unto my Lord, sit thou on my right hand, until I make thine enemies thy footstool.' If David then call him Lord, how is he his son?" No one was able to answer him, neither durst any man from that day forth [saith the record] ask him any question (cf. Matt. 22:42-44).

The above question can only be answered by the plain truth, that the first Lord (the Father) said unto the second Lord (the Son, Jesus Christ), "sit thou on my right hand, until I make thine enemies thy footstool"; and the second Lord could become the "Son of David" only on the maternal side, Mary being a descendant of David. The Jews dare not answer, nor make further inquiry about this seeming mystery without admitting that the Anointed One, their Messiah, was to be veritably the "Son of God."

---

3. <Ms III* "the right hand of the Power"—*Ed.*>

JESUS CHRIST IS TO BE WORSHIPPED, HENCE GOD

Jesus Christ, according to the New Testament scriptures, is to be worshipped by men and angels, and worship is an honor to be paid only to true Deity. The angels of heaven refuse the adoration we call worship. When an angel appeared to the Apostle John while on the Isle of Patmos, and the apostle, awed by the brightness of his glory, fell upon his face to worship him, the angel said:

> See thou do it not, for I am thy fellowservant and of thy brethren . . . worship God (Rev. 19:10).

Again,

> Unto which of the angels said He [God] at any time, "Thou art my Son, this day have I begotten thee!" And again, "I will be to him a Father, and he shall be to me a Son." . . . When he bringeth in the firstborn into the world [who is Jesus], He [God] saith, "Let all the angels of God worship him" (Heb. 1:5-6).
>
> Wherefore, God also hath highly exalted him and given him a name which is above every name: that at the name of Jesus every knee should bow, of things in heaven, and things in earth, and things under the earth; and that every tongue should confess that Jesus Christ is Lord, to the glory of God the Father (Philip. 2:9-11).

JESUS CHRIST IS THE CREATOR, HENCE GOD

Evidence of this is found in the testimony of John in the opening verses of his great gospel, as we have already seen:

> In the beginning was the Word, and the Word was with God, and the Word was God. . . . All things were made by him, and without him was not any thing made that was made. In him was life and the life was the light of man (John 1:1, 3-4).
>
> The Father . . . hath translated us into the kingdom of his dear Son . . . who is the image of the invisible God, the firstborn of every creature: for by him were all things created, that are in heaven, and that are in earth, visible and invisible, whether they be thrones, or dominions, or principalities, or powers: all things were created by him, and for him; and he is before all things, and by him all things consist (Col. 1:12-13, 15-17).

So also the writer of the Epistle to the Hebrews:

> God, who at sundry times and divers manners spake in times past unto the fathers by the prophets, hath in these last days spoken unto us by His Son, whom He hath appointed heir of all things, by whom also He made the worlds (Heb. 1:1-2).

That is to say, under the direction of the Father, Jesus Christ as pre-existent spirit created the worlds.

JESUS CHRIST EQUAL WITH GOD THE FATHER, HENCE GOD

After his resurrection Jesus appeared to his disciples on a mount in Galilee, and said:

> All power is given unto me in heaven and in earth. Go ye therefore and teach all nations, baptizing them in the name of the Father, and the Son, and the Holy Ghost, teaching them to observe all things whatsoever I have commanded you; and lo, I am with you always, even unto the end of the world (Matt. 28:18-20).

Observe in this passage, that this Jesus Christ is placed upon a footing of equality with God the Father and with the Holy Ghost. This brings to mind the scripture of St. Paul, who speaking of Jesus said, "Who, being in the form of God, thought it not robbery to be equal with God" (Philip. 2:6). Also, the Son of God, Jesus Christ, is declared to be in "the brightness of His [the Father's] glory, and the express image of His person, and upholding all things by the word of His power, when he had by himself purged our sins, sat down at the right hand of the Majesty on High" (Heb. 1:3). So Paul to the Corinthians, "Christ, who is the image of God" (2 Cor. 4:4). And again, in his letter to the Colossians, "who is the image of the invisible God, the firstborn of every creature" (Col. 1:15). Being the "express image of his person," then the "image of the invisible God," Jesus becomes a revelation of the person of God to the children of men as well as a revelation of God's attributes, for "it pleased the Father that in him [the Lord Jesus Christ] should all fullness dwell. . . . For in him dwelleth all the fullness of the Godhead bodily" (Col. 1:19; 2:9). All there is then of God, there is in Jesus Christ, and all is revealed through him. All that Jesus Christ is, God is; and Jesus Christ, after his resurrection, is an immortal man of flesh and bone and spirit united; and who, with his Father and the Holy Ghost, reigns eternally in the heavens, our Godhead. "Great is the mystery of Godliness;" and yet "God was manifest in the flesh,[4] justified in the Spirit, seen of angels, preached unto the Gentiles, believed on in the world, received up into glory" (1 Tim. 3:16).

GOD REVEALED TO THE WORLD IN THE PERSON OF JESUS CHRIST

The world stands in need of a revelation of God. He whom Babylonians, Assyrians, and Egyptians sought for in their pantheism must be made known. God whom Confucius would have man respect, but keep at a distance, must draw near.

---

4. <The earliest textual form of this verse does not affirm the deity of Jesus. For explanation of how the original *hos* "who" developed to *theos* "God," see Bruce M. Metzger, *The Text of the New Testament: Its Transmission, Corruption, and Restoration*, 2d ed. (New York: Oxford University Press, 1968), 187—*Ed.*>

The "Alfader" of the Goths and Huns and Scythians,[5] mysterious and incomprehensible to them, must be brought out of the northern darkness into a glorious light. The God-idea that prevailed among the Greek philosophers must be brought from out the midst of their idle speculations and made to stand before the world. Him whom they ignorantly worshipped must be preached unto them. He whom the Jews were seeking to deny and forsake, because of their misunderstanding, must be revealed, and that concretely, to the children of men. And lo! when the veil falls, and the darkness moves back through the revelation that God gives of Himself, what form is that which steps forth from the background of the world's ignorance[6] and mystery? A man, as God lives! Jesus of Nazareth, the great Peasant Teacher of Judea! And He is God revealed henceforth to the world!

Those who thought upon God as impersonal, without form, must know Him henceforth as a person in the sense of being an individual, in the form of man—or, more properly, man in His form; for in the image of God was man created. Those who held Him to be "without quality" must henceforth know Him as possessed of the qualities of Jesus of Nazareth. Those who have regarded Him as infinitely "terrible" must henceforth know Him as infinitely gentle. Those who would hold him at a distance will now permit him to draw near.

This is the world's mystery revealed. This is "God manifested in the flesh." This is the Son of God, who comes to reveal the Father, for he is the "express image" and likeness of the Father's person, and the revealer of the Father's mind. Henceforth, when men[7] shall say "show us the Father," Jesus, as when he answered Philip, will point to himself as the complete revelation of the Father and say, "He that hath seen me hath seen the Father" (John 14:8-9). Henceforth, when men shall dispute about the "being" and "nature" of God, it shall be a perfect answer to uphold Jesus Christ as the complete and perfect revelation and manifestation of God; and through all the ages it shall be so—eternally so. For there shall be no excuse for men saying that they know not God, for all may know Him from the least to the greatest, so tangible, so real a revelation has God given of Himself in the person, character, and attributes of Jesus Christ. Jesus lived his life on earth, a life of sorrow, its pathway strewn with actions fraught with mercy, kindness, and love. A man he was approved of God among men by miracles and wonders and signs which God did by him. But him men took, and by wicked hands crucified, and slew. God raised him up, however, having loosed the pains of death, because

---

5. <Ms III "Syphians"—*Ed.*>
6. <Ms III[*] "from the background from the world's ignorance"—*Ed.*>
7. <Ms III[c] adds "men"—*Ed.*>

it was not possible that he should be holden of them;[8] and exalted him on high, at the right hand of God, whence he shall come to judge the quick and the dead.

Mark you, in all this there is not a word about the "mysterious, ineffable generation of the Son of God" from the Father; and nothing about any other of the many mysteries that men indulged in their learned disquisitions about God. Yet the foregoing is the revelation of God as seen in Jesus Christ, according to the New Testament scriptures.

8. <Ms III[*] "he should be holden of it"—*Ed.*>

CHAPTER XX

Departure of the Church from the True Doctrine of God

SCRIPTURE READING LESSON

Analysis

I. The Revealed God.

II. The Christian Doctrine of God.

III. The Christian Godhead.

IV. First Authoritative Formula on Doctrine of God.

V. "The Apostles' Creed."

VI. Patristic View of the Divinity of Christ.

VII. Paganization of the New Testament Doctrine of Christ.

VIII. Doctrine of Trinities.

IX. The Nature and Relations of the Christ.

X. "The Nicene Creed."

XI. "Athanasian Creed."

XII. Pagan Origin of the Creedal Doctrine of God Conceded.

XIII. The Call "Back to God."

References

All the scriptures and works cited in the body of the text of this chapter and the contexts thereto.

All the standard church and ecclesiastical histories. I have usually followed Augustus Neander, *General History of the Christian Religion and Church*, 5 vols. (New York: Hurd and Houghton, 1871); John Lawrence von Mosheim, *Institutes of Ecclesiastical History, Ancient and Modern, in Four Books*, 3 vols., trans. James Murdock (New York: Harper and Brothers, 1839); Joseph Milner, *The History of the Church of Christ*, 4 vols. (London: T. Cadell, 1834); Henry Hart Milman, *The History of Christianity from the Birth of Christ to the Abolition of Paganism in the Roman Empire*, 2 vols. (New York: A. C. Armstrong and Son, 1881); Eusebius, for the first three Christian centuries, and the apostolic Christian fathers. Also, on the Catholic side, Dr. Heinrich Brück, *History of the Catholic Church for Use in Seminaries and Colleges*, 2 vols., trans. E. Pruente (New York: Benziger Brothers, 1884-85).

As a sort of handbook on the subject, I recommend B. H. Roberts, *Outlines of Ecclesiastical History* (Salt Lake City: George Q. Cannon and Sons, 1893), and the citations to authorities therein.

CHAPTER XX

Departure of the Church from the True Doctrine of God

THE REVEALED GOD

In the revelation of God through Jesus Christ our Lord, set forth in the last chapter, the true doctrine of God as to his nature, attributes, and physical form is established from the scriptures (Old and New Testament). That vision of Him on the "Mount" in Galilee, where he had appointed a meeting with his eleven apostles, is the true vision of God (Matt. 28:16). The resurrected Christ, a spirit and body in human form, indissolubly united, never more to be separated: spirit and body fused into a sole being, the true God-type; and in the case of the Christ is God absolutely revealed, for "in him dwelleth all the fullness of the Godhead bodily" (Col. 2:9).

This is not the revelation of God ridiculed by those who have a scorn of anthropomorphic notions of God, and who they claim is represented as an "old man with a grey beard," and whom they scornfully reject as God. But the revelation of God presented here is the immortal and eternal, youthful Christ; resurrected at the age of thirty-three years, the height of gloriously developed manhood, and caught at that age and made eternal, by a union of a perfect body with a perfect spirit, in eternal youth and youthfulness. God as perfected man, and manifested in the flesh for all time as the God-type of the universe, God blessed[1] forever more!

This is the revelation of God through Jesus Christ, of which the apostles were to bear witness to the world; of which the church is to bear witness in all time.[2] The apostles were faithful throughout their age to make known this revelation of God to the world; but the church after the death of the apostles and those associated with them—the Apostolic Fathers—were not so faithful and successful. Rather like the Hebrew race, they failed to maintain the truth committed to them; and it is our

---

1. <Ms III[c] adds "ed" to make "blessed"—*Ed.*>
2. <Ms III[*] "bear witness in all the world"—*Ed.*>

business in this chapter to trace the melancholy story of the departure of the primitive church from this great doctrine of the Christ and of the apostles.

THE CHRISTIAN DOCTRINE OF GOD

The existence of God both Jesus and the apostles accepted as a fact. In all the teachings of the former he nowhere seeks to prove God's existence. He assumes that and proceeds from that basis with his mission. He declares the fact that God was his Father and frequently calls himself the Son of God (John 10; Matt. 27; Mark 14:61-62). After his resurrection and departure into heaven, the apostles taught that he, the Son of God, was with God the Father in the beginning; that he, as well as the Father, was God; that under the direction of the Father he was the creator of worlds; that without him was not anything made that was made (for all of which, see John 1:1-4, 14; Heb. 1:1-3). That in him dwelt all the fullness of the Godhead bodily (Col. 1:15-19; 2:9); and that he was the express image of the Father's person (Heb. 1:2-3). Jesus himself taught that he and the Father were one (John 10:30; 17:11-22); that whosoever had seen him had seen the Father also (John 14:9), that it was part of his mission to reveal God the Father through his own personality; for as was the Son, so too was the Father (John 1:18; 14:1-9). Hence, Jesus was God manifested in the flesh—a revelation of God to the world (1 Tim. 3:16). That is, a revelation not only of the being of God, but of the kind of being God is.

Jesus also taught and prayed (and in doing so showed in what the "oneness" of himself and his Father consisted) that the disciples might be one with him, and also one with each other, as he and the Father were one (John 14:10-11, 19-20; also, John 17:11-23). Not one in person, of course—not all merged into one individual, and all distinctions of personality and individuality lost—but one in mind, in knowledge, in love, in will; one by reason of the indwelling in all of the one Spirit, even as the mind and will of God the Father was also in Jesus Christ (Eph. 3:14-19).

The Holy Ghost, too, was upheld by the Christian religion to be God (Acts 5:1-11).[3] Jesus ascribed to him a distinct personality; as proceeding from the Father; as sent forth in the name of the Son; as feeling love; <as> experiencing grief; as forbidding; as abiding; as teaching; as bearing witness; as appointing to work; and as interceding for men. All of which clearly establishes for him, too, a personality (John 14:16–15:27).

The distinct personality of these three individual Deities (united, however, into one Godhead, or Divine Council) was made apparent at the baptism of Jesus; for

3. To lie to the Holy Ghost is to lie to God, because the Holy Ghost is God.

as he, God the Son, came up out of the water from his baptism at the hands of John, a manifestation of the presence of the Holy Ghost was given in the sign of the dove, which rested upon Jesus; while out of the glory of heaven surrounding the personage in the scene, the voice of God the Father was heard, saying, "This [referring to Jesus] is my beloved Son, in whom I am well pleased" (Matt. 3:16).

The distinctness of the personality of each member of the Godhead is also again shown by the commandment to baptize those who believe the gospel in the name of each person of the Holy Trinity; that is, "in the name of the Father, and of the Son, and of the Holy Ghost" (Matt. 28:19). And again, also in the apostolic benediction, viz., "The grace of the Lord Jesus Christ, and the love of God, and the communion of the Holy Ghost, be with you all" (2 Cor. 13:14).

THE CHRISTIAN GODHEAD[4]

These three personages constitute the Christian Godhead, the Holy Trinity. In early Christian theology they were regarded as the supreme governing and creating power in heaven and in earth. Of which Trinity the Father was worshipped in the name of the Son, while the Holy Ghost bore record of both the Father and the Son. And though the Holy Trinity was made up of three distinct personages as being individuals, yet did they constitute but one Godhead, or supreme governing power.

This outline of the doctrine of God derived from the New Testament represents God as being anthropomorphic; that is, like man in form; or, rather, it reaffirms the old doctrine found in the book of Genesis, viz., that man is created in the image of God and after His likeness. The outline of New Testament doctrine also ascribes to God what are called human mind qualities and feelings; but as in the foregoing we first say that God is represented as being in human form, and then to get the exact truth say, "or, rather, man was created in the image and likeness of God"; so in this latter case, when we have said that the doctrine of the New Testament ascribes human mind qualities and feelings to God, to get the exact truth we should say: or, rather, man possesses in lower degree the mind qualities of God—the power of knowing, willing, judging, loving, etc.—though it should be stated, of course, that man does not possess these attributes in their perfection, as God does. The same may also be said of the physical perfections. While man has been created in the image and very likeness of God, yet our bodies in their present state of imperfection—sometimes stunted in growth, deformed, diseased, subject to sickness, wasting decay, and death—can not be said to be like God's glorious,

4. <Ms III[c] adds "The Christian Godhead"—*Ed.*>

perfect, physical, but also spiritual, body. Yet we have the Divine word that our bodies finally shall be made like unto His body:

> For our conversation is in heaven; from whence also we look for the Savior, the Lord Jesus Christ: who shall change our vile body, that it may be fashioned like unto his glorious body, according to the working whereby he is able even to subdue all things unto Himself (Philip. 3:20-21).

So also the attributes of the spirit of man—the attributes of the mind—now imperfect and limited in the range of vision and apprehension of things, owing largely to the conditions in which man finds himself placed in this earth-life (and all for a wise purpose in God's economy); yet the time will come that it will be with the mind as with the body; for God shall change our perhaps vile mind that it may be fashioned like unto his own glorious mind, "according to the working whereby he is able even to subdue all things unto himself." That whereas "now we may see only as through a glass darkly," but when that more perfect state is come, we shall see as we are seen; that whereas now we know but in part, then we shall know even as we are known (1 Cor. 13:9-12).

FIRST AUTHORITATIVE FORMULA ON DOCTRINE OF GOD[5]

Perhaps the finest formula of an expression of faith as to God and which was a truly authoritative Christian creed came from the famous conversation of St. Peter with the Christ. "Whom do ye say that I am?" inquired Jesus of the apostles, and Simon Peter answered: "Thou art the Christ, the Son of the Living God." Whereupon, the Master declared that his Father had revealed this truth to the apostle, and upon that truth he would build his church. The Christ's benediction also went with St. Peter's confession: "Blessed art thou, Simon Bar-jona, for flesh and blood hath not revealed it unto thee, but my Father which is in heaven" (Matt. 16:17). Incidentally, it should be noted here that the Christ not only accepts this declaration of himself as the "Son of the Living God," but proclaims that "Living God" as his "Father in Heaven."

As an instance of the felt need of some form of a confession as warranting entrance into the church, we may take the case of the officer of the court of Queen Candace, instructed from the scriptures on the redemptive mission of the Christ by Philip, one of the seven evangelists:

> *Officer*: "What doth hinder me to be baptized?"
> *Philip*: "If thou believest with all thine heart, thou mayest."
> *Officer*: "I believe that Jesus Christ is the Son of God" (Acts 8:36-37).

---

5. <Ms III^{c} adds "First Authoritative Formula On Doctrine of God"—*Ed.*>

The chariot was halted straightway and the baptism performed.

St. Paul represented the "word of faith" which we preach to be that "if thou shalt confess with thy mouth the Lord Jesus and shall believe in thine heart that God hath raised him from the dead, thou shalt be saved" (Rom. 10:8-9).

THE APOSTLES' CREED

According to a tradition in the early Christian church, before the apostles disbursed to go upon their world-wide mission they met and formulated what stands in ecclesiastical history as the "Apostles' Creed." The genuineness, however, of this tradition is doubted, indeed it is strongly denied by respectable authority. Dr. Mosheim doubts of the apostles formulating it in the following language:

> There is indeed extant a brief summary of Christian doctrines, which is called the "Apostles' Creed," and which from the fourth century onward was attributed to Christ's ambassadors themselves. But at this day all who have any knowledge of antiquity confess unanimously that this opinion is a mistake and has no foundation.[6]

To this also substantially agrees Dr. Neander. The creed itself is as follows:

> I believe in God, the Father Almighty, and in Jesus Christ, His only begotten Son, our Lord, who was born of the Virgin Mary by the Holy Ghost, was crucified under Pontius Pilate, buried, arose from the dead on the third day, ascended to the heavens, and sits at the right hand of the Father; whence he will come, to judge the living and the dead; and in the Holy Spirit; the Holy Church; the remission of sins; and the resurrection of the body.[7]

While in the face of the historical evidence to the contrary we may not believe this "creed" was formulated by a council of the apostles; and also certain inconsistencies therein would bar one from believing this "creed" to be of apostolic origin, still, emphasizing as it does, belief "in God, the Father Almighty, and in Jesus Christ, His only begotten Son, our Lord, . . . and in the Holy Spirit" (i.e., the Holy Ghost)—in all this, since it became so widely accepted by the church during the early Christian centuries, it is a valuable Christian document on the belief in God, especially as expressed in the Holy Trinity.

> The Apostolic Fathers [Christian writers contemporaneous with some of the

---

6. John Lawrence von Mosheim, *Institutes of Ecclesiastical History, Ancient and Modern, in Four Books*, trans. James Murdock (New York: Harper and Brothers, 1839), bk. i, cent. i, part ii, chap. 3, p. 79.

7. Augustus Neander, *General History of the Christian Religion and Church*, trans. Joseph Torrey (New York: Hurd and Houghton, 1871), 1:306-307.

> Apostles] . . . attempted no speculative construction of the doctrine of the Trinity. They merely repeat[ed] the biblical phraseology, without endeavoring to collect and combine the data of revelation into a systematic form. They invariably speak of [the] Christ as Divine and make no distinction in their modes of thought and expression between the Deity of the Son and that of the Father. These immediate pupils of the apostles enter into no speculative investigation of the doctrine of the Logos [the "Word"], but content[ed] themselves with the simplest and most common expressions respecting the Trinity.[8]

THE PATRISTIC VIEW OF THE DIVINITY OF CHRIST

The following brief excerpts from the early Fathers of the church will be sufficient to indicate the freedom with which the Fathers apply the term of God to the second person, who is most commonly conceived of as the God-man and called Jesus Christ by them. "Brethren," says Clement of Rome (and bishop; lived 30-100 A.D.), "we ought to conceive of Jesus Christ as of God, as of the judge of the living and the dead."[9] Ignatius addresses the church at Ephesus "as united and elected by a true passion, according to the will of the Father, and of Jesus Christ, our God."[10] Writing to the church Ignatius of Antioch[11] describes the saints there in his greeting as "illuminated by the will of him who willeth all things that are according to the love of Jesus Christ, our God."[12] In somewhat like manner he <Clement of Rome> makes reference to the Holy Trinity: "Have we not one God, and one Christ? Is there not one Spirit of Grace, who is poured out upon us?"[13] Polycarp (bishop of Smyrna, lived 69-155 A.D.) closed his prayer at the stake by saying: "I praise Thee [God the Father] for this, . . . together with the eternal and heavenly Jesus, Thy beloved Son, with whom [and] to Thee, and the Holy Ghost, be glory, both now, and to all succeeding ages."[14]

The foregoing doctrine of God, taught to the Christians in apostolic times,

---

8. William G. T. Shedd, *A History of Christian Doctrine*, 10th ed. (New York: Charles Scribner's Sons, 1891), 1:264-65.

9. Clement of Rome, Second Epistle to the Corinthians, chap. 1. <For a discussion of the spuriousness of this letter and its probable second century date, see Michael W. Holmes, ed., *The Apostolic Fathers*, 2d ed., trans. Joseph B. Lightfoot and John R. Harmer (Grand Rapids, MI: Baker Book House, 1989), 65-67–*Ed.*>

10. <Ignatius of Antioch, Epistle to the Ephesians, heading–*Ed.*>

11. <Ms III "Clement of Rome," which is corrected to "Ignatius of Antioch"–*Ed.*>

12. <Ignatius of Antioch, Epistle to the Romans, heading–*Ed.*>

13. <Clement of Rome, First Epistle to the Corinthians, chap. 46–*Ed.*>

14. Shedd, *History of Christian Doctrine*, 1:267. <The quotation is from the Martyrdom of Polycarp, chap. 14–*Ed.*>

awakened their pious reverence without exciting their curiosity. They dealt with no metaphysical abstractions, but were contented to accept the teachings of the apostles in humble faith, and believed that Jesus Christ was the complete manifestation of Deity, and the express image of God, His Father; and hence, a revelation to them of God; while the Holy Ghost they accepted as God's witness and messenger to their souls for the truth about God and the gospel.

PAGANIZATION OF THE NEW TESTAMENT DOCTRINE OF GOD

But primitive Christianity, as is well known, came in contact with other doctrines concerning Deity. It was almost immediately brought in touch with the mysticism of the Orient, and also with the philosophy of the Greeks, who took so much delight in intellectual subtleties. In the Oriental philosophies, and in the Greek, there was conceived the idea of a trinity in Deity; an idea which possibly may have come down from the doctrines revealed to the patriarchs concerning the Godhead, but which had been corrupted and rendered unintelligible by the vain philosophizings of men. In some of the Oriental systems the trinity or trimurti consisted of Brahma, the creator; Vishnu, the preserver; and Siva, the destroyer. It will be seen, however, that this trinity is not necessarily one of persons, or individuals, but may be one of attributes, qualities, or even a trinity of functions in one being; and in this way it is usually understood.[15]

DOCTRINE OF TRINITIES[16]

Plato's trinity is sometimes stated in the terms, "First Cause; Reason or Logos; and Soul of the Universe"; but more commonly in these: "Goodness, Intellect, and Will." The nature of the Greek trinity has long been a matter of contention among the learned, and one indeed that is not settled to this day. Is there indicated in his system "a true and proper tri-personality, or merely a personification of three impersonalities," a trinity of attributes or functions? The answers to these questions are varied, and would require too much space for consideration here. Christians having been taught to accept the New Testament doctrine of the Father, Son, and Holy Spirit, as constituting one Godhead, no sooner came in contact with the philosophies of the Greeks and Egyptians than there was an effort made to identify the Christian trinity with that of the Greek and other philosophies.

The temptation to do this was very great. Christianity was a proscribed

---

15. Shedd, *History of Christian Doctrine*, 1:244 et seq. and note.

16. <Ms III^c adds "Doctrine of Trinities"—*Ed.*>

religion[17] and its followers detested. Whenever it could be shown, therefore, that under new symbols the church was really teaching the same doctrines that the old philosophers did, it was regarded as a distinct gain to Christianity. The mere fact of Christianity teaching a trinity of any kind was a sufficient basis of comparison, under the temptation offered, and hence in a short time we have the alleged followers of Christ involved in all the metaphysical disputations of the age. The chief difficulty in those speculations was to define the nature of the "Logos," or "Word" of God—a title that is given to our Savior by the Apostle St. John, be it remembered (John 1:1-5, 14).

THE NATURE AND RELATIONS OF THE CHRIST[18]

Adopting absolute "being" as the postulate of their conception of God, absolute oneness, and therefore absolute singleness, their difficulties arose in trying to reconcile the existence of three persons in the Godhead to the postulate of unity. The disputations were carried on chiefly concerning the Christ, the "Word" in his relationship to the Godhead; and the disputants concerned themselves with such questions as these: "Is Jesus the Word?" "If he be the 'Word,' did he emanate from God in time, or before time?" "If he emanated from God, is he co-eternal and of the same, that is, identical substance with Him, or merely of a similar substance?" "Is he distinct from the Father, that is, separate from Him, or is he not?" "Is he made or begotten?" "Can he beget in his turn?" "Has he paternity, or productive virtue without paternity?"

Similar questions were asked as to the other person of the Godhead—the Holy Ghost. These questions were violently agitated at Alexandria by the bishop of that city, Alexander, and one of the presbyters, Arius, 318-321 A.D.; thence, the contention spread throughout Christendom, and culminated finally in the Council of Nicea, 325 A.D. Arius held the doctrine that the Logos or "Word" was a dependent or spontaneous production created out of nothing by the will of the Father; hence, the Son of God, by whom all things were made, begotten before all worlds; but there had been a time when the Logos was not; and also he was of a substance, however similar it might be, different from the Father. This doctrine, in the minds of the opponents of Arius, detracted from the divine nature of Christ; in fact, denied him true Deity, and relegated him to the position of a creature (i.e., a created being) against which the piety of a large number of Christians rebelled. After six years of hot disputation and frequent appeals by the contestants to the emperor Constantine, the council of Nicea was assembled and the mysteries of the

---

17. <Ms III[*] "a prescribed religion"—*Ed.*>

18. <Ms III[c] adds "The Nature and Relations of the Christ"—*Ed.*>

Christian faith submitted to public debate, a portion of the time, at least, in the presence of the emperor, who to some extent seemed to exercise the functions of president over the assembly. The doctrine of Arius was condemned, and after "long deliberations, among struggles, and scrupulous examinations," the following "creed" was adopted:

THE NICENE CREED

> We believe in one God, the Father Almighty, Creator of all things visible and invisible; and in one Lord Jesus Christ, the Son of God, only begotten of the Father, that is, of the substance of the Father; God of God, Light of Light, very God of very God; begotten, not made; being of the same substance with the Father, by whom all things were made in heaven and in earth; who for us men and for our salvation came down from heaven, was incarnate, was made man; suffered, rose again the third day, ascended into the heavens; and he will come to judge the living and the dead; and in the Holy Ghost. Those who say there was a time when he was not, and he was not before he was begotten, and he was made of nothing [he was created], or who say that he is of another hypostasis, or of another substance [than the Father], or that the Son of God is created, that he is mutable, or subject to change, the Catholic church anathematizes.

Arius himself was condemned as a heretic and banished into one of the remote provinces, Ilyricum, his friends and disciples branded by law, with the odious name of "Porphyrians," because it is supposed that Arius like Porphyr,[19] had sought to injure Christianity. His writings (i.e., of Arius) were condemned to the flames and a capital punishment was pronounced against those in whose possession they should be found. Three years later, however, through the influence of the women at the imperial court, Constantine softened in his demeanor towards Arius and his followers. The exiles were recalled and Arius himself was received at court and his faith approved by a synod of prelates and presbyters at Jerusalem; but on the day that he was to be publicly received in the cathedral church at Constantinople, by the order of the emperor, who by the way received the sacrament at the hands of Arians, he expired under circumstances which have led many to believe that other means than the prayers of the orthodox against him were the cause of his death. The leaders of the orthodox party, Athanasius of Alexandria, Eustathius of Antioch, and Paul of Constantinople, were now to feel the wrath of the first

---

19. <Ms III* "with the odious name of 'Porphyr,'" but due to skipping from "Porphyr-ians" to "Porphyr" the wording "ians because it is supposed that Arius like Porphyr" from the earlier draft was omitted and these are reinserted above and below the line in Ms III^c^—*Ed.*>

Christian emperor. They were deposed on various occasions and by the sentences of numerous councils and banished into distant provinces. In fact, so far from the adoption of the Nicene creed ending the conflict which had arisen, it was more like the opening of that controversy which agitated Christendom for so long, and resulted in so many shameful conflicts. Councils were arrayed against councils, and though they never could convince one another of error, they never failed, in the spirit of such Christian charity as was then extant, to close their decrees with anathemas. Votes were bartered for and purchased in those councils, and the facts justify the latent sarcasm in Gibbon's remark that "the cause of truth and justice was promoted by the influence of gold."[20] There were persecutions and counter-persecutions, as now one party and then the other prevailed; there were assassinations and bloody battles over this doctrine of Deity, the accounts of which fill, as they also disgrace, our Christian annals. The creed which was adopted at Nicea, however, became the settled doctrine of orthodox Christendom, and remains so to this day.

It may be thought that this historical setting has no place in this writing, but how else than by the setting down of these historical facts—well-attested by the highest authority—shall the spirit of this controversy be known?

THE ATHANASIAN CREED

It is doubtful if the creed called Athanasian was really formed by Athanasius, bishop of Alexandria, and in the fourth century. The more authoritative opinion seems to be that[21] "the creed used in the Catholic, Lutheran, and English churches, and called the Nicene Creed, is in reality the creed set forth by the Council of Constantinople"[22] in the fourth century,[23] but however much doubt may be thrown upon its authorship, no one hesitates to accept it as the explanation of the orthodox Christian doctrine of Deity; and, in fact, it is accepted as one of the important symbols of the Christian faith, and is as follows:

> We worship one God in Trinity, and Trinity in Unity, neither confounding the persons nor dividing the substance. For there is one person of the Father, another of the Son, and another of the Holy Ghost. But the Godhead of the Father, Son, and

---

20. <Edward Gibbon, *The History of the Decline and Fall of the Roman Empire*, ed. John B. Bury (London: Methuen and Co., 1909-14), chap. 21, 2:390—*Ed.*>

21. <Ms III* "seems to be that it was composed by"; after the words "it was composed by" were deleted, Ms III[c] adds the quotation from Mosehim—*Ed.*>

22. Mosheim, *Institutes of Ecclesiastical History*, bk. ii, cent. iv, pt. ii, chap. 5, p. 291, n. 22.

23. <Ms III "and in the fif [*sic*] century," which is corrected to "fourth"—*Ed.*>

> Holy Ghost is all one: the glory equal, the majesty co-eternal. Such as the Father is, such is the Son, and such is the Holy Ghost. The Father uncreate, the Son uncreate, and the Holy Ghost uncreate. The Father incomprehensible, the Son incomprehensible, and the Holy Ghost incomprehensible. The Father eternal, the Son eternal, and the Holy Ghost eternal. And yet there are not three eternals, but one eternal. As also there are not three incomprehensibles, nor three uncreate, but one uncreate and one incomprehensible. So likewise the Father is almighty, the Son almighty, and the Holy Ghost almighty; and yet they are not three almighties, but one almighty. So the Father is God, the Son is God, and the Holy Ghost is God; and yet there are not three Gods, but one God.

As already stated, this creed of St. Athanasius is quite generally accepted as one of the symbols of the orthodox Christian faith. It is understood that these creeds—the Apostles', the Nicene, and Athanasian—teach that God is incorporeal, that is to say, an immaterial being. The Catholic Church says: "There is but one God, the Creator of heaven and earth, the Supreme, incorporeal, uncreated Being, who exists of Himself and is infinite in all His attributes."[24] While the Church of England teaches in her articles of faith "that there is but one living and true God, everlasting, without body,[25] parts, or passions, of infinite power, wisdom, and goodness."[26] This view of God as an incorporeal, immaterial, bodiless, partless, passionless being is now, and has been from the days of the great apostasy from God and Christ in the second and third centuries, the doctrine of Deity generally accepted by Christendom. The simple doctrine of the Christian Godhead, set forth in the New Testament is corrupted by the jargon of these creeds and their explanations. The learned who profess a belief of them are wandering in the darkness of the mysticisms of the old pagan philosophies. No wonder that Athanasius himself, whom Gibbon with a quiet sarcasm calls the most sagacious of the Christian theologians:

> Candidly confessed that, whenever he forced his understanding to meditate on the divinity of the Logos [and which, of course, involved the whole doctrine of the Godhead], his toilsome and unavailing efforts recoiled on themselves; that the more he thought, the less he comprehended: and the more he wrote, the less capable was he of expressing his thoughts![27]

---

24. Joseph Faà di Bruno, *Catholic Belief; or, A Short and Simple Exposition of Catholic Doctrine*, ed. Louis A. Lambert (New York: Benziger Brothers, 1884), 25.

25. I.e., without materiality—non-material.

26. Book of Common Prayer, Articles of Religion, article 1.

27. <Gibbon, *Decline and Fall*, 2:360—*Ed.*>

It is a fine passage with which Gibbon closes his reflections upon this subject, and hence I shall give it place here:

> In every step of the inquiry, we are compelled to feel and acknowledge the immeasurable disproportion between the size of the object and the capacity of the human mind. We may try to abstract the notions of time, of space, and of matter, which so closely adhere to all the perceptions of our experimental knowledge. But, as soon as we presume to reason of infinite substance, of spiritual generation;[28] as often as we deduce any positive conclusions from a negative idea, we are involved in darkness, perplexity, and inevitable contradiction.[29]

Recurrence to the New Testament doctrine of God, and a comparison of it with the doctrine of Deity set forth in the Nicene and Athanasian creeds, will exhibit the wide departure—the absolute apostasy—that has taken place in respect of this most fundamental of all doctrines of religion—the doctrine of God. Truly "Christians" have denied "the Lord that bought them" (2 Pet. 2:1), and turned literally to fables. They have enthroned a conception of a negative idea of "being," which can stand in no possible relationship to man, nor man to it; and to this they ascribe divine attributes and give it title, knee and adoration and worship which belong to God alone.

One does not have far to seek to find the origin of those ideas which led the early Christians away from the plain anthropomorphism of the New Testament revelation of God through Jesus Christ. It has already been referred to in this chapter, but further consideration of it is deemed necessary to a full presentation of the case.

THE PAGAN ORIGIN OF THE CREEDAL DOCTRINE OF GOD CONCEDED

In his great work on the *History of Christian Doctrine*, Mr. William G. T. Shedd says:

> The early Fathers, in their defenses of Christianity against the[ir] pagan opponent[s], contend that the better pagan writers themselves agree with the new religion in teaching that there is one Supreme Being. Lactantius (*Institutiones*, i, 5), after quoting the Orphic Poets, Hesiod, Virgil, and Ovid, in proof that the heathen poets taught the unity of the supreme deity, affirms that the better pagan philosophers agree with them in this. "Aristotle," he says, "although he disagrees with himself and says many things

28. <Ms III "or spiritual generation," but Gibbon's text has "of spiritual generation"—*Ed.*>

29. Gibbon, *Decline and Fall*, chap 21, 2:360-61.

that are self-contradictory, yet testifies that one supreme mind rules over the world. Plato, who is regarded as the wisest philosopher of them all, plainly and openly defends the doctrine of a divine monarchy, and denominates the supreme being, not ether, nor reason, nor nature, but as he is, God; and asserts that by him this perfect and admirable world was made. And Cicero follows Plato, frequently confessing the deity, and calls him the Supreme Being, in his treatise on the Laws."[30]

It is conceded by Christian writers that the Christian doctrine of God is not expressed in New Testament terms, but in the terms of Greek and Roman metaphysics, as witness the following from the very able article in *The Encyclopædia Britannica* on "Theism," by the Rev. Dr. Flint, Professor of Divinity, University of Edinburgh:

> The proposition<s> constitutive of the dogma of the Trinity—the propositions in the symbols of Nice, Constantinople, and Toledo relative to the immanent distinctions and relations in the Godhead—were not drawn directly from the New Testament and could not be expressed in New Testament terms. They were the product<s> of reason speculating on a revelation to faith—the New Testament representation of God as a Father, a Redeemer, and a Sanctifier . . . were only formed through centuries of effort, only elaborated by the aid of the conceptions and formulated in the terms of Greek and Roman metaphysics.[31]

The same authority says:

> The massive defense of theism erected by the Cambridge school of philosophy against atheism, fatalism, and the denial of moral distinctions was avowedly built on a Platonic foundation.[32]

Guizot,[33] the eminent statesman and historian of France, in one of his lectures of which this is a subdivision of the title—"Of the Transition from Pagan Philosophy to Christian Theology"—says in concluding his treatment of this theme:

> I have thus exhibited the fact which I indicated in the outset, the fusion of pagan philosophy with Christian theology, the metamorphosis of the one into the other. And it is remarkable that the reasoning applied to the establishment of the spirituality of the soul is evidently derived from the ancient philosophy, rather than from Christianity, and that the author <Mamertius Claudienus> seems more especially to aim at

30. Shedd, *History of Christian Doctrine*, 1:55-56.

31. <Robert Flint, "Theism," in *The Encyclopædia Britannica: A Dictionary of Arts, Sciences, and General Literature*, 9th ed. (New York: The Werner Co., 1900), 23:240—*Ed.*>

32. <Ibid., 23:245—*Ed.*>

33. <Ms III "Quizot"—*Ed.*>

convincing the theologians, by proving to them that the Christian faith has nothing in all this which is not perfectly reconcilable with the results derived from pure reason.[34]

In method of thought also, no less than in conclusions, the most influential of the Christian fathers on these subjects followed the Greek philosophers rather than the writers of the New Testament. Shedd, the author of the *History of Christian Doctrine*, says:

> Platonism and Aristotelianism . . . exerted more influence upon the intellectual methods of men, taking in the whole time since their appearance, than all other systems combined. They certainly influenced the Greek mind, and Grecian culture, more than all the other philosophical systems. They reappear in Roman philosophy—so far as Rome had any philosophy. We shall see that Plato, Aristotle, and Cicero exerted more influence than all other philosophical minds united, upon the greatest of the Christian Fathers, upon the greatest of the Schoolmen, and upon the theologians of the Reformation—Calvin and Melanchthon. And if we look at European philosophy, as it has been unfolded in England, Germany, and France, we shall perceive that all the modern theistic schools have discussed the standing problems of human reason, in very much the same manner in which the reason of Plato and Aristotle discussed them twenty-two centuries ago. Bacon, Descartes, Leibniz, and Kant, so far as the first principles of intellectual and moral philosophy are concerned, agree with their Grecian predecessors. A student who has mastered the two systems of the Academy and the Lyceum, will find in modern philosophy (with the exception of the department of natural science) very little that is true, that may not be found for substance, and germinally, in the Greek theism.[35]

It is hoped that enough is said here to establish the fact that the conception of God as "pure being," "immaterial," "without form," or "<without> parts or passions," as held by orthodox Christianity, has its origin in pagan philosophy, not in Jewish nor Christian revelation.

THE CALL—"BACK TO GOD"[36]

In view of all this that is here set forth, we can understand how it is that to St. John when given the vision of an angel in the hour of God's judgment, in the last days, coming with the "everlasting gospel" to be preached to every nation and

---

34. <François P. G. Guizot, *The History of Civilization, from the Fall of the Roman Empire to the French Revolution*, trans. William Hazlitt (New York: D. Appleton and Co., 1867), vol. 2, lecture 6—*Ed.*>

35. <Shedd, *History of Christian Doctrine*, 1:51-52—*Ed.*>

36. <Ms III^{c} adds "The Call—'Back to God'"—*Ed.*>

kindred and tongue and people, would make as part of that message this ringing call of back to God:

> FEAR GOD, AND GIVE GLORY TO HIM, FOR THE HOUR OF HIS JUDGMENT IS COME; AND WORSHIP HIM THAT MADE HEAVEN, AND EARTH, AND THE SEA, AND THE FOUNTAINS OF WATER (Rev. 14:7).

Evidently in the hour or time of God's judgment men would not be worshipping God "that made heaven and earth and the sea"—hence, the angel warning them and calling upon them to the worship of the true, and living, and personal God; the Father, Son, and Holy Ghost; three personal beings united in one Godhead, or Divine Council, in which all fullness and perfection dwells.

CHAPTER XXI

Of Kindred Subjects to the Knowledge of God Which Men Have Misapprehended

SCRIPTURE READING LESSON

Analysis

I. Creation.

II. Philosophers on Creation.

III. Bible Meaning of "Create."

IV. The Origin of Man.

V. Purpose of God in the Earth-Life of Man—Not Known.

VI. Several "Origins of Man" Have No Warrant of Scripture.

References

All the Bible texts and works cited in the text of this chapter, and often the context of the quoted scripture or works.

The standard biblical dictionaries and commentators under subjects here treated.

Joseph Smith, *The King Follett Discourse; The Being and Kind of Being God Is; The Immortality of the Intelligence of Man*, annotated by B. H. Roberts (Salt Lake City: Magazine Printing Co., 1926), pamphlet.

B. H. Roberts, "Man's Relationship to Deity," published in *The Gospel: An Exposition of Its First Principles*, 3d ed. (Salt Lake City: The Deseret News, 1901).

CHAPTER XXI

Of Kindred Subjects to the Knowledge of God Which Men Have Misapprehended

CREATION

It was not alone in the matter of departing from the revealed God of the Old and the New Testament that the Jewish and the Christian world turned from the path direct respecting the knowledge of God. Kindred things—the creation of the world, and the origin and nature of man are among the things of revealed knowledge that have been lost. The Christians converted into dogma the false notion of the creation of the universe out of "nothing," assuming God's transcendence of the universe. They accepted the idea that "creation" meant absolutely bringing from non-existence into existence, and ultimately pronounced anathema upon those who might attempt to teach otherwise. While it is true that the use of the word "create" is applied to the idea of bringing forth something from nothing, from non-existence into existence, yet there is nothing in the word itself, we are assured on good authority, that demands any such interpretation of its use in Holy Scripture. On the contrary, "fashioned" or "formed" from pre-existent materials[1] is just as consistent an interpretation of "create" or "creation" as the idea of creation from nothing. After conceding that most of the Jewish philosophers find in Gen. 1:1 that "creation" meant "creation out of nothing," *The Jewish Encyclopedia* says that the etymological meaning of the verb ("create") "is 'to cut out and [to] put into shape' [fashion], and thus presupposes the use of material."[2] It is significant that in Gen. 1:1 it is the verb that is used—"in the beginning God created" etc.—that is "cut out," "put into shape," or fashioned out of pre-existent material, the heaven and the earth.

Even Roman Catholic authorities—and thus the Roman Catholic Church may be regarded as the staunchest proponent of the doctrine of "creation from

---

1. <Ms III* "material"—*Ed.*>

2. Emil G. Hirsch, "Creation," in *The Jewish Encyclopedia: A Descriptive Record of the History, Religion, Literature, and Customs of the Jewish People from the Earliest Times to the Present Day*, ed. Isidore Singer (New York: Funk and Wagnalls Co., 1903), 4:336.

nothing"—concedes that the idea of "creation from nothing" is "the implicit, rather than specifically explicit, statement of the Bible."[3] It is only fair to say, however, that this authority holds that her deductions from the implication of scripture on the creation of the universe from nothing is warranted. It is important, however, that this authority should admit that the "creation from nothing" idea is implicitly rather than explicitly found in the Bible. The Protestant division<s> of Christendom have generally been in substantial agreement with both Jews and Catholics on this subject.

A word in evidence of what was said a moment since as to good authority sustaining the view that there is nothing in the word "create" itself that requires its interpretation to mean "create out of nothing." This in addition to what is quoted above from the Jewish and Roman Catholic encyclopedias.

The Reverend Baden Powell of Oxford University, writing for Kitto's *Cyclopædia of Biblical Literature*, says:

> The meaning of this word [create] has been commonly associated with the idea of "making out of nothing." But when we come to inquire more precisely into the subject, we can of course satisfy ourselves as to the meaning only from an examination of the original phrases.

The professor then proceeds to say that three distinct Hebrew verbs are in different places employed with reference to the same divine act, and may be translated, respectively, "create," "make," "form or fashion." The professor continues:

> Now though each of these has its shade of distinction, yet the best critics understand them as so nearly synonymous that, at least in regard to the idea of making out of nothing, little or no foundation for that doctrine can be obtained from the . . . first of these words.[4]

And, of course, if no foundation for the doctrine can be obtained from the first of these words—viz., the verb translated "create," then the chances are still less for there being any foundation for the doctrine of creation from nothing in the verb<s> translated "made," "formed," or "fashioned."

Prof. Powell further says:

> The idea of "creation," as meaning absolutely "making out of nothing," or

3. Francis P. Siegfried, "Creation," in *The Catholic Encyclopedia: An International Work of Reference on the Constitution, Doctrine, Discipline, and History of the Catholic Church*, ed. Charles G. Herbermann et alia (New York: Robert Appleton Co., 1908), 4:471.

4. <Baden Powell, "Creation," in John Kitto, ed., A *Cyclopædia of Biblical Literature* (New York: Mark H. Newman, 1845), 476-77—Ed.>

> calling into existence that which did not exist before, in the strictest sense of the term . . . is not a doctrine of scripture; but it has been held by many on the grounds of natural theology, as enhancing the ideas we form of the divine power, and more especially since the contrary must imply the belief in the eternity and self-existence of matter.[5]

Dr. William Smith's great *Dictionary of the Bible* (Hackett edition, 1894) has no article on the term "create" or "creation," but in the article "earth" we have reference to the subject, and really an implied explanation as to why his work contains no treatise on "create" or "creation":

> The act of creation itself, as recorded in the first chapter of Genesis, is a subject beyond and above the experience of man; human language, derived, as it originally was, from the sensible and material world, fails to find an adequate term to describe the act; for our word "create" and the Hebrew *br'*, though most appropriate to express the idea of an original creation, are yet applicable and must necessarily be applicable to other modes of creation; nor does the addition of such expressions as "out of things that were not" . . . or "not from things which appear" . . . contribute much to the force of the declaration.[6]

PHILOSOPHERS ON CREATION[7]

The philosophers with equal emphasis sustain the contention as to the facts of science being against the idea of "creation from nothing." Herbert Spencer, in his *First Principles*, says:

> There was once universally current, a notion that things could vanish into absolute nothing, or arise out of absolute nothing. . . . The current theology, in its teaching<s> respecting the beginning and end of the world, is clearly pervaded by it. . . . The gradual accumulation of experiences . . . has tended slowly to reverse this conviction; until now, the doctrine that matter is indestructible has become a commonplace. All the apparent proofs that something came out of nothing, a wider knowledge has one by one cancelled.[8]

John Fiske follows Spencer and in his *Cosmic Philosophy* sums up the matter

---

5. <Ibid., 479—*Ed.*>

6. <William L. Bevan, "Earth," in Horatio B. Hackett and Ezra Abbot, eds., *Dr. William Smith's Dictionary of the Bible, Comprising Its Antiquities, Biography, Geography, and Natural History* (Boston: Houghton, Mifflin and Co., 1894), 1:631—*Ed.*>

7. <Ms III^{c} adds "Philosophers On Creation"—*Ed.*>

8. Herbert Spencer, *First Principles* (New York: D. Appleton, 1896), 172-73.

in these words: "It is now inconceivable that a particle of matter should either come into existence or lapse into non-existence."[9]

BIBLE MEANING OF "CREATE"[10]

Turning to the Bible, and we have in the chapter which is supposed to dispose of the matter of creation (Gen. 1:1-2) three things given as existing when the work of the creation began:

(1) "In the beginning God . . .";

(2) "The earth, without form and void; and darkness upon the face of the deep" (chaos or earth-material in chaotic existence);

(3) The Spirit of God—"and the Spirit of God moved upon the face of the water."

These three things we have and then the work of "creation" or "fashioning" began. "And God said, Let there be light and there was light" (Gen. 1:3).

This <is> the first creative act; and it occurred on the first of the six creative days. "And God saw the light that it was good and divided the light from the darkness. . . . And the evening and the morning were the first day" (Gen. 1:4-5). Thence followed the other creative acts, climaxed by the creation of man in God's own likeness and in God's own image; and in giving man dominion over the earth.

Two things should here be observed with reference to this sublime account of creation. First, that the whole introduction to the drama of creation (Gen. 1:1) should be rendered in the light thrown upon the whole subject of creation by Genesis 2:4; viz., "These are the generations of the heavens and of the earth *when* they were created, in the day that the Lord God made the earth and the heavens." This rendering of Genesis 1:1-2 will then be, "In the beginning, when God created the heavens and the earth, the earth was without form and void, and darkness was upon the face of the deep." On this rendering creation is not out of nothing, but out of pre-existing material in a state of chaos.

The second thing referred to as necessary to remember in the exposition of the creation story is to note the fact that the creation of the heaven and the earth mentioned in Genesis 1:1—"In the beginning God created the heaven and the earth," etc.—"creation" mentioned there did not precede the work of the six days, but comprised it. The creation did not begin until the first of the six days, when God said on that first day or period, "Let there be light, and there was light."

---

9. John Fiske, *Outlines of Cosmic Philosophy*, in *The Miscellaneous Writings of John Fiske, with Many Portraits of Illustrious Philosophers, Scientists, and Other Men of Note* (Boston and New York: Houghton, Mifflin and Co., 1902), 1:94.

10. <Ms III^{c} adds "Bible Meaning of 'Create'"—*Ed.*>

In addition to the fact that there is no explicit, direct authority from the Bible itself that "creation" is "creation from nothing to something," but on the contrary the etymology of the verb "create" implies creation from pre-existing materials,[11] the theologians of the "creation from nothing" school have to meet the stern facts presented by science on the eternal existence of the universe, manifested both by the uncreatability and the indestructibility of matter and force—and hence, the necessary eternity of the universe. There is a possibility of ceaseless and infinite changes within the universe, and this under the direction of Eternal Intelligences operating within the universe—but no possibility of absolute beginning or absolute end. These subjects have been dealt with in previous pages, to which the attention of the reader is again invited.[12]

We next turn to the second subject mentioned at the beginning of this chapter, viz., the origin and nature of man. These remarks will be addressed only to those people who have supposedly built their faiths upon the revelations of God found in the Old and in the New Testament; and it should be observed that the people having access to the revelations of God and professing belief in them, could more reasonably be expected to have the clearest and most accurate ideas on this subject; but I shall make bold to say that they are without clear-cut, definite ideas upon this important subject; and nowhere is there authoritative statement pointed to by them in the scriptures, or to be found in their creeds in the interpretation of the scriptures, anything that is satisfactory upon this subject.

THE ORIGIN OF MAN

David exclaimed, addressing himself unto God:

> When I consider Thy heavens, the work of Thy fingers, the moon and the stars which Thou hast ordained, What is man, that Thou art mindful of him, and the son of man that Thou visitest him? For Thou hast made him a little lower than the angels, and hast crowned him with glory and honor; Thou madest him to have dominion over the works of Thy hands. Thou hast put all things under his feet. . . . O Lord, our Lord, how excellent is Thy name in all the earth (Ps. 8:3-6, 9).

Paul in substance quotes these words of David (Heb. 2:6-8), but neither David nor Paul answers the questions propounded, nor have others in the Jewish or Christian world given definite, authoritative answer to them. While both Jews and

---

11. <Francis Brown, Samuel R. Driver, and Charles A. Briggs, *A Hebrew and English Lexicon of the Old Testament* (Oxford: Clarendon Press, 1907), 135, translates *b r '* as "shape, fashion, create, always of divine activity"—*Ed.*>

12. See chapters 7 and 8.

Christians[13] may refer man's origin to God, as their "Creator," yet a divided conception is held with reference to the manner of his creation. These views are expressed usually under what is known as "Creationism" or "Traducianism."

Creationism is generally defined as the doctrine that the universe was originally brought into existence without pre-existent material, by the word of God, and also that new species or forms of being have been successively produced by the direct formative exercise of the divine wisdom and power; and as applied to the creation of man's soul, or spirit, that God creates a new soul whenever a human being begins to live. This is the Roman Catholic view, and so far as Protestant divisions commit themselves on the subject, the general Protestant Christian view also. That this is the Catholic view is sustained by their footnote[14] comment on Genesis 2:2, which is as follows: "He still worketh . . . by conserving and governing all things, and creating souls;" and, of course, from the Catholic viewpoint of creating, creates out of nothing new souls, each time that a human being is begotten by act of generation. Professor Draper in his *Conflict between Religion and Science* suggests that "to many devout persons there is something <very> revolting in the suggestion that the Almighty is a servitor to the caprices and lusts of man, and that after a certain term after its origin, it is necessary for Him to create for the embryo a soul."[15]

The other theory of the origin of man already mentioned, "Traducianism," the doctrine that human souls (spirits) are propagated by generation along with human bodies, is opposed, as will be seen, to "Creationism." This theory consigns to man, except as to the first, a purely human origin.

There remains one other theory as to man's origin, but it has no general standing among Jews, Roman Catholics, or Protestants, namely, "Infusionism"; the doctrine that the soul is pre-existent to the body, and infused into it at conception or birth.[16] This is sometimes called "Pre-existentism," meaning that

---

13. <Ms III "both Jewish and Christians"—*Ed.*>

14. <Ms III[c] adds "foot-note"—*Ed.*>

15. John William Draper, *History of the Conflict between Religion and Science*, 6th ed. (New York: D. Appleton and Co., 1875), 127.

16. <Since there exists no official First Presidency statement on this issue, the committee report of May 1930 "questions the advisability of stating any given time when the spirit unites with the body." Roberts does not state a personal preference whether this union of body and spirit occurs at conception or at birth, but five chapters later he expresses a definite opinion in favor of birth, based on the pre-existent Christ's statement to Nephi in the Book of Mormon that the next day he would be born ("Doctrinal Points Questioned by the Committee Which Read the Manuscript of Elder B. H. Roberts, Entitled The Truth, The Way, The Life," attached to Rudger Clawson, Letter to Heber J. Grant, [15 May 1930], in David J. Buerger Collection, Manuscript 622, Bx 10, Fd 8, Manuscripts Division, Marriott

every soul has been in existence either from all eternity or from the creation of the world.[17] The birth of the individual being viewed as the conjoining of the soul and the body in one person. The theory was held by Origen, a Greek Christian Father of the third century. It seems to have been adopted by him from the speculations of Plato and of the Pythagoreans. It has emerged occasionally in modern theology, but as before stated it has had no wide acceptance.

PURPOSE OF GOD IN THE EARTH-LIFE OF MAN[18]

With reference to the purpose of God in the earth-life of man there appears no clear-cut ringing statement to be found in either the Old or the New Testament. As far as that revelation is contained in these books, the best statement on the subject is to be found in St. John's Revelation:

> Thou art worthy, O Lord, to receive glory and honor and power, for Thou hast created all things; and for Thy pleasure they are and were created (Rev. 4:11).

And let this be considered, for the purpose of emphasis, in connection with Proverb 16:4, "The Lord hath made all things for Himself," and again, for enlargement of the view:

> For by Him all things were created that are in heaven and that are in earth, visible or invisible, whether they be thrones, or dominions, or principalities, or powers: all things were created by Him and for Him (Col. 1:16).

And, of course, including man. And this also is quoted by those who seek to know the purpose of God in the creation from the Bible: "For of Him, and through Him, and to Him are all things; to whom be glory for ever" (Rom. 11:36). This is as far as the revelation contained in either the Old or New Testament gives light upon the subject. And it must be confessed that this light is not very clear; these statements are not very definite. They amount simply to this, that God has created all things for His pleasure, for Himself; for His glory; but as to how this creation is to contribute pleasure to him, or glory, nothing definite is stated: and as to man's part in it—what knowledge may he gather as to God's purpose with reference to him—there is only silence; and that, it must be confessed in this case, is not "golden"—not of value!

Library, University of Utah, Salt Lake City)—*Ed.*>

17. <For Origen's views about man in the pre-existence, see John Clark Smith, *The Ancient Wisdom of Origen* (Lewisburg, PA: Bucknell University Press, 1992), 38-39, 281n9—*Ed.*>

18. <Ms III^{c} adds "Purpose of God in the Earth-life of Man"—*Ed.*>

The creeds of Jews and Christians so far as they have expressed themselves on this subject have been under the necessity of doing so by such deductions as may be made from these unsatisfactory passages of scripture; or else by their conjectures merely.

The Westminster confession of faith, which stands for the Presbyterian subdivisions of Christendom generally, ascribes the purpose of all the creative acts of God to be "the manifestation of the glory of His eternal power, wisdom, and goodness."[19] In an authoritative explanation of this part of the creed it is said: "The design of God in creation was the manifestation of His own glory." And again: "Our confession very explicitly takes the position that the chief end of God in His eternal purposes, and in their temporal execution in creation and providence is the manifestation of His own glory. . . . The scriptures explicitly assert that this is the chief end of God in creation–the manifestation of His own glory is[20] intrinsically the highest and worthiest end that God could propose to Himself."[21] The commentator refers for proof of his assertions both for his comment and for the substance of his creed to the scripture passages quoted above, and those passages are the only warrant for the statement in the Westminster Confession.

The great Protestant body of Christians, known as the Episcopal Church, English and American, whose doctrines are set forth in the *Book of Common Prayer*, are silent on the purpose of God for man's existence, except that their creed proclaims faith in God, "the maker and preserver of all things, both visible and invisible"; but nowhere does it declare the purpose of that creation and, consequently, they have no word as to the object of man's existence.

The Roman Catholic view is perhaps best explained in their catechism, the "Douay Catechism," as follows:

> *Ques.* What signifies the words creation of heaven and earth?
>
> *Ans.* They signify that God made heaven and earth and all creatures in them of nothing by His word only.
>
> *Ques.* What moved God to make them?
>
> *Ans.* His own goodness, so that He may communicate Himself to angels and to man for whom He made all other creatures.

Referring again to man's creation the following occurs:

---

19. Westminster Confession of Faith, chap. 4, "Of Creation," sect. 1.

20. <Ms III[c] adds "is"–*Ed.*>

21. Rev. Archibald A. Hodge, D.D., *A Commentary on the Confession of Faith, with Questions for Theological Students and Bible Classes* (Philadelphia: Presbyterian Board of Publication, 1869).

Ques. Do we owe much to God for creation?

Ans. Very much, because He made us in such a perfect state, creating us for Himself and all things else for us.[22]

From all this it may be summarized that the purpose of God in the creation of man, according to the Catholic view is: (1) that God might communicate Himself to them; (2) that they might be partakers of His glory; (3) that He created them for Himself and all things else for them.

While this may be in part the truth, and so far excellent, it has no higher warrant of authority than human deduction based upon rather indefinite scripture; and it certainly falls short of giving to man that "pride of place" in existence to which his higher nature and his dignity as an intelligence entitles him.

SEVERAL "ORIGINS" OF MAN HAVE NO WARRANT OF SCRIPTURE[23]

It is not my purpose in this chapter to undertake an extended discussion of man's origin, nor the purpose of God in his earth-life, but the development of our theme to this point, and the intended conclusion of this Part I—which approaches—seemed to require that something be said as to the doctrine taught in the revelation of the Old Testament and of the New Testament in regard to man's origin. Moreover, that it should be considered from the scriptural viewpoint rather than from any discoveries that may obtain in the world of science. There is nothing in scripture, let me be bold enough to say, that warrants the idea of "Creationism," namely, that God with every new human physical life begotten, creates at conception or at birth a soul for each such person; nor is there scripture warrant for "Traducianism," the doctrine that man—spirit and body—is the product of his parents by act of propagation, giving to man no higher origin than a merely human, physical origin—mental and spiritual—except as to the first man.

It will be seen from the above that the revelation-believing world are far removed from a strong scriptural doctrine of man's origin. The fuller treatment of this theme, however, belongs to a subsequent chapter. It is merely to note the world's limited and unsatisfactory knowledge on the subject that it is mentioned here.

---

22. Douay Catechism, chap. 3.

23. <Ms III[c] adds "Several 'Origins' of Man Have No Warrant Of Scripture"—*Ed.*>

CHAPTER XXII

Revelation: Our Revelation Local, Pertaining to Our Earth and Its Heavens

SCRIPTURE READING LESSON

Analysis

I. As to Revelation in Modern Times.

II. No Scripture Limitations to Revelations.

III. Future Dispensations of Revelations Promised.

IV. The Holy Ghost as a Source of Revelation.

V. The Modern World's Need of Revelation.

VI. Limited Victory of Christianity.

VII. Our Revelations Local.

VIII. God's Revelation to Moses in the Mosaic Fragment.

References

The citations of scripture and works in the text of this chapter.

Book of Moses and Book of Abraham (here and there).

Orson Pratt, "Divine Authenticity of the Book of Mormon," in *A Series of Pamphlets on the Doctrines of the Gospel*, cover title, *Orson Pratt's Works* (Salt Lake City: Juvenile Instructor Office, 1899).

Chap. 1: "To expect more revelation not unscriptural . . . not unreasonable."

Chap. 2: "More revelation indispensably necessary."

Chap. 3: "Bible . . . without further revelation an insufficient guide."

CHAPTER XXII

Revelation: Our Revelation Local, Pertaining to Our Earth and Its Heavens

AS TO REVELATION IN MODERN TIMES

It is quite generally the understanding that while God "at sundry times and in divers manners spake in times past to the fathers by the prophets" (Heb. 1:1), and by the ministering of angels and by His own voice from heaven, and some two thousand years ago gave a supreme revelation through His Son, Jesus Christ—it is the general understanding now that revelation in modern times has not only ceased, but is no more to be expected. The volume of revelation is alleged to have been completely closed and the awful voice of God in revelation has been heard for the last time. Since what we have to say in the remaining chapters of this work will rest largely upon revelation in recent times, it is quite necessary that we should call attention to this prevailing belief about the cessation of revelation.

Let the reader be reminded in the first place, that there is nothing in the nature of revelation itself that would lead us to think that revelation from God in modern times is impossible, or improbable. If it be conceded that God in past ages spoke to chosen men whom He made His prophets, seers, and apostles; and sent them with a message to mankind, it would be vain to argue that it would be impossible for Him to do the same now. To think of revelation as now impossible would be to deny God's power to do what He afore time did. Belief in God at all will certainly include belief in His power to reveal Himself when and how will please Him.

Moreover, there is nothing in the revelations that have been given, and that are contained in the Old and New Testament that gives any warrant for saying that revelation would ever cease. True, God has cautioned men at various places in His revelation that they must not "add to" or "take from" the particular revelation given of God. One such caution was given to ancient Israel, wherein God said:

> Ye shall not add unto the words which I command you, neither shall ye diminish ought from it, that you may keep the commandments of the Lord your God, which I command you (Deut. 4:2).

But this was no general proclamation that revelation would cease. Indeed, we know that the great volume of Israel's revelation was given after those days.

Written in the last book of the New Testament, as at present compiled in the last chapter, and in the closing verses, is St. John's solemn warning:

> I testify to every man that heareth the words of the prophecy of this book, if any man shall add unto these things, God shall add unto him the plagues that are written in this book (Rev. 22:18).

Per contra:[1]

> And if any man shall take away from the words of the book of this prophecy, God shall take away his part out of the book of life, and out of the holy city, and from the things which are written in this book (Rev. 22:19).

This, being within one of the last verses of the Bible, has been held by expositors to represent the formal closing up of the whole volume of revelation! The inhibitions, however, are limited to the book of St. John's revelation—the few leaves that make up the book of that prophecy, and has no reference to the whole Bible, or the whole volume of revelation. St. John's Book of Revelation is well known to have been written before his Gospel, and if John's Gospel is to be held as an inspired book, containing a revelation, then the apostle himself would be guilty of violating his own prohibition of further revelation from God, if the inhibition of adding to the word of God contained in the last chapter of the revelation is held to mean a prohibition of all further revelation from God.

There is the further consideration also, namely, the language of St. John's book is "if any *man* shall add to the words of the prophecies of this book," then calamity shall follow. This merely forbids man to add to God's word, it makes no attempts to forbid God to add to his own revelations for the enlightenment of the children of men.

The reader may fix it in his mind as a settled conviction, founded upon reason that (1) there is nothing in the nature of revelation itself to prevent God from giving revelation in modern times as well as in times past; and (2) there is no inhibition pronounced in what has been revealed in past ages that would estop God from giving revelation in modern times, or in any times, however far in the future. The power and the right to give revelation is within the sovereign power and will of God. God will speak when He will, and how He will; and it is vain in man to undertake to set limitations for God in the matter of His giving revelations.[2]

All the implications of the scriptures are to the effect that we may look for revelations in dispensations later than those whose history is given in the Bible,

---

1. <Ms III[*] "and Per contra"—*Ed.*>
2. <Ms III[c] adds an "s" to make the plural "revelations"—*Ed.*>

later than the dispensation of two thousand years ago,[3] namely, the Christian or Meridian[4] dispensation. St. Peter, for instance, addressing himself to the Jews on a somewhat momentous occasion, in which he witnessed that Christ had fulfilled the things predicted by the previous prophets, gives then this admonition to the listening multitude of the Jews:

> Repent ye, therefore, and be converted, that your sins may be blotted out, when the times of refreshing shall come from the presence of the Lord; and He shall send Jesus Christ, which before was preached unto you, whom the heaven must receive[5] until the times of restitution of all things, which God hath spoken by the mouth of all His holy prophets since the world began (Acts 3:19-21).

Mark the words of this chief of the apostles—"whom the heaven must receive," this referring to Jesus Christ, "until the times of restitution of all things." This is clearly a promise of some future unfolding and enlargement of God's work of revelation in the earth. The "time of restitution of all things" that God had in mind, which He has committed to His servants the prophets and seers; and all these things in the future, God here promises to gather together and unite in one splendid whole, which will disclose His purposes with reference to the whole earth and the inhabitants thereof. A prominent feature of this future dispensation will be that God will again send Jesus Christ, which before had been preached unto the Jews, but whom now the heaven must receive until the time promised—"the time of the restitution of all things." This unquestionably has reference to some mighty revelation subsequent to the apostolic days of St. Peter.

St. Paul is no less emphatic in prophesying of a similar dispensation to this—the same in fact—in these terms:

> God . . . having made known unto us the mysteries of His will, according to His good pleasure which He hath purposed in Himself; that, in the Dispensation of the Fullness of Times, He might gather together in one all things in Christ, both which are in heaven and which are on earth, even in Him (Eph. 1:3, 9-10).

The "Dispensation of the Fullness of Times" corresponds admirably with St. Peter's "Times of Restitution of All Things" of which God had spoken by the mouth of all His holy prophets.

---

3. <Ms III* "the dispensations of two thousand years ago"—*Ed.*>
4. <Ms III^{c} adds "or Meridian"—*Ed.*>
5. <Ms III* "whom the heavens must receive"—*Ed.*>

THE HOLY GHOST AS A SOURCE OF REVELATION[6]

It should be noticed also, in passing, that the chief source and means of God's revelation to man is through the Holy Ghost, which is declared in the scriptures to be the very "spirit of prophecy" (Rev. 19:10). And the spirit of prophecy can be no other than the spirit of revelation also. St. Peter officially opening the mission of himself and his fellow apostles upon the day of Pentecost, bore witness to the people that if they would repent of their sins and be baptized for the remission of them, they should receive the gift of the[7] Holy Ghost; that the promise of receiving this spirit of prophecy–the Holy Ghost–was to all those who heard his word, to their children, "to all that are afar off, even to as many as the Lord . . . should call" (Acts 2:39). Take note that the Spirit of inspiration and revelation–the spirit of prophecy–was promised unto all who should receive the gospel. After that pledge of God to argue for the cessation of inspiration and revelation from God is illogical, and leads to the denial of the perpetuation of the powers of the Holy Ghost himself as well as to a denial of the power of God the Father.

Great emphasis was laid upon the powers of the Holy Ghost in this line by the Savior himself. He promised to send to his disciples "another Comforter," that "He might abide with them forever, even the Spirit of Truth" (cf. John 14:16-17), which later he identifies as the Holy Ghost. He continues:

> The Comforter, which is the Holy Ghost, whom the Father will send in my name, he shall teach you all things and bring all things to your remembrance whatsoever I have said unto you (John 14:26).

Again:

> When the Comforter is come, whom I will send unto you from the Father, even the Spirit of truth, which proceedeth from the Father, he shall testify of me (John 15:26).

And still again:

> When he, the spirit of truth, is come [identified as the Holy Ghost, be it remembered], he will guide you into all truth; for he shall not speak of himself, but whatsoever he shall hear that shall he speak, and he will show you things to come! (John 16:13).

Identified again as the spirit of prophecy, and the chief source of prophecy is necessarily revelation. And hence, it must be that revelation and prophecy will be perpetual where the gospel of the Christ, and the Church of Christ is; and where

---

6. <Ms III^{c} adds "The Holy Ghost as a Source of Revelation"–*Ed.*>
7. <Ms III^{c} adds "gift of the"–*Ed.*>

these spiritual powers cease to be in manifestation, there neither the gospel, nor the Church of Christ has been perpetuated. So that when so-called Christianity repudiates continuous revelation in the churches, they do but proclaim their own departure from God and the truth of God.

THE MODERN WORLD'S NEED OF REVELATION

Is there anyone who will question the world's need for revelation in these days on the great fundamental questions concerning God, the Christ, the Christ's nature, and relationship to God, and to man; the origin of man and his relationship to whatever creative power has produced him; the purpose of his earth-life; his future, whether there is tangible, personal immortality for him in a wider, deeper, and larger existence? Or only an endless sleep in oblivion—extinction? In respect of positive, authoritative enlightenment the world is in doubt and ignorance in relation to all these questions. Christianity set forth in the New Testament, I know, is supposed to have furnished revealed knowledge concerning these things. But does it? Cite chapter and verse. Review the various interpretations given to such revelations as are therein contained by the several divisions of Christendom, and see what you have. Where is there in any of these divisions and subdivisions of Christendom a clear-cut, outstanding word or interpretation of these subjects that can be accepted as authoritative and final? Why are such divisions in Christendom, if there is clearness in the original revelation in which they are supposed to have their origin and commission? Why this multitude of "lo heres" and "lo theres" concerning one revelation, the one gospel, and supposedly the one church? Confusion is confounded in this multitude of various voices proclaiming many faiths and shades of faith over this supposed revealed religion and interpreting the Christ and his mission.

THE LIMITED VICTORY OF CHRISTIANITY[8]

Then again there is the very limited victory of Christianity, even if we should consent to regard it as essentially one religious movement and one church. After two thousand years of existence Christianity counts in its membership—and that is its nominal membership only, not active membership—less than one-third of the earth's inhabitants![9] During that time—two thousand years—though in constant contact with the Jews, Christianity has been unsuccessful in persuading that branch

8. <Ms III[c] adds "The Limited Victory of Christianity"—*Ed.*>

9. <The current 1.833 billion Christians are still one-third of the earth's total population of 5.48 billion—*Ed.*>

of the house of Israel (Judah) to accept the Christ as their Messiah; and Judah is as much in rebellion against acceptance of Jesus of Nazareth as their manifested Jehovah in the flesh, as they were two thousand years ago. And the great mass of humanity are still strangers to God as revealed in Jesus Christ.

All these considerations loudly plead for some further word of God that shall make clear the revelations that have been given; and for such additions to them as will unfold the fullness of truth that shall make it clear to the understanding of men, the meaning of this world of ours, God's purpose in creating it, man's life upon it, and man's future. The world was never more in need of revelation than now. What an infinite pity, if no word of God is spoken to meet the world's need!

OUR REVELATION LOCAL[10]

The first thing to be observed with reference to those things which are to occupy our attention in these closing chapters of Part I, is to note the important fact that such revelations as God has given to man on our earth, pertain to our earth alone, and the heavens immediately associated with it. That is to say, the limited family of worlds to which our earth belongs. This important truth is made known in the Book of Moses, the fragment of revelation brought to light by Joseph Smith, as already stated, early in his ministry, shortly after the church was organized in 1830 (Moses 1).

GOD'S REVELATION TO MOSES

God in this fragment is represented as saying to Moses:

> Worlds without number have I created, and I also created them for mine own purpose; and by the Son [Jesus Christ] I created them, which is mine Only Begotten. . . . For behold there are many worlds that have passed away, by the word of my power. And there are many that now stand; and innumerable are they unto man; but all things are numbered unto me, for they are mine, and I know them. But only an account of this earth [the earth whereon Moses stood] and the inhabitants thereof, give I unto you (Moses 1:33, 35b, 35a).

Then Moses:

> Be merciful unto Thy servant, O God; and tell me concerning this earth and the inhabitants thereof, and also the heavens, and then Thy servant will be content (Moses 1:36).
>
> And the Lord God spake unto Moses, saying, "The heavens, they are many, and they can not be numbered unto man, but they are numbered unto me, for they are

---

10. <Ms III* "Our Revelation Social"—*Ed.*>

> mine. And as one earth shall pass away, and the heavens thereof, even so shall another come; and there is no end to my works, neither to my words. . . . And now Moses, my son, I will speak unto thee concerning this earth upon which thou standest; and thou shalt write the things which I shall speak" (Moses 1:37-38, 40).

And again:

> It came to pass that the Lord spake unto Moses, saying, "Behold, I reveal unto you concerning this heaven and this earth; write the words which I speak. I am the Beginning and the End, the Almighty God; by mine Only Begotten I created these things; yea, in the beginning I created the heaven and the earth upon which thou standest. And the earth was without form and void, and I caused darkness to come upon the face of the deep; and my Spirit moved upon the face of the water; for I am God. And I, God, said, Let there be light; and there was light" (Moses 2:1-3).

Then follows the account of the creation, substantially in the first chapter of Genesis.

This is a wonderful item of information,[11] this fact that God's revelations which He gave through Moses, and subsequently of course to all the prophets, are limited to the earth and the immediate heavens[12] with which the earth is associated. The revelations pertain to our earth, to the inhabitants thereof, and to the Divine Intelligences which constitute its Godhead, its Creator, its Redeemer, its Witness—the Holy Ghost. The revelations which God has given to our earth-prophets undertake no treatment of the entire universe—the hundreds of millions of suns and their attendant planetary systems with the inhabitants thereof, all which make up the tremendous galaxy of our universe; much less a revelation that attempts to account for those other innumerable galaxies out in the space depths.[13]

What science discovers helps us to realize the greatness and wonderfulness of this revelation in the new fragment of the revelation of God to Moses, wherein we are told that "there are many worlds," so many that they are innumerable to man; "the heavens—they are many, and they cannot be numbered unto man" (Moses 1:35, 37). Many worlds have passed away, by the word of God's power. "And as one earth shall pass away, and the heavens thereof, even so shall another come" (Moses 1:38); and there is no end to God's works!

Let it be remembered that these wonderful statements were made by a confessedly unlearned youth, unschooled in the sciences, even of his time,

---

11. <Ms III[*] "a wonderful bit of information"—*Ed.*>

12. <Ms III[c] adds an "s" to make the plural "heavens"—*Ed.*>

13. <Ms III[*] "galaxies out in the space depths, which through the discovery of science we are just now beginning to find out"—*Ed.*>

unlearned in the lore of astronomy, and the speculations as to origins; and it is not until recent developments that modern science and modern instruments of science have brought to light such fullness of knowledge concerning the universe and the extent of it as is here proclaimed by the Prophet of the New Age of revelation in the Dispensation of the Fullness of Times. That is to say, a knowledge of the immensity of the universe, and the notion of worlds passing away and others created to take their place, or the re-creation of those which had passed away coupled with the notion, already referred to, that all this obtains under a reign of law in the universe, holding that the destructive forces—so called—as well as the creative forces in the universe are under the dominion of law, which will conserve and perpetuate through eternity the orderly cosmos.

The thing which I wish to emphasize here, however, in referring to the Mosaic fragment,[14] is the limitation of revelation to our earth and its heavens and its affairs and relationships; all which will have an important influence in understanding the great truths we hope to unfold; the importance of which, however, can only be realized as we proceed with the application of the thought to the facts as they are passed in review.

---

14. <Ms III* "referring to the Mosaic fragments"—*Ed.*>

CHAPTER XXIII

Revelation: Abrahamic Fragment

SCRIPTURE READING LESSON

Analysis

I. Revelation: The Book of Abraham.

II. The Abrahamic System of the Heavens:

(1) The World of God's Residence;

(2) Kolob;

(3) Oliblish;

(4) Kae-e-vanrash;

(5) Hah-ko-kau-beam;

(6) Ko-kau-beam.

III. Comments on the Indicated System.

IV. Value of the Knowledge That Revelations Are Local.

V. Of God in the Light of Revelations Being Local.

VI. The Earth as a Local Kingdom.

VII. Empires of Kingdoms.

VIII. The Spirit of God–God Immanent.

IX. The Holy Ghost.

X. Of the Godhead.

XI. Unity of the Godhead: the Nature of.

XII. The Holy Ghost: Deity of.

XIII. Summary.

References

The scriptures and works cited in the twenty-four <39> footnotes of this chapter and others in the body of the text. Reading the context of the specific citations will also be helpful.

The Pearl of Great Price: The Book of Moses and the Book of Abraham.

B. H. Roberts, *The Mormon Doctrine of Deity; The Roberts-[Cyrill] Van Der Donckt Discussion, to Which Is Added a Discourse, Jesus Christ, The Revelation of God* (Salt Lake City: The Deseret News, 1903). This will be especially useful in studying this chapter. It is recommended with all the more confidence because the manuscript before publication was read to the late Presidents Joseph F. Smith and Anthon H. Lund, and approved by them.

CHAPTER XXIII
Revelation: Abrahamic Fragment

THE BOOK OF ABRAHAM

Here also will be the proper place to take note of those things which God revealed to Abraham, and which are to be found in the fragment of Abraham's writings in the Book of Abraham, brought to light by Joseph Smith, and published just previous to his death.

The knowledge on the subject of the heavens and the earth was imparted to Abraham by means of the Urim and Thummim, a divine instrument through which God gave revelations in ancient times to his seers, of which Abraham was one (Abr. 3:1).

It may be admitted that there is some lack of clearness in what is revealed, owing to the fragmentary character of the Book of Abraham, and only the partial interpretation that our prophet gives of it; but somewhat of the immensity of the universe is made out. Abraham reports:

> I saw the stars and they were very great. . . . And I talked with the Lord, face to face, as one man talks with another; and He told me of the works which His hands had made; and He said unto me, "My son (and His hand was stretched out), behold I will show you all these." And He put His hands upon my eyes, and I saw those things which His hands had made, which were many, and they multiplied before mine eyes, and I could not see the end thereof (Abr. 3:2, 11-12).

Then God told the patriarch the names of some of these creations:

> He said unto me, ". . . Shinehah, which is the sun"; and He said unto me, "Kolob, which is star"; and He said unto me, "Kokaubeam, which signifies stars," or all the great lights which are in the firmament of heaven, [that is, the universe] (Abr. 3:13).

It was on this occasion that the Lord said unto Abraham that he would be greatly multiplied, and that his seed after him should be <as> numerous as the stars, or as the sands upon the seashore. And the Lord said unto Abraham:

> I show these unto thee before ye go into Egypt, that ye may declare all these words (Abr. 3:15).

And now to throw what God had revealed unto Abraham into something like systematic form as it may be gathered from this fragment of the patriarch's writings:

ABRAHAMIC SYSTEM OF THE "HEAVENS" WITH WHICH OUR EARTH AND SOLAR SYSTEM SEEM TO BE CONNECTED

(1) "The World of God's Residence." A great celestial orb where God resides, where the throne of God is (Abr. 3:2-9). "And there are many great stars which are near unto it" (cf. Abr. 3:2).

(2) "Kolob." A sun nearest to the celestial residence of God, a mighty governing and controlling center; the first creation (i.e., of the group); also first in government in that subdivision of the universe–the "heavens" to which our earth belongs. Kolob is first in government, but last, or slowest, in the measurement of time. Kolob's time is celestial time, after the reckoning of the Lord's time, one day in the Lord's Residence-World and in Kolob being equal to one thousand years of time upon our earth. Kolob is the controlling center of all those worlds which belong to the same order as our earth (Abr. 3:3-9).

(3) "Oliblish." A great star, also near to the celestial world–home of God, and second only to Kolob in governing power, holding the key of light and power to other planets. Oliblish is equal to Kolob in the measurement of time–one day being as a thousand years of time upon our earth. The fact that Kolob and Oliblish are both near the celestial world where God resides, that both are said to be governing centers over other suns and their planetary systems, that they both have the same time measurements, rather suggests that they may be "twin," or "binary stars," of which there are several hundred known to exist in our galaxy.[1] The binary stars are double stars, whose members have a revolution around their common center. In this case of Kolob and Oliblish, the great celestial residence-world of God, binary stars are accounted as among the most interesting and beautiful phenomena of the heavens.

(4) "Kae-e-vanrash." This is one of the governing stars also and controls fifteen of the so-called fixed stars, or suns, including in the number our own sun and the earth; and, of course, the whole solar system. This noble center of fifteen other stars–suns–with their planetary systems, as in the case of our own sun, receive light and power from and through–

(5) "Hah-ko-kau-beam," a group of stars in the sidereal system of our galaxy,

---

1. See T. E. R. Phillips and Dr. W. H. Steavenson, *Splendour of the Heavens: A Popular Authoritative Astronomy*, 2 vols. (New York: Robert M. McBride and Co., 1925).

receiving light and power from the controlling force of Kolob, which in turn receives conserving power and dynamic force from–

(6) "Ko-kau-beam," which signifies stars in general, the whole universe or all the great lights which are in the firmament of heaven.[2]

COMMENT ON THE SYSTEM[3]

As already stated it may be that this Abrahamic system is not completely set forth, owing to the fragmentary character of the Book of Abraham itself, and also for the reason that some portions of it were not completely translated by the Prophet of the New Dispensation, which appears from the explanation he gives and which will be found opposite the Egyptian disk no. 2 in the Book of Abraham, several items of which[4] it was unlawful for him to reveal unto the world, and is to be had only in the temple of God. But even though confessedly fragmentary, one may discern in this grouping of worlds and their relations to each other, a worked-out system of a section of the universe with which our earth and our solar system is connected; for the statements of the patriarch include our sun in this grouping, all which is under the controlling force exerted by the master star of these associated worlds, Kolob.

It is only a cursory view, that this Book of Abraham gives us of the structure of that section of the universe with which it deals, and our prophet gives but a partial translation of that fragment. Nevertheless, it is important,[5] this fragment and its partial translation, in that it discloses the fact that in ancient times some considerable knowledge was had as to the immensity of the universe, and the orderly system on which it was constructed: that God was the power within it; creating power, conserving power, and governing power–God in His Templed Universe! All shall be well with the Universe!

VALUE OF THE KNOWLEDGE THAT REVELATIONS TO OUR EARTH ARE LOCAL[6]

This important truth has already been referred to as having been imparted

---

2. See Book of Abraham, plate 2 and its accompanying explanation; also Abraham, chap. 3. <For additional information on Facsimile No. 2, see Michael D. Rhodes, "A Translation and Commentary of the Joseph Smith Hypocephalus," *Brigham Young University Studies* 17 (Spring 1977): 259-74–*Ed.*>

3. <Ms III[c] adds "Comment On the System"–*Ed.*>

4. <Ms III[*] "some of which"–*Ed.*>

5. <Ms III[*] "It is important, however"–*Ed.*>

6. <Ms III[c] adds "Value of The Knowledge That Revelations To Our Earth Are

to Moses concerning the revelations given to him, and, of course, by implication, to other and in fact to all our world seers; that is, they pertain to our earth and its heavens,[7] and chiefly to our earth and its affairs. So enlightened we shall be able to approach the revealed knowledge of our world scriptures from new viewpoints, and with a better prospect of understanding the things whereof they treat.

OF GOD IN THE LIGHT OF REVELATION BEING LOCAL

The first, as it is also the most important theme to be considered in the light of our new information—the limitation of revelation to our earth and its heavens[8]—is God. As matters now stand in our consciousness, we are facing a pluralistic universe, a universe made up of many things, of many beings, among them personal intelligences; kingdoms—meaning worlds and world-systems—wherein is present dominant, creating, conserving, perpetuating, and governing Mind; in a sense, universal Mind, made up of harmonized, individual intelligences, united in perfect knowledge, wisdom, purpose, and will. So perfectly united are these intelligences, and so all-powerful, that the universe under their control and direction is secure in its power to persist and in its power to hold the good dominant. The welfare of the whole is secured by perfect wisdom, founded upon and rising out of perfect knowledge; with truth as the solvent of all problems; with justice as the end of all relations; with mercy and her handmaid patience, rising from love, as the bond of union among all intelligences; with righteousness as the crowning glory of individual and community life. These qualities, and the attributes from which they spring, make up the "Divine Nature" in which the highly-developed intelligences participate; and by partaking of this "Divine Nature," they become One with all such similar intelligences throughout the universe and throughout eternity.[9] Let us go more into detail through the means of illustration.

Local"—*Ed.*>

7. <Ms III* "For practical use, this knowledge that comes to us from the Mosaic and Abrahamic fragments of revelation centers in the important fact that the revelations given to Moses, and, of course, by implication, to other of our world seers, are local; that is, they pertain to our earth and its heavens"—*Ed.*>

8. <Ms III[c] adds an "s" to make the plural "heavens"—*Ed.*>

9. <According to Van Hale, "Defining the Mormon Doctrine of Deity: What can theological terminology tell us about our own beliefs?" *Sunstone* 10 (Jan. 1985): 24, this is a type of Mormon monotheism, because B. H. Roberts and Orson Pratt (though opposed by Brigham Young) "believed in an impersonal power or attributes which is the 'Divine Nature'

THE EARTH AS A LOCAL KINGDOM[10]

Let us contemplate our earth as a distinct planet, inhabited by our human race, which is, though perhaps slowly, fulfilling the divine injunction to subdue the earth and have dominion over it. Accepting the fact of progress made in the past as a prophecy for its continuance for the future, we may think of our earth with its inhabitants as attaining to very great heights of development in all things that make for worthwhileness and glory. And if in some way there could be vouchsafed for the world an immortality—continuance, as a glorified, celestialized world; and likewise vouchsafed immortality for its inhabitants, or for such portion of them as would qualify for habitancy on such a world—we would then have a world with something like real meaning to it, and it doubtless would develop a governing council of intelligences which would put the world into a class of redeemed and sanctified, and in a way, self-governing, celestial kingdoms.

EMPIRES OF KINGDOMS

Perhaps also the same thing could happen to the other planets of our solar system, each world having for its Presiding Council or Presidency a number[11] of divine, and of course harmonized Intelligences. Then the solar system itself as an empire of kingdoms—redeemed and sanctified and glorified—would have its Grand Presidency constituting a unit in a group of related worlds; being one of a number of solar systems grouped into still greater empires than a solar system would form an empire of empires! And so on, and up, through the heights until we might contemplate the whole galaxy that comprises our universe, consisting as it does of its thousands of millions of suns and their planetary systems; and all the universe of the space-depths as organized worlds and world-kingdoms presided over by the organized and harmonized intelligences of eternity: each group or Council of Intelligences acting in its place and station and appointed office; and organizing what would doubtless be patriarchal and theo-democratic order of government, constituting as a whole the Priesthood of the Cosmos.

We used above the term "theo-democratic order of government." We do so for the reason that it will appear in subsequent discussions of these matters that things in the orderly government of the universe will be done on the principle of common consent, expressed in the form of consent of those who must submit to the authority which obtains; for we shall find this government obtaining in the

---

shared by all who are gods"—*Ed.*>

10. <Ms III[*] "The Earth As A Local God's Kingdom"—*Ed.*>

11. <Ms III[c] adds "a number"—*Ed.*>

universe largely, if not entirely, moral government; government based upon love and persuasion, truth and wisdom, mercy and justice, rather than upon force; for after all these are the stronger elements in government, even as we know it among the higher forms of government, even in the imperfect conditions and the broken harmonies which obtain in this our present world.

THE SPIRIT OF GOD—GOD IMMANENT

One other great truth should here be noted. The stellar system is made up of self-luminous suns, that shine, we say, by virtue of their own nature. They emit rays of light that extend from their own bodies into the space depths. The sun of our own system, 92,000,000 <92,900,000> of miles away, sends forth from its surface the light and the heat waves, which, striking our atmosphere, burst into sunshine, and the warmth and the light of the sun and his vital force visit our earth and render it habitable and splendid. In like manner the rays of our sun pass beyond our earth and visit the other planets of our solar system. Before reaching us these rays fell upon Mercury, 36,000,000 miles from the sun; and then upon Venus, 67,000,000 miles from the sun; passing us at 92,000,000 <92,900,000> miles, they go on to Mars, 141,000,000 <142,000,000> miles distant from the sun; thence to Jupiter, 463,000,000 <483,000,000> miles distant; to Saturn, 886,000,000 miles distant; thence to Uranus, 1,781,000,000 <1,784,000,000> miles distant from the sun; and to Neptune—the outermost planet of our system[12]—2,791,000,000 <2,793,000,000> miles distant from the sun. The same is true as to the light of all the suns of our universe, they are self-luminous by nature, they shine of their own power and send out waves of light and warmth and vital force to the respective groups of planets which encircle them, until from all these great stars or suns there is radiated forth and blended into the universe the cosmic light and warmth and vital force that come from all these great centers.[13]

And now as from these self-luminous suns there radiates forth these light waves and heat waves and vital force waves, so there proceeds forth from the Divine Intelligences inhabiting the universe, the Spirit of these Intelligences, which moves throughout the universe as in the beginning of the creation of our earth, "the Spirit of God moved upon the face of the waters" (Gen. 1:2). These radiations are of the same nature and qualities and attributes as are the mind of Divine Intelligences from which they proceed, and extend the Spirit of these Intelligences who have

12. <Pluto, 3.7 billion miles from the sun, was discovered in February 1930. See William Graves Hoyt, *Planets X and Pluto* (Tucson, AZ: University of Arizona Press, 1980), and A. J. Whyte, *The Planet Pluto* (Oxford, Eng.: Pergamon Press, 1980)—*Ed.*>

13. <Ms III* "until from all these great centers of light and heat and vital force"—*Ed.*>

attained unto the Divine Nature—hence Gods—into all the space-depths, filling the "immensity" of space with the Spirit of the Gods, bearing with that Spirit knowledge, wisdom, truth, holiness, justice, mercy, judgment, and love—all these blended into One Divine Essence, constituting the Spirit of the Gods and spoken of in the revelations of God to our Prophet of the New Dispensation, as being for us "the light of Christ." This Light, he goes on to say, is in the sun and his retinue of worlds,[14] and is[15] the power by which they were created or made; also the "Light which shineth,"[16] which gives to men light is through him who enlighteneth their eyes, and is "the same light[17] that quickeneth their understanding"; therefore, the intelligence-inspiring power as well as creative and world-sustaining power, "The Light which lighteth every man that cometh into the world" (John 1:9; cf. D&C 6:6-13). Also, the power which giveth "life to all things," hence, vital force; also "the law by which all things are governed, even the power of God," proceeding from the Gods, One Spirit Essence in which all are united. This is God immanent in the universe; Omnipresent, and present with power; Omniscient, all-knowing; Omnipotent, almighty (D&C 88:1-13 and context). This united force and power of all the Gods of the universe; from whose all-seeing eye there is no escape; from whom the darkness can not hide evil thoughts or evil deeds; from whose judgment there is no escape;[18] the Universal Consciousness that holds all things in an eternal Present; the Power that holds in balance the stars, and judges the thoughts "and weighs[19] the deeds of men"; the Spirit that moves throughout the space-depths—throughout the immensity of space—and executes the decrees of the Councils of Divine Intelligences, from whom this Spirit proceeds! Thus, the harmonized Intelligences of the universe—the Gods. Thus, the One Spirit of the Gods—God immanent.

THE HOLY GHOST

Let no one here confound this universal everywhere-present Spirit of the Gods—proceeding forth from their presence to fill the immensity of space—the Light which lighteth every man that cometh into the world—and for us of this world called the Light of Christ—let no one confound this Spirit with the Holy Ghost, which is a Spirit Personage of the Godhead, and from whose immediate personal presence

14. <Ms III[*] "The Light of our sun and his retinue of worlds"—*Ed.*>
15. <Ms III[c] adds "is"—*Ed.*>
16. <Ms III[*] "also as the 'Light which shineth'"—*Ed.*>
17. <Ms III[*] "which gives to men light, which is the same light"—*Ed.*>
18. <Ms III[c] adds "from whose judgment there is no escape"—*Ed.*>
19. <Ms III[c] adds "weighs"—*Ed.*>

there goes forth a special, spiritual, witnessing power—pure spirit of Intelligence—which brings to those brought into contact with it a witness of the Truth, of all Truth; for "by the power of the Holy Ghost ye may know the truth of all things" (Moro. 10:5). This is the very "Spirit of Truth" of the discourse of Jesus—"the Comforter . . . which is the Holy Ghost"; the Spirit that will "teach" the disciples "all things," "bring all things to their remembrance," and "guide them[20] into all truth" (for all the above expressions of the Christ, see John 14:16–15:26). But "whom the world cannot receive, because it seeth him not, neither know him; but ye [the disciples] know him, for he dwelleth with you and shall be in you" (John 14:17). This is the special gift to those who receive, in obedience, the gospel. "Repent and be baptized, . . . for the remission of your sins," said St. Peter on the day of Pentecost, "and ye shall receive the gift of the Holy Ghost" (i.e., the Holy Ghost as a gift); and this "promise" was unto "as many as the Lord our God shall call" (Acts 2:38-39). "We are his [the Christ's] witnesses of these things," said St. Peter, "and so is also the Holy Ghost, whom God hath given to all that obey him" (cf. Acts 5:32), and not otherwise. Thus, then stands the truth as to these two things:

(1) There is a universal Spirit which proceeds forth from the presence of Divine Intelligences to "fill the immensity of space," a creative and upholding power and vital force—intelligence-inspiring power—"the light which lighteth every man that cometh into the world"—the common heritage of man.

(2) There is another Spirit, the Holy Ghost, whom the world cannot receive, but is given as a gift to those who obey the gospel—"Whom God giveth to them that obey him"; and the Holy Ghost possesses and imparts to those who by obedience are in fellowship with him, the special gifts and spiritual power ascribed to him above.[21]

---

20. <Ms III[c] adds "them"—*Ed.*>

21. <B. H. Roberts in the 1888 edition of *The Gospel* described the Holy Ghost in non-personal terms as "that most subtle, powerful, sensitive, and intelligent of all influences" and "this great spiritual force in the universe." He quoted D&C 130 concerning the Holy Ghost being a personage of Spirit and then added that the tabernacle of the Holy Ghost is omnipresent "in the elements of the universe, giving life and light and intelligence to all things, and is the grand medium of communication between God the Father and his Son Jesus Christ and their vast creations" (B. H. Roberts, *The Gospel: An Exposition of Its First Principles* [Salt Lake City: The Contributor Company, 1888], 212, 215). However, in the 1901 3d. ed. of the *Gospel*, published after James E. Talmage's *Articles of Faith* (Salt Lake City: The Deseret News, 1899), the Holy Ghost has been significantly revised to become a person: instead of the Holy Ghost being a "subtle, powerful, sensitive, and intelligent . . . influence" the Holy Ghost exists on his own and from him influences proceed. Also at this

OF THE GODHEAD

We must turn again to the fact that such revelations, as God has given to our earth's seers and prophets, are local; that is, they pertain to our earth and its heavens and the affairs thereof; and to our Godhead.[22]

This Godhead consists of three Divine Personages—the Father, the Son, and the Holy Ghost.[23] Each separate and distinct as persons in the sense of being separate, individual Divine Intelligences. Three Deities united in One Council, participating in the One Divine Nature; having the same perfect knowledge, and perfect wisdom, that can only arise from perfect knowledge;[24] being alike in the attributes of holiness, justice, mercy, judgment; one in purpose and united in one will.

Let us consider the scriptures on these matters, first, as to the Trinity of the[25] Godhead, in four separate incidents. The fact of the Trinity is made apparent: (1) At the baptism of Jesus. As Jesus, who is God the Son, came forth from his baptism at the hands of John, the baptizer, a manifestation of the presence of God, the Holy Ghost, was given in the sign of the dove, which rested upon Jesus; and at the same time the voice from heaven, the voice of God the Father was heard, saying: "This is my beloved Son, in whom I am well pleased." Here is a complete and simultaneous[26] manifestation of the three distinct personages of the Trinity: Father, Son, and Holy Ghost (Matt. 3:16-17).

---

time the Holy Ghost became a *he* not an *it*. The earlier statement that the Holy Ghost's tabernacle exists "in the elements of the universe" was revised to the Holy Ghost's "power and influence are in the elements of the universe" (B. H. Roberts, *The Gospel: An Exposition of Its First Principles; and Man's Relationship to Deity*, 3d ed. [Salt Lake City: The Deseret News, 1901], 195, 199). Thomas G. Alexander has observed that Roberts, Talmage, and John A. Widtsoe undertook "a reconstruction which carried doctrine far beyond anything described in the 'Lectures on Faith' or generally believed by church members prior to 1835" (Thomas G. Alexander, "The Reconstruction of Mormon Doctrine: From Joseph Smith to Progressive Theology," *Sunstone* 5 [July-August 1980]: 29; reprinted in *Line upon Line: Essays on Mormon Doctrine*, ed. Gary James Bergera [Salt Lake City: Signature Books, 1989], 62)—*Ed.*>

22. <Ms III[*] "to our Godhead. Of this Godhead we are now to speak."—*Ed.*>

23. <For the changing role of the Holy Ghost, see Vern G. Swanson, "The Development of the Concept of a Holy Ghost in Mormon Theology," in *Line upon Line*, 1989), 89-101—*Ed.*>

24. <Ms III[*] "from perfect knowledge; and perfect wisdom," but the words "and perfect wisdom" unintentionally repeat the same words on the previous line—*Ed.*>

25. <Ms III[c] adds "the"—*Ed.*>

26. <Ms III[c] adds "and simultaneous"—*Ed.*>

(2) In the commission given to the apostles by the Lord Jesus himself[27] to teach all nations:

> And Jesus came and spake unto them, saying, "All power is given unto me in heaven and in earth. Go, therefore, and teach all nations, baptizing them in the name of the Father, and of the Son, and of the Holy Ghost" (Matt. 28:18-19).

There can be no question as to the distinctiveness of the three personages here named by Jesus.

(3) In the vision of St. Stephen when the mob rushed upon him at the close of his arraignment of the Jews for the crucifixion of the Christ:

> But he, being full of the Holy Ghost, looked steadfastly into heaven, and saw the glory of God, and Jesus standing on the right hand of God (Acts 7:55).

Two of the three visible, the other consciously present in the martyr.

(4) In the apostolic benediction, viz., "the grace of the Lord Jesus Christ, and the love of God, and the communion of the Holy Ghost, be with you all" (2 Cor. 13:14).

This Godhead of three divine personages is also[28] emphatically proclaimed in the Book of Mormon: speaking of those who must come to the judgment of God, it is written that they shall be "arraigned before the bar of Christ the Son, and God the Father, and the Holy Spirit, which is one Eternal God, to be judged according to their works" (Alma 11:44). Again, in the instructions on baptism it is written: "After this manner shall ye baptize, in the name of the Father, and of the Son, and of the Holy Ghost. . . . For verily I say unto you, that the Father, and the Son, and the Holy Ghost are one" (cf. 3 Ne. 11:25, 27). Equivalent statements repeatedly occur in this American volume of scripture. So also is there testimony to the same effect in the Book of Doctrine and Covenants, a collection of revelations given in our own times (D&C 20:17-28). Also, the statement of Joseph Smith, the prophet, recorded in the same volume: "The Father hath a body of flesh and bones as tangible as man's; the Son also; but the Holy Ghost has not a body of flesh and bones, but is a personage of spirit" (D&C 130:22).

UNITY OF THE GODHEAD:THE NATURE OF IT

Both the unity and the distinctiveness of these personages is apparent from these scriptures. The existence of God the Father, both Jesus and the apostles

---

27. <Ms III^c adds "by the Lord Jesus himself"—*Ed.*>

28. <Ms III^c adds "also"—*Ed.*>

accepted as a reality. Jesus repeatedly declares the fact that God was his Father and frequently calls himself, the Son of God, and prays to the Father in that capacity:

> As the Father knoweth me, even so know I the Father. . . . Therefore doth my Father love me, because I lay down my life for the sheep. . . . This commandment have I received from my Father. The works that I do in my Father's name, they bear witness of me. . . . Say ye of him, whom the Father hath sanctified and sent in the world "thou blasphemest," because I said, I am the Son of God? (cf. John 10:15, 17-18, 25, 36).

All these sayings are recorded in St. John's gospel. John also represents Jesus as saying in his prayer in Gethsemane:

> Father, the hour is come; glorify Thy Son, that Thy Son also may glorify thee. . . . And now, O Father, glorify thou me with Thine own self, with the glory which I had with Thee before the world was. . . . Holy Father, keep through Thine own name those whom Thou hast given me, that they may be One as we are; . . . that they all may be one, as Thou, Father, art in me, and I in Thee (John 17:1, 5, 11, 21).

Then after the resurrection Jesus said to Mary of Magdala: "Touch me not, for I have not yet ascended to my Father; but go to my brethren, and say unto them, I ascend unto my Father and your Father; and to my God and your God" (John 20:17). The separate and distinct existence of God the Father, and of the Son, and of the Holy Ghost could not be more emphatically represented than in these scriptures.

The proof which set off the Father and the Son as separate and distinct personalities, also present the Holy Ghost as a separate and distinct personality; for whether we contemplate these Divine Personages when the three are presented together, as at the baptism of Jesus, or in the vision of St. Stephen, or in the baptismal formula, or in the apostolic benediction—they are always presented in a manner that implies distinctiveness as persons, however closely they may be united in purpose and will. Jesus clearly ascribes to the Holy Ghost as a distinct personality. He represents the Holy Ghost as "proceeding from the Father"[29] (John 15:26); as sent forth in the name of the Son (John 14:26); as abiding (John 14:16); as teaching and as bearing witness (John 14:26; 15:26-27); as reproving the world of sin, and of righteousness, and of judgment (John 16:8).

The apostles also referred to the Holy Ghost in much the same manner. St.

---

29. <Ms III* "Jesus clearly ascribes to the Holy Ghost as 'proceeding from the Father,'" but due to skipping from "the Holy Ghost" to "the Holy Ghost" the words "as a distinct personality. He represents the Holy Ghost" from the earlier draft were accidentally omitted and these are reinserted above the line—*Ed.*>

Peter represents the Holy Ghost as speaking by the mouth of David concerning the treachery of Judas (Acts 1:16-17); he also represents Ananias as having lied to the Holy Ghost, and hence also he had lied to God (Acts 5:3); also he represents the Holy Ghost as bearing witness, with himself and his fellow apostle John, to the divinity of the Christ (Acts 5:29-32); also the Holy Ghost is represented as sending forth men to the ministry: "The Holy Ghost said, 'Separate me Barnabas and Saul for the work whereunto I have called them.' . . . So they, being sent forth by the Holy Ghost, departed unto Seleucia" (Acts 13:2, 4). The Holy Ghost is represented as forbidding Paul and Timothy preaching in Asia and Bithynia. After they were gone to Phrygia and the region of Galatia, they "were forbidden of the Holy Ghost to preach . . . in Asia. After they were gone to Mysia, they assayed to go into Bithynia, but the Spirit [the Holy Ghost] suffered them not" (cf. Acts 16:6-7). "The fruit of the Spirit" (the Holy Ghost) is said to be "love, joy, peace, longsuffering, gentleness, goodness, faith, meekness, temperance" (Gal. 5:22-23); and as these things can only proceed from a being possessed of attributes that produce them, we must needs think of the Holy Ghost as being loving, merciful, patient, meek, temperate; as having judgment. All which, with the other things preceding here set forth of Him, clearly establishes personality for the Third Person of the Godhead.

THE HOLY GHOST: DEITY OF

There remains to be considered the question, Is the Holy Ghost God—Deity in his own right? The proof is in the fact that the Holy Ghost is an equal member of the Holy Trinity. Also in the fact that Jesus makes blasphemy against the Holy Ghost a greater sin than blasphemy against himself, for he said:

> All manner of sin and blasphemy shall be forgiven unto men, but the blasphemy against the Holy Ghost shall not be forgiven unto men. Whosoever speaketh a word against the Son of Man, it shall be forgiven him, but whosoever speaketh against the Holy Ghost, it shall not be forgiven him, neither in this world, neither in the world to come (Matt. 12:31-32; cf. Mark 3:28-29).

This could not be unless the Holy Ghost were Deity, and in some peculiar way so related to men, that makes this sin of blasphemy against the Holy Ghost especially heinous. It may come from the fact that the Holy Ghost has especially the function of Chief Witness for Divine Truth in the Holy Trinity. And from the fact that he, the Holy Ghost, while a personage of Spirit,[30] and remaining a[31] spirit,

---

30. <Ms III* "while a personage of Spirit, as the Christ was previous to his taking on a tabernacle of flesh and bones"—*Ed.*>

31. <Ms III^c adds "a"—*Ed.*>

that in some way he may more effectually make connection with man's spirit, after man's special preparation by acceptance of the gospel in baptism for the remission of his sins (cf. Acts 2:37-40 and John 14:17)[32] and that he[33] may receive such a connection and infusion to his soul of the radiating power from the Holy Ghost that there is born in him an additional spiritual life, something added to his own spirit, that to sin up to the point of blaspheming against the Holy Ghost, would be to commit a spirit-murder, more terrible than a physical, bodily murder; and hence, the darker and deeper sin, the sin that may not be forgiven in this world or in the world to come.

THE SUM OF THE MATTER

So much for the distinctiveness and the Deity of each[34] of these Divine Beings as personages and as also constituting an organized unit, a body that is a Divine Council. It should be kept in mind that their Oneness consists in moral unity, not physical unity, or identity of substance, or essence even.[35] In other words, while they are distinct and separate personages in the sense of being distinct individuals,[36] their unity consists in agreement of purpose, and unity of will and action for the accomplishment of certain definite ends pertaining to creation, conserving, and governing in the universe; and in bringing peace and salvation and the possibility of eternal progress to men. Our prophet of the New Dispensation says:

> An everlasting covenant was made between three personages before the organization of this earth relating to their dispensation of things to men[37] on the earth. These personages . . . are called God the first, the Creator; God the second, the Redeemer; and God the third, the Witness or Testator.[38]

These three united are the Godhead to which man owes his allegiance. This

---

32. In the latter <scripture> "The Spirit of Truth"—identified with the Holy Ghost—"whom the world"—the unbaptized—"can not receive," etc.

33. <Ms III^c adds "and that he"—*Ed.*>

34. <Ms III^c adds "and the Deity of each"—*Ed.*>

35. <Ms III^c adds "even"—*Ed.*>

36. <Ms III* "being distinct and individuals"—*Ed.*>

37. <Ms III "man," which is corrected to "men"—*Ed.*>

38. Franklin D. Richards and James A. Little, *A Compendium of the Doctrines of the Gospel*, rev. ed. (Salt Lake City: Deseret Book Co., 1925), 272. <The source of this *Compendium* statement, including the words "according to Abraham's record" (omitted by Roberts), is a section entitled "By Joseph" in William Clayton's "Private Book"; see George D. Smith, ed., *An Intimate Chronicle: The Journals of William Clayton* (Salt Lake City: Signature Books in association with Smith Research Associates, 1991), 517—*Ed.*>

Godhead constitutes the creating, sustaining, redeeming, and witnessing power of the universe, the Supreme God. In this Godhead righteousness and holiness and truth and knowledge and wisdom and power and glory and justice and mercy and love—all that we do recognize or can recognize as belonging to the Divine Nature are incarnated in these personages in their perfection. This Godhead is the source of spiritual light and power and life.[39]

39. <Ms III[c] adds "light and power and life"—*Ed.*>

CHAPTER XXIV

Creation: The Time and Manner of the Earth's Creation I

SCRIPTURE READING LESSON

Analysis

I. Causation.

II. Time Element in Creation.

III. The Manner of Creation.

IV. Definition of Evolution.

V. The Gloomy Outcome of Evolution.

References

This chapter, involving as it does consideration of various theories of creation, including evolution, makes all the standard authorities on these subjects sources of reference. I have found the following works helpful. Charles Darwin, *On Origin of Species by Means of Natural Selection* (London: J. Murray, 1859), and his *Descent of Man and Selection in Relation to Sex* (London: J. Murray, 1871), of course; though one needs to keep in mind that there have been many modifications of the theory of evolution since his day.

Herbert Spencer, *A System of Synthetic Philosophy*, 9 vols., especially *First Principles*; John Fiske, *Outlines of Cosmic Philosophy*, 4 vols., an interpretation of Spencer (largely), *passim*; J. Arthur Thomson, ed., "Story of Evolution," in *The Outline of Science: A Plain Story Simply Told*, 4 vols.; vol. 1 is chiefly devoted to evolution. Ernst Haeckel, *The Riddle of the Universe at the Close of the Nineteenth Century* (New York and London: Harper and Bros., 1901), 54, 239, 243; his *Life and Work*, 114, 130, 279, 310; also his *Anthropogenie*, 5th ed., translated into English as *The Evolution of Man*.

Will Durant, *The Story of Philosophy* (New York: Simon and Schuster, 1926), *passim*. B. H. Roberts, "Man's Relationship to Deity," published in *The Gospel*, 6th ed., 1926. All references given in analysis of chapter 25.

CHAPTER XXIV

Creation: The Time and Manner of the Earth's Creation I

CAUSATION

From what has heretofore been said, it will be remembered that we hold the universe to be self-existent and eternal. Duration, space, matter, force, mind—each infinite after its kind—are its prime and included factors. The universe is comprised of these.

Such a universe can have no first cause, since that would imply a time when there was no cause, and there has been and can be no such time. Causation is eternal, and in the eternal and infinite universe there has been operating always Eternal Cause. The cause which produces all action, all movements that produce events, changes; the creation of, or forming of, world-systems, and worlds within world-systems; causing also the passing away of worlds and world-systems, whenever they may have fulfilled some special purpose for which they were created, and hence are ready to pass away, to be reformed into more desirable worlds or world-systems. For in a universe where Intelligence united with goodness and power obtains and prevails, even changes which may have disintegrating or destructive aspects, can only be conceived as having a beneficent purpose in them, changing from a good to a better status: or, to be more exact, and to place the physical as well as the moral and spiritual notion into the betterment wrought by the apparently destructive changes—better say that the changes move from telestial to terrestrial; and from terrestrial to celestial orders of worlds.[1]

Of the creation of our earth and its heavens—worlds with which our earth-revelations deal—it need only be said that they were formed or fashioned from pre-existing world-stuff, which "in the beginning" was formless, unorganized, and darkness covered all its depths. Then God spake and "the Spirit of God" moved

1. <Roberts alludes to the "telestial kingdom" (D&C 76:81-109; 88:21-31), which in Mormon cosmology is the lowest state in the hereafter—increasing in glory from telestial, to terrestrial, to celestial—*Ed.*>

in the chaos, and in due time an orderly world arose from the chaos and became the habitat of man as we now know it.

Two things have mainly occupied the attention of intellectual men with respect of this creation: first, the time of it; second, the manner of it.

TIME ELEMENT IN CREATION

As to the time element of creation for our earth a great variety of views have been held. The Bible story of creation was held to mean, by the theologians, that the creation was effected some six thousand years ago by fiat word of God, and within six days as measured by the rotation of the earth upon its axis—just six ordinary days! Then came the message derived from developed scientific knowledge, which indicated that the earth was of much greater antiquity than this, extending from hundreds of thousands to millions of years since its beginning. Scientists pointed to the record found in the earth's crust for the evidence of its slow formation and its great antiquity. Fossil remains of its extinct forms of life in its various strata; its well-defined glacial periods of scores of thousands of years ago; the submerged portions of present large land areas uplifted by slow process into great desert tablelands and mountain ranges; and in recent years the accumulative evidence for the existence of man in the earth in a remote antiquity, amounting to scores and to even hundreds of thousands of years, has rapidly increased and is of sufficient clearness apparently to be generally accepted by the scientific world. All these discoveries and developments with their accepted implications have led to attempts at revision of the theological interpretation of the first chapter of Genesis. Some accepting as a cue the casual statement of St. Peter "that one day is with the Lord as a thousand years, and a thousand years as one day" (2 Pet. 3:8); and the Psalmist's expression of nearly the same import (Ps. 90:4). They have held that the "day" of Genesis was after the Lord's method of computing time; which would make the "creation day" a period of a thousand years of earth time. But even this is insufficient to meet the demands of the creation time periods of science.

Again, theologians have suggested that the "creation days" in Genesis are not even after the Lord's measurement of "days" of a thousand years of earth time, but the "creation days" of Genesis are periods of indefinite time, and may be understood as representing thousands, or even millions of years. Other interpreters call attention to the significant language of the first verse of Genesis, which says, "In the beginning God created the heavens and the earth," and point out that there is no indication in the revelation itself when "the beginning" was; holding that "the sacred writer in Genesis does not commit himself to any definite limits of time [at all], but simply speaks of the 'creation' as taking place 'in the beginning,' and [holding that] this phrase is elastic enough to cover the modern scientific position,"[2] that is, as to the time period in which the earth was created.

Our own position with reference to the time element in creation is that, while there is no definite time fixed by revelation as to the "beginning" of the creation of our earth and its heavens, yet the revelation does limit the time of creation to the beginning "when" God created our earth and its heavens; this "beginning," and not an absolute beginning of the universe, is the meaning of the first verse of Genesis. So that the rendering of Genesis 1:1 would be: "In the beginning 'when' God created the heavens and the earth, the earth was without form," and so following. This does not fix any period in terms of years for the beginning of the creation of our world; but it does make it possible to accord to science whatever antiquity its demonstrations[3] may require for the duration of the earth, and hence, approximately—with very wide latitude—the "beginning of creation." Of this more will be said later.

THE MANNER OF CREATION

As already stated the theologians held creation to be by fiat word of God, quoting in support of the theory the scripture:[4]

> By the word of the Lord were the heavens made; and all the hosts of them by the breath of His mouth. . . . For He spake, and it was done; He commanded, and it stood fast (Ps. 33:6, 9).

Against this fiat theory of creation, however, science has presented the view that the order and beauty of the world are not the result of one direct creative act, nor even of a series of directly creative acts; but it is the outcome of a gradual process continued through immense periods of time, from many lower forms and stages of life; and perhaps ultimately from only one life substance.[5] There are, it is said, some eighty odd chemical elements known in the earth today,[6] and "it is now much more than a suggestion that these are the outcome of an inorganic evolution,

---

2. "The Creation Story and Science," in John R. Dummelow, ed., *A Commentary on the Holy Bible by Various Writers, Complete in One Volume* (New York: The Macmillan Co., 1922), xxx.

3. <Ms III[c] adds an "s" to make the plural "demonstrations"—*Ed.*>

4. <Ms III[*] "quoting in support the theory of the scripture"—*Ed.*>

5. <Ms III "from one only life substance"—*Ed.*>

6. <Ninety naturally-occurring elements have now been discovered, and scientists have made another nineteen, for a total of 109. See James E. Brady and John R. Holum, *Chemistry: The Study of Matter and Its Changes* (New York: John Wiley and Sons, 1993), 35—*Ed.*>

element giving rise to element, going back and back to some primeval stuff, from which they were all originally derived infinitely long ago,"[7] and out of which has been differentiated all life forms that now inhabit the earth or that ever have lived upon it. This is the evolution theory of accounting for the existence of life forms in the earth.

DEFINITION OF EVOLUTION[8]

It is described by one of the master architects of the theory, Herbert Spencer, as follows:

> Evolution is an integration of matter and a concomitant dissipation of motion; during which the matter passes from an indefinite, incoherent homogeneity to a definite, coherent heterogeneity; and during which the retained motion undergoes a parallel transformation.[9]

After reading this definition, we can appreciate what Will Durant, author of *The Story of Philosophy* (1926), meant when he says that Spencer "made the intellect of Europe gasp for breath," when the author of the *Synthetic Philosophy* gave out that definition of evolution; nor are we surprised when he tells us that it "required ten volumes and forty years for its explanation." Durant himself asks the question, "What does this definition mean?" and follows it with an explanation that is nearly as difficult as Spencer's own. We may here only give part of Durant's answer; sufficient, however, we trust, to set forth the theory of evolution somewhat clearly, though only in headlines.

> The primeval nebulae [cosmic dust] is homogeneous, i.e., it consists of parts that are alike [with that simple stuff, nebulae dust, evolution starts]; but soon it is differentiated into gases and liquids and solids; the earth becomes here green with grass, there white with mountain tops [snow-capped], or blue with the multitudinous sea; evolving life begets, out of a relatively homogeneous protoplasm [i.e., stuff relatively simple], the varied organs of nutrition, reproduction, locomotion, and perception; a single language fills whole continents with its multiplying dialects; a single science breeds a hundred, and the folklore of a nation flowers into a thousand forms of literary art; individuality grows, character stands out uniquely, and every race and people develops its peculiar genius. Integration and heterogeneity, aggregation of parts into ever larger wholes, and differentiation of parts into every more varied forms. These are

7. J. Arthur Thomson, "Introduction," *The Outline of Science: A Plain Story Simply Told* (New York and London: G. P. Putnam's Sons, 1922), 1:4.

8. <Ms III[c] adds "Definition of Evolution" before the beginning of the quote from Spencer, but it is here placed before Roberts's introduction to the quote—*Ed.*>

9. Herbert Spencer, *First Principles* (New York: D. Appleton, 1896), 253.

the foci of the orbit of evolution. Whatever passes from diffusion to integration and unity, and from a homogeneous simplicity to a differentiated complexity, is in the flow of evolution. Whatever is returning from integration to diffusion, and from complexity to simplicity, is caught in the ebb of dissolution.[10]

THE GLOOMY OUTCOME OF EVOLUTION

Here perhaps is as suitable a place as any to set down the horribly dark future which the theory of evolution sets out as the future of the world. Mr. Durant says, commenting upon the theory of evolution as set forth by Spencer:

> Finally and inescapably comes "equilibration." Every motion, being motion under resistance, must sooner or later come to an end; every rhythmic oscillation (unless externally reinforced) suffers some loss of rate and amplitude. The planets ride through a lesser orbit, or will ride, than once they rode; the sun will shine less warmly and brightly as the centuries pass away; the friction of the tide will retard the rotation of the earth. This globe that throbs and murmurs with a million motions, and luxuriates into a million forms of riotously breeding life, will some day move more leisurely in its orbit and its parts; the blood will run cooler and more slowly in our desiccated veins; we shall not hurry any more; like dying races we shall think of heaven in terms of rest and not of life; we shall dream of Nirvana. Gradually, and then rapidly, "equilibration" will become dissolution, the unhappy epilogue of evolution. Societies will disintegrate, masses will migrate, cities will fade into the dark hinterland of peasant life; no government will be strong enough to hold the loosened part together; social order will cease to be even remembered. And in the individual, too, integration will give way to disruption; and that coordination which is life will pass into that diffuse disorder which is death. The earth will be a chaotic theater of decay, a gloomy drama of energy in irreversible degradation; and it will itself be resolved into the dust and nebula from which it came. The cycle of evolution and dissolution will be complete. The cycle will begin again, and endless times again; but always this will be the denouement. *Memento mori* is written upon the face of life, and every birth is a prelude to decay and death.[11]

Such <is> the gloom of evolution! What is the use of these repeated cycles of life and death? Though endless the repetition of such cycles of life, could one say that existence is better than non-existence?

---

10. Will Durant, *Story of Philosophy: The Lives and Opinions of the Greater Philosophers* (New York: Simon and Schuster, 1926), 399.

11. Ibid., 400-401.

CHAPTER XXV

Creation: The Time and Manner of the Earth's Creation II

SCRIPTURE READING LESSON

Analysis

I. "Creation" and God.

II. Earth-life by Migrations from Other Worlds.

III. The Development of Life Forms.

IV. Kinds of Evolution.

V. The Great Law of Life.

VI. Bible Creation: Progressive Creation in Genesis.

VII. Power of Life in Earth and Sea and Air.

VIII. Creative Development Sustained by Some Scientists.

IX. The "Terror" of Anthropomorphism.

References

All scripture quotations in this and the preceding lesson.

All the works cited in references of Chapter 24.

Robert K. Duncan, *The New Knowledge: A Popular Account of the New Physics and the New Chemistry in Their Relation to the New Theory of Matter* (New York: A. S. Barnes and Co., 1905), *passim*; Frederick W. Headley, *Problems of Evolution* (New York: T. Y. Crowell and Co., 1901).

Francis W. Rolt-Wheeler, ed., *Science-History of the Universe*, 10 vols. (New York: The Current Literature Publishing Co., 1909),. See *passim*, vol. 5, *Biology*, vol. 7, *Anthropology*, vol. 10, *Philosophy*.

George H. Howison, University of California, *The Limits of Evolution and Other Essays Illustrating the Metaphysical Theory of Personal Idealism*, 2nd ed., rev. and enl. (New York: The Macmillan Co., 1904).

B. H. Roberts, "Man's Relationship to Deity," published in *The Gospel*, 6th ed. (Salt Lake City: Deseret Book Co., 1926).

Samuel Kinns, Ph.D., *Moses and Geology; or, The Harmony of the Bible with Science*, 2nd ed. (1882).

Henri Bergson, *Creative Evolution*, authorized translation from the French into English by Arthur Mitchell, Ph.D. (New York: Henry Holt & Co., 1911).

CHAPTER XXV

Creation: The Time and Manner of the Earth's Creation II

"CREATION" AND GOD

As in the case of the time period of creation, so in the "manner" of creation, we may not wholly accept either of the theories or any of the variations of them proposed. We start, of course, with God as the creator of the earth and its heavens. They were created at his command, and by his power, and under the operation of laws of creation. All which, however, does not require us to believe that the creation of the earth and its heavens were made instantly, as by magic, or by an absolutely new process; nor that the things "created," any more than the order, were new and for the first time produced. Both the things created and the order of their production must have been many times repeated in the multitudinous worlds of the universe, where creations in some manner have been going on eternally.

If, as we have presented the case in previous chapters, there are older worlds than ours in existence, inhabited by myriads of forms of life, vegetable and animal, such as live in the seas and fly in the air and roam over the plains and through the forests; and if, as we have set forth in previous chapters, the superior Intelligences of older worlds have mastered the problems not only of interplanetary and inter-solar-system communication, but also of interplanetary transportation, indeed universal communication and transportation throughout the universe–then it is possible that some method of transportation may have been employed in conveying life in varied forms from other worlds to ours.

EARTH-LIFE BY MIGRATION FROM OTHER WORLDS[1]

This theory of bringing life forms from outside our earth to the earth[2] is not without the support of scientific names of high standing. It is held by both

---

1. <Ms III^{c} adds "Earth-life by Migration from Other Worlds"–*Ed.*>
2. <Ms III* "from outside our earth to it"–*Ed.*>

<Hermann von> Helmholtz and Lord Kelvin, and others in good scientific standing, viz., that minute living creatures may have come to the earth from elsewhere in the cracks of meteorites or among cosmic dust. The author of *The Outline of Science* says:

> It must be remembered that seeds can survive prolonged exposure to very low temperatures; and spores of bacteria can survive high temperature; that seeds of plants[3] and germs of animals in a state of "latent life" can survive prolonged drought and absence of oxygen. It is possible, according to Berthelot, that as long as there is no molecular disintegration, vital activities may be suspended for a time and may afterwards recommence when appropriate conditions are restored. Therefore, one should be slow to say that a long journey through space is impossible. The obvious limitation of Lord Kelvin's theory [just what is stated above] is that it only shifts the problem of the origin of organisms (i.e., living creatures) from the earth to elsewhere.[4]

All that need be said in answer to this alleged limitation of Lord Kelvin's theory is that in an eternal universe, where neither life nor life forms may[5] have any absolute beginning, all life and many forms of life being equally eternal with the eternal universe, the supposed limitations named by Thomson have no existence, and consequently no problem of the origin of life or of forms of life, both being eternal.

THE DEVELOPMENT OF LIFE FORMS

The transportation of a few forms of life, varieties from other worlds, would doubtless be sufficient from which to develop all our earth-life forms; for it is certain that development of varied forms of life goes on in the vegetable and animal kingdoms of our world—a limited development, however, of life forms; each within the limits of its kind; so that from a comparatively few forms of life there may have arisen all the multitudinous forms that have inhabited the earth. This theory of development within certain group-forms, rather than by absolute mechanical or creative evolution starting with one primeval substance or life "stuff"—the protoplasm of the scientists—may have been the process from which has been produced and differentiated all forms of life, even up to production of the human race—meaning, as to the last, production from one primeval pair.

The difference here set forth in what we shall call "The Development Theory" and the theory of the generally accepted evolution of science, consists in this. The

---

3. <Ms III "seeds of planets," but Thomson's text has "seeds of plants"—*Ed.*>

4. J. Arthur Thomson, ed., *The Outline of Science: A Plain Story Simply Told* (New York: G. P. Putnam's Sons, 1922), 1:61.

5. <Ms III^c adds "may"—*Ed.*>

development theory above outlined leaves room for the operation of the great propagative and "development law," namely, that each great kingdom or subdivision of life named in Genesis 1, produces after its kind, whereas evolution in all its forms destroys that thought and holds that all the varied forms of life have been absolutely produced by evolutionary processes, and leaves no line of estoppage between the kingdoms, orders, families, genera, classes, or the species[6] of vegetable and animal life forms.

KINDS OF EVOLUTION

In the interest of clearness a further word as to various kinds of evolution is necessary. Three kinds are usually recognized. (1) Materialistic evolution. This denies everything but matter and motion in the evolutionary process. This I refer to as "mechanical evolution." (2) Agnostic evolution. This "postulates an 'unknown' and 'unknowable' as the basis and explanation of the process." This <is> the evolution basis (or lack of basis) of the <Herbert> Spencer, <Thomas Henry> Huxley, and <John> Fiske school of evolutionists—the general school of evolutionists. (3) "Theistic evolution," which assumes God or Mind in some way back of all working, with results along the unalterable line of natural law, "and by physical force exclusively"; but working, perhaps, towards some definite far-off, though unknown end or event. This is sometimes regarded as purposeful evolution. Also, it is referred to as "creative evolution," of which Henri Bergson is perhaps the most prominent proponent.[7]

THE GREAT LAW OF LIFE

The development theory, which I am setting forth as the biblical story of creation, differs from both agnostic and creative or theistic evolution (mechanical or materialistic evolution is not considered at all) in this: that both of these forms of evolution start with an homogeneous substance which is differentiated into gases and liquids and solids (inorganic evolution, thence into life substance and simple forms of life; thence into more complex life forms, until there is produced by an ever-differentiating process all the life forms known: whereas the development theory of this chapter and work recognizes and starts with the eternity of life—the life force; and the eternity of some life forms, and the possibilities of these forms—perhaps in embryonic status, or in their simplest forms (save as to man) are

---

6. <Ms III* "between even the kingdoms, the classes or the species"—*Ed.*>

7. Henri Bergson, *Creative Evolution*, the French original is translated into English by Arthur Mitchell, Ph.D. (New York: Henry Holt and Co., 1911).

transplanted to newly created worlds there to be developed each to its highest possibilities, by propagation, and yet within and under the great law of life of Genesis 1, viz., each "after," and within, "its kind."

BIBLE CREATION: PROGRESSIVE CREATION IN GENESIS[8]

The revelation of God on creation contained in Genesis, chapters one and two, gives evidence of the existence of creation by propagative and development processes, which let us now consider. To begin with there is in the whole first chapter of Genesis[9] a succession of creative acts that shows the developing process:

First: the existence of chaos, material in chaotic state, void, and with darkness brooding over it. Then the Spirit of God moves throughout the watery, vapory mass, and God speaks and says: "Let there be light" and there is light; and he divides the light from the darkness, and this was the work of the first creative day or period (Gen. 1:1-5).

Second: and God said, Let there be a firmament (i.e., division) in the midst of the waters which are under the firmament, from the waters which are above the firmament (necessarily expanse between) and the firmament was called heaven. This was the work of the second creative day or period (Gen. 1:6-8).

Third: God also said, Let the waters under the heaven (or firmament) be gathered together unto one place, and let the dry land appear; and it was so. The dry land was called earth, and the gathering together of the waters, sea. God also said in this period "let the earth bring forth grass, the herb yielding seed, and the fruit tree yielding fruit after his kind, whose seed is in itself. . . . And the earth brought forth the grass, and the herb yielding seed after his kind, and the tree yielding fruit, whose seed was in itself, after his kind" (Gen. 1:11-12). And this was the third creative day or period (Gen. 1:9-13).

Fourth: in the fourth creative period our earth was brought into such relationships or changed conditions as[10] to other spheres that the great lights in the world-system to which our earth belongs, produced our ordinary day and night.[11] The light period being called day, and the darkness night (Gen. 1:14-19).

Fifth: in the fifth period God said, Let the waters bring forth abundantly the moving creature that hath life; and let the flying creatures that fly above the earth

---

8. Compare creation account<s> in Book of Moses and the Book of Abraham; also in allusions to <creation> in other revelations of the New Dispensation, Doctrine and Covenants, *passim*: they will be found in agreement with the Bible.

9. <Ms III "the whole chapter of first Genesis"—*Ed.*>

10. <Ms III^c adds "as"—*Ed.*>

11. <Ms III* "our ordinary day and night was produced"—*Ed.*>

in the open firmament of heaven appear. The living creatures of both the waters and the fowls of the air were to reproduce after their kind, and this "abundantly." And God in this fifth period made the beast of the earth after his kind;[12] and cattle after their kind, and every thing that creepeth on the earth after his kind, and God saw that it was good (Gen. 1:20-25).

Sixth: then came the sixth creative period in which man was created–that is, be it remembered, formed or fashioned. And in man's production there seems to have been something special or peculiar; for God said, "Let Us make man in Our image, after Our likeness" (Gen. 1:26). This is not said of any of the other creations; and the proposition further was that to man should be given dominion over all the rest of the creation; over the fish of the sea, the fowl of the air, the cattle, and over all the earth. "So God created man in His own image, in the image of God created He him, male and female created He them. And God blessed them, and God said unto them, Be fruitful and multiply and replenish the earth and subdue it" (Gen. 1:27-28). Every herb, vegetable, and the animal creation the Lord also gave unto man for his food. "And God saw everything that He had made, and behold, it was very good" (Gen. 1:31). Thus closed the sixth creative period (Gen. 1:26-31), followed by a seventh period, designated as a day of rest, the creation having been sufficiently completed to meet the purposes of God at that time (Gen. 2:1-3).

Thus, from chaos to the production of man in an orderly unfolding development from lower to higher forms, from simple to constantly-increasing complexity, but running throughout the whole course of such development is the iteration and reiteration that the forms of life are to produce each after his kind. When we arrive at the creation of man, undoubtedly the same creative law is followed–he is produced after his kind. "And God said, Let Us make man in Our image, after Our likeness"; which is only equivalent to saying, after Our kind. This "after his kind," the law of creation, is iterated and reiterated nine times in this short chapter on creation! The emphasis must be important.[13]

POWER OF LIFE IN THE EARTH, AND SEA, AND AIR[14]

One other thing to be observed. The creation account says:

---

12. <Ms III "the beasts of the earth, after his kind," but the singular "beast" is used in order to agree with "his kind" and with Gen. 1:25–*Ed.*>

13. The treatment of the creation of man for earth, and especially of Adam and the kind of being he was at his advent upon the earth, is considered in chapters 30, 31, 33, part II.

14. <Ms III[c] adds "Power of Life in the Earth, and Sea, and Air"–*Ed.*>

> Let the earth bring forth grass, the herb yielding seed, and the fruit tree yielding fruit after his kind, whose seed is in itself, upon the earth (Gen. 1:11).

"Let the earth bring forth!" As if a power was in the earth to produce life of varied forms. This in the third creative period.[15] Let it be observed also that in this first period such mandate goes as to grasses, herbs, and fruit trees—the lower forms of life (i.e., vegetable life).

Then in the fifth period:[16]

> Let the waters bring forth abundantly the . . . creature that hath life, and fowl that they may fly above the earth in the firmament (cf. Gen. 1:20).

As if power were in the sea to produce life, and in the air to produce the living creature, and God blessed them saying, Be fruitful and multiply and fill the waters in the seas and let the fowl multiply in the air. Turning again to the earth, in the twenty-fourth[17] verse—after God had said in the eleventh verse, "Let the earth bring forth grass," etc.—He now says, contemplating a larger earth-life, "Let the earth bring forth the living creature," the creeping thing, the lower forms of earth animal life, and beasts of the earth, including cattle—higher forms of animal life—"after their kind." This address to earth, and sea, and again to earth would rather indicate that these had productive life powers of varied kinds within them.

CREATIVE DEVELOPMENT SUSTAINED BY SOME SCIENTISTS

As already stated such a theory as to origin of living creatures upon the earth is not without advocates of sufficient high standing to command respect. Under the heading of "Origin of Living Creatures upon the Earth" as a third answer to the question of how life originated, J. Arthur Thomson, author of *The Outline of Science*, points out that some have held:

> That living creatures of a very simple sort may have merged on the earth's surface from not-living material, e.g., from some semi-fluid carbon compounds activated by ferments. The tenability of this view is suggested by the achievements[18] of the synthetic chemists, who are able artificially to build up substances such as oxalic acid, indigo, salicylic acid, caffeine, and grape-sugar.[19]

---

15. <Ms III "the second creative period," which is corrected to "third"—*Ed.*>

16. <Ms III "the fourth creative period," which is corrected to "fifth"—*Ed.*>

17. <Ms III "thirty-fourth"—*Ed.*>

18. <Ms III* "by the adjustments," but Ms III[c] "by the achievements" coincides with Thomson's text—*Ed.*>

19. Thomson, *Outline of Science*, 1:61.

Mr. Thomson continues in his comment:

> We do not know . . . what in Nature's laboratory would take the place of the clever synthetic chemists, but there seems to be a tendency to complexity. Corpuscles form atoms, atoms form molecules, small molecules larger ones. . . . So far as we know of what goes on today, there is no evidence of spontaneous generation; organisms seem always to arise from pre-existing organisms of the same kind; where any suggestion of the contrary has been fancied, there have been flaws in the experimenting. But it is one thing to accept the verdict (all life from life)[20] as a fact, to which experiment has not yet discovered an exception, and another thing to maintain that this must always have been true or must always remain true.[21]

This statement Mr. Thomson follows with the sympathetic paragraph, which I here quote:

> If the synthetic chemists should go on surpassing themselves, if substances like white of egg should be made artificially, and if we should get more light on possible steps by which simple living creatures may have arisen from not-living materials, this would not greatly affect our general outlook on life, though it would increase our appreciation of what is often labelled as "inert" matter. If the dust of the earth did naturally give rise very long ago to living creatures, if they are in a real sense born of her and of the sunshine, then the whole world becomes more continuous and more vital, and all the inorganic groaning and travailing becomes more intelligible.[22]

Let this be as it may as to the origin of life in the earth, or at least as to some forms of it,[23] it need not affect our view here set forth as to life, and especially as to the higher forms of life;[24] and especially of human forms of life, which beyond doubt were transplanted[25] from some of the older and more highly-developed worlds. And from a few other transported forms of life to the earth,[26] there could be development of varied kinds of life, yet adhering closely to the great law of creation, so constantly repeated—"each after his kind." Not necessarily rigidly limited to stereotyped individual forms, but developing the kinds from the

---

20. <The words in parentheses are Roberts's translation of Thomson's Latin *omne vivum e vivo—Ed.*>

21. Thomson, *Outline of Science*, 1:61-62.

22. Ibid., 1:62.

23. <Ms III[c] adds "or at least as to some forms of it"—*Ed.*>

24. <Ms III[*] "here set forth that life, and especially the higher forms of life"—*Ed.*>

25. <Ms III[*] "and again, especially human forms of life, may have been transplanted"; notice that in the revision of the text Roberts has changed the original possibility of "may have been transplanted" to the certainty of "beyond all doubt were transported"—*Ed.*>

26. <Ms III[*] "from a few such forms transported to the earth"—*Ed.*>

subdivisions of vegetable and animal kingdoms into various species through development from primeval forms; and for man a divine origin after his kind, bearing the image of God—his Father.

THE "TERROR" OF ANTHROPOMORPHISM

Theologians, in their efforts to provide means of escape from a too rigid anthropomorphism would fain interpret this "image" of God to mean, not the full-length portrait or image of God, but a so-called "moral image." "The likeness to God," says one commentator, "lies in the mental and moral features of man's character, such as reason, personality, free will, the capacity for communion with God."[27] But this is pure assumption on the part of the theologians—this limitation of the "image of God" to these mental and moral qualities. We have a right from the scripture record to the inclusion of the physical features as well as to the mental and moral qualities, and do not have to yield anything to the "terror of anthropomorphism," which is affected by the theologians and philosophers to maintain the conceptions of God as immaterial being, which their antecedents of bygone ages adopted from the pagan philosophies current two thousand years ago. It is no more dishonoring to God to think of Him as having impressed His physical likeness upon man, than to have impressed upon him a mental and moral image. The highest development of spiritual manifestation in our earth is by a spirit in association with a body—in a word, with man.

Where is spirituality more highly developed than in the case of the Lord Jesus Christ? And especially after his resurrection, when spirit and body had become indissolubly united, never again to be separated, not now separated, but still living in union, spirit and body united as it was on that sun-kissed hill in Galilee, when in that resurrected form he appeared to his disciples and stretching forth his arms, as if to embrace the heavens as well as the earth, he cried:

> All power is given unto me in heaven and in earth. Go ye, therefore, and teach all nations, baptizing them in the name of the Father, and of the Son, and of the Holy Ghost. . . . And, lo, I am with you alway, even unto the end of the world (Matt. 28:18-20).

That moment God, through the Christ, was most perfectly manifested unto man; and beyond that occasion there has been no superior spiritual manifestation, no higher type given of spirit life and form than in that well-attested incident in

---

27. John R. Dummelow, ed., *A Commentary on the Holy Bible by Various Writers, Complete in One Volume* (New York: The Macmillan Co., 1922), at Gen. 1:26.

the life of the Christ. This <is> the manifestation or revelation of God in the flesh: for such was Jesus Christ—God manifested in the flesh. Witness the scripture:

> Without controversy great is the mystery of godliness; God was manifest in the flesh, justified in the Spirit, seen of angels, preached unto the Gentiles, believed on in the world, received up into glory (1 Tim. 3:16).

All in plain allusion to the Christ.

On this showing we may conclude that the highest development of the spiritual is in its connection with the physical, and always will be so in God's creation of man in His own image and in His own likeness, male and female. This is what God is working at in creation—as we shall see later—the bringing to pass the indissoluble union of spirit and element, in which union man can attain to his highest development and greatest joy.

And why should it be thought incredible that God should be in human form? Or derogatory to His dignity or nature? Of all life forms man's unquestionably is the[28] most excellent in all things; most beautiful; most convenient; most noble. Shakespeare did not overdraw the picture of man, when he exclaimed of him:

> How noble in reason! How infinite in faculty! In form and moving how express and admirable! In action, how like an angel! In apprehension, how like a God![29]

The crowning glory of the "creation" also is he; begotten after his kind—a son of God!

---

28. <Ms III[c] adds "the"—*Ed.*>
29. <William Shakespeare, "Hamlet," act 2, scene 2, line 306—*Ed.*>

CHAPTER XXVI

Man: Pre-existence of Spirits, Eternal Existence of Intelligences

SCRIPTURE READING LESSON

Analysis

I. Of the "Creation" of Man.

II. The Pre-earth Existence of the Christ.

III. Jesus as the Firstborn.

IV. Jesus, "Elder Brother" to Men.

V. Jesus, the Only Begotten Son of God in the Flesh, and the First Begotten of the Dead.

VI. Eternal Intelligences.

VII. The Book of Abraham on the Eternity of Intelligences.

VIII. Of Words Used Interchangeably in the Scriptures.

IX. Joseph Smith on the Eternity of Intelligences.

X. Value of the Doctrine of the Eternity of Intelligences.

References

Suggest careful consideration of all the citations of scripture in the text with context.

Joseph Smith, *The King Follett Sermon; The Being and Kind of Being God Is; The Immortality of the Intelligence of Man*, annotated by B. H. Roberts (Salt Lake City: Magazine Printing Co., 1926).

B. H. Roberts, *Joseph Smith, the Prophet-Teacher*, 2d ed. (Salt Lake City: Deseret Book Co., 1927).

D&C 93.

Also, B. H. Roberts, *Seventy's Course in Theology, Second Year*, lessons 1-4; *Third Year*, lessons 1-4, and *passim* throughout the course.

Also, B. H. Roberts, "The Prophet's Work—Mormonism a System of Philosophy," chap. 55 of "History of the 'Mormon' Church," *Americana* 6 (October 1911): 993-1019.

This subject, being more especially a doctrine of the New Dispensation, does not admit of a wide range of references.

CHAPTER XXVI

Man: Pre-existence of Spirits, Eternal Existence of Intelligences

OF THE "CREATION" OF MAN

It will be observed that the word "creation" in the side heading is enclosed in quotation marks. This is done advisedly, because it will be held in this work that there is something more to the origin of man than the word "creation" describes in its ordinary sense. It has already been noted (chapter 21) that the doctrine of "Creationism" and "Traducianism" as describing the origin of man is not in harmony with the doctrine to be upheld in this writing. The doctrine of "Creationism" as applied to man is that each time a human being is begotten by parents, God creates "out of nothing" a soul for that body. "Traducianism," on the contrary, assigns the origin of both soul and body to generation by the earthly parents. The view to be maintained in this writing, however, is that the mind, the spirit of man, has a pre-existence to his earth-life; and that there is a taking possession of the body by this pre-existent spirit at birth.[1]

THE PRE-EARTH EXISTENCE OF THE CHRIST

St. John in the colorful preface to his gospel declares that in the beginning

---

1. The definite statement of the text as to the time of the spirit taking possession of the body is justified, as the writer believes, from the Book of Mormon: "And it came to pass that he cried mightily unto the Lord . . . ; and behold, the voice of the Lord came unto him, saying, 'Lift up your head and be of good cheer; for behold, the time is at hand, and on this night shall the sign [i.e., of the Christ's birth] be given, and on the morrow come I into the world'" (3 Ne. 1:12-13). This the pre-existent, personal Spirit of the Christ speaking to the Nephite prophet the night previous to the Christ's birth; and hence he had not yet entered into the infant body to be born of Mary; but "on the morrow"—the day of his birth—"come I into the world." And as it was in the case of the Christ, undoubtedly it is as to all the spirits of men, who take possession of the bodies provided for them—they take possession of them at the moment of birth—when they catch the breath of life, and begin a separate existence. <For a discussion of this question, see Jeffrey E. Keller, "When Does the Spirit Enter the Body?" *Sunstone* 10 (Mar. 1985): 42-44—*Ed.*>

was the "Word" which was with God, "and that was God"—in him was life, "and the life was the light of men"—he declared this "Word was made flesh, and dwelt" among men, that they "beheld His glory, even the glory of the only begotten of the Father," thus identifying this pre-existent "Word," that was God, with Jesus of Nazareth (cf. John 1:1, 4, 14). Under this scripture the divisions and subdivisions of Christendom believe that in some way, not very clearly defined, however, the "Word" identified with Jesus Christ had a pre-existence with God.[2] The Christ, however, spirit and body, as he went about his mission in his earth-life, closely resembled man both in mental and physical qualities. He was warmed by the same fire, chilled by the same winter's blast, subject to hunger and fatigue; he required the same food and rest; pre-eminently he was the man of sorrows, having affections, ties of friendship, experiencing pity, and at times angered by manifestations of injustice and hypocrisy; and finally was subject to death as all men are. The question arises, if the Christ resembled man in all these points, may not man resemble the Christ in the matter of a pre-existence? That if the Christ, as a spirit personage, was "in the beginning" with the Father, may not the spirits of men have had such an existence also? It is written in scripture that "he that sanctifieth [having in mind the Christ] and they who are sanctified [men][3] are all of one: for which cause he is not ashamed to call them brethren"[4] (Heb. 2:11).

From the above considerations it surely can be reasonably argued that if Christ's spirit, pre-existing as the "Word," was "in the beginning with God," may there not have been likewise a pre-existence of the spirits of men from the beginning with God?

In further evidence of the pre-existence of the Christ to his earth-life, we have him in his Gethsemane prayer, saying:

> And now, O Father, glorify Thou me with Thine own self, with that same glory that I had with Thee before the world was (cf. John 17:5).

Again in Hebrews:

> God . . . who spake in times past unto the fathers, by the prophets, hath in these last days spoken unto us by his Son, whom He hath appointed heir to all things, by whom also He made the worlds (Heb. 1:1-2).

From this it is clear that the Christ not only had a pre-mortal life existence, but also that life was of such majesty that he was employed by the Father in the creation of "worlds"!

---

2. <Ms III[*] "had a pre-existence with His Father"—*Ed.*>
3. <Ms III[c] adds "[men]"—*Ed.*>
4. <Ms III[*] "to call them (men) brethren"—*Ed.*>

Often the Christ bewildered the Jews that entered into controversy with him as to his mission and himself. On one occasion he said to them:

> "Your father Abraham rejoiced to see my day; and he saw it, and was glad." Then said the Jews unto him, "Thou art not yet fifty years old and hast thou seen Abraham?" Jesus said unto them, "Verily, verily, I say unto you, Before Abraham was, I Am" (John 8:56-58).

Which could only be true, of course, because the spirit of the Christ had a pre-mortal life existence with God. This doctrine seems to have been too much for some of his disciples to accept; for on expounding it to them under the statement that he was "the bread of life which came down from heaven," they turned away from him with the remark that this was "a hard saying; who can hear it?" Whereupon the Christ, knowing their murmuring, said, "Does this offend you? What and if ye shall see the Son of man ascend up where he was before?" (cf. John 6:58, 60-62).

From all these texts it can only be concluded that the Christ had a pre-existence in a glorified state with his Father before the world was; that under the Father's direction he even created worlds, and hence was creator—Father of heaven and earth.[5]

MEN AND JESUS OF THE SAME ORDER OF BEINGS

The scriptures teach that Jesus Christ and men are of the same order of beings; that men are of the same race with Jesus, of the same nature and essence; that he is indeed our "elder brother."

> For it became him, for whom are all things, and by whom are all things, in bringing many sons unto glory, to make the captain of their salvation perfect through suffering. For both he that sanctifieth [the Christ] and they who are sanctified [men] are all of one: for which cause he is not ashamed to call them brethren (cf. Heb. 2:10-11).

Also, the newly-risen Christ said to Mary Magdala as she approached him on the resurrection morning:

> Touch me not, for I have not yet ascended to my Father; but go to my brethren and say unto them, I ascend unto my Father and your Father; to my God and to your God (John 20:17).

A sweeter statement of the fatherhood of God, and the brotherhood of the

---

5. Alma 11:38-39: "'Is the Son of God the very Eternal Father?' And Amulek said, ... 'Yea, he is the very Eternal Father, [Creator] of heaven and earth, and all things that in them are.'"

Christ to men, may not be found. Hence, while very far removed from us in that the Christ is perfect in all righteousness, and more highly developed in intellectual and spiritual powers than we, yet these differences are of degree, not of kind; so that what is revealed concerning Jesus the Christ may be of infinite helpfulness in throwing light upon the nature of man and the several estates he has occupied and will occupy hereafter.

The co-eternity of Jesus Christ with God the Father is quite universally held to be set forth in the preface of St. John's gospel, which is so familiar that it need not be repeated here. Moreover, to those who accept the New Dispensation of the gospel, through the revelations of God to the Prophet Joseph Smith, the doctrine of John's preface comes with increased emphasis by reason of the proclaimed extension of the principle of the co-eternity of God the Father and Jesus Christ to men also;[6] and by asserting also the fact that the intelligent entity in man, the mind, intelligence, was "not created or made, neither indeed can be" (D&C 93:29).

In the following we have the co-eternity of Jesus and of all men most emphatically stated:

> I was in the beginning with the Father, . . . Ye were also in the beginning with the Father; that which is spirit [that is, that part of man that is spirit] . . . ; man [that is, all men, the term is generic, includes the race] was . . . in the beginning with God (D&C 93:21, 23, 29).

And then mark what follows: "Intelligence"—the part that was with God in the beginning, the entity in man which cognizes truth, that perceives that which is, mind, say—"intelligence, or the light of truth, was not created or made, neither indeed can be" (D&C 93:29).

JESUS AS THE FIRSTBORN IN THE SPIRIT LIFE[7]

Sure it is that God the Father is the Father of the spirits of men. Paul says:

> We have had fathers of our flesh which corrected us, and we gave them reverence: shall we not much rather be in subjection unto the Father of spirits and live? (Heb. 12:9).

Also, "Our Father which art in heaven, hallowed be Thy name" (The Lord's Prayer, Matt. 6:9)—the relationship expressed can not be meaningless.

According to this, then, there is a "Father of spirits." It follows, of course, that "spirits" have a father—they are begotten—not made. The difference being that the

---

6. <Ms III[c] adds "also"—*Ed.*>
7. <Ms III[c] adds "In The Spirit Life"—*Ed.*>

thing which is begotten partakes of the very nature of him who begets while that which is made may not. It should be remarked that the term "spirits" in the above passage can not refer to self-existent, unbegotten intelligences of the revelations, considered in the above, except as intelligences inhabiting spirit bodies, and certainly this relationship of fatherhood to spirits is not one brought about in connection with generation of human life in this world. Paul makes a very sharp distinction between "fathers of our flesh" and the "Father of spirits,"[8] in the above. Fatherhood to spirits is manifestly a relationship established independent of man's earth-existence; and, of course, in an existence which preceded earth-life, where the uncreated intelligences were begotten spirits. Hence, the phrase, "shall we not be in subjection[9] to the Father of spirits and live?"

Christ is referred to by the writer of the Epistle to the Colossians, as the "firstborn of every creature" (Col. 1:15) and the Revelator speaks of him as "the beginning of the creation of God" (Rev. 3:14). And in the revelation already quoted so often Jesus represents himself as being in the "beginning with the Father" and as "the Firstborn" (D&C 93:21).

The reference to Jesus as the "firstborn of every creature" cannot refer to his birth into earth-life, for he was not the firstborn into this world; therefore, "firstborn" here referred to must have reference to the birth of his spirit before his earth-life. The reference to Jesus as the "beginning of the creation of God" cannot refer to his creation or generation in earth-life; for manifestly he was not the beginning of the creations of God in this world; therefore, he must have been the "beginning" of God's creation (begetting)[10] elsewhere, viz., in the spirit-world, where he—an intelligence from eternity—was begotten a spiritual personage; a son of God.

JESUS, "ELDER BROTHER" TO MEN

The reference to Jesus as the "firstborn"—and hence the justification for our calling him our "Elder Brother"—can not refer to any relationship that he established in his earth-life, since as to the flesh, he is not our "Elder Brother"; any more than he is the "firstborn" in the flesh; there were many born as to the flesh before he was, and older brothers to us in the flesh than he. The relationship of "Elder Brother" can not have reference to that estate where all were self-existent, uncreated and unbegotten, eternal intelligences; for that estate admits of no such

---

8. <Ms III* "and the 'Fathers of spirits'"—*Ed.*>

9. <Ms III* "shall we not be subject," while Ms III[c] adds "in," it omits to change "subject" to "subjection," as in Heb. 12:9—*Ed.*>

10. <Ms III[c] adds "(begetting)"—*Ed.*>

relation as "elder" or "younger"; for as to the succession in time, the fact on which "younger" and "elder" depends, the intelligences are equal, that is, equal as to their eternity. Therefore, since the relationship of "Elder Brother" was not established by any possible fact in that estate where all were self-existing intelligences, it must have been established in the spirit life, where Jesus, with reference to the hosts of intelligences designed to our earth, was the "firstborn spirit," and by that fact became our "Elder Brother," the "firstborn of every creature," "the beginning of the creations of God," as pertaining to our order of existence.

JESUS, THE ONLY BEGOTTEN SON OF GOD IN THE FLESH, AND THE FIRST BEGOTTEN OF THE DEAD

As to his earth-life—his existence in it—Jesus bears two marked distinctions: first, he is the "only begotten of the Father" in the flesh; and, second, he is "the first begotten of the dead." He is designated as the "only begotten of the Father" by St. John in the following passages:

> And the Word [the pre-existing Christ of the preface to St. John's gospel] was made flesh, and dwelt among us, and we beheld his glory, the glory as of the only begotten of the Father, full of grace and truth (John 1:14).

Again:

> God so loved the world, that He gave His only begotten Son, that whosoever believeth on him might not perish. . . . But he that believeth not is condemned already, because he hath not believed in the name of the only begotten Son of God (John 3:16, 18; same in 1 Jn. 4:9).

As in the second distinction, the "first begotten of the dead," that is also ascribed to him by St. John in the Revelation, where he refers to Jesus as "the Faithful Witness, and the First-begotten of the dead" (Rev. 1:5). And Paul in his discourse on the resurrection—speaking of the order of it—says "but every man in his own order: Christ the firstfruits, afterwards they that are Christ's at his coming" (1 Cor. 15:23).

ETERNAL INTELLIGENCES

There is something deeper, however, to this matter of man's origin than his pre-existence to this earth-life; a deeper truth to be found—there is the intelligence of spirits to be accounted for. In one of our modern revelations through the prophet of the New Dispensation, Joseph Smith, it is said: "Intelligence, or the light of truth, was not created or made, neither indeed can be" (D&C 93:29). "Intelligence, or the light of truth"—evidently meaning by that the light by which truth is discerned, or cognized; and that intelligence which cognizes truth, is not made, nor can it be made, because it is eternal. Wonderful Truth! Let us see what comes of it.

Theologians regard it as a very wonderful discovery that Christ, the second Personage in the Trinity, the "Word" which was "with God in the beginning," "and which was God," was co-eternal with the Father; though they had to leave it as among the unsolvable mysteries. In a modern revelation this same truth is stated, but in a somewhat different terminology, which may help to clarify it. The revelation represents the Christ as saying:

> And now, verily I say unto you, I was in the beginning with the Father, and am the Firstborn. . . . Ye [meaning Joseph Smith and the Elders who were present with him when the revelation was received]–Ye were also in the beginning with the Father, that which is spirit, even the spirit of truth. . . . Man [i.e., the race] was also in the beginning with God. Intelligence, or the light of truth, was not created or made, neither indeed can be (D&C 93:21, 23, 29).

This undoubtedly means that the intelligence of spirits–of spirit personages–is equally eternal with Christ and with God.[11] Of the nature of intelligence in general and of individual intelligences as inhabiting the universe, we have already spoken in a previous chapter (10), and it is only necessary to emphasize here the existence of such an entity in every individual spirit. Let us recapitulate, for the importance of the truth is worthy of it.

First is affirmed the co-eternity of the Christ and God the Father–"in the beginning, before the world was." Then the like co-eternity of the spirits of men present when the revelation above quoted was given is affirmed. Afterwards the like co-eternity of "man" used in the generic sense, meaning the race, is affirmed, followed by the declaration that "intelligence, or the light of truth [the power which cognizes truth], was not created or made" (D&C 93:29). Then, of course, it follows

---

11. <In his monumental work, *The Comprehensive History of the Church*, Roberts has a chapter on Joseph Smith's philosophical thought, and he coined the term "eternalism," as the best description of the LDS outlook (Truman G. Madsen, *Eternal Man* [Salt Lake City: Deseret Book Co., 1966], 24n). Roberts explains the term as follows: "*Eternalism* is the term I would select as the best descriptive word for New Dispensation philosophy; for that term best represents its concepts: an eternal universe, with no beginning and no end; eternal intelligence, working in eternal duration, without beginning or ending, and without ultimates, and hence eternal progression running parallel with eternal lives; and and eternal or 'everlasting' gospel, offering eternal opportunities for righteousness; eternal existence of mercy, justice, wisdom, truth, and love; all accompanied by eternal relations, associations, unions–eternal youth, and eternal glory!" (B. H. Roberts, *A Comprehensive History of the Church of Jesus Christ of Latter-day Saints, Century I* [Salt Lake City: Church of Jesus Christ of Latter-day Saints, 1930], 2:410-11)–*Ed.*>

that such intelligences are eternal, self-existing beings. It may be urged, however, that the word "intelligence" in the revelation quoted above is used in the singular not in the plural form; and hence may refer to intelligence in general, en masse,[12] as being uncreated and uncreatable, and not to the eternity of individual intelligences. But immediately preceding the words "intelligence . . . was not created or made" is the declaration "man was in the beginning with God," and the word "intelligence" in the passage quoted is governed as to its meaning by "man" in the sentence "man was also in the beginning with God"; and now, "intelligence" (i.e., in man), hence an individual intelligence–hence intelligent entities–were "not created or made, neither indeed can be." In other words, these intelligences are as eternal as God is, or as the Christ is, or the Holy Spirit. This becomes more apparent when we learn in a subsequent verse of the revelation, that "man is spirit," that is, in the inner fact of him, in the power and glory of him, man is not so many pounds avoirdupois of bone, muscle, lime, phosphate, water, and the like; but in the great fact of him, he is spirit–spirit substance and intelligence.[13]

So far as human or revealed knowledge can aid one to something of a conclusion, there is no intelligence existing separate and apart from persons, from intelligent entities. Either intelligence exists as individual persons, or as proceeding from such persons as a power, or force, such as the Spirit of God when it "moved upon the face of the waters" (Gen. 1:2). But this Spirit of God is never separated from its source, any more than rays of light are separated from the luminous bodies whence they proceed. So that if any affirm a Universal Intelligence, or "Cosmic Mind," or "Over-Soul," as existing in the universe, it is a spirit, proceeding either from an individual intelligence, or from harmonized individual intelligences–as mind atmosphere proceeding from them–a projection of their mind–into the universe, as our sun and all the suns project light and warmth into the space-depths,

---

12. <Bruce R. McConkie, *Mormon Doctrine*, 2d ed. (Salt Lake City: Bookcraft, 1966), 387, takes this view, saying, "The intelligence or spirit element became intelligences after the spirits were born as individual entities"–*Ed.*>

13. "That is the more real part of a man in which his characteristics and his qualities are. <All> the facts and phenomena of life confirm the doctrine that the soul [spirit] is the real man. What makes the qualities of man? What gives him character as good or bad, small or great, lovable or detestable? Do these qualities pertain to the body? Everyone knows that they do not, but they are qualities of the mind. Then the real man is not the body, but the living soul" (Samuel M. Warren, "The Soul and Its Future Life," in *The World's Parliament of Religions: An Illustrated and Popular Story of the World's First Parliament of Religions, Held in Chicago in Connection with the Columbian Exposition of 1893*, ed. John H. Barrows [Chicago: The Parliament Publishing Co., 1893], 1:480). <In the next to last sentence of the quote Warren's text has "but they are the qualities of the man"–*Ed.*>

so from harmonized intelligences proceeds that Spirit force we recognize as the "Spirit of God," extending God and all His powers throughout the immensity of space.

THE BOOK OF ABRAHAM ON THE ETERNITY OF INTELLIGENCES[14]

In further evidence of the eternal existence of individual intelligences, I quote from the Book of Abraham, which is of equal authority with any portion of the Bible.

> If two things exist and there be one above the other, there shall be greater things above them. . . . If there be two spirits, and one shall be more intelligent than the other, yet these two spirits, notwithstanding one is more intelligent than the other, have no beginning; they existed before, they shall have no end, they shall exist after, for they are "gnolaum" or eternal (Abr. 3:16, 18).

OF WORDS USED INTERCHANGEABLY IN THE SCRIPTURES[15]

Before making another quotation, in further proof of the eternity of each individual intelligence, I must needs make a brief detour and say something in regard to the use of words interchangeably. It is often the case that misconceptions arise through a careless use of words, and through using words interchangeably, without regard to shades of differences that attach to them; and this <occurs> in the scriptures as in other writings. Indeed, this fault is more frequent in the scriptures perhaps than in any other writings; for the reason that for the most part, the scriptures were composed by men who did not aim at scientific exactness in the use of words. They were not in most cases equal to such precision in the use of language in the first place; and in the second place they depended more upon the general tenor of what they wrote for making truth apparent than upon technical precision in a choice of words; ideas, not exactness of expression, was the burden of their souls; thought, not its dress. Hence, in scripture a large dependence upon the general tenor of what is written to convey the truth is characteristic of the writers of it. Thus, the expressions, "Kingdom of God," "Kingdom of Heaven," "the Whole Family in Heaven," "The Church of Christ," "The Church of God" are often used interchangeably for the "Church of Christ," when they are not always equivalents. So, too, are used the terms "Spirit of God" and "Holy Ghost"; "Spirit of Christ" and the "Holy Ghost"; "spirit" and "soul"; "intelligences" and "spirits," and "angels." I mention this now because I believe many of the differences of

---

14. <Ms III[c] adds "The Book of Abraham on the Eternity of Intelligences"–*Ed.*>

15. <Ms III[c] adds "Of Words Use [*sic*] Interchangeably in the Scriptures"–*Ed.*>

opinion and much of the confusion of ideas that exists arise out of our not recognizing, or our not remembering, these facts.

And now, as to the quotation of which these remarks on the interchangeable use of words was deemed necessary before giving it.

JOSEPH SMITH ON THE ETERNITY OF INTELLIGENCES[16]

The quotation is from a discourse by the Prophet of the New Dispensation, Joseph Smith, generally known as the "King Follett Sermon."[17] It was delivered at Nauvoo in April 1844, a little more than two months before the prophet's martyrdom. It was taken down in longhand and published from the notes of those who wrote it down: Willard Richards, counselor to the prophet; Wilford Woodruff, one of the Twelve Apostles; Thomas Bullock, the secretary of the prophet; and William Clayton, also a secretary to the prophet.[18] It was not reported stenographically, and hence some verbal errors in the reporting may exist. For instance, in the sermon as printed several times in church publications,[19] the prophet is represented as saying: "The intelligence which man possesses is co-equal with God himself." There can be no question, but what this "co-equal" is an error. From the whole tenor of the discourse, the word used must have been "co-eternal" with God, not "co-equal."[20]

---

16. <Ms III[c] adds "Joseph Smith On The Eternity of Intelligences"—*Ed.*>

17. <T. Edgar Lyon, "Doctrinal Development of the Church During the Nauvoo Sojourn, 1839-1846," *Brigham Young University Studies* 15 (Summer 1975): 445, says that in this discourse Joseph Smith for the first time described the "ultimate potential of human beings"—*Ed.*>

18. <These four contemporary accounts of the King Follett Discourse were amalgamated in 1855 by Jonathan Grimshaw. More recently there has been a new amalgamation, based solely on the extant manuscripts in the editor's "The King Follett Discourse: A Newly Amalgamated Text," *Brigham Young University Studies* 18 (Winter 1978): 193-208—*Ed.*>

19. The King Follett Sermon was published, at least a large section of it, in the *Times and Seasons* of August 15, 1844, two months following the martyrdom of the prophet; next it appeared in the *Journal of Discourses* 6 (1859): 1-11; and on many various occasions since. The last publication of it was in the *Improvement Era* 12 (January 1909): 169-91, with references and footnotes by the present writer; now published as a pamphlet, *The King Follett Discourse; The Being and Kind of Being God Is; The Immortality of the Intelligence of Man*, annotated by B. H. Roberts (Salt Lake City: Magazine Printing Co., 1926).

20. <There was disagreement among the church's general authorities about whether men and women are co-eternal with God. Accordingly, at the very last moment some unidentified apostle(s) ordered the Deseret News to delete the King Follett Discourse from

With the explanation here set forth, we shall take the liberty of placing in brackets the right word, where a wrong one has clearly been used; and, in cases where "spirit" and "intelligence" have been used interchangeably, we shall indicate that in the same manner. And now the excerpt from the King Follett Sermon:

> The soul—the mind of man—the immortal spirit [intelligence][21]—where did it come from? All learned men and doctors of divinity say that God created it in the beginning, but it is not so; the very idea lessens man in my estimation. I do not believe the doctrine. I know better. Hear it, all ye ends of the world, for God has told me so. If you don't believe me, it will not make the truth without effect. . . . We say that God Himself is a self-existent being. Who told you so? It is correct enough, but how did it get into your head<s>? Who told you that man did not exist in like manner, upon the same principles? Man does exist upon the same principles. God made a tabernacle and put spirit into it, and it became a living soul. How does it read in the Hebrew? It does not say in the Hebrew that God created the spirit of man. It says, God made man out of the earth, and put into him Adam's spirit, and so became a living body. The mind or the intelligence which man possesses is co-equal [co-eternal] with God himself. I know my testimony is true. . . . I am dwelling on the immortality of the spirit [intelligence] of man. Is it logical to say that the intelligence of spirits is immortal, and yet that it [i.e.,

---

B. H. Roberts' edition of volume six of *The History of the Church*. The King Follett Discourse, occupying an entire chapter, had already been set in type and the pages numbered but not yet printed when the decision came to delete the discourse. The pagination in the 1912 edition skips from 301 to 318; the missing sixteen pages do not appear until the second edition of 1950 (Donald Q. Cannon, "The King Follett Discourse: Joseph Smith's Greatest Sermon in Historical Perspective," *Brigham Young University Studies* 18 [Winter 1978]: 191). Donald Q. Cannon states that the discourse was "removed as the book was ready to be bound," but since 301 and 318 are on both sides of the same sheet, it is more precise to say "printed" than "bound." It is not known who ordered that the discourse be removed from *The History of the Church*, but George Albert Smith wrote to Samuel O. Bennion, "I have thought that the report of that sermon might not be authentic and I have feared that it contained some things that might be contrary to the truth" (George Albert Smith to Samuel O. Bennion, 30 Jan. 1912, George A. Smith Family Collection, Manuscript 36, Bx 32, Fd 2, Manuscripts Division, Marriott Library, University of Utah, Salt Lake City). This action disturbed Roberts and later he had the King Follett Discourse privately published, along with his own notes and references (Joseph Smith, *The King Follett Discourse; The Being and Kind of Being God Is; The Immortality of the Intelligence of Man*, annotated by B. H. Roberts [Salt Lake City: Magazine Printing Co., 1926])—*Ed.*>

21. <This reference to "the immortal spirit" Roberts interprets as the "intelligence," but Madsen says that "the remarks apply also to the begetting of the spirit" (Madsen, *Eternal Man*, 33n)—*Ed.*>

> the intelligence] had a beginning? The intelligence of spirits had no beginning, neither will it have an end.[22] That is good logic. That which has a beginning may have an end. There never was a time when there were no spirits [intelligences] for they are co-equal[23] [co-eternal] with our Father in heaven. . . . Intelligence is eternal and exists upon a self-existent principle. It is a spirit [intelligence] from age to age, and there is no creation about it. . . . The first principles of a man [his intelligence] are self-existent with God.[24]

The difference between "spirits" and "intelligences" as herein used is this. Intelligences are uncreated entities; some inhabiting spiritual bodies—bodies composed of fine spirit elements; others are intelligences unembodied in either spirit bodies or other kinds of bodies.[25] They are uncreated, self-existent entities, necessarily self-conscious, and otherwise consciousness—they are conscious of the "me" and the "not me." They possess powers of comparison and discrimination without which the term "intelligence" would be a solecism. They discern between evil and good; between good and better; they possess will or freedom—within certain limits at least. The power, among other powers, to determine upon a given course of conduct as against any other course of conduct. The individual intelligence can think his own thoughts, act wisely or foolishly; do right or wrong. To accredit an intelligence with fewer or less important powers than these would be to deny him intelligence altogether.

---

22. <In a new amalgamation of the King Follett Discourse, the two previous sentences appear as: "Is it logical to say that a spirit is immortal and yet have a beginning? Because if a spirit of man had a beginning, it will have an end" (see the editor's "King Follett Discourse," 204). Notice that both instances of "the intelligence of spirits" in the traditional King Follett text used by Roberts are replaced by "a spirit" and "a spirit of man," respectively. Joseph Smith used the terms "spirit" and "intelligence" interchangeably.>

23. <Ms III[c] adds "co-equal"—*Ed.*>

24. <Joseph Smith, *King Follett Discourse*, 18-21—*Ed.*>

25. <On 6 February 1907 B. H. Roberts read to the First Presidency and six apostles his discussion concerning the pre-existence of men and women. Roberts's position was that "the elements of man [the intelligence] became a spirit—a child to God—through pre-mortal birth." He strengthened his case by using the example of the brother of Jared seeing the pre-mortal spirit body of Jesus Christ (Ether 3:6-16). The brethren approved his explanation with only minor revision, and this view was incorporated in the 1909 statement of the First Presidency. In August 1911 Roberts read to the First Presidency his essay on the philosophy of Joseph Smith. He explained that intelligences were self-existent entities before the time they became spirits (Thomas G. Alexander, "The Reconstruction of Mormon Doctrine: From Joseph Smith to Progressive Theology," *Sunstone* 5 [July-Aug. 1980]: 30; this information not included in the 1989 reprint of Alexander's article)—*Ed.*>

VALUE OF THE DOCTRINE OF THE ETERNITY OF INTELLIGENCES

It may be asked, what value is this doctrine of the eternal existence of uncreated intelligences, regarding each man as possessed of something within him, and the chief thing about him, as an eternal entity? In what way does it contribute to the better apprehension of that which is THE TRUTH? How better show THE WAY? How better lead to THE LIFE? These considerations are really to underlie all our discussion of the general scheme of things in this earth of ours, and concerning the race of sentient and intelligent beings who inhabit it.

This conception of the eternity of the mind, the intelligence of man, affects in a very vital way the general scheme of things. As matters now stand the usually accepted "Christian doctrine" in the matter of man's origin is that God of His free will "created out of nothing" the spirit[26] and body of man. That men are as He would have them, since in His act of creation He could have had them different had He so minded. Then why should He—being infinitely wise and powerful and good—for so the creeds represent Him—why should He create by mere act of volition beings such as men are, not only capable of, but prone to moral evil? Which, under the theory of God creating man, spirit and body, absolutely, and "out of nothing" in the last analysis of things, in spite of all special pleadings to the contrary, leaves responsibility for moral evil in the world with God.

God's creative acts culminating thus, the next pertinent questions are: then what of the decreed purpose of God to punish moral evil? And what of the much-vaunted justice of God in that punishment? Wherein lies the responsibility of man, if he was so created as to love evil and to follow it? Is it not revolting to reason, as it is shocking to piety, to think that God of His own free will created some men, not only inclined to wickedness, but desperately so inclined; while others, He of His own volition created with dispositions naturally inclined toward goodness? In like manner stands it with man in relation to his inclination to faith, and to disbelief: and yet, under the orthodox "Christian" belief all are included under one law for judgment, and that eternal judgment!

On the other hand, under the conception of the existence of independent, uncreated, self-existent intelligences, who by the inherent nature of them are of various degrees of intelligence and moral quality, differing from each other in many ways, yet alike in their eternity and their freedom—how stands it under this conception of things? Let us so far anticipate consideration of the purposes of God in the earth-life of man as to suppose that God's purpose is the betterment of the condition of these intelligences, and as men to provide progress for them to higher levels of being and power through change. Under this conception of things how

---

26. <Ms III* "the spirits"—*Ed.*>

would matters stand? There is the begetting of these intelligences, <that is to say> the begetting of spirits, the spirits of men; and finally bringing men forth as resurrected immortal[27] personages of infinite possibilities.[28] At each change increased powers for development are added to intelligences; yet ever present through all the processes of betterment is the self-existent entity, the "intelligence" with the tremendous fact of its, or his—for always he is personal—consciousness and moral freedom and indestructibility. He has his choice of moving upward or downward in every estate he occupies; often defeating, for a time at least, the benevolent purposes of God respecting him, through his own perverseness. He passes through dire experiences, suffers terribly, yet learns by what he suffers, so that his very suffering becomes a means to his improvement. He learns, quickly or slowly according to the inherent nature of him, obedience to law. He learns that:

> That which is governed by law is also preserved by law and perfected and sanctified by the same; and that which breaketh law and abideth not by law, but seeketh to become a law unto itself, and willeth to abide in sin, and altogether abideth in sin, cannot be sanctified by law, neither by mercy, justice, or judgment. Therefore, <they> must remain filthy still (D&C 88:34-35).

This conception of things relieves God of the responsibility for the nature and status of intelligences in all stages of their development; their inherent nature and their volition make them, primarily, what they are. This nature they may change, slowly perhaps, yet change it they may. God has put them in the way of changing it by enlarging their intelligence through increase of knowledge and change of environment, through experiences.[29] The only way God effects these self-existent beings is favorably; He creates not their inherent nature; He is not responsible for the use they make of their freedom to choose good or evil—their free moral agency;

---

27. <Ms III[c] adds "immortal"—*Ed.*>

28. <John A. Widtsoe also distinguished between intelligences and spiritual birth. The 1915 publication of Widtsoe's *Rational Theology*, in which he "had included a discussion of intelligences, which he said had existed as separate entities before men became spirit beings, and he included an explicit statement that there was a time when there was no God" (Alexander, "Reconstruction," 31; this information not included in the reprint). The First Presidency had all these statements deleted in the published version. Even with these deletions, Widtsoe still expressed the view that "man has existed 'from the beginning,' and that, from the beginning, he has possessed distinct individuality impossible of confusion with any other individuality among the hosts of intelligent beings" (John A. Widtsoe, *Rational Theology As Taught by the Church of Jesus Christ of Latter-day Saints* [Salt Lake City: Published for the Use of the Melchizedek Priesthood by the General Priesthood Committee, Church of Jesus Christ of Latter-day Saints, 1915], 16)—*Ed.*>

29. <Ms III[*] "change of environment, through change, through experiences"—*Ed.*>

nor is He the author of their sufferings when they fall into sin; that arises out of the violation of law and must be endured until its lessons are learned. But meantime, each for himself, intelligence, spirit, or man—the last all three combined—is responsible for his own status—not God.

CHAPTER XXVII

Purpose of God in the Earth-Life of Man

SCRIPTURE READING LESSON

Analysis

I. God's Work and Glory:
   a. Testimony of Moses;
   b. Testimony of the Book of Mormon.
   c. Testimony of the Prophet of the New Dispensation.

II. The Larger View of Man's Life.

III. Exposition of the Larger View of Man's Life.

IV. Moriancumer's Vision of the Christ in His Spirit-body.

V. The Essential Qualities of Intelligences.

VI. The Completed Thought on the Purpose of God in Man's Earth-life.

VII. And This "Joy!" What is It?

VIII. The Truth in Respect of Man.

References

The Book of Moses, *passim*, especially chap. 1.

The Book of Abraham, *passim*, but especially chap. 3.

Book of Mormon, *passim*, especially 2 Ne. 2:1-30.

Doctrine and Covenants, *passim*, but especially D&C 93.

Joseph Smith, *King Follett Discourse*, annotated by B. H. Roberts (Salt Lake City: Magazine Printing Co., 1926), on the "Immortality of Man."

See also B. H. Roberts, "The Prophet's Work—Mormonism a System of Philosophy," chap. 55 of "History of the 'Mormon' Church," *Americana* 6 (October 1911): 993-1019.

B. H. Roberts, *Seventy's Course in Theology, Second Year*, lessons 1-4, *passim*, *Fourth Year*, lessons 1-4, *passim*.

B. H. Roberts, "Immortality of Man," *Improvement Era* 10 (April 1907): 401-23.*

*This article was really a report of a committee appointed by the First Presidency to answer a number of questions that had been submitted to them on the nature of man's immortality. The committee was Elder Francis M. Lyman of the Twelve Apostles and Elder B. H. Roberts of the First Council of the Seventy. The report was submitted to the First Presidency and a number of the Twelve. An editorial note in the *Era*, above referred to, makes the following statement: "Elder Roberts submitted the following paper to the First Presidency and a number of the Twelve Apostles [seven were present] none of whom found anything objectionable in it, or contrary to the revealed word of God, and therefore, favored its publication—Editors."

CHAPTER XXVII[1]

Purpose of God in the Earth-Life of Man

We are now prepared to consider the purpose of God in the "creation" of man and in a broader way than in the allusion to it in the twenty-first chapter, where it was briefly considered merely to show the wrong and the inadequate conceptions entertained upon the subject in the current theology of the churches. Also, we are to consider such purpose in the light of that fuller knowledge of the subject, which has been made of it through the revelations of God which have come to men in the New Dispensation. It has already been pointed out that there is no clear-cut knowledge to be found on the purpose of God in creation in any of the revelations in the Old Testament or in the New. The question, therefore, is what new light has been thrown upon said purpose in the supplemental revelations of the New Dispensation. Here we are most happy in finding both clear-cut and adequate word of God upon the subject.

GOD'S WORK AND GLORY:

(a) Testimony of Moses[2]

In the Mosaic fragment before referred to in these pages comprising the Book of Moses, we have this as word of God to Israel's great prophet:[3] "This is my work and my glory, to bring to pass the immortality and the eternal life of man" (Moses 1:39).

To appreciate the full value of that brief statement, we will suppose that from some catacomb or pyramid or temple of Egypt, an imperishable parchment had been found, which undeniably was a lost fragment of the writings of Moses, and was the word of God to him, so that this could be regarded by Jew and Christian alike, as a veritable utterance of God. What value would Jew and Christian assign

1. <Ms III* "CHAPTER XVI"–*Ed.*>

2. <Ms III[c] adds "God's Work And Glory: (a) Testimony of Moses," placing this section heading after the introductory sentence and just before the quote from Moses 1:39–*Ed.*>

3. <Ms III* reading appears to be "great prophet Moses"–*Ed.*>

to it, especially in view of the fact that there is no such adequate utterance in any reputed revelation in the Old Testament or in the New, on the purpose of God with reference to the creation of man? Would it not be hailed as a pearl beyond price? A flash from the inner fact of things, driving back the mysteries and the blackness from the horizon of man's vision as to why he is here in this, God's world? It is the purpose of God "to bring to pass the immortality and the eternal life of man"—as man, of course. As immortal man! Immortal as the Christ was and is after his resurrection from the dead—spirit and body indissolubly united; one "soul"; for in the light of our new knowledge, "the spirit and the body is the soul of man, and the resurrection of the body is the redemption of the soul" (cf. D&C 88:15-16). To this first completed "soul" (the Christ)[4] had been given all power in heaven and in earth, and he began the radiation of that "all power," by giving commission to his apostles—his officially accredited witnesses for the whole truth of the gospel scheme of things, with an injunction that they were to teach all nations and administer the gospel ordinances of salvation[5] to them. As with the Christ[6] so shall it be with men in varying degrees as to the glory and power of the immortal existence we are assured will come to them.

But let us not outrun the development of our theme. Let us confine ourselves for the moment to this thought: "This is my work and my glory—to bring to pass the immortality and eternal life of man" (Moses 1:39).

(b) Testimony of the Book of Mormon[7]

This utterance from the Mosaic fragment of revelation is not the only word, nor the completed word that has come to the world through the revelation of God in the New Dispensation. Another word is found, and an additional purpose given—to the one already above set forth—viz., in the American volume of scripture, the Book of Mormon, there one of the old prophets of the ancient American race is represented as saying:

> All things have been done in the wisdom of Him who knoweth all things. Adam fell that men might be, and men are that they might have joy (2 Ne. 2:24-25).

"Adam fell that man might be"; that is, that men might have existence as men; and the design in bringing about the existence of man through Adam's fall is ultimately that he might have joy, exist in a sphere or realm of joy, a world and state of joy. A world where joy shall obtain and persist and go on, and on!

---

4. <Ms III[c] adds "(the Christ)"—*Ed.*>
5. <Ms III[*] "administer its ordinances of salvation"—*Ed.*>
6. <Ms III[c] adds "As with the Christ"—*Ed.*>
7. <Ms III[c] adds "(b) Testimony of the Book of Mormon"—*Ed.*>

Not for dole and sorrow is God bringing man into an existence that is to be immortal—deathless. But for joy; something greater than happiness—joy![8] Of which more later, when we shall contemplate it, and revel in it; after we get[9] into the reader's mind the fullness of this unfolding truth of the purpose of God in the creation of man.

(c) Testimony of the Prophet of the New Dispensation

We have brought into this consideration a word from Moses, God's masterful, prince-like prophet, who knew his God "face to face." We have brought a word from Lehi, the faithful prophet of another branch of the House of Israel, which dwelt in America—the Book of Mormon passage. We have yet another word, and a deeper reason given on the same theme; and this time direct from God to the prophet of the New Dispensation. Let us hear him. Jesus, the Christ, is speaking to the prophet.

THE LARGER VIEW OF MAN'S LIFE[10]

> I was in the beginning with the Father, and am the Firstborn. . . . Ye [the prophet and the brethren with him when the revelation was given][11] were also in the beginning with the Father, that which is spirit. . . . Man [the race—all men][12] was also in the beginning with God. Intelligence, or the light of truth, was not created or made, neither indeed can be. All truth is independent in that sphere in which God hath placed it, to act for itself, as all intelligence also; otherwise there is no existence [i.e., no place where these conditions do not obtain].[13] Behold, here is the agency of man, and here is the condemnation of man; because that which was from the beginning is plainly manifest unto them, and they receive not the light. And every man whose spirit receiveth not the light is under condemnation, for man is spirit. The elements are eternal, and spirit and element, inseparately connected, receive a fullness of joy. And when separated, man cannot receive a fullness of joy. The elements are the tabernacle of God; yea, man is the tabernacle of God, even temples; and whatsoever temple is defiled, God shall destroy that temple. The glory of God is Intelligence, or in other words, light and truth (D&C 93:21, 23, 29-36).

A prose-poem that, on a profoundly spiritual subject, the most exalted that

---

8. <Ms III* "But for joy; not happiness - but something greater - Joy!"—*Ed.*>

9. <Ms III* "when we get"—*Ed.*>

10. <Ms III^{c} adds "The Larger View of Man's Life"—*Ed.*>

11. <Ms III^{c} adds "[the prophet and the brethren with him when the revelation was given]"—*Ed.*>

12. <Ms III^{c} adds "[the race—all men]"—*Ed.*>

13. <Ms III^{c} adds "[i.e. no place where these conditions do not obtain]"—*Ed.*>

man can contemplate—the purpose of man's earth-life.[14] Had the prophet of the New Dispensation left no other word to the world than that word, he would have been a prophet, a seer; one who sees, and sees truly; and teaches God's truth, for that prose-poem is true. Let us contemplate it, let us give it exposition step by step as it unfolds to our thought.

EXPOSITION OF THE LARGER VIEW OF MAN'S LIFE

First, Jesus, who gives the revelation, is declared to be in the beginning with God, co-eternal with God; that part of him which matters most, Intelligence, the Intelligent Entity, which was not created, and was not made, but which is eternal, as all intelligences are.[15] The "Thing," the "Entity" which starts out on its career of progress, not each of the same quality or degree, but various; not all as the "Word," who is the Christ, was; but whether of low or of high degree, nevertheless, equal in this one thing, their eternity;[16] and they are what they are in virtue of what their varied intelligence itself is. Not being of the same capacity, they will go forward swiftly, or slowly, or stand still, as they choose. Some intelligences as spirits[17] will

---

14. <Ms III^{c} adds "the purpose of man's earth-life"—*Ed.*>

15. <Speaking of intelligences, Paul Nolan Hyde, "Intelligences," in *Encyclopedia of Mormonism*, ed. Daniel H. Ludlow (New York: Macmillan Publishing Co., 1992), 2:692, says that "the term has received two interpretations by writers within the Church: as the literal spirit children of Heavenly Parents and as individual entities existing prior to their spirit birth"—*Ed.*>

16. In proof of this I quote what the Lord said to Abraham: "The Lord said unto me, . . . If two things exist, and there be one above the other, there shall be greater things above them; . . . Now, if there be two things, one above the other, and the moon be above the earth, then it may be that a planet or a star may exist above it; . . . as also, if there be two spirits, and one shall be more intelligent than the other, yet these two spirits, notwithstanding one is more intelligent than the other, have no beginning; they existed before, they shall have no end, they shall exist after, for they are *gnolaum*, or eternal" (Abr. 3:15-18).

17. <The review committee objected that Roberts's use of the terms Intelligence and Spirit is confusing, saying that an Intelligence was an uncreated "eternal entity" and that only after intelligences become begotten spirits could they rebel. Roberts' handwritten responses were that this objection was "of no substance or importance" and that there was a "misapprehension here," since Intelligence was "that which perceives truth." However, in response to (and in accordance with) the committee's suggestion Roberts revised his text of TWL by adding Ms III^{2} "intelligences as spirits," with the word "intelligences" also added in the left margin ("Doctrinal Points Questioned by the Committee Which Read the Manuscript of Elder B. H. Roberts, Entitled The Truth, The Way, The Life," attached to Rudger Clawson, Letter to Heber J. Grant, [15 May 1930], located in David J. Buerger Collection, Manuscript 622, Bx 10, Fd 8, Manuscripts Division, Marriott Library, University

rebel against the order of things in the universe as did Lucifer and his following, but they will not prevail against the order of the universe, that shall stand secure, because there will always be enough, and enough of sufficient power, to hold things in their course of progress, and to the attainment of the higher things, the best things. But these rebellious ones, may if they so choose, persist in their rebellion against the higher Intelligences—even against God and the orderly universe; but they must endure the consequences. So much for the initial thought of the passage, and now the next step.

"I was in the beginning with the Father, and am the Firstborn." Is not that "Firstborn" incompatible with the idea of the eternity of the Christ-Intelligence? Who from the beginning was with God, and *was* God? Why "Firstborn"? It can be no other than this: that mighty, self-existent Intelligence, which was the "Word," and was in the beginning with God the Father, was begotten a Spirit; and in the order of our earth, and the spirit[18] Intelligences connected and associated with it, was the "firstborn" of the spirits[19]—the "firstborn" of many brethren[20]; and the Christ illustrates[21] what takes place with all intelligent entities of the divine human species. Intelligences are begotten spirits, and these spirits no doubt[22] are more definite personalities, and of[23] greater tangibility, and possessed of higher powers than many suppose them to be. It is written in Hebrews that God had revealed Himself to men through the Son, who was "the brightness of His glory, and the express image of His person; . . . by whom also He made the worlds" (Heb. 1:3a, 2b). This making of worlds was previous to the earth-life of the Christ, and hence was a work accomplished when he was a spirit-personage,[24] in which spirit-life he was the Firstborn.[25]

---

of Utah, Salt Lake City)—*Ed.*>

18. <Ms III[c] adds "spirit"—*Ed.*>

19. <Ms III[*] "'firstborn' of the spirits of that sub-division of the universe"—*Ed.*>

20. Rom. 8:29, where Jesus, the Son of God, is referred to as "the firstborn among many brethren." Again, in Col. 1:15 it is written, speaking of the Christ, "who is the image of the invisible God—the firstborn of every creature." In Heb. 1:6 "And again, when he bringeth in the First Begotten into the world, he saith, And let all the angels of God worship him."

21. <Ms III[*] "and he illustrates"—*Ed.*>

22. <Ms III[c] adds "no doubt"—*Ed.*>

23. <Ms III[c] adds "and of"—*Ed.*>

24. <Ms III[c] adds "personage"—*Ed.*>

25. See all the citations under #6 <i.e., footnote 20>.

MORIANCUMER'S VISION OF THE CHRIST IN HIS SPIRIT-BODY[26]

Fortunately, too, we have a very great message on this point from a revelation in the Book of Mormon, where the pre-existent Spirit of the Christ appeared to an ancient prophet among the Jaredite people. This prophet was Moriancumer, the brother of Jared.[27] He besought the Lord, according to the Book of Mormon account of the vision, to make luminous certain stones which were to give light to the barges in which the people of Moriancumer were to cross the seas from the "Old World" to the "New." And as the hand of the Spirit-Christ was outstretched[28] to touch the stones, the vision of Moriancumer was so quickened that he beheld the finger of the Lord, and fell down before him stricken in fear, and said: "'I knew not that *the Lord had flesh and blood,*' for the finger was as the finger of a man, *like* unto flesh and blood. And the Lord said unto him: 'Because of thy faith thou hast seen that *I shall take upon me flesh and blood*'" (cf. Ether 3:8, 6b, 9) not that he was then flesh and blood. And then was given to this prophet a full view of the Lord, as later such a view[29] was given unto Moses and other leaders[30] of the House of Israel.[31]

> And the Lord said: "*Behold, this body, which ye now behold, is the body of my spirit*; and man have I created after the body of my spirit; and even as I appear unto thee to be in the spirit, will I appear unto my people in the flesh" (Ether 3:16).

Not in flesh and blood, then, did Moriancumer behold the Lord, but in the body of the Lord's spirit, or the spirit body;[32] the spirit body begotten of the Father, inhabited by the intelligent entity, the "Word" that was with God in the beginning, and from all eternity, and "that was God," and "that was [finally][33] made flesh," and "dwelt among men."[34]

Now to resume our comment in the more direct line: "Ye were also in the

---

26. <Ms III[c] adds "Moriancumer's Vision of the Christ in His Spirit-body"—*Ed.*>
27. <Ms III[c] adds "the brother of Jared"—*Ed.*>
28. <Ms III[*] "the hand of God was outstretched"—*Ed.*>
29. <Ms III[c] adds "such a view"—*Ed.*>
30. <Ms III[*] "unto Moses and other members"—*Ed.*>
31. See vision of Moses, Aaron, and seventy of the Elders, Ex. 24:9-11.
32. <Ms III[*] "or the spiritual body"—*Ed.*>
33. <Ms III[c] adds "[finally]"—*Ed.*>
34. <The review committee objected that Roberts did not make clear whether Christ's "spirit body" and "the Word" refer to his "Intelligence" or to his "begotten spirit." Roberts's handwritten response was: "clarify" ("Doctrinal Points Questioned by the Committee," located in Buerger)—*Ed.*>

beginning with the Father," continued the Christ, speaking to the Prophet Joseph Smith and the brethren who were with him when the revelation was received[35]—"Ye were also in the beginning with the Father, that which is spirit." And, of course, as the spirit nature of the Christ was, so too was their nature: intelligences, begotten spirits, and capable of immense activities and great achievements.

THE ESSENTIAL QUALITIES OF INTELLIGENCES[36]

Connected with this eternal existence of intelligences is the agency, or moral freedom, of them; which carries with it the condemnation of man when disobedient to righteous laws. "Because that which was from the beginning is plainly manifest unto them," as intelligences; "and they received not the light, and every man whose spirit receiveth[37] not the light is under condemnation, for man is spirit [intelligence within a spirit body]" (D&C 93:31-33); and this "spirit" is native to the "light of truth"; that is, it has natural affinity for that light of truth. Even as flame leaps towards flame and blends with it, so truth, proclaimed and striking the hearing spirit of man, finds entrance there, and understanding; unless he by perverseness[38] holds back the will to believe, and with that holding back comes condemnation because he receives not the light which comes to his understanding—his[39] intelligence.

THE COMPLETED THOUGHT ON THE PURPOSE OF GOD IN MAN'S EARTH-LIFE[40]

Again: "For man is spirit. The elements are eternal, and spirit and element, inseperably connected,[41] receive a fullness of joy" (D&C 93:33).

Here our circle completes itself. Moses told us that the purpose of God was to bring to pass the immortality and the eternal life of man; the Nephite prophet told us that Adam fell that man might be, or exist as man; and that men are that they might have joy. And now, in this prose-poem of our prophet of the New Dispensation comes out this same truth under new form:

---

35. <Ms III[c] adds "when the revelation was received"—*Ed.*>

36. <Ms III[c] adds "The Essential Qualities of Intelligences"—*Ed.*>

37. <Ms III[*] "whose spirit [i.e., intelligence] receiveth"—*Ed.*>

38. <Ms III[*] "unless men by perverseness"—*Ed.*>

39. <Ms III[c] adds "—his"—*Ed.*>

40. <Ms III[c] adds "The Completed Thought On the Purpose of God in Man's Earth-life"—*Ed.*>

41. <Ms III "inseparately connected"—*Ed.*>

> Man is spirit [he has the native power to cognize truth].[42] The elements are eternal, and spirit and element inseparably connected receive a fullness of joy, and when separated man cannot receive a fullness of joy (D&C 93:33-34).

And that is what God is working at through this earth-life of man.[43] Man shall come to that immortality of which Moses speaks, shall come to that inseparable connection between elements and spirit—which shall be wrought ultimately through the resurrection from the dead, of which the Christ is the type and the power.[44] And through that indissoluble union of spirit and element thus wrought[45] an immortal man shall be brought into being, with full equipment for that advancement over God's great highway of progress universe-wide, and long, and deep, and high; and running through all the ages that know no limitations. This the purpose of God in the earth-life of man—man's eternal progress, and in that, and growing out of it, man's everlasting joy.

AND THIS "JOY"—WHAT IS IT?[46]

What is meant by this: "Man is that he might have joy" (cf. 2 Ne. 2:25)? Have we here the reappearance of the old Epicurean doctrine, "pleasure is the supreme good and chief end of life?" No, verily! Nor any form of ancient or modern Hedonism[47] whatsoever. For mark, in the first place, the different words "joy" and "pleasure." They are not synonymous. The first does not necessarily arise from the second. Joy may arise from quite another source than "pleasure," even from pain, when the endurance of pain is to eventuate in the achievement of some good: such as the travail of a mother in bringing forth her offspring; the weariness and pain and danger of toil by a father to secure comforts for loved ones. Moreover, whatever apologists may say, it is very clear that the "pleasure" of the Epicurean philosophy,

---

42. <Ms III^{c} adds "he has the native power to cognize truth"—*Ed.*>

43. <Ms III* "this earth-life for man"—*Ed.*>

44. <Ms III^{c} adds "and the power"—*Ed.*>

45. <Ms III^{c} adds "thus wrought"—*Ed.*>

46. <Ms III^{c} adds "And This 'Joy'—What Is It"—*Ed.*>

47. "Hedonism: the doctrine of certain Greek philosophers <Aristippus and the Cyrenaics>; in ethics, gross self-interest. Hedonism is the form of eudemonism that regards pleasure (including avoidance of pain) as the only conceivable object in life, and teaches that as between the lower pleasures of sense and the higher enjoyments of reason, or satisfied self-respect <Ms III "or satisfactory satisfied-respect"—*Ed.*>, there is no difference except in the degree, duration, and hedonic value of the experience, there being in strictness no such thing as ethical or moral value" (*A Standard Dictionary of the English Language*, ed. Isaac K. Funk [New York: Funk and Wagnalls Co., 1895], 832).

hailed as "the supreme good and chief end of life," was to arise from agreeable sensations, or whatever gratified the senses, and hence was, in the last analysis of it–in its roots and branches–in its theory and in its practice–"sensualism." It was to result in physical ease and comfort, and mental inactivity–other than a conscious, self-complacence–being regarded as "the supreme good and chief end of life." We judge this to be the net result of this philosophy, since these are the very conditions in which Epicureans describe even the gods to exist; and surely men could not hope for more "pleasure," or greater "happiness" than that possessed by their gods. Cicero even charges that the sensualism of Epicurus was so gross that he represents him as blaming his brother, Timocrates, "'because that brother would not allow that everything which had any reference to a happy life was to be measured by the belly,' nor has he," continues Cicero, "said this once only, but often."[48]

This is not the "joy," it is needless to say, contemplated in our text. Nor is the "joy" there contemplated the "joy" of mere innocence–mere innocence! Which, say what you will of it, is but a negative sort of virtue: a virtue that is colorless, never quite sure of itself, always more or less uncertain, because untried. Such a virtue–if mere absence of vice may be called virtue–would be unproductive of that "joy," the attainment of which is set forth in the context of the Book of Mormon passage above quoted, as the purpose of man's existence. It is written, "They [Adam and Eve] would have remained in a state of innocence, having no joy, for they knew no misery; doing no good, for they knew no sin" (2 Ne. 2:23). From which it appears that the "joy" contemplated herein is to arise from something more than mere innocence, which is impliedly unproductive of "joy." The "joy" contemplated herein is to arise out of man's knowledge of evil, of sin; through knowing misery, sorrow, pain, and suffering; through seeing good and evil locked in awful conflict; through a consciousness of having chosen in that conflict the better part, the good (which will include the true and the beautiful); and not only in having chosen it, but in having wedded it by eternal compact; made it his by right of conquest over evil. It is the "joy" that will arise from a consciousness of having "fought the good

---

48. In Cicero's description of the Epicurean conception of the gods, he says: "That which is truly happy cannot be burdened with any labor itself, nor can it impose any labor on another, nor can it be influenced by resentment or favor, because things which are liable to such failings must be weak and frail. . . . Their life [i.e., of the gods] is most happy and the most abounding with all kinds of blessings which can be conceived. They do nothing. They are embarrassed with no business; nor do they perform any work. They rejoice in the possession of their own wisdom and virtue. They are satisfied that they shall ever enjoy the fullness of eternal pleasure. . . . Nothing can be happy that is not at ease" (*Cicero's Tusculan Disputations; also Treatises on the Nature of the Gods and on the Commonwealth*, trans. Charles D. Yonge [New York: Harper, 1894], "The Nature of the Gods," 266-68).

fight," of having "kept the faith" (2 Tim. 4:7). It will arise from a consciousness of moral, spiritual, and physical strength. Of strength gained in conflict. The strength that comes from experience; from having sounded the depths of the soul; from experiencing all the emotions of which mind is susceptible; from testing all the qualities and strength of the intellect. A "joy" that will come to man from a contemplation of the universe, and a consciousness that he is an heir to all that is—a joint heir with Jesus Christ and God the Father; from knowing that he is an essential part of all that is. It is a "joy" that will be born of the consciousness of existence itself—that will revel in existence—in thoughts of realization of existence's limitless possibilities. A "joy" born of the consciousness of the power of eternal increase. A "joy" arising from association with the Intelligences of innumerable heavens—the Gods of all eternities. A "joy" born of a consciousness of being, of intelligence, of faith, knowledge, light, truth, mercy, justice,[49] love, glory, dominion, wisdom, power; all feelings, affections, emotions, passions; all heights and all depths. "Men are that they might have joy"; and that "joy" is based upon and contemplates all that is here set down.

THE TRUTH IN RESPECT OF MAN[50]

Here, then, stands the Truth so far as it may be gathered from God's revelations and the nature of things respecting man.[51] There is in man an eternal, uncreated, self-existing entity, call it "intelligence," "mind," "spirit,"—for these terms are often used interchangeably in the scriptures—but call it[52] what you will, so long as you recognize it, and regard its nature as in the main intelligent and[53] eternal.[54] There came a time when in the progress of things (which is another way of saying in "the nature of things"), an earth-career, or earth-existence, because of the things it has to teach, was necessary to the enlargement, to the advancement of these "Intelligences." Hence, an earth is prepared; and One, sufficiently advanced[55] and able,

---

49. <Ms III[c] adds "justice"—*Ed.*>

50. <Ms III[c] adds "The Truth In Respect of Man"—*Ed.*>

51. <Ms III[c] adds "respecting man"—*Ed.*>

52. <Ms III[c] adds "for these terms are often used interchangeably in the scriptures—but call it"—*Ed.*>

53. <Ms III[c] adds "in the main intelligent and"—*Ed.*>

54. <The review committee objected that Roberts's "use of 'mind,' 'spirit,' and 'soul' appears confusing," but Roberts's argument is that these terms, as well as the word "intelligence," are used synonymously ("Doctrinal Points Questioned by the Committee," located in Buerger)—*Ed.*>

55. <Ms III* "One, as we have seen, sufficiently advanced"—*Ed.*>

by the nature of him to bring to pass the necessary event and the spirit in which he proposed to work found satisfactory,[56] is chosen to act as Redeemer to the race.

As to the second part of the great truth—"men are that they might have joy"—viewed in the light of the "intelligence" in man,[57] being an eternal, uncreated, self-existing entity, and remembering what has already been said[58] as to the nature of this "joy," which it is the purpose of earth existence to secure; remembering also from what this joy is to arise—from the highest possible development—the highest conceivable enlargement of physical, intellectual, moral, and spiritual powers—remembering all this[59]—what other conceivable purpose for existence in earth-life could there be for eternal intelligences than this attainment of "joy" arising from progress? Man's existence for the "manifestation of God's glory,"[60] as taught by the creeds of men, is not equal to it. That view represents man as but a thing created, and God as selfish and vain of glory. True, the Book of Mormon idea of the purpose of man's existence—that he might have joy—is accompanied by a manifestation of God's glory; for with the progress of intelligences there must be an ever-widening manifestation of the glory of God. It is written that "the glory of God is Intelligence" (D&C 93:36); and it must follow, as the day follows night, that with the enlargement, with the progress of intelligences, there must ever be a constantly-increasing splendor in the manifestation of the glory of God. But in our doctrine, the manifestation of that glory may be said to be incidental.[61] The primary purpose is not in that manifestation but in the "joy" arising from the progress of intelligences. And yet that fact adds to the glory of God, since it represents God as seeking the enlargement and "joy" of kindred intelligences to Himself though more lowly, rather than the mere selfish manifestation[62] of His own personal glory. "This is my work and my glory," said the Lord, "to bring to pass the immortality and eternal life of man" (Moses 1:39); and therein is God's "joy." A "joy" that comes from the progress of others. Not the immortality of the "spirit" of man, mark you, for that immortality is already existent; but to bring to pass the immortality of the spirit and body in a united status, and which together constitutes "man," the "soul"—the completed man; for "the spirit and the body is the soul of man" and "the resurrection of the dead is the redemption of the soul" (D&C 88:15-16)—the

56. <Ms III[c] adds "found satisfactory"—*Ed.*>
57. <Ms III[*] "the 'intelligence' or 'spirit' in man"—*Ed.*>
58. <Ms III[*] "what I have already said"—*Ed.*>
59. <Ms III[c] adds "remembering all this"—*Ed.*>
60. <Ms III[*] "manifestation alone of God's glory"—*Ed.*>
61. <Ms III[*] "that glory is incidental"—*Ed.*>
62. <Ms III[*] "the mere selfish manifestations"—*Ed.*>

whole man. And the noble purpose of all this is that man might have joy; that joy which, in the last analysis of things, should be even as God's joy, and God's glory, namely, the bringing to pass the progress, enlargement, and joy of others.

CHAPTER XXVIII

A Review of Part I

SCRIPTURE READING LESSON

Analysis

I. What Man Knows of Truth.

II. Large Questions.

III. Nature of Universe Intelligences.

IV. Interplanetary Communication.

V. The Reign of Law.

VI. The World's Great Religions. Report of Seekers after God.

VII. The Hebrew-Christian Revelation.

VIII. Revelation: Modern.

IX. God and the Godhead.

X. Of Creation and Purpose of God in Man's Earth-Life.

References

All of Part I, and all the references in the lesson analyses.

CHAPTER XXVIII
A Review of Part I

We have now before us the treatment of themes it was my purpose to consider under the first division of this work—the Truth.

WHAT MAN KNOWS OF TRUTH

We began by a brief treatise of what Truth is, finding that truth is knowledge of things as they are, and as they were, and as they are to come. We went in search of what knowledge, in a general way, man possesses. Beginning with man's knowledge of himself, and his knowledge of other selves and things. Moving from man's childhood knowledge of things immediately about him, we extended our account of his knowledge outward to his country, to other countries, and finally to the whole world he inhabits. Thence to what knowledge he has acquired of the solar system to which his earth belongs. Here a diversion was made to the consideration of the ideas of the existences of space, time, matter, force, mind, and the reign of law. We reached knowledge of these important things both by inductions and by deductions, and by arriving at "necessary truths" concerning them: viz., by becoming conscious of the inability of the mind to conceive the contrary to the conclusions made.

Thence we sought knowledge concerning the solar system; something concerning the planets and their satellites of which it consists; the immense distances within it, and the mass and greatness of its respective planets, and of the sun, the center of the system. Thence we glanced at the sidereal system, our galaxy, the immensity of it, composed as it is of hundreds of millions of suns; one billion, at least; and yet, great as it is, not comprising all the universes that exist, if we may be permitted to use words that once would have been fiercely paradoxical, but now accepted quite understandingly; for our galaxy is but one out of many others, faintly discernable by man's improved scientific instruments to be in existence; and how many galaxies exist in boundless space is a matter of conjecture merely—but it is quite apparent that they may extend to infinity.

LARGE QUESTIONS

Then came the question, do these other suns than our own that make up our galaxy, and other galaxies, have groups of planets revolving about them, as our sun has? No positive answer could be made to that question from human knowledge. It was here that we adopted the principle of "reasoning from what we know" to possibility, to probability, and likelihood. Thus: knowing that our own sun has his retinue of planets moving in their respective orbits about him, it is possible, nay, probable, that the other suns also have their planetary systems. There exists no known reason why it should not be so; for the forces that produced planets for the orb of our own system would most likely produce planets to other similar suns.

Then came the further question: are other planets of our own solar system, and the planetary systems of other suns inhabited by sentient intelligences? We know that our own is, and again, "reasoning from what we know," it seems probable that other planets of our solar system and the planets of like systems throughout the universe would be inhabited by sentient intelligences. It seems unreasonable to think that our little speck of an earth in our own solar system and in the universe should be the only one so inhabited; and what a waste of creative energy there must have been if these billions of worlds are tenantless of intelligent and joyous inhabitants!

Then the question: may not many of these worlds in other planetary systems be vastly older[1] than our own? And since time is often a factor in development, may not the inhabitants of these older worlds be superior intelligences, and more highly developed than those of our own world inhabitants? With superior community life, and higher stages of civilization in their worlds than exists in ours?

NATURE OF UNIVERSE INTELLIGENCES[2]

Further we asked: may not these superior intelligences be possessed of altruistic sentiments and impulses, which would lead them to have interests in other worlds than their own and the inhabitants thereof? Again, applying the principle of "reasoning from what we know," we found that superior intelligences in our own earth possessed such altruistic sentiments; and that they were led to seek the development and general welfare through uplift of undeveloped peoples, leading even to self-sacrifice and the elimination of selfish interests in order to attain the welfare of the undeveloped, or the reformation of the fallen. Knowing this, it led us to the conclusion that the superior intelligences of more highly developed worlds might be led to do something akin to this by means of communicating knowledge to the less developed worlds, to draw them into higher stages of development, to the increase of their well-being and joy.

---

1. <Ms III* "systems be immensely [*sic*] older"—*Ed.*>
2. <Ms III^c adds "Nature of Universe Intelligences"—*Ed.*>

INTERPLANETARY COMMUNICATION

The question of interplanetary communication, however, came into consideration as a possible barrier to such communications. But investigation of man's progressive mastery over the difficulties of communication and transportation over the earth he inhabits—his triumph over distances between islands and continents, and the establishment of all but instant communication over the whole earth, led to the conclusion that interplanetary communication and visitation by the intelligences of other worlds might have been so mastered as to form no insuperable obstacle to communication and visitation to the earth, and hence, the possibility of interplanetary communication and visitation might be regarded as the ground of possible revelation.

REIGN OF LAW[3]

The order of the universe, the evident existence of a reign of law throughout, was considered as evidence of intelligence presiding within the universe and in some way conserving and governing therein. Evidently an orderly universe proclaims the reign of mind over matter—enthroning somehow Intelligence as in control of the universe.

This it was concluded might have given rise to those traditions about God which the fathers from the earliest ages communicated to succeeding generations. And this in turn inspired spiritual souls to seek after God, until at least they supposed they had found him, and reported as from him their findings—their revelations of him. From this point began a brief review of those reports of the great teachers to their respective peoples on what they had found regarding God and the universe and life and the meaning and the intent of it.

THE WORLD'S GREAT RELIGIONS: REPORTS OF SEEKERS AFTER GOD[4]

Briefly we considered the Babylonian-Assyrian religion; the religion of the Egyptians; also of the Persians, the Medes, and Phoenicians; of the Greeks and the Roman; and the religions of Northern Europe. Also, the Mohammedan religion; the religions of India—Brahmanism and Buddhism; the religions of China: (a) Buddhism, (b) Confucianism, (c) Taoism. Finally we came to the Hebrew revelation and religion.

In all this, of course, there could be only a cursory review; and yet, as before

---

3. <Ms III^{c} adds "Reign of Law"—*Ed.*>

4. <Ms III^{c} adds "The World's Great Religions: Reports of Seekers After God"—*Ed.*>

stated, some sort of a review of all these religions was necessary to the completion of our theme, and in order to get before the reader the reports of the seekers after God.

THE HEBREW-CHRISTIAN REVELATION

Of the reports on God delivered to the world, that which came through the prophets of the Hebrew race and its proper supplement found in the Christian development of two thousand years ago, we judged to be of sufficient importance to call for special consideration; and from that revelation considered, both from the Old Testament and the New, we discovered the revelation of God in the person and character of Jesus of Nazareth, who through his life and resurrection to immortality became God's revelation of himself—God incarnate—a complete manifestation of Deity—of the Godhead bodily.

Thence we traced in history the misapprehension and final rejection or misunderstanding of this revelation through one of the divine intelligences sent from another world, a son of God, to enlighten the inhabitants of our world as to God, to redeem and to sanctify earth's inhabitants.

Also, we considered the misapprehension of men concerning the creation of the world; how even those who believed the revelation supposed the worlds to have been created out of nothing. Likewise, briefly we examined the misapprehension of men concerning the origin of man and the purpose of God in his creation.

REVELATION: MODERN

At this point we took up the consideration of revelation, especially with reference to modern revelation, the reasonable expectation that the modern world may have that the spirit of revelation would function in these modern days as in ancient times; and the modern world's need of revelation for guidance; and the important fact that the revelations given to our earth from the beginning are local; that they pertain to our earth and its heavens—its associated worlds and world-systems, and their inhabitants, past and present and those yet to be.

All which is made known from a fragment of scripture brought to light in the New Dispensation by revelation to its prophet Joseph, and called the Book of Moses. The Book of Moses is followed by another fragment of scripture, also brought forth in the New Dispensation and by the same prophet, known as the Book of Abraham, containing knowledge which God revealed to the Hebrew patriarch in Egypt; knowledge concerning the earth and its heavens. In outline may be discerned an Abrahamic system of that part of the universe to which our earth and solar system belong—a section of the universe. The Book of Abraham like the Book of Moses is but a fragment, and our prophet has given a translation of but part of it, but even so it is of highest importance to our knowledge as to what the ancients knew concerning the universe and God and man and the pre-existent spirits of men, their rank and station in the spirit world, and God's purpose with reference to the creation of the earth and of man's life upon it. These fragments of ancient revelation contribute enlightening facts to the whole realm of thought relating to the earth and the heavens, to creation and to God; to man and his relationship to God; to time and to eternity—to the dramatic whole of existences. This enlightenment supplies the keys of the universe.

GOD AND THE GODHEAD

Next was taken up the theme of God and the Godhead, under the conception of our revelations being local—pertaining to our earth and its heavens; of God and the spirit of God—the everywhere-present Deity; of the Holy Ghost; and the essential unity of God in all incarnations—the participations in the One Divine Nature.

OF CREATION AND THE PURPOSE OF GOD IN MAN'S EARTH-LIFE

Creation was our next theme; the time and manner of the earth's creation. A discussion of causation—First or Eternal cause? The Bible story of creation. Then the creation of man—the various theories of his origin, and finally the purpose of God in man's creation, and the possibilities that may come with a life everlasting—immortality—eternal youth—and the way of progress—progress in the knowledge of the Truth.

Such the road we have traversed. Such the milestones we have marked along the journey so far. The background of our theme is inlaid. But our task is but half finished. We must follow through. There lies before us yet, THE WAY, THE LIFE.

PART II
THE WAY

"I am The Way. . . .
No Man Cometh to the Father
but by Me."

JESUS, ST. JOHN 14:6

CHAPTER XXIX

The Way of Eternal Life—The Everlasting Gospel

SCRIPTURE READING LESSON

Analysis

I. Sources of Authority.

II. The One and Only Gospel; This Everlasting.

III. Dispensation, Meaning of.

IV. The War in Heaven.

V. The Great, Noble, and Good.

VI. The Plan Proposed.

VII. The Savior Chosen.

VIII. More Light on the War in Heaven.

IX. What God's Plan of Man's Eternal Life Includes.

X. A Supposed Purpose of "the World's Author" by a Philosopher.

References

All the citations in the text of this chapter, with the contexts of same.

The Books of Moses and of Abraham in the Pearl of Great Price.

Discourse of Joseph Smith on "Creation," "Priesthood," "Adam," etc., *History of the Church of Jesus Christ of Latter-day Saints: Period I: History of Joseph Smith, the Prophet by Himself*, 3:385-92.

B. H. Roberts, "History of the 'Mormon' Church," *Americana* 6 (September-October 1911): 891-910, 993-1019, chaps. 54-55.

William James, *Pragmatism: A New Name for Some Old Ways of Thinking: Popular Lectures on Philosophy* (New York: Longmans, Green, and Co., 1908); also *A Pluralistic Universe: Hibbert Lectures at Manchester College on the Present Situation in Philosophy* (New York: Longmans, Green and Co., 1909), *passim*.

D&C 29, 76, 84, and 88.

CHAPTER XXIX

The Way of Eternal Life–The Everlasting Gospel

Having now as background the knowledge that may be had of the universe, somewhat of its nature, extent, and grandeur; some knowledge of its inhabitants and the controlling power of harmonized, divine Intelligences within it, some knowledge of the origin of man and his nature; likewise some knowledge of the purpose of God in relation to man's earth-life; we are prepared to consider THE WAY to, and THE WAY of, that eternal life.

SOURCES OF AUTHORITY

We again take occasion to remind the reader that we shall discuss this part of our treatise in the light of all the knowledge that is to be had from all the revelations of God given in all ages, in all dispensations of the gospel, and from among all people who have received any dispensation of the word of God in relation to this subject. That will at least include all that is to be found in the Old Testament and the New; the fragments of the writings from Moses as revealed to Joseph Smith, known as the Book of Moses; and the fragments from the writings of Abraham, known as the Book of Abraham; both <of> which fragments are found in the Pearl of Great Price. Also, we shall appeal to the Book of Mormon, which contains the revelations of God to the ancient inhabitants of America, and also the revelations given directly of God to Joseph Smith, the prophet of this New Dispensation of the gospel; which revelations received by him are collected and published in the Doctrine and Covenants. All these books are accepted as scripture by the Church of Jesus Christ of Latter-day Saints.[1] All these scriptures will be freely quoted in what we have to say in relation to THE WAY in which God has designed to bring to pass His purposes with reference to man in his earth-life and his eternal life; and all this without further explanation for using as authoritative reference works, these ancient and modern revelations of God. To the writer these scriptures are all of equal authority, all of them dependable sources of knowledge. Also, we remind

1. For a treatise on these several books, the reader or student may consult the *Seventy's Course in Theology: First Year, Outline History of the Seventy and A Survey of the Books of Holy Scripture* (Salt Lake City: The Deseret News, 1907).

the reader again that we shall depend upon the reasonableness, the beauty, the order, the exactness, and the wholeness of God's planned way to bring to pass the immortality and the eternal life of man, to carry conviction of its truth to the mind of the reader, rather than an appeal to any special texts, however apropos to the subject they may be.

Let it be our first concern, then, to present a larger view of this WAY than is ordinarily entertained, keeping in mind, however, that such revelations as our prophets and seers have received are limited in their application to our earth and its heavens; and that they concern intelligences, spirits, angels, men—the human race—that pertain to our earth and its heavens.

THE ONE AND ONLY GOSPEL: THIS EVERLASTING

Already we have quoted the scripture in the letter of Paul to Titus, giving out the fact that St. Paul lived "in hope of eternal life, which God, that can not lie, promised before the world began" (Titus 1:2). This at once declares the existence of God's plan for the eternal life of man before the world began, so that we may say that God's plan of THE WAY for man's eternal life is older than the earth. This "plan of eternal life" or WAY is referred to in other scriptures as the "everlasting gospel." St. John so speaks of it, in describing the coming of a new dispensation of that gospel subsequent to his own day, and as coming forth in "the hour of God's judgment"—therefore, in the last days. He said:

> I saw another angel flying in the midst of heaven, having the everlasting gospel to preach to them that dwell upon the earth. . . . Saying with a loud voice, "Fear God and give glory to Him, for the hour of His judgment is come" (Rev. 14:6-7).

The only use we make of this quotation here is to show that the gospel is referred to as the "everlasting gospel." The plan of eternal life which God promised before the world began. In the Epistle to the Hebrews the blood of the Christ is referred to as "the blood of the everlasting covenant" (Heb. 13:20). In Revelation[2] Jesus is spoken of as "the Lamb slain from the foundation of the world" (Rev. 13:8). Also, a war in heaven is spoken of where:

> Michael and his angels fought against the dragon [the devil], and the dragon fought and his angels and prevailed not; neither was their peace found any more in heaven (Rev. 12:7-8).

Undoubtedly, this "war in heaven" was Lucifer's rebellion in the spirit world, before the earth-life of man began, and had some relationship to man's earth-life

2. <Ms III "In Revelations"—*Ed.*>

and to the purposes of God[3] in regard to that life. All which will have further consideration later on. Enough perhaps is set forth here to establish the great antiquity of "the everlasting gospel," God's planned way for man's eternal life.

Let us now get the important fact established that there exists but one WAY for the bringing to pass of that eternal life plan of God, in other words, but one gospel; and that there has been, and never can be, but one WAY.[4] So sure was St. Paul of this, that in writing the church at Galatia, where certain schisms and divisions appeared, that he reproved them by saying sarcastically:

> I marvel that ye are so soon removed from him that called you into the grace of Christ unto another gospel: which is not another; but there be some that trouble you and would pervert the gospel of Christ. But though we, or an angel from heaven, preach any other gospel unto you than that which we preach unto you, let him be accursed. As we said before, so I say now again, If any man preach any other gospel unto you than that ye have received, let him be accursed (Gal. 1:6-9).

And to the schismatic factions at Corinth he wrote, reproving them for saying, as these factions did say, "We are of Paul," "We are of Apollos," and others "We are of Cephas," and others "We are of Christ"; and then came this thundering question, "Is Christ divided, was Paul crucified for you, or were ye baptized in the name of Paul?" (1 Cor. 1:12). All this makes it clear that there is but one gospel and ever shall be but one, and that "the everlasting gospel," God's one plan for man's salvation. God's promise[5] of eternal life to be wrought out in all ages by various dispensations of that one gospel plan.

DISPENSATION: THE MEANING OF

This brings us to the necessity of defining a dispensation. The word in the revelations of God is used in its ordinary meaning of "giving out," as dispensing food to the hungry, clothing to the needy, or dispensing just judgments to violators of the law; giving out. So as to the gospel, giving out knowledge of its truths by revelation from God; revealing it in whole or in subdivisions or part of it,[6] by bestowing through the administration of angels, or otherwise divine authority upon men, the Priesthood, by which man may be authorized to teach and preach in the authority of God, or administer in its ordinances, baptisms for the remission of sins,[7] or the laying on of hands for reception of the Holy Ghost,

---

3. <Ms III* "the purpose of God"—*Ed.*>
4. <Ms III* "but one gospel, one WAY"—*Ed.*>
5. <Ms III* "God promised"—*Ed.*>
6. <Ms III^{c} adds "revealing it in whole or in sub-divisions or part of it"—*Ed.*>
7. <The review committee objected to Roberts's use of the plural "baptisms"

or consecrate the emblems of the Holy Sacrament, which represent the crucified body and the shed blood of the Christ for the redemption of man. These are the outgivings comprising knowledge of gospel truth, and outgivings of authority to administer to man the ordinances of that gospel. All the while, however, let it be held in mind, that there is but the one gospel and these dispensations are but acts of God directly or indirectly giving out knowledge and authority with reference to that one gospel.

Sometimes also a dispensation marks off an epoch in the continuous stream of God's providence towards man; as the Adamic Dispensation, meaning by that all the dispensations of God's truth which may take place during Adam's lifetime, or with extension beyond Adam's life, so long as there is unbroken succession as to those things instituted during his lifetime. The Noachian Dispensation or the dispensation of God's truth and authority to Noah and succeeding prophets until some developing event required a still further dispensing of some part of the one gospel, as in the matter of the dispensation which called Abraham and set him apart to bring to pass some special purpose of God; the Mosaic Dispensation and the Christian Dispensation, comprising that wonderful era made glorious by the personal ministry of the Christ, the offering of the supreme sacrifice which was to redeem and save a world—the very heart of the whole gospel scheme. And beyond that is mentioned another dispensation—a Dispensation of the Fullness of Times spoken of by the apostle Paul in Ephesians, in which it is promised that God will "gather together in one all things in Christ, both which are in heaven and which are on earth, even in Him" (Eph. 1:10); indicating that there will be a dispensation of dispensations, a dispensation of the fullness of all times; and of all dispensations both in heaven and in earth, a dispensation which will include all that has gone before, and which figuratively may be represented as all the streams of earth flowing into the ocean,[8] to be held by that ocean in one great union of all the river systems and all the seven seas. So with the dispensation of the fullness of times; as all rivers to the ocean trend, so all dispensations come into and are included in this one last and completed dispensation, in which all things both in heaven and in earth shall be gathered together in one, even in Christ. Such <is> the meaning of a dispensation of the gospel; and such the meaning also[9] of the dispensation of the

("Doctrinal Points Questioned by the Committee Which Read the Manuscript of Elder B. H. Roberts, Entitled The Truth, The Way, The Life," attached to Rudger Clawson, Letter to Heber J. Grant, [15 May 1930], in David J. Buerger Collection, Manuscript 622, Bx 10, Fd 8, Manuscripts Division, Marriott Library, University of Utah, Salt Lake City)—*Ed.*>

8. <Ms III[*] "may be presented as the gathering together of all the streams of earth and emptying them into the ocean"—*Ed.*>

9. <Ms III[c] adds "also"—*Ed.*>

fullness of times, the dispensation to which we now have come, and in which we labor for the achievement of God's great purpose in all the labor and travail of our earth and its heavens; and all the human race that have been or shall be associated with our earth and its heavens, and with all the intelligences and the angels and spirits that have or shall belong to it, all entering into this dispensaton,[10] which unites and completes all dispensations.

THE WAR IN HEAVEN

The "War in Heaven" described by St. John in his book of Revelation, and briefly referred to above, requires more detailed consideration. I give St. John's account of it in full:

> And there was war in heaven: Michael and his angels fought against the dragon; and the dragon fought and his angels, and prevailed not; neither was their place found any more in heaven. And the great dragon was cast out, that old serpent, called the Devil, and Satan, which deceiveth the whole world: he was cast out into the earth and his angels were cast out with him. And I heard a loud voice saying in heaven, Now is come salvation, and strength, and the kingdom of our God, and the power of his Christ: for the accuser of our brethren is cast down, which accused them before our God day and night. And they overcame him by the blood of the Lamb, and by the word of their testimony; and they loved not their lives unto the death (Rev. 12:7-11).

There is liable to be confusion arising from St. John's description of this "war in heaven" on account of connecting it with persecuting earth-powers to which the "dragon" of "the war in heaven"—the Devil and Satan—gives his power and wrath and vindictiveness in efforts made to destroy the Church of God. This Dragon, or Satan, being the underlying force and inspiration of those earthly powers which persecuted the saints and chiefly, in John's time, the persecuting Roman emperors. The "war in heaven," however, in reality took place in heaven before the advent of man on the earth; and it was doubtless on that occasion to which Jesus referred when he said to the triumphantly returning Seventy from their mission, "I beheld Satan as lightning fall from heaven!" (Luke 10:18). The whole circumstance of this rebellion, as before stated, took place before man's advent to the earth and among the pre-existent spirits of the spirit world.

One naturally wonders why there should be rebellion and war in heaven; and what it could be all about. Satan—as we shall see—was with his angels overwhelmed;[11] and all were cast out into the earth for seeking to overthrow the plans of God. It is significant that in an earlier verse of the chapter from which we quoted

---

10. <Ms III* "into this one dispensaton"—*Ed.*>

11. <Ms III* "was overwhelmed with his angels"—*Ed.*>

John's account of the "war in heaven," that the great Dragon drew after him "the third part of the stars of heaven and did cast them to the earth" (Rev. 12:4). Doubtless meaning the number of those who in the "war in heaven" fought on the Dragon's side.

Again, why this "war in heaven" and what was it all about? The book of Revelation supplies no definite answer to that question, nor is there any enlightenment in the Old Testament or the New. By revelation in modern days, however, in this New Dispensation of the gospel in which all things are being gathered together in Christ, important additions of knowledge are brought to light concerning this great event. In the fragment, the Book of Abraham, it is said that the Lord revealed to Abraham the existence of the intelligences that were organized before the world was. Meaning, doubtless, the intelligences which had been begotten spirits. Therefore, he beheld in his vision these pre-existent spirits destined for habitancy on the earth.[12] And among all these:

> There were many of the noble and great ones, and God saw these souls that they were good, and He stood in the midst of them and He said, "These I will make my rulers," for He stood among those that were spirits, and He saw that they were good, and He said unto Abraham, "Abraham, thou art one of them; thou wast chosen before thou wast born!" (cf. Abr. 3:22-23).

THE GREAT, NOBLE, AND GOOD[13]

In addition to the fact of pre-existence so clearly stated here, there are two other facts that deserve emphasis, viz., (1) that certain spirits at least are chosen before they are born, and their earth-missions assigned to them; (2) the other fact that is to be emphasized is that the basic reason for the selection of these special spirits for leadership in their projected earth-life and missions is that they are "great" souls, that they are "noble" souls, and that they "are good"; and does not this make up the sum of all virtues that enter into leadership? They are great, they are noble, they are good! Under these generalizations may be assembled all the virtues; and these, God decreed, should be his "rulers"; more especially chosen, doubtless, as his representatives in the earth as prophets, seers, teachers, inspired of God. Abraham was one of them, and doubtless a type of the class whom God would use for the unfolding of His truth and His purposes in the earth.

12. <For a survey of the Mormon concept of pre-existence, see Blake T. Ostler, "The Idea of the Pre-existence in the Development of Mormon Thought," *Dialogue: A Journal of Mormon Thought* 15 (Spring 1982): 59-78–*Ed.*>

13. <Ms III[c] adds "The Great, Noble and Good"–*Ed.*>

THE PLAN PROPOSED

We resume our quotation from the Book of Abraham:

> And there stood one among them [the Great, Noble, and Good spirits] that was like unto God, and he said unto those who were with him, "We will go down, for there is space there, and we will take of these materials, and we will make an earth whereon these may dwell. And we will prove them herewith, to see if they will do all things whatsoever the Lord their God shall command them. And they who keep their first estate shall be added upon; and they who keep not their first estate shall not have glory in the same kingdom with those who keep their first estate; and they who keep their second estate shall have glory added upon their heads forever and ever" (Abr. 3:24-26).

It will be seen that the purpose of the creation of the proposed earth is that these spirits which existed before the world was, which the Lord revealed to Abraham and among whom Abraham was, is that the spirits might be "added upon," if they kept their first estate, which was their pre-existent spirit-life, and those who did keep their earth-life, these will have added upon them glory forever and forever–in other words, will be put in the way of eternal progress. This <is> God's covenant with these spirits, which established "the hope of eternal life" referred to by St. Paul when he said that he lived in such hope of eternal life, "which God that cannot lie promised before the world began" (Titus 1:2).

THE SAVIOR CHOSEN

To resume again our quotation:

> And the Lord said, "Whom shall I send?" And one answered like unto the Son of Man, "Here am I, send me." And another answered . . . , "Here am I, send me." And the Lord said, "I will send the first." And the second was angry and kept not his first estate, and at that day many followed after him (Abr. 3:27-28).

"Whom shall I send?" Why it was necessary to send anyone does not appear in the Book of Abraham, but from other revelations we learn both the significance of the question and the answer to it. First, from the Book of Moses, where the Lord in revealing unto Moses the things pertaining to our earth and its heaven and concerning his purposes with reference to man's life on the earth, is given an account of Satan and his rebellion and the "war in heaven" that is illuminating; for early in his career as a prophet Moses had come in contact with Lucifer and had successfully resisted him and his temptations; and then God said:

> That Satan, whom thou hast commanded in the name of my Only Begotten, is the same which was in the beginning, and he came before me, saying, "Behold, here am I, send me, I will be Thy son, and I will redeem all mankind, that one soul shall not be lost, and surely I will do it; wherefore, give me Thine honor."

> But behold, my Beloved Son, which was my Beloved and Chosen from the beginning, said unto me, "Father, Thy will be done, and the glory be Thine forever." Wherefore, because that Satan rebelled against me and sought to destroy the agency of man, which I, the Lord God, had given him, and also that I should give unto him mine own power; by the power of mine Only Begotten, I caused that he should be cast out. And he became Satan, yea, even the devil, the father of all lies, to deceive and to blind men and to lead them captive at his will, even as many as would not hearken unto my voice (Moses 4:1-4).

The controversy in heaven then and Lucifer's ultimate rebellion concerned the plan, THE WAY, in which should be carried out the purposes of God with reference to the earth-life of man, and what was to be attained through it; that is, the manner in which the hosts of spirits existing before the world was should receive those additions to their spirit life that would put them in the way of being "added upon"; increase of intelligence and power and glory without limitation; how they should be put in the way of eternal progress; and how, in some way, there would be a redemption for them from the complications that might arise in carrying out that scheme of things. And hence, One must needs be chosen[14] as a Redeemer. That bright spirit, a Son of the Morning, called "Lucifer," because of his high intelligence—"Light Bearer"—proposed to save all men—spirits when incarnate in human bodies—irrespective of what they might do. "Behold," said he, "here am I, send me! I will be Thy son, and I will redeem all mankind, that one soul shall not be lost, and surely I will do it; wherefore, give me Thine honor!" (Moses 4:1). Pride, inordinate ambition revealed in every word of this proposal! Also, Lucifer's proposal would strike down the agency of man, and save him on compulsion—not one should be lost. "Give me," however, "Thy glory" is the spirit in which he spake. And then the Beloved Son, chosen from the beginning—determined upon of God—spake! Listen to him and contrast his spirit with the spirit of Lucifer: "Father, Thy will be done, and the glory be Thine forever." The answer to Lucifer was not obscure. Already it was known that the Father had decreed that those who kept not their first and second estates should not have glory in the same kingdom with those who kept those estates. That was the will of the Father, and, therefore, the Christ's answer: "Father, Thy will be done, and the glory be Thine forever"; and with this he offered himself as the Redeemer. The agency of man in this offer was preserved; and likewise the glory of God.

And this was the One, the pre-existent Spirit of the Christ, who in earth-life shall be known as Jesus of Nazareth, "Immanuel"—"God with us." He was chosen to be the Redeemer of men. And because Lucifer and his scheme of salvation for

---

14. <Ms III* "One must needs come"—*Ed.*>

man was rejected, he rebelled against God the Father and Jesus Christ, <who was> chosen to be the Redeemer. But Lucifer and the hosts which followed him were overwhelmed, and were cast out of heaven, and took up their abode on earth, there to resist and defeat, if possible, the designs of God in bringing to pass the immortality and eternal life of man—as man; as spirits, united with earth elements, that they might have power to receive a fullness of joy, and which, as we have already seen, they could not receive without forming this inseparable connection with material elements.

MORE LIGHT ON "THE WAR IN HEAVEN"

There still remain other enlightening utterances about this "war in heaven," and these given by direct revelation from God to the prophet of the New Dispensation:

> And it came to pass that Adam, being tempted of the devil—for, behold, the devil was before Adam, for he rebelled against me, saying, "Give me Thine honor, which is my power"; and also a third part of the hosts of heaven turned he away from me because of their agency [the "third part of the stars of heaven" of St. John's Revelation]. And they were thrust down, and thus came the devil and his angels. And behold, there is a place prepared for them from the beginning, which place is hell. And it must needs be that the devil should tempt the children of men, or they could not be agents unto themselves; for if they never should have bitter, they could not know the sweet. Wherefore, it came to pass that the devil tempted Adam, and he partook of the forbidden fruit and transgressed the commandment, wherein he became subject to the will of the devil, because he yielded unto temptation (D&C 29:36-40).

In this quotation we see repeated some of the former elements entering into the rebellion of Lucifer, with the added item that one-third of the hosts of heaven followed Lucifer, because of their agency, because they were free even as spirits to accept or reject the things proposed of God, subject, of course, to consequences.

One other, and the final quotation on this head, and from the same source of authority—a revelation of God given to the prophet of the New Dispensation. It occurs in the noted vision given to the prophet in February 1832, in which is set forth, as nowhere else, both the past and the future of pre-existent spirits; of spirits in earth-life, and the glory it is possible for them to attain through obedience to the gospel. In that part of the revelation which accounts for Lucifer's rebellion and the "war in heaven," the prophet says:

> And this we saw also, and bear record, that an angel of God who was in authority in the presence of God, who rebelled against the Only Begotten Son, whom the Father loved and who was in the bosom of the Father, was thrust down from the presence of God and the Son and was called Perdition, for the heavens wept over him—he was Lucifer, a son of the morning. And we beheld, and lo, he is fallen! is fallen, even a son

> of the morning! And while we were yet in the Spirit, the Lord commanded us that we should write the vision; for we beheld Satan, that old serpent, even the devil, who rebelled against God and sought to take the kingdom of our God and his Christ—wherefore, he maketh war with the saints of God, and encompasseth them round about (D&C 76:25-29).

Then follows the statement as to the condition of those whom he overcomes by his wiles, but upon which, at this point, it is not pertinent to our developing theme to say more.

WHAT GOD'S PLAN OF MAN'S ETERNAL LIFE INCLUDES

We now have before us, from divine authoritative sources, the reason of Lucifer's rebellion and the war in heaven. By the development of the reasons for that war we have come to know the solemn covenant of God with the pre-existent spirits of men, the promise to give to them eternal life—life everlasting—immortality; and under circumstances that would make for their eternal progression—to make it possible for those who keep both their first and their second estates to have glory added upon their heads forever and ever; and this through acceptance of and obedience to the one and only gospel. This gospel will include the fall of Adam, to bring about the broken harmonies in which man must learn his lessons in good and evil; in joy and sorrow; in hope and disappointment; in sickness and in health; in life and death; learning to appreciate the sweet by tasting the bitter; having wisdom with the passing years by the lessons that things in conflict and opposition have to teach. It will include his spiritual death—separation from God; for man's spiritual life depends upon his sustained union with God; that union broken spiritual death results.[15] It will include reunion with God, the rebirth of the spirit

---

15. The statement scarcely needs the support of argument. Spiritual life means relation to and participation in all the higher and better things—the good, the true, the beautiful, the pure, the refined, the noble, the courageous, the unselfish, the merciful; united with truth, justice, knowledge, wisdom, power, intelligence. The heart of all this—the very center and circumference of it, and the life of it, is and must be God; and to so deport one's self that he is thrown out of harmony with all this, severed from fellowship with God by separation from him who is the life of all this volume of higher and better things, this body of soul-quality, this ocean of righteousness—is death indeed—spiritual death; death as real as physical death—the separation of spirit and body. Following is an inspired statement of the spiritual death: "Wherefore, it came to pass that the devil tempted Adam, and he partook of the forbidden fruit and transgressed the commandment, wherein he became subject to the will of the devil, because he yielded unto temptation. Wherefore, I, the Lord God, caused that he should be cast out from the Garden of Eden, from my presence, because of his transgression, wherein he became spiritually dead, which is the first death, even that same

into fellowship with God; it will include resurrection from the dead; a reunion of the spirit with such elements of the body as may be necessary for its everlasting garment. All this to get the equipment—the indissoluble union of spirit and element in one sole being, eternal, deathless; with God's highway opening at each soul's feet for the journey of progress up through the heights of being in an endless and inexhaustible universe of progress.

Such the plan of God for the advancement of intelligences. First, through their habitancy of a spirit body; second, habitancy of a human, mortal body, by birth into this earth-life; third, habitancy of an immortal body by a greater birth, resurrection from the dead into a deathless life. Such <is> the plan which the wisdom of God has devised for bringing to pass "the immortality and eternal life of man"—the everlasting joy of man.

A SUPPOSED PURPOSE OF "THE WORLD'S AUTHOR" BY A PHILOSOPHER

The late Mr. Wm. James in his *Pragmatism* has a very wonderful passage bearing upon the whole thought of this chapter, and so pregnant with suggestion relative to our theme, so supported by philosophical thought and analysis of human nature, both strong and weak, that one marvels at so close a parallel of our doctrine, given to the Church of the Latter-day Saints—in large part[16]—in the very early years of her existence. The following is the passage from Mr. James:

> Suppose that the world's Author put the case to you before creation, saying: "I am going to make a world not certain to be saved, a world the perfection of which shall be conditional merely, the condition being that each several agent does its own 'level best.' I offer you the chance of taking part in such a world. Its safety, you see, is unwarranted. It is a real adventure, with real danger, yet it may win through. It is a social scheme of cooperative work genuinely to be done. Will you join the procession? Will you trust yourself and trust the other agents enough to face the risk?"
>
> Should you in all seriousness, if participation in such a world were proposed to you, feel bound to reject it as not safe enough? Would you say that, rather than be part and parcel of so fundamentally pluralistic and irrational a universe, you preferred to relapse into the slumber of non-entity from which you had been momentarily aroused by the tempter's voice?[17]

---

death which is the last death, which is spiritual, which shall be pronounced upon the wicked when I shall say, Depart, ye cursed" (D&C 29:40-41; cf. 2 Ne. 9:10-11).

16. <Ms III^c adds "—in large part—"—*Ed.*>

17. Of course, this proposition of relapsing into "non-entity" is no part of our (Latter-day Saint) <Ms III^c adds "(Latter-day Saint)"—*Ed.*> scheme of thought, since the actual proposition of our revelations was made to intelligences alike uncreated and uncreatable,

Of course, if you are normally constituted, you would do nothing of the sort. There is a healthy-minded buoyancy in most of us, which such a universe would exactly fit. We would, therefore, accept the offer—"Top! und schlag auf schlag!" It would be just like the world we practically live in; and loyalty to our old nurse Nature would forbid us to say no. The world proposed would seem "rational" to us in the most living way.

Most of us, I say, would, therefore, welcome the proposition and add our fiat to the fiat of the Creator. Yet perhaps some would not; for there are morbid minds in every human collection, and to them the prospect of a universe with only a fighting chance of safety would probably make no appeal. There are moments of discouragement in us all, when we are sick of self and tired of vainly striving. Our own life breaks down, and we fall into the attitude of the prodigal son. We mistrust the chances of things. We want a universe where we can just give up, fall on our father's neck, and be absorbed into the absolute life as a drop of water melts into the river or the sea.

The peace and rest, the security desiderated at such moments is security against the bewildering accidents of so much finite experience. Nirvana means safety from this everlasting round of adventures of which the world of sense consists. The Hindoo and the Buddhist, for this is essentially their attitude, are simply afraid of more experience, afraid of life! . . .

I find myself willing to take the universe to be really dangerous and adventurous, without, therefore, backing out and crying "no play." I am willing to think that the prodigal-son attitude, open to us as it is in many vicissitudes, is not the right and final attitude towards the whole of life. I am willing that there should be real losses and real losers, and no total preservation of all that is. I can believe in the ideal as an ultimate, not as an origin, and as an extract, not the whole. When the cup is poured off, the dregs are left behind for ever, but the possibility of what is poured off is sweet enough to accept.

As a matter of fact, countless human imaginations live in this moralistic and epic kind of a universe, and find its disseminated and strung-along successes sufficient for their rational needs. There is a finely translated epigram in the Greek anthology, which admirably expresses this state of mind, this acceptance of loss as unatoned for, even though the lost element might be one's self:

> "A shipwrecked sailor, buried on this coast,
> Bids you set sail.

---

and alike indestructible; so that while in the exercise of their freedom these intelligences might decline participation in the scheme of things proposed, they could not sink back into non-entities, they would merely remain *status quo*. <However, Wilford Woodruff records that Brigham Young taught on 17 February 1856: "For the Gods & all intelligent Beings would never scease [*sic*] to learn except it was the Sons of perdition they would continue to decrease untill they became dissolved back into their native Element & lost their Identity"; see Scott G. Kenney, ed., *Wilford Woodruff's Journal: 1833-1898 Typescript* (Midvale, UT: Signature Books, 1983), 4:402—*Ed.*>

> Full many a gallant bark, when we were lost,
> Weathered the gale."

> It is, then, perfectly possible to accept sincerely a drastic kind of a universe from which the element of "seriousness" is not to be expelled. Whoso does so is, it seems to me, a genuine pragmatist. He is willing to live on a scheme of uncertified possibilities, which he trusts; willing to pay with his own person, if need be, for the realization of the ideals which he frames.[18]

A STARTLING PARALLEL

Such <is> the voice of a modern and, without disparagement of others, we may venture to say, one of our foremost American philosophers. In this statement, as we said in introducing it, Professor James puts the case of the proposed earth-existence of man in a close parallel to that set forth in the early revelations to the Church of the Latter-day Saints. So closely a parallel that it is startling. The proposition put to intelligences before the earth was made, in each case; an earth-life full of adventure and danger, safety not guaranteed in each case; the counter plan proposed that would guarantee safety rejected; and yet the existence of some "morbid minds" among the spirits—found "in every human collection," to whom "the prospect of a universe with only a fighting chance" made no appeal, and accordingly their rejection of it; in both cases enough heroic souls to accept the adventurous proposition of a scheme of things involving real losses.

We may thank God that the Christ in the great council prevailed, as also he prevailed in the War of the Rebellion in Heaven, which followed upon that council's decision. The Christ's spirit stood for freedom of man in that great controversy. He stood for a serious earth-life for intelligences, in which though there would be some losses, many losses in fact, yet also there would be great gain and glory. Gain, however, that could not be obtained but through great strivings; the exercise of all the great virtues, of trust and patience, endurance and courage, wisdom and temperance, together with faith and hope and charity. Thank God, we say, that Jesus the Christ in the pre-existence stood for all those things which make earth-life worthwhile, and existence itself endurable—for the moral freedom of man.

---

18. William James, *Pragmatism: A New Name for Some Old Ways of Thinking: Popular Lectures on Philosophy* (New York: Longmans, Green, and Co., 1908), 290-92, 296-98.

CHAPTER XXX

The Earth-Life of Man Opened

SCRIPTURE READING LESSON

Analysis

I. The Two Creation Stories of Genesis.
II. A Key to the Mystery.
III. Spiritual and Temporal Creations.
IV. Progressive Movement in Spiritual and Temporal Creations.
V. The Place of Man in the Second Creation Story.
VI. The Second Creation Story, An Incident in the Earth's Creative Phases.
VII. Reality of the Spiritual Creation.
VIII. As This Theory of Creation Affects Man.
IX. Of Other Forms Than of Human Life.

References

The subject matter of this chapter stands so apart that it is difficult to find authorities to which the student may be directed for corroborative material. It is, therefore, urged that special attention be paid to the scriptures and other works cited in the body of the text.

CHAPTER XXX
The Earth-Life of Man Opened

THE TWO CREATION STORIES

The next task before us is to open the earth-life of man. To get him from the pre-existent spirit estate into the commencement of the human race life. This requires a back reference to the creation story as we have it in Genesis. So far as we have considered that story of creation we confined ourselves to the first chapter of Genesis, and that chapter treats creation as a developing, unbroken series of events from chaotic material without form and void to the creation of man and woman in the image of God—begotten after their kind.

(a) The First[1]

The creation story in Genesis, first chapter, is complete and worthily grand; without flaw or blemish, poetical, and sublime;[2] but when we take up the second chapter of Genesis, we are puzzled by having on our hands seemingly, another account of creation, different in form, and rather puzzling to the Bible theologians as well as to the laymen Bible readers. Such is the difference between the creation account in the first chapter of Genesis and the second, that modern Bible scholarship comes to the conclusion that the story of creation in the second chapter must be altogether from a different source than the account in the first chapter; and holds that there is a serious cleavage that gives reason for the belief that they must have come from separate documents.[3]

---

1. <Ms III[c] adds "(A) The First"—*Ed.*>

2. The story of this creation in the first chapter of Genesis should include the first three verses of the second chapter. And the second chapter properly should begin at the present fourth verse of that chapter, if the sense and spirit of the creation story is to be regarded.

3. J. Paterson Smyth, *How God Inspired the Bible: Thoughts for the Present Disquiet*, 5th ed. (London: Sampson, Low, Marston, 1910), chap. 6, esp. 196-97. Also, Samuel R. Driver, *An Introduction to the Literature of the Old Testament*, new ed., rev. (New York: Scribner, 1910), chap. 1, 8.

(b) The Second[4]

In the second account of the creation, the whole story seems to be reversed from that which is given in the first. The second account says:

> These are the generations of the heavens and of the earth, when they were created, in the day that the Lord God made the earth and the heavens, and every plant of the field before it was in the earth, and every herb of the field before it grew: for the Lord God had not caused it to rain upon the earth and there was not a man to till the ground (Gen. 2:4-5).

We naturally wonder what has become of the grasses, herbs, and trees, spoken of in the first chapter of Genesis? What of the fishes of the sea, the fowls of the air, the beasts of the field? What of man—male and female—of whose creation we read in the first chapter? And what of the commandment "to multiply and replenish the earth" (Gen. 1:28)? Is it not strange that after reading of the creation of man in the first chapter, that we should be told in the second that "there was not a man to till the ground"?

Proceeding with this second account of the creation, the Bible says:

> But there went up a mist from the earth and watered the whole face of the ground. And the Lord God formed man from the dust of the ground and breathed into his nostrils the breath of life; and man became a living soul. And the Lord God planted a garden eastward in Eden, and there He put the man whom He had formed. And out of the ground made the Lord God to grow every tree that is pleasant to the sight, and good for food; the Tree of Life also in the midst of the garden, and the Tree of Knowledge of Good and Evil. And a river went out of Eden to water the garden; and from thence it was parted and became into four heads. . . . And the Lord God took the man and put him into the Garden of Eden to dress it and to keep it. . . . And out of the ground the Lord God formed every beast of the field and every fowl of the air, and brought them unto Adam [the name he had given to the man he had created] to see what he would call them: and whatsoever Adam called every living creature, that was the name thereof (Gen. 2:6-10, 15, 19).

What is especially difficult in this second account of the creation, as before remarked, is that it seems to reverse the order of creation as given in the first chapter. The first account commences with the formation of the earth from chaotic matter; and then records the various steps of progress in succinct and, one would think, natural order up to completion; the last in the order of creation being man. The second account begins with the creation of man, the planting of a garden, as the beginning of vegetable and tree life; and there God places the man to keep it. Then comes the creation of the fowls of the air and the beasts of the field.

---

4. <Ms III[c] adds "(B) The Second"—*Ed.*>

A KEY TO THE MYSTERY

There is one significant remark in this second story of the creation in Genesis which may prove to be a key that will unlock the seeming mystery of this difference in the account of the creation without accepting the conclusion adopted by modern criticism, which is that these two creation stories come from different sources and most likely from distinct documents. This significant remark referred to is:

> These are the generations of the heavens and of the earth . . . in the day that the Lord God made the earth and its heavens, *and every plant of the field before it was in the earth*, and every herb of the field *before it grew*; for the Lord God had not caused it to rain upon the earth and *there was not a man to till the ground,*[5] but there went up a mist from the earth and watered the whole face of the ground. . . . And the Lord God planted a garden eastward in Eden (Gen. 2:4-6, 8).

Let it be remembered that this passage is in Genesis 2, though the italics in the quotation are mine. This passage standing alone, it is conceded, does not solve the mystery, something more is required; and in our Book of Moses[6] the necessary increase of light is given. After giving an account of the creation, much as it stands in the first chapter of Genesis, the revelation in this book proceeds,[7] in its third chapter, to say:[8]

> And now, behold, I say unto you, that these are the generations of the heaven and of the earth when they were created, in the day that I, the Lord God, made the heaven and the earth, and every plant of the field before it was in the earth, and every herb of the field, before it grew. For I, the Lord God, created all things of which I have spoken, spiritually, before they were naturally upon the face of the earth. For I, the Lord God, had not caused it to rain upon the face of the earth. And I, the Lord God, had created all the children of men; and not yet a man to till the ground; for in heaven created I them; and there was not yet *flesh*[9] upon the earth, neither in the water, neither in the air; but I, the Lord God, spake, and there went up a mist from the earth and watered the whole face of the ground. And I, the Lord God, formed man from the dust of the ground, and breathed into his nostrils the breath of life; and man became a living soul, the first flesh upon the earth, the first man also. Nevertheless, all things were before created, but spiritually were they created and made according to my word (Moses 3:4-7).

---

5. <Emphasis added by Roberts–*Ed.*>

6. <Ms III[*] "and in our Mosaic fragment of a revelation–The Book of Moses–"–*Ed.*>

7. <Ms III[*] "the revelation in this fragment proceeds"–*Ed.*>

8. <Ms III[c] adds "in its second chapter, to say"; the word "second" has been corrected to "third"–*Ed.*>

9. <Emphasis added by Roberts–*Ed.*>

SPIRITUAL AND TEMPORAL CREATION[10]

Still another word from modern revelation is given upon this subject of the two creations, the spiritual and the physical, called in the revelation, however, the "spiritual and the temporal."[11] And now the passage:

> And as the words have gone forth out of my mouth, even so shall they be fulfilled, that the first shall be last, and that the last shall be first in all things whatsoever I have created by the word of my power, which is the power of my Spirit. For by the power of my Spirit created I them; yea, all things both spiritual and temporal. First spiritual, secondly temporal, which is the beginning of my work; and again, first temporal, and secondly spiritual, which is the last of my work—speaking unto you that you may naturally understand; but unto myself my works have no end, neither beginning (D&C 29:30-33).

PROGRESSIVE MOVEMENT IN SPIRITUAL AND TEMPORAL CREATION[12]

An important thought arises out of this statement, in addition to the confirmation of the word from the Book of Moses passage, that things were created spiritually before they were created temporally (i.e., physically). We are given the idea of a process, a movement in creation, which suggests from lower to higher and from higher to still higher: first, from an imperfect spiritual state, to a union with the temporal—the birth of man into earth-life. Thence from the imperfect temporal (imperfect because the life is mortal) to the higher spiritual status—spirit being indissolubly united to its physical counterpart, the physical body, by the resurrection from the dead—raised to spiritual life—to the "immortality" God designed for man from the beginning through this process—from spiritual-temporal to temporal-spiritual; the completion or perfection of God's work.

---

10. <Ms III[c] adds "Spiritual and Temporal Creation"—*Ed.*>

11. <Sterling M. McMurrin, *The Theological Foundations of the Mormon Religion* (Salt Lake City: University of Utah Press, 1965), 25, points out that "Mormonism holds a double-creation doctrine that is reminiscent of Philo, who argued that the two accounts of the creation set forth in Genesis (chapters 1 and 2), which are often taken by modern scholarship as evidence of a compound documentary structure of Genesis, are accounts of a first creation of the Platonic ideas or universals, the 'intelligible' world, and a second creation of the world of material particulars which exemplify those universals"—*Ed.*>

12. <Ms III[c] adds "Progressive Movement in Spiritual and Temporal Creation"—*Ed.*>

THE PLACE OF MAN IN THE SECOND CREATION STORY[13]

It appears from the second creation story that man is the first creation instead of the last; that he is not only the first man, but the "first flesh" upon the earth also; and then comes the act of creation of woman, the planting of the garden, the placing of man in it, the creation of animal life, the fish of the sea, and fowls of the air. The question is, How can these things be? And how can the second story be made to harmonize with the first? In the second creation story man seems to get his earth-heritage in a barren state, as if some besom of destruction had swept the earth; and it must be newly fitted up as a proper abode for him from desert barrenness to a fruitful habitat.[14]

THE SECOND CREATION STORY, AN INCIDENT IN THE EARTH'S CREATIVE PHASES[15]

This "second creation story" may be regarded as one of a developing series of phases through which the planet earth is passing in its course towards a final celestial state of being. For example, had our revelations pertaining to the earth begun with Noah instead of Adam, and at the close of the cataclysm of the flood, when all animal life had been destroyed, except that which was especially preserved in the ark with Noah, we could clearly understand the procession of events leading out from Noah and his family into a world development under the commandment which God gave to Noah and his sons, when He said to them: "Be fruitful and multiply and replenish [refill] the earth" (Gen. 9:1); and then renewing with the family of Noah the covenant of mastery over all things in the earth, even as He had covenanted with Adam. May it not be that some such condition as this, which we have supposed in the case of Noah, really happened in regard to the "beginning" of things with Adam? And that what is recorded in the second creation story is

---

13. <Ms III[*] of section heading "The Second Creation Story in Genesis"—*Ed.*>

14. <The review committee gave the following objection to Roberts's interpretation: "The place of man in the order of creation is questioned, as it is taught in this chapter. The expression, 'the first flesh upon the earth also,' is not interpreted by members of the committee as you have expressed it here. We feel that the arguments as given contradict the accounts given in all our scriptures, and more especially in the temple ceremonies" ("Doctrinal Points Questioned by the Committee Which Read the Manuscript of Elder B. H. Roberts, Entitled The Truth, The Way, The Life," attached to Rudger Clawson, Letter to Heber J. Grant, [15 May 1930], in David J. Buerger Collection, Manuscript 622, Bx 10, Fd 8, Manuscripts Division, Marriott Library, University of Utah, Salt Lake City)—*Ed.*>

15. <Ms III[c] adds "The Second Creation Story An Incident in the Earth's Creative Phases"—*Ed.*>

merely an account of the preparation of the earth for the occupancy of it by Adam; and the account also of his advent upon the earth with Eve, his wife? That is to say, previous to the advent of Adam upon the earth, some destructive cataclysm, a universal glacial period or an excessive heat period left the earth empty and desolate, and it became the mission[16] of Adam to "replenish" the earth with inhabitants.

That there were pre-Adamite races in the earth, and that man's habitancy of it is of greater antiquity than the period which begins with Adam, is quite generally accepted by the scientific world, and for them, admits of no doubt;[17] but if the account of things through the Bible revelations begins with Adam, as merely the opening of a dispensation[18] of God's providences with the human race on the earth since that time,[19] then matters take on a form much more understandable, and makes possible the solving of many problems.

REALITY OF THE SPIRITUAL CREATION[20]

In using the phraseology of "spiritual creation" and "temporal" and "natural" creation in the foregoing quotations and comments upon them, their use must not be thought to imply that the spiritual creation was not a real creation. It was doubtless as tangible and actual as the creation on which we walk; but in the process of creation it appears that there are two parts: first, a spiritual creation and second, a temporal or natural one, what in our modern phraseology would be called the physical creation.

Though we may not fully[21] understand the nature of this spiritual creation, yet to learn that the first account of the creation in the Bible is of a spiritual creation, and the second of a natural one, gives some relief from the apparent contradiction from the fact that it removes all appearance of inconsistency or contradiction

---

16. <Ms III[*] "it came the mission"—*Ed.*>

17. This subject is considered somewhat at length in the chapter following this. <Roberts's position in "The Truth, The Way, The Life" is in contrast with his earlier statement that "if the researches of scientists prove beyond all question that there were pre-Adamic races, then doubtless they were inhabitants of that world which was destroyed, . . . Though, in this connection, I must say that so far as I have examined the works of those who treat on the subject of pre-historic man, or pre-Adamic races, they have hung the heaviest weights on the slenderest of threads: and I am inclined to the opinion that Adam was the progenitor of all races of men whose remains have yet been found" (B. H. Roberts, "Man's Relationship to Deity," *The Contributor* 10 [May 1889]: 267)—*Ed.*>

18. <Ms III[*] "as the merely opening of a dispensation"—*Ed.*>

19. <Ms III[c] adds "since that time"—*Ed.*>

20. <Ms III[c] adds "Reality of the Spiritual Creation"—*Ed.*>

21. <Ms III[c] adds "fully"—*Ed.*>

between the two accounts. For since they are descriptions of two different things instead of a conflicting account of one thing, there is nothing in the law of consistency requiring the account in the first chapter of Genesis—the account of spiritual creation—<there is nothing in the first chapter of Genesis> but what[22] could be safely accepted as the announcement of the general plan of the creation of worlds not only of our own planet but of all worlds; and in it will be found ample scope for the belief that the earth came into existence, as our scientists generally insist, by the accretion of nebulous matter; that it took millions of years for the concentration and solidification of that matter, granting as long periods as geologists may demand for the formation of the earth's crust followed by the changes which were wrought during the six great periods named in Genesis; beginning with the production of light, the dividing of the water, the appearing of land, then vegetation, animals, man.[23]

The temporal or physical creation of our planet, however, and of all planets, would doubtless correspond to the spiritual creation of it. The spiritual creation standing in the same relationship to the natural or physical creation, as the well-devised plan of the architect—the mind creation of his building—does to the material erection of a building, so that the account given of the spiritual creation of our earth may as well be regarded as the account of the natural or physical creation of it. But this conclusion would leave all the difficulties between the two accounts of the creation in the Bible untouched, unless we accept the second creation story as describing an incident, and one of many, that has happened in the long history of our planet; and in this case regard the second creation story of Genesis as the account of preparing the earth for the advent of Adam and Eve, his wife, on their mission to bring forth the human race upon earth as already suggested.

AS THIS THEORY OF CREATION AFFECTS MAN

Let us contemplate the foregoing conception of creation as it affects man. First, according to what has already been set forth—there is the self-existent, intelligent entity—and intelligence is not created or made, be it remembered, neither indeed can it be. This entity is begotten spirit—an intelligent entity united to a spirit-body, in some way begotten of God, and by some method of self-sundering, near or

22. <Ms III^{c} adds "but what"—*Ed.*>

23. The order of creation in the second account of creation in Genesis, it will be remembered, is somewhat reversed: 1. man; 2. vegetation; 3. animals; 4. woman; instead of from lower forms of life to higher—from simple to more complex, as given in Gen. 1. <Ms III^{c} adds "instead of from lower forms of life to higher—from simple to more complex, as given in Gen. 1"—*Ed.*>

remote—but sufficiently direct and near to impart something of the divine nature to the spirit which is to become man, and near enough to establish fatherhood of God to it.

This fulfills the "firstly spiritual" of the revelation. This spiritual personage is begotten a man in earth-life and fulfills the "secondly temporal" of the revelation. This man, so created or begotten, exists on the earth for a time to learn the lessons which earth-life amid broken harmonies has to teach; and in that earth-life appears the beginning of the second creative movement as the "again firstly temporal" of the revelation (D&C 29:32).

After a time the man dies; then again after a time, the man undergoes what might with some justification be called a greater birth. He undergoes resurrection from the dead. The spirit and body, which were separated at death and by death, are reunited by the resurrection from death; the spirit and the body become truly "soul" (also "sole")—spirit and body inseparably connected, deathless. This second creative movement fulfills the requirement of the "secondly spiritual," which is the last of God's work (D&C 29:32)—that is, the last of God's creative acts with reference to man as a "soul," the indissoluble union of a spirit with earth elements. God has attained his purpose in bringing about the immortality of man.

This, as our principle is applied to man, clearly sets forth this double action movement in creation, in bringing to pass the completed creation of man, and just how that created movement takes place from "spiritual" to "temporal"; and then from "temporal" to "spiritual"; which, however, is seen to be both temporal and spiritual united, or the union of what we usually call material element with spirit, which when perfectly and indissolubly united, is the highest attainment in creation.

OF LESSER FORMS THAN HUMAN LIFE

How the creation of lesser forms of life are affected by creation first spiritually and then temporally is not so definitely indicated in the revelations of God; and we are under the necessity of confessing that we do not know of anything that is directly and fully revealed concerning the matter, and so must needs let it pass without an attempted exposition; accepting it, however, on the word of God, as being true, that "all things" are created spiritually before they are created temporally, or take on a material body.

CHAPTER XXXI
An Adamic Dispensation

SCRIPTURE READING LESSON

Analysis

I. Further Localization.

II. The Antiquity of Man in the Earth:

(a) The Once "Orthodox Christian" View of Creation.

(b) The Science View on the Antiquity of Man in the Earth.

III. "The Rock Record."

IV. Alleged Evidence of Man's Antiquity in the Earth:

(a) The Java Man.

(b) The Heidelberg Man.

(c) The Neanderthal Man.

(d) The Piltdown or "Dawn" Man.

(e) The Cro-Magnon Man.

V. A Catholic Cardinal's Comment on This Class of Evidence.

VI. The Author's Comment

<Sections V and VI in the text of the chapter were later marked by Roberts to be deleted–*Ed.*>

References

The standard works on anthropology.

Prof. Richard Swann Lull's lecture on "The Antiquity of Man," published in George Alfred Baitsell, ed., *The Evolution of Man* (New Haven: Yale University Press, 1923), chap. 1.

Prof. J. Arthur Thomson, *The Outline of Science: A Plain Story Simply Told*, 4 vols. (New York and London: G. P. Putnam's Sons, 1922), vol. 1 considers the evolution topics taken up in this chapter.

The Bible, Book of Genesis; also, Book of Moses and Book of Abraham in the Pearl of Great Price.

CHAPTER XXXI
An Adamic Dispensation

FURTHER LOCALIZATION OF REVELATION[1]

We have already seen that the revelations of God given through Moses pertain to our earth and the heavens[2] with which it is connected, and have noted the effect of that localization of revelations to our earth and its heavens.[3] Now it is proposed to consider a still further localization of our revelations to an Adamic Dispensation in the world's history. We begin then with Adam, and the procession of events from his time; which, with reference to the whole period of the earth's existence, may be set down as comparatively recent, and even very recent times, within historic time in fact, if we accept the Bible account of the commencement of things as historic.[4] This would admit of a very long period of time beyond the advent of Adam, to the absolute beginning of the physical existence[5] of the earth, during which time pre-Adamite races, less developed than he, may have existed. They may have lived and died through various long ages through which the earth passed, of which we have no information supplied by revelation concerning them; but who have provided all the fossil and other evidences of man's existence in the earth discovered by the researches of science, and which so disturb the Bible account of things, when an attempt is made to stretch the Bible account to cover all the possible human life[6] events that have happened in all periods of time since the physical or temporal existence of the earth began.[7]

---

1. <Ms III^{c} adds "of Revelation"—*Ed.*>

2. <Ms III^{c} adds an "s" to make the plural "heavens"—*Ed.*>

3. <Ms III^{c} adds an "s" to make the plural "heavens"—*Ed.*>

4. <Ms III^{c} adds "as historic"—*Ed.*>

5. <Ms III^{c} adds an "s" to make the plural "existences," but the singular Ms III* "existence" is followed, because it also occurs at the end of the paragraph and because it seems more appropriate—*Ed.*>

6. <Ms III^{c} adds "possible human life"—*Ed.*>

7. <The review committee gave the following objection to Roberts's interpretation about pre-Adamites: "This doctrine is not taught by the Church; it is not sustained in the scriptures. It can only be treated as an hypothesis, and the result will be uncertain, confusing,

THE ANTIQUITY OF MAN IN THE EARTH[8]

Let us briefly consider some of the evidences of man's greater antiquity[9] in the earth than the Bible account warrants. Of course, we shall not be able to go deeply into the subject, and can only present the conclusions at which scientific investigators have arrived.

THE ONCE[10] "ORTHODOX CHRISTIAN" VIEW OF CREATION

In the first place, let us present the once orthodox conception of the date of creation as fixed by an interpretation of the Mosaic account of creation. The most definite statement on this head, and one that is very frequently referred to in controversial writings on the subject, is the interpretation of the Mosaic account by Dr. John Lightfoot, said to be a profound Biblical scholar. He was vice-chancellor of Cambridge University in 1654. As a result of careful searching of scripture, Dr. Lightfoot was led to declare that "heaven and earth, center and circumference, were made in the same instant[11] [of time], and clouds full of water . . . and man was created by the Trinity on the 23rd of October, 4004 B.C., at 9 o'clock in the morning."[12]

Of course, this represents the definiteness of extreme methods of interpretation followed by biblical students of Dr. Lightfoot's days. It is now recognized that even the accepted dates of creation and other biblical events by the chronologers, <James> Ussher, <William> Hales, and the Jewish reckoning, are to be regarded ap-

---

for after all is said it is speculation leading to endless controversy. We are aware that one of the brethren (Orson Hyde) in an early day advocated this teaching; however, we feel that the brethren of the general authorities cannot be too careful, and should not present as doctrine that which is not sustained in the standards of the Church. It appears to us that all which has been revealed is contrary to this teaching, especially that given in the Temple." Roberts's handwritten responses were that he had "not so presented" this teaching and that Orson Hyde's teaching "was approved also by Pres. Young" ("Doctrinal Points Questioned by the Committee Which Read the Manuscript of Elder B. H. Roberts, Entitled The Truth, The Way, The Life," attached to Rudger Clawson, Letter to Heber J. Grant, [15 May 1930], in David J. Buerger Collection, Manuscript 622, Bx 10, Fd 8, Manuscripts Division, Marriott Library, University of Utah, Salt Lake City)—*Ed.*>

8. <Ms III[*] "The Antiquity of Man in the Earth: The Science View"—*Ed.*>

9. <Ms III[*] "the evidences Science gives of man's greater antiquity"—*Ed.*>

10. <Ms III[c] adds "Once "—*Ed.*>

11. <White's text has "were created all together, in the same instant"—*Ed.*>

12. <Andrew D. White, *A History of the Warfare of Science with Theology in Christendom* (New York: D. Appleton and Co., 1896), 1:9—*Ed.*>

proximate only.[13] Since the computations made by those chronologers, the researches of Oriental scholars are bringing forth other evidence bearing upon the subject. While these researches are confirming the historical character of Abraham and other Hebrew patriarchs as quite definite, in their extensive excavations on the sites of ancient cities, they are tracing back a more remote period for the history of Near-Eastern peoples. The Babylonian tablets discovered in these researches give the world a message out of the past which antedates that of Christ up to about 5,500 to 6,000 years instead of 4,004; adding more than a thousand years to the Bible account of creation, as interpreted by Dr. Lightfoot and others of the orthodox school.

A MODIFICATION OF THE ORTHODOX VIEW[14]

Here it will be suitable to present a modification of this supposed scripture account of the advent of Adam, as given in the sayings of Joseph Smith.[15]

> As the Father hath life in Himself, so hath He given to the Son to have life in Himself (John 5:26).
>
> As the Father knoweth me, even so know I the Father; and I lay down my life for the sheep. . . . Therefore doth my Father love me, because I lay down my life, that I might take it up again. No man taketh it from me, but I lay it down of myself. I have power to lay it down and I have power to take it again. This commandment have I received from my Father (John 10:15-18).
>
> Verily, verily, I say unto you, the Son can do nothing of Himself, but what He seeth the Father do; for what things soever He doeth, these also doeth the Son likewise. For the Father loveth the Son and showeth Him all things that Himself doeth (John 5:19-20).

Having these scriptures in mind, the Prophet of the New Dispensation, in commenting upon the substance of them said:

> What did Jesus say?[16] . . . The scriptures inform us that Jesus said, "As the

---

13. <James Ussher's dates for biblical events first appeared in the margin of the Oxford edition of the King James Version of 1701; see Jack P. Lewis, *The English Bible/From KJV to NIV: A History and Evaluation* (Grand Rapids, MI: Baker Book House, 1981), 39—*Ed.*>

14. <This section is a later, four-page insertion by Roberts, which at the top of the page had the wording "ADD AT P. 3 before 3/2." This was crossed out and replaced by Ms III[c] "A Modification of the Orthodox View." This four-page addition is in the Buerger Collection—*Ed.*>

15. <Ms III[*] "this supposed scripture account of the creation of man"—*Ed.*>

16. <Ms III "What did John say?" but the King Follett Discourse correctly has "What did Jesus say?" See the editor's "The King Follett Discourse: A Newly Amalgamated Text," *Brigham Young University Studies* 18 (Winter 1978): 201—*Ed.*>

> Father hath power in Himself, even so hath the Son power"–to do what? Why, what the Father did. The answer is obvious–in a manner to lay down his body and take it up again. Jesus, what are you going to do? "To lay down my life as my Father did, and take it up again." Do you believe it? If you do not believe it, you do not believe the Bible.[17]

Moreover, if the Father of Jesus Christ had done that, viz., laid down his life which Jesus was also about to do, following out what the Father before him had done, then it is not inconceivable that that Father's Father had done the same thing. And such is the argument in one of the Prophet's notable discourses, namely, one which was delivered in Nauvoo on June 16, 1844. In the body of his discourse the Prophet repeated his text: "And hath made us kings and priests unto God and His Father" (Rev. 1:6). Here, before quoting the Prophet, I may be permitted to exclaim–God had a Father then. And now the Prophet's comment:

> I learned a testimony concerning Abraham and he reasoned concerning the God of heaven; . . . said he, "Suppose we have two facts: that supposes another fact may exist–two men on the earth, one wiser than the other, would logically show that a<nother who is> wiser than the wisest [i.e., of these two] may exist. Intelligences exist one above another, so that there is no end to them." If Abraham reasoned thus–If Jesus Christ was the Son of God, and John discovered[18] that God, the Father of Jesus Christ, had a Father, you may suppose that He [i.e., the <Grand>Father of Jesus Christ] had a Father also. Where was there ever a son without a father? And where was there a father without first being a son? . . . And everything comes in this way. Paul says that which is earthly is in the likeness of that which is heavenly. Hence, if Jesus had a Father, can we not believe that *He* [i.e., the Father of Jesus] had a Father also? . . . I want you to pay particular attention to what I am saying. Jesus said that the Father wrought precisely in the same way as His Father had done before Him, as the Father had done before Him. He laid down His life and took it up, the same as His Father had done before He [Jesus] did, after He was sent to lay down His life and take it up again. And then was committed to Him the keys.[19]

---

17. <Joseph Smith, *The King Follett Discourse; The Being and Kind of Being God Is; The Immortality of the Intelligence of Man*, annotated by B. H. Roberts (Salt Lake City: Magazine Printing Co., 1926), 9-10–*Ed.*>

18. <Ms III "and God discovered"–*Ed.*>

19. Joseph Smith, "The Christian Godhead–Plurality of Gods," *History of the Church of Jesus Christ of Latter-day Saints, Period I: History of Joseph Smith, the Prophet by Himself* (Salt Lake City: Deseret News, 1912), 6:476-77. <In the next to last sentence Roberts has changed the wording from the way it appears in the following two sentences of the *History of the Church*: "He laid down His life, and took it up the same as His Father had done before. He did as He was sent, to lay down His life and take it up again." This sentence appears in the Thomas Bullock transcript, which is printed in Andrew F. Ehat and Lyndon W. Cook, eds.,

The thing to be noted here, however, is that this laying down of the lives of these Fathers was not upon this earth, but must have taken place on other worlds, together with their resurrection also: so that there was life and death before Adam's time, at least on other worlds.

The conclusion I wish to present here is, that life and death were not new and original things to our planet, and only peculiar to Adam and since his time. They were from of old, and should not be considered as inconceivable as happening not only on other worlds but in our earth also in pre-Adamite times.

In further confirmation of this line of thought the Prophet Joseph is represented as saying: "Everlasting covenant was made between three personages before the organization of this earth and relates to their dispensation of things to men[20] on the earth. These personages according to Abraham's record are called God the first, the creator; God the second, the Redeemer; and God the third, the Witness or Testator."[21]

And again, from the same source, "The world and earth are not synonymous terms. The world is the human family. This earth was organized or formed out of other planets which were broken up and remodeled and made into the one on which we live. The elements are eternal. . . . In the translation 'without form and void' it should read 'empty and desolate.' The word 'created' should be 'formed' or 'organized.'"[22]

It must be admitted that Elder Franklin D. Richards, compiler of this *Compendium*, does not cite precisely the source whence these items were obtained nor have I been able to trace them to other sources than this *Compendium*, but then it should be remembered that Elder F. D. Richards, one of the Twelve Apostles and in his day historian of the church and a contemporary with the Prophet himself, is an important authority in such matters.[23]

The Words of Joseph Smith: The Contemporary Accounts of the Nauvoo Discourses of the Prophet Joseph (Provo, UT: Religious Studies Center, Brigham Young University, 1980), 380, as: "he laid down his life & took it up same as his Far. had done bef—he did as he was sent to lay down his life & take it up again"—*Ed.*>

20. <Ms III "man," which is corrected to "men"—*Ed.*>

21. Franklin D. Richards and James A. Little, "Gems from the History of Joseph Smith," *A Compendium of the Doctrines of the Gospel*, rev. ed. (Salt Lake City: Deseret Book Co., 1925), 272.

22. Ibid., 271.

23. <Richards's source for these two *Compendium* statements is William Clayton's "Private Book," the sections entitled "By Joseph, January 5th, 1841, Answer to the question, was the Priesthood of Melchizedeck [*sic*] taken away when Moses died" and "By Joseph," which are printed in George D. Smith, ed., *An Intimate Chronicle: The Journals of William Clayton* (Salt Lake City: Signature Books in association with Smith Research Associates,

It will be noted here that in the first of the above quotations the covenant of the Three Personages mentioned *relates to their dispensation of things to men on the earth.* And in the second quotation the statement is made that this earth was organized or formed out of other planets which were broken up and remolded and made into the one on which we live. Were those planets out of which ours was made inhabited by pre-Adamic races? Who shall say? But if so, the commandment to Adam to multiply and *re*-plenish the earth would not have been inappropriate any more than it was for Noah to be commanded to go forth and "multiply and replenish the earth" (Gen. 9:1).[24]

ORIGIN OF THE EARTH AS VIEWED BY SCIENCE[25]

In contrast to this (supposed) Bible view of creation, I place in contrast the scientific view.[26] This begins with part of the generally accepted nebulae hypothesis;[27] that is, that our solar system, to extend the brief statement no further, was brought into existence by some great sun many millions of years ago, passing so near to our sun that it whipped from the gravitational grip of the sun large masses of the sun's substances and set them whirling separately into space.[28]

1991), 515-17–*Ed.*>

24. <Here there is a sentence beginning a discussion of "replenish," which discussion is inserted several pages later in this chapter–*Ed.*>

25. <This section is another four-page insertion, which Roberts placed after p. 3 of chapter 31 and gave the numbers of "3/2," "3/3," "3/4," and "3/5." Since Roberts quotes from the December 1929 printing of Sir James Jeans's book, *The Universe around Us*, this section can be dated to 1930–*Ed.*>

26. <For an up-to-date discussion of modern cosmology, see Barry Parker, *The Vindication of the Big Bang: Breakthroughs and Barriers* (New York: Plenum Press, 1993)–*Ed.*>

27. <For the nebular hypothesis, see Ronald L. Numbers, *Creation by Natural Law: Laplace's Nebular Hypothesis in American Thought* (Seattle: University of Washington Press, 1977)–*Ed.*>

28. "New <now> planets are very rare. They come into being as the result of the close approach of two stars, and stars are so sparsely scattered in space that it is an inconceivably rare event for one to pass near to a neighbor. Yet exact mathematical analysis shows that planets cannot be born except when two stars pass within about three diameters of one another. As we know how the stars are scattered in space, we can estimate fairly closely how often two stars will approach within this distance of one another. The calculation shows that even after a star lived its life of millions of millions of years, the chance is still about 100,000 to 1 against its being a sun surrounded by planets" (Sir James Jeans, *The Universe Around Us* [New York: The Macmillan Co.; Cambridge, England: The University Press, December 1929], 320-21). <For the planetesimal hypothesis (which Roberts and Jeans describe), see Stephen G. Brush, "A Geologist among Astronomers: The Rise and Fall of

In time these whirling, fiery masses took their respective places in orbits around the sun according to the minor planets of our system. In reference to our own planet, to again limit our consideration to that which more nearly concerns our inquiry, in time—and how long is unknown[29]—the fiery mass that was finally to constitute our earth began condensing until the mass was covered over by a thin rocky coating: this thickened sufficiently to confine the heat beneath the incrustation, while the hydrogen and oxygen united to form vapors about it. These became condensed and descending on all sides of the earth completely enveloped it with water, something as a universal ocean would do. Also, in time an atmosphere gathered about it.

Ages upon ages passed and the Laurentian, the Cambrian, and the Silurian rocks were gradually formed under the water. Then intermittently came great upheavals of the earth's crust, the foldings of it into mountain chains, carrying with them even to the summits of mountains remains of marine animal life, which had lived at the bottom of seas.[30] Then land upheavals rising above the

---

the Chamberlin-Moulton Cosmology," *Journal for the History of Astronomy* 9 (Feb./June 1978): 1-41, 77-104—*Ed.*>

29. The lapses of time of recent geological estimates concerning the age of the earth and life upon it is stated by Sir James Jeans in his recent work, *The Universe around Us* (1929), 13, is given in tabulated form as follows:

Age of the earth.	about 2,000,000,000 of years
Age of life on the earth	300,000,000 of years
Age of man on the earth	300,000 of years

As an indication of the great age of the earth's crust the following note from John William Draper, *History of the Conflict between Religion and Science*, 6th ed. (New York: D. Appleton and Co., 1875), 190-91, gives substantial and irresistible evidence of its immense age: "The coal-bearing strata in Wales by their gradual submergence have attained a thickness of 12,000 ft.; in Nova Scotia of 14,750 ft. So slow and so steady was this submergence that erect trees stand one above another on successive levels; seventeen such repetitions may be counted in a thickness of 4,515 ft. The age of the trees is proved by their size, some being 4 ft. in diameter. Round them as they gradually went down with their subsiding soil, calamities grew at one level after another. In the Sydney coal fields fifty-nine fossil forests occur in superposition." <According to Steven M. Stanley, *Earth and Life through Time* (New York: W. H. Freeman and Co., 1986), 239, the current scientific estimate is that the earth was formed about 4.6 billion years ago—*Ed.*>

30. "Marine shells, found on mountain tops far in the interior of continents, were regarded by theological writers as an indisputable illustration of the Deluge [in the days of Noah, says Draper], but when, after geological studies became more exact, it was proved that in the crust of the earth vast fresh water formations are repeatedly interrelated <intercalated> with vast marine ones, like the leaves of a book, it became evident that no single cataclysm was sufficient to account for such results; that the same region, through gradual variations

water divided them and formed separate oceans and seas; meantime gradual subsidances of some parts of the earth's crust and the elevation of other parts gave form to the land areas—to continents and islands. Low forms of plant life appeared—mosses, ferns, grasses, flowering plants, shrubbery and trees began to appear. The dense vapors which had shrouded the earth in these ages began to disappear and the sun shone on the earth's surface to quicken and enlarge life, in sea, earth, and air; these thrived in all their varied forms, and ultimately man came and began his wonderful career.

This is not a chapter on geology, even in outline much less a work on that subject; so that I am not concerned in tracing even in tabulated form the several periods and strata of the earth's formation from first to last. I only wish to mention enough of these to make intelligible the scientific conceptions of the antiquity of man in the earth. So I pass by the primary and secondary parts of geological formations in the textbooks and other works on the subject. But in the Tertiary and Quaternary period we have the epochs where the emergence of man, or near-man, occurs; and, therefore, these are in the geological period of immense import and to our own subject. These geological periods include what are called the Eocene and Oligocene times or epochs, in which arise the higher mammals of the ancient species; the Miocene and Pliocene times, in which man emerges; and finally, preceding recent times, the Pleistocene epoch, which is identical with the last great Ice Age. These epochs in geological formations correspond with the following periods of time.

The Miocene, within the Tertiary period, to 900,000 years ago; Pliocene, within the Tertiary period,[31] to 500,000 years ago; Pleistocene or last great Ice Age, in which ancient articrafts of man with his remains are found and ranging from 400,000 years down to twenty or thirty thousand years ago, which marked the retreat of the great glaciers from the present northern temperate zones.[32] So that within the Tertiary and Quaternary geological periods, within which it is claimed

---

of its level and changes in its topographical surrounding<s>, had sometimes been dry land, sometimes covered with fresh and sometimes with sea water. It became evident also that, for the completion of these changes, ten<s> of thousands of years were required" (John William Draper, *History of the Conflict between Religion and Science*, 6th ed. [New York: D. Appleton and Co., 1875], 191).

31. <Ms III "within the Quatenary period," which is corrected to "Tertiary"—*Ed.*>

32. <Modern discovery has pushed the dates for these epochs back further. For example, according to Steve Jones, Robert Martin, and David Pilbeam, ed., *The Cambridge Encyclopedia of Human Evolution* (Cambridge, Eng.: Cambridge University Press, 1992), 467, 469, the Miocene covers 23.3 to 5.2 millions years ago, the Pliocene covers 5.2 to 1.64 million years ago, and the Pleistocene covers 1.64 million to 10,000 years ago—*Ed.*>

that fossil remains of man and his articrafts and weapons are found, there is room for a very great antiquity for man, and certainly a pre-Adamite period of human existences.

THE[33] SCIENCE VIEW[34] ON THE ANTIQUITY OF MAN IN THE EARTH

Meantime science submits its deductions on the subject of the antiquity of man in the earth.[35] These come from a number of sources, among them through the fixing of time by the discovery made through the articrafts[36] which man has used in various periods of time. For instance, there is the age of iron and steel, our own age, in which man uses these materials in manufactures and building. This was preceded by the age of bronze, and that by the stone age. This last-named age is divided into three periods: first, the Neolithic or "new stone age"; this was preceded by the Paleolithic or the "older stone age"; and this again by the Eolithic. This third period is supposed to be the very oldest period in which man began the use of anything like implements in his ways of life. There is some doubt if the so-called "stone implements" of this age were "purposeful manufactures" at all. Some hold that such implements as were used were merely nature-shaped stones, as were more convenient than others for various uses; and it was these rude nature-shaped implements that suggested the purposeful manufactures of the Paleolithic or old stone age. The crude implement manufactures of this period merged into the more artistically prepared and the greater variety of implements of the new stone age, or Neolithic period. The antiquity of man in the earth is attested first by the undoubted existence and use of these implements, and the slow development of their form and multiplied uses, coupled with calculations based on the glacial periods that are known to have overwhelmed portions of the earth's surface and under which drifts these articrafts of early man have been found, and[37] to scientists justify the conclusion that man has lived upon the earth very many thousands of years longer than the interpretations given of the Mosaic account of creation by the orthodox chronologers. The conclusion based upon these even limited[38] facts carry back the antiquity of man from 25,000 to 30,000 years in his

33. <Ms III^c adds "The"—*Ed.*>

34. <Ms III^c adds "View"—*Ed.*>

35. Prof. Richard Swann Lull, "The Antiquity of Man," a lecture in George Alfred Baitsell, ed., *The Evolution of Man* (New Haven, CT: Yale University Press, 1923), 1-38.

36. <Ms III* "the artifacts," but Ms III^c crosses out the "f" and adds a supralinear "cr" to form an intended "articrafts"—*Ed.*>

37. <Ms III^c adds "and"—*Ed.*>

38. <Ms III^c adds "even limited"—*Ed.*>

occupancy of the earth, and hence tend to establish the probability of pre-Adamite races in the earth.

THE ROCK RECORD[39]

The author of *The Outline of Science* asks:[40]

> How do we know when the various classes of animals and plants were established on the earth? How do we know the order of their appearance and the succession of their advances? The answer is: by reading the "Rock Record." In the course of time the crust of the earth has been elevated into continents and depressed into ocean-troughs, and the surface of the land has been buckled up into mountain ranges and folded in gentler hills and valleys. The high places of the land have been weathered by air and water in many forms, and the results of the weathering have been borne away by rivers and seas, to be laid down again elsewhere as deposits, which eventually formed sandstones, mud-stones, and similar sedimentary rocks. . . . When the sediments were accumulating age after age, it naturally came about that remains of the plants and animals living at the time were buried, and these formed the fossils by the aid of which it is possible to read the story of the past. By careful piecing together of evidence the geologist is able to determine the order in which the different sedimentary rocks were laid down, and thus to say, for instance, that the Devonian period was the time of the origin of Amphibians. In other cases the geologist utilizes the fossils in his attempt to work out the order of the strata when these have been much disarranged. For the simpler fossil forms of any type must be older than those that are more complex. There is no vicious circle here, for the general succession of strata is clear, and it is quite certain that there were fishes before there were amphibians [from amphibia, one of the classes of vertebrates, a marsh frog is of the type], and amphibians before there were reptiles, and reptiles before there were birds and mammals. In certain cases, e.g., of fossil horses and elephants, the actual historical succession has been clearly worked out.[41]

Running parallel with this line of evidence and confirming it is the evidence that comes from the discovery of human remains in various old earth strata, which represent geological formations of hundreds of thousands of years ago. It is held that human remains have been found in the Pliocene strata of the earth's surface, preced-

---

39. <Ms III* has the words "The Rock Record" and the quotation from Thomson as a footnote. However, in the left margin Ms III^c adds "(make into body of text)–(not note)"–*Ed.*>

40. <Ms III^c adds "asks the author of the Outline of Science" between the first and second sentences of the quotation from Thomson–*Ed.*>

41. J. Arthur Thomson, *The Outline of Science: A Plain Story Simply Told* (New York and London: G. P. Putnam's Sons, 1922), 1:88-89.

ing the Pleistocene strata[42] and corresponding with the earlier glacial periods, and immediately preceding the present surface formation. The Pliocene strata corresponds in terms of years to about 500,000 years ago; and it follows that, if human remains are found in that strata, then man lived upon the earth that long ago.[43]

I give the following abbreviated account of these various discoveries of human remains in these strata with the corresponding time period in years:[44]

EVIDENCE OF MAN'S ANTIQUITY IN THE EARTH[45]

(a) *The Java Man*

The finds in relation to this so-called man consist of a small top of the skull (skull cap), a thigh bone, and two back teeth. There is some dispute among authorities as to whether these remains are really of man or some pre-human ape-man; others hold that they are relics of a primitive man, but off the main line of "the ascent of man." Sir Arthur Keith holds this creature was "a being, human in nature, human in gait, human in all its parts, save its brain." In scientific phraseology they call him *Pithecanthropus*. He is supposed to have been about 5'7" in height, somewhat less than the average height of man today. The skull cap indicates low-cut forehead, beetling brows, and a brain capacity of about two-thirds of the modern man. The remains were found by Dr. E. Dubois, a Dutch army surgeon at Trinil, central Java, 1894. The Java man is supposed to have lived from four hundred thousand to five hundred thousand years ago.

(b) *The Heidelberg Man*

The remains of this fossil are a lower jawbone and its teeth. It was discovered in Heidelberg in 1907 by Dr. <Otto> Schoetensack. With the relic were bones of various mammals long since extinct in Europe, such as the elephant, rhinoceros, bison, and lion. There were also some crude flint implements with these finds. "But the teeth are human teeth," says Professor Thomson, author of *The Outline of Science*, "but," he adds, "the relic is of a primitive type, off the main

---

42. <Ms III* "the Pleistocene strata of the earth surface"–*Ed.*>

43. Thomson, *Outline of Science*, 1:92, 162, et seq. and illustrated plates.

44. <For a modern account on the origin of humankind, see Ian Tattersall, *The Human Odyssey: Four Million Years of Human Evolution* (New York: Prentice Hall, 1993); for an atlas of fossil man, see Clark Spencer Larsen, Robert M. Matter, and Daniel L. Gebo, *Human Origins: The Fossil Record*, 2d ed. (Prospect Heights, IL: Waveland Press, 1991)–*Ed.*>

45. <Ms III^{c} adds "Alleged Evidence of Man's Antiquity in the Earth" and then later the word "Alleged" was deleted–*Ed.*>

line of human ascent."[46] The reconstructed man from this jawbone received the scientific name of *Homo heidelbergensis*. The age of this fossil is claimed to be three hundred thousand years.

(c) The Neanderthal Man[47]

The fossils of this man were recovered from the Neanderthal ravine, near Dusseldorf, Germany, 1856. According to some authorities the Neanderthal man was living in Europe a quarter of a million years ago. He was the "cave man" of that period. It is claimed "he used fire, . . . buried his dead reverently,[48] and furnished them with an outfit for a long journey, <and he> had a big brain, . . . great beetling, ape-like eyebrows." Professor Huxley was of the opinion that "the Neanderthal man represents a distinct species off the main line of ascent."[49]

(d) The Piltdown Man or "Dawn Man"

The remains of this man consist of two pieces of skull bone, a small piece of jawbone, and a canine tooth. Found in Sussex, England, 1912, it is thought by some that the two little bits–jawbone and canine tooth–may not belong to the skull at all. The conclusion is that the skull indicates a large brain, a high forehead without the beetling eyebrows. The time period of these fossil remains date from one hundred thousand to five hundred thousand years ago.[50]

(e) The Cro-Magnon Man

This is the cave man, or race we hear so much about, existing between the third and fourth ice ages of the earth, extending back from thirty to fifty thousand years ago. The evidence for the existence of such a race is much more satisfactory than the fossil remains of the other periods, and it is held by scientists quite

---

46. <Thomson, *Outline of Science*, 1:169–*Ed.*>

47. <In this section of Ms III and in the chapter synopsis Roberts refers to this man with the spelling "Meanderthal"–*Ed.*>

48. <Ms III "buried his dead reverent," but Thomson's text has "buried his head [*sic*] reverently"–*Ed.*>

49. <Thomson, *Outline of Science*, 1:169. Roberts has telescoped Thomson's discussion, since Thomas Henry Huxley believed Neanderthal man "as a low form of the modern type," while the quotation in the text is William King's view, expressed in 1864–*Ed.*>

50. <Roberts was, of course, not aware that the "Piltdown Man" was a fraud, which was discovered in 1953. See Charles Blinderman, *The Piltdown Inquest* (Buffalo, NY: Prometheus Books, 1986), and Frank Spencer, *Piltdown: A Scientific Forgery* (Oxford: Natural History Museum Publications, Oxford University Press, 1990)–*Ed.*>

generally that this man approaches more nearly the modern man than any of the other supposed races.[51]

<TWO DELETED SECTIONS>[52]

---

51. Thomson, *Outline of Science*, 1:155-80. Prof. Lull's lecture, "The Antiquity of Man," in *The Evolution of Man*, chap. 1. <According to Erik Trinkaus, "Cro-Magnon People," in *McGraw-Hill Encyclopedia of Science and Technology*, 7th ed., ed. Sybil P. Parker (New York: McGraw-Hill, Inc., 1992), 4:527-28, "early modern humans emerged between 50,000 and 100,000 years ago," while the Cro-Magnon group in western Europe date from about 32,000 years ago—*Ed.*>

52. <The two sections which are printed in this footnote are part of Ms III*, and both these sections are included in the synopsis at the beginning of chap. 31. However, Roberts later indicated that the sections entitled "A Catholic Comment" and "The Author's Comment," both of which relate to the Piltdown Man, should be eliminated from Ms III* of TWL—*Ed.*>

"*A Catholic Comment.* On the remains of the Piltdown, or Dawn Man, we have a recent interesting comment made by Cardinal <William H.> O'Connell, American Cardinal of the Roman Catholic Church. The remains of the Dawn Man are in the American Museum of Natural History, New York, in the hall of the 'Age of Man.' 'In that hall,' said the Cardinal, 'the popular feature arranged by Dr. Henry Fairfield Osborn is an exhibition of what might be justly termed the grotesque gullibility of so-called scientists. There is the Piltdown man; two bits of skull-bone, a very small piece of jawbone, and a canine tooth. All these bones were found in different places in a sandpit of Sussex and at long intervals. Now for the scientific process out of these scraps of bone which you could conceal in the hollow of your hand, by pure, unproven assumption, is constructed an ape-man and labeled *Eoanthropus*, or the 'Dawn Man,' out of the pure imagination and false assumption, not backed by a single spark of evidence, science produces a purely fake skeleton and bids the world to come to the Natural History Museum for educational instruction! (from synopsis of speech of Cardinal O'Connell, *New York World*, 1 February 1926)."

<Then follows Roberts's own remarks, which were also marked to be eliminated from Ms III* of TWL—*Ed.*>

"*The Author's Comment.* Of course, there seems to be telling effect in the sarcastic comment of the Roman Cardinal on these bits of alleged <Ms III^{c} adds "alleged"—*Ed.*> fossil human remains; but notwithstanding these sarcasms, comparative structural anatomy has to its credit some very wonderful achievements, and one must not attempt to settle the whole controversy on one item of evidence. All the fossil discoveries must be considered, not only those from the Pliocene and Pleistocene strata of the earth's crust, but with them there must be accounted the human remains found in the various glacial periods of scores and hundreds of thousands of years ago, together with the written historical evidences which are pushing back the line of man's antiquity in the earth far beyond the 4004 years B.C. of the supposed Bible account of creation. The stone ages of man alone give greater antiquity to man than the Bible account of creation, and establish, one may feel very safe in saying, evidences of pre-Adamite races in the earth, and justifies the assumption we are about to test out, that so

If it shall be urged that this conception of things with reference to the earth and its inhabitants only pushes back the problem of human origin to an earlier date, and by no means settles the question of human origins, we shall concede that such is the case, and answer that it is not our purpose to deal with these pre-Adamite conditions and questions, but only to account for man's origin as we know man now and with special reference to the purpose of God in this present Adamic Dispensation, leaving the disposal of the beginning and the end of pre-Adamite races to still further revealed knowledge from God or to future knowledge ascertained by the researches of man.[53]

FURTHER CONSIDERATION OF THE WORD "REPLENISH"[54]

Attention has already been called (in the preceding chapter) to the use of the word "replenish" in connection with the commandment to Adam to be fruitful and "replenish" the earth. The derivation of the word "replenish" comes from the Old French[55] *replenir:* <derived from Latin> *re-*, "again," and *plenus*, "full."[56] Hence, in all the leading dictionaries the primary meaning of "replenish" is given "to fill again as something that has been emptied." In the intransitive sense the primary meaning is also "to fill again and to recover former fullness." It should be noted, however, that there are secondary definitions which render the word "to finish,

---

far as the revelations of God to the human race is concerned, they relate to the advent of man to the earth in very recent times to begin a dispensation of human life for the attainment of some special purpose with reference to the earth-life of man—of man as we know him, in <Ms III^{c} adds "of man as we know him, in"—*Ed.*> the Adamic Dispensation merely."

<Notice that in this comment by Roberts, he had added the handwritten word "alleged" to the typewritten text of Ms III* "bits of fossil human remains"—*Ed.*>

53. <This paragraph was originally the ending to chap. 31, then when the previous sections on "A Catholic Comment" and "The Author's Comment" were marked to be deleted, this concluding paragraph was also so marked. Then even later the words "Page out" at the top of the page of Ms III^{c} were themselves crossed out. Consequently, the final intention of Roberts was that this paragraph be printed in the text—*Ed.*>

54. <This section, not included in the synopsis for the chapter, is a three-page addition placed at the end of the chapter and given the page numbers 10-12—*Ed.*>

55. <Ms III "Latin," which is corrected to "Old French"—*Ed.*>

56. A *Standard Dictionary of the English Language*, ed. Isaac K. Funk (New York: Funk and Wagnalls Co., 1895), 1512. <Roberts considers only the meaning of the English term "replenish." However, the book of Genesis was written in Hebrew, and he should have researched into the meaning of the Hebrew verb used at Gen. 1:28. Joseph Fielding Smith opposes Roberts (who is following Orson Hyde) in the interpretation of "replenish" at Gen. 1:28 as meaning "to fill again." Smith correctly points out that the Hebrew *mālē'*, also used at Gen. 1:22, means simply "to fill"—*Ed.*>

perfect"; "to fill by occupying," etc. And these do not necessarily include the meaning "to regain a state of former development," but if the biblical use of the word be considered as used in the case of Noah and his sons (as already suggested) to whom God said, as well as to Adam, "multiply and replenish the earth" (Gen. 9:1), we shall find "to fill again" or "refill" most nearly the mission given to Noah and his sons, viz., to again fill the earth with inhabitants; and this same word used in the commission to Adam, "to replenish the earth" in the event of some cataclysm having swept away pre-Adamite races, may have the same significance as when the word was[57] said to Noah.

In this connection it is interesting to note that one of the original apostles of the New Dispensation, a contemporary of the Prophet Joseph Smith and President Brigham Young, ventured to advance the doctrine of a pre-Adamite race and the above interpretation of "replenish." Also his doctrine was publicly approved by President Brigham Young when the discourse was delivered. This was at the general conference of the church on the 6th of October 1854, at which Orson Hyde, the apostle referred to, had been appointed to deliver a special lecture, from which I quote the following:

> I will go back to the beginning and notice the commandment that was given to our first parents in the Garden of Eden. The Lord said unto them, "Multiply and replenish the earth." I will digress here for a moment from the thread of the subject and bring an idea that may perhaps have a bearing upon it.
>
> The earth, you will remember, was void and empty [having in mind the description of the earth in Genesis 2], until our first parents began at the Garden of Eden. What does the term "replenish" mean? This word is derived from the Latin *re-* and *plenus*. The *re* denotes repetition, [or] iteration; and *plenus* signifies full, complete; then the meaning of the word "replenish" is to refill, recomplete. If I were to go into a merchant's store and find he had got a new stock of goods, I should say, "you have *replenished* your stock, that is, <you have> filled up your establishment, for it looks as it did before." "<Now> go forth," says the Lord, "and replenish the earth," for it was covered with gloomy clouds of darkness excluded from the light of heaven, and darkness brooded upon the face of the deep. *The world was peopled before the days of Adam, as much so as it was before the days of Noah. It was said that Noah became the father of a new world*, but it was the same old world still, and will continue to be, though it may pass through many changes.
>
> When God said, Go forth and "replenish" the earth, it was to replenish the inhabitants of the human species and make it as it was before.[58]

57. <Ms III^{c} adds "the word was"–*Ed.*>

58. Orson Hyde, "The Marriage Relations," *Journal of Discourses* 2 (1855): 79. <Emphasis added by Roberts–*Ed.*>

At the close of Elder Hyde's discourse, President Brigham Young arose and said:

> *I do not wish to eradicate any items from the lecture Elder Hyde has given us this evening,* but simply give you my views in a few words on the portion touching Bishops and Deacons [on the matter of their being married men]. . . . We have had a splendid address from Brother Hyde, for which I am grateful. . . . *I say to the congregation, treasure up in your hearts what you have heard tonight and at all other times.*[59]

EVIDENCES OF MAN'S ANTIQUITY IN THE EARTH[60]

Of course, we can not here go into extensive treatment of the subject outlined; the volume of evidence and the extent of the argument are too great for that in these chapters; but it is possible to give citations and conclusions of those who have treated the subject at length.

SIR CHARLES LYELL[61]

Among those who recognized in the discoveries that were being made midway of the nineteenth century that man was not only contemporary with long-extinct animals of past geological epochs, but that he had already developed in those epochs,[62] into a stage of culture above pure savagery, was Sir Charles Lyell, M.A., F.R.S., the celebrated and all but father of the science of modern geology. In his earlier works on geology Sir Charles long opposed the idea of the great antiquity of man in the earth, but in 1863 he published the first edition of his *Geological Evidence of the Antiquity of Man.*[63] "And the fact," remarks Andrew D. White, author of the two volumes of *A History of the Warfare of Science with Theology* (1896), "that he had so long opposed the new idea<s> gave force to the clear and conclusive

59. Ibid., 88, 90. <Emphasis added by Roberts–*Ed.*>

60. <This section, not included in the synopsis at the beginning of the chapter, is an eighteen-page addition placed at the end of the chapter and given the page numbers 13-30. The latest datable quotation is 14 December 1930, which indicates that this chapter was considerably expanded and updated in preparation for Roberts's presentation to the Quorum of the Twelve Apostles on 7 January 1931–*Ed.*>

61. <Ms III^{c} adds "SIR JAMES [*sic*] LYELL"; in this heading and in the two instances in the following paragraph, the incorrect "James" of Ms III has been corrected to "Charles"–*Ed.*>

62. <Ms III* "he had already developed, at that time"–*Ed.*>

63. <Charles Lyell, *The Geological Evidences of the Antiquity of Man, with Remarks on Theories of the Origin of Species by Variation* (London: J. Murray, 1863)–*Ed.*>

argument which led him to renounce his early scientific beliefs."[64] Continuing, our author, White, says:

> Research among the evidences of man's existence in the early Quaternary, and possibly in Tertiary period [hundreds of thousands of years ago], was now pressed forward along the whole line. . . . These investigations went on vigorously in all parts of France and spread rapidly to other countries. The explorations which Dupont began in 1864, in the caves of Belgium, gave to the museum at Brussels 80,000 flint implements, 40,000 bones of animals of the Quaternary period, and a number of human skulls and bones found mingled with these remains. From Germany, Italy, Spain, America, India, and Egypt similar results were reported.[65]

ANDREW D. WHITE[66]

White devotes three chapters of his great work to this subject under the title "From Genesis to Geology," "The Antiquity of Man, Egyptology, and Assyriology," and "The Antiquity of Man and Prehistoric Archaeology."[67] In his concluding pages of chapter 7, he says:

> Human bones had been found under such circumstances as early as 1835 at Cannstadt near Stuttgart, and in 1856 in the Neanderthal near Dusseldorf; but in more recent searches they had been discovered in a multitude of places, especially in Germany, France, Belgium, England, the Caucasus, Africa, and North and South America. Comparison of these bones showed that even in that remote Quaternary period [several hundred thousand years ago] there were great differences of race, and here again came in an argument for the yet earlier existence of man on the earth; for long previous periods must have been required to develop such racial differences. Considerations of this kind gave a new impulse to the belief that man's existence might even date back into the Tertiary period [a half a million years ago]. The evidence for this earlier origin of man was ably summed up, not only by its brilliant advocate, Mortillet, but by a former opponent, one of the most conservative of modern anthropologists, Quatrefages; and the conclusion arrived at by both was that man did really exist in the Tertiary period. The acceptance of this conclusion was also seen in the more recent work of Alfred Russel Wallace, who, though very cautious and

---

64. See Andrew D. White's work referred to above <i.e., on the previous page>, *A History of the Warfare of Science with Theology in Christendom*, 1:275. In a footnote on this page White cites the works of eleven writers on various phases of this subject, research workers and scientists all, who support the theory of man's great antiquity in the earth.

65. Ibid., 1:275-76.

66. <Ms III[c] adds "ANDREW D. WHITE"–*Ed.*>

67. These chapters are in vol. 1, chaps. 5-7, where he cites many authorities. In his last pages of chapter 7, he cites more than a score of scientific works on the subject.

conservative, placed the origin of man not only in the Tertiary period, but in an earlier stage of it than most had dared assign—even in the Miocene. . . .

Of attempts to make an exact chronological statement throwing light on the length of the various prehistoric periods, the most notable have been those of M. Morlot, on the accumulated strata of the Lake of Geneva; by Gilliéron, on the silt of Lake Neufchâtel; by Horner, in the delta deposits of Egypt; and by Riddle, in the delta of the Mississippi. . . . The period of man's past life upon our planet, which has been fixed by the universal Church [he refers here to the Roman Catholic Church], "always, everywhere, and by all," is thus perfectly proved to be insignificant compared with those vast geological epochs during which man is now known to have existed.[68]

DR. JOHN W. DRAPER

In his work on *Conflict between Religion and Science* (1875), John W. Draper, M.D., LL.D., author of *The Intellectual Development of Europe*, also has an important and exhaustive chapter on "The Age of the Earth and the Antiquity of Man." In his closing pages of that chapter, he says:

> So far as investigations have gone, they indisputably refer the existence of man to a date remote from us by many hundreds of thousands of years. . . . We are thus carried back immeasurably beyond the six thousand <years> of patristic chronology. It is difficult to assign a shorter date for the last glaciation of Europe[69] than a quarter of a million years, and human existence antedates that period. But not only is it this grand fact that confronts us, we have to admit also a primitive animalized state, and a slow, a gradual development.[70]

---

68. As to the evidence of man in the Tertiary period, see works already cited, especially <Armand de> Quatrefages <de Bréau>, <Émile> Cartailhac, and <Gabriel> Mortillet. For an admirable summary, see <Samuel> Laing, *Human Origins*, chap. 8. See also, for a summing up of the evidence in favor of man in the Tertiary period, Quatrefages, *Histoire Générale des Races Humaines*, in the <series> Bibliothèque Ethnologique (Paris, 1887), chap. 4. As to the earlier view, see <Karl C.> Vogt, *Lectures on Man* <(London, 1864), lecture 11. For a thorough and convincing> refutation of Sir J. W. Dawson's attempt to make the old and new Stone periods coincide, see H. W. Haynes, in chap. 6 of the *History of America*, edited by Justin Winsor. For development of various important points in the relation of anthropology to the human occupancy of our planet, see <Paul> Topinard, *Anthropology* (London, 1890), chap. 9. <In the text Roberts is quoting from White, *Warfare of Science with Theology*, 281-83, and this footnote is Roberts's quotation of White's footnote on p. 283; Roberts also adds a marginal, handwritten Ms III^{c} "omit reading of," which is his note to himself to not read this footnote during his presentation to the Twelve Apostles on 7 January 1931—*Ed.*>

69. <Ms III* "the last glaciation period of Europe"—*Ed.*>

70. John William Draper, *History of the Conflict between Religion and Science*, 6th ed. (New York: D. Appleton and Co., 1875), 199. <In the Ms III footnote Roberts incorrectly

DR. RICHARD SWANN LULL[71]

A more recent authority, Richard Swann Lull, Professor of Vertebrate Paleontology, Yale University, 1921-22, in a lecture symposium published by the Yale University Press (1923), says in his discussion about the Piltdown or Dawn Man and the geological structure in which he was found that:

> The British authorities, Lewis Abbott and J. Reid Moir, both refer the older gravels to the Pliocene, but the more widely accepted belief is that the Piltdown man is Lower Pleistocene, of Second or Third Interglacial time, so that in terms of years his age [i.e., of the Piltdown Man] is from 200,000 to 300,000 years.[72]

In the concluding paragraphs of Professor Lull's lecture he says:

> All of our evidence points to central Asia as the birthplace of mankind, and to the Miocene [period] 1,000,000 to 2,000,000 years ago, as the time of his origin. The antiquity of man has thus been made known by *direct* evidence in the form of human relics, the greatest age of which can hardly be less than half a million years. *Corroborative* evidence lies in the great variation, not alone between the several species of prehistoric man, but also among the many races of *Homo sapiens* himself, of which <William K.> Gregory recognizes twenty-six, with a number of sub-races. And that the major divisions are very old is attested by ancient murals and other documents of the Egyptians and other oriental peoples.[73]

LATER UTTERANCES: SIR ARTHUR KEITH[74]

Still later utterances by scientists of prominence in current periodicals abundantly sustain these authorities I have been quoting. For instance, in the Magazine Section of the *New York Times*, for October 12, 1930, Sir Arthur Keith, the eminent anthropologist and world distinguished scholar, describes what he considers to be "one of the greatest triumphs that has ever been accomplished by patient, exact archaeological inquiry," in the discovery that "about 20,000 years ago in Europe a race of white men—primitive Cro-Magnon men—displaced[75] an earlier and inferior type, [the] Neanderthal man"; and then at length discusses the question, "Whence did Cro-Magnon man come?" And this at some length. I may only quote briefly:

---

gave the title as *Warfare of Science with Theology*—*Ed.*>

71. <Ms III[c] adds "DR. RICHARD SWANN LULL"—*Ed.*>

72. <Lull, "Antiquity of Man," in Baitsell, *Evolution of Man*, 22—*Ed.*>

73. Ibid., 38.

74. <Apparently Ms III[c] adds "LATER UTTERANCES; SIR ARTHUR KEITH"—*Ed.*>

75. <Ms III "a race of white, non-primitive Cro-Magnon man — displaced," but Keith's wording is followed—*Ed.*>

We have grown up with the belief that Europe has always been the home of white men: we never knew until recently that what has happened in North America and Australia during recent times—the replacement of one race by another—also occurred in the continent of Europe some 20,000 years ago, according to our present mode of reasoning[76] prehistoric time. . . . At the present day the white man is replacing the aborigines of Australia. What is our evidence for asserting that some 20,000 years earlier a similar replacement occurred in Europe—a primitive type of white man, men of the Cro-Magnon type, migrating into Europe, colonizing it, and ultimately taking complete possession of the continent? . . .

We infer the date[77] of the colonization from its relationship to the last Ice Age. We know that Neanderthal Man lived in Europe before the last Ice Age set in. We have found his fossil remains and his culture under its oldest deposits. Then there came an interlude—a temperate interval—in the Ice Age. It was in this interlude that the Cro-Magnon appeared in Europe and in which the Neanderthalians either died out or were exterminated. So far we have found no evidence of cross-breeding[s], but it may have occurred. Then after the temperate interlude, which saw the arrival of the Cro-Magnons, arctic conditions returned and continued until the dawn of the modern climate of Europe. By painstaking investigations the geologists of Scandinavia have been able to calculate approximately the number of centuries which have elapsed since arctic conditions came to an end in Europe. Their estimate is 12,000 years. . . . We estimate that at least 8000 years must be added to the 12,000 to give the date of the glacial interlude which saw the first arrival of the forerunners of the modern inhabitants of Europe. The date of their arrival may very well be much earlier, it cannot be later.[78]

He then presents the claims made by those who regard the migration of the Cro-Magnon people as coming from Africa. The advocates of this idea, Sir Arthur claims:

Can produce irrefutable evidence that the Sahara—the whole of North Africa—was then inhabited by man, for in deposits which have been laid down by its[79] ancient rivers and streams, man's stone implements have been found.

English geologists (Messrs. Sanford and Arkell), working for the government of Egypt, have proved (1929) that in the lower valley of the Nile there are deposits which contain the same succession of stone implements as occur in the valleys of the Seine and of the Thames. In the valleys of tributary streams issuing from the Libyan Desert, the same deposits are found with the same succession of implements.

In these early times the basin of the Faiyum, which lies to the southwest of Cairo,

76. <Ms III "reasoning," but Keith's text has "reckoning"—*Ed.*>

77. <Ms III "time," but Keith's text has "date"—*Ed.*>

78. <Arthur Keith, "Whence Came the White Race?" *The New York Times*, Magazine section, 12 Oct. 1930, 1—*Ed.*>

79. <Ms III "those," but Keith's text has "its"—*Ed.*>

> was filled by the water of the Nile. In the beaches of this old lake, Messrs. Sanford and Arkell found evidence that the desiccation of North Africa and of the Sahara began to set in during the period of Aurignacian culture—the period at which Cro-Magnon people appear in Europe [20,000 years ago]. In Tunis and Algiers, French archaeologists have discovered and examined many of the workshops of Aurignacian man.
>
> On the strength of this evidence, the pro-African school of anthropologists assume that it was the flaming sword of drought which compelled the Cro-Magnon people to emigrate from the Sahara and seek a home in Europe.[80]

Sir Arthur Keith himself, however, finds the Asiatic origin of the Cro-Magnon race most convincing, which he argues at length, but assigns about the same period of time for the Cro-Magnon advent into Europe.

> What I have been seeking to show is that they [i.e., these Cro-Magnon migrations] are but repetitions of migratory movements which are as old as the evolution of human races. The Australians of today are but repeating what their ancestors did in Europe 20,000 years ago.

And after lengthy argument he says:

> The seizure of Europe by pioneer bands of white settlers was a slow process; it probably extended over several thousand years; there were migrations. The European pioneers made a clean sweep in their new country; the original natives, Neanderthal men, disappeared from Europe just as completely as the native race did from Tasmania in the 19th century.[81]

SIR JAMES JEANS[82]

In the November 23, 1930,[83] number of *The Times*, is another exhaustive argument on the age of the earth, in which it is stated by Wm. L. Laurence, who discusses the question, that:

> Sir James Jeans, dealing with this same subject in *The Universe around Us*, published in 1929, gives the age of the earth as 2,000,000,000 years;[84] the age of life on the earth as 300,000,000 years; and the age of man on earth as 300,000 years. The

---

80. <Keith, "Whence," *The New York Times*, 12 Oct. 1930, 1-2—*Ed.*>

81. Ibid., 22.

82. <Ms III^c adds "SIR JAMES JEANS"—*Ed.*>

83. <Ms III^c adds "(1930)"—*Ed.*>

84. <Sir James Jeans, *The Universe around Us* (New York: The Macmillan Co.; Cambridge, Eng.: University Press, 1929), 11, 13, has 2 billion, but by the time his book was reprinted in 1944 the age of the earth was raised to 3 billion—*Ed.*>

first of these figures would seem to have been corroborated now by the latest findings of Professor <Alois> Kovarik.[85]

SIR ARTHUR KEITH AGAIN: EVIDENCE IN SOUTH AFRICA[86]

In the *Times*, Magazine Section of November 23, Sir Arthur Keith again made an important contribution to the subject of man's antiquity on the earth. This time under the title of "Supermen—of the Dim Past and Future." This article was based upon recent discoveries in South Africa led by one J. B. Botha, a farmer at Boskop in the Transvaal. Many discoveries of the remains of ancient man went on until finally representatives of the British Association for the Advancement of Science visited South Africa in 1929. Sir Arthur Keith says:

> An<other> important addition was made to our knowledge of these large-brained <ancient> inhabitants of South Africa. Local archaeologists had been busy searching caves and river deposits in Cape Colony, the Transvaal, and Rhodesia for traces of ancient man and were able to demonstrate to their visitors that there was strange parallelism between ancient South Africa and ancient Europe. In both of these widely separated parts of the world men had lived and had shaped stone tools for hundreds of thousands of years—ever since the beginning of the last geological age, the Pleistocene period of the earth's history.
>
> In South Africa, as in Europe, one method of shaping stone tools, after having been in fashion for a long time, was succeeded by another method of "culture." The strange thing was that although the South African stone cultures were never at any time identical with the European, yet there were many resemblances not only between individual cultures but in the sequence with which these cultures followed one another. Cave art flourished both in Europe and in South Africa. South Africa was even more rich than Europe in its rock and cave paintings. The British visitors were also surprised to learn that the rock paintings and rock engravings which were known to be the oldest were also the finest from an artistic point of view. As time went on, the hand of the South African artist lost its cunning.[87]

Sir Arthur Keith also gives an account of the recent discoveries of a fossilized skeleton of a man at what is called Skildegat Cave, of which he gives the following account:

> The floor of the cave was nearly 100 feet wide; they ran sections across it and had,

---

85. *The New York Times*, 23 November 1930.

86. <Ms III[c] adds "SIR ARTHUR KEITH AGAIN; EVIDENCE IN SOUTH AFRICA"—*Ed.*>

87. <Arthur Keith, "Supermen—of the Dim Past and Future," *The New York Times*, Magazine section, 23 Nov. 1930, 4—*Ed.*>

by the autumn of 1929, dug down to a depth of fourteen feet, passing through five distinct strata, every one of them rich in traces of humanity—hearths, implements, and burials. Above the fifth stratum and at a depth of nine feet they came across an ancient grave containing a complete skeleton. The bones were fossilized: the strata over the skeleton were intact. Now the stone tools of the stratum in which the skeleton lay were all of a kind which have been named "Still Bay"—because it was in a deposit at Still Bay, 200 miles to the east of Fish Hoek, that this culture was first discovered. A beautiful stone lance-head of the Still Bay type lay under the skeleton; all the evidence pointed to the fact that the Still Bay culture was the handiwork of the kind of man found in the Skildegat Cave. It was the first time a human skeleton had been found in South Africa amid the tools which in life the man had fabricated and used.

Now the Still Bay culture of South Africa has its parallel in Europe; it is known as the Solutrean, and prevailed toward the end of the last Ice Age—having an antiquity of at least 15,000 years. There is every reason to suppose that the Still Bay culture of South Africa is just as ancient as the Solutrean of Europe. The skeleton found in the Skildegat Cave is that of a man who inhabited South Africa some 15,000 years ago, or perhaps more. The man whose skeleton Messrs. Peers[88] discovered has been named the Fish Hoek Man.[89]

H. S. HARRISON, PRESIDENT OF THE BRITISH ASSOCIATION FOR THE ADVANCEMENT OF SCIENCE

In the New York Times of November 30, 1930, there is an article by H. S. Harrison, president of the Anthropological Section of the British Association for the Advancement of Science, in which he says:

> There is less inclination than there was to regard all known fossil human or humanoid forms as being ancestral types to modern man, and they are now welcomed as distant collaterals rather than as forefathers. Neanderthal man of the Mousterian epoch,[90] Heidelberg man of a rather earlier period, and the still more remote men or apemen of Piltdown <*sic*> in England, of Java and of Peking, are placed in different genera or species, as the case may be, from *Homo sapiens;* to this are assigned all existing men, and all those who have lived since the end of Mousterian times, say 20,000 years ago.[91]

THE PEKING MAN[92]

In December 1929 scientists reported the discovery of one skull and several

88. <A father and son team, Bert Peers, Sr., and Bert Peers, Jr.—*Ed.*>

89. Keith, "Supermen," *The New York Times*, Magazine section, 23 Nov. 1930, 5.

90. <Ms III "the most Mousterian epoch," an instance of accidental doubling—*Ed.*>

91. H. S. Harrison, "Is Man an Accident? A Startling View," *The New York Times*, Magazine section, 30 Nov. 1930, 5.

92. <Ms III^{c} adds "THE PEKING MAN"—*Ed.*>

skeletons found in the stone quarries at Chow Cutien, 30 miles from Peking, China. The skull was unearthed by Chinese geologists who claimed it belonged to a species of the famous Peking man, the *Sinanthropus pekinensis*, said to be associated with the period of the Piltdown <*sic*> skull and the Java ape-man. The dispatch making the announcement said that "while the scientists who knew of the discoveries were sworn to secrecy, it was understood here (Peking), that they regarded them as perhaps the greatest human finds ever made." The discoveries were made in the same limestone quarries where a very primitive type of men was found in 1928. The location of the more recently discovered skeletons was said to have convinced the discoverers that the ancient home of a distinctive type of primitive man had been discovered. The dispatch continued so:

> It was understood, that the scientists believed, with the various skeletons as well as the complete skull, they have material enough to reconstruct the entire drama of the life of the prehistoric colony or at least to sketch a portrait of man as he existed in the region of Peiping [near Peking][93] more than a million years ago. In addition to the human skull and skeletons, the fossil skull of a rhinoceros has been found in the quarry. Also there were uncovered heaps of bones believed to be those of other animals. Many of the bones were clearly broken as if by human hands, possibly, the scientists believe, by hungry men, seeking marrow as food.

DR. J. G. ANDERSON[94]

Dr. J. G<unnar> Anderson, Swedish adviser to the Chinese Geological Survey and others continued searching eagerly for the heads of the headless skeletons found. The first trace of the Peking man was discovered—1920—by Dr. <Otto> Zdansky, a Russian, who found a tooth near the site where the latest recoveries have been reported.

DR. DAVIDSON BLACK[95]

Dr. Davidson Black, an American at Peiping [Peking] Union Medical College, placed the Peking man on a stage of development between the modern human and more ancient human or semi-human creatures. The time estimate of a million years ago as the period in which the Peking man inhabited the district was based on recent advances in geology whereby the age of the earth and that of its living creatures is calculated at far higher figures than it was a few years ago; by that scale

---

93. <Ms III[*] "Peiping (Peking)"—*Ed.*>

94. <Ms III[c] adds "DR. J. G. ANDERSON"—*Ed.*>

95. <Ms III[c] adds "DR. DAVIDSON BLACK"—*Ed.*>

the Peking man is believed to include the Neanderthal man and to be about contemporaneous with the Heidelberg man of Europe.

Such <was> the dispatch concerning the discovery of December 15, 1929, to the press of America. On July 30, 1930, a second dispatch was received from Peking, announcing the discovery of still another human skull in the same vicinity, in which it was announced that Dr. Davidson Black had been lent to the survey by the Rockefeller Foundation to devote his entire time to the first skull of the Peking man. He announced the decision in this second dispatch that the first find was a female skull and the second a male skull, and goes on with a lengthy statement of the new discovery. There came at the same time a cable from London to the *New York Times*, in which Professor G. Elliot Smith—one of the foremost geological authorities of England and connected with the University of London—who declared <that> the discovery of a second skull of the Peking race of antiquity was of great importance as dealing with the fossil remains of extinct types of living creatures.

Still later, namely, December 14, 1930, a dispatch from New Haven, Connecticut, to the *New York Times*, giving an account of Professor G. Elliot Smith of the University of London, delivering a lecture at Yale University on the Peking man, who in the meantime had visited Peking to participate in the discoveries made at that distinct point, said "that instead of one Peking man there were now available parts of the skulls of ten individuals, and that at least one is the skull of a female."

Professor Smith said:

> It is certain that the pre-historic man of 500,000 years ago [the age assigned to these Peking finds] could speak. The skull of the Peking man, he said, bridges the gap between the *Pithecanthropus erectus* and the Piltdown <*sic*> man, which had been considered heretofore two distinct types and representative of two entirely separate eras in the development of man. The skulls which have been found in China disclose a relationship between the two types.[96]

Of course, such statements as these from leading scientists could be multiplied almost indefinitely, but surely sufficient is here set forth to show that the unbroken thread of researches made concerning the antiquity of man establishes so far as such researches and human knowledge can establish anything, the great antiquity of the human race on the earth; and certainly that man's life on the earth goes further back than any time fixed by the Bible sources of information; which, at best, as to the advent of Adam and his race, goes no further back than from 6,000 to 8,000 years, and the lesser date is the one usually accepted by orthodoxy. In references made to the existence of man in the earth in our modern revelation, say

---

96. Dispatch from New Haven to *The New York Times*, December 14, 1930, second division of news section.

in Section 84 of the Doctrine and Covenants, no earlier existence for man is given than the Bible revelation; and sure it is that the archaeological evidences for man's existence, even if all the claims of a great antiquity may not be allowed, still go far beyond anything that is set down in our sacred chronology, ancient or modern; and therefore, far beyond Adam's period; which forces the recognition of the existence of pre-Adamite races, if there is to be any adjustment between man's discoveries[97] and the records of scripture; and therefore, I am urging the recognition of the advent of Adam to the earth as merely the introduction of an Adamic Dispensation of man's existence, all which will tend to account for all the facts forced upon our attention, and give reasonable standing for what has been revealed with what man by his searching has found out.

There is no other way to account for the stone ages, old and new, than to say that they began in a culture far beyond the period of Adam's advent. The facts of revelation contained in the Bible and our modern revelation, which accepts and coalesces with them, do not fit in with the facts of man's evident prolonged existence before the Adamic period on any other basis.[98] Here is a fine opportunity for the development of a great truth.

A mighty stride forward in truth was made when it became known that the revelation given to Moses had reference not to the whole, vast universe, but to just this earth on which man lived and to its immediate heavens associated with it (see Moses 1); and now with the evidence of life and death on the earth so indisputably evident, including the pre-Adamite life and death of man, in various stages of a successive race-life, why not recognize that truth and see that which is inevitable, that in the advent of Adam the time had come for the achievement of some special purpose in relation to man—some spiritual relationship—that brought about the introduction of the Adamic Dispensation? Otherwise the whole volume of facts as they are disclosed are thrown into confusion; and the revealed truths themselves for most men rendered doubtful, being out of harmony with the facts ascertained as to man's antiquity.

Moreover, by giving this interpretation to Bible facts and the evident truths science has discovered, we shall be doing just now not only a service to our own church, especially to youth of it, but a service to all Christendom and to humanity in general, in that we shall make it possible to all Christendom and the world to see a Way to Harmony between the Bible facts of revelation and the truths revealed by science, which is but the facts discovered by human research placed in orderly array.

On the other hand, to limit and insist upon the whole of life and death to this

97. <Ms III* "to be any reconciliation between man's discoveries"—*Ed.*>

98. <Ms III[c] adds "on any other basis"—*Ed.*>

side of Adam's advent to the earth, some six or eight thousand years ago, as proposed by some, is to fly in the face of the facts so indisputably brought to light by the researcher of science in modern times, and this as set forth by men of the highest type in the intellectual and moral world; not inferior men, or men of sensual and devilish temperament, but men who must be accounted as among the noblest and most self-sacrificing of the sons of men—of the type whence must come the noblest sons of God, since "the glory of God is intelligence" (D&C 93:36); and that too the glory of man. These searchers after truth are of that class. To pay attention to and give reasonable credence to their research and findings is to link the church of God with the highest increase of human thought and effort. On that side lies development, on the other lies contraction. It is on the former side that research work is going on and will continue to go on, future investigation and discoveries will continue on that side, nothing will retard them, and nothing will develop on the other side. One leads to narrow sectarianism, the other keeps the open spirit of a world movement with which our New Dispensation began. As between them which is to be our choice?

CHAPTER XXXII

Life Status of Adam and Eve at Their Earth Advent

SCRIPTURE READING LESSON

Analysis

I. The Coming of Adam.
II. The "Royal Planters"—Adam and Eve.
III. The Kind of Beings Adam and Eve Were When Brought to Earth.
IV. Translation and Translated Beings.
V. Translation of Enoch and His City.
VI. The Prophet of the New Dispensation on Translated Beings.
VII. Immortality Means Deathless: Testimony of the Book of Mormon.
VIII. The Process of Becoming Immortal.

References

Parley P. Pratt, *Key to the Science of Theology: Designed as an Introduction to the First Principles of Spiritual Philosophy, Religion, Law, and Government, as Delivered by the Ancients, and as Restored in This Age, for the Final Development of Universal Peace, Truth, and Knowledge*, 5th ed. (Liverpool: John Henry Smith, 1883), chap. 6.

Sir Oliver Lodge, F.R.S., *Science and Immortality* (New York: Moffat, Yard, and Co., 1908), sect. 3, chaps. 8-9.

Brigham Young, "Self-Government—Mysteries—Recreation and Amusements Not in Themselves Sinful—Tithing—Adam, Our Father and Our God," *Journal of Discourses* 1 (1854): 50, 9 April 1852.

Discourse of the Prophet Joseph Smith on "Priesthood," *History of the Church of Jesus Christ of Latter-day Saints, Period I: History of Joseph Smith, the Prophet by Himself* (Salt Lake City: Deseret News, 1908), 4:207-12, 425-26.

Book of Mormon, *passim*—especially Mosiah 18, Alma 11; also, Alma 40.

CHAPTER XXXII

Life Status of Adam and Eve at Their Earth Advent

THE COMING OF ADAM

The outcome of reflections inspired by the last two chapters would lead us to the acceptance of all that has proceeded from the days of Adam as an Adamic Dispensation of the things of God with reference to the earth and its inhabitants; and not an entire and complete record of all the happenings upon the earth from the beginning of its first physical creation.

Let us consider how this works out in the long course of the earth's existence. Some cataclysm, some excessive heat period, or some overwhelming glacial calamity emptied the earth of all its forms of life—including the human and near-human life. And perhaps in preparation of a better order of things; then comes to pass conditions under which the desolated earth may be replenished with life—vegetable and animal life—in sea, and air, and earth. When this is so, the Intelligences of some more highly developed world conclude to bring this to pass, and one from among their number, physically and in every way fitted to fulfill such a mission, is brought to the earth and with him his spouse, whose mission together it will be to "replenish" the earth, as it was in the case of Noah after the cataclysm of the flood. A man is brought, and a woman;[1] a garden is planted in a desolate earth, and many forms of life are brought to the earth, and take on existence and spread until the whole earth is abundantly supplied with life in all its varied forms; and human life begins as set forth in the revelations of God in the Bible—especially as recorded in the second chapter of Genesis.

THE "ROYAL PLANTERS"—ADAM AND EVE

As for the man and his spouse, Adam and Eve, in the account of their origin that is given under the symbols of procreation. Man <was> created from the dust of the earth, and a human pre-existent spirit infused into him. Woman produced

1. <Ms III* "A man is created, and a woman"—*Ed.*>

truly of man, so also man was produced of man and woman; but symbols of the phallic generation of woman are used in the account of her creation. The body of man is created from the dust of the earth, and so with woman, and that is true today through the process of generation, and the slowly gathered material from the earth integrating through food and the digestion of it, and growth to the attainment of the appointed height and frame of man. So, indeed, it was with reference to Adam and Eve, generated in the same way (under nature's law), as men and women are generated today, but upon another world than this we inhabit and where they grew to the state of physical and spiritual development, which fitted them for the mission assigned to them on this earth. Let it be remembered that they came out of an eternal universe, where this process of creation from spiritual to temporal (material or physical),[2] and from temporal up to a higher spiritual, has been going on eternally; without beginning, and will continue without end, going on in one everlasting present. For the God-mind all distinctions of time as to past and present and future, so stand that they live and work in the eternal "now." So there is nothing mysterious—only as all existence is mysterious—in the matter of Adam and Eve being created by act of generation, the process here suggested, and then, when they had attained suitable development to receive this mission appointment to open a dispensation with reference to the purposes of God on the earth, they came to plant their race in a desolate earth, and to become patriarch and matriarch[3] to earth's future teeming millions in that dispensation they were honored to begin.[4]

THE KIND OF BEINGS ADAM AND EVE WERE WHEN BROUGHT TO EARTH

Further consideration is necessary as to Adam and Eve, an inquiry into their degree of development in the process of life, when they came to the earth; that is to say, had they attained unto resurrection in some former world, or had they in the process of life that has been already described in these pages halted somewhat this side of resurrection and immortality? This is mentioned here because it has

2. <Ms III[c] adds "or physical"—*Ed.*>

3. <Ms III[*] "and become Patriarch and Mother"—*Ed.*>

4. <The review committee gave the following objection to Roberts's view that Adam and Eve came to a desolate earth: "This is questioned by the committee. According to the revelations bearing on the question, the earth was fully prepared for Adam and pronounced 'good,' before he was placed upon it, and was full of life and beauty" ("Doctrinal Points Questioned by the Committee Which Read the Manuscript of Elder B. H. Roberts, Entitled The Truth, The Way, The Life," attached to Rudger Clawson, Letter to Heber J. Grant, [15 May 1930], in David J. Buerger Collection, Manuscript 622, Bx 10, Fd 8, Manuscripts Division, Marriott Library, University of Utah, Salt Lake City)—*Ed.*>

been suggested that when Adam came into the Garden of Eden, he came into it with a "celestial body"; and that would mean an immortal body—he would be a resurrected personage. This is sustained by a subsequent explanation of the theory here referred to as follows: "When Adam and Eve had eaten of the forbidden fruit, their bodies became mortal from its effects, and therefore their offspring were mortal."[5] It would appear from this conception of things pertaining to Adam's status in life that he came to the earth with a "celestial body," that is, an immortal body, and then became mortal by partaking of the forbidden fruit, and this in order that he might beget children that would be mortal, in order to accomplish the purpose of God with reference to man's earth-life, that he might have his experiences in broken harmonies, ending in death—separation of spirit and body—to be followed by resurrection and an immortal life, as set forth in previous pages. But there is an inconsistent thing in such a conception of Adam's status in life when brought to the Garden of Eden. Immortality means "exempt from liability to die," "imperishable," "undying," "lasting forever," "having unlimited or eternal existence"—it means deathless! To say that a person is "immortal," and then claim that by eating forbidden fruit, or anything else, he can become subject to death is a solecisim, a rank misunderstanding of terms. *If a person is immortal, then he can not die under any circumstances.* If one supposed to be immortal should die, you have conclusive evidence that he was not immortal.

TRANSLATION AND[6] TRANSLATED BEINGS

There is nothing in the scriptures, or any utterances equivalent to scripture, that requires us to believe that when Adam was brought to the earth he was an immortal personage; the fact that he died is proof positive that he was not immortal. On the other hand, the scriptures give an account of an order of men in whom the process of death is suspended by the power of God, that there might be[7] an order of beings capable of performing such special missions to worlds where by the nature of them they would be fitted to such work as might be assigned to them.[8]

---

5. Discourse of Brigham Young, "Self-Government—Mysteries—Recreation and Amusements Not in Themselves Sinful—Tithing—Adam, Our Father and Our God," *Journal of Discourses* 1 (1854): 50. This discourse was delivered April 9, 1852. <Roberts omits any quotations from this discourse which reveal Young's controversial Adam-God Doctrine; see David J. Buerger, "The Adam-God Doctrine," *Dialogue: A Journal of Mormon Thought* 15 (Spring 1982): 14-58—*Ed.*>

6. <Ms III[c] adds "Translation and"—*Ed.*>

7. <Ms III[*] "in order that there might be"—*Ed.*>

8. <The review committee gave the following objection to Roberts's view that Adam was a translated being: "The doctrine that Adam came here a 'translated' being from some

These are "translated" personages, such for instance as Elijah, who, we are told, was taken into heaven without tasting death (2 Kgs. 2:11). Also, we are told in the Bible that Enoch "walked with God: and he was not, for God took him" (Gen. 5:24). This is explained by St. Paul, who said: "By faith Enoch was translated that he should not see death; and was not found, because God had translated him" (Heb. 11:5); which is generally understood that, as in the case of Elijah, he was taken to heaven without tasting death.

TRANSLATION OF ENOCH AND HIS CITY[9]

Through modern revelation we obtain further knowledge as to Enoch and his translation, viz., in the fragment of the writings of Moses, known as the Book of Moses, in the Pearl of Great Price. Here is given an extended account of the ministry of Enoch as a preacher of righteousness. Those whom his ministry brought to a knowledge of the truth were gathered together into a Holy City called "Zion," which signifies, among other things, the "pure in heart," or the "city of holiness." We are also told that "Zion in process of time was taken up into heaven"; so that not only was Enoch translated, but his whole city, for not only did Enoch walk with God, "but Enoch and all his people walked with God, and he [Enoch] dwelt in the midst of Zion; and it came to pass that Zion was not, for God received it up into His own bosom, and from thence went forth the saying, 'Zion is fled'" (Moses 7:18-19,69).[10]

THE PROPHET OF THE NEW DISPENSATION ON TRANSLATED BEINGS

The prophet of our New Dispensation, Joseph Smith, also had something of importance to say concerning this principle of translation. In an article presented and read to the conference of the Church of Jesus Christ of Latter-day Saints at Nauvoo, October 3, 1840,[11] the prophet said, commenting on Genesis 5:24, which deals with the translation of Enoch:

---

other world is not accepted as a doctrine of the Church. The theory that he came here from some other world a 'translated' being does not take care of the element of 'death' as that condition came into the world, for translated beings are subject to death according to the teaching of the Book of Mormon." They also added that the Fall of Adam "brought death into the world" ("Doctrinal Points Questioned by the Committee," in Buerger)–*Ed.*>

9. <Ms III[c] adds "Translation of Enoch and His City"–Ed.>

10. For the whole ministry of Enoch, see Book of Moses, chapters 6 and 7, Pearl of Great Price.

11. <Andrew F. Ehat and Lyndon W. Cook, eds., *The Words of Joseph Smith: The Contemporary Accounts of the Nauvoo Discourses of the Prophet Joseph* (Provo, UT: Religious Studies Center, Brigham Young University, 1980), 38, 50, date this "Priesthood" discourse

> Now this Enoch God reserved unto Himself, that he should not die at that time, and appointed unto him a ministry unto a terrestrial body,[12] of whom there has been but little revealed. He [Enoch] is reserved also unto the Presidency of a Dispensation,[13] and more shall be said of him and terrestrial bodies in another treatise. He [Enoch] is a ministering angel, to minister to those who shall be heirs of salvation. . . .
>
> Now the doctrine of translation is a power which belongs to this Priesthood [i.e., the Melchizedek]. There are many things which belong to the powers of the Priesthood and the keys thereof that have been kept hid from before the foundation of the world. They are hid from the wise and prudent to be revealed in the last times.
>
> Many have supposed that the doctrine of translation was a doctrine whereby men were taken immediately into the presence of God, and into an eternal fullness, but this is a mistaken idea. Their place of habitation is that of the terrestrial order, and a place prepared for such characters He held in reserve to be ministering angels unto many planets, and who as yet have not entered into so great a fullness as those who are resurrected from the dead.[14]

This means that translated persons have not altogether escaped from death; for it is most solemnly declared that "as in Adam all die, even so in Christ shall all be made alive" (1 Cor. 15:22). And if this hold true, then Elijah, Enoch, and Enoch's people, all who have been translated, in fact, must also pass through the change that is wrought by physical death.

Later, namely at the church conference of October 3, 1841, the Prophet on this same subject said: "Translated bodies cannot enter into rest until they have undergone a change equivalent to death. Translated bodies are designed for future missions."[15]

With these facts and principles relative to translation[16] before us, established upon authoritative sources of knowledge accepted by the Church of Jesus Christ of Latter-day Saints, as authoritative teachings on this subject of translated beings, and the possible missions to which they may be assigned, we are prepared to apply this principle to the commencement of things in this earth-life of man under the

---

to 5 October 1840—*Ed.*>

12. <Ms III* "a ministry unto a terrestrial body [i.e. terrestrial world]," but the text of the sermon on "Priesthood" has "a ministry unto terrestrial bodies"—*Ed.*>

13. Shall we say, even as Adam was reserved to the Presidency of the Dispensation he opened on our earth? <In line with this note by Roberts, there is a handwritten marginal Ms III^{c} "same as Adam"—*Ed.*>

14. Joseph Smith, "Priesthood," *History of the Church of Jesus Christ of Latter-day Saints, Period I: History of Joseph Smith, the Prophet by Himself* (Salt Lake City: Deseret News, 1908), 4:209-210.

15. Joseph Smith, *History of the Church*, 4:425.

16. <Ms III^{c} adds "relative to translation"—*Ed.*>

Adamic Dispensation. We have pointed out that it would be inconsistent to say that immortal beings came to the earth to start things as Adam and Eve did and then to say that by partaking of forbidden fruit they were so changed in their immortal nature that they died, since a person who is once become immortal can not again be subject to death; and on this we have the most positive testimony from the Book of Mormon.

IMMORTALITY MEANS "DEATHLESS": BOOK OF MORMON TESTIMONY[17]

Speaking of the Christ, the Prophet Mosiah says:

> He is the light and the life of the world; yea, a light that is endless, that can never be darkened; yea, and also a life which is endless, that *there can be no more death*. Even this mortal shall put on immortality, and this corruption shall put on incorruption (Mosiah 16:9-10).[18]

If this be true of the resurrected Christ, it is true of all resurrected personages. The prophet Amulek[19] is represented as saying:

> Now there is a death, which is called temporal death; and the death of Christ shall loose the bands of this temporal death, that all shall be raised from this temporal death. The spirit and the body shall be reunited again in its perfect form; both limb and joint shall be restored to its proper frame, even as we now are at this time. . . . Now behold, I have spoken unto you concerning the death of the mortal body, and also concerning the resurrection of the mortal body. I say unto you that this mortal body is raised to an immortal body, that is, from death, even from the first death unto life, that They Can Die No More; their spirits uniting with their bodies—never to be divided; thus the whole becoming spiritual and immortal, that They Can No More See Corruption (Alma 11:42-43, 45).

THE PROCESS OF BECOMING IMMORTAL[20]

The only way of obtaining immortality is in accordance with God's plan in bringing about the immortality of man, namely, they are begotten mortal men into an earth-life; they die and are resurrected to their immortality, and when so made immortal then it happens to them according to the above teaching of the Book of Mormon, they become immortal, that is, *deathless! They can not die under any*

17. <Ms III^c adds "Testimony"—*Ed.*>
18. <Emphasis added by Roberts—*Ed.*>
19. <Ms III* "The prophet Zeezrom"—*Ed.*>
20. <Ms III^c adds "The Process of Becoming Immortal"—*Ed.*>

circumstance. They have become "soul," and also "sole," a single thing—a spiritual being, compounded of a union of imperishable earth elements, and imperishable intelligent and spirit elements, that admit of no possible tearing apart or sundering or dissolution. They are deathless—immortal! Proof against all possibility of dissolution; so that if Adam came to this earth a "celestial," an "immortal being," he could not have died, and since he did die the conclusion must be that he was not immortal when he came to the earth, but was possibly a translated being, such as Elijah or Enoch and the people of Enoch's city were.[21] In that state he could be brought to this earth to people it with offspring that would be mortal, subject to death as he himself was, and subject also to resurrection from the dead as he himself was; and brought by that resurrection to a glorious immortality.

Thus, we have our start of the human race in the earth through Adam and Eve, children of God from some other world, begotten in the image of God, after His kind, and now to beget offspring after their kind, and perpetuate the race of God's children in this earth in order that they might attain, ultimately, to immeasurable heights of power and glory and honor and immortality—eternal life—physical and spiritual.

---

21. <Joseph Fielding Smith labels the idea that Adam was a translated being as "absurd" (Joseph Fielding Smith to Rudger Clawson, 14 Jan. 1931); later Joseph Fielding Smith, *Answers to Gospel Questions* (Salt Lake City: Deseret Book Co., 1966), 5:171, argues strongly that "Adam was not a translated being from another planet"—*Ed.*>

CHAPTER XXXIII
The Problem of Evil

SCRIPTURE READING LESSON

Analysis

I. The Garden of Eden.
II. Symbols of Knowledge and Life:
   (a) The Tree of Death,
   (b) The Tree of Life.
III. The World's Great Mystery—the Existence of Evil.
IV. Testimony of the Book of Mormon—Eternity of Evil.
V. This Doctrine Unique to Modern Revelation.
VI. Evil among the Eternal Things.
VII. Testimony of a Modern (Harvard) Philosopher.
VIII. Summary of Fiske's Contribution.
IX. God Did Not Create Evil.
X. The Answer of Epicurus.

References

The Bible: Gen. 1-3.

Book of Mormon: 2 Ne. 2; also, Alma 42.

Dean Henry L. Mansel, *The Limits of Religious Thought, Examined in Eight Lectures Delivered before the University of Oxford, in the Year MDCCCLVIII, on the Bampton Foundation* (Boston: Gould and Lincoln, 1875).

The American philosopher, Ralph Waldo Emerson's Essay "Compensation," in *Essays: First and Second Series* (Boston and New York: Houghton Mifflin Co., 1921), 91-127.

Sabine Baring-Gould, *The Origin and Development of Religious Belief* (London: Rivingtons, 1869-1870), 2:22-23.

John Fiske, section on "The Mystery of Evil," *Studies in Religion* in *The Miscellaneous Writings of John Fiske, with Many Portraits of Illustrious Philosophers, Scientists, and Other Men of Note* (Boston and New York: Houghton, Mifflin and Co., 1902), 9:225-67.

For fuller treatise than this chapter affords, see author's *The Seventy's Course in Theology: Second Year, Outline History of the Dispensations of the Gospel* (Salt Lake City: Skelton Publishing Co., 1908), lesson 10.

CHAPTER XXXIII
The Problem of Evil

THE GARDEN OF EDEN

In the garden of God's planting, mentioned in Genesis, second chapter, and into which man was brought and made the keeper, were two special trees—the Tree of Life and the Tree of the Knowledge of Good and Evil. Of this tree—the Tree of the Knowledge of Good and Evil—the Lord said to Adam:

> Of every tree of the garden thou mayest freely eat; but of the Tree of the Knowledge of Good and Evil thou shalt not eat of it: for in the day that thou eatest thereof, thou shalt surely die (Gen. 2:16-17).

Thus, God's commandment to man. Thus, the challenge of law to man's obedience, the application of God's pre-determined test:

> We will make an earth whereon these [pre-existent spirits of men] may dwell, and we will prove them herewith, to see if they will do all things whatsoever the Lord their God shall command them; and they who keep their first estate [i.e., pre-existent spirit estate] shall be added upon; . . . and they who keep their second estate [man's earth estate] shall have glory added upon their heads forever and ever (Abr. 3:24-26).

SYMBOLS OF KNOWLEDGE AND LIFE: TREE OF DEATH AND THE TREE[1] OF LIFE

In the above symbols, together with the announced penalties to follow disobedience, we have assembled the great mysteries of this world—Life, Death, Good, Evil, the fact of man's agency—power to order his own course, to obey or disobey God;[2] continued life for obedience, which is but conformation to the law of life; and death for disobedience, or departure from the conditions on which life is predicated. The Tree of Life was the symbol of Eternal Life, for later when man had partaken of the fruit of the Tree of Death—the Tree of the Knowledge of Good and Evil—God is represented as saying, in effect, Behold, the man is become as one of us, to know good and evil; and now lest he put forth his hand and partake

1. <Ms III^{c} adds "The Tree"—*Ed.*>
2. <Ms III^{c} adds "God"—*Ed.*>

also of the Tree of Life, *and eat and live forever*, let us send him forth from the Garden of Eden to till the ground, and guard the Tree of Life by cherubim[3] with flaming sword. And so it was ordered (Gen. 3:22-24).

Death was symbolized in the Tree of the Knowledge of Good and Evil—in the day thou eatest of it, thou shalt surely die—hence, the Tree of Death. Death, we learn from other scriptures than Genesis, is both temporal and spiritual. What is here called temporal death is physical death, separation of the spirit and body, the dust returning to the earth whence it came; but the spirit, being a thing immortal, survives in conscious life and goes to the world of spirits. "Dust thou art, and to dust thou shalt return" (Gen. 3:19) was not written of the spirit of man. The spiritual death is disruption of the union of the soul of man with God, and hence spiritual death, since union with God is the source of man's spiritual life. But while partaking of the fruit of the Tree of Knowledge would bring death, both spiritual (separation from God—hence, from good)[4] and temporal (separation of spirit and body—physical death),[5] yet it would bring also the knowledge that would make men as Gods,[6] to know good and evil, and so far become like God.

THE WORLD'S GREAT MYSTERY—THE EXISTENCE OF EVIL[7]

Here let us face this world's great mystery—the existence of evil, especially moral evil, which one high in religious and philosophical thought speaks of as "the real riddle of existence—the problem which confounds all philosophy, aye, and all religion, too." He represents that the real riddle is "that evil should exist at all"! He continues:

> Against this immovable barrier of the existence of evil, the waves of philosophy have dashed themselves unceasingly since the birthday of human thought, and have retired broken and powerless, without displacing the minutest fragment of the stubborn rock, without softening one feature of its dark and rugged surface.[8]

TESTIMONY FROM THE BOOK OF MORMON LEHI[9]

In the Book of Mormon, which here we hold to be an ancient volume

3. <Roberts's Ms III and Gen. 3:24 incorrectly have the plural as "cherubims"—*Ed.*>

4. <Ms III[c] adds "(separation from God—hence, from good)"—*Ed.*>

5. <Ms III[c] adds "(separation of spirit and body—physical death)"—*Ed.*>

6. <Ms III[*] "would make men as God"—*Ed.*>

7. <Ms III[c] adds "The Existence of Evil"—*Ed.*>

8. Dean Henry L. Mansel, *The Limits of Religious Thought, Examined in Eight Lectures Delivered before the University of Oxford, in the Year* MDCCCLVIII, *on the Bampton Foundation* (Boston: Gould and Lincoln, 1875), 197.

9. <Ms III[c] adds "Lehi"—*Ed.*>

of American scripture written by the inspiration of God in its prophets and seers, and translated also by the inspiration of God, is a master stroke of philosophy, as also an authoritative theological doctrine of highest value—the doctrine of necessary opposition in all things, the antinomies of the universe. This Book of Mormon treatise on necessary opposite existences, boldly carries the necessity of such existences to such an extreme that the sacred writer Lehi (of the first part of the sixth century B.C.),[10] makes existence itself, and even the existence of God, to depend upon the fact of things existing in duality: "things that act and things that are acted upon" (cf. 2 Ne. 2:14). Opposite physical forces are seen in attraction and repulsion—the centripetal and centrifugal forces, the action and reaction of which hold the worlds in balance; in chemistry the composing and decomposing substances; in electricity the positive and negative forces; and in the whole universe is to be seen what is called the antinomy, or opposites, of light and darkness, movement and repose, energy and matter, heat and cold, life and death; "the one and the multiple"; in the moral order, good and evil, joy and sorrow, courage and cowardice, righteousness and wickedness. And now Lehi's statement of the case and his reasoning thereon and his startling conclusion:

> For it must needs be that there is an opposition in all things. If not so, . . . righteousness could not be brought to pass; neither wickedness; neither holiness nor misery; neither good nor bad. Wherefore, all things [i.e., in that event][11] must needs be a compound in one; wherefore, if it should be one body, it must needs remain as dead, having no life neither death, nor corruption nor incorruption, happiness nor misery, neither sense nor insensibility.
>
> Wherefore, it must needs have been created for a thing of naught; wherefore, there would have been no purpose in the end of its creation. Wherefore, this thing must needs destroy the wisdom of God, and His eternal purposes; and also the power, and the mercy, and the justice of God.
>
> And if ye shall say there is no law, ye shall also say there is no sin. If ye shall say there is no sin, ye shall also say there is no righteousness. And if there be no righteousness, there is no happiness. And if there be no righteousness nor happiness, there is no punishment nor misery. And if these things are not, there is no God. And if there is no God, we are not, neither the earth; for there could have been no creation of things, *neither to act nor to be acted upon*; wherefore, all things must have vanished away (2 Ne. 2:11-13).[12]

---

10. <Ms III "the first part of the fifth century B.C.," which is corrected to "sixth"—*Ed.*>
11. <Ms III[c] adds "[i.e., in that event]"—*Ed.*>
12. <Emphasis added by Roberts—*Ed.*>

THIS DOCTRINE UNIQUE TO MODERN REVELATIONS

The antinomies of the universe–things in necessary duality–essential to the existence of things at all, is the doctrine of this passage. Who before this in ancient times taught this doctrine? Who of modern times, prior to 1830, the year in which the Book of Mormon was published, ever taught it? And especially whoever either in ancient or modern times ever carried the daring thought to the height of making existences of the universe and the universe itself, and even the existence of God, depend upon the existence of things in duality–in a necessary opposition in all things? I shall make bold to claim this as a uniqueness of the Nephite scripture. But pride of it is not in its uniqueness, but in the self-evident truth of it, and in the tremendous consequences that draw with it, and the light it throws athwart the world's mystery of the existence of evil; the aid it is to philosophy; the aid it is to religion; the assistance it will afford in our exposition of the fall of man.

EVIL AMONG THE[13] ETERNAL THINGS

We can be assured from the Book of Mormon doctrine that evil as well as good is among the eternal things. The existence of evil did not begin with its appearance on our earth. Evil existed even in heaven; for Lucifer and many other spirits sinned there, rebelled against heaven's matchless King, waged "war," and were thrust out into the earth for their transgression.

Evil is not a created quality. It has always existed as the background of good. It is as eternal as goodness; it is as eternal as law; it is as eternal as the agency of intelligences. Sin, which is evil, is transgression of law,[14] and so long as the agency of intelligences and law have existed, the possibility of the transgression of law has existed; and as the agency of intelligences and law have eternally existed, so, too, evil has existed eternally, either potentially or active, and will always so exist. Evil may not be referred to God for its origin. He is not its creator. Evil is one of those independent existences that is uncreate, and stands in the category of qualities of eternal things.[15] The good cannot exist without the antithesis of evil–the foil on

---

13. <Ms III[c] adds "The"–*Ed.*>

14. <Ms III[*] "Sin, which is active, is transgression of law"–*Ed.*>

15. Lest some text-proofer should retort upon me and cite the words of Isaiah–"I make peace *and create evil*" <emphasis added by Roberts–*Ed.*>–the only text of scripture ascribing the creation of evil to God–I will anticipate so far as to say that it is quite generally agreed that no reference is made in the words of Isaiah to "moral evil"; but to such evils as may come as judgments upon people for their correction, such as famine, or tempest, or war; such an "evil" as would stand in natural antithesis to "peace," which word precedes "I create evil" in the text–"I make peace and create"–the opposite of peace–"The evil of afflictions

which it produces itself and becomes known. The existence of one implies the existence of the other; and conversely, the non-existence of the latter would imply the non-existence of the former. It is from this basis that Lehi reached the conclusion that either his doctrine of the existence of opposites is true, or else there is no existence.

Lehi's conclusion is woven into the very fabric of the things of the universe. It cannot be otherwise. The opposite, the absence of one or the other member in a given series of antitheses is unthinkable. The fact of the reality of opposite existences[16] must be recognized as a necessary truth–a truth the opposite of which is inconceivable.

THE TESTIMONY OF A MODERN (HARVARD) PHILOSOPHER

Since the publication of the Book of Mormon (spring of 1830) consideration of this subject of evil has been more frequent and fuller, but in none of these more recent discussions is to be found those who in consideration of the theme take on the coloring of Lehi's conclusions, until you come to John Fiske, professor, historian, and philosopher of Harvard fame, from whose writings is to be obtained full warrant for all that the Book of Mormon passage on opposite existences set forth, and this in his great treatise on the "Mystery of Evil" (1899) and published in his *Studies in Religion*.[17] Mr. Fiske says:

> Whatever exists is part of the dramatic whole, and this can quickly be proved. The goodness in the world–all that we love and praise and emulate–we are ready enough to admit into our scheme of things, and to rest upon it our belief in God. The misery, the pain, the wickedness, we would fain leave out. But if there were no such thing as evil, how could there be such a thing as goodness? Or to put it somewhat

---

and punishments, but not the evil of sin" (Catholic Bible comment on Isa. 45:7). Meantime we have the clearest scriptural evidence that moral evil is not a product of God: "Let no man say when he is tempted, I am tempted of God; for God cannot be tempted with evil, neither tempteth he any man" (James 1:13). That is to say, God has nothing to do with the creation of moral evil. "But every man is tempted, when he is drawn away of his own lust and enticed. Then when lust hath conceived, it bringeth forth sin; and sin, when it is finished, bringeth forth death" (James 1:14-15). "The evil and the good are necessary correlatives" (Sir Oliver Lodge, "Christianity and Science: The Divine Element in Christianity," *The Hibbert Journal* 4 [Apr. 1906]: 657).

16. <Ms III* "the existence of opposite existences"–*Ed.*>

17. John Fiske, "The Mystery of Evil," *Studies in Religion, Being The Destiny of Man, The Idea of God, Through Nature to God, Life Everlasting*, vol. 9 in *The Miscellaneous Writings of John Fiske, with Many Portraits of Illustrious Philosophers, Scientists, and Other Men of Note* (Boston and New York: Houghton, Mifflin and Co., 1902).

differently, if we had never known anything but goodness, how could we ever distinguish it from evil? How could we recognize it as good? How would its quality of goodness in any wise interest or concern us? This question goes down to the bottom of things, for it appeals to the fundamental conditions according to which conscious intelligence exists at all. Its answer will, therefore, be likely to help us. It will not enable us to solve the problem of evil, enshrouded as it is in a mystery impenetrable by finite intelligence, but it will help us to state the problem correctly; and surely this is no small help. In the mere work of purifying our intellectual vision there is that which heals and soothes us. To learn to see things without distortion is to prepare one's self for taking the world in the right mood, and in this we find strength and consolation.

Again:

It is an undeniable fact that we cannot know anything whatever, except as contrasted with something else. The contrast may be bold and sharp, or it may dwindle into a slight discrimination, but it must be there. If the figures on your canvas are indistinguishable from the background, there is surely no picture to be seen. Some element of unlikeness, some germ of antagonism, some chance for discrimination is essential to every act of knowing. I might have illustrated this point concretely without all the foregoing explanation, but I have aimed at paying it the respect due to its vast importance. I have wished to show how the fact that we cannot know anything whatever except as contrasted with something else is a fact that is deeply rooted in the innermost structure of the human mind. It is not a superficial but a fundamental truth, that if there were no color but red it would be exactly the same thing as if there were no color at all. . . .

If our palates had never come in contact with any tasteful thing save sugar, we should know no more of sweetness than of bitterness. If we had never felt physical pain, we could not recognize physical pleasure. For want of the contrasted background, its pleasurableness would be non-existent. And in just the same way it follows that, without knowing that which is morally evil, we could not possibly recognize that which is morally good. Of these antagonist correlatives, the one is unthinkable in the absence of the other. In a sinless and painless world, human conduct might possess more outward marks of perfection than any saint every dreamed of: but the moral element would be lacking; the goodness would have no more significance in our conscious life than that load of atmosphere which we are always carrying about with us.

We are thus brought to a striking conclusion, the essential soundness of which cannot be gainsaid. In a happy world there must be sorrow and pain; and in a moral world the knowledge of evil is indispensable. The stern necessity for this has been proved to inhere in the innermost constitution of the human soul. It is part and parcel of the universe. To him who is disposed to cavil at the world which God has in such wise created, we may fairly put the question whether the prospect of escape from its ills would ever induce him to put off this human consciousness and accept in exchange some form of existence unknown and inconceivable! The alternative is clear: on the one hand, a world with sin and suffering; on the other hand, an unthinkable world in which conscious life does not involve contrast.

The profound truth of Aristotle's remark is thus more forcibly than ever brought home to us. We do not find that evil has been interpolated into the universe from without; we find that, on the contrary, it is an indispensable part of the dramatic whole.[18]

SUMMARY OF FISKE'S CONTRIBUTION

There can be no doubt that this is strong and direct support to the essential things in Lehi's philosophy. Let me throw the evidence of it in sight:

> Whatever exists is part of the dramatic whole. . . . This question goes down to the bottom of things, for it appeals to the fundamental conditions according to which conscious intelligence exists at all; . . . It is an undeniable fact that we cannot know anything whatever except as contrasted with something else; . . . If the figures on your canvas are indistinguishable from the background, there is surely no picture to be seen. . . . It is not a superficial but a fundamental truth that if there were no color but red, it would be exactly the same thing as if there were no color at all [so as to the[19] good]. . . . If we had never felt physical pain, we could not recognize physical pleasure. . . . Without knowing that which is morally evil, we could not possibly recognize that which is morally good. . . . In a happy world there must be sorrow and pain, and in a moral world the knowledge of evil is indispensable. . . . We do not find that evil has been interpolated into the universe from without; we find that, on the contrary, it is an indispensable part of the dramatic whole.

GOD DID NOT CREATE EVIL: NOR IS HE RESPONSIBLE FOR IT

From this view of things we get a new conception of evil. It is not a created thing, it exists in the sum of things, in the constitution of things. It is "part of the dramatic whole." As already suggested God is not the creator of evil. It is repulsive to every worthy thought of Deity to think so; and contrary to the unity and consistency of His attributes of righteousness and true holiness and justice and love that He should be the author of evil, or the creator of the devil to produce evil, and be responsible for it in our world or in any other world, for in that case God would still be responsible for the existence of evil.

Evil rests upon the eternal nature of things, of existences in both their eternal positive and negative forms. God did not create space (i.e., expanse or extension in which things exist); God did not create duration—limitless time; God did not create matter[20]—the stuff that things are made of and that occupies space; God did

---

18. <Ibid., 9:242-43, 249-52—*Ed.*>

19. <Ms III[c] adds "the"—*Ed.*>

20. <Ms III[*] "God did create matter," but Ms III[c] adds the word "not" after "God"—*Ed.*>

not create force or energy or mind (intelligence)—the thing in Lehi's philosophy which "acts." All these are eternal things, and God working among these brings to pass changes and ordains events, these his creative acts. God is not the author of evil or wickedness; neither did he create the devils of this or of other worlds; such devils as exist are intelligences possessed of free moral agency, who chose to do evil and rebelled against good and against God, and have had perverse inclination to seek to induce other intelligences to follow their evil course. There is no more mystery about the existence of devils, than there is about the existence of evil men.[21] Meanwhile, but apart from devils or evil-minded wicked men, evil exists eternally, active or potential, in the very constitution of things. By the side of the virtue of courage lurks the evil of danger, without which courage would be unknown. In the same way, good must have its background of evil, else it would never be known; to employ Fiske's illustration: "If the figures on your canvas are indistinguishable from the background, there is surely no picture to be seen." So it stands that evil is as eternal as good; as eternal as space or duration or matter or force. God did not create any of these things, nor is He responsible for them. He found Himself, so to speak, co-eternal with these other eternal things, and so works out His creative designs in harmony with those existences; not creating intelligences, but begetting intelligences, spirits. God is not responsible for the inner fact of them—the entity which ultimately determines the intellectual and moral character of spirits and of men, which are but spirits incarnate in human bodies. God is not responsible for their nature, as if He had created them absolutely of nothing—intelligences, spirits, men; and created them as He would have them, measuring to each severally as He pleased to have them in intellectual degree and intensity of moral value. Had He so absolutely created them, He could have made the man of lowly degree the same as the man of highest degree; the man of brute mind and nature the same as the man of refined sentiment and aesthetic instincts. Why this inequality, if God absolutely created men—intelligence, spirit, body; and created them as he willed to have them, and could have had them different had He so willed? Why then did He not have them of higher grade all round? Why were not all the men made brave and all the women fair? The answer to all this is that God did all that could be done as the immanent, eternally active, and creating, and causing power in the universe under the limitations of other eternal existences, such as we have previously enumerated, and including consideration of the intractableness of the material with which the Creator had to work. If that did not

21. <Ms III* "about the existence of evil men," but due to skipping from "about the existence of" to "about the existence of" the words "of devils, than there is about the existence" from the earlier draft were accidentally omitted and these are reinserted above the line—*Ed.*>

eventuate in the best conceivable of worlds under the limitations of our human thinking, we may be assured that it has resulted in the best of possible worlds. And while this best possible world presents apparent limitation to the power of its Creator, such as He may not create space, nor matter, nor force, nor intelligence; nor annihilate evil, yet all the power that is—creative, or destructive, or controlling—is His; He holds it, and hence, He is all-powerful; all the might that exists is His; hence, He is the Almighty; all the good that exists is His; hence, He is the All-Good; and the All-Benevolent, and the All-Loving One, for the same reason that He is the Almighty.

These are matters that affect our conceptions of God, and have now of a long time puzzled the minds of men, leading to such troublesome questions as these.

TROUBLESOME PROBLEMS: ANTITHESES OF EPICURUS[22]

If God is absolutely omnipotent, why does he not prevent evil? The fact that evil exists and persists generally in the economy of the world leads to the conclusion that the Deity is limited in power. If God is absolutely benevolent or good, why has He created a world where pain, sorrow, suffering, and death are the common lot of men? And the conclusion formed from such a question is that either the Creator is not benevolent, or that again He is limited in power.

The most celebrated formula of these time-worn problems is known as "The Antitheses of Epicurus," namely:

(1) "Is God willing to prevent evil, but not able? Then He is impotent."

(2) "Is He able, but not willing? Then He is malevolent!"

(3) "Is He both able and willing? Then why is evil?"

These questions are supposed to present an impasse to any harmony in the nature of Deity on the basis of His omnipotence, benevolence, and the existence of evil. Yet in the light of our reflections in this chapter on evil, and especially in the light of the philosophy of Lehi in the Book of Mormon and John Fiske's faultless reasoning, the antitheses of Epicurus are not so formidable as might otherwise appear.

ANSWER TO EPICURUS

God may not be able to prevent evil and destroy the source of it, but He is not impotent, for He guides intelligences, notwithstanding evil, to kingdoms of peace and security.[23] Evil is a means of progress, for progress is overcoming evil.

---

22. <Ms III^{c} adds "Antitheses of Epicurus"—*Ed.*>

23. <Davis Bitton, "The Truth, The Way, The Life: B. H. Roberts' Unpublished

God may not be able, nor willing if He were able, to prevent evil, and yet He is not malevolent. For knowing that evil exists in the whole scheme of things as the necessary antithesis of good, and that one may not be destroyed without destroying both, why wreck the universe in order to prevent evil? And which if achieved would be the greatest of evils, since all things else would go with it.

"Why then is evil?"–the last of the questions of Epicurus? The answer is that it is a necessary and eternal part of "the dramatic whole," as set forth in both Lehi's philosophy and John Fiske's reasoning.[24] And the kingdom of righteousness wherein dwelleth peace–the beatific vision and hope of the faithful is the kingdom to be won by the conquest over evil; and which never may be realized but by that conquest.

Masterwork," 4 (in David J. Buerger Collection, Manuscript 622, Bx 10, Fd 7, Marriott Library, University of Utah, Salt Lake City), says that "although he did not say so explicitly, Roberts was defending God's wisdom and power but not his omnipotence, for even God was subject to the 'whole scheme of things'"–*Ed.*>

24. <Ms III[*] "John Fiske's faultless reasoning"–*Ed.*>

CHAPTER XXXIV

The Affair in Eden—The "Fall" of Man

SCRIPTURE READING LESSON

Analysis

I. The Symbol Trees: The Tree of Death, The Tree of Life.

II. The Tree of Knowledge Not an Evil Tree.

III. The Doctrine of the "Fall" according to the Book of Mormon.

IV. The Dilemma: What Shall Adam Do?

V. The Effect of the "Fall."

VI. The Attitude of Christendom on the "Fall":

(a) The Roman Catholic View.

(b) The Protestant View.

(c) Presbyterian Modification of the Protestant View of the "Fall."

VII. Views of John Fiske on Life in Eden without the "Fall."

VIII. Adam Fell That Men Might Be.

References

Gen. 2-3.

Moses 5-7.

Book of Mormon, 2 Ne. 2, Alma 12:19-25; 42:1-31.

D&C 29:26-50.

All the scriptural citations in the footnotes of this lesson and their contexts.

John Fiske, section on "The Mystery of Evil," *Studies in Religion, Being The Destiny of Man, The Idea of God, Through Nature to God, Life Everlasting,* in *The Miscellaneous Writings of John Fiske, with Many Portraits of Illustrious Philosophers, Scientists, and Other Men of Note* (Boston and New York: Houghton, Mifflin and Co., 1902), 225-67.

All the references given in lesson analysis of Chapter 33.

CHAPTER XXXIV

The Affair in Eden—The "Fall" of Man

With the doctrine of a necessary opposition in all things set forth as essential to any existence at all; that good can only exist and be known in antithesis with evil; that both joy and sorrow are essential to a happy world; and recognizing evil as among the eternal things not created or made but existing as part of the "dramatic whole," we are prepared to approach the affair in Eden—"the Fall of Man"—with larger assurance of understanding than could otherwise be hoped for.

THE SYMBOL TREES: THE TREE OF DEATH, THE TREE OF LIFE

The story of the "fall" is well known; we shall have small need of entering upon its details. In the garden of God's planting, Eden, were two symbol trees. (1) The Tree of the Knowledge of Good and Evil; to eat of its fruit meant death to the life then known to man—the life of innocence and the physical life.[1] This tree, then, could also be known as "The Tree of Death." (2) Opposite to this, and in the midst of the garden, was "The Tree of Life." Here in the last analysis are the symbols of the necessary "opposition in all things"—The Tree of Life, The Tree of Death—symbols of the antinomies of the universe!

With the necessity of knowing both good and evil in order to know anything, it can scarcely be expected that man was placed in the Garden of Eden to refrain from partaking of the fruit of the Tree of Knowledge. Notwithstanding the commandment not to partake of the forbidden fruit, why is he there if not to partake of it? And may not the "commandment" respecting the Tree of the Knowledge of Good and Evil, saying, "Thou shalt not eat of it; for in the day that thou eatest thereof thou shalt surely die" (Gen. 2:17)—may not this be regarded more as announcing the nature of the fruit of the tree and the consequence of eating it, than an expected and effective prohibition of partaking of this fruit?

Back of all this iterated "commandment" "thou shalt not eat of the fruit of this tree, for in the day thou eatest thereof thou shalt surely die" is felt the fact of the agency of man; his power to choose for himself—to eat or not to eat. Only know the consequences, O Man! If you eat of it, death to your life of innocence will

1. <Ms III* "and the temporal physical life"—*Ed.*>

follow; death to your physical life will follow; for "dust thou art, and to dust shalt thou return" (Gen. 3:19). It is full of risk, this eating of the forbidden fruit! It is full of danger. There are real losses to face. It means adventure. It will inaugurate a new order of things. Man, thou art forewarned, but thou art free!

THE TREE OF KNOWLEDGE NOT AN EVIL TREE[2]

Let it be observed that the Tree of Knowledge, even though the Tree of Death, is nowhere called an "Evil Tree," or its fruit bad.

> And out of the ground made the Lord God to grow every tree that is pleasant to the sight and good for food; the Tree of Life also in the midst of the garden; and the Tree of Knowledge of Good and Evil (Gen. 2:9).

No intimation of this Tree of Knowledge being in itself evil. Rather to the contrary: it is included among the "trees pleasant to the sight and good for food," in the same verse in which it is named (cf. Gen. 2:9). The observation of Eve[3] in the commencement of her conversation with Lucifer (symboled by the serpent) may have been wholly true[4] of the fruit of the Tree of Knowledge of Good and Evil:[5] "And when the woman saw that the tree was good for food, and that it was pleasant to the eye, and a tree to be desired to make one wise" (Gen. 3:6), she was not merely echoing something that Lucifer had suggestively infused into her mind, but was uttering a truth respecting the tree itself, and what it stood for. It is good to know; and since the good may not be known without also knowing the evil, it is good—since from the constitution or nature of things it can not be otherwise—it is good to know both.

Besides throughout the whole narrative of Genesis, it is taken for granted that to eat the forbidden fruit "will make men as Gods, knowing good and evil" (cf. Gen. 3:5, 22); and is it not good for men to be as Gods, knowing good and evil—in any way to be[6] as Gods? Who shall say nay? "The Fall of Man!" Is it not here that man begins to rise? True, it is Lucifer, who in the Genesis narrative[7] first suggests, and doubtless with evil intent, that eating the fruit would open the eyes of man, "and make him as God." Yet it was a truth; for God Himself is represented as saying later,[8] after Adam and Eve had eaten the forbidden fruit:

---

2. <Ms III[c] adds "The Tree of Knowledge Not An Evil Tree"—*Ed.*>
3. <Ms III[*] "The observation respecting Eve"—*Ed.*>
4. <Ms III[*] "may have been really and wholly true"—*Ed.*>
5. <Ms III[c] adds "of Good and Evil"—*Ed.*>
6. <Ms III[c] adds "to be"—*Ed.*>
7. <Ms III[*] "the Genesis narration"—*Ed.*>
8. <Ms III[c] adds "later"—*Ed.*>

> Behold, the man has become as one of us [the Gods], to know good and evil. And now, lest he put forth his hand, and take also of the Tree of Life, and eat and live for ever, therefore, the Lord God sent him forth from the Garden of Eden, to till the ground. . . . And He placed . . . cherubims and a flaming sword . . . to keep the way of the Tree of Life (Gen. 3:22-24).

Which only means that the time had not then come for man to attain immortality; nor then to know the way to the Tree of Life. Opportunity to reap the full harvest from eating[9] of the Tree of the Knowledge of Good and Evil must be granted; not only to Adam and his spouse, but to their posterity, also to the race; a testing period and a testing place is provided, where the whole drama of Good and Evil in conflict shall work out the purposes of God in the planned earth-life of man.

But for man to become as God, in any respect, in any way, and by any means, must be great gain, and surely embraced from the beginning in God's general and positive plan for man's advancement. It[10] must have been included in the covenant of "eternal life, which God that cannot lie promised before the world began" (Titus 1:2);[11] and not an incident that surprised the purposes of God and provoked His anger.

THE DOCTRINE OF THE FALL ACCORDING TO THE BOOK OF MORMON

And now as to the effects of the Fall according to the account of it given in the Book of Mormon. If Adam had not fallen:

> He would have remained in the garden of Eden. And all things which were created must have remained in the same state which they were, after they were created; and they must have remained forever and had no end. And they [Adam and Eve] would have had no children; wherefore, they would have remained in a state of innocence, having no joy, for they knew no misery; doing no good, for they knew no sin. But behold, all things have been done in the wisdom of Him who knoweth all things (2 Ne. 2:22-24).

The parts to emphasize in these statements are: (1) but for the "fall" all things must have remained in the same state in which they were created without end: no change, hence, no progression; (2) the state of man's innocence before the "fall" would have brought no joy, for in it man knew no misery; (3) Adam and Eve could do no good, for they knew no sin.

---

9. <Ms III^c adds "from eating"—*Ed.*>

10. <Ms III^c adds "It"—*Ed.*>

11. <In Ms III Roberts cites this scriptural quotation as coming from 1 Tim. 3:16—*Ed.*>

THE DILEMMA: WHAT SHALL ADAM DO?[12]

What then? Shall the creation in which they stand remain static? Know no good because, forsooth, to know good and to do good, evil must also be experienced! And that because of the eternal nature of things, for which no one is responsible, no, not God. No one has created that "eternal nature of things" any more than any one has created space, duration, matter, force, or intelligences: these are eternal things. So, too, are good, beauty, truth, righteousness, life, peace, joy. These latter,[13] however, as we have seen, may be known only in duality—they are known only in contrast with their respective opposites; good by its opposite or antinomy of evil; joy by its opposite of sorrow; life by its opposite of death, and so following. To know any one of these you must experience its opposite.[14] The question resolves itself into this: is the knowledge of the good, the beautiful, and the true, the realization of life—even immortal life—worthwhile? Is conscious existence better than non-existence? Even when conscious existence involves misery and suffering, but is attended by the hope that sometime, somewhere, there will be relief; such as "weeping may endure for a night, but joy cometh in the morning" (Ps. 30:5)?

These were the principles involved in the "fall." These the issues set before man in Eden. And Adam and his spouse chose the way of life, even the way of immortal and eternal life, though the way led through the valley and the shadow of temporal death; and though by necessity they must experience the mingled joys and sorrows of a world of broken harmonies, with good and evil, life and death in conflict—and fiercely in conflict—disclosing the pain of the universe. Yet in all this Book of Mormon doctrine, there is no complaint of the hard condition the "fall" imposes on the participants or on their descendants who fall heirs to their woes; no upbraiding of the Creator as being responsible for the evil. No, on the contrary, the affirmed assurance is:

> All things have been done in the wisdom of Him who knoweth all things (2 Ne. 2:24).

---

12. <Ms III[c] adds "The Dilemma: What Shall Adam Do?"—*Ed.*>

13. <Ms III[c] adds "latter"—*Ed.*>

14. <The review committee gave the following objection: "This thought raises some questions. While it is necessary that there be opposition in all things, yet a man does not have to sin, or come in contact with wickedness by partaking of it, to know it. We may have failed in grasping the meaning here" ("Doctrinal Points Questioned by the Committee Which Read the Manuscript of Elder B. H. Roberts, Entitled The Truth, The Way, The Life," attached to Rudger Clawson, Letter to Heber J. Grant, [15 May 1930], in David J. Buerger Collection, Manuscript 622, Bx 10, Fd 8, Manuscripts Division, Marriott Library, University of Utah, Salt Lake City)—*Ed.*>

Later, when prophetically the coming of Messiah in the fullness of time is made known to Adam and the men who by now were with him, and the purpose of Messiah's coming and mission is declared to be the redemption of "the children of men from the fall" (2 Ne. 2:26), then listen to the full organ-tones of the joy in which these things are recounted, and it will not be difficult to understand how the "fall" is really held to be "the beginning of the rise of man":

> And the Messiah cometh in the fullness of time, that he may redeem the children of men from the fall. And because that they are redeemed from the fall, they have become free forever, knowing good from evil; to act for themselves, and not to be acted upon, save it be by punishment of the law at the great and last day, according to the commandments which God hath given.
>
> Wherefore, men are free according to the flesh; and all things are given them which are expedient unto man. And they are free to choose liberty and eternal life, through the great mediation[15] of all men, or to choose captivity and death, according to the captivity and power of the devil; for he seeketh that all men might be miserable like unto himself (2 Ne. 2:26-27).

EFFECT OF THE FALL

I shall doubtless be told, however, that this rejoicing is over the "redemption from the fall," rather than rejoicing over the "fall"; but it was the "fall" which brought forth the need of the "redemption"; and, therefore, mediately, if not immediately, the cause of the rejoicing. Moreover, it is the things brought about by the "fall" that are mentioned as the occasion for the rejoicing: men have a new-found freedom—"they have become free forever"; they know now "good from evil"; that knowledge came through the "fall"; henceforth, they will be free "to act, and not merely to be acted upon," save to meet the consequences of their acts in judgments. A great change has been wrought in their status. Henceforth, they will be self-centers of free agency, agents of self-determining power, centers of intelligent force with power of initiative. They are awakened to a knowledge of good and evil; they have become as God, at least so far as to know good and evil, and have become conscious of the power to choose between them.

This affair in Eden, the "fall," is something more, allow me to repeat, than a thing "permissively embraced in the sovereign purpose of the Deity,"[16] which He

---

15. <The important textual reading "the great mediator" in the Printer's Manuscript of the Book of Mormon for 2 Ne. 2:27 was discussed in the editor's "Textual Variants in Book of Mormon Manuscripts," *Dialogue: A Journal of Mormon Thought* 10 (Autumn 1977): 19, and then four years later the 1981 edition of the Book of Mormon corrected this text to "the great Mediator"—*Ed.*>

16. <Archibald A. Hodge, A *Commentary on the Confession of Faith, with Questions for*

designed "to order <it> to his own glory."[17] The necessity of its taking place was something that is imbedded[18] in the very constitution of things. The only way by which man could come to knowledge of good, and to do good, was by partaking of the fruit of the "Tree of the Knowledge of Good and Evil." This is the only way to be "as God," in respect of knowing good and evil; which knowledge is the source of man's free agency; the consciousness of the freedom of the human will; of true morality; and of self-given loyalty to God. With so many things of high import and precious to man and dear to God, there can be no doubt but what the "fall" was as much a part of God's earth-planned life for man as the "redemption" provided for him; indeed, there would have been no need of redemption but for the "fall," and no redemption would have been provided[19] but for anticipation of that "fall."

THE ATTITUDE OF CHRISTENDOM ON THE FALL

Though all this seems so clearly set forth, or is very reasonable implied from the story of the "fall" in Genesis, yet the attitude of Christendom, both in Roman Catholic and Protestant divisions, on the doctrine of the "fall" of man seems to be one of profound regret that the "fall" ever happened. As self-constituted interpreters of the event these churches deplore the "fall" and strongly hold that man and the world would have been better off had the thing never happened. And upon Adam is laid a heavy burden of responsibility. It was he, they complain, who "brought death into the world, and all our woe."

(a) The Roman Catholic View

The Roman Catholic doctrine of the "fall" is set forth straight-forwardly in the Douay Catechism, from which I quote:

> Q. How did we lose original justice?
>
> A. By Adam's disobedience to God in eating the forbidden fruit.
>
> Q. How do you prove that?
>
> A. Out of Romans 5:12: "By one man sin entered into the world, and by sin death; and so unto all men death did pass, in whom all have sinned."
>
> Q. Had man ever died, if he had never sinned?
>
> A. He would not, but would live in a state of justice and at length would be translated alive to the fellowship of the angels.[20]

Theological Students and Bible Classes (Philadelphia: Presbyterian Board of Publication, 1869), 147—*Ed.*>

17. <Westminster Confession, chap. 6, sect. 1—*Ed.*>

18. <Ms III* "was something rather that is imbedded"—*Ed.*>

19. <Ms III* "and none would have been provided"—*Ed.*>

20. Douay Catechism, 13.

Again, Joseph Faà di Bruno, D.D., says:

> The Catholic Church teaches that Adam by his sin [has] not only caused harm to himself, but to the whole human race; that by it he lost the supernatural justice and holiness, which he received gratuitously from God, and lost it, not only for himself, but also for all of us; and that he, having stained himself with the sin of disobedience, has transmitted not only death and other bodily pains and infirmities to the whole human race, but also sin, which is the death of the soul.[21]

And again:

> Unhappily, Adam, by his sin of disobedience, which was also a sin of pride, disbelief, and ambition, forfeited, or more properly speaking, rejected that original justice; and we, as members of the human family, of which he was the head, are also implicated in that guilt of self-spoliation, or rejection and deprivation of those supernatural gifts; not indeed on account of our having willed it with our personal will, but [by] having willed it with the will of our first parent, to whom we are linked by nature as members to their head.[22]

(b) The Protestant View

For the Protestant view I quote the following from Buck's *Theological Dictionary*, published in 1844, American edition. It was the Protestant encyclopedia on Protestant theology at the period of publication:

> In the fall of man we may observe: (1) the greatest infidelity, (2) prodigious pride, (3) horrid ingratitude, (4) visible contempt of God's majesty and justice, (5) unaccountable folly, (6) a cruelty to himself and to all his posterity. . . . That man is a fallen creature is evident, if we consider his misery as an inhabitant of the natural world; the disorders of the globe we inhabit, and the dreadful scourges with which it is visited; the deplorable and shocking circumstances of our birth; the painful and dangerous travail of women; our natural uncleanliness, helplessness, ignorance, and nakedness, the gross darkness in which we naturally are, both with respect to God and a future state; the general rebellion of the brute creation against us; the various poisons that lurk in the animal, vegetable, and mineral world, ready to destroy us; the heavy curse of toil and sweat to which we are liable; the innumerable calamities of life, and the pangs of death.
>
> God, it is said, made man upright (Eccl. 7:29), without any imperfection, corruption, or principle of corruption in his body or soul; with light in his understanding, holiness in his will, and purity in his affection. This constituted his original

---

21. Joseph Faà di Bruno, *Catholic Belief; or, A Short and Simple Exposition of Catholic Doctrine*, ed. Louis A. Lambert (New York: Benziger Brothers, 1884), 30. The work carries the approval of Cardinal Henry E. Manning, Archbishop of Westminster, England.

22. Ibid., 337-38.

> righteousness, which was universal, both with respect to the subject of it, the whole man, and the object of it, the whole law. Being thus in a state of holiness, he was necessarily in a state of happiness. He was a very glorious creature, the favorite of heaven, the lord of the world, possessing perfect tranquility in his own breast, and immortal. Yet he was not without law; for the law of nature, which was impressed on his heart, God superadded a positive law, not to eat of the forbidden fruit (Gen. 2:17) under the penalty of death—natural, spiritual, and eternal. Had he obeyed this law, he might have had reason to expect that he would not only have had the continuance of the natural and spiritual life, but have been transported to the upper paradise. . . . Man's righteousness, however, though universal, was not immutable, as the event has proved. How long he lived in a state of innocence cannot easily be ascertained, yet most suppose it was but a short time. The positive law which God gave him he broke, by eating the forbidden fruit. The consequence of this evil act was that man lost the chief good; his nature was corrupted; his powers depraved, his body subject to corruption, his soul exposed to misery, his posterity all involved in ruin, subject to eternal condemnation, and for ever incapable to restore themselves to the favor of God, to obey his commands perfectly and to satisfy his justice.[23]

From another Protestant source:

> The tree of <the> knowledge of good and evil revealed to those who ate its fruit secrets of which they had better have remained ignorant; for the purity of man's happiness consisted in doing and loving good without even knowing evil.[24]

(c) Presbyterian Modification of the Protestant View of the Fall

All this severity is relieved but by one division of Christendom of any considerable numbers and standing; and by that division the modification is but slight. This is by the Presbyterian Church in its Westminster Confession of Faith and an authoritative comment upon it by A. A. Hodge. The confession dealing with the "fall" concedes that "God was pleased, according to His wise and holy counsel, to permit it [the "fall"] having purposed to order it to his own glory."[25]

In the authoritative exposition of this chapter, it is set forth:

> That this sin[26] [the "fall"] was permissively embraced in the sovereign purpose of God. . . . Its purpose being God's general plan,[27] and one eminently wise and

23. Charles Buck, *A Theological Dictionary, Containing Definitions of All Religious Terms* (Philadelphia: Woodward, 1844), 182, 335-36.

24. William Smith, LL.D., *The Old Testament History from the Creation to the Return of the Jews from Captivity* (New York: Harper and Bros., 1899), 26.

25. Westminster Confession, chap. 6, sect. 1.

26. <Ms III "That this aim," but Hodge's text has "sin"—*Ed.*>

27. <Hodge's text has "It appears to be God's general plan"—*Ed.*>

> righteous, to introduce all the new-created subjects of moral government into a state of probation for a time, in which he makes their permanent character and destiny depend upon their own action.[28]

Still, this "sin" described as being "permissively embraced in the sovereign purpose" of the Deity and that God designed "to order it to his own glory," nowhere appears to be of any benefit to man. The only thing consulted in the theory of this creed seems to be the manifestation of the glory of God—a thing which represents God as a most selfish being—but just how the glory of God even[29] can be manifested by the "fall," which according to this creed results in the eternal damnation of the overwhelming majority of his "creatures," is not quite apparent.

Those who made this Westminster Confession, as also the large following which accept it, concede that their theory involves them at least in two difficulties which they confess it is impossible for them to meet. These are, respectively: first, "How could sinful desires or volitions originate in the soul of moral agents created holy like Adam and Eve?"; second, how can sin be permissively embraced in the eternal purpose of God, and not involve Him as responsible for the sin?

They say:

> If it be asked why God, who abhors sin, and who benevolently desires the excellence and happiness of His creatures, should sovereignly determine to permit such a fountain of pollution, degradation, and misery to be opened, we can only say, with profound reverence, "Even so, Father, for so it seemed good in Thy sight."[30]

Such <is> the theology of yesterday, and also of today in official creeds and their expositions, but rapidly these are becoming obsolete to the thoughtful, who are doubtful if this lauded life of innocence in Eden would have been as desirable as the theologians of past generations would have us think. Dr. John Fiske of Harvard, in his *Studies in Religion* challenges it squarely, and on the "Fall," as in the matter of the necessity of "opposite existences" in order to exist at all,[31] is in strict accord with both the theology and with the philosophy of Lehi, the Book of Mormon prophet.

VIEWS OF JOHN FISKE ON LIFE IN EDEN WITHOUT "THE FALL"

> What would have been the moral value or significance of a race of human beings ignorant of sin, and doing beneficent acts with no more consciousness or volition than the deftly contrived machine that picks up raw material at one end, and turns out some

28. <Hodge, *Commentary on the Confession*, 147-48—*Ed.*>

29. <Ms III[c] adds "even"—*Ed.*>

30. Hodge, *Commentary on the Confession*, 148, 151.

31. <Ms III "in order to existences at all"—*Ed.*>

> finished product at the other? Clearly, for strong and resolute men and women an Eden would be but a fool's paradise. How could anything fit to be called character have ever been produced there? But for tasting the forbidden fruit, in what respect could man have become a being of higher order than the beasts of the field? An interesting question is this, for it leads us to consider the genesis of the idea of moral evil in man. . . . We can at least begin to realize distinctly that unless our eyes had been opened at some time, so that we might come to know the good and the evil, we should never have been fashioned in God's image. We should have been denizens of a world of puppets, where neither morality nor religion could have found place or meaning.[32]

In this passage the Harvard philosopher unwittingly supports the sober doctrine of the Book of Mormon that partaking of the fruit of the tree of the knowledge of good and evil was an absolute necessity to a life worthwhile; for thereby was brought to pass the broken harmonies of the world out of which would be forged the experiences that would lead to virile manhood, high character, human freedom, morality, and loyalty to righteousness; and, therefore, the "fall" is not an incident to be deplored. Again, it was "the beginning of the rise of man."

ADAM FELL THAT MEN MIGHT BE

One item mentioned in the passages quoted from the Book of Mormon on the "fall" has not yet been mentioned in these comments, but it is worthy of a paragraph. The item is:

> And all things . . . must have remained forever and had no end. And they would have had no children. . . . Adam fell that men might be; and men are that they might have joy (2 Ne. 2:22-23, 25).

From this we learn that in some way, the "fall" seems to be associated with the having of children, and also we learn that the purpose of man's existence is that "he might have joy." That is God's good intent towards him. Tentatively I suggest the following as a possible solution of this phase of the "fall."

Paul in his first letter to Timothy, referring to the experience in Eden, said, "Adam was not deceived; but the woman being deceived was in the transgression" (1 Tim. 2:14).

Reference to the order of the happenings in Eden verifies the truth of this statement. Eve was persuaded to eat of the forbidden fruit, and undertook the persuasion of Adam to the same act of disobedience.[33] Eve was already in "the

32. John Fiske, "The Mystery of Evil," *Studies in Religion*, in *The Miscellaneous Writings of John Fiske, with Many Portraits of Illustrious Philosophers, Scientists, and Other Men of Note* (Boston and New York: Houghton, Mifflin and Co., 1902), 252, 266.

33. <Ms III* "Eve was persuaded to eat of the forbidden fruit, and undertook the

transgression," and stood in the shadow of the penalty of the law–banishment from Eden, union broken with God, separation from God, death! Under these circumstances what shall Adam do? Conjointly they had received this mission to "replenish the earth" (Gen. 1:28)–refill it with inhabitants. If this penalty falls upon Eve alone there will be separation of the pair, and the high purpose of their conjoint mission will be defeated. Again, what shall Adam do? Shall he draw about him the consciousness of his own innocence, and let his spouse bear the burdens of her violations of the law pertaining to the knowledge of good and evil? I refrain from what my comment would be could I think the progenitor of the human race guilty of such procedure. But no! Our Prince Michael did no such thing. Not deceived, but with eyes open and knowing all the consequences, he ate the forbidden fruit offered by a loving hand–one who so loved him that she would have him as "God, knowing good and evil" (Gen. 3:5). He resolved upon fulfilling the major part of his mission, which might not be fulfilled in separation from Eve. And hence "Adam fell that men might be, and men are that they might have joy" (2 Ne. 2:25). Despite the "fall"? Nay, rather because of it! He has partaken of the Tree of the Knowledge of Good and Evil, he has become as God that far; he shall yet[34] find his way to the Tree of Life!

---

persuasion of Adam to the forbidden fruit, and undertook the persuasion of Adam to the same act of disobedience," which illustrates the error of accidental doubling (skipping up a line in the earlier draft from the occurrence of "the" in the phrase "the same act of disobedience" back to the occurrence of "the" in the phrase "the forbidden fruit") so that the accidentally-doubled words are now deleted from this text–*Ed.*>

34. <Ms III[c] adds "yet"–*Ed.*>

CHAPTER XXXV

After the "Fall": The First Dispensation of the Gospel

SCRIPTURE READING LESSON

Analysis

I. Penalties:
   (a) Upon Adam;
   (b) Upon Eve;
   (c) Upon Lucifer.

II. The "Decrees" Written in the Book of Experience.

III. The Veil of Forgetfulness.

IV. Adam's World under the "Fall."

V. The Two Deaths:
   (a) Spiritual Death;
   (b) Physical Death.

VI. The Mystery of Sacrifice.

VII. The First Revelation after the "Fall"—"The Morning Breaks!"

VIII. A Dispensation of the Gospel to Adam.

IX. Rejoicing:
   (a) Of Adam;
   (b) Of Eve.

X. The Earth Antiquity of the Gospel.

References

Gen. 3-4.

Moses 5-8.

2 Ne. 2:14-30, Mosiah 4:4-12, Alma 11:38-46; 42:1-31.

D&C 29, 84, *passim*.

Note: Any of the standard dictionaries of the Bible or commentaries can be consulted sometimes with profit on these subjects, although they may not be relied upon as sustaining the views of the text of this work, which is so largely influenced by the "new knowledge" brought to light by the prophet of the New Dispensation, Joseph Smith.

CHAPTER XXXV

After the "Fall": The First Dispensation of the Gospel

The "fall" has become reality. The judgments have been pronounced. Adam, Eve, and Lucifer know their earth-fate. Broken union with God for both man and woman; banishment from Eden—guarded away from the Tree of Life. No access to it—yet. It must have been a comfort to the stricken pair to know of its existence in the midst of God's garden—a ray of hope, which would linger in blurred memories of Eden. Cherubim and gleaming sword now barred "the way to it"; but would it always be so?

PENALTIES

(b) Upon Adam

For Adam as a result of his special part in the changed conditions through partaking of the fruit of the Tree of Knowledge:

> Cursed is the ground for your sake; in sorrow shalt thou eat of it all the days of thy life. Thorns also and thistles shall it bring forth unto thee; . . . by the sweat of thy face shalt thou eat bread, till thou return to the ground; . . . for dust thou art, and to dust shalt thou return [physical death] (Gen. 3:17-19).

(b) Upon Eve

To the woman:

> I will greatly multiply thy sorrow and thy conception: in sorrow thou shalt bring forth children, and thy desire shall be to thy husband and he shall rule over thee (Gen. 3:16).

Let it be remembered that these were but announced consequences of the "fall," resulting from the changed conditions following the new order brought about by it, not vindictive cruelties invented from the anger of God. This, parenthetically, now to return.

(c) Upon Lucifer

To Lucifer (symboled by the serpent), the Lord God said:

> Because thou hast done this thing [his part in the drama of early days in Eden and with evil intent towards man, and malice towards God], thou art cursed above all cattle, and above every beast of the field: upon thy belly shalt thou go, and dust shalt thou eat all the days of thy life: and I will put enmity between thee and the woman, and between thy seed and her seed; it [the woman's seed] shall bruise thy head, and thou shalt bruise his heel (Gen. 3:14-15).

Victory shall be with the seed of the woman; for, mark you, while Lucifer shall have power to bruise his (the woman's seed) heel; he (the woman's seed)[1] shall have power to bruise Lucifer's head—wound him in a vital part.[2]

THE "DECREES" WRITTEN IN THE BOOK OF EXPERIENCE

It is worthy of remark that these decrees forecasting what should befall man and woman are as truly written in human experience as well as in the book of Genesis. And as for Lucifer, the sign and symbol and personification of evil, and in rebellion against God—who so despised, dreaded, feared, hated, as he? Well symbolized in the serpent—cold, sinuous, clammy, noiseless in approach, fascinating, cunning, strong to crush in coils, deadly to strike with fang and poison with tooth, and merciless withal! And dreaded and repulsive above all animals living, his symbol—the serpent.[3] And as the symbol is, so the spirit of incarnate evil is—Lucifer! Of which "serpent" is the fitting sign.

THE VEIL OF FORGETFULNESS

So man went forth from Eden bowed by the weight of sorrow, to his life and toil and death. His "vision splendid" not yet risen, and as it was later said of a more glorious "Adam," "in his humiliation, his judgment [knowledge on which judgment is based] was taken from him" (Acts 8:33), also may we say of this our first Adam—and more abundantly—"in his humiliation his judgment was taken from him"—a veil of forgetfulness cast over him, shutting out most memories of the creation days on this earth, and of the former home and friends and associates of the home-world, where he had come to translation development to prepare him for this earth-dispensation.[4] He perhaps remembered some little of the glory and

---

1. <Ms III^{c} adds "(the woman's seed)"—*Ed.*>

2. <Ms III* "wound him in a vital part—bruise his head!"—*Ed.*>

3. <Ms III^{c} adds "his symbol—the serpent"—*Ed.*>

4. <The review committee again objected to Roberts's use of the term "translation" in reference to Adam: "The question of 'translation' comes in here, and is questioned as in <chapter> 32" ("Doctrinal Points Questioned by the Committee Which Read the Manuscript of Elder B. H. Roberts, Entitled The Truth, The Way, The Life," attached to

splendor of the Lord God. Some recollection of the "Tree of Life" in the midst of the garden—did the memory carry with it a gleam of hope? Some remembrance, too, may have survived from that half-veiled promise that the seed of the woman should bruise the serpent's head. Perhaps a memory of the Lord God's kindness survived, seen in the gracious act of God making and giving to Adam and his wife coats of skin to "clothe them," better covering than the fig-leaved aprons they had made to hide their nakedness in the first confusion following their disobedience. This was the parting act at the portals of Eden when they were driven forth. They would likely remember that and cherish it. Surely it portended good will. It was an act of mercy.

ADAM'S WORLD UNDER THE FALL

But Adam had come into no mere make-believe world, where there was to be no real hardships, only mock sorrows and sins that did not hurt, and that would have no lasting effects; where punishments would be light and all would be well in the end. Surely the Lord God had not framed such a thing as this for the earth-planned life of man! Charge not such folly to the Lord Omniscient, and the Lord Omnipotent!

Adam and Eve and all their posterity, numerous as the stars of heaven, or as the sand upon the seashore, were to learn that earth-life was to be tremendously real; and in it would be real losses. There would be sorrows heart-breaking; suffering both mental and physical; severe tests of painful endurance to the point of blood-sweat and terror; disappointments to be endured that would stretch the heart strings to the point of breaking; death universal, and cruel, and pitiless, without remorse, without respect of persons, falling upon the young as upon the aged, upon the innocent as upon the sinful; striking quite recklessly, sinking some by slow and painful decay, cutting others off with the flash of lightening or the tempest's fierceness, or the earthquake's horror; by slow famine, or the shock of red battle—by any and all means by which life can be snuffed out or crushed out—and so permanently! This <is> a world where hope pales, faith falters, love weeps! Things are so obscure, so uncertain, so apparently meaningless; the light so dim and far away, the mists so recurrent and dense—they shut out the pathway to the Tree of Life. Scarce need to guard it, one would think, by cherubim and flaming sword!

Such was Adam's world into which he was driven from his Eden. How long

---

Rudger Clawson, Letter to Heber J. Grant, [15 May 1930], in David J. Buerger Collection, Manuscript 622, Bx 10, Fd 8, Manuscripts Division, Marriott Library, University of Utah, Salt Lake City)—*Ed.*>

it lasted so no one knows. Long enough to teach him the lessons to be derived from the knowledge of good and evil, no doubt. He is said to have lived nine hundred and thirty years in this world of broken harmonies! Cain's, Lamech's and other wickedness appeared within his own days; his life doubtless approached sufficiently near the wickedness of Noah's times for him to see that the wickedness would be so great that "every imagination of the thought of his [man's] heart was only evil continually" (Gen. 6:5).

THE TWO DEATHS

Under the "fall" Adam was confronted by two phases of death: spiritual death and physical death. The first, a broken union with God; the second, the separation of the spirit from the body, and the passing of the body back to dust, whence it came. Both these deaths Adam realized in experience.

(a) The Spiritual Death

The first or spiritual death was experienced when Adam and his wife were driven from Eden, and shut out from the presence of God, the source of his spiritual life, the fountain that fed his spirit with love of the true, the good, and the beautiful. Separated from that source of spiritual life his spirit would languish into sluggish dullness and brutality; hope all but fled, faith strained to the breaking point, desire for righteousness fading–Adam wandering further and ever further from God! Let it but continue long enough and without renewal of conscious fellowship with the source of spiritual life, and there could be no doubt but that it would end in completely placing him beyond the power to repent, or desire for forgiveness–spiritual death.

The spiritual death consists of separation from God; and, with the banishment from Eden, is thus described in a modern revelation:

> It came to pass that the devil tempted Adam, and he partook of the forbidden fruit and transgressed the commandment, wherein he became subject to the will of the devil, because he yielded unto temptation. Wherefore, I, the Lord God, caused that he should be cast out from the Garden of Eden, from my presence, because of his transgression, wherein he became spiritually dead, which is the first death, even that same death which is the last death, which is spiritual, which shall be pronounced upon the wicked when I shall say, "Depart, ye cursed" (D&C 29:40-41).
>
> The last death, which is spiritual, . . . "Depart, ye cursed!" (D&C 29:41).
>
> Then will I confess unto them, "I never knew you; depart from me, ye that work iniquity" (cf. Matt. 7:23).
>
> Then shall he say also unto those on his left hand, "Depart from me, ye cursed, into everlasting fire, prepared for the devil and his angels" (Matt. 25:41).

In each case separation from God; and in each case[5] spiritual death; banished "into outer darkness, where shall be weeping and gnashing of teeth" (Matt. 25:30).[6]

(b) Physical Death

The dreadful reality and mystery of physical death came into man's experience first through a greater calamity than death itself—through a murder. By this the first pair were shocked into a realization of the sentence passed upon them while yet in Eden, upon their posterity—upon the race—as well as upon themselves, and of this they had stern evidence in the death of their second son, Abel,[7] murdered by his brother Cain. It must have been mysterious and doubly painful, this first death. First, because inflicted by a brother's hand; second, because falling upon one least deserving of it; one strong, manly, gentle withal, a keeper of sheep—righteous, for he is so alluded to in the scriptures in many places (Heb. 11:4; also 1 Jn. 3:12), and according to the story in Genesis, he and his offering were acceptable to God, while Cain and his offering was rejected. Why should thus fall the righteous—the innocent—this first recorded[8] instance of death? But here it was, this physical death, the very palpable evidence of it, thrown into the trembling arms of Adam and Eve[9]—a strange silence and coldness!

THE MYSTERY OF SACRIFICES

Sometime before the death of Abel, something significant happened, but one gets only slight knowledge of it in Genesis, and nothing directly. Nothing may be learned from Genesis on the origin of sacrifices, either of first fruits or animal, that is to say, blood sacrifices.[10] They are simply referred to as an established thing with

---

5. <Ms III^{c} adds "separation from God; and in each case"—*Ed.*>

6. <In Ms III Roberts cites "Matthew 13:49-50," but the quotation is closer to Matt. 8:12 and Matt. 25:30—*Ed.*>

7. <The review committee objected to Roberts's referring to Abel as Adam's "second son": "We question this in the light of the writings of Moses. Adam may have had many sons and daughters before Cain was born, so it appears" ("Doctrinal Points Questioned by the Committee," in Buerger)—*Ed.*>

8. <Ms III^{c} adds "recorded"—*Ed.*>

9. <Ms III^{c} adds "of Adam and Eve"—*Ed.*>

10. "In tracing the history of sacrifice, from its first beginning to its perfect development in the Mosaic ritual, we are at once met by the long-disputed question, as to the origin of sacrifice; whether it arose from a natural instinct of man, sanctioned and guided by God, or whether it was the subject of some distinct primeval revelation. . . . The great difficulty in the theory which refers it to a distinct command of God, is the total silence of Holy Scriptures—a silence the more remarkable, when contrasted with the distinct reference made in Gen. 2, to the origin of the Sabbath. Sacrifice, when first mentioned, in the case of Cain

the first sons of Adam: "In the process of time"—"at the end of days" is the marginal rendering of the text, as if it were at the end of some fixed period of days, that the time of sacrifice recurred, and so at the end of that recurring period:[11]

> It came to pass that Cain brought of the fruit of the ground an offering unto the Lord. And Abel, he also brought[12] of the firstlings of his flock, and of the fat thereof. And the Lord had respect unto Abel and to his offering. But unto Cain and to his offering he had not respect. And Cain was very wroth, and his countenance fell (Gen. 4:3-5).

Such <is> the first mention of the offering of sacrifice in Genesis. What its origin or purpose or significance we may not know from this introduction to it.[13] Also, the account is silent as to why the offering of the lamb by Abel—a blood sacrifice—was acceptable to the Lord God; and why the fruit offering by Cain was not acceptable. But while Genesis is strangely silent on this subject the fragment of the writings of Moses, brought to light by the prophet of the New Dispensation, supplies the much-needed information.

THE FIRST REVELATION AFTER "THE FALL": "THE MORNING BREAKS!"

This revealed fragment of the writings of Moses[14] makes it known that after the banishment from Eden, Adam and Eve amidst their toil and labors in cultivating the earth and subduing the animal kingdom to their dominion, they begot both sons and daughters:

> And they began to multiply and replenish the earth. And from that time forth the

---

and Abel, is referred to as a thing of course; it is said to have been 'brought' by men; there is no hint of any command given by God. This consideration, the strength of which no ingenuity has been able to impair, although it does not actually disprove the formal revelation of sacrifice, yet at least forbids the assertion of it, as of a positive and important doctrine" (Alfred Barry, "Sacrifice," in Horatio B. Hackett and Ezra Abbot, eds., *Dr. William Smith's Dictionary of the Bible, Comprising Its Antiquities, Biography, Geography, and Natural History* [Boston: Houghton, Mifflin and Co., 1894], 4:2770-71).

11. <The review committee said: "There is a question as to the time the law of sacrifice was given, whether it was in or out of the Garden" ("Doctrinal Points Questioned by the Committee," in Buerger)—*Ed.*>

12. <Ms III[c] adds "sacrifice, but" to produce the wording "he also brought sacrifice, but of the firstlings"; however, these two added words were later deleted (probably when it was realized that the text was part of a scriptural quotation)—*Ed.*>

13. <Ms III[*] "from this one introduction to it"—*Ed.*>

14. <Ms III[*] "of the writing of Moses"—*Ed.*>

> sons and daughters of Adam began to divide two and two in the land, and to till the land, and to tend flocks, and they also begat sons and daughters (Moses 5:2-3).

Then it would appear that, moved by their recollections of the Lord God in Eden, both Adam and his wife Eve "called upon the name of the Lord" (and apparently for the first time since being driven from Eden) and:[15]

> They heard the voice of the Lord from the way toward the Garden of Eden, speaking unto them, (and they saw Him not, for they were shut out from His presence). And He gave unto them commandments, that they should worship the Lord their God, and should offer the firstlings of their flocks, for an offering unto the Lord. And Adam was obedient unto the commandments of the Lord (Moses 5:4-5).

Observe, however, in all this there is no explanation as to "why" the sacrifice should be offered; but its kind was designated. It was to be of the firstlings of the flocks—a blood sacrifice. Perhaps that was the reason Cain's offering was not acceptable to the Lord God. He brought that for an offering which the Lord God had not appointed. He apparently set aside that which God had appointed and substituted something of his own devising, and insulted the majesty of God therewith. A fruit offering did not symbolize the sacrifice to be offered up finally by the Christ.[16]

COMMUNICATION WITH GOD ESTABLISHED—REVELATION

But what a joy for Adam, this renewal of contact with the Lord God must have been! God's silence was broken: "From the way toward the Garden of Eden" they had heard the voice of the Lord speaking to them. He had given a commandment, no matter what. The important thing was that communication with God had been resumed. The darkness in which Adam and Eve had lived, relieved only by fragment recollections,[17] was breaking up and shadows were fleeing. Of course, they will obey the commandment, nor even ask the reason why. Blind obedience this? Nonsense! Intelligent obedience, under the circumstances; the unquestioning obedience was but natural obedience—the obedience which sprung from their joy—joyful obedience which forgot to ask the reasons why from the haste to obey.

---

15. <Ms III* "and O, Joy!"—*Ed.*>

16. <Ms III^c adds "A fruit offering did not symbolize the sacrifice to be offered up finally by the Christ"—*Ed.*>

17. <Ms III* "relieved only by fragment recollection"—*Ed.*>

A DISPENSATION OF THE GOSPEL TO ADAM[18]

Then:

> After many days an angel of the Lord appeared unto Adam, saying, "Why dost thou offer sacrifices unto the Lord?" And Adam said unto him, "I know not, save the Lord commanded me." And then the angel spake, saying, "This thing is a similitude of the sacrifice of the Only Begotten of the Father, which is full of grace and truth. Wherefore, thou shalt do all that thou doest in the name of the Son, and thou shalt repent and call upon God in the name of the Son forevermore." And in that day the Holy Ghost fell upon Adam, which beareth record of the Father and the Son, saying, "I am the Only Begotten of the Father from the beginning, henceforth and forever, that as thou hast fallen thou mayest be redeemed, and all mankind, even as many as will" (Moses 5:6-9).

REJOICING

(a) Of Adam

What a sermon of enlightenment is here! What a gospel revealed! No wonder that the record quoted goes on to say:

> And in that day Adam blessed God and was filled, and began to prophesy concerning all the families of the earth, saying, "Blessed be the name of God, for because of my transgression my eyes are opened, and in this life I shall have joy, and again, in the flesh I shall see God" (Moses 5:10).

(b) Of Eve

And Eve, too, sent forth her paean of praise:

> And Eve, his wife, heard all these things and was glad, saying, "Were it not for our transgression, we never should have had seed, and never should have known good and evil, and the joy of our redemption, and the eternal life which God giveth unto all the obedient." And Adam and Eve blessed the name of God, and they made all things known unto their sons and their daughters (Moses 5:11-12).

This original pair of the earth's inhabitants in their joy were breaking into the harmonies that had prevailed in the heavens when God "laid the foundations of the earth. . . . When the morning stars sang together, and all the sons of God shouted for joy" (Job 38:4, 7) at the prospects opening before them for an earth-planned life. They would now live in hope of that "eternal life, which God that cannot lie promised before the world began" (Titus 1:2). A dispensation of

---

18. <Ms III^c adds "To Adam"—*Ed.*>

the gospel had been imparted to them, and they delivered knowledge of it unto their posterity.

THE EARTH ANTIQUITY OF THE GOSPEL

Quite contrary to the general belief of Christendom, now and of old, knowledge was had of the gospel from the earliest ages—from Adam. Our enlightening fragment from the writings of Moses, brought to light by modern revelation, closes the fifth chapter I have been quoting with this declaration:

> Thus the gospel began to be preached, from the beginning, being declared by holy angels sent forth from the presence of God, and by His own voice, and by the gift of the Holy Ghost. And thus all things were confirmed unto Adam, by an holy ordinance, and the gospel preached, and a decree sent forth, that it should be in the world, until the end thereof; and thus it was (Moses 5:58-59).

CHAPTER XXXVI

Further Development of the Gospel in the Adamic Dispensation

SCRIPTURE READING LESSON

Analysis

I. Exposition of the Gospel by Direct Word of God.

II. Adam's Baptism—Born of the Water and of the Spirit.

III. Adam Made an High Priest.

IV. Priesthood: God's Authority Given to Man.

V. The Last Days of Adam.

VI. Cain and His Descendants.

VII. Josephus on the People of Cain.

VIII. Cain and His Relationship to Lucifer.

IX. League and Covenant between Cain and Lucifer.

References

Moses 4-6.

D&C 84, 107, and elsewhere, *passim.*

Discourse by Joseph Smith on "Priesthood," *History of the Church of Jesus Christ of Latter-day Saints, Period I: History of Joseph Smith, the Prophet by Himself* (Salt Lake City: Deseret News, 1905), 3:385-92.

Flavius Josephus, *The Works of Flavius Josephus: Antiquities of the Jews,* trans. William Whiston (Baltimore: Armstrong and Berry, 1837), bk i, chaps. 1-3.

CHAPTER XXXVI

Further Development of the Gospel in the Adamic Dispensation

In addition to the knowledge concerning Adam and the hand-dealings of God with him and his posterity, learned from the Book of Moses,[1] and set forth in the preceding chapter, we have still further knowledge revealed concerning him from the same source. Full knowledge was given to Adam concerning the whole plan of salvation as it had been wrought out in the council of Divine Intelligences, when they contemplated the creation of the world and the mission to be given to the Christ as Redeemer; and doubtless the mission of Adam to the then-desolate world; and we are told in this revelation to Adam concerning these things that the Lord said by His own voice to him:

EXPOSITION OF THE GOSPEL BY DIRECT WORD OF GOD

> I am God; I made the world and men before they were in the flesh. . . . If thou wilt turn unto me and hearken unto my voice and believe, and repent of all thy transgressions and be baptized, even in water, in the name of mine Only Begotten Son, who is full of grace and truth, which is Jesus Christ, the only name which shall be given under heaven, whereby salvation shall come unto the children of men—ye shall receive the gift of the Holy Ghost, asking all things in his name and whatsoever ye shall ask, it shall be given you (Moses 6:51-52).

And the Lord further said unto him:

> Inasmuch as thy children are conceived in sin, even so when they begin to grow up, sin conceiveth in their hearts, and they taste the bitter that they may know to prize the good. And it is given unto them to know good from evil; wherefore, they are agents unto themselves, and I have given unto you another law and commandment. Wherefore, teach it unto your children, that all men, everywhere, must repent, or they can in nowise inherit the kingdom of God, for no unclean thing can dwell there or dwell in his presence; for, in the language of Adam, Man of Holiness is his name, and

1. <Ms III* "learned from our Mosaic fragment, the Book of Moses"—*Ed.*>

the name of his Only Begotten is the Son of Man, even Jesus Christ, a righteous judge, who shall come in the meridian of time. . . .

By reason of transgression cometh the fall, which fall bringeth death, and inasmuch as ye were born into the world by water, and blood, and the spirit, which I have made, and so became of dust a living soul, even so ye must be born again into the kingdom of heaven, of water, and of the Spirit, and be cleansed by blood, even the blood of mine Only Begotten; that ye might be sanctified from all sin, and enjoy the words of eternal life in this world, and eternal life in the world to come, even immortal glory; for by the water ye keep the commandment; by the Spirit ye are justified, and by the blood ye are sanctified. Therefore, it is given to abide in you; the record of heaven; the Comforter; the peaceable things of immortal glory; the truth of all things; that which quickeneth all things; which maketh alive all things; that which knoweth all things and hath all power, according to wisdom, mercy, truth, justice, and judgment. And now, behold, I say unto you: this is the plan of salvation unto all men, through the blood of mine Only Begotten, who shall come in the meridian of time (Moses 6:55-57, 59-62).

ADAM'S BAPTISM—BORN OF THE WATER AND OF THE SPIRIT[2]

And it came to pass, when the Lord had spoken with Adam, our father, that Adam cried unto the Lord, and he was caught away by the spirit of the Lord, and was carried down into the water, and was laid under the water, and was brought forth out of the water. And thus he was baptized, and the Spirit of God descended upon him, and thus he was born of the Spirit, and became quickened in the inner man. And he heard a voice out of heaven saying: "Thou art baptized with fire and with the Holy Ghost. This is the record of the Father and the Son from henceforth and forever; and thou art after the order of Him who was without beginning of days or end of years, from all eternity to all eternity. Behold, thou art one in me, a son of God; and thus may all become my sons" (Moses 6:64-68).

ADAM MADE AN HIGH PRIEST

Thou art after the order of Him who was without beginning of days or end of years, . . . thou art one in me, a Son of God (Moses 6:67-68).

From other sources of knowledge, through revelation, we have reason to believe that these words carry with them peculiar significance; namely, that Adam was made an High Priest of God, after the order of the Son of God. This was the same order of priesthood as that which later was held by Melchizedek (Gen. 14:18-20), of whom Paul said that he was king of righteousness, also king of peace; that he was "made like unto the Son of God, and abideth a priest continually" (Heb. 7:2-3).

---

2. <Ms III^{c} adds "Born of the Water and of the Spirit"—*Ed.*>

PRIESTHOOD–GOD'S AUTHORITY GIVEN TO MAN[3]

Priesthood, it may be well to remark here, is that power which God gives to men by which they become representatives of, or agents of, God; by reason of which they are authorized to act for God, that is to say, in His stead, in delivering the word of God unto men, preaching righteousness, and conveying to men from time to time such messages as God may have to send into the world. Also to administer in the ordinances pertaining to the salvation of men. This Priesthood[4] conferred upon Adam is after the order of that priesthood which the Son of God held.

Thus, early in the Adamic Dispensation the priesthood[5] after the order of the Son of God was conferred upon men, and was designed to be perpetuated among them that there might always be priests of the Most High God to minister in things pertaining to God, even as described by Paul:

> For every High Priest taken from among men is ordained for men in things pertaining to God, that he may offer both gifts and sacrifices for sins; . . . and no man taketh this honor unto himself, but he that is called of God (Heb. 5:1, 4).

Even as Adam, Noah, Melchizedek, Abraham, and as[6] many others were called.

This priesthood, we are assured by the prophet of the New Dispensation:

> Was first given to Adam; he obtained the first Presidency and held the keys of it from generation to generation. He obtained it in the creation. . . . He had dominion given him over every living creature. He is Michael, the Archangel, spoken of in the scriptures. . . . The Priesthood is an everlasting principle, and existed with God from eternity, and will to eternity, without beginning of days or end of years.[7] The keys have to be brought from heaven whenever the Gospel is sent [i.e., to the earth].[8]

---

3. <Ms III^c adds "Priesthood–God's Authority Given to Man"–*Ed.*>

4. <Ms III* "The degree of this Priesthood"–*Ed.*>

5. <Ms III* "in the Adamic dispensation this priesthood"–*Ed.*>

6. <Ms III^c adds "as"–*Ed.*>

7. This supplies the material for an explanation of Paul's somewhat mysterious saying when speaking of Melchizedek, he says: "Without father, without mother, without descent, . . . neither beginning of days nor end of life; but made like unto the Son of God; abideth a priest continually" (Heb. 7:3). But it was the priesthood which Melchizedek held that was without father or mother, without beginning of days or end of life, not the man Melchizedek.

8. Joseph Smith, "Discourse on Priesthood," *History of the Church of Jesus Christ of Latter-day Saints, Period I: History of Joseph Smith, the Prophet by Himself* (Salt Lake City: Deseret News, 1905), 3:385-86.

THE LAST DAYS OF ADAM[9]

The closing scene with reference to the ministry of Adam upon the earth is described in the following revelation to the Prophet of the New Dispensation:

> Three years previous to the death of Adam, he called Seth, Enos, Cainan, Mahalaleel, Jared, Enoch, and Methuselah, who were all high priests, with the residue of his posterity who were righteous, into the valley of Adam-ondi-Ahman, and there bestowed upon them his last blessing. And the Lord appeared unto them, and they rose up and blessed Adam, and called him Michael, the prince, the archangel. And the Lord administered comfort unto Adam, and said unto him, "I have set thee to be at the head; a multitude of nations shall come of thee, and thou art a prince over them forever." And Adam stood up in the midst of the congregation; and, notwithstanding he was bowed down with age, being full of the Holy Ghost, predicted whatsoever should befall his posterity unto the latest generation. These things were all written in the Book of Enoch,[10] and are to be testified of in due time (D&C 107:53-57).

CAIN AND HIS DESCENDANTS

Running parallel with these events, which make up the development of the dispensation of the gospel given to Adam, is the continued opposition to the way of righteousness, set up and perpetuated by Cain and his coadjutors. Cain's wickedness did not end with the murder of his brother Abel. By direct decree of God he was cursed as to the earth which had opened her mouth to receive his brother's blood from his hand. The earth would no more yield her strength to his tillage—a fugitive and a vagabond should he become. He complained that under this decree his punishment was greater than he could bear: also he feared that everyone that should find him would slay him. Whereupon, God set a mark upon him[11] and decreed that whosoever should slay Cain, vengeance should be taken

---

9. <Ms III[*] "Days of Adam's Life"—*Ed.*>

10. Jude makes reference also to this Book of Enoch wherein he says, after speaking of certain vicious characters and what would befall them: "And Enoch also, the seventh from Adam, prophesied of these, saying, Behold, the Lord cometh with ten thousands of His saints, to execute judgment upon all and to convince all that are ungodly among them of all their ungodly deeds which they have ungodly committed and of all their hard speeches which ungodly sinners have spoken against him" (Jude 1:14-15).

11. <Ms III[*] "a mark upon him (doubtless the mark of a black skin)"; notice that Roberts's identification of the mark as "a black skin" has been deleted in Ms III[c]. For the interpretation which connects Cain and his descendants with the present-day Black people, see Newell G. Bringhurst, *Saints, Slaves, and Blacks: The Changing Place of Black People within Mormonism* (Westport, CT: Greenwood Press, 1981), 10, 41-45, 124—*Ed.*>

upon him sevenfold (Gen. 4:9-15). He naturally would withdraw himself from the more righteous of the descendants of Adam, and Genesis recounts his living eastward from Eden, where he founded a city which he named for a son born to him—Enoch. And here the Genesis account of Cain ends, save that a descendant of Cain—Lamech—fifth in the direct line of descent, also became a murderer, killing most likely two men, for in his confession to his wives, he said: "I have slain a man to my wounding, and a young man to my hurt; if Cain shall be avenged seven fold, truly Lamech seventy and seven fold" (Gen. 4:23-24).[12]

While the account of Cain in Genesis is brief, the historian Josephus doubtless following Hebrew tradition gives a very much fuller account of his life and of the character of the people who followed him.

JOSEPHUS ON THE PEOPLE OF CAIN

> When Cain had travelled over many countries, he with his wife built a city named Nod, which is a place so called, and there he settled his abode; where also he had children. However, he did not accept of his punishment in order to amendment, but to increase his wickedness; for he only aimed to procure every thing that was for his own bodily pleasure, though it obliged him to be injurious to his neighbors. He augmented his household substance with much wealth, by rapine and violence; he excited his acquaintance to procure pleasure and spoils by robbery, and became a great leader of men into wicked courses. . . . He changed the world into cunning craftiness. . . . Even while Adam was alive, it came to pass that the posterity of Cain became exceeding wicked, every one successively dying, one after another, more wicked than the former. They were intolerable in war, and vehement in robberies: and if anyone were slow to murder people, yet was he bold in his profligate behavior, in acting unjustly, and doing injuries for gain.[13]

CAIN AND HIS RELATIONSHIP TO LUCIFER

All this is in harmony with the further knowledge we have of Cain in the Mosaic fragment familiar to us now as the Book of Moses. Here Cain is represented as loving "Satan more than God" (Moses 5:18), and this even before the murder of his brother. Could it be that Satan had suggested the offering of a sacrifice that God had not appointed, the offering of "first fruits of the ground" rather than the

12. <In suggesting that Lamech may have killed two men, Roberts misinterprets the Hebraic parallelism in the first two clauses. Here, "and" is the equivalent of "even"; that is, Lamech, like Cain, had committed murder. See Umberto Cassuto, *A Commentary on the Book of Genesis* (Jerusalem: The Magnes Press, Hebrew University, 1961), 1:241—*Ed.*>

13. Flavius Josephus, *The Works of Flavius Josephus: Antiquities of the Jews*, trans. William Whiston (Baltimore: Armstrong and Berry, 1837), bk i, chap. 2.

"firstlings of his flock"?[14] A fruit offering rather than a "blood offering"—such as would symbolize the offering to be made by the Son of God, who is called "the Lamb slain from the foundation of the world" (Rev. 13:8)? Nothing could be more insulting to the majesty of God than this, and nothing could be more gratifying to Lucifer than through Cain to offer such an insult to God—it would be mockery to his liking! A similar passage occurs in the Genesis account of the conversation between God and Cain in the matter of Cain's rejected sacrifice:

> And the Lord said unto Cain, "Why art thou wroth? And why is thy countenance fallen? If thou does well, shalt thou not be accepted? And if thou doest not well, sin [Sin, i.e., Satan] lieth at the door. And unto thee shall be his desire, and thou shalt rule over him" (Gen. 4:6-7).

This passage has given the commentators[15] much trouble, and many and various explanations have been suggested for it. Light from the Book of Moses,[16] however, makes complete understanding clear. The conversation on the matter of the rejected sacrifice is enlarged to read:

> "And if thou doest not well, sin [Sin] lieth at the door, and Satan desireth to have thee; and except thou shalt hearken unto my commandments, I will deliver thee up, and it shall be unto thee according to his desire, and thou shalt rule over him; for from this time forth thou shalt be the father of his lies; thou shalt be called Perdition; for thou wast also before the world. And it shall be said in time to come—that these abominations were had from Cain; for he rejected the greater counsel which was had from God; and this is a cursing which I will put upon thee, except thou repent." And Cain was wroth, and listened not any more to the voice of the Lord, neither to Abel, his brother, who walked in holiness before the Lord. And Adam and his wife mourned before the Lord, because of Cain and his brethren (Moses 5:23-27).

Something like this could well be supported from the text in Genesis:

> And if thou doest not well, sin lieth at the door. And unto thee shall be his desire, and thou shalt rule over him (Gen. 4:7).

If "Sin" be regarded as one of the many names of Satan, then the reading becomes simple. Then it would stand: If thou doest not well, Sin (Satan) lieth (or

---

14. <The review committee objected to Roberts's reference to Cain's sacrifice as not what God had appointed and his statement that it was not accepted because Cain offered first fruits: "It was not because he offered fruits, but because he hearkened unto Satan rather than unto God" ("Doctrinal Points Questioned by the Committee," in Buerger)—*Ed.*>

15. <Ms III* "commentator"—*Ed.*>

16. <Ms III* "from the Mosaic fragment, the Book of Moses," but Ms III^c only deletes "fragment"—*Ed.*>

standeth) at the door. And unto thee shall be his desire (he will hope to possess thee); and then—strangely enough—"Thou [Cain] shalt rule over him [Satan]." Cain shall rule over Satan!

LEAGUE AND COVENANT BETWEEN CAIN AND LUCIFER

Turning again to the Book of Moses[17] the account is given of the league and covenant of evil between Cain and Lucifer:

> And Satan said unto Cain: "Swear unto me by thy throat, and if thou tell it, thou shalt die; and swear thy brethren by their heads, and by the living God, that they tell it not; for if they tell it, they shall surely die; and this that thy father may not know it; and this day I will deliver thy brother Abel into thine hands." And Satan sware unto Cain that he would do according to his commands. And all these things were done in secret. And Cain said: "Truly I am Mahan, the master of this great secret, that I may murder and get gain." Wherefore, Cain was called Master Mahan, and he gloried in his wickedness (Moses 5:29-31).

All this is in character with both Lucifer and Cain, and especially in keeping with that account of Cain and his following given by both the Bible and Josephus, and in harmony with the development of that wickedness in the ante-diluvian world, which finally justified its destruction.

Of Cain and his place in the scheme of things we shall have occasion to speak in a future chapter. What is said here is merely to show how was launched that stream of evil in the world which ran counter to the plan of righteousness inaugurated by the introduction of the Way through the dispensation of the gospel given to Adam, the progenitor of the race.

Taking this chapter with the two immediately preceding it, chapter 33 on "The Problem of Evil"; and chapter 34 on "The Affair in Eden—The Fall of Man"; and now the preceding chapter and[18] this on events "After the Fall" and the first dispensation of the gospel as it was revealed to Adam[19]—all this covers the transition period from men as spirits existing before the beginning of earth-life, and the launching of the race into earth-life as the progeny of Adam and Eve. We may now consider the gospel—the Way—at the commencement of its earth career.

---

17. <Ms III* "again to our Mosaic fragment"—*Ed.*>

18. <Ms III[c] adds "the preceding chapter and"—*Ed.*>

19. <Roberts's wording indicates that originally chapters 35 and 36 were a single chapter on the Adamic Dispensation—*Ed.*>

CHAPTER XXXVII

The Gospel in the Patriarchal Ages

SCRIPTURE READING LESSON

Analysis

I. The Line of Righteous Patriarchs.
II. The Dispensation of Enoch.
III. Enoch and the City of "Zion."
IV. The Dispensation of Noah.
V. Cause of the Flood.
VI. The "Sons of God" and the "Daughters of Men."
VII. Earth-Life a Sphere of Rewards for Conduct in Previous States of Existence.
VIII. The Limitations of Certain Races.
IX. Progenitor of the Less Noble.
X. Descendants of Cain through the Flood.

References

Moses 5-8.

Abr. 1-3.

Gen. 4-10, *passim.*

D&C 76, *passim.* D&C 45:54 and context.

Observe Note in Reference Column, Lesson 35.

CHAPTER XXXVII

The Gospel in the Patriarchal Ages[1]

THE PATRIARCHS

This dispensation of the gospel opening with the experiences and revelations imparted to Adam, and the events proceeding from such introduction, was continued through a line of ten patriarchs down to and including Noah, in whose days came the flood. These patriarchs were in their order: Adam, Seth, Enos, Cainan, Mahalaleel, Jared, Enoch, Methuselah, Lamech, Noah. Lamech, the father of Noah, according to the <James> Ussher Bible[2] chronology, was fifty-six years of age when Adam died at nine hundred and thirty years of age. So that nine of these patriarchs were all living in the earth together. And according to the Book of Moses, "they were preachers of righteousness and spake and prophesied and called upon all men everywhere to repent, and faith was taught unto the children of men" (Moses 6:23). Also, in tracing this genealogy in the Book of Moses, it is run through from Enoch back to Adam, "who was the son of God, with whom God Himself conversed" (Moses 6:22).

DISPENSATION OF ENOCH

In tracing the dispensations from Adam, we will begin with the Patriarch Enoch, since Adam's life overlapped into the life of Enoch, Adam's Dispensation would be joined to that of Enoch's. Enoch is represented in the Mosaic fragment of revelation (Book of Moses) as both a prophet and a seer; for he beheld the spirits that God had created, and he beheld also the things which were not visible to the natural eye, and from thence forth came the saying abroad in the land, "A seer hath the Lord raised up unto his people" (Moses 6:36). In the course of his preaching Enoch recapitulates much that had been revealed unto Adam, also his vision extended into the future, even forward to the time when the purposes of God would culminate in the salvation of men and the complete redemption of the earth. The writer of the Book of Jude bears witness to some of this, for in describing

1. <Ms III[*] "THE PATRIARCHAL AND PROPHETIC AGES"–*Ed.*>
2. <Ms III[c] adds "Bible"–*Ed.*>

some of evil mind, who would follow in the way of Cain, <and> become "as wandering stars to whom is reserved the blackness of darkness forever," he says:

> Enoch, the seventh from Adam, prophesied of these, saying, "Behold, the Lord cometh with ten thousand of his saints, to execute judgment upon all and to convince all that are ungodly among them of all their ungodly deeds" (Jude 1:13-15).

All which has reference to the glorious coming of the Lord Jesus in the clouds of heaven and in great glory in the commencement of that righteous reign on earth that is testified of in the scriptures as "the millennium"—the thousand-year reign of righteousness.

ENOCH AND HIS CITY "ZION"[3]

Enoch made a special gathering together of the people, whom he converted to his doctrines and established them in a city, and they were called "the people of Zion," because they were of one heart, and one mind, and dwelt in righteousness; and there were no poor among them, also this "city" was called "the city of holiness, even Zion" (Moses 7:18-19). "And lo, Zion in process of time was taken up into heaven" (Moses 7:21), that is to say, it was translated, together with the inhabitants thereof, including Enoch. These translated persons, as we have before seen were preserved for special work and missions,[4] which the Lord had in mind.

THE DISPENSATION OF NOAH

Noah was the next prominent member of this patriarchal group. In his day came the flood, which cataclysm emptied the earth of its inhabitants, only Noah and his family being preserved to perpetuate inhabitants in the earth under the commandment of God. This commandment was given to him as it had previously been given to Adam—"multiply and replenish the earth" (Gen. 9:1). So that Noah may be regarded as a "second Adam," from whom a new "beginning" of things started. It should be remembered that with Noah in the post-diluvian world all the traditions received from Adam and succeeding patriarchs, and a knowledge of all the dispensations of the gospel were retained and taught to the new generations of men following the flood.

CAUSE OF THE FLOOD

Much speculation has been indulged in with reference to the cause of the

3. <Ms III[c] adds "Enoch And His City 'Zion'"—*Ed.*>
4. <Ms III[c] adds "and missions"—*Ed.*>

flood, which resulted in the destruction of the antique world, excepting Noah and his family. It is represented in Genesis (Authorized Version) that it was occasioned by the "utter wickedness of man in the earth," "and every imagination of the thoughts of his heart was only evil continually"; and so great was this wickedness and so universal, that "it repented the Lord that He had made man on the earth, and it grieved Him at His heart" (cf. Gen. 6:5-7).

This would lead one to believe that the great wickedness in Noah's period had quite surprised God, and was not present to his foreknowledge of things. It is certainly unthinkable that God would repent of having made man; as surely nothing had happened up to this time that God had not foreseen.[5] The rendering of the text in the Book of Moses is "and it repented Noah, and his heart was pained that the Lord had made man on the earth, and it grieved him at his heart" (Moses 8:25). This rendering is certainly more in conformity with reason than the rendering of the Authorized Version.

THE "SONS OF GOD" AND THE "DAUGHTERS OF MEN"[6]

It is also written in Genesis that:

> The sons of God saw the daughters of men, that they were fair, and they took them wives of all which they chose. And the Lord said, "My spirit shall not always strive with man, for that he also is flesh" (Gen. 6:2-3).

That is to say, perishable; and so He shortened the years of man's life; evidently to curtail wickedness.

> Also after that, when the sons of God came in unto the daughters of men, and they bear children to them, the same became mighty men which were of old, men of renown (Gen. 6:4).

Then follows the declaration of the race's universal wickedness, Noah's regret that God had made man, and the decree of God is entered for their destruction. These paragraphs—Genesis 6:1-7—have perplexed the commentators and a number of solutions for the difficulties they present have been discussed, among them that we have here a trace of the stories of unions between deities and the women of earth, which resulted in gigantic, monstrous, and cursed races. Others have suggested that the "sons of God" were evidently the angels, and that they had carnal[7] union with the women of earth. None of these suggested explanations,

---

5. <Ms III^{c} adds "as surely nothing had happened up to this time that God had not foreseen"—*Ed.*>

6. <Ms III^{c} adds "The 'Sons of God' And The 'Daughters of Men'"—*Ed.*>

7. <Ms III^{c} adds "carnal"—*Ed.*>

however, is the truth. Running parallel with the descendants of Adam—through Seth—in the earth was also the race of Cain, and they were known as the "sons of men," in contradistinction to the descendants of Adam, and the succeeding patriarchs of that line, who were called "the sons of God." The descendants of Adam were forbidden to intermarry with the descendants of Cain, the "sons of men"; and the violation of this commandment by which a mongrel race was being produced by the intermarriage of descendants of Cain and the "sons of God" was part of the wickedness which prepared ante-diluvian world for its destruction.

EARTH-LIFE A SPHERE OF REWARDS FOR CONDUCT IN PREVIOUS STATES OF EXISTENCE[8]

Reference to our chapter dealing with the "War in Heaven" (chapter 29) will recall the fact that Lucifer in that controversy drew away with him one-third of the hosts of heaven, and that they with him became the "fallen angels," and by their rebellion forfeited their right of participation in the earth-planned life of man. They kept not their first estate—their spirit-life estate. And of those who remained and were not cast out, there were doubtless among them a variety of degrees as to greatness of soul, nobility of character, and moral value. God Himself showed unto Abraham such distinctions among the intelligences that were to inhabit the earth.

> The Lord had shown unto me the intelligences that were organized before the world was; and among all these there were many of the noble and great ones. And God saw these souls that they were good; and He stood in the midst of them, and He said, "These I will make my rulers" (Abr. 3:22-23).

If there were such outstanding intelligences as these among those destined for habitancy of the earth, then by plain implication there were many who possessed the qualities of greatness, nobility, and of goodness in less varying degrees than these whom God declared He would make his "rulers." And doubtless this all but infinite variety of intelligence, greatness, and goodness would lead to a corresponding variety in faith and action in the "war in heaven," calling again for corresponding variety of capacity for service, as also[9] of rights and opportunities granted in earth-life as rewards for faith and demonstrated loyalty[10] in the spirit-life. Hence, the endless variety of opportunity and apparent privileges granted to some races, tribes, families, and individuals in earth process of events and changes making up the earth-life of man.

---

8. <Ms III^{c} adds "Earth-Life A Sphere of Rewards For Conduct in Previous States of Existence"—*Ed.*>

9. <Ms III^{c} adds "of capacity for service, as also"—*Ed.*>

10. <Ms III* "as rewards for capacity, faith, action, and demonstrated loyalty"—*Ed.*>

THE LIMITATIONS OF CERTAIN RACES[11]

One of these distinctions in the earth-life of man is to be observed in this marked difference between Cain and his descendants and the descendants of Adam through Seth, and the distinguished line of patriarchs to Noah: the "sons of men" and the "sons of God." The distinction rests primarily upon the difference in the intrinsic nature of the eternal, uncreated intelligences[12] themselves, who were begotten spirits;[13] and then what their faith and actions were as spirits[14] in the pre-existent spirit life.[15] Evidently there were some who so demonstrated their worthiness in that life—pre-earth-life—in[16] greatness, nobility, and goodness, that God could entrust them with His power to act for Him as His representatives and agents; and in this special way and sense become "Sons of God"[17] by holding appointed power from Him—His priesthood, which is God's authority in man.[18]

And now among the hosts of the spirit world destined for earth-life were many[19] who would be unworthy of the distinction[20] of holding this power from God—"the priesthood"—and yet had not so far transgressed as to have forfeited all right to an earth-life, albeit under limitations, one of which might well be the right to hold power from God, to represent God and act in His name. These the less "noble," and "great," and "good," whom God would not, and could not, in justice, make His rulers. Hence, their limitations in this respect in the earth-life.[21]

---

11. <Ms III^c adds "The Limitations of Certain Races"—*Ed.*>

12. <Ms III* "intrinsic nature or soul-value of the intelligences"—*Ed.*>

13. <Ms III* "who were begotten men"—*Ed.*>

14. <Ms III^c adds "as spirits"—*Ed.*>

15. <For a 1949 First Presidency statement explaining that the denial of the priesthood to the blacks was due to their conduct in the pre-existence, see "Authoritative Statements on the Status of Blacks," in Lester E. Bush, Jr., and Armand L. Mauss, eds., *Neither White nor Black: Mormon Scholars Confront the Race Issue in a Universal Church* (Midvale, UT: Signature Books, 1984), 221—*Ed.*>

16. <Ms III^c adds "life—pre-earth life—in"—*Ed.*>

17. <Ms III* "become his Sons"—*Ed.*>

18. <LDS theology has changed since Roberts wrote in the 1920s. Karl C. Sandberg, "Modes of Belief: David Whitmer, B. H. Roberts, Werner Heisenberg," *Sunstone* 12 (Sept. 1988): 14, says that "Roberts developed an elaborate scheme whereby those who were less valiant in a pre-existence, i.e., the blacks, would be denied access to the priesthood. This priesthood policy was supposedly written into the very structure of the cosmos, but the change of policy in 1978 unhinged this particular theological notion"—*Ed.*>

19. <Ms III* "destined for the world were doubtless many"—*Ed.*>

20. <Ms III* "unworthy of this distinction"—*Ed.*>

21. <For the Mormon folklore justifying denial of priesthood to blacks, see Armand L. Mauss, "Mormonism and Minorities," Ph.D. diss., University of California, Berkeley,

THE PROGENITOR OF THE LESS NOBLE[22]

Yet they are worthy, under such limitations as God's justice may provide, to participate in earth-life. Through what lineage shall they come? Obviously through those worthy only to be the progenitors of such classes as these less noble ones. Hence, Cain, Lamech, Ham—this <is> the line of progenitors whose progeny are worthy only to be called "the sons of men"; while those who God has decreed He would make His "rulers" come of a line of progenitors worthy to be accounted in a special sense the "sons of God." Hence, Cain, jealous, evil-minded, covetous, murderous, loving Satan more than God—perhaps closely and dangerously allied with Lucifer in that "War in Heaven"—became the earth progenitor of those least noble and valiant spirits who were permitted to come to earth, but under very serious and painful limitations, denial of right to the priesthood being among them; they are to be known merely as the "sons of men."[23]

It was doubtless to check this mingling of races between the descendants of Cain—"the sons of men"—and the race descending from the line of Seth to Noah—men of racial and character fitness to receive the priesthood—having right in this special way to be "sons of God," that the flood was sent to cut off a growing mongrel race, unsuited to the purpose of God.

THE DESCENDANTS OF CAIN PRESERVED THROUGH THE FLOOD

It will be of interest to note in what way provision was made to carry someone through the flood by whom fit ancestry could be provided for the less noble spirits of the spirit world. This was through Ham, the least noble of the sons of Noah. And now, after the flood, the numerical adjustment was so made that there would never be likelihood of the descendants of a forbidden race menacing the existence of the race competent to perpetuate those among them who could become, in the special way pointed out, the "sons of God."

1970, 131-33—*Ed.*>

22. <Ms III^{c} adds "The Progenitor of the Less Noble"—*Ed.*>

23. For these distinctions see and cf. D&C 76:50-60, where those who receive the priesthood "after the order of the Son of God"—the Melchizedek Priesthood—are declared to be "the sons of God." Moses 6:67-68 <gives> account of Adam's becoming a son of God (cf. D&C 84:6-7, 17; 107:39-53; Adam referred to with other patriarchs as "High Priests"). Also, Moses 8:13, where Noah and his sons are called "the sons of God," and the daughters of these "sons of God" are reproved for having sold themselves to "the sons of men." See also Moses 5:51-53, where descendants of Cain through Lamech are "the sons of men" and cursed of God—i.e., deservedly limited in opportunities granted to others. <Ms III^{c} adds "—i.e., deservedly limited in opportunities granted to others"—*Ed.*> See also Abraham 3.

Of the low character of Ham we have the evidence in the unfortunate circumstance of his father Noah's drunkenness after the flood, and Ham's exposure of both his father's weakness and his shamefulness to his father's nakedness,[24] but which the nobler sons of Noah, Shem, and Japheth, covered and[25] with becoming delicacy. And when the patriarch of the two worlds–ante-diluvian and post-diluvian–awoke from his drunken sleep, and learned what shame his youngest son had put upon him, he cursed the posterity of Ham through Ham's son, declaring an inferiority for him, saying:

> "Cursed be Canaan; a servant of servants shall he be unto his brethren." And he said, "Blessed be the Lord God[26] of Shem; and Canaan shall be his servant. God shall enlarge Japheth, and He shall dwell in the tents of Shem; and Canaan shall be his servant" (Gen. 9:25-27).

In addition to his low character exhibited in the shameful exposure of his father's plight during his intemperance, Ham had also married into the forbidden race of Cain. The name of his wife was "Egyptus,"[27] which interpreted means "forbidden." Evidence of the race whence she came–the forbidden race of Cain. And thus was the race of Cain perpetuated in the earth after the flood. The descendants of Ham were settled in Egypt by his daughter, also named "Egyptus," after her mother; and who named the land in which she settled her sons, Egypt,[28] either in honor of herself or of her mother. "And thus," says the authority I am following, "from Ham, sprang that race which preserved the curse in the land" (Abr. 1:24).

Our authority, however, speaks well of the eldest[29] son of Egyptus, daughter of Ham, who founded the first government in the land. This government was[30] patriarchal in form and character, "imitating" the order of the patriarchal forms of his forefathers, including Noah, who, we are informed, "blessed him with the

24. <Ms III "to his brother's nakedness"–*Ed.*>

25. <Ms III^{c} adds "and"–*Ed.*>

26. <Ms III* "And he blessed the Lord God"–*Ed.*>

27. <Walter L. Whipple, "An Analysis of Textual Changes in 'The Book of Abraham' and in the 'Writings of Joseph Smith, the Prophet' in the Pearl of Great Price," M.A. thesis, Brigham Young University, 1959, 22, shows that the two manuscripts he used had the reading of "Zeptah" for Abr. 1:23. The manuscript in the handwriting of Willard Richards shows the stages of change as "Geptah" to "Egeptah" to "Egeptus" to "Egyptus"–*Ed.*>

28. <Ms III^{c} adds "in" to make "she settled her sons in Egypt," but Ms III* is followed, since it explains the origin of the name "Egypt" for the land–*Ed.*>

29. <Ms III^{c} adds "eldest"–*Ed.*>

30. <Ms III^{c} adds "government was"–*Ed.*>

blessings of the earth, and with the blessings of wisdom, but cursed him as pertaining to the priesthood" (Abr. 1:26).

Enoch, the patriarch seventh from Adam and preeminently a seer, in the pre-vision God gave him of things to happen in generations future from his time, throws much light upon what would be the status of this Canaanitish race in the world.

The Lord said to this seer, "Look, and I will show unto thee the world for the space of many generations" (Moses 7:4). And among the things fore-visioned to him were the movements and some of the wars waged by the Canaanites:

> And the people of Canaan shall divide themselves in the land, and the land shall be barren and unfruitful, and none other people shall dwell there but the people of Canaan. For behold, the Lord shall curse the land with much heat, and the barrenness thereof shall go forth forever; and there was a blackness came upon all the children of Canaan, that they were despised among all people (Moses 7:7-8).[31]

And here we may leave that "forbidden race"—forbidden to intermarry with those races whence may arise those who are not cursed by denial of the priesthood to them, but from whose midst may arise those who in a special way may become the sons of God through receiving the priesthood—the power of God—by which they may be accounted sons of, or multiples of, God.

OTHER LIMITATIONS

Among other limitations to the descendants of Ham, and to some other races, might be named the tardy appearance of civilized enlightenment and knowledge of truth among them, because of their incapacity for, and their unworthiness of, these things; and so they live their earth-lives under necessary and deserved[32] limitations. And yet this present earth-life will and does hold high values for them, in that it affords them the necessary union of spirit and element essential to such "joy" as they may be capable of; and they shall be heirs, too, of salvation; for it is made known in our modern revelations that the inhabitants of the higher kingdoms of glory shall minister to the kingdoms of lower degrees of glory; and speaking of the angels who in the hereafter shall minister to those of "the telestial glory"—the very lowest of the kingdom<s>—whose inhabitants come not forth until "the last resurrection"—even these shall be "heirs of salva-

31. The land occupied by descendants of Cain was northern Africa, and the barren land referred to as cursed with excessive heat was, doubtless, the desert of Sahara.

32. <Ms III[c] adds the letters "ser" above the letters "cei" of Ms III[*] "deceived," thus intending the reading "deserved"—*Ed.*>

tion" (D&C 76:88). And of the heathen nations—"they that knew no law"—it is written:

> The heathen nations shall be redeemed, and they that knew no law shall have part in the first resurrection; and it shall be tolerable for them (D&C 45:54).

CHAPTER XXXVIII

The Post-Diluvian Dispensations

SCRIPTURE READING LESSON

Analysis

I. Melchizedek, Priest of the Most High God.
II. The "Call" of Abraham.
III. The Gospel Preached to Abraham.
IV. The Mosaic Dispensation.
V. The Priesthood under the Mosaic Dispensation.
VI. Vision of God under Moses.
VII. Melchizedek Priesthood Held by the Prophets of Israel.
VIII. Melchizedek–Shem?
IX. Note: Melchizedek–Shem–Elias Identical?

References

On Melchizedek, Priest of God: Gen. 14:18, 20; Ps. 110:4; Heb. 5:6-10; 6:20; 7:1.

Also, *The Jewish Encyclopedia: A Descriptive Record of the History, Religion, Literature, and Customs of the Jewish People from the Earliest Times to the Present Day*, 12 vols., ed. Isidore Singer (New York: Funk and Wagnalls Co., 1901), articles "Melchizedek" and "Abraham."

Also, other standard Bible commentaries and dictionaries, especially John Kitto, *A Cyclopædia of Biblical Literature*, 2 vols. (New York: Mark H. Newman, 1845), articles "Melchizedek" and "Abraham."

Flavius Josephus, *The Works of Flavius Josephus: Antiquities of the Jews*, trans. William Whiston (Baltimore: Armstrong and Berry, 1837), bk i, chap. 10.

D&C 84:1-28.

All the citations in the text and footnotes of this chapter and their context.

B. H. Roberts, *Seventy's Course in Theology, Second Year, Outline History of the Dispensations of the Gospel* (Salt Lake City: Skelton Publishing Co., 1908), lesson 17.

Author's notes end of this chapter.

CHAPTER XXXVIII
The Post-Diluvian Dispensations

MELCHIZEDEK, PRIEST OF THE MOST HIGH GOD

Noah after the flood lived three hundred and fifty years, being nine hundred and fifty years old when he died (Gen. 9:28-29).

Standing out in bold relief among the patriarchs of the post-diluvian period is Melchizedek, described in Genesis as the king of Salem, who met Abraham after his conquest of several of the petty kings in the land of Canaan. This Melchizedek was "Priest of the Most High God," and he brought forth bread and wine and administered it to Abraham, saying: "Blessed be Abram of the Most High God, possessor of heaven and earth, and blessed be the Most High God, which hath delivered thine enemies into thy hand" (Gen. 14:19-20). And Abraham gave Melchizedek tithes of all—that is, one-tenth of the spoils taken from the kings he had conquered.

Paul in the Book of Hebrews makes reference to this high priest of the early post-diluvian age as being a priest-type after the order of the Son of God, saying:

> Christ glorified not himself to be made an high priest, but He [God] . . . said unto him, "Thou art my Son, this day have I begotten thee; . . . thou art a priest for ever after the order of Melchizedek; . . . called of God an high priest after the order of Melchizedek" (Heb. 5:5-6, 10).

It must ever be that the Christ, being the Word that was in the beginning with God, and that was God, and afterwards "was made flesh" and dwelt among men (John 1:1-14) must have precedence over Melchizedek; and the question then arises, how comes it that the Christ is spoken of as being a "priest forever after the order of Melchizedek"? The mystery disappears when we come to the knowledge that it is Melchizedek who is a high priest after the order of the Son of God, rather than the Son of God an high priest after the order of Melchizedek; and this is learned from a revelation to the prophet of the New Dispensation in the following language:

> There are, in the church, two priesthoods, namely, the Melchizedek and Aaronic. . . . Why the first is called the Melchizedek Priesthood is because Melchizedek was such a great high priest. Before his day it was called the Holy Priesthood after the order of the Son of God. But out of respect or reverence to the name of the Supreme Being, to

> avoid the too frequent repetition of his name, they, the church, in ancient days called that priesthood after Melchizedek, or the Melchizedek Priesthood (D&C 107:1-4).

This changing of the name of the priesthood, however, from "the Holy Priesthood after the Order of the Son of God" (who was to come in the meridian of time) to the "Melchizedek Priesthood" did not change the nature of the priesthood itself, and it was still after the change of the name "the Holy Priesthood after the Order of the Son of God"; and the Son of God, of course, takes precedence over Melchizedek, and it is Melchizedek that derives his priesthood from the Son of God, rather than the Son of God deriving aught from Melchizedek. Melchizedek was merely a prototype of that high priest that was to be developed in the Christ, the Son of God, when he should appear in the earth in the meridian of time.

Much speculation has been indulged in regard to Melchizedek–who was he?[1] Little doubt can exist, however, but that he was Shem, the son of Noah,[2] and therefore in the direct line of both the post-diluvian patriarch Noah, and through him in the line of ante-diluvian patriarchs back to Adam. It is most appropriate, therefore, that Abraham, who was to become the great head of the Hebrew race, should receive blessing from him, and take his place in the line of the patriarchs from Adam to his own day, and then pass on that same connection through his descendants Isaac and Jacob, whence sprang the Hebrew race and nation, destined to become God's witness, par-excellent, in the earth.

THE "CALL" OF ABRAHAM

This connection established between the patriarch Shem (Melchizedek) and Abraham, the head of the Hebrew race, introduces the Abrahamic Dispensation of things in the earth, for in addition to this connection with the patriarch Shem, God also directly revealed Himself to Abraham and called him to the special work unto which he had been appointed, even in the spirit world before his earth-life began (Abr. 3:23). The genealogy of Abraham and some of his history, is given in the eleventh chapter of Genesis and from it we learn that he originally dwelt in the land of Ur of the Chaldees and here the Lord spake unto Abraham commanding him to leave that country and his kindred and go into a land that the Lord had appointed unto him–the land of Canaan. The Lord said:

> And I will make of thee a great nation, and I will bless thee and make thy name great; and thou shalt be a blessing; and I will bless them that bless thee, and curse him that curseth thee, and in thee shall all families of the earth be blessed (Gen. 12:2-3).

---

1. <Ms III* "in regard to who Melchizedek was"–*Ed.*>

2. See note at close of chapter. <Roberts is referring to the last two sections of this chapter–*Ed.*>

This is generally referred to in theological writings as the "Call of Abraham."

A famine diverted him from immediately possessing Canaan and hence came Abraham's sojourn in Egypt, from which he afterwards returned and settled in Canaan, where came his contact with Shem (Melchizedek). God's reason for calling Abraham is thus given:

> I know him, that he will command his children and his household after him, and they shall keep the way of the Lord, to do justice and judgment; that the Lord may bring upon Abraham that which He hath spoken of him (Gen. 18:19).

That is, make of him the head of a people and nation and that all the nations of the earth shall be blessed in him and in his seed. Also, the patriarch received the further compliment of being called "the friend of God" (cf. 2 Chr. 20:7), and "I have chosen the seed of Abraham, my friend" (Isa. 41:8).

"THE GOSPEL" PREACHED TO ABRAHAM[3]

We learn from another scripture that a dispensation of the gospel was given to Abraham. This is the passage:

> The scripture, foreseeing that God would justify the heathen through faith, preached before the gospel unto Abraham, saying, "In thee shall all nations be blessed" (Gal. 3:8).

Let it be remembered that there is but one gospel, but one plan for man's salvation, one covenant which God made of eternal life, and though an angel should preach any other than this one gospel, he is under apostolic anathema (Gal. 1:6-9; Titus 1:2). Paul himself asks the question, "Wherefore then serveth the law?" (Gal. 3:19)–having reference to the law of Moses, given, of course, subsequently to this gospel, which had been preached unto Abraham: and which was "the law of carnal commandments" (Heb. 7:16; 9:10), under which Israel lived, and of which we shall say something more later–but the question again–"wherefore then serveth the law," if the gospel was preached to Abraham? The answer of Paul to that question is:

> It was added because of transgressions, till the seed [the Christ] should come in whom the promise was made; and it was ordained by angels in the hands of a mediator. . . . Wherefore, the law [again referring to the law of Moses] was our schoolmaster to bring us unto Christ, that we might be justified by faith. But after that faith is come, we are no longer under a schoolmaster. For ye are all the children of God, by faith in Christ Jesus[4] (Gal. 3:19, 24-26).

---

3. <Ms III[c] adds "'The Gospel' Preached to Abraham"–*Ed.*>

4. <Ms III[*] "faith in Jesus Christ"–*Ed.*>

Which simply means that the gospel was preached unto Abraham, but later, when his posterity had developed into a people who proved themselves unfaithful and inadequate to live in harmony with the gospel as it had been revealed to Abraham (and later to Moses), because of transgression, an inferior law, called in the scriptures "the law of carnal commandments," a law of symbols and ceremonies for their training, was given to them in place of the gospel of faith and grace and the higher spiritual life and union with God. But the gospel as known from of old was given to Abraham and also to Moses[5] before the law, known as the law of Moses, was given.

MOSAIC DISPENSATION

This course of events brings us now to Moses, the next great prophet following after the patriarchal period, which seems to have closed with Abraham, and Isaac, and Jacob, and Joseph, son of Jacob. And we now enter the prophetic period in the development of God's purpose in the earth.

To Moses and to Israel under Moses the gospel was first presented before a coming in of the law of Moses. This is evident from the scriptures. It is written by Paul:

> Moreover, brethren, I would not that ye should be ignorant, how that all our fathers were under the cloud, and all passed through the sea; and were all baptized unto Moses in the cloud and in the sea; and did all eat the same spiritual meat; and did all drink the same spiritual drink; for they drank of that spiritual Rock that followed them: and that Rock was Christ (1 Cor. 10:1-4).

It is written, and here let me say, in quoting this <following> passage from Hebrews, I take no note of the fact, except for this remark, that the passage is made up of the closing verses of chapter three and the opening verses of chapter four. It must be remembered that the inspired writers of the scriptures are not responsible for these divisions of their writings into chapters and verses, and sometimes passages of scripture that relate to one thing and ought not to be divided by so much as a period, are nevertheless sometimes torn apart by being placed in separate chapters.[6] The passage I am about to quote is an instance of this kind. Paul speaking of Israel, part of whom provoked God by their transgressions, as they were led out of Egypt by Moses, says:

---

5. <Ms III[c] adds "and also to Moses"—*Ed.*>

6. <Stephen Langton divided the Latin Vulgate into chapters in the thirteenth century, while versification first appeared in the 1557 edition of the Greek New Testament by Robert Stephanus—*Ed.*>

> But with whom was He grieved forty years? Was it not with them that had sinned, whose carcasses fell in the wilderness? And to whom sware He that they should not enter into His rest, but to them that believed not? So we see that they could not enter in because of unbelief. Let us therefore fear, lest a promise being left us of entering into His rest, any of you should seem to come short of it. For unto us was the gospel preached, as well as unto them [ancient Israel under Moses mentioned above], but the word preached did not profit them, not being mixed with faith in them that heard it (Heb. 3:17-19; 4:1-2).

And so the gospel was preached not only to Abraham, but also to Israel under Moses, before the law was given; but not being equal to living in harmony with its excellence, and because of their transgression, God gave them the law of carnal commandments. The fact that the gospel was first offered to Israel through Moses established by the above scriptures, makes clear also the knowledge that Moses evidently had knowledge of the Christ to come in the future, for it is written of him:

> By faith Moses, when he was come to years, refused to be called the son of Pharaoh's daughter; choosing rather to suffer affliction with the people of God, than to enjoy the pleasure<s> of sin for a season; esteeming the reproach of Christ greater riches than the treasures of Egypt; for he had respect unto the recompense of the reward (Heb. 11:24-26).

THE PRIESTHOOD UNDER THE MOSAIC DISPENSATION

Again, the fragment which we call the Book of Moses, revealed to Joseph Smith, contains the evidence that the gospel was made known unto Moses from the council in heaven to the full development of the gospel as it had been revealed unto Adam after the "fall," and to Enoch, and also to Noah. Also, Moses organized the priesthood after the order of the Son of God, the same that is known as the Melchizedek Priesthood or priesthood after the order of Melchizedek. And in our modern revelation to the Prophet of the New Dispensation it is made known that Moses received this priesthood under the hands of his father-in-law Jethro, the priest of Midian (Ex. 3:1), who received this priesthood through a line of men reaching back to Abraham, and thence to Melchizedek, who conferred that priesthood upon Abraham, and thence back to Noah, and from Noah back[7] to Adam, through the line of the ten patriarchs to Adam, who is the first man. "Which priesthood," says this revelation, "continueth in the church of God in all generations, and is without beginning of days or end of years" (D&C 84:17). In this revelation also is mentioned the fact that the Lord confirmed a priesthood upon

7. <Ms III[c] adds "back"—*Ed.*>

Aaron and his seed, throughout all their generations. Why it is called the lesser priesthood is because it is an appendage to the greater, or the Melchizedek, priesthood and has power in administering chiefly[8] outward ordinances. This priesthood also continueth and abideth forever with the priesthood which is after the holiest order of God, i.e., "after the order of the Son of God."

Referring again to this higher order of priesthood–the Melchizedek–the revelation continues:

> And this greater priesthood administereth the gospel and holdeth the key of mysteries of the kingdom, even the key of the knowledge of God. Therefore, in the ordinances thereof, the power of godliness is manifest. And without the ordinances thereof,[9] and the authority of the priesthood, the power of godliness is not manifest unto men in the flesh; for without this no man can see the face of God, even the Father, and live.
>
> Now this Moses plainly taught to the children of Israel in the wilderness, and sought diligently to sanctify his people that they might behold the face of God; but they hardened their hearts and could not endure His presence. Therefore, the Lord in His wrath, for His anger was kindled against them,[10] swore that they should not enter into His rest while in the wilderness, which rest is the fullness of His glory.
>
> Therefore, He took Moses out of their midst, and the Holy Priesthood [i.e., the priesthood after the order of the Son of God] and the lesser priesthood [i.e., which he had conferred upon Aaron] continued, which priesthood holdeth the key of the ministering of angels and the preparatory gospel; which gospel is the gospel of repentance and of baptism, and the remission of sins, and the law of carnal commandments, which the Lord in His wrath caused to continue with the house of Aaron among the children of Israel until John [i.e., the Baptist], whom God raised up, being filled with the Holy Ghost from his mother's womb. For he was baptized while he was yet in his childhood, and was ordained by the angel of God at the time he was eight days old unto this power, to overthrow the kingdom of the Jews, and to make straight the way of the Lord before the face of His people, to prepare them for the coming of the Lord, in whose hand is given all power (D&C 84:19-28).

VISIONS OF GOD UNDER MOSES

Notwithstanding what is written above about the failure of Moses to bring his people into full and sustained contact with God, because of the hardening of their hearts, which made it impossible for them to endure the presence of the Lord, and that ultimately resulted in the Lord taking Moses and the[11] higher priesthood as

---

8. <Ms III^c adds "chiefly"–*Ed.*>

9. <Ms III "without it the ordinances thereof," but D&C 84:21 is followed–*Ed.*>

10. <Ms III "for his anger was enkindled against them"–*Ed.*>

11. <Ms III^c adds "the"–*Ed.*>

an organization out of their midst, still there are some bright spots during that time when Moses was seeking to induce his people to live in harmony with the higher law of the gospel, and he was able to bring some part of his people into visible and actual communion with God. As for instance we read in Exodus:

> And He [the Lord] said unto Moses, "Come up unto the Lord, thou, and Aaron, and Nadab, and Abihu, and seventy of the elders of Israel, and worship ye afar off. And Moses alone shall come near the Lord, but they shall not come nigh, neither shall the people go up with him" (Ex. 24:1-2).

This commandment Moses delivered to assembled Israel, and:

> Then went up Moses, Aaron, Nadab, and Abihu, and seventy of the elders of Israel, and they saw the God of Israel, and there was under His feet as it were a paved work of a sapphire stone, and as it were the body of heaven in his clearness. And upon the nobles of the children of Israel He laid not His hand; also they saw God and did eat and drink (Ex. 24:9-11).

Above in this chapter it has been set forth that without holding the Melchizedek Priesthood—the priesthood after the order of the Son of God—man may not see the face of God and live. But since this number of men out of Israel could be brought into the presence of the Lord and eat and drink in His presence—was it a sacramental eating and drinking on that occasion?—it is evident that they must have held the priesthood after the order of the Son of God,[12] and to that extent, at least, that Moses succeeded in bringing his people into that intimate relationship, which he would have brought all Israel into, had it not been for the hardening of their hearts; but because of "transgression," the gospel which had been preached to Abraham, and which was given to Moses to introduce to Israel, but which they were unworthy of and unable to live, therefore, this holy priesthood[13] was taken from them as an organization, and also Moses, who held the keys of it. And Israel was left with the lesser priesthood and the law of carnal commandments to be their schoolmaster to prepare them finally for the coming of that great high priest himself, from whom all others in the world in ancient times, in meridian times, and in the last days shall derive whatsoever of priesthood they may hold.

Taking away Moses and the Melchizedek Priesthood, and leaving for the purpose named the lesser priesthood, left Israel also with only the lesser law. Later the gospel dispensation, graced by the presence of the Christ, the great high priest, who offered himself as a sacrifice for the redemption of the world, was ushered in—then the higher priesthood again assumed the direction of things, the lesser

---

12. <Ms III* "after the order of the Son of God, after the order of Melchizedek"—*Ed.*>
13. <Ms III* "this holy priesthood after the order of Melchizedek"—*Ed.*>

priesthood occupying its proper subordinate relationship, and the law was supplanted by the gospel, with its higher spiritual powers and life.

MELCHIZEDEK PRIESTHOOD HELD BY THE PROPHETS OF ISRAEL

There remains but one thing more to be accounted for, namely, that some of the prophets in Israel between the departure of Moses and the coming of the Christ seem to function in a manner that could only be warranted by their possessing the Melchizedek Priesthood, as for instance, where Isaiah had the face to face vision of God:

> In the year that King Uzziah died I saw also the Lord sit upon a throne, high and lifted up, and His train filled the temple. Above it stood the seraphims, . . . and one cried unto another and said, "Holy, holy, holy, is the Lord of hosts: the whole earth is full of His glory." And the posts of the door moved at the voice of him that cried, and the house was filled with smoke. Then said I, "Woe is me, for I am undone, for I am a man of unclean lips, and I dwell in the midst of a people of unclean lips: for mine eyes have seen the King, the Lord of hosts" (Isa. 6:1-5).

The explanation of this must be, that while the priesthood as an organization, together with Moses, was taken away from Israel, from time to time individual prophets received direct individual ordination from God in order to accomplish His purposes in the earth. We have such an instance as this in the case of Esaias, where the revelation of God to our prophet of the New Dispensation traces back the line of Jethro's priesthood (father-in-law of Moses and of whom Moses received the ordination to the priesthood), through four predecessors in the line of his priesthood to Esaias, who also lived in the days of Abraham and of whom it is said, "and Esaias received it [the priesthood] under the hand of God" (D&C 84:12). Since Esaias lived in the days of Abraham and Abraham was blessed of him, is it not quite possible that this "Esaias" under that name[14] was Melchizedek[15] and that he was the one to whom the priesthood of Jethro is traced in this revelation here considered, for Jethro, Moses' father-in-law, received his priesthood from one Caleb, "who received the priesthood from Elihu, who received the priesthood under

---

14. <Ms III[c] adds "under that name"—*Ed.*>

15. <The review committee objected to Roberts's identification of Esaias as Melchizedek: "We question the statement that Esaias and Melchizedek are the same, based on what is written in D. and C. 84" ("Doctrinal Points Questioned by the Committee Which Read the Manuscript of Elder B. H. Roberts, Entitled The Truth, The Way, The Life," attached to Rudger Clawson, Letter to Heber J. Grant, [15 May 1930], in David J. Buerger Collection, Manuscript 622, Bx 10, Fd 8, Manuscripts Division, Marriott Library, University of Utah, Salt Lake City)—*Ed.*>

the hand of Jeremy, and Jeremy received the priesthood under the hand of Gad, and Gad under the hand of Esaias" (cf. D&C 84:8-11), who is also the one who received his priesthood under the hand of God, and Esaias also lived in the days of Abraham and blessed him. He doubtless was the Melchizedek[16] and this name, which he appears under here ("Esaias"), accounts for the variation perhaps of this Elias who appeared in the Kirtland Temple.

This brief historical sketch made possible by reason of the revelations[17] given in the New Dispensation to Joseph Smith, and quoted in this chapter, unites the dispensations of Moses and the prophets of Israel with Abraham on the one hand, and with Christ, the Messiah, on the other, which dispensation we are to consider in the next chapter.

NOTE: MELCHIZEDEK = SHEM

That Melchizedek was Shem is recognized by the "Palestinian Targum" and also by Jerome of the fourth and fifth centuries in his comments on Isaiah 41.[18] It may be interesting to record also that it was Shem who offered the sacrifices[19] after Noah and his family came out of the ark (cf. Gen. 8:20), since tradition has it that Noah had been crippled by the lion, and was therefore unfitted for the priestly office; Noah gave Shem the priestly garments also which he had inherited from Adam (see Num. 4:6). This, too, confirms the tradition held in relation to Shem being the successor to Noah in the patriarchal line.[20] The Samaritans also identified the city of Samaria with the city of Salem,[21] and their sanctuary on Mt. Gerizim.[22]

---

16. <Identifying Esaias with Melchizedek and then Melchizedek with Noah's son, Shem (which Roberts does in the next section) is impossible to reconcile with D&C 84:13-14 (which Roberts does not quote): "Esaias also lived in the days of Abraham, and was blessed of him–which Abraham received the priesthood from Melchizedek, who received it through the lineage of his fathers, even till Noah"–*Ed.*>

17. <Ms III[c] adds an "s" to make the plural "revelations"–*Ed.*>

18. William R. Smith and Stanley A. Cook, "Melchizedek," in *The Encyclopædia Britannica: A Dictionary of Arts, Sciences, Literature and General Information*, 11th ed. (Cambridge and New York: Cambridge University Press, 1910-1911), 18:92.

19. <Ms III[*] "offered the sacrifices on the earth"–*Ed.*>

20. *The Jewish Encyclopedia: A Descriptive Record of the History, Religion, Literature, and Customs of the Jewish People from the Earliest Times to the Present Day*, 12 vols., ed. Isidore Singer (New York: Funk and Wagnalls Co., 1901), article "Shem."

21. <The review committee objected to Roberts's identification of Salem with Samaria: "We also question the statement that Salem and Samaria are the same" ("Doctrinal Points Questioned by the Committee," in Buerger)–*Ed.*>

22. <Ms III "Geriziam"–*Ed.*>

The rabbis of later generations also identified Melchizedek with Shem, the ancestor of Abraham.[23]

<John M'Clintock and James Strong say:>

In one of the Messianic Psalms it is foretold that the Messiah would be a priest "after the order of Melchizedek" (Ps. 110:4),[24] which the author of the Epistle to the Hebrews cites as showing that Melchizedek was a type of Christ (Heb. 6:20), and the Jews themselves, certainly, on the authority of this passage of the Psalm<s>, regarded Melchizedek as a type of the regal priesthood, higher than that of Aaron, to which the Messiah should belong. . . .[25]

A mysterious supremacy came also to be assigned to [Melchizedek] (. . . Philo, *Opp.* ii, 34), [but] by reason of his having received tithes from the Hebrew patriarch [Abraham]; and on this point [the author of] the epistle to the Hebrews expatiates strongly (Heb. 7:1-7). But the Jews in admitting this official or personal superiority[26] of Melchizedek to Abraham sought to account for it by alleging that the royal priest[27] was no other than Shem, the most pious of Noah's sons, who according to the shorter chronology [Ussher's] might have lived at the time of Abraham [according to that chronology Shem's life overlapped into the life of Abraham over one hundred and fifty years]. [Shem] as a survivor of the deluge is supposed to have been authorized by the superior dignity of old age to bless even the father of the faithful, and entitled as a paramount lord of Canaan (Gen. 9:26) to convey his light to Abraham (Gen. 14:19).

[This opinion, i.e., that Shem was Melchizedek] was . . . embraced by [Martin] Luther, [his strong supporter and learned friend] <Philipp> Melanchthon, by H<ugh> Broughton, <John> Selden, [Bishop] <Joseph> Lightfoot, <William> Jackson, and many others.

Jerome [of the fourth and fifth centuries] in his epistle [written in Rome] (lxxiii, *ad Evangelum*, in *Opp.* i, 438), which is entirely devoted to consideration of the person and dwelling-place of Melchizedek, states that this [i.e., that Melchizedek is Shem] was the prevailing opinion of the Jews in his time, and it was [also] ascribed to the Samaritans.[28]

Also, it is interesting to note that in an editorial in the *Times and Seasons*,

---

23. *Jewish Encyclopedia*, article "Shem."

24. <Ms III has "Ps. 90:4," and this error can be attributed to Roberts, who by transposition read the Roman-numeral reference "cx,4" in the *Cyclopædia* as if it were "xc,4"—*Ed.*>

25. John M'Clintock and James Strong, "Melchizedek," *Cyclopædia of Biblical, Theological, and Ecclesiastical Literature* (New York: Harper and Bros., 1891), 6:57.

26. <Ms III "popular superiority," but M'Clintock's text has "personal superiority"—*Ed.*>

27. <Ms III* "the royal priesthood," but M'Clintock's text has "the royal priest"—*Ed.*>

28. <M'Clintock and Strong, *Cyclopædia*, 6:57-58—*Ed.*>

December number for 1844, published in Nauvoo, Illinois, the statement is made that Melchizedek was Shem: "And with the superior knowledge of men like Noah, Shem (who is Melchizedek), and Abraham, the father of the faithful, . . . holding the keys of the highest order of the priesthood," etc.[29]

Other conjectures in relation to Melchizedek, on account of the mystery that shadows his name and career, are that he was an impersonal power, virtue, or substance of God personified; that he was the son of God, appearing in human form; that he was the Messiah (Jewish opinion); also that he was Ham, which, of course, in the light of what we have already said of Ham would be obviously[30] ridiculous.

SHEM, MELCHIZEDEK, AND ELIAS IDENTICAL

The establishment of the identity of Shem and Melchizedek leads to the likelihood of an important fact connected with the New Dispensation. We read in the Doctrine and Covenants, Section 110, of the appearing in the Kirtland Temple to the Prophet Joseph Smith and to Oliver Cowdery: first the Savior; then Moses,[31] who restored to the prophet the keys of the gathering of Israel from the four parts of the earth and the leading of the ten tribes from the land of the North; then of Elias, who appeared and committed the dispensation of the gospel of Abraham, saying to Joseph and Oliver that in them "and in their seed all generations after them should be blessed" (cf. D&C 110:12). Then follows the account of the appearing of Elijah the prophet, who was taken to heaven without tasting death.

The question arises, Who is this "Elias," who committed the dispensation of the gospel of Abraham? Why is it that in all our modern revelations Abraham never appears as coming with the keys of a dispensation, since he is so prominent a figure of antiquity? The answer, of course, would be that a greater than Abraham lived in his day, and held the keys of that dispensation; and who ordained Abraham to his special work of perpetuating the patriarchal line after the departure of that greater one, who held the keys of the dispensation in which Abraham was started upon his career in the priesthood. Between Noah and the appearance of Abraham on the scene, the one intervening great character that looms large is Melchizedek, and with the fact established that he was Shem, we have a beautiful and unbroken line of God's great servants from ante-diluvian patriarchs through Noah into the post-diluvian period in which period Noah continued his life for three hundred

---

29. <This editorial entitled "Ancient Ruins" was printed in the *Times and Seasons* 5 (15 Dec. 1844): 746; at this time the editor was John Taylor—*Ed.*>

30. <Ms III^{c} adds "obviously"—*Ed.*>

31. <Ms III* "afterwards Moses"—*Ed.*>

and fifty years. Shem continuing to live contemporaneously with him through that period, meeting with Abraham, conferring the priesthood upon him, and thence the line continuing until Israel arose to be enlarged into a nation to perpetuate the work of God through the earth. This conception of the course of things arising out of the identification of Elias, who appeared in the Kirtland Temple to the Prophet Joseph Smith and Oliver Cowdery, with Melchizedek, and Melchizedek with Shem, perpetuates the patriarchal line of the priesthood, and it was doubtless that patriarchal feature of the priesthood and the work of God linking the generations of men together in the patriarchal line that Elias—or Melchizedek—came to restore.

> Elias appeared and committed the dispensation of the gospel of Abraham, saying that in us and our seed, all generations after us should be blessed (D&C 110:12).

CHAPTER XXXIX
The Meridian Dispensation

SCRIPTURE READING LESSON

Analysis

I. Mission of the Christ, Outline of.
II. The Christian Sacraments:
   (a) Water Baptism;
   (b) Spirit Baptism.
III. The Sacrament of the Lord's Supper: The Prayer of Consecration.
IV. The Prayer of Consecration Expounded.
V. The Resurrection.
VI. The Testimony of the Judean Apostles.
VII. Testimony of a Modern Prophet.
VIII. The Testimony of the Book of Mormon.
IX. Assurance of the Resurrection.

References

All the citations in the text and notes of this chapter and their contexts.

D&C 76, all; D&C 20, 45, *passim*.

Moro. 4-5, on the sacrament.

On the resurrection, see closing chapter of each of the four gospels; cf. 1 Cor. 15; Acts of Apostles and Epistles, *passim*.

Sermon by Joseph Smith on "Life, Death, and the Resurrection," *History of the Church of Jesus Christ of Latter-day Saints, Period I: History of Joseph Smith, the Prophet by Himself* (Salt Lake City: Deseret News, 1908), 4:553-57.

CHAPTER XXXIX

The Meridian Dispensation

THE MISSION OF THE CHRIST IN OUTLINE

We come now to the dispensation of the gospel that is to be graced by the advent of the Son of God and the performance of his great mission. That mission is to reveal in person God the Father, and all that is or can be called God in the universe: "for in him shall all fullness dwell, . . . even the fullness of the Godhead bodily" (Col. 1:19; 2:9; cf. Col. 1:12-18). To redeem man from the consequences of Adam's transgression, from the "fall." To introduce the element of mercy into the divine economy, by making it possible under a reign of moral and spiritual law to forgive the personal sins of men without violence to justice; also bringing men from their alienation from God back to fellowship and union with him; by which they are redeemed from spiritual death, and restored to spiritual life. To bring to pass the resurrection from physical death, by which shall be established immortality–a deathless, physical life.

Lastly, the Christ came to stand as a witness for the truth of all the foregoing things; for he said unto Pilate, when brought before the Roman procurator by the Jews:

> To this end was I born, and for this cause came I into the world, that I should bear witness unto the truth (John 18:37).

These several things constituted the very heart and life of the mission of the Christ, and, of course, of the gospel, the whole plan of God for the establishment of both thy physical immortality of man and also the eternal spiritual life of man.

THE TWO GREAT CHRISTIAN SACRAMENTS[1]

We pass over the historical features of the Meridian Dispensation, as being too well-known to require restatement: viz., the coming and mission of the forerunner of the Messiah, John the Baptist; and the birth and youth and early ministry of the Messiah himself. It should be noted, however, that to set forth in

1. <Ms III^{c} adds "The Two Great Christian Sacraments"–*Ed.*>

concrete form and perpetuate the main features of his mission, the Christ established two sacraments; each having two parts, viz., first, baptism; and second, the Lord's supper. Baptism, as stated above, consists of two parts: (a) baptism, or birth of the water; and (b) baptism, or birth of the spirit.

(a) Water Baptism

Water baptism is to be performed by immersion, or complete burial, of the candidate in water. The official formula for this ordinance, as given by the risen Christ to the Nephites in America, was as follows:

> Behold, ye shall go down and stand in the water; . . . and now behold, these are the words which ye shall say, calling them [the candidates] by name . . . : "Having authority given me of Jesus Christ, I baptize you in the name of the Father, and of the Son, and of the Holy Ghost. Amen." And then shall ye immerse them in the water, and come forth again out of the water (3 Ne. 11:23-26).

This ordinance is to be preceded by a confession of faith in God the Father, in Jesus Christ his Son, and in the Holy Ghost. In baptism is represented symbolically the death, burial, and resurrection of Jesus Christ; as the Christ died and was buried, so the candidate dies to his old life of sin, by separating himself from it by repentance; and he is buried with Christ in baptism. And as the Christ rose from the grave to "newness of life" (Rom. 6:4) to immortal life—so the immersed candidate rises from the watery grave of baptism to a newness of life in righteousness. The symbolism is complete.

Through this ordinance comes remission of sin by visible acceptance of the atonement of the Christ, and the cleansing power of his sacrificial blood in that atonement made for sin. Also, it is partial entrance, or a preparation for entrance, into the kingdom of heaven—the Church of Christ. Also, this water baptism is a preparation for the other part of baptism—the baptism, or birth, of the spirit: this by cleansing from sins, by forgiveness of them, through the grace of God (John 3:3; Mark 1:4; Acts 2:37-39; Rom. 6:4).

(b) The Baptism of the Spirit—The Holy Ghost

The second part of this one baptism—the baptism of the spirit—is administered by the laying on of the hands by those having authority to minister the spirit, by which the properly prepared water-baptized convert receives an immersion of the Holy Ghost to his soul. He is born again into a union with God—into a renewal of spiritual life. This baptism of the spirit completes his entrance into the kingdom of God. He is born both of the water and of the spirit, without which he could neither see nor enter into the kingdom of God—the Church of Christ. This baptism brings him to possession of that spirit which guides him into all truth; which takes the things of God and makes them known to him; by which he may know that

Jesus is the Christ (John 3:3-4; 14:16-26; Acts 2:37-39; 8:14-24), by which also he may know the truth of all things (John 14:16-17; 1 Cor. 12:3; Moro. 10:4-5). Blessed baptism into a union with God, and to a knowledge of all the things of God.

THE SACRAMENT OF THE LORD'S SUPPER

The nature of this sacrament will best be learned from the prayer of consecration of the bread and the wine of the supper. This is to be found both in the Book of Mormon as given by the Christ among the ancient Nephites, and to the prophet of the New Dispensation by revelation (Moro. 4:1-3; D&C 20:75-77). Moroni, describing the manner in which it was administered among his people, says:

The manner of their elders and priests administering the flesh and blood of Christ unto the church; and they did administer it according to the commandment<s> of Christ; wherefore, we know the manner to be true (Moro. 4:1).

Consideration of the prayer over the broken bread will be sufficient for the present purpose.

Prayer of Consecration

> O God, the Eternal Father, we ask Thee in the name of Thy Son, Jesus Christ, to bless and sanctify this bread to the souls of all those who partake of it; that they may eat in remembrance of the body of Thy Son, and witness unto Thee, O God, the Eternal Father, that they are willing to take upon them the name of Thy Son, and always remember him, and keep his commandments which he hath given them, that they may always have his Spirit to be with them. Amen (D&C 20:77).

A similar prayer to this with only slight variations to make it appropriate as representing the blood of the Christ instead of his broken body is given in the same revelations. These prayers of consecration are the most perfect forms of sacred literature to be found. So perfect they are that one may not add to them or take ought from them without marring them. One may say of these prayers of consecration what Archdeacon Paley says concerning the Lord's Prayer, namely that:

> For a succession of solemn thoughts, for fixing the attention upon a few great points, for suitableness . . . , for sufficiency, for conciseness without obscurity, for the weight and real importance of its petitions—[it] is without an equal or a rival.[2]

---

2. <William Paley, *A View of the Evidences of Christianity*, ed. E. A. Litton (London: Society for Promoting Christian Knowledge, 1871), pt. ii, chap. ii, 360; in the ellipsis Roberts deleted Paley's words "to every condition"—*Ed.*>

And as representing a few great fundamental and all-comprehensive truths concerning religion, these prayers of consecration form a rallying point—raise a standard that will make for the holding together in union and fellowship the followers of the Master, beyond all other formulas known to man; and for that purpose, beyond all doubt, were they given, as well as to call up to man's consciousness the sacrifice God made for man's redemption, and man's covenant to remember and to keep God's commandments, that he might always be in union with God.

THE PRAYERS OF CONSECRATION EXPOUNDED

These prayers of consecration are a "creed," as well as sacramental prayers. This will sufficiently appear, if we analyze the prayer over the bread.

"O God, the Eternal Father." Here, in addition to being the most solemn form in which Deity can be addressed, is expressed faith in God as "Eternal Father"—remembering that the first fact of fatherhood is creation through begetting, and next is watching over and guiding to proposed ends, loving watchfulness over the creation—fathering! We have God recognized as the Father of men, and the Eternal Creator of all things, and the eternal sustaining power of all things—"the very Eternal Father of heaven and earth" (Mosiah 15:4; cf. Alma 11:38-39), not as "first cause," but as "eternal," continuing cause, and "eternal," sustaining power. How fortunate the form of that address, "O God, the Eternal Father"!

"We Ask Thee, in the Name of Thy Son, Jesus Christ." This is an assertion of faith in Jesus Christ, and in Jesus Christ as the Son of God, as Son of the "Eternal Father." He was the "first begotten" of the spirits destined to come to the earth, called "first begotten" by the Father himself (Heb. 1:6; cf. Rom. 8:29); and hence "Elder Brother" to all that host of spirits. Also, he is "the only begotten of the Father," of all the sons of men born into the world (John 1:14)—having reference, of course, to the Christ's birth of Mary and as "the Son of the Highest—the Son of God" (Luke 1:35). So that indeed God is the Father of our Lord Jesus Christ, both of his spirit and of his body, and in this respect the Christ is uniquely "the Son of God."

"We Ask Thee . . . To Bless and Sanctify This Bread." And what is this bread? It is broken when blessed and presented to the communicants, and is the symbol of the broken body of the Christ. Symbol of the fulfillment of the prophecy: "He was wounded . . . for our iniquities" (cf. Isa. 53:5).[3] Symbol of the broken body of the Christ; broken when the crown of hard thorns was pressed upon his brow,

3. And the serpent was given power to "bruise" the heel of the woman's seed (Gen. 3:15).

and blood streamed down his face; broken when the cruel nails were driven through the quivering flesh of hands and feet; broken when the Roman soldier's spear pierced his side and shed the life's blood that was to save a world. The Christ's suffering in Gethsemane, where in agony he sweat blood at every pore; and his suffering on the cross, where hung his broken body in unspeakable pain. This was the price of suffering[4] paid for man's salvation and the broken bread is the symbol of it.

"Bless and Sanctify This Bread to the Souls of All Those Who Partake of It." The broken bread is to be a soul-food, then, not bodily food; an appeal to remembrance, to gratitude, to moral obligation.

In the prayer of consecration, then, faith is declared in God as Eternal Father; in Jesus Christ as the only begotten Son of God (in the flesh); in the atonement of Jesus Christ for the sins of men (as a race and as individuals), and this by accepting the symbols of the broken body of the Christ in the broken bread. These are three great fundamentals of the gospel, which if a man accepts in his convictions, all else of the gospel will follow as matter of course.

The second part of the sacrament deals with the renewal of covenant with God on the part of man:

"That They May Witness unto Thee, O God, the Eternal Father: (a) That They Are Willing to Take upon Them the Name of Thy Son." Become Christ's men and Christ's women—Christians.

(b) "And Always Remember Him." Every day remember him, every month, and through all the years—always.

(c) "And Keep His Commandments Which He Hath Given Them." In human weakness men may not always "keep" perfectly his commandments; but they may keep alive in their souls their "willingness" to keep his commandments; and by affirming and reaffirming that willingness, the memory of the obligation "to keep his commandments" will be ever present to consciousness.

And the end of all this? The climax? The purpose of it?

"That They May Always Have His [the Christ's] Spirit To Be with Them." What an end to be attained! The spirit of the Christ to be with men always! The perpetuation of the spiritual life into which they were born when they accepted the gospel of Jesus Christ. What could be more desirable? What more admirable? What more profitable for the individual and for the community life, than that men should always have the spirit of the Christ to be with them "to live and move and have their being" (cf. Acts 17:28) and work and serve in that spirit—the spirit of the Master—the Christ!

---

4. <Ms III[c] adds "of suffering"—*Ed.*>

THE RESURRECTION OF THE DEAD

It is fitting that a word should be spoken here in relation to one other stupendous fact connected with the Dispensation of the Meridian of Times, namely, the Christ's resurrection from the dead. And his resurrection, it[5] should be remembered, is a prototype of the resurrection of all men, the actual, physical resurrection of the body of all men, and the immortality of the individual so raised from the dead, in fulfillment of God's covenant made to the spirits of men before the foundation of the world, namely, the covenant of eternal life (Titus 1:2). I waive all discussion as to the physical possibility of such a resurrection. We have God's assurance in his revealed word that it shall be so, and such is the manifest power of God in creation, in the miracle of man's mortal life, in the miracle of the existence of all animal and plant life, the miracle of existence of the earth itself, sun, moon, and stars, that it is not worthwhile carping over the alleged "impossibility" and "improbability" of the physical resurrection of men.

It is no more difficult for God to bring to pass the physical immortality through the reunion of spirit and body, than it is impossible for God to bring to pass the mortal life of man; and in the presence of all the "miraculous" things known to men about life and its wonders. We might repeat, even to this scientific age, proud of its acquired knowledge yet confusedly ignorant of the mystery of life in general, and human life in particular, we could still say to them, as Paul did to King Agrippa, "Why should it be thought a thing incredible with you, that God should raise the dead?" (Acts 26:8). This resurrection to physical, immortal life is the great unique thing of the Christian religion as founded by the Christ, and developed by the ministry of the apostles.

Other faiths have presented more or less dimly the idea of a continued consciousness of being in some form or other, some spirit essence kind of existence, or some absorption back into the being whence the individual has been called into existence, some survival of ethereal existence, as the perfume of the rose after her petals are fallen, or else some pilgrimage of the soul through transmigration into varied forms of life, sometimes in the way of retribution visited upon the spirit because of the absence of some perfection or failure to fulfill purposes of existence in granted life periods, a procession of chastisements until the right is purchased to escape the painful consciousness of personal existence, and there comes the alleged blessed period of Nirvana, or rest from the weary round of struggle and effort.

It is the Christian religion alone out of all the faiths that raises up as a standard this proclamation that "as in Adam all die, even so in Christ shall all be made

---

5. <Ms III[c] adds "it"—*Ed.*>

alive" (1 Cor. 15:22). And the promise of the Christ himself, "If a man believe in me, though he were dead, yet shall he live"; and also his solemn words, "I am the resurrection and the life" (cf. John 11:25); and again the Master's words near the close of his mortal life's ministry:

> Verily, verily, I say unto you, The hour is coming, and now is, when the dead shall hear the voice of the Son of God; and they that hear shall live. For as the Father hath life in Himself, so hath He given to the Son to have life in himself. . . . Marvel not at this: for the hour is coming in the which all that are in the graves shall hear his voice, and shall come forth; they that have done good, unto the resurrection of life, and they that have done evil unto the resurrection of damnation (John 5:25-26, 28-29).

The resurrection of the just and also of the unjust. God's covenant to his spirit children before the earth-life of man began was that He would give unto men immortality—deathless physical existence, in the union of spirit and element; and we are assured of the possibility of such a thing by reason of the existence of accomplished things all about us equally miraculous with the fulfillment of this promise of resurrection from the dead.

THE TESTIMONY OF THE JUDEAN APOSTLES

The fact of the resurrection of the Christ from death is witnessed by the apostles in their discourses in the New Testament scriptures; and is also used by them as proof positive of the divinity of the Christian scheme of things, as witnessed in Paul's speech in Athens, where he represents that God hath given assurance that He hath called all men to repentance under the Christian scheme of things—"in that He hath raised him [the Christ] from the dead" (Acts 17:31 and context).

To all this is to be added the testimony of each of the writers of the four gospels, who represent the resurrection of the Christ as a most literal resurrection of the personal Christ by the reunion of his body and spirit. The reality of this reunion is most emphatically given perhaps in St. John's Gospel, where on his second appearance to the apostles he gives the assurance of the reality of his resurrection to Thomas, who had said to his brethren who reported the first visitation of the risen Christ, "Unless I see the wounds in his hands and in his side and thrust my hand into his side, I will not believe." On the second visitation the Master called "Doubting Thomas" to him and said unto him, "Reach hither thy finger, and behold my hands; and reach hither thy hand, and thrust it into my side. And be not faithless, but believing." And Thomas answered and said to the risen Christ, "My Lord and my God!" And the Christ reproved him for his previous lack of faith (cf. John 20:25-29).

On the first visit of the risen Lord, when the disciples were affrighted at his appearing among them, supposing that they had seen a spirit, he said unto them:

"Why are ye troubled? And why do thoughts arise in your hearts? Behold my hands and my feet, that it is I myself; handle me and see; for a spirit hath not flesh and bones, as ye see me have." And when he had thus spoken, he showed them his hands and his feet. And while they yet believed not for joy, and wondered, he said unto them, "Have ye here any meat?" And they gave him a piece of broiled fish, and of an honeycomb. And he took it, and did eat before them (Luke 24:38-43).

Peter in the course of his ministry was wont to refer to this and other circumstances of physical contact with the risen Christ, an example of which is found in the discourse in the home of Cornelius, saying—"we" referring to himself and brethren that were with him on that occasion:

We are witnesses of all things which he [the Christ] did, both in the land of the Jews and in Jerusalem. Whom they slew and hanged on a tree, him God raised up the third day and showed him openly; not to all the people, but unto witnesses chosen before of God, even to us, who did eat and drink with him after he rose from the dead (Acts 10:39-41).

THE TESTIMONY OF A MODERN PROPHET

This is the testimony of the Jewish scripture, more especially of the New Testament, although through the whole course of the scriptures there is abundance of witness to this great truth, and especially in our modern revelation given through the prophet of the New Dispensation. This prophet said:

And now, after the many testimonies which have been given of him, this is the testimony last of all which we give of him; that he lives, for we [referring to himself and his early associate, Sidney Rigdon] saw him, even on the right hand of God, and we heard the voice bearing record that he is the Only Begotten of the Father (D&C 76:22-23).[6]

THE TESTIMONY OF THE BOOK OF MORMON

Also, in the Book of Mormon is given a most dramatic and soul-thrilling testimony to the resurrection of the Christ by the appearance of the risen Redeemer to a multitude of people in America, shortly after the resurrection of the Christ; for to the people of America, no less than to the people of the Eastern Hemisphere, did God give assurances through their ancient prophets from time to time of the existence of His gospel and of its power unto salvation; and lastly, the risen Christ

---

6. The whole great revelation in this section of the Doctrine and Covenants—one of the greatest outgivings of God to man in any age of the world—is based upon this testimony of the risen and present-living Christ, the Son of God, and we commend that whole revelation to the consideration of the reader.

came to them to assure them of the verities of the plan of salvation and especially of this feature of it, the resurrection from the dead, by his own glorious appearance among them, and his quite extended ministry among them.[7]

Here the resurrected Christ according to the Nephite record descended out of heaven and appeared to the multitude, proclaiming himself to be the Son of God, the Redeemer of the world; and the multitude blessed the name of "the Most High God, and they did fall down at the feet of Jesus and did worship him" (3 Ne. 11:17).

ASSURANCE OF THE RESURRECTION

No incident in the gospel history is more emphatically proven than this great truth, the resurrection of the Son of God, and the promise of the resurrection of all men. It was the center, around which all the hopes of the early Christians was grouped—the hope of immortality, of eternal life. It is the vital force of the Christian religion. It is the hope of the world, the only kind of a future life that can meet the aspiring, uplifting desires of the human soul. If such a life as that which is promised through the resurrection, as taught in the Christian religion, is not to be realized, then the future hopes for any existence worthwhile fall in dark confusion about the feet of men.

---

7. For all which, see Book of Mormon, 3 Nephi, the whole book, but especially chapter 11.

CHAPTER XL

The Atonement I—The Revealed Fact of the Atonement

SCRIPTURE READING LESSON

Analysis

I. Introductory to Fact of Atonement.

II. Prophecy of the Atonement.

III. The Paschal Sacrifice.

IV. The Sin Offering.

V. Fact of Atonement in History.

VI. The Witness of the New Testament:

(a) Testimony of the Angel Gabriel.

(b) Testimony of John the Baptist.

(c) Testimony of the Christ.

(d) Testimony of St. Peter.

(e) Testimony of St. Paul.

(f) Testimony of St. John.

VII. Book of Mormon Prophecies of the Atonement.

VIII. Book of Mormon Historical Utterances on the Atonement.

IX. Testimony of the Prophet of the New Dispensation.

References

The four gospels of the New Testament and the Epistles and Acts, *passim*.

The Book of Mormon, especially in 3 Nephi, chaps. 9 and 11, and throughout 3 Nephi, *passim*. Also, Mosiah, chaps. 3-5. See collection of references on "atonement" in the index of current edition of Book of Mormon.

D&C 19, and throughout the book, *passim*.

All the quotations and citations in this chapter with study of context in each case.

CHAPTER XL

The Atonement I—The Revealed Fact of the Atonement

NOTE: I must ask at the outset of this treatise on the atonement—comprising six chapters—that there be a suspension of judgment on the respective parts of the theme until all shall have been read; as knowledge of the whole, I am sure, will be necessary to the complete understanding of the parts.

INTRODUCTORY[1]

It is fitting that the atonement should receive doctrinal exposition when considering the dispensation of the gospel in which the sacrifice comprising it was made. What has already been set forth in this work as to the plan of man's redemption from spiritual and physical death, together with the knowledge of what took place in the heavenly council among pre-existent spirits before man's earth-life in the Dispensation of Adam began, relieves us of the necessity of a full statement and a long discussion in the introduction of the atonement. Under our plan we have been able from the very first to proceed with the consciousness of the purpose of man's earth-life and redemption all the while present. It still remains, however, to consider the atonement from the scriptural and philosophical side of it, and deal with the necessity for it, and the nature of it; and first of all to be convinced as to the revealed fact of it. Upon the established fact of it by revelation is where we begin our discussion; and first by noting briefly the testimony of prophecy for the promise of it.

PROPHECY OF THE ATONEMENT

St. Paul says:

> When Moses had spoken every precept to all the people according to the law, he took the blood of calves and of goats, with water, and scarlet wool, and hyssop, and sprinkled both the book and all the people, saying, "This is the blood of the testament which God hath enjoined unto you." Moreover, he sprinkled with blood both the

1. <Ms III[*] of section heading "The Revealed Fact Of It"—*Ed.*>

> tabernacle and all the vessels of the ministry. And almost all things are by the law purged with blood, and without the shedding of blood is no remission (Heb. 9:19-22; cited from Ex. 24:8).

It is very generally conceded that the sacrifices and oblations of the Mosaic ritual have a direct relationship to the great atoning sacrifice to be made by the Christ. From the ninth and tenth chapters of the epistle to the Hebrews it is evident that "the law" was "a shadow of good things to come." The law's sacrifices for sin and reconciliation with God but figured forth the greater and more efficient sacrifice to be made by the Son of God; nay, whatever of virtue there was in the sacrifices of the law were dependent upon the greater sacrifice to follow. Of themselves, the sacrifices of the law had no virtue at all unconnected with the sacrifice to be made by the Christ; they were but symbols showing forth that sacrifice, in which the virtue was the sacrifice of the Christ himself.

THE PASCHAL SACRIFICE

In some respects the paschal sacrifice more perfectly than any other, perhaps, foreshadowed the future sacrifice of the Son of God for the deliverance of his people—those who would trust the sign of deliverance in his blood. The institution of the sacrifice and the accompanying feast were as follows. When all other judgments upon Pharaoh failed to persuade him to let God's people go, then said the Lord to Moses:

> All the firstborn in the land of Egypt shall die, from the firstborn of Pharaoh that sitteth upon his throne, even unto the firstborn of the maidservant that is behind the mill; and all the firstborn of beasts. . . . But against any of the children of Israel shall not a dog move his tongue, against man or beast; that ye may know how that the Lord doth put a difference between the Egyptian<s> and Israel (Ex. 11:5, 7).

When this terrible judgment was about to be executed the Lord provided the following means of deliverance for his people. Each family in Israel was commanded at a given time to take a lamb without blemish, a male of the first year, for a "passover offering," and it was to be killed in the evening.

> And they shall take of the blood and strike it on the two side-posts, and on the upper door-post of the houses, wherein they shall eat it. And they shall eat the flesh in that night, roast with fire, and unleavened bread; and with bitter herbs they shall eat it. . . . And the blood shall be to you for a token upon the houses where ye are: and when I see the blood, I will pass over you, and the plague shall not be upon you to destroy you, when I smite the land of Egypt. And this day shall be unto you for a memorial; and ye shall keep it a feast to the Lord throughout your generations; ye shall keep it a feast by an ordinance for ever (Ex. 12:7-8, 13-14).

Of course, it cannot be doubted that this festival of the passover was instituted as a great memorial of the deliverance from Egyptian bondage, and the birth of the nation of Israel; and there are not wanting those who maintain that this was its primary and only significance. But the leading feature of the festival, the paschal lamb, "a male without blemish"; the killing of it; the blood sprinkled upon the door post, the sign of safety to God's people; the eating of the lamb in preparation of the journey; the subsequent honoring of this feast by the Christ with his disciples; the substitution of the Sacrament of the Lord's Supper for the Passover festival at the very time and on the very occasion of celebrating the feast of the Passover among the Jews; together with the subsequent inspired reference to Christ as the "Paschal Lamb" of the Christians, are circumstances too numerous and too nearly related to doubt of the significance of the Passover festival having reference to the great sacrifice to be made by the Son of God through the shedding of his blood in atonement for, and the deliverance of, his people.

THE SIN OFFERING[2]

Other sacrifices of the Mosaic law which shadowed forth the future atonement to be made by the Son of God was the "Sin Offering." Of Mosaic sacrifices in general and of this sacrifice in particular, the author of the article on "Sacrifices" in *Dr. Wm. Smith's Dictionary of the Bible* (this is Rev. Alfred Barry, Fellow of Trinity College, Cambridge) says:

> All [sacrifices] had relation, under different aspects, to a covenant between God and man. The "Sin Offering" [described in detail in Lev. 4] represented that covenant as broken by man, and as knit together again, by God's appointment through the shedding of blood. . . . The shedding of blood, the symbol of life, signified that the death of the offender was deserved for sin, but that the death of the victim was accepted for his death by the ordinance of God's mercy.[3]

To the same effect our author sets forth the ceremonial of the "Day of Atonement," (detail of which is given in Lev. 16:7-10). A number of the early and later "Christian Fathers" take the same view.[4]

---

2. <Ms III^{c} adds "The Sin Offering"–*Ed.*>

3. Alfred Barry, "Sacrifice," in *Dr. William Smith's Dictionary of the Bible, Comprising Its Antiquities, Biography, Geography, and Natural History*, ed. Horatio B. Hackett and Ezra Abbot (Boston: Houghton, Mifflin and Co., 1894), 4:2774.

4. See B. H. Roberts, *The Seventy's Course in Theology: Fourth Year, The Atonement* (Salt Lake City: The Deseret News, 1911).

THE FACT OF THE ATONEMENT IN HISTORY

The first intimation of an atonement in the earth-history of man was doubtless the statement in Genesis that the serpent–standing for, and symbolizing in the narrative, Lucifer–would bruise the heel of the woman's seed; while "the seed of the woman"–meaning the Christ–"would bruise the serpent's [or Lucifer's] head" (cf. Gen. 3:15). This and the institution of sacrifice, early in Adam's and his sons' lives, with the explanation which some time afterwards was given of the significance of the sacrificial offering–all taken together–is our earliest historical data on the atonement. It will perhaps be remembered that the revealed purpose of the sacrifice was (see chapter 35):

> "This thing is a similitude <of the sacrifice> of the Only Begotten of the Father, which is full of grace and truth. Wherefore, thou shalt do all that thou doest in the name of the Son . . . forevermore." And in that day the Holy Ghost fell upon Adam, which beareth record of the Father and the Son, saying: "I am the Only Begotten of the Father from the beginning, henceforth and forever, that as thou hast fallen thou mayest be redeemed, and all mankind, even as many as will" (Moses 5:7-9).

WITNESS OF THE NEW TESTAMENT

We turn next to the testimony of the New Testament writers on the fact of the atonement.

(a) Testimony of the Angel Gabriel

In Matthew we read what the angel said to Joseph, when warning him not to put away Mary, his betrothed wife, because of her being found with child:

> Joseph, thou son of David, fear not to take unto thee Mary, thy wife: . . . she shall bring forth a son, and thou shalt call his name Jesus, for he shall save his people from their sins (Matt. 1:20-21; cf. Luke 1:26-35).

Such <is> the testimony of an angel of God as to the mission of the Christ.

(b) Testimony of John the Baptist

John the Baptist said to his own disciples as Jesus passed:

> Behold, the Lamb of God that taketh away the sin[s] of the world . . . and I saw and bear record that this is the Son of God (John 1:29, 34).

(c) Testimony of the Christ

The Christ's own testimony is recorded as follows:

> And as Moses lifted up the serpent in the wilderness, even so must the Son of Man be lifted up: that whosoever believeth in him should not perish, but have

> everlasting life. . . . For God sent not his Son into the world to condemn the world, but that the world through him might be saved (cf. John 3:14-15, 17).

And again the Christ:

> When ye have lifted up the Son of Man, then shall ye know that I am he [i.e., the one that taketh away the sins of the world] (John 8:28).

And again the Christ at the Paschal Supper, preceding his betrayal:

> Jesus, having blessed the bread, brake it and gave it to his disciples and said, "Take, eat; this is my body." And he took the cup and gave thanks and gave it to them, saying, "Drink ye all of it, for this is my blood, which is the new testament, which is shed for many for the remission of sins" (cf. Matt. 26:26-28).[5]

After the resurrection Jesus, overtaking two of the disciples on their way to Emmaus, engaged them in conversation respecting the crucifixion of Jesus, and in the course of their narrative about the crucifixion and the missing body of the Christ, the risen Lord said to them:

> "Ye fools and slow of heart to believe all that the prophets have spoken. Ought not Christ to have suffered these things and to enter into his glory?" And beginning with Moses and all the prophets, he expounded unto them in all the scriptures the things concerning himself (Luke 24:25-27).

Subsequently, appearing to the twelve, he opened their understanding that they might understand the scriptures and said unto them:

> Thus it is written, and thus it behooveth Christ to suffer and to rise from the dead [on] the third day; and that repentance and remission of sins should be preached in his name in all nations beginning at Jerusalem. And ye are witnesses of these things (Luke 24:46-48).

(d) Testimony of St. Peter

St. Peter, chief of the apostles, bears witness of this same truth when he says:

> Christ also hath once suffered for sins, the just for the unjust, that he might bring us to God, being put to death in the flesh, but quickened by the Spirit (1 Pet. 3:18).

Again:

> Christ also suffered for us, leaving us an example, that ye should follow his steps; who did no sin, neither was guile found in his mouth; . . . who his own self bare our

---

5. Luke and Mark practically give the same account of the incident; and St. Paul in his account of the resurrection states "Christ died for our sins according to the scriptures" (1 Cor. 15:3).

sins in his own body on the tree, that we, being dead to sins, should live unto righteousness: by whose stripes ye were healed (1 Pet. 2:21-22, 24).

Again:

Elect ... through the sanctification of the Spirit, unto obedience and sprinkling of the blood of Jesus Christ. Grace unto you, and peace, be multiplied. ...Forasmuch as ye know that ye were not redeemed with corruptible things, as silver and gold, from your vain conversation, received by tradition from your fathers; but with the precious blood of Christ, as of a lamb without blemish and without spot, who verily was foreordained before the foundation of the world, but was manifest in these last times for you (1 Pet. 1:2, 18-20).

(e) Testimony of St. Paul

All have sinned, and come short of the glory of God; being justified freely by His grace, through the redemption that is in Christ Jesus, who<m> God hath set forth to be a propitiation through faith in his blood, to declare his righteousness for the remission of sins that are past, through the forbearance of God (Rom. 3:23-25).

When we were yet without strength, in due time Christ died for the ungodly. . . . But God commendeth His love toward us, in that, while we were yet sinners, Christ died for us. Much more then, being now justified by his blood, we shall be saved from wrath through him. ...And not only so, but we also joy in God through our Lord Jesus Christ, by whom we have now received the atonement (Rom. 5:6, 8-9, 11).

(f) Testimony of St. John

So St. John, in his epistles:

And if any man sin, we have an advocate with the Father, Jesus Christ the righteous; and he is the propitiation for our sins; and not for ours only, but also for the sins of the whole world (1 Jn. 2:1-2).

In this was manifested the love of God toward us, because that God sent His only begotten Son into the world, that we might live through him. ... Not that we loved God, but that He loved us, and sent His Son to be the propitiation for our sins (1 Jn. 4:9-10).

And so throughout the New Testament, in an unbroken harmony the witnesses testify to the fact of the atonement; and the "propitiation" for man's sins through that atonement.

The same is true also as to the Book of Mormon witnesses, both when speaking through the voice of prophecy and the voice of history.

BOOK OF MORMON PROPHECIES OF THE ATONEMENT

Before the birth of Christ, early in the sixth century B.C.,[6] in the small colony Lehi led from Jerusalem to the promised land of America, it was declared:

> The Messiah cometh in the fullness of time, that he may redeem the children of men from the fall. And because that they are redeemed from the fall, they have become free forever, knowing good from evil. . . . Wherefore, men are free according to the flesh; and all things are given to them which are expedient unto man. And they are free to choose liberty and eternal life, through the great mediation of all men,[7] or to choose captivity and death according to the captivity and power of the devil (2 Ne. 2:26-27).

Passing over many such prophecies, we come to[8] one written near the close of the second century B.C., <which> is peculiarly emphatic: speaking of children who die in childhood before the years of accountability for sin, the Nephite prophet Benjamin says:

> I say unto you that they are blessed; for behold, as in Adam, or by nature, they fall, even so the blood of Christ atoneth for their sins. . . . But men [who have come to an age to understand] drink damnation to their own souls, except they humble themselves and become as little children, and believe that salvation was, and is, and is to come, in and through the atoning blood of Christ, the Lord Omnipotent (Mosiah 3:16, 18).

There are many more such prophetic passages in the Book of Mormon.

BOOK OF MORMON HISTORICAL UTTERANCES ON THE ATONEMENT

The most important utterances that can come to man on any subject would be what the Lord Jesus Christ himself would say upon those subjects. For that reason I am limiting the historical statements of the Book of Mormon on the atonement, to such words as are alleged to have been spoken by the risen Lord Jesus:

> Behold, I am Jesus Christ, the Son of God. . . . I was with the Father from the

---

6. <Ms III "the fifth century B.C.," which is corrected to "sixth"–*Ed.*>

7. <Roberts was not aware that the Printer's Manuscript of the Book of Mormon at 2 Ne. 2:27 has the much more significant reading "the great mediator of all men" and in 1981 the Book of Mormon text was corrected to the manuscript reading. See the editor's "Textual Variants in Book of Mormon Manuscripts," *Dialogue: A Journal of Mormon Thought* 10 (Autumn 1977): 19–*Ed.*>

8. <Ms III[c] adds "we come to"–*Ed.*>

> beginning; . . . and in me the Father hath glorified His name. . . . The scriptures concerning my coming are fulfilled. And as many as have received me, to them have I given to become the sons of God; and even so will I to as many as <shall> believe on my name, for behold, by me redemption cometh, and in me is the law of Moses fulfilled. I am the light and the life of the world. I am Alpha and Omega, the beginning and the end. . . . Behold, I have come unto the world to bring redemption unto the world, to save the world from sin. . . . Therefore, repent and come unto me, ye ends of the earth, and be saved (3 Ne. 9:15-18, 22).

Again, he said to a multitude of Nephites, when appearing to them as the resurrected Christ:

> Behold, I am Jesus Christ, whom the prophets testified should come into the world. And behold, I am the light and the life of the world; and I have drunk out of that bitter cup which the Father hath given me, and have glorified the Father in taking upon me the sins of the world, in the which I have suffered the will of the Father in all things from the beginning (3 Ne. 11:10-11).

Centuries later, a Nephite teacher <Mormon> said to his people:

> Ye shall have hope through the atonement . . . and the power of his [the Christ's] resurrection, to be raised unto life eternal, and this because of your faith in him according to the promise (Moro. 7:41).

TESTIMONY OF THE PROPHET OF THE NEW DISPENSATION ON THE ATONEMENT OF CHRIST

The revelations to the prophet of the New Dispensation of the gospel as they are published in the Doctrine and Covenants are all founded upon the atonement of the Christ as a fact, as a reality. One passage being of special emphasis[9] and particularization is here quoted in proof of the above. It occurs in a revelation reproving one of the early disciples for his unbelief and a disposition to swerve from the faith. And now the word of the Lord to him through the prophet:

> I command you to repent—repent, lest I smite you by the rod of my mouth, and by my wrath, and by my anger, and your sufferings be sore—how sore you know not, how exquisite you know not, yea, how hard to bear you know not. For behold, I, God, have suffered these things for all, that they might not suffer, if they would repent. But if they would not repent, they must suffer even as I; which suffering caused myself, even God, the greatest of all, to tremble because of pain, and to bleed at every pore, and to suffer both body and spirit—and would that I might not drink the bitter cup, and shrink—nevertheless, glory be to the Father, and I partook and finished my preparations unto the children of men (D&C 19:15-19).

---

9. <Ms III* "One passage as of special emphasis"—*Ed.*>

After the consideration of these scriptures, we shall regard the fact of the atonement as a reality established by the revelations of God.

CHAPTER XLI

The Atonement II—In Harmony with a Reign of Law

SCRIPTURE READING LESSON

Analysis

I. The Law.
II. The Essence of Law.
III. The Quality of Regularity of Law, How Secured.
IV. Where Then Is Mercy?
V. Seeming Modifications in Accordance with Law.
VI. Sense of Security under a Reign of Law.
VII. The Inexorableness of Law Required the Atonement.
VIII. Harmony under a Reign of Law.
IX. The Propitiation for Sin.
X. Man Freed from "the Law of Sin and Death."
XI. The Atonement Infinite.

References

A careful examination of all the citations of scripture in the text and the footnotes of this lesson with their context is suggested.

Henry Drummond, *Natural Law in the Spiritual World* (New York: The Columbian Publishing Co., 1893); see introduction and the whole work, *passim*.

Alfred Lord Tennyson, *In Memoriam*, *passim*.

John Fiske, "Through Nature to God," *Studies in Religion*, in *The Miscellaneous Writings of John Fiske* (Boston and New York: Houghton, Mifflin and Co., 1902), 9:215-373.

Herbert Spencer, *First Principles* (New York: D. Appleton, 1896), 53, 59; uniformity of the reign of law, 203; universality of, 347 and note, 384; developing systems of, 589-91.

Sir Oliver Lodge, *Science and Immortality* (New York: Moffat, Yard, and Co., 1908), chap. 3.

John William Draper, *History of the Conflict between Religion and Science*, 6th ed. (New York: D. Appleton and Co., 1875), chap. 9.

Andrew D. White, A *History of the Warfare of Science with Theology in Christendom* (New York: D. Appleton and Co., 1896), 2 vols., *passim*, but especially vol. 1, chap. 4, "From 'Signs and Wonders' to Law in the Heavens."

CHAPTER XLI

The Atonement II–In Harmony with a Reign of Law

In a former chapter we said somewhat respecting the universe being under a reign of law (see chapter 6). That brief mention[1] had to do chiefly with physical laws; while the atonement deals with moral and spiritual laws. However, it will be found that the physical universe and the spiritual universe are alike in this—both are under the dominion of law. And hence I am holding here that the atonement is in harmony with a reign of law, which obtains in the moral and spiritual kingdoms of the universe.

THE LAW

> Verily I say unto thee, Thou shalt by no means come out thence [from prison], until thou hast paid the uttermost farthing (Matt. 5:26).
>
> Think not <that> I am come to destroy the law. . . . I am not come to destroy, but to fulfill. For verily I say unto you, Till heaven and earth pass, one jot or one tittle shall in no wise pass from the law, till all be fulfilled (Matt. 5:17-18).

THE ESSENCE OF LAW

First, it is necessary to remark somewhat upon the nature of the law. Inexorableness is of the essence of law. There can be no force in law, only as it is inexorable. What effect is to cause in the physical world, so penalty or consequence must be to violation of law in the moral and spiritual kingdom. The inexorableness of law is at once both its majesty and glory; without it neither majesty nor glory could exist in connection with law; neither respect, nor sense of security, nor safety, nor rational faith. If the idea of the "reign of law" be set aside and there be substituted for it the "reign of God" by His sovereign will, independent of law, even then we must postulate such conception of the attributes of God that regularity will result from His personal government, not capriciousness, today one thing, tomorrow another. Hence, one of old viewing God's government from the side of

---

1. <Ms III* "That brief treatise"–*Ed.*>

its being a direct, personal reign of God, rather than a reign of God through law, wrote his message from God as follows: "I am the Lord, I change not; therefore, ye sons of Jacob are not consumed" (Mal. 3:6).[2] And another, holding the same point of view, said: "Every good gift and every perfect gift is from above, and cometh down from the Father of lights"–and then he adds immediately, "with whom is no variableness, neither shadow of turning" (James 1:17).

THE QUALITY OF REGULARITY OF LAW–HOW SECURED

View the matter, then, from whichever[3] standpoint you may, government of the world by the personal, sovereign will of God; or the government of God through the reign of law, the quality of regularity, that can only come of inexorableness–arising either from the quality of God's attributes or the inherent nature of law–is necessary to a sense of security, to right mental attitude, to rational thinking, and right conduct. All this becomes apparent if the matter is thought upon conversely. If a reign of law is supposed to exist and the law is not inexorable, but may be set aside, suspended, abridged, enlarged, or its penalties modified or annulled altogether; and these changes affected not by the operation of any fixed principle, or by some controlling higher law, but capriciously through the interposition of some sovereign will, call it "special providence" or what not, then, of course, you have no reign of law at all; but the reign of a sovereign will that operates independent of law. Under such government–if, indeed, it could be called government–all would be confusion, uncertainty, perplexity, doubt, despair. Happily no such condition exists; but instead there exists, paralleling a reign of law in the physical universe, a divine moral and spiritual government in the universe, operating through a reign of law; and the virtue and value of that government arises from the inexorableness of the laws of which it consists.

WHERE THEN IS MERCY?

If, however, the inexorableness[4] of law is to be insisted upon up to this degree of emphasis, where then does mercy, which is supposed to mitigate somewhat the severity and inexorableness of law; and, furthermore, is supposed in some way to represent the direct and gracious act of God when mitigating the law's severity–where does mercy appear? At what point does she enter into the moral and spiritual economy? A large question, this, and one not to be considered just yet, except to

---

2. For the notion expressed in the text that Malachi viewed God's government from the side of a personal government, see the preceding verses of the chapter cited.

3. <Ms III[c] adds "ever" to make "whichever"–*Ed.*>

4. <Ms III[c] adds "in" to make "inexorableness"–*Ed.*>

say that the entrance of mercy into the economy of the moral and spiritual kingdom is not in violation of law, but in harmony with it. In fact, as we shall see somewhat later, mercy takes her part in the economy of the moral and spiritual kingdoms because of the existence of a reign of law, rather than in derogation of it.

SEEMING[5] MODIFICATION OF LAW IN THE MORAL AND SPIRITUAL WORLD, IN ACCORDANCE WITH LAW

When a reign of law is conceived as governing in the physical world, then the conception must also include the destructive or disintegrating forces, as well as the integrating forces, else your reign of law in not universal, and would be imperfect. Moses stood with God and beheld the vastness of his numberless creations:

> And the Lord God said unto Moses, "For mine own purpose have . . . I created them. . . . And worlds without number have I created; and I have created them for mine own purpose. . . . Behold, there are many worlds that have passed away by the word of my power. And there are many that now stand, and innumerable are they unto man. . . . And as one earth shall pass away, and the heavens thereof, even so shall another come, and there is no end to my works, neither to my words" (Moses 1:31-33, 35, 38).

This passage implies constant movement in the universe. The statement—"As one earth shall pass away, and the heavens thereof, even so shall another come"—corresponds somewhat to the modern scientist's notion of "evolution and devolution"; the operation of integrating and disintegrating forces; but the thing to be noted here is that not only is God represented as having created these worlds and world-systems "by the word of His power," but also that "there are many worlds that have passed away by the word of His power." By which we are to understand that destructive as well as creating forces in the physical world operate under law.[6]

So also should we understand that in the moral and spiritual world, where there appears to be a modification of the inexorableness of law, such as comes in

5. <Ms III[c] adds "Seeming"—*Ed.*>

6. <The review committee objected to Roberts's use of the phrase "evolution and devolution" and that by his word God destroys as well as creates: "Evolution and devolution of worlds, as stated here, is questioned. Worlds pass away, just as this earth shall, but go on through the resurrection, or renewing, to continue their existence in permanent, or immortal form." In the margin Roberts placed an exclamation mark ("Doctrinal Points Questioned by the Committee Which Read the Manuscript of Elder B. H. Roberts, Entitled The Truth, The Way, The Life," attached to Rudger Clawson, Letter to Heber J. Grant, [15 May 1930], in David J. Buerger Collection, Manuscript 622, Bx 10, Fd 8, Manuscripts Division, Marriott Library, University of Utah, Salt Lake City)—*Ed.*>

a manifestation of mercy in the modification, or suspension, or the obliteration, of the penalty of a law, say by forgiveness of sins, "for sin is the transgression of the law" (1 Jn. 3:4).[7] All this must not be thought upon as capriciousness, the arbitrary act of Deity in the interests of special favorites. No; the manifestation of mercy, which seems to set aside the severity of the law, which seems to soften its inexorableness by allowing an escape from its penalty–by forgiveness of sins–this must be viewed as the result of the operation of law as much so as when the law proceeds to the utmost of its severity, to the extreme manifestation of its inexorableness in the exaction of the utmost farthing of its penalty.

It is not by special and personal favor that men shall have forgiveness of sins, and find shelter under the wings of mercy. That must be obtained, if obtained at all, under the operation of law governing the application of mercy in the economy of the moral and spiritual world; by law that operates upon all alike. Forgiveness of sins, like other blessings, is predicated upon the obedience to law, and is not based upon personal favor. "There is a law, irrevocably decreed in heaven before the foundation<s> of the world," says the prophet of the New Dispensation, "upon which all blessings are predicated; and when we obtain any blessing from God, it is by obedience to that law upon which it is predicated" (D&C 130:20-21)–forgiveness of sins with the rest. It is because we live under this reign of law that the scriptures teach that God is no respecter of persons.

> God . . . regardeth not persons, nor taketh reward (Deut. 10:17).
>
> Neither doth God respect any person; yet doth He devise means, that His banished be not expelled from Him (2 Sam. 14:14).
>
> Peace to every man that worketh good, to the Jew first, and also to the Gentile; for there is no respect of persons with God (Rom. 2:10-11).
>
> Call on the Father, who without respect of persons judgeth according to every man's work (1 Pet. 1:17).

SENSE OF SECURITY UNDER A REIGN OF LAW

Men stand under the reign of law, then, before God, who administers the moral and spiritual law. No one may hope to escape the penalty due to violation of law through favor; no one will fall under the condemnation of the law through lack of favor with God, by reason of capriciousness in Him, much less through vindictiveness, which is unthinkable in God. God will make no infraction of the law, in the interests of supposed favorites; such "blessings," whether in the providing of permanent opportunities for individuals, families, or races, as may reach through the apparent complexity of things to men; or occasional blessings

7. <Ms III incorrectly cites the gospel "St. John 3:4"–*Ed.*>

such as seem to come to some individuals as special acts of providence; all will come in accordance with the laws upon which such blessings were predicated before the foundations of the world were laid; and this notwithstanding inequalities and diversity of fortunes and misfortunes that exist among individuals, families, nations, races or men.[8] Underneath all the diversities and inequalities that exist, so difficult to account for in some of their aspects, there law is operating despite all seeming incongruities; and out of all these diversities and complexities of experiences, at the last, will come justice—God's justice; and men will be satisfied that it is so.

Meanwhile, this reign of law, with all its inexorableness—nay, rather because of it—present and operating, present in the manifestations of mercy and special "acts of providence"; as also in manifestations of severity—how splendid it all is! How satisfying! What assurance, what confidence it gives! No wonder that John Fiske, remarking upon the idea of the reign of law, said:

> So beautiful is all this orderly coherence, so satisfying to some of our intellectual needs, that many minds are inclined to doubt if anything more can be said of the universe than that it is a "Reign of Law," an endless aggregate of coexistences and sequences.[9]

But the deeper and truer view of things will be, not to accept this "reign of law" as God; nor mistake it for Deity—for mistake it would be if confounded with, or mistaken for, God. Let the reign of law be conceived rather as the means through which God is working to the achievement of His high purposes—God in the world and working through law, "reconciling all things unto Himself"[10] (Col. 1:20).[11] God, the administrative power in a perfect reign of law.

---

8. <Ms III[*] "races of men"—*Ed.*>

9. <John Fiske, *Studies in Religion*, in *The Miscellaneous Writings of John Fiske, with Many Portraits of Illustrious Philosophers, Scientists, and Other Men of Note* (Boston and New York: Houghton, Mifflin and Co., 1902), 9:338—*Ed.*>

10. <Ms III[c] adds "reconciling all things unto himself"—*Ed.*>

11. It is only just to John Fiske to say that such is his conception of the matter; for, commenting upon the effect upon the thinker who has this conception of the reign of law in the world, he says: "The thinker in whose mind divine action is thus identified with orderly action [and reign of law], and to whom a really irregular phenomenon would seem like a manifestation of sheer diabolism, foresees in every possible extension of knowledge a fresh confirmation of his faith in God. From this point of view there can be no antagonism between our duty as inquirers and our duty as worshippers. To him no part of the universe is godless. In the swaying to and fro of molecules and ceaseless pulsations of ether, in the secular shifting<s> of planetary orbits, in the busy work of frost and raindrop, in the mysterious sprouting of the seed, in the everlasting tale of death and life renewed, in the dawning of the babe's intelligence, in the varied deeds of men from age to age, he finds that

THE INEXORABLENESS OF LAW REQUIRED THE ATONEMENT[12]

It is this quality of inexorableness in law,[13] that made the atonement of the Christ necessary to the salvation of man. The condition was this: a law was broken. The penalty must be paid. The majesty of law has been violated; the law must be vindicated. It must be conceded that the law is just; for to suppose that the law itself is defective, would be to challenge the whole moral system of the universe. If the law be conceded to be just, then its penalty must be executed by rigid enforcement or a propitiation made,[14] "The soul that sinneth, it shall die" (Ezek. 18:4).[15]

But the law must not be unjust; for injustice is not and cannot be law. And if in the nature of eternal things–such as a necessary opposition in all things, and the eternal existence of evil as well as of good be allowed, so that the good, the true, the beautiful, and the harmonious may not be realized in the consciousness of intelligences but by setting into action the opposites of the good, the true, the beautiful, and the harmonious; and if the conditions to full equipment for eternal life and progress–such as eternally and deathlessly uniting elements of matter and spirits into immortal personages–then necessity would demand that such a program be inaugurated as would bring to pass the full achievement of these ends; and the obstacles which would hinder intelligences awaiting that opportunity for progression must be removed. And yet in bringing about these conditions the violation of a law is involved–the law for the perpetuation of innocence. The fruit of the tree of knowledge, if eaten, will bring consciousness of evil as well as good; and with that new and strange consciousness of evil, innocence will depart; the law on which her perpetuation depended has been violated. A new order of things will have to be brought in; a new order based upon a knowledge of good and evil. The new righteousness–for there must be righteousness–will be based upon virtue instead of upon mere innocence. It will be a righteousness founded upon experience, upon tested experimentation, an intelligent righteousness.

---

which awakens the soul to reverential awe; and each act of scientific explanation but reveals an opening through which shines the glory of the Eternal Majesty" (Fiske, *Studies in Religion*, in *Writings of John Fiske*, 9:167-68).

12. <Ms III^c adds "The Inexorableness of Law Required The Atonement"–*Ed.*>

13. <Ms III* "exorableness in law," but Ms III^c adds a marginal "in" to make "inexorableness"–*Ed.*>

14. <Ms III^c adds "or a propitiation made"–*Ed.*>

15. The declaration is several times repeated in the same chapter, and the whole chapter should be studied to get the whole majesty of the doctrine.

HOW HARMONY MAY BE OBTAINED IN A REIGN OF LAW[16]

But again the violation of the law? How shall the harmony of a reign of law be maintained, if a law be broken and no penalty inflicted[17] which vindicates it? The consequences of violated law, however, did fall upon those guilty of the violation. Adam and Eve by eating of the forbidden fruit did come to the knowledge of good and evil; and spiritual death—banishment from the presence of God—followed; and in due time physical death—the dissolving of the union of spirit and element—followed. Owing to the conditions under which they are born, these consequences fell also upon all the posterity of the first pair. So that the situation requires a vindication of the law that there may be redemption for the race subject to its consequences. Let the developing thought of this paragraph at this point be suspended for the moment, until other data are brought into view.

THE PROPITIATION FOR SIN[18]

When God, according to the Book of Moses,[19] was instructing Adam on the means provided for his redemption, Adam asked the question: "Why is it that men must repent and be baptized in water?" And the Lord answered: "Behold, I have forgiven thee thy transgression in . . . Eden." "Hence came the saying around among the people," says the sacred writer of the text, "that the Son of God hath atoned for original guilt,[20] wherein the sins of the parents cannot be answered upon the heads of the children, for they are whole from the foundation of the world" (Moses 6:53-54)—i.e., under the conditions provided, of course, by the atonement. Taking this full text into account it is evident that God had forgiven Adam his transgression in the Garden of Eden, not arbitrarily, as an act of sovereign will, but "because the Son of God hath atoned for original guilt." Propitiation had been—or would be—made for "original guilt"—eating the forbidden fruit in Eden, which violated the law of innocence and of life. It brought forth the consciousness of guilt and the certainty of death—but "the Son of God hath atoned for original guilt"—he would satisfy the claims of the law. But how? By the Son of God, who was in the beginning with God and who was God, "being made flesh," and dwelling among men, and in that human life keeping in behalf of man the law of absolute obedience to God. Living man's life, but yielding to no temptation. Suffering, but

16. <Ms III[c] adds "How Harmony May Be Obtained In a Reign of Law"—*Ed.*>

17. <Ms III "inflected"—*Ed.*>

18. <Ms III[c] adds "The Propitiation For Sin"—*Ed.*>

19. <Ms III* "according to the Mosaic fragment—the Book of Moses"—*Ed.*>

20. Or that he "would" atone for "original guilt" when the fullness of the time would have come; for necessarily the matter was at this time prophetic.

not for his own transgressions, for he was without sin (Heb. 4:15; cf. Heb. 7:26). Such is the whole tenor of the scriptures respecting the Christ:

> For what the law could not do, in that it was weak through the flesh, God sending His own Son in the likeness of sinful flesh, and for sin, condemned sin in the flesh, that the righteousness of the law might be fulfilled in us, who walk not after the flesh, but after the Spirit (Rom. 8:3-4).

This passage is undoubtedly to be understood as follows. For what man could not do under the law in that he was weak because of the flesh (human nature), God sent His Son in the likeness of sinful flesh to do; and condemned sin in that he in the flesh kept the law of perfect obedience, and thus "for sin condemned sin in the flesh." That the righteousness of the law might be fulfilled in them who thereafter should walk not after the flesh, but after the spirit.

> We have not an high priest which cannot be touched with the feeling of our infirmities; but was in all points tempted like as we are, yet remained without sin (cf. Heb. 4:15).
>
> Christ also suffered . . . who did no sin, neither was guile found in his mouth (1 Pet. 2:21-22).
>
> For He hath made him [the Christ] to be sin for us, who knew no sin; that we might be made the righteousness of God in him (2 Cor. 5:21).

The Christ suffered for Adam's transgression, not for his own; and for the transgression of all men; for the sins of the world. He suffered for all men, that they might not suffer on certain conditions–the condition of repentance and acceptance of the Christ[21] (D&C 19:16-17). And that by reason of his stripes men might be healed (Isa. 53:5, and Isa. 53:1-4). He made "propitiation" for men's sins (1 Jn. 2:2), and thus satisfied the claims of the law to the uttermost–even unto death–the death of the cross. But it was not "possible that he should be holden of it" (Acts 2:24)–i.e., of death; for he was Lord of life and of death. He had power to lay down his life, and to take it up again.

> I lay down my life for the sheep [men]. . . . Therefore doth my Father love me, because I lay down my life, that I might take it again. No man taketh it from me, but I lay it down of myself. I have power to lay it down, and I have power to take it again. This commandment have I received of my Father (John 10:15, 17-18).

The Christ's suffering and death, then, wherein consists his sacrifice, will be voluntary. But since he may not "be holden of death," he will take up his life again in a resurrection from the dead; and so will all men, and that by the power of the

---

21. <Ms III^{c} adds "the condition of repentance and acceptance of the Christ"–*Ed.*>

Christ imparted unto them;[22] "for as in Adam [through one] all die, so in Christ [by one] shall all be made alive" (1 Cor. 15:22).

MAN FREED "FROM THE LAW OF SIN AND DEATH" (ROM. 8:2)

It should be observed,[23] in passing, that in the matter of original sin, the atonement of the Christ arrested the permanent[24] visitation of that sin of the fathers upon the children. The Lord said to Adam:

> "Behold, I have forgiven thee thy transgression in the Garden of Eden." Hence came the saying . . . the Son of God hath atoned [speaking prophetically] for original guilt, wherein the sins of the parents cannot be answered upon the heads of the children, for they are whole from the foundation of the world (Moses 6:53-54).

That is to say, that while death as a result of Adam's transgression will come upon all men, in that all must die, yet it will not be permanent, there is redemption from it, and free redemption. There is no condition[25] precedent necessary to this redemption, except only, of course, the atonement made by the Christ.[26] For though death may have reigned from Adam to Moses, and from Moses until now, "over those who have not sinned after the similitude of Adam's transgression" (Rom. 5:14), yet:

> Not as the offense, so also is the free gift; . . . and not as it was by one that sinned, so is the gift; for the judgment was by one unto condemnation, but the free gift is of many offenses unto justification (Rom. 5:15-16).

From all which it appears, that while death came as a result of Adam's transgression, there came also free and universal redemption from death through the atonement and resurrection of Jesus Christ. In view of this the Church of the Latter-day Saints say in their summary of faith: "We believe that [all] men will be punished for their own sins, and not for Adam's transgression" (A of F 2).

THE ATONEMENT INFINITE

Take note again that this atonement is made by the Son of God, who "was in the beginning with God, and was God" (cf. John 1:1-2). It was, then, an atonement made by God; and by virtue of that fact it was the highest atonement that could in

22. <Ms III[*] "and so will all men by this means, and by the power of the Christ"—*Ed.*>
23. <Ms III[*] "It should also be observed"—*Ed.*>
24. <Ms III[c] adds "permanent"—*Ed.*>
25. <Ms III[*] "that is, there is no condition"—*Ed.*>
26. <Ms III[c] adds "except only, of course, the atonement made by the Christ"—*Ed.*>

any way be made–a supreme sacrifice indeed! And that is why, no doubt, it is so frequently referred to as "an infinite atonement" (2 Ne. 9:7; Alma 34:12). It is a supreme sacrifice because it was made by a Deity, and because it also embraced all that could be given even by Deity; and that done, the law that was broken in Eden must stand vindicated at the bar of the reign of law.

As to whether the sacrifice by an innocent person can atone for the sin of a guilty one; or whether vicarious suffering for sin can be admitted in the scheme of things at all under a reign of law, I shall postpone the consideration of to the last chapter dealing with this subject of the atonement (chapter 45).

CHAPTER XLII

The Atonement III—Its Relation to the Attributes of God

SCRIPTURE READING LESSON

Analysis

I. Attributes Ascribed to God. First group—Attributes of Power and Majesty:
   1. Eternity;
   2. Immutability;
   3. Omnipotence;
   4. Omniscience;
   5. Omnipresence;
   6. Intelligence;
   7. Wisdom.

II. Comments on Above Attributes.

III. Second Group—Moral and Spiritual Attributes:
   1. Holiness;
   2. Truth;
   3. Justice;
   4. Mercy;
   5. Love.

IV. The Harmony of God's Moral and Spiritual Attributes.

V. The Relation of the Atonement to the Attributes of God.

References

See the citations in the body of this chapter, both in the text and in the footnotes.

The "Lectures on Faith," published in all editions of the Doctrine and Covenants previous to the edition of 1921, have a fine treatise on the attributes of God.

See also collection of Bible passages (and comment) in Oxford and Cambridge Bible Helps (concordance) and William Wright, ed., *The Illustrated Bible Treasury* (New York: Thomas Nelson and Sons, 1896) (concordance).

CHAPTER XLII

The Atonement III—Its Relation to the Attributes of God

THE ATTRIBUTES ASCRIBED TO GOD

As the attributes of God are necessarily involved in the philosophy of the atonement, we think it proper here to make brief allusion to them, especially to those more immediately involved in the atonement. The attributes usually ascribed to God, either upon the ground of scripture or the supposed necessity of His nature, we shall consider as falling into two groups. First group—attributes of power: eternity, immutability, omnipotence, omniscience, omnipresence, intelligence, wisdom. These seven attributes we shall consider as one group, out of which grows the power of God. The second group we shall regard as the moral attributes, the spiritual forces or powers in the nature of God. They consist[1] of holiness, truth, justice, mercy, love. Let it be remembered that in the main we are dependent upon God for our knowledge of Him and His attributes, and, therefore, we quote the scriptures freely in relation to Him. And now a very brief description of the first group.

ATTRIBUTES OF POWER: ETERNITY

By "eternity," regarded as an attribute of God, is meant God's eternal existence. We may not in rational thought assume a time when God was not—or when He did not exist. God's eternity is sustained by such scripture as David's Ninetieth Psalm:

> Before the mountains were brought forth, or thou hadst formed the earth and the world, even from everlasting to everlasting, thou art God (Ps. 90:2).

Also, St. Paul bears the same witness:

---

1. <Ms III[*] "The second group which we shall regard as the moral attributes, the spiritual forces or powers in the nature of God, consist," but since Ms III[c] adds "They" to make a new sentence, it has been necessary to drop the "which" in the previous clause to make an independent sentence—*Ed.*>

> And, Thou, Lord, in the beginning hast laid the foundation of the earth; and the heavens are the works of Thine hands. They shall perish; but Thou remainest; and they all shall wax old as doth a garment; and as a vesture shalt Thou fold them up, and they shall be changed; but Thou art the same, and Thy years shall not fail (Heb. 1:10-12; cf. Ps. 102:24-27).

Immutability

God's "immutability," his unchangeableness, is sustained in such passages of both ancient and modern scriptures as follow:

> Every good gift and every perfect gift is from above, and cometh down from the Father of lights, with whom is no variableness, neither shadow of turning (James 1:17).
>
> For I am the Lord, I change not; therefore, ye sons of Jacob are not consumed (Mal. 3:6).
>
> For God does not walk in crooked paths, neither does He turn to the right hand nor to the left, or vary from that which He has said; therefore, His paths are straight, and His course is one eternal round (D&C 3:2).
>
> Listen to the voice of the Lord your God, even Alpha and Omega, the beginning and the end, whose course is one eternal round, the same yesterday, today, and forever (cf. D&C 35:1).

These remarks are subject to modification as noted under the discussion which follows this first group of attributes in a subsequent paragraph.

Omnipotence

By "omnipotence" is meant all-powerfulness. This attribute is essential to all rational thinking upon God. We may not think upon God and then think upon Him as being overruled by a higher power, and still have Him remain to our thought as God. The scriptures in their whole spirit present this view of the omnipotence of Deity.

> In the beginning God created the heavens and the earth. . . . And God said, "Let there be light," and there was light. . . . And God said, "Let the waters . . . be gathered together in one place, and let the dry land appear," and it was so (Gen. 1:1, 3, 9).

In this manner the work proceeds throughout the creation periods.

Of this attribute David sings:

> The heavens shall praise Thy wonders, O Lord; . . . for who in the heavens can be compared unto the Lord? . . . O Lord God of Hosts, who is a strong Lord like unto Thee? . . . Thou rulest the raging of the sea: when the waves arise, Thou stillest them. . . . The heavens, they are Thine, the earth also is Thine: as for the world and the fullness thereof, Thou hast founded them. . . . Thou hast a mighty arm: strong is Thy hand, and high is Thy right hand (Ps. 89:5-6, 8-9, 11, 13).

To the same effect sang Isaiah (Isa. 11:10-15), also Jeremiah (Jer. 27:17), and Daniel (Dan. 4:35).

In the New Testament the Christ teaches that "with God all things are possible" (Matt. 19:26) and negatively, "with God nothing shall be impossible" (Luke 1:37). The Revelation uses the term "omnipotent" direct:

> And I heard as it were the voice of a great multitude, and as the voice of many waters, and the voice of the mighty thunderings, saying, "Alleluia, for the Lord God Omnipotent reigneth" (Rev. 19:6).[2]

Omniscience

By "omniscience" is meant all-knowing. "Known unto God are all His works from the beginning of the world," said the Holy-Spirit-inspired council of the apostles and elders of the early Christian church (Acts 15:18).

> Remember the former things of old. . . . I am God, and there is none like me, declaring the end from the beginning, and from ancient time the things that are not yet done, saying, My counsel shall stand, and I will do all my pleasure (Isa. 46:9-10).

A sparrow falls not without the Father's notice (Matt. 10:29).

Omnipresence[3]

"Omnipresence" means everywhere present; and perhaps the best description of this attribute of God is in David's passage:

> Whither shall I go from Thy spirit? Or whither shall I flee from Thy presence? If I ascend up into heaven, Thou art there; if I make my bed in hell, behold, Thou art there. If I take the wings of the morning, and dwell in the uttermost parts of the sea, even there shall Thy hand lead me, and Thy right hand shall hold me. If I say, Surely darkness shall cover me; even the night shall be light about me. Yea, the darkness hideth not from Thee: but the night shineth as the day: the darkness and the light are both alike to Thee (Ps. 139:7-12).

"Will God indeed dwell on the earth?" asked Solomon in dedicating the first temple. "Behold the heaven, and heaven of heavens, cannot contain Thee; how much less this house that I have builded" (1 Kgs. 8:27). And Paul, in teaching the nearness of God to men, said that God "had made of one blood all nations of

---

2. Also "Lectures on Faith," Doctrine and Covenants <before 1921>, Lecture 3; so, too, in the Book of Mormon, Mosiah 3:17-18, 21.

3. <In Ms III* the section on "Intelligence" precedes the section on "Omnipresence," but at the beginning of each section there is a marginal Ms III[c] instruction by Roberts to switch their positions—*Ed.*>

men," and had given to all the privilege of seeking "the Lord, if haply[4] they might feel after Him, and find Him, though He be not far removed from every one of us, for in Him we live, and move, and have our being" (cf. Acts 17:26-28).

Under the attribute of "omnipotence"–all powerful–I include "power," which is sometimes, and usually, treated separately as an attribute of God: and under "omniscience" I include "knowledge," which is also usually regarded separately as an attribute of Deity; but both these terms–"power" and "knowledge"–may very appropriately fall under the larger terms–"omnipotence" and "omniscience."

Intelligence

In reasoning with Abraham upon the Intelligences in heaven, and the fact that they varied in degree of intelligence, the Lord said that where there were two intelligences and the one was more intelligent than the other, "there shall be another more intelligent than they: I am the Lord, Thy God, I am more intelligent than them all" (Abr. 3:19). By which is meant, as we think, not that God is more intelligent than any other one of the Intelligences, but more intelligent than all of them together. On this head the prophet of the New Dispensation gave to the world that wonderful announcement, all-comprehensive in its greatness, glorifying God as no other sentence in the language in all the ages has ever glorified him, saying: "The glory of God is intelligence" (D&C 93:36). This is the force and power that holds in right balance and union all the attributes of God, in their application and in the working out of the purposes of God.

Wisdom

Wisdom that arises from knowledge seems essentially an attribute of Deity; as well from the nature of the attribute as from the declaration of scripture. God as unwise is unthinkable; unpossessed of this attribute, He could not appeal to the consciousness of man as God as all. Therefore, it is agreeable to think with Elihu in Job that God "is mighty in strength and wisdom" (Job 36:5). Also with David: "O Lord, how manifold are Thy works! In wisdom Thou hast made them all: the earth is full of Thy riches" (Ps. 104:24). And again, David: "Great is our Lord, and great of power; His understanding is infinite" (Ps. 147:5). So Paul: "To God, only wise, be glory through Jesus Christ forever" (Rom. 16:27); "the wisdom of the world is foolishness with God" (1 Cor. 3:19). He says, again, so high above the wisdom of men does he esteem the wisdom of God, that even "the foolishness of God is wiser than men" (1 Cor. 1:25). We may fittingly close his testimony with his prayer: "Now unto the King eternal, immortal, invisible, the only wise God, be honor and glory for ever and ever. Amen" (1 Tim. 1:17).

---

4. <Ms III "happily," but the King James Version text is "haply"–*Ed.*>

Worthy to go with this testimony is that of Joseph Smith, in which is found the same spiritual music:

> The Lord is God, and beside Him there is no Savior. Great is His wisdom, marvelous are His ways, and the extent of His doings none can find out. His purposes fail not, neither are there any who can stay His hand (D&C 76:1-3).

COMMENTS ON THE LIMITATIONS IN THE ATTRIBUTES OF GOD

We may now consider somewhat the limitations of the attributes so far named.[5]

The eternity of God may be regarded as absolute. "I am that I Am," the Eternal One, the self-existent, admits of no modification.

His immutability should be regarded as stability, adherence to principle. What stands among men under the name of "constitutional morality," fixed devotion to law; and working through law to the achievement of His divine purposes, rather than by caprice, or by arbitrary, personal action. But God's immutability should not be so understood as to exclude the idea of advancement or progress even of God. Thus, for example, God's kingdom and glory may be enlarged, as more and more redeemed souls are added to His kingdom: as worlds and world-systems are multiplied and redeemed and enrolled with celestial spheres, so God's kingdom is enlarged and His glory increased. So that in this sense there may come change, enlargement, and progress, even for God. Hence, we could not say of God's immutability, as we do of his eternity, that it is absolute, since there may come change through progress, even for God; but an absolute immutability would require eternal immobility—which would reduce God to a condition eternally static, which for the nature of things would bar Him from participation in that enlargement of kingdoms and increasing glory that comes from redemption and the progress of men. And is it too bold a thought, that with this progress, even for the Mightiest, new thoughts and new vistas may appear, inviting to new adventures and enterprises that will yield new experiences, advancement, and enlargement, even for the Most High.[6] It ought to be constantly remembered that terms absolute to

---

5. <For a discussion of how Mormon meanings differ from traditional Catholic and Protestant terminology, see Kent E. Robson, "Omnis on the Horizon [Omniscience, Omnipotence, Omnipresence]," *Sunstone* 8 (July-Aug. 1983): 21-23—*Ed.*>

6. On this point Sir Oliver Lodge has a passage at once advanced and bold, and yet for which he claims Christian warrant. It is, however, far removed from modern Christian orthodoxy, though splendidly true: "The universe is not a 'being' but a 'becoming'—an ancient but light-bringing doctrine when realized. It is in change, in development, in movement, upward and downward, that activity consists. A stationary condition, or stagnation, would to us be simple non-existence; the element of progression, of change, of

man may be relative terms to God, so far above our thinking is His thinking; and His ways above our ways (cf. Isa. 55:9).[7]

The attribute "omnipotence" must needs be thought upon also as somewhat limited. Even God, notwithstanding the ascription to Him of all-powerfulness in such scripture phrases as "with God all things are possible" (Matt. 19:26), "nothing shall be impossible with God" (Luke 1:37)—notwithstanding all this, I say,[8] not even God may have two mountain ranges without a valley between. Not even God may place Himself beyond the boundary of space: nor on the outside of duration. Nor is it conceivable to human thought that He can create space or annihilate matter. These are things that limit even God's omnipotence. What, then, is meant by the ascription of the attribute "omnipotence" to God? Simply that all that may or can be done by power conditioned by other eternal existences—duration, space, matter, truth, justice, reign of law—God can do. But even He may not act out of harmony with the other eternal existences, which condition or limit even Him.

So with the all-knowing attribute, "omniscience." That must be understood somewhat in the same light as the other attributes just considered: not that God is

---

activity, must be as durable as the universe itself. Monotony, in the sense of absolute immobility, is unthinkable, unreal, and cannot anywhere exist: save where things have ceased to be. Such ideas, the ideas of development and progress, extend even up to God Himself, according to the Christian conception. So we return to that with which we started. The Christian idea of God is not that of a being outside the universe, above its struggles and advances, looking on and taking no part in the process, solely exalted, beneficent, self-determined, and complete: no, it is also that of a God who loves, who yearns, who suffers, who keenly laments the rebellious and misguided activity of the free agents brought into being by Himself as part of Himself, who enters into the storm and conflict, and is subject to conditions as the Soul of it all; conditions not artificial and transitory, but inherent in the process of producing free and conscious beings, and essential to the full self-development even of Deity. It is a marvelous and bewildering thought, but whatever its value, and whether it be an ultimate revelation or not, it is the revelation of Christ (Sir Oliver Lodge, *Science and Immortality* [New York: Moffat, Yard, and Co., 1908], 292).

7. <The review committee objected to Roberts's view that God progresses in knowledge: "Progression of God in knowledge. This thought is not accepted by members of the committee. We do not feel that it is wise to express a thought limiting God in this manner, which will cause needless controversy. While we believe in eternal progression and that God is progressing, it is not in quest of hidden truth or laws yet undiscovered to Deity." Roberts wrote in the margin that this objection was "meaningless" ("Doctrinal Points Questioned by the Committee Which Read the Manuscript of Elder B. H. Roberts, Entitled The Truth, The Way, The Life," attached to Rudger Clawson, Letter to Heber J. Grant, [15 May 1930], in David J. Buerger Collection, Manuscript 622, Bx 10, Fd 8, Manuscripts Division, Marriott Library, University of Utah, Salt Lake City)—*Ed.*>

8. <Ms III* "all this, we say"—*Ed.*>

omniscient up to the point that further progress in knowledge is impossible to Him; but that all the[9] knowledge that is, all that exists, God knows. All that shall be He will know. The universe is not so much a "being" as a "becoming," an unfolding. Much more is yet to be. God will know it as it "becomes," or as it unfolds; for He is universal consciousness, and Mind–He is the "All-knowing One," because He knows all that is known, and all that shall yet be to become known–He will know it.[10]

"Omnipresence" is the everywhere-present attribute. This must be so far limited as to be ascribed to God's Spirit, or influence, or power: but may not be affirmed of God as a person or individual, for in these latter respects even God is limited by the law that one body cannot occupy two places at one[11] and the same time. But radiating from His presence, as beams of light and warmth radiate from our sun, is God's Spirit, penetrating and permeating space, making space and all worlds in space vibrate with His life and thought and presence: holding all forces–dynamic and static–under control, making them to subserve His will and purposes.

God also uses other agencies to reflect Himself, His power, or authority, also His wisdom, goodness, justice, and mercy–angels and archangels, both in heaven and on earth; and in the earth prophets, apostles, teachers–all that make for uplift, for righteousness; all that catch some ray of the Divine Spirit in poem, music, painting, sculpture, stagecraft,[12] or mechanical arts–all these but reflect God and are a means of multiplying and expressing Him, the Divine. And in a special way, as witness for God, and under very special conditions, the Holy Ghost, that Being accounted the third person of the Godhead–he reflects and stands for God, His power, and wisdom; His justice, truth, and mercy–for all that can be, or is called God, or is God.[13] All these means, direct and indirect, convey God into the

9. <Ms III[c] adds "the"–*Ed.*>

10. <Roberts qualifies the usual superlative which attributes omniscience to God. Roberts accepted that God is perfect, but his knowledge is not absolute and his foreknowledge is not complete–he does not know the future until it happens. Since the universe itself is continually unfolding, God himself does not know its precise end. God can know everything in general, but not every detail. Brigham Young and Wilford Woodruff agree with this view. David L. Paulsen, "Omnipotent God; Omnipresence of God; Omniscience of God," in *Encyclopedia of Mormonism*, ed. Daniel H. Ludlow (New York: Macmillan Publishing Co., 1992), 3:1030, points out that "some [LDS] have thought that God increases endlessly in knowledge as well as in glory and dominion. Others hold to the more traditional view that God's knowledge, including the foreknowledge of future free contingencies, is complete"–*Ed.*>

11. <Ms III[*] "two places at once"–*Ed.*>

12. <Ms III "state-craft"–*Ed.*>

13. <There has been a wide diversity of opinions among LDS leaders about the

universe, and keep Him everywhere present in all His essentials of wisdom, power, and goodness, while His bodily presence remains as the moving center of it all.

MORAL AND SPIRITUAL ATTRIBUTES OF GOD[14]

There is yet to be considered the second group of attributes: holiness, truth, justice, mercy, love; and these are the attributes which are more immediately involved in the doctrine of the atonement.

Holiness

"Holiness," as an attribute of God, is equally as indispensable as any other of the attributes of Deity. Equally unthinkable is it that Deity should not possess it, as it is that He should not possess intelligence or wisdom. No marvel that Moses

---

distinction between God's spirit and the Holy Ghost. The "Lectures on Faith," bound with the 1835 Doctrine and Covenants, was accepted by the church as authoritative scripture. The fifth lecture states the following about the Godhead of two personages and the relationship to the Holy Spirit or Holy Ghost: "There are two personages who constitute the great matchless, governing and supreme power over all things. . . . They are the Father and the Son—the Father being a personage of spirit, glory and power, possessing all perfection and fullness: The Son, who was in the bosom of the Father, a personage of tabernacle, made, or fashioned like unto man . . . possessing the same mind with the Father, which mind is the Holy Spirit." All subsequent editions also contained the "Lectures on Faith," until 1921 when they were deleted. In 1855 Parley P. Pratt published his *Key to the Science of Theology*, which described "a non-personal Holy Ghost who was an omnipresent spirit" (Vern G. Swanson, "The Development of the Concept of a Holy Ghost in Mormon Theology," in *Line upon Line: Essays on Mormon Doctrine*, ed. Gary James Bergera [Salt Lake City: Signature Books, 1989], 92). Swanson adds that in the 1915 edition of Pratt's *Key to the Science of Theology* "without noting his alterations, [Charles W.] Penrose deleted or changed passages describing the Holy Ghost as a non-personal 'spiritual fluid' pervading the universe" (Swanson, "Development," 95). Roberts continued to use and quote the earlier version of Pratt's text. Franklin D. Richards expressed the view that there was one Holy Spirit and many holy spirits to assist (see Rudger Clawson, *A Ministry of Meetings: The Apostolic Diaries of Rudger Clawson* [Salt Lake City: Signature Books in association with Smith Research Associates, 1993], 21). George Q. Cannon, "commenting on the ambiguity existing in our printed works concerning the nature or character of the Holy Ghost, expressed his opinion that the Holy Ghost was in reality a person, in the image of the other members of the Godhead—a man in form and figure; and that what we often speak of as the Holy Ghost is in reality but the power or influence of the Spirit" (James E. Talmage Diary, 5 Jan. 1894, James E. Talmage Collection, Manuscript 229, Archives and Manuscripts, Harold B. Lee Library, Brigham Young University, Provo, Utah)—*Ed.*>

14. <Ms III^{c} adds "Moral And Spiritual Attributes of God"—*Ed.*>

sang, "Who is like unto Thee, O Lord, among the gods? <Who is like Thee>, glorious in holiness?" (Ex. 15:11). "I am the Lord your God; . . . ye shall be holy: for I am holy" was God's word to ancient Israel (Lev. 11:44). Throughout the scriptures God is spoken of as the "Holy One of Israel."

> Thou art holy, O thou that inhabitest the praises in Israel (cf. Ps. 22:3).
> Sing unto the Lord . . . at the remembrance of His holiness (Ps. 30:4).
> God that is holy shall be sanctified in righteousness (Isa. 5:16).
> And one cried unto another and said: "Holy, holy, holy is the Lord God of Hosts; the whole earth is full of His glory" (Isa. 6:3).

Both the Old and the New Testaments are replete with the doctrine. In one of the prophets it is written:

> O Lord, . . . Thou art of purer eyes than to behold evil, and canst not look on iniquity (Hab. 1:12-13).

And again in the scripture: "I the Lord cannot look upon sin with the least degree of allowance" (D&C 1:31),[15] which, perhaps more than any other utterance of holy writ, asserts the holiness of God.

Truth

The attribute of "truth" is ascribed to God; and here we again come in touch with the absolute, as when speaking of God's eternity. God can be no other than absolute in this quality. An untruthful God! The thought is blasphemy!

> God is not a man, that He should lie; neither the son of man, that He should repent (Num. 23:19).
> Mercy and truth shall go before Thy face (Ps. 89:14).
> A God of truth and without iniquity, just and right is He (Deut. 32:4).
> Thou hast redeemed me, O Lord God of truth (Ps. 31:5).
> Abundant in goodness and truth (Ex. 34:6).

So our modern scriptures:

> God does not walk in crooked paths, neither does He turn to the right hand nor the left, or vary from that which He has said, therefore His paths are straight, and His course is one eternal round (cf. D&C 3:2).

---

15. "Nevertheless," continues the passage, "he that repents and does the commandments of the Lord shall be forgiven" (D&C 1:32); showing that while God may not compromise with sin by looking upon it with any degree of allowance, yet He has compassion upon the sinner who repents.

It cannot be emphasized too strongly–God is a God of Truth; and does not, and could not lie, without ceasing to be God. It would wreck the moral universe for God to lie. He must be–He is Truth!

A God of truth, without iniquity, just and right is He (cf. Deut. 32:4).

Justice

"Justice," as an attribute, is of the same quality as the attribute of truth–it must be conceived as absolute in Deity. God not just! The thought would be unbearable. Of course, we have scripture warrant for the doctrine:

> Justice and judgment are the habitation of Thy throne (Ps. 89:14).
> There is no God beside me: a just God and a Saviour (cf. Isa. 45:21).
> The just God is in the midst thereof (Zeph. 3:5).
> Behold, thy King cometh unto thee: he is just and having salvation (Zech. 9:9).

Mercy

"Mercy," as an attribute of God, is in a class with truth and justice and holiness. A God without compassion–only another name for mercy–would be a monstrosity. No, God must be merciful! Else what shall become of man? God not merciful! It is unthinkable, that is all. The testimony of the psalmist is:

> Mercy and truth shall go before His face (cf. Ps. 89:14).
>
> And the Lord passed by before him, and proclaimed, "The Lord, the Lord God, merciful and gracious" (Ex. 34:6).
>
> But thou art a God ready to pardon, gracious and merciful (Neh. 9:17).

Love

"Love"! The crowning glory of all the attributes of God! We may revel in this attribute.

> He that loveth not, knoweth not God; for God is love! (1 Jn. 4:8).
>
> God is love, and he that dwelleth in love dwelleth in God, and God in him (1 Jn. 4:16).
>
> Every one that loveth is born of God (1 Jn. 4:7).
>
> In this was manifested the love of God towards us, because that God sent His only begotten Son into the world, that we might live through him. Herein is love, not that we loved God, but that He loved us, and sent His Son to be the propitiation for our sins (1 Jn. 4:9-10).
>
> God so loved the world, that He gave His only begotten Son, that whosoever believeth in him should not perish, but have everlasting life (John 3:16).

THE HARMONY OF GOD'S MORAL AND SPIRITUAL[16] ATTRIBUTES

These attributes of the second group, as well as those considered in the first group, must be thought upon as constituting a harmony; those—the first group—in harmony with the existences as real and eternal as the attributes;[17] and these—the second group—in a harmony within or among themselves. Thus justice may not deny the claims of mercy. Mercy may not rob justice. Even love may not allow God to intrude upon justice, or wisdom, or truth. At the same time it must be remembered that mercy and love, no less than justice, are attributes of God, and somehow and somewhere must find entrance into the divine economy, must get themselves expressed and that worthily; worthy of their intrinsic nature and value, and worthy of God in whom they inhere in perfection, and all in perfect balance. And while "all must be law"; all must also be "love"—i.e., in harmony with love; for God, from first to last, is love. The attributes of God must be preserved in perfect accord, if the moral and spiritual harmony of the universe is to be maintained. And the matters relating to man must conform to the moral and spiritual attributes of God, or they can not be conceived as substantially placed, and eternally secure. It is these considerations which unite the attributes of God with the subject of the atonement. If God's moral government of the universe is, like His physical government, one of law, then law, not personal, arbitrary caprice, will and must rule. And if God's attributes constitute a moral and spiritual harmony and are united perfectly with His attributes of power and majesty, then again, in the devising of any scheme for redemption of men from the consequences of the violation of law, that scheme must take into account the attributes of God; and plan its scheme of "salvation" in accordance with the attributes of Deity and their harmonious action and reaction upon one another.

It may be thought that our exposition of the attributes of God in this chapter is unnecessarily elaborate, especially since but two or three paragraphs are devoted directly to a treatment of their relationship to the atonement; but I am sure that a realization, through consciousness of the majesty and beauty and glory of those attributes, is necessary to a full appreciation of their relations to the atonement, hence the space devoted to their consideration; and I offer it as all worthwhile.

THE RELATION OF THE ATONEMENT TO THE ATTRIBUTES OF GOD

We have already said, in the chapter preceding this, that it is the quality of inexorableness in law that made the atonement of the Christ necessary; and now at the conclusion of the consideration of the attributes of God—which are His

16. <Ms III[c] adds "Moral and Spiritual"—*Ed.*>
17. <Ms III[*] "as real and eternal as themselves"—*Ed.*>

perfections–they also make the atonement of the Christ necessary to the salvation of man, if harmony be maintained within them. For the perfections of God's attributes correspond precisely with a reign of perfect law. Maintenance of the harmony of God's attributes and maintenance of a reign of perfect law is essentially the same thing; for each demands that when there is transgression there shall be atonement for it; which is but the vindication of the law, in the one case; and reaction to the harmony of the attributes of God in the other. So when the attributes of God are brought to bear on squaring human conduct with either a reign of law or the attributes of God, the quality of the attributes–say of wisdom and justice, mercy and love–and their harmonious relations must needs be so taken into account that any adjustment that can make redemption from the consequences of a broken law possible, must be of a character that will make no break in the sustained harmony and interplay of God's attributes, as well as in the maintenance of perfection in the application of mercy and justice and love in a reign of law.

These are the considerations which make the ethic of the gospel so absolute. "For therein is the righteousness of God revealed from faith to faith" (Rom. 1:17). The only way to achieve an absolute standard of "oughtness" of righteousness is to accept the immutable ethic founded upon the attributes of God, as the true standard of the law of righteousness.

CHAPTER XLIII

The Atonement IV—Could Other Means Than the Atonement Have Brought to Pass Man's Salvation?

SCRIPTURE READING LESSON

Analysis

I. The Question Proposed.
II. Summary of Principles Affecting the Atonement
III. The Testing Place and Period.
IV. What Can Man or God Do by Way of Atonement?
V. Arbitrary Power May Not Nullify Law.
VI. If Other Means Were Possible—?
VII. Helplessness of Man under Broken Law.
VIII. The Capacity to Do, as well as Willingness to Do, Needful.
IX. The Atonement a Voluntary Act.
X. The Severity of the Atonement Considered.
XI. The Lesson Taught by the Severity of the Atonement.

References

All the scripture passages, both in the text and in the footnotes of this chapter with their contexts and parallel passages.

All four books of our scripture—Bible, Book of Mormon, Doctrine and Covenants, and Pearl of Great Price—*passim*. Diligent use of indexes and cross references therein.

Since this treatise of the atonement is derived from the "New Knowledge" that is peculiar to the New Dispensation of the gospel, the treatise<s> of Catholic and Protestant Christendom are of little use in the development of the theme. However, in B. H. Roberts, *The Seventy's Course in Theology: Fourth Year, The Atonement* (Salt Lake City: The Deseret News, 1911), is an appendix in which is given "Other Views of the Atonement," Catholic, Protestant, and Liberal views and is valuable for comparison and contrast.

CHAPTER XLIII

The Atonement IV—Could Other Means Than the Atonement Have Brought to Pass Man's Salvation?

THE QUESTION PROPOSED

The next question to be considered is: Could any other means than the atonement of Christ have been devised to bring to pass man's salvation? Let it be kept in mind what that term means—salvation. The declaration of the Christ concerning his mission was, "The Son of Man is come to save that which was lost" (Matt. 18:11).[1] And we have already in previous chapters shown what it was that was lost: (1) man's spiritual life, his union with God; (2) man's physical life, separation of spirit and body. And so, when considering the means of restoring that which was lost, we must have in mind these two things.

Our present inquiry is: Could this salvation have been secured by any other means than the atonement made by the Christ? Perhaps a brief summary of some of the principles previously discussed will help us approach this important theme more understandingly. We say "important" because many doubt of the necessity of the atonement, and argue that, if a forgiveness of Adam's transgression in Eden was needed, or if man's individual sins need a pardon, then God of His sovereign will, without any expiation for the one or the other of these sins, could have forgiven these transgressions. And now the proposed summary:

SUMMARY OF PRINCIPLES AFFECTING THE ATONEMENT

Violations of law, whether ignorantly done or deliberately planned, even for right ends, destroy the steady maintenance of law, and also involve the transgressors in the penalties inseparately connected with law, and without which law would be

1. <The incorrect scriptural reference given by Roberts in Ms III is "Matt. 19:10," which appears to be an unintentional amalgamation of references to Matt. 18:11 and the textually more strongly attested synoptic parallel at Luke 19:10, which reads "The Son of man is come *to seek and* to save that which was lost"—*Ed.*>

of no force at all. A reign of law subsists throughout the universe; as well in the moral and spiritual kingdoms as in the physical world; and this perfect reign of law, and reign of perfect law, is in strict harmony with, and the concomitant of, God's perfect attributes. The attributes of God, complete as they are and perfect, must exist in harmony with each other, no one supplanting another or intruding upon its domain.

Any manifestations of mercy or special providence, prompted even by love, must not violate the conception of the universal reign of law or justice; or violate the harmony subsisting in the attributes of Deity. Love and mercy, however, must also enter into the economy of the earth order of things; they must get themselves in some way worthily expressed; no divine economy can exist without them, and without expression of them. Justice cries aloud for their presence in the divine government. To get love and mercy adequately expressed in the earth order of things, in harmony with all the attributes of God present and active, and in harmony with a universal reign of law, is the burden and mission of the Christ through the atonement. And now to take up our present inquiry.

THE TESTING PLACE AND PERIOD

According to what is set forth in previous pages, God has created our earth and provided for the existence of man upon it. He designs man's earth-life to be a testing period for man. His aim is to provide a means of eternal progression. His words in the great council, where this purpose was planned, are—speaking of the spirits that were to come to the earth as men: "And we will prove them herewith, to see if they will do all things whatsoever the Lord their God shall command them" (Abr. 3:25); and those who would prove their integrity by their obedience were "to have glory added upon their heads forever and forever" (cf. Abr. 3:26). In other words, a pathway was to be opened to them for eternal progress. To open such a highway, however, it is necessary to create a testing period in the midst of broken harmonies.

We say this is necessary, and we emphasize that word "necessary" up to the standard of being absolute, and this necessity becomes the pivot, on which this whole idea of atonement turns. The end proposed by the Lord God can not be achieved in any other way than through[2] a temporal life, for the manifestation of the necessary opposition in all things. To bring that to pass "necessity" demanded the "fall" of man, attended by the veiling of his memory[3] between his spirit life and his earth-life, that he might learn to walk by faith, to master the lessons that broken

2. <Ms III[c] adds "through"—*Ed.*>

3. <Ms III[*] "attended by the falling of the veil over his memory"—*Ed.*>

harmonies have to teach, that he may learn important truths acquired by actual experience in seeing things as through a glass darkly and in conflict; learning to know things also by seeing them in sharp contrast; light and darkness, truth and error, joy and sorrow, sickness and health, life and death. And so on, and on, throughout the whole category of antinomies which earth experience has to teach. To get all this expressed and man brought into contact with it, harmonious conditions must be violated, to produce which law must be broken and hence the "fall."

In that "fall," however, law is broken and penalties must be enforced, else the reign of law is at an end.[4] Its integrity is destroyed unless penalties follow. The penalties made and provided in this case, however, do follow. Those penalties are found in the events actually following the "fall"—"in the day thou eatest thereof, thou shalt surely die" (Gen. 2:17). And that is what happened. Union with God was severed; this was spiritual death; and it happened as God decreed it would, in the day that man partook of the fruit that was forbidden. Later came the second part of the penalty, men began to die physically; nine-hundred-thirty years after the "fall" Adam died; and having begotten children while in mortality, they became heirs to that mortality, and death has reigned in the earth from Adam until now. The race has found in its experience the decree of God to be true. Man's physical life consists of a union of spirit and element; man's body is of the dust, and true to the decree of God in the event of disobedience—to dust it returns.

THE LAW GIVEN AS TO AN IMMORTAL BEING

It should be observed also that this commandment given to man is addressed, of course, to his understanding, to the intelligent entity; therefore, to the already immortal part of man, to the thing within him which can not die! The prophet of the New Dispensation says:

> All things whatsoever God in His infinite wisdom has seen fit and proper to reveal to us, while we are dwelling in mortality, in regard to our mortal bodies, are revealed to us in the abstract and independent of affinity with this mortal tabernacle; but are revealed to our spirits, precisely as though we had no bodies at all; and those revelations which will save our spirits will save our bodies.[5] God reveals them to us in view of no eternal dissolution of the body or tabernacle.[6]

---

4. <Ms III* "at an end or it is a mockery"—*Ed.*>

5. <This clause in the editor's "The King Follett Discourse: A Newly Amalgamated Text," *Brigham Young University Studies* 18 (Winter 1978), 204, is stronger: "and those revelations which must of necessity save our spirits will save our bodies"—*Ed.*>

6. Sermon at April Conference, Nauvoo, 1844, known as the "King Follett Sermon," published in the sixth volume, *Journal of Discourses*. Also in the *Improvement Era* 12 (January

And again the Lord said to this prophet:

> Not at any time have I given unto you a law which was temporal; neither Adam your father, whom I created. Behold, I gave unto him that he should be an agent unto himself, and gave unto him commandment, but no temporal commandment gave I unto him, for my commandments are spiritual, they are not natural nor temporal neither carnal, nor sensual (D&C 29:34-35).

Such then was the commandment of God to Adam, a commandment addressed to an eternal intelligent being, the penalty as well as the commandment being part of the law, was so addressed to him.

WHAT CAN MAN OR GOD DO IN FACE OF THESE CONDITIONS?

And now, in the presence of these facts, what can man do to mend this breach in the law? What can God do? Forgive man his transgression out of hand, as becomes the true sovereign of the universe? An ancient, and we could well say, a time-honored suggestion. Origen, the theologian of the third Christian century, and held to be the greatest Christian mind of the ante-Nicene age, held forth the possibility of such procedure; for in his view:

> The remission of sin is made to depend upon arbitrary will, without reference to retributive justice, as is evidenced by his assertion[7] that God might have chosen milder means to save man than He did; e.g., that He might by a sovereign act of His will have made the sacrifices of the Old Testament [ritual] to suffice <for an atonement> for[8] man's sin.[9]

Shedd's commentary on Origen's doctrine says:

> But logic could not stop . . . at this point. For . . . if the . . . provision for ratifying the broken law is resolved[10] . . . into an optional act on the part of God, it follows that . . . an atonement might be dispensed with altogether.

1909): 169-91; and now in pamphlet form, *The King Follett Discourse; The Being and Kind of Being God Is; The Immortality of the Intelligence of Man*, annotated by B. H. Roberts (Salt Lake City: Magazine Printing Co., 1926).

7. <Ms III "by his version," but Shedd's text has "assertion"–*Ed.*>

8. <Ms III "the sacrifices of the Old Testament ritual to suffice for," but due to skipping from one "for" to another "for" the words "for an atonement" from the earlier quotation were accidentally omitted and these are restored to the text–*Ed.*>

9. William G. T. Shedd, *A History of Christian Doctrine* (New York: Charles Scribner's Sons, 1891), 2:234. He cites Ernst R. Redepenning, *Origenes: eine Darstellung seines Lebens und seiner Lehre* (Bonn: E. Weber, 1841-1846), 2:409, for his authority.

10. <Shedd's text has "the whole provision for satisfying justice is resolved"–*Ed.*>

He continues:

> For the . . . arbitrary and Almighty Will that was competent to declare the claims of justice to be satisfied by the finite sacrifice of bulls and goats would be competent also to declare that those claims should receive no satisfaction at all.[11]

The views of Origen are all the more surprising from the fact that the Epistle to the Hebrews makes clear all the inadequacy of the sacrificing of animals for the satisfaction of the claims of justice for man's transgression of the law (Heb. 9:10-15). On this point the Book of Mormon prophet, Alma <Amulek>—among the greatest of the ancient American prophets—is very clear:

> Behold, I say unto you, that I do know that Christ shall come among the children of men to take upon himself the transgressions of his people, and that he shall atone for the sins of the world; for the Lord God has spoken it. For it is expedient [necessary] that an atonement should be made; for according to the great plan of the eternal God, there must be an atonement made or else all mankind must unavoidably perish [i.e., remain in the condition that the "fall" of Adam brought upon them—alienated from God, under the doom of spiritual death—and subject also to physical death]. Yea, all are hardened; yea, all are fallen[12] and are lost and must perish, except it be through the atonement, which it is expedient [necessary][13] should be made. For it is expedient that there should be a great and last sacrifice; yea, not a sacrifice of man, neither of beast, neither of any manner of fowl, for it shall not be a human sacrifice; but it must be an infinite and eternal sacrifice. . . . And behold, this is the whole meaning of the law [i.e., of Moses, in which only symbols of the true sacrifice obtained]; every whit pointing to that great and last sacrifice; and that great and last sacrifice will be the Son of God, yea, infinite and eternal (Alma 34:8-10,14).

It should be remembered that the doctrine of the reign of law in the moral and spiritual government of the world, excludes arbitrary action—action independent of law—even though beneficent; and if this as to a reign of law in the spiritual world were not true, even then God must act in harmony with His own attributes. Mercy must not be at variance with justice. Even God's omnipotence must conform to the attributes of truth and wisdom, and justice and mercy.[14] Satisfaction for violated law, satisfaction to divine justice, is a claim that may no more be set aside than the pleadings of mercy. A way shall be found out of these

---

11. Shedd, *History of Christian Doctrine*, 260-61.

12. <Ms III* "Yea, all are fallen," but due to skipping from "all are" to "all are" the words "hardened; yea, all are" from the quotation were accidentally omitted and these are reinserted above the line in Ms III^c—*Ed.*>

13. <Ms III^c adds "[necessary]"—*Ed.*>

14. <Ms III^c adds "and justice and mercy"—*Ed.*>

difficulties, but it must not be by a "chasm in the Deity," or a conflict between or among the divine attributes.

ARBITRARY POWER[15] MAY NOT NULLIFY LAW

It can be readily understood that not even God's omnipotence could make it possible for Him to act contrary to truth and justice. It ought to be no more difficult to understand that God's omnipotence would not permit Him to set aside a satisfaction to justice, any more than to grant an arbitrary concession to mercy. Mere power has not the right to nullify law, nor even omnipotence the right to abolish justice. Might in Deity is not more fundamental than right. God, we must conclude, will act in harmony with all His attributes, else confusion in the moral government of the world.

These reflections lead to the inevitable conclusion that there must be a satisfaction made to justice before there can be redemption for man. They also lead to the conclusion that the necessity of expiation in order to pardon both Adam's transgression and secure forgiveness of man's individual sins arise from the nature of the case, an existing reign of law, and harmonious reactions to the attributes of God, and not from arbitrary action. Justice is of such an absolute character that it would be as impossible to save the guilty without an antecedent satisfaction to God's attribute of justice as it would be for God to lie; and for God to lie would wreck the moral government of the universe, and result–if such a thing were possible–in His dethronement.

IF OTHER MEANS WERE POSSIBLE–?

We have already seen that the necessity for the atonement is established by an appeal to the revelations of God. The absolute necessity of the atonement as it stands would further appear by the confidence one feels that if milder means could have been made to answer as an atonement, or if the satisfaction to justice could have been set aside, or if man's reconciliation with the divine order of things could have been brought about by an act of pure benevolence without other consideration, it undoubtedly would have been done; for it is inconceivable that either God's justice or His mercy would require or permit more suffering on the part of the Redeemer than was absolutely necessary to accomplish the end proposed. Any suffering beyond that which was absolutely necessary would be cruelty, pure and simple, and unthinkable in a God of perfect justice and mercy.

Much has been said, and much that is vicious has been said, about the severity of the suffering of the Christ in the atonement; and all the more because he who

---

15. <Ms III* "Mere Power"–*Ed.*>

is sacrificed is innocent of any transgression, and suffered vicariously for man, all which seems to make the Christ's part so pitiful. It is through suffering, however, and pain, that men are most powerfully moved and influenced, so that suffering possesses highly influential appeal. Oxenham says:

> Pain is one of the deepest and truest things in our nature; we feel instinctively that it is so, even before we can tell why. Pain is what binds us most closely to one another and to God. It appeals most directly to our sympathies as the very structure of our language indicates. To go no further than our own, we have English words such as "condolence" to express sympathy with grief; we have no one word to express sympathy with joy. So, again, it is a common remark that if a funeral and wedding procession were to meet, something of the shadow of death would be cast over the bridal train, but no reflection of bridal happiness would pass into the mourners' hearts. Scripture itself has been not inaptly called "a record of human sorrow." The same name might be given to history. Friendship is scarcely sure till it has been proved in suffering, but the chains of an affection riveted in the fiery furnace are not easily broken. So much, then, at least, is clear, that the passion of Jesus was the greatest revelation of his[16] sympathy: "Greater love hath no man than this, that a man lay down his life for his friends"[17] (John 15:13). And hence Fathers [i.e., of the Christian Church] and schoolmen alike conspire to teach, that one reason why He [God] chose the road of suffering, was to knit us more closely to Himself. For this He exalted His head, not on a throne of earthly glory, but on the cross of death. It is, indeed, no accident of the few, but a law of our present being, which the poet's words express:
>
> That to the cross the mourner's eye should turn,
> Sooner than where the stars of Christmas burn.
>
> For all, in their several ways and degrees, are mourners. The dark threads are woven more thickly than the bright ones into the tangled skein of human life; and as time passes on, the conviction that it is so is brought home to us with increasing force.[18]

The Christ doubtless was aware of the force that attached to suffering when he, contemplating his mission, said: "And I, if I be lifted up, will draw all men unto me" (cf. John 12:32). "Crowns of roses fade, crowns of thorns endure."[19] "The man of sorrows" and the one "acquainted with grief," who knows the pain and struggle of the universe, is more powerful than the man of joys only, and the

16. <Ms III[c] adds "his"—*Ed.*>

17. <Ms III[*] "for a friend"—*Ed.*>

18. Henry N. Oxenham, *The Catholic Doctrine of the Atonement*, 2nd ed. (London: W. H. Allen, 1869), 290-92, quoted by Sabine Baring-Gould, *The Origin and Development of Religious Beliefs* (London: Rivingtons, 1869-1870), 2:307-308.

19. <Abram J. Ryan, foreword to "A Land without Ruins," in *Poems: Patriotic, Religious, Miscellaneous*, 18th ed. (New York: P. J. Kennedy, 1899)—*Ed.*>

death of the testator alone[20] is accepted as the effectual seal to the testimony of the testator (Heb. 9:17).

HELPLESSNESS OF MAN UNDER BROKEN LAW

Admittedly man, as the transgressor of law, is powerless to make satisfaction to the law. True, it is conceivable that he might repent of his transgression, and through struggle may maintain himself in righteousness for the future, but that does not reach the past. If he should by struggle maintain himself in righteousness for the future, that is no more than he ought to do; man owes that duty every day in the present and in the future; and also he owed it as his duty in the past. It is the breach in the law that must be mended. Man is under the sentence of death for a past transgression of the law of God, keeping the law is his duty in the present, and will be his duty in the future, and will not make satisfaction for the past. Man is helpless in the presence of that broken law; no act of his can atone for his own individual sins, nor for the transgression of Adam, or stay the effects of the "fall" upon the race, or redeem them from the penalty of death. Man has started something by his transgression and by begetting a race that is mortal. He can not arrest the progress of it, the mischief is larger than his power to undo. Adam's sin was against a divine law, and the "first judgment," as <Jacob> one of the Nephite prophets expresses it:

> The first judgment, which came upon man [the judgment of death, spiritual and physical] must needs have remained to an endless duration. And if so, this flesh must have laid down to rot, . . . to rise no more (2 Ne. 9:7).

Again:

> Because of the fall of Adam all mankind were fallen, and they were in the grasp of justice; yea, the justice of law, which consigned them forever to be cut off from God's presence (cf. Alma 42:14).

And also they were subject to physical death.[21]

THE CAPACITY TO DO AS WELL AS WILLINGNESS TO DO, NEEDFUL[22]

To redeem man from this condition must be the work of one who has the power to do it. It is not only a matter of willingness, but a matter also of capacity

20. <Ms III[*] "the death of the testator only"–*Ed.*>
21. <Ms III[*] "subject to the physical death"–*Ed.*>
22. <Ms III[c] adds "Needful"–*Ed.*>

to do it. The effects of the sin, unless some means of escape should be found, are eternal; and in this, "like must meet like, and measure answer measure." As just suggested it is a question of power, of capacity. Not only must there be made satisfaction to eternal justice, but there must be the power of Deity exercised, if man is to be saved from death; there must be a power of life so that that which was lost may be restored, both as to the spiritual life of man and the physical life. A restoration through union of the spirit to the body, on which, as we have seen in preceding chapters, the joy and progress that God has designed for man depends. Man, it should be always remembered, in the greater fact of him, is spirit, but it requires spirit and element inseparately connected in order to receive a fullness of joy (D&C 93:33-34). Hence, the importance of man's physical life, the union of his deathless spirit with a body that is to be made equally immortal; and since the fall brought to man this physical death, as well as the spiritual death, his redemption to be complete must reestablish that physical life by reuniting the essential elements of the body of man and his spirit, through a resurrection from the dead, and the atonement and the power of it must be as universal as the fall; as in Adam all die, so through the Redeemer of men must all be made alive.

The atonement must be sufficient for all this; and this, doubtless, is what our Nephite prophets mean when they say, in speaking of the atonement, "it must needs be an infinite atonement" (2 Ne. 9:7). The Redeemer must be a Lord of Life, hence Deity. He must not only have the power of life within himself, but the power to impart it to others—a Godlike power! And to inspire faith in his possession of such power, the manner of the atonement must be such as to include demonstration of that fact, else how shall man have faith in him? All these considerations left the Redeemer and the atonement that must be made far above man and what man can do. Truly the redemption of man is to be the work of God—by His power—hence truly, the gospel "is the power of God unto salvation" (Rom. 1:16).

THE ATONEMENT A VOLUNTARY ACT

Scripture warrant for the above is abundant. The Christ said:

> I lay down my life for the sheep [men]. . . . Therefore doth my Father love me, because I lay down my life, that I might take it again. No man taketh it from me, but I lay it down of myself. I have power to lay it down and I have power to take it again. This commandment have I received of my Father (John 10:15, 17-18).
>
> Destroy this temple and in three days I will raise it up (John 2:19).

He spake of the temple of his body—"when therefore he was risen from the dead, his disciples remembered that he had said this unto them" (John 2:22).

> Thus it behooved Christ to suffer and to rise from the dead the third day (Luke 24:46).

> In him was life, and the life was the light of men (John 1:4).
>
> Verily, verily, I say unto you, The hour is coming, and now is, when the dead shall hear the voice of the Son of God; and they that hear shall live. For as the Father hath life in himself; so hath he given to the Son to have life in himself. And hath given him authority to execute judgment also, because he is the Son of Man. Marvel not at this: for the hour is coming, in the which all that are in the graves shall hear his voice, and shall come forth; they that have done good, unto the resurrection of life; and they that have done evil, unto the resurrection of damnation (John 5:25-29).
>
> Verily, verily, I say unto you, The Son can do nothing of himself, but what he seeth the Father do: for what things soever He doeth, these also doeth the Son likewise. For the Father loveth the Son and sheweth him all things that Himself doeth: and He will shew him greater works than these, that ye may marvel. For as the Father raiseth up the dead, and quickeneth them; even so the Son of Man quickeneth whom he will (cf. John 5:19-21).

But to return now to the thought that "God" must make atonement for man's transgression in order to have it adequate. It will be necessary to keep in mind that Jesus the Savior is God, the Son of God, and God as Atoner. There is that which smacks of justice in a God making the atonement. A God proposed the whole plan. His plan for man's progress could only be accomplished by breaking the world's harmonies. There was no other way. It had to be. Necessity dominated in the case, and God so desired that man should have this opportunity for progress, and He so loved man that if man himself would take his part of the risk, God's covenant with him was that His Son, who also was God, would make the necessary atonement; and hence, the covenant of eternal life was made, as Paul says, "before the world began" (Titus 1:2). We come back to that thought, namely, that a God must make the atonement, with increased conviction after considering the element of "power" or "capacity" to do the thing, to make the atonement; the ability to restore that which was lost, life spiritual and life physical. The work truly of Deity, not of man; a Lord of Life—"God himself must redeem man." That, or justice must take its course and man be left to satisfy justice in endless misery under the sentence of law, without union with God, and without physical, immortal life, the thing necessary to his progress. Justice must not be left to take its course, else a greater injustice will be done to man who was promised eternal life, if he would enter into the scheme of things proposed by God, for his progression.

Moreover, the atonement must be made by Deity, living man's life, enduring man's temptations, yet remaining without sin, that the sacrifice might be without spot or blemish; just as the animals used in ancient times as the types indicating the sacrifices were not only to be the firstlings of the flock—firstborn of the flock—but without spot or blemish. He must give the world its illustration and demonstration of the one perfect life. A life in which "the will" shall be wholly subjected to the will of God the Father. The atonement must be made by a Deity who shall die man's death; but who shall not be holden of it; but break its bands, and demonstrate the power of the resurrection of which he will be the first fruits, and ever after the Lord of Life and the power of the resurrection.

In view of all that is here set forth, it must be clear that no other means than the atonement of the Christ, as it was made, could have been devised for the salvation of man.

THE SEVERITY OF THE ATONEMENT CONSIDERED

Here is doubtless the place where a further word may most appropriately be said in relation to the severity of the atonement already mentioned in this chapter. And this with reference to what the atonement purchased for man, and the effect it was doubtless designed to have in forever fixing in the minds of men the values upon certain great things. Hereafter, and because of the atonement, we must have exalted conceptions of the value of that stately fabric known as the moral government of the world, for it was for the preservation of its integrity that the Christ suffered and died. When the plan of redemption is contemplated with reference to what it cost the Christ, then we must have exalted notions ever after of the majesty and justice of God, for it was to make ample satisfaction to that majesty and justice of God that the Christ suffered and died.

We must set a higher value even upon physical life hereafter, for it was in order to bring to pass the resurrection of man to physical life, and to make that life immortal, that the Christ suffered and died. New glory must attach hereafter to spiritual life—perpetual union between soul of man and soul of God—for it was to bring to pass that spiritual life, that indissoluble union with God on which it depends for existence, that the Christ suffered and died.

We must henceforth have a higher regard for God's attribute of mercy, for it was that mercy might be brought into the earth-scheme of things, and claim her own, that the[23] Christ suffered and died. We must have a deeper reverence for the love of God and the love of Christ for man, and a higher regard for man himself, since God so loved him—for it was to give a manifestation of that love that the Christ suffered and died.

If it be true, and it is, that men value things in proportion to what they cost, then how dear to them must be the atonement, since it cost the Christ so much in suffering that he may be said to have been baptized by blood-sweat in Gethsemane, before he reached the climax of his passion, on Calvary. "Behold, he

---

23. <Ms III^{c} adds "the"—*Ed.*>

suffereth the pains of <all men, yea the pains of> every living creature,[24] both men, women, and children, who belong to the family of Adam" (2 Ne. 9:21).

Again, but in a modern revelation:

> Surely every man must repent or suffer [i.e., the eternal consequences of sin]. . . . For behold, I, God, have suffered these things for all, that they might not suffer, if they would repent; but if they would not repent, they must suffer even as I, which suffering caused myself, even God, the greatest of all, to tremble because of pain, and to bleed at every pore, and to suffer both body and spirit, and would that I might not drink the bitter cup (D&C 19:4, 16-18).

Advantages to be realized in eternal life purchased at such a cost as this, should indeed be regarded by men as pearls of great price, to obtain which a man would be justified in selling all that he hath, that he might buy them.

But on the other hand, if the great and important things enumerated above–redemption of a world from death–spiritual and physical; and salvation of men as individuals from the consequences of their own sins–if all this could only be secured by the severity of suffering that attended upon the atonement made by the Christ, then, we say, and we trust with becoming reverence, that it was worth all that the Christ by his suffering paid for them; and make bold to add: what an infinite pity it would be, if in the moral and spiritual economy of the universe there had been such means of salvation possible! And I further add, what a commentary it would be upon the strength, and courage, and sympathy, and altruism, and love of the divine Intelligences of the universe if none–no, not one–could have been found to come, under the conditions prescribed, to save a world–a race, his brethren!

THE LESSON TAUGHT BY SEVERITY OF THE ATONEMENT

Let the severity of the atonement impress men with one very important truth, viz., that breaking up the harmony of the moral government of the world is a serious, adventurous, and dangerous business, even though when necessary to bring about conditions essential to the progress of intelligences; and more serious when man in his presumption and apostasy from God, of his own perverse will, to gratify his ambition, or pride, or appetite, or passions, violates the law of God and breaks the union between himself and Deity. That is serious; and how difficult it is to reestablish that union, to purchase forgiveness for that sin! How hard it is to make amends to God, dishonored by man's individual transgression of divine

---

24. <Ms III "he suffereth the pains of every living creature," but due to skipping from "the pains of" to "the pains of" the words "all men, yea the pains of" from the quotation were accidentally omitted and these are now added–*Ed.*>

law—let the severity of the Christ's atonement for man's sin bear witness to that, for it required all that the Christ gave in suffering and agony of spirit and body to lay the grounds for man's forgiveness and reconciliation with God.

The severity of the atonement should impress men with the fact that we live in a world of stern realities; that human actions draw with them tremendous consequences that may not be easily set aside, if the actions in which they have their origin are wrong. Moral laws have their penalties as physical laws have their consequences; there could be no moral laws without penalties; and the penalties of laws must be enforced, else laws are mere nullities. Violations of moral law are attended by shame and suffering. Suffering is the consequence or the penalty of violating divine, moral law; and the penalty must be paid, either by the one sinning or by another who shall suffer vicariously for him, and make satisfaction to the law.

This brings us to one of the great questions inseparably connected with the atonement. Can there be such a thing as vicarious suffering? And can the vicarious suffering of an innocent victim pay the debt to justice due from one who is guilty of the transgression of moral and spiritual law?

CHAPTER XLIV

The Atonement V—The Atonement of Broader Scope Than Making Satisfaction for Adam's Sin

SCRIPTURE READING LESSON

Analysis

I. Sins of the Individual.

II. Distinction between Adam's Transgression and Individual Sins.

III. Men Dependent upon the Atonement for Salvation from Individual Sin.

IV. Identical Principles Operative in Man's Redemption from Individual Sins as in Redemption from Adam's Sin.

V. Motive Force in the Atonement.

VI. Man's Cooperation with God Necessary to Salvation.

VII. The Work of Salvation a Work of Sanctification as Well as of Justification.

VIII. Spiritual and Moral Growth.

IX. Phases of the Atonement Peculiar to the New Dispensation:

(1) Redemption from Adam's Sin Unconditional, from Individual Sin Conditional.

(2) Free and Complete Redemption of Little Children.

(3) Redemption of Those Who Die without Law.

(4) Salvation for the Dead.

References

Such is the nature of the treatise in this chapter that chief dependence will have to be placed upon the authorities quoted in the text or cited in the footnotes; and these are chiefly from the scriptures; but the references may be greatly extended by the student.

See also the appendix to B. H. Roberts, *The Seventy's Course in Theology: Fourth Year, The Atonement* (Salt Lake City: The Deseret News, 1911), 135-60, especially "Anselm's Theory of Satisfaction."

The seven chapters devoted to soteriology (doctrine of the work of Christ in the atonement) by William G. T. Shedd, in his *History of Christian Doctrine*, 2 vols., 10th ed. (New York: Charles Scribner's Sons, 1891), are very illuminating in a general way on the atonement, but do not deal with the topics of this chapter. See Shedd, vol. 2, book 5, chaps. 1-7, inclusive.

A fine treatise on the atonement in Augustus Neander's great work (5 vols.) *General History of the Christian Religion and Church*, trans. Joseph Torrey (New York: Hurd and Houghton, 1871), 4:497-508.

CHAPTER XLIV

The Atonement V—The Atonement of Broader Scope Than Making Satisfaction for Adam's Sin

SINS OF THE INDIVIDUAL

The atonement is of much broader scope than redemption from Adam's transgression for "original guilt." Not only was satisfaction to be made for the transgression of Adam, that the integrities of the moral government of the world might be preserved, but a redemption was also to be provided from the effects of the individual sins of man. Man, when he sins by breaking the laws of God, sins, of course, against divine law; commits a crime against the majesty of God, and thereby dishonors Him. And man is just as helpless to make adequate satisfaction to God as Adam was for his sin in Eden; and is just as hopelessly in the grasp of inexorable law as Adam and his race were after the first transgression. For individual man from the beginning was as much in duty bound to keep the law of God as Adam was; and if now, in the present, and for the future he observes the law of God and remains righteous, he is doing no more than he ought to have done from the beginning; and doing his duty now and for the future can not free him from the fact and the consequences of his past violations of God's law. The individual man, then, is in need of a satisfaction being made to the justice of God for his individual transgression of divine law.

DISTINCTION BETWEEN ADAM'S TRANSGRESSION AND INDIVIDUAL SIN[1]

The difference between the sin of Adam and the sin of the individual man is this:

First, Adam's sin, which the scriptures call the "fall," was racial, in that it involved all the race of Adam in its consequences, bringing upon them both a spiritual and a physical death, the nature of which has already been explained. Man's individual sin is more limited in its consequences, though for a time his

1. <Ms III* "Between Adam's Sin and Individual Sin"—*Ed.*>

personal sin may involve the happiness of others in its consequences, yet ultimately they will be limited to personal results; affecting the actual sinner's personal relationship to God, to righteousness, to truth, to progress, to sustained joy.

Second, Adam's sin was necessary to the creation of those conditions under which man could obtain the experiences of earth-life necessary to the union of his spirit with earth elements; necessary to his progress as a divine intelligence; necessary to his knowledge of good and evil in actual conflict; joy and sorrow; pleasure and pain; life and death; in a word, necessary that man might become acquainted with these opposite existences,[2] their nature, and their values; all which was essential to, and designed for, man's progress, for his ultimate development in virtue and power and largeness and splendor of existence. But man's individual sins are not necessary to these general purposes of God. That is, the fall of Adam was necessary to the accomplishment of the general purposes of God; but it was not necessary to those purposes that Cain should kill Abel, his brother; or "that every imagination of the thoughts of man's heart" should be "evil continually" (cf. Gen. 6:5).

The "fall" of Adam, we say, was necessary to the attainment of these possibilities of progress for man, and hence the atonement made for Adam's sin is of universal effect and application without stipulations, or conditions, or obedience, or any other act as a condition precedent to participation in the full benefits of release from the consequences of Adam's transgression. Hence, it is written:

> Therefore, as by the offense of one judgment came upon all men to condemnation; even so by the righteousness of one the free gift came upon all men to the justification of life (Rom. 5:18).

Free redemption from the consequences of Adam's transgression, but not so with reference to man's individual sins. Salvation from the consequences of those sins is another story. All men sin:

> All have sinned, and come short of the glory of God (Rom. 3:23).
>
> And so death passed upon all men, for that all have sinned (Rom. 5:12).
>
> There is none righteous, no, not one; . . . They are all gone out of the way; . . . there is none that doeth good, no, not one (Rom. 3:10, 12).

But while all sin—except those who die in infancy or early childhood—it is not necessary to any of the general purposes of God, or to the interests of the race, that

2. See 2 Ne. 2; also B. H. Roberts, *New Witnesses for God* (Salt Lake City: Deseret News Press, 1909), 3:219-27.

men should sin; and hence, they may be held fully accountable to the justice of God for their individual transgression of law, and are so held accountable.

The penalty for the individual sins of men is a second spiritual death, not a physical death, not a separation of the spirit and the body of man after the resurrection, for what is achieved for man's physical life by the resurrection remains. He will not again be subject to physical death. But for his own individual sins (and this constitutes the third distinction between Adam's "original sin" and the personal sins of men)[3] the individual is subject to a second spiritual death, to banishment from the presence of God; his spiritual union and communion with God is broken, and spiritual death ensues–his death to righteousness. The Lord, in speaking of Adam and his first transgression, says:

> I, the Lord <God>, caused that he should be cast out from the Garden of Eden, from my presence, because of his transgression, wherein he became spiritually dead, which is the first death, even that same death, which is spiritual, which shall be pronounced upon the wicked when I shall say–depart, ye cursed (D&C 29:41).

So Alma, the Nephite prophet, explaining the "fall" of man and how God gave unto men commandments, after having made known unto them the plan of redemption, even in the days of Adam, says:

> God conversed with men, and made known unto them the plan of redemption, which had been prepared from the foundation of the world; and this He made known unto them according to their faith and repentance and their holy works.
>
> Wherefore, He gave commandments unto men, they having first transgressed the first commandments as to things which were temporal, and becoming as Gods, knowing good from evil, placing themselves in a state to act, or being placed in a state to act according to their wills and pleasures, whether to do evil or to do good–
>
> Therefore, God gave unto them commandments, after having made known unto then the plan of redemption, that they should not do evil, the penalty thereof being a second death, which was an everlasting death as to things pertaining unto righteousness; for on such the plan of redemption could have no power, for the works of justice could not be destroyed, according to the supreme goodness of God.
>
> But God did call on men, in the name of His Son, (this being the plan of redemption which was laid), saying: If ye will repent, and harden not your hearts, then will I have mercy upon you, through mine Only Begotten Son.
>
> Therefore, whosoever repenteth, and hardeneth not his heart, he shall have claim on mercy through mine Only Begotten Son, unto a remission of his sins; and these shall enter into my rest.
>
> And whosoever will harden his heart and will do iniquity, behold, I swear in my wrath that he shall not enter into my rest (Alma 12:30-35).

---

3. <Ms III* "and the sins of other men"–*Ed.*>

Furthermore, he says–speaking of the wilfully impenitent:

> They shall be as though there had been no redemption made; for they cannot be redeemed according to God's justice; and they cannot die, seeing there is no more corruption [i.e., physical decay of death of the resurrected body] (Alma 12:18).

MEN DEPENDENT[4] ON THE ATONEMENT FOR SALVATION FROM INDIVIDUAL SINS

As already remarked, men, having transgressed the law of God by their own personal violations of it, are helpless of themselves to make satisfaction to the justice of God, or of the law; and are just as dependent upon a Redeemer to rescue them from the spiritual effects of their personal transgression of the divine law, as from the effects of Adam's "fall." Also, under a reign of law, God may not pardon men for their individual sins by arbitrary act of sovereign will. He may no more set aside the claims of justice unsatisfied in the case of men's personal sins than in the case of Adam's first sin. In both cases "a necessary attribute of Deity" stands in the way of the non-infliction of the penalty due to sin, viz., the attribute of justice, which not even the attribute of mercy may displace or rob. God must act in harmony with His own attributes.

IDENTICAL PRINCIPLES OPERATIVE IN MAN'S INDIVIDUAL SINS AS IN ADAM'S SIN

In the case of man's individual violations of law, as in Adam's sin, the inexorableness of law holds good (Hel. 14:17-18). Thus, satisfaction to justice in the case of man's individual sins, like the satisfaction to justice for Adam's "original sin," must be rendered by one competent to make such satisfaction. The same necessity for one not only willing but able to make the atonement, by suffering the penalty due to the sins of all men. He must suffer for them; for the groundwork of their forgiveness and restoration to union with God must be that the penalty due to their sin has been paid. This or justice goes unsatisfied–mercy robs justice. This satisfaction must be rendered to justice by an atonement or else the law must take its course and punishment be actually inflicted upon the transgressors, which leaves man to a life of eternal misery, alienated from God, separated from the source of spiritual excellence. Man, under such circumstances, would indeed be spiritually dead, and dead eternally, since he is helpless to extricate himself from such conditions, as a sinner can not justify his sin, nor a criminal pardon his own crime.

But to leave the punishment to be actually inflicted upon man would thwart

---

4. <Ms III* "Individual Men Dependent"–*Ed.*>

the purpose of God with reference to man's earth-life; for God designed that man's earth-life should eventuate in joy, in the union of man with God. "Men are that they might have joy" (2 Ne. 2:25). By other Book of Mormon teachers the plan for man's redemption is called "the plan of happiness," "the great plan of happiness" (Alma 42:8, 16); and as this "happiness" depends upon union and communion with God, which is but another way of saying "in harmony with the true, the good, and the beautiful," it is proper to think of the gospel as contemplating the spiritual union of man with Deity.

We conclude, then, that for man's individual sins, as for Adam's transgression, though differing in some respects already noted, involve the same necessity of atonement. There is the same inexorableness of law; the same helplessness on the part of man to make satisfaction for his sin; hence, man's dependence upon a vicarious atonement, if he is to find redemption at all. There is the same need for ability on the part of the one making the atonement to make full satisfaction to justice by paying the uttermost farthing of man's obligations to the law; the idea of satisfaction necessarily involves that of penal suffering. This couples together the two ideas, satisfaction through expiation; or satisfaction to justice through expiation. Whosoever redeems man from his individual sins must pay the penalty due to sin by suffering in man's stead. No merely human sacrifice will be adequate. As put by Alma, the Nephite prophet:

> If a man murder, behold, will our law, which is just, take the life of his brother? I say unto you, Nay. But the law requireth the life of the murderer. Therefore, there can be nothing which is short of an infinite atonement which will suffice for the sins of the world (cf. Alma 34:11-12).

What man is equal to the whole world's sin, and the suffering due to it? Who can bear it? The answer is obvious: no man. But there remains God. What man cannot do, what no human brother can do, it may be that God can do. And that is the basis of the gospel doctrine, the doctrine of the atonement–God will atone for the sins of man.[5] Man, incapable of saving himself, may be saved of God. God may find and save that which was lost. As it was said in the matter of atoning for Adam's "original sin," so in atoning for man's individual sins, it must be a supreme sacrifice.[6] It must be by the sacrifice of the Highest–God! And hence, an infinite sacrifice. It must be all that can be given in sacrifice–there must be no more that

---

5. <Ms III* "the sin of man"–*Ed.*>

6. <Ms III* "of atoning for man's individual sins, it must be a supreme sacrifice," but due to skipping from "atoning for" to "atoning for" the words "Adam's 'original sin,' so in atoning for" from the earlier draft were accidentally omitted and then (since it was immediately noticed) the above line with the error was crossed out. Then Ms III* continued with "of atoning for Adam's 'original sin,' so in atoning for man's individual sins, it must

can be given in sacrifice for sin. Hence, it is the last and is final. As we concluded in our reflections on the atonement of the Son of God as applied to the sin of Adam, so here. The atonement is made by the Son of God, "who was in the beginning with God, and who was God" (cf. John 1:1-2). It is, then, an atonement that was made by God, the highest atonement that can be made. A supreme sacrifice, indeed! And all that could be given in sacrifice it embraces, and meets the demands of justice. Men were "bought with a price" (1 Cor. 7:23), but:

> Not redeemed with corruptible things, as silver and gold, from their vain conversation, received by tradition from their fathers; but with the precious blood of Christ, as a lamb without blemish and without spot; who verily was <fore>ordained before the foundation of the world (cf. 1 Pet. 1:18-20).

MOTIVE FORCE IN THE ATONEMENT

What shall prompt a Deity to make such an atonement? The answer is: two attributes of the Deity now of a long time kept in the background, viz., love and mercy. They will supply motive for atonement. We have seen and considered at some length the helplessness of man in the midst of those earth conditions necessary to his progress, viz., knowledge of good and evil. God saw[7] man's helplessness from the beginning; and:

> So loved the world, that He gave His only begotten Son, that whosoever believeth on him might not perish but have everlasting life. For God sent not His Son into the world to condemn the world, but that the world through him might be saved (John 3:16-17).

This love prompts the Son of God to suffer for the individual sins of men as well as for the sin of Adam in Eden. He undertook to pay the penalty due to each man's sin, that there might be ground for man's justification under the law; that mercy might claim the sinner upon conditions that love may prescribe. And so Paul says:

> By grace are ye saved through faith; and that not of yourselves; it is the gift of God (Eph. 2:8).
>
> The law entered that the offense might abound.[8] But where sin abounded, grace did <much> more abound; that as sin hath reigned unto death, even so might grace reign through righteousness, unto eternal life by Jesus Christ our Lord (Rom. 5:20-21).

---

be a supreme sacrifice"—*Ed.*>

7. <Ms III[c] adds "God saw"—*Ed.*>

8. <Ms III "entered that sin might abound"—*Ed.*>

And in harmony with this a Book of Mormon Prophet—the first Nephi—declares:

> We know that it is by grace we are saved, after all that we can do (2 Ne. 25:23).

MAN'S COOPERATION WITH GOD NECESSARY TO SALVATION

Notwithstanding this doctrine of being "saved by grace after all that men can do," yet in securing redemption from the consequences of man's individual sins, the cooperation of man is required; his acceptance, through faith, of God's plan for his salvation; acceptance of Jesus Christ and his redemptive work—obedience to him manifested by baptism, or burial in water for the remission of sin. The baptism being the symbol of the death, burial, and the resurrection of the Christ, and also the sign of the convert's acceptance of the Christ and the atonement he has made for the sins of men. Then also the acceptance of confirmation into membership of the Church of Jesus Christ by the laying on of hands, by which comes also the baptism of the Spirit—the Holy Ghost—bringing the convert into fellowship and union with God, by which he becomes spiritually alive—"born of the spirit," by reason of which he has become united to the spirit life of God, and hence put in THE WAY of eternal progress.

The gospel so far as the individual man is concerned is the "power of God unto salvation" (Rom. 1:16) to everyone that believes it, and obeys its prescribed ordinances, and its covenant of thereafter continuing righteousness. In the difference between the redemption from the transgression of Adam and redemption from man's personal sins, the one being free, unconditional, and universal; and the other being free, possible to all, but conditional, and therefore limited to those who comply with the conditions, there is to be observed nice discriminations in the justice of God. Free and universal redemption comes from the consequences of Adam's "fall," because that "fall" is absolutely necessary to the accomplishment of the purposes of God with reference to man's progress; without it nothing may be done for his progress. He must know the distinctions between good and evil in order to make progression,[9] though that knowledge may not be acquired but by a "fall" from a state of innocence. Therefore, since that fall is necessary to these ends, justice demands that there be provided free and universal and complete and unconditional redemption from its consequences. But in the case of man's personal sins they are not absolutely necessary to the accomplishment of any general purposes of God. Of course, the earth-environment of man, including the broken harmonies as he finds them, may be necessary to the individual experience of man;

---

9. <Ms III* "in order to progress"—*Ed.*>

but all that will abundantly come once men are at the same time free to choose, and good and evil is set before them. But what is here meant is that it is not an absolute necessity that individual men should sin, or that they sin without limit. Men can refrain from sin, if they will; the power is in them. They are brought into earth-life able to stand, "yet free to fall." They have power to choose good and to follow that instead of evil, if they so elect. Therefore, while it is eminently proper that the atonement of the Christ should be made to include satisfaction to justice for the personal sins of men, and the debt of suffering due to them should be paid, and paid vicariously, since man is powerless to offer expiation for himself, and it is needful that ample provision be made for the justification of man's pardon; yet it is also in accordance with justice that man shall cooperate with God in bringing about the blessed result of his deliverance from the consequences of his personal sins; and that conditions shall be required as necessary to participation in the forgiveness provided, such conditions as belief in and acceptance of the terms of atonement; repentance of sin, and a hearty cooperation with God in overcoming the evil, and its effects, in the human soul.

THE WORK OF SALVATION A WORK OF SANCTIFICATION AS WELL AS OF JUSTIFICATION

Moreover, this salvation from the effects of personal sins is not only a matter of forgiveness of past sins; a matter of justification before God; a matter of reestablishing union with God, which is spiritual life; but it is a matter of sanctification of the soul; and of power to maintain the renewed spiritual life with God. It is a matter that involves human desires and human will. Surely it is unthinkable that God would hold man in union with Himself against man's desire, or against his will. Such a condition would not be "union" but "bondage." The cooperation of man then in this work of his personal salvation becomes an absolute necessity, and hence the conditions of individual salvation already noted, and which may be summed up in the fact of man's self-surrender unto God, manifested by his obedience to God under the divine law; and the declared intention of that obedience by receiving the symbols of the atonement, to be found in the ordinances of the gospel, especially in baptism of both the water and the spirit, and the sacrament of the Lord's Supper.

SPIRITUAL AND MORAL GROWTH

The attainment of the condition of Christian righteousness is a matter of character building under the favorable conditions provided by the gospel; and character building, even under favorable conditions, is a matter of slow, self-conquest. It means to follow the admonition of the chief Judean apostle, St. Peter:

> Add to your faith, virtue; and to virtue, knowledge; and to knowledge, temperance; and to temperance, patience; and to patience, godliness; and to godliness, brotherly kindness; and to brotherly kindness, charity. For if these things be in you, and abound, they make you that ye shall neither be barren nor unfruitful in the knowledge of our Lord Jesus Christ (2 Pet. 1:5-8).

To be fruitful in that knowledge means to be growing in grace, in knowledge of the truth, in righteousness. It means development according to <the> type of the Christian spiritual life, which type is Christ Jesus, our Lord. "If you wish to go where God is," said the prophet of the New Dispensation, "you must be like God, or possess the principles God possesses." All of which, of course, may not be possessed without divine help, as well as by human effort. "He that lacketh these things"—the virtues above enumerated by St. Peter, and the disposition to build them up by his own effort, as well as by divine grace—"is blind and cannot see afar off," continues that apostle:

> And hath forgotten that he was purged from his old sins. Wherefore the rather, brethren, give diligence to make your calling and election sure: for if ye do these things, ye shall never fall: for so an entrance shall be ministered unto you abundantly into the everlasting kingdom of our Lord and Savior Jesus Christ (2 Pet. 1:9-11).

PHASES OF THE ATONEMENT PECULIAR TO THE NEW DISPENSATION OF THE GOSPEL

(1) Redemption from Adam's Sin Unconditional, from Individual Sins Conditional

It may be remarked, in passing, that the distinction noted in the foregoing paragraphs of this chapter on applying the Christ's atonement to Adam's sin and man's personal sins—in the first case unconditional, and in the second conditional—is a doctrine, in modern times, peculiar to the New Dispensation of the gospel revealed to Joseph Smith; and is derived almost wholly from the teachings of the Book of Mormon (see 2 Ne. 2, 9, Alma 34, 42,[10] Morm. 9). In that distinction the beauty and glory of the atonement, the balanced claims of justice and mercy, shine forth as no where else, even in holy writ—much less in uninspired writings of men. It may be regarded as the New Dispensation's contribution to views of the atonement of Christ, for it is to be found nowhere else except in the New Dispensation literature. But there, in the chief summary of the things the church

10. <Ms III has "Alma 34:42," but there are only 41 verses in this chapter, so it is here interpreted to refer to both chapters 34 and 42—*Ed.*>

of the New Dispensation believes, it is written: "We believe that [all] men will be punished for their own sins and not for Adam's transgression."[11]

(2) The Free and Complete Redemption of Little Children

From the foregoing distinction in the application of the atonement of Christ, there arises another, viz., if redemption from the consequences of Adam's "fall" in Eden is to be absolutely unconditional, and universal, and that entirely through the atonement of the Christ, and without any cooperation on the part of man, then it logically follows that if man himself remains absolutely without sin, he would stand in need of no satisfaction being made for his personal sin, and no forgiveness of personal[12] sins would be necessary, since in that case sins would have no existence; and, therefore, the atonement of the Christ for the sin of Adam would be all-sufficient to redeem man from the power of death and restore him to union with God. It follows that if any part of the human race die in this state of personal innocence, then they are redeemed by virtue of the atonement of Christ without any other consideration whatsoever. Children dying in infancy are in this status, and, therefore, the host of them so dying are saved by virtue of the atonement of the Christ for Adam's transgression. In view of this splendid truth, listen to the words of the Christ himself to <Mormon> one of the ancient American prophets:

> Behold, I came into the world not to call the righteous but sinners to repentance; the whole need no physician, but they that are sick; wherefore, little children are whole, for they are not capable of committing sin; wherefore, the curse of Adam is taken from them in me, that it hath no power over them; . . . Little children need no repentance, neither baptism. . . . Little children are alive in Christ, even from the foundation of the world (Moro. 8:8, 11-12).

No less explicit is the word of the Lord through the prophet Joseph Smith:

> But behold, I say unto you, that little children are redeemed from the foundation of the world through mine Only Begotten. Wherefore, they cannot sin, for power is not given unto Satan to tempt little children, until they begin to become accountable before me (D&C 29:46-47).

---

11. See summary in the Prophet Joseph Smith's letter to Mr. <John> Wentworth, *History of the Church of Jesus Christ of Latter-day Saints, Period I: History of Joseph Smith, the Prophet by Himself* (Salt Lake City: Deseret News, 1908), 4:540. <In this quotation, which was later canonized as the second "Article of Faith," Robert adds the word "all"—*Ed.*>

12. <Ms III^{c} adds "personal"—*Ed.*>

(3) The Redemption of Those Who Die without Law: "The Heathen" Nations And Races

Moreover, it appears that mercy has especial claims upon the nations and the races of men who have not known the gospel, the so-called "heathen" races. The first Nephi <Jacob>, in speaking of the atonement of Christ and its effects where no law exists,[13] says:

> Wherefore He [God] has given a law; and where there is no law given there is no punishment; and where there is no punishment, there is no condemnation; and where there is no condemnation, the mercies of the Holy One of Israel have claim upon them, because of the atonement; for they are delivered by the power of him [the Christ]. For the atonement satisfieth the demands of His justice upon all those who have not the law given to them, that they are delivered from that awful monster, death and hell, and the devil, and the lake of fire and brimstone,[14] which is endless torment; and they are restored to that God who gave them breath, which is the Holy One of Israel (2 Ne. 9:25-26).

And again:

> For the power of redemption cometh on all them that have no law (Moro. 8:22).

To this also agree the teachings of St. Paul:

> For as many as have sinned without law shall also perish without law: and as many as have sinned in the law shall be judged by the law (Rom. 2:12).

I venture the assertion, basing it upon the sense of the whole passage, that the above passage should read "shall be judged without law."

In the adjustment of things connected with the placing of men and nations and races in and during the first resurrection, it is declared in modern revelation that it shall be tolerable, at that time, for the heathen, meaning those who lived and died without law or knowledge of the gospel: "Then shall the heathen nations be redeemed," saith the Lord, "and they that knew no law shall have part in the

---

13. <Ms III* "its effects where proclaimed and rejected"—*Ed.*>

14. The torments of the ungodly sinners are likened unto a lake of fire and brimstone by this writer, Nephi <Jacob>. Not that the sinners are plunged into a lake of fire and brimstone, as so-called orthodox Christians teach. Indeed, in the above passage there is a definition of what the lake of fire is—it is "endless torment," which "endless torment" ever exists for the punishment of impenitent sinners—each one partaking of it to such a degree and for such time as is necessary to satisfy the demands of justice. In this very chapter above quoted Nephi <Jacob> says of the wicked: "And their torment is as a lake of fire and brimstone, whose flames ascend up forever and have no end" (2 Ne. 9:16). See also Alma 12:17.

first resurrection, and it shall be tolerable for them" (D&C 45:54). Not that these will rise at once to the full height and perfect glory of God's celestial kingdom; but they shall be "heirs of salvation" (D&C 76:88). They are not irredeemably lost, as false teachers and their falser creeds, though regarded as Christian and orthodox, hold. On the contrary, they will come forth in the first resurrection as stated above, as also again declared in the great revelation on the various degrees of glory to which men shall attain in and through the resurrection from the dead,[15] and to them will be accorded the advantages of "the everlasting gospel," the gospel which endures through all the ages to bless with opportunity of progression, the children of God.

(4) Salvation for the Dead

The principles of the immediately preceding paragraphs bring us to the fourth great distinctive feature of the atonement peculiar in modern times to the New Dispensation of the gospel, viz., the application of the atonement and the whole gospel scheme to all who may not have heard it, or even heard of it; or who having heard of it in their blindness, or semi-blindness, or ignorance have rejected it. This in the New Dispensation literature is generalized as "salvation for the dead." It has its inception first in the fact that the gospel is an "everlasting gospel"; one that endures through the ages, and that to bless and save men, when they shall turn to it for its saving grace and power. Second, in the fact that the revelations of God give warrant for the belief that there is provided such a means of salvation for those who may have missed fair opportunity to understand and receive the gospel. Fuller development of this doctrine, however, belongs to a place in a future chapter (chapter 47, part II) where the discussion of it takes place.

---

15. This is one of the greatest revelations of the New Dispensation, and is one of the greatest monuments to the inspiration of the Prophet Joseph Smith; see D&C 76.

CHAPTER XLV

The Atonement VI—The Efficacy of Vicarious Atonement

SCRIPTURE READING LESSON

Analysis

I. The Law of Righteousness.
II. Spirit Suffering.
III. Men Suffer because of the Sins of Others.
IV. Men Suffer with Each Other on account of Sin.
V. Willingness of Men to Suffer for Each Other.
VI. Vicarious Suffering.
VII. Intimations of Great Possibilities.
VIII. The Reign of Law and Love.

References

The quotations of the text and footnotes in this chapter.

There is little else to give in way of references, except to suggest that all that was given under "References" in Lesson 44 could be adopted here.

CHAPTER XLV

The Atonement VI–The Efficacy of Vicarious Atonement

Herein is love, not that we loved God, but that He loved us, and send His Son to be the propitiation for our sins

(1 Jn. 4:10).

THE LAW OF RIGHTEOUSNESS

All sin against moral law is followed by suffering. At first glance that statement may not be accepted without qualification; but it is true. "Sin is <the> transgression of the law" is scriptural definition of sin (1 Jn. 3:4; Rom. 4:15). No difficulty will arise from that definition, but there might arise difference of opinion as to what constitutes the "law," which to violate would be sin. Of course, moral law, or the law of righteousness, varies among different races and nations; and indeed varies in the same race and nation in different periods of time; but no matter how variant the law may be among different races or nations; or how variant it may be among individuals, the principle announced that suffering follows sin will hold good. Of course, between the Christian whose conscience is trained in the moral law of the doctrine of Christ, and the heathen, "who know not God," there is a wide difference. Many things which are sin to the Christian conscience are not sin to the heathen races, unenlightened by the ethics of the Christian religion; but, nevertheless, what I say is true; and if heathen peoples do not have the same moral standards that prevail in Christian lands, they have some moral standards; and whenever they violate what to them is the "rule of righteousness," it is followed by chagrin, by sorrow, by mental suffering for them; and so with the Christian people who are instructed in the high, moral principles of the Christian religion. When they fall below their ideals, when they consciously violate their "rule of righteousness," it is followed by suffering, by a sense of shame, by sorrow; and, indeed, the great volume of the sorrows of this world spring from sin, the transgression of the moral law.

SPIRIT SUFFERING[1]

It is just as real, this suffering of the spirit for the violation of the moral law, as the suffering of physical pain. The mind no less than the body may be hurt, wounded as deeply as the body, and carry its scars as the evidence of its wounds as long. Guizot says:

> And it often happens that the best men, that is, those who have best conformed their will to reason, have often been the most struck with their insufficiency, the most convinced of the inequality between the conduct of man and his task, between liberty and law [and, therefore, have they suffered most].[2]

It is possible, and men do suffer for their own sins.

MEN SUFFER BECAUSE OF THE SINS OF OTHERS

This we know, also, it is possible for men to suffer because of the sins of others, and they often do. You can scarcely conceive of a man being so far isolated, so far outside the sympathies of the world, that it can be said of him that he lives unto himself alone; that his sinning and his suffering concerns only himself. Men are so knit together in a network of sympathies–not seen, but real[3] nevertheless–that they suffer *because* of each other. It is easily proven. Take the case of an honorable father and mother who have led, we will say–and there are such fathers and mothers–ideal lives. They have lived in honor; they have met their obligations to the world with reasonable fidelity; they have lived lives of righteousness; they have set good examples to their children and neighbors; they have taught the Christian truths at the fireside; they have surrounded their family with every advantage that would prepare them for honorable stations among men. They have taken pride as they have seen their children grow from infancy to manhood, and their souls have hoped that a sort of immortality would subsist in the perpetuation of their race through their children. Then out of this family group, over which the parents have watched with such anxious solicitude, there comes forth a reprobate youth, in whom there seems to be scarcely any moral sense. He violates all the conventions of society and of moral living; he destroys all his prospects by his excesses, and he becomes a vagabond and outcast among men, a degenerate;

1. <Ms III* "Possibility of the Spirit Suffering"–*Ed.*>

2. <François P. G. Guizot, *The History of Civilization, from the Fall of the Roman Empire to the French Revolution*, trans. William Hazlitt (New York: D. Appleton and Co., 1867), vol. 2, lecture 5–*Ed.*>

3. <Ms III^c adds "real"–*Ed.*>

perhaps finds his way through the sewers of sin, into the prison house, and at last, perchance, may go to the very gallows itself.

And what is the condition of that righteous father and mother the while, when they look upon this sad mischance in their household? Sorrow! The one who has led this shameful life, though he may suffer somewhat for his sins, has not suffered the one-thousandth part of the shame and humiliation and disgrace that has been experienced by this father and mother. They suffer because of the sins of this wayward son. They illustrate in their experience the fact that men can suffer because of each other; the innocent are involved in the sins and crimes of the guilty.

From this confessedly extreme case all down the line of human experiences and relationships in constantly varying degrees men suffer because of each other.

MEN SUFFER WITH EACH OTHER ON ACCOUNT OF SIN

Again, men suffer with each other on account of sin. An outsider, looking at this scene I have presented—I mean one not a member of the grief-stricken family—witnessing the sorrow of the father, and the inconsolable grief of the mother; the mental distress and shame experienced by brothers[4] and sisters; the outsider, the near friend, or neighbor, witnessing all this is distressed with the sorrowing father and mother; he suffers *with* them through common, human sympathy.

WILLINGNESS OF MEN TO SUFFER FOR EACH OTHER

There is still another phase of this suffering on account of sin, and one that draws very near to the point I am trying to establish. There is among men, and especially among men of highly sensitive natures, a willingness to suffer *for* others. Take the case, for instance, of David and Absalom.[5] Absalom was the most worthless of all David's sons; he had planned rebellion against the old king; he would have clutched the crown from the hoary head of David and put it upon his own. In every way he had warred against the honor and the interests of his father. Yet when news was brought to the king that the worthless young man had been caught in the battle and slain, the old king was stricken with sorrow, and gave vent to the father-cry that rings through all the ages—"Oh Absalom, my son! Would to God I had died for thee!" (cf. 2 Sam. 18:33). In this experience of David we see the willingness of one to suffer for another. Nor is this willingness confined to parents alone who would so often and so willingly take upon themselves the consequences of their children's sins, though those consequences involved death. The same willingness exists on the part of the children, but perhaps is less

4. <Ms III[c] adds an "s" to make the plural "brothers"—*Ed.*>

5. <In this section Ms III has the spelling "Absolom"—*Ed.*>

frequently manifested, to suffer for their parents. The same is true also as to brothers and sisters, and among friends, where no tie of consanguinity exists; and even among strangers, on the occasion of great, imminent danger, this impulse in man, this willingness to risk his own life for others is frequently manifested. Such experiences make up the history of heroism, which is the chief glory of our human race.

THE PITY OF IT, IF–![6]

Here let it be understood that I am not introducing the question as to whether men can suffer one for another in breaches of the moral law. I am inclined to doubt that, as it might lead to the thwarting of justice[7] rather than to the promotion of it in our human life; but I am discussing the evident willingness of men to suffer for the sins of others, if they could, up to the point of laying down their lives for them; and with Browning I hold that:

> 'Tis not what man does which exalts him, but what man would do.[8]

I am pointing out the existence of such an impulse, inclination, or principle in men, in human nature, in order to argue from what we know of this well-attested fact,[9] that there being such a disposition in man, it may be reasonably concluded that such a disposition, but[10] more abundantly, and more perfectly, and more intensely, and quite effectively[11] will be found in the Divine Intelligences, or Gods; and who at need, as in the case of redeeming man from the "fall" through Adam,[12] and from the consequences of personal sins–would, through love, make the necessary sacrifice for the sins of a world, as did the Christ. For if this disposition exists more intensively in Gods than in men, what an infinite pity it would be should there be no means in the moral economy of things for such expression of self-sacrificing love!

---

6. <Ms III[c] adds "The Pity Of It, If–!"–*Ed.*>

7. <Ms III[*] "the thwarting of injustice"–*Ed.*>

8. <Robert Browning, "Saul," stanza xviii, in *Browning: Poetical Works, Complete from 1833 to 1868 and the Shorter Poems Thereafter* (London: Oxford University Press, 1967), 231–*Ed.*>

9. <Ms III[*] "this well-attested fact, (and the reader will observe that our old method of earlier chapters abides with us still)"–*Ed.*>

10. <Ms III[c] adds "but"–*Ed.*>

11. <Ms III[*] "and quite effectively–the same willingness and inate [*sic*] disposition"–*Ed.*>

12. <Ms III[*] "through an Adam"–*Ed.*>

VICARIOUS SUFFERING NECESSARY TO SUPREME LOVE-MANIFESTATION

"Vicarious suffering," says some now-forgotten author, "seems supremely unjust, yet it is blessed and glorious; for in no other way can love so intensely be expressed—that one suffer for his friend through love." And I will add the suffering victim being himself innocent, would make his sacrifice all the more impressive.[13]

The apostle said:

> Hereby perceive we the love of God,[14] because he laid down his life for us (1 Jn. 3:16).

And again:

> In this was manifested the love of God toward us, because that God had sent His only begotten Son into the world, that we might live through him. Herein is love, not that we loved God, but that He loved us, and sent His Son to be the propitiation for our sins (1 Jn. 4:9-10).

It is through this means, self-sacrifice, that love gets expressed, and this leads to manifestations of mercy in the divine moral and spiritual economy; and in no other way can they become expressed—this love and mercy! But a divine moral and spiritual economy cannot exist without the manifestation of them. Therefore, to make the scheme of things perfect, there must be place and means of bringing in these two brightest and best elements of such economy, else both a reign of law and the attributes of Deity stand broken and inharmonious in our consciousness. From the very nature of things, then, there must be a means of expressing love, and of expressing it supremely, by sacrifice, else mercy shall not appear, for mercy springs from love as wisdom rises from knowledge.

It is from the above basis of thought that the poet Browning, worked out his conception of vicarious suffering in his "Saul." This poem is the story of David's love for the melancholy, obsessed king of Israel, and David's willingness out of this love, to suffer for the king, even to die for him, if only that would restore Saul to his best and maintain him there.

> Could I help thee, my father,
> inventing a bliss, [says David,]
> I would add, to that life of the past
> [which he had just glorified in song],

---

13. <Ms III* "the more impressive and effective"—*Ed.*>

14. <The words "of God" are in italics in the King James Version, indicating that there are no corresponding words in the original Greek—*Ed.*>

both the future–and this;
I would give thee new life altogether,
as good, ages hence,
As this moment–had love but the warrant,
love's heart to dispense.[15]

And then the thought: if he, David, being but a man would do this for the restoration of Saul, would not God do as much? Or, as the poet makes David say:

Do I find love so full in my nature . . .
That I doubt God's own love can compete with it?
Would I fain in my impotent yearning
do all for this man,
And dare doubt he alone shall not
help him, who yet alone can?
Would I suffer for him that I love?
So would God, [he concludes]–so wilt thou! . . .
See the Christ stand![16]

INTIMATIONS OF GREAT POSSIBILITIES

Does this fact of willingness to suffer for others, so abundantly attested in human experiences, bear witness to the existence of no great and eternal principle, that may be of incalculable benefit in the moral economy of the universe? Is it meaningless? I think not. On the contrary, it suggests the existence of a great and effective truth, namely, that Divine Intelligences of the universe are so bound together in sympathetic relations that at need they can suffer for each other, as well as with each other, and because of each other.

> Greater love hath no man than this, that a man lay down his life for his friends (John 15:13).

The same would doubtless be true of God. Shall those Intelligences we must needs think of as Divine, as making up David's "Congregation of the Mighty," the Gods among whom God, the greatest of all the Intelligences, stands and judges (Ps. 82:1)–shall these be denied the privilege of love-manifestation which goes with this

15. <Browning, "Saul," stanza xv, in *Browning: Poetical Works*, 230–*Ed.*>

16. I commend the whole poem to the reader. It is too long to insert here and less than the whole would do an injustice to a masterpiece of thought and composition. It will richly repay the half-score readings that will be required to master it. <Browning, "Saul," stanzas xvii-xviii, in ibid., 231–*Ed.*>

giving of all? And shall this suffering for others in such cases have no benefiting effect upon those others for whom the suffering is endured? Shall this love-force of Divine Intelligences be mere waste of the highest and most refined of all forces—spiritual love-force? Not so, if reason answers the question. Certainly not so if the scriptures answer it. The scriptures abundantly confirm the declaration made that Divine Intelligences are not denied the power of giving the highest love manifestation for others by suffering for them; and in that love manifestation giving all they can give, even to taking upon themselves the consequences of the sins of others and making effective atonement for them; suffering that others might have placed within their reach the means of eternal progression, and escape the eternal consequences of sin, if only they would accept such means as are provided for such escape. Otherwise, of course, the sinners themselves must suffer all the consequences due to their sins; for nothing is clearer in the revealed word of God, developed in this treatise, than that satisfaction must be made to justice whenever the domain of law and justice is trespassed upon, else all is confusion in the moral government of the world; so that if men will not avail themselves of means which love provides for their redemption, then they themselves must meet the inexorable demands of justice.

VICARIOUS SUFFERING: ITS REALITY AND ITS EFFECTIVENESS THE DOCTRINE OF THE GOSPEL

This, then, is the especial doctrine of the gospel, on which the earth-life mission of the Christ is based. One Divine Intelligence at need can suffer for others, and vicariously endure suffering for another's sins;[17] make a satisfaction to justice, and bring the quality of love, and mercy its consequent, into the moral economy of the world, and give it legitimate standing under a reign of law, softening somewhat the otherwise harsh aspect of things in this, God's world.

THE REIGN OF LAW AND LOVE

To this then our inquiry and discussions lead us; to recognize in the gospel of Jesus Christ, the central truth of which is the atonement, a reign of law and love; and that to preserve this law, and to manifest this love, was the purpose of the earth-life mission of the Christ. To teach and to demonstrate, first of all, God-love for man, by a sacrifice that tasks God <in order> that man might be

17. <Ms III[*] "and for such an one to stand responsible for another; and vicariously endure suffering for another's sins"—*Ed.*>

saved; and second, to inspire man-love for God, by the demonstration that God first loved man, and how deeply God loved him; and third, to teach man-love for man. "For beloved," says the apostle,[18] "If God so loved us, we also ought to love one another" (1 Jn. 4:11). In this love for one another the children of God are manifest, he contends.

> Whosoever doeth not righteousness is not of God, neither he that loveth not his brother. For this is the message that ye heard from the beginning, that we should love one another. . . . We know that we have passed from death into life, because we love the brethren. He that loveth not his brother abideth in death. . . . Hereby perceive we the love of God, because he laid down his life for us; and we ought to lay down our lives for the brethren (1 Jn. 3:10-11, 14, 16).

It is not to be marveled at that this same apostle declared that "He that loveth not knoweth not God; for God is love" (1 Jn. 4:8), or that Paul, accepting the same principle, should say, "he that loveth another, hath fulfilled the law. . . . Therefore, love is the fulfilling of the law" (Rom. 13:8, 10).

Jesus, however, teaches the matter most perfectly. Accepting the love of God for man as assured, then the great commandment for man is:

> Thou shalt love the Lord thy God with all thy heart and with all thy soul, and with all thy mind. This is the first and great commandment. And the second is like unto it, Thou shalt love thy neighbor as thyself. On these two commandments hang all the law and the prophets (Matt. 22:37-40).

"Love is the fulfilling of the law." Love exists in the earth-scheme of things, in the moral government of the world, in harmony with the universal reign of law. It is not born of some caprice, or mere impulse, howsoever beneficent; but interwoven it is into the very web and woof of things. It is immanent in them, an indestructible Presence. It is because love reigns in harmony with law that we mortals can be so sure of it; and rest so secure in it. For as it was not born of caprice, so, too, it will not depart from the world, nor from individuals on caprice; but will endure as space itself endures—from the very nature of it; as truth abides; as law itself subsists; as God lives; for it is of the eternal things—the things that do not pass away.

---

18. <Ms III* "says the apostle whom Jesus loved pre-eminently"—*Ed.*>

CHAPTER XLVI

Departure from "The Way"

SCRIPTURE READING LESSON

Analysis

I. Breaking of the Covenant; Changing of the Ordinances.
II. Contentions among the Leading Officers of the Primitive Church.
III. Law and Gospel Controversy.
IV. Character of Church Membership in Apostolic Times.
V. Two Parties in the Church of the First Century.
VI. Evidence of Early Dissensions among Primitive Christians.
VII. St. Peter's Prophecies on Apostasy.
VIII. Testimony of St. John on Apostasy.
IX. Purpose of This Review.
X. Effect of Early Persecutions on the Church.
XI. Paul's Great Prophecy on Universal Apostasy.
XII. The Sum of the Matter.

References

Joseph Priestley, LL.D., F.R.S., *An History of the Corruptions of Christianity*, 2 vols. (London: J. Johnson, 1782). A most scholarly and masterful treatise.

Dr. John Lawrence von Mosheim, *Institutes of Ecclesiastical History*, 3 vols., trans. James Murdock (New Haven, Connecticut: A. H. Maltby, 1839). Follow through the three volumes the chapters on "Adverse Events" and the chapters on "Schisms and Heresies."

Other church histories may be consulted with advantage: Augustus Neander, *General History of the Christian Religion and Church*, 5 vols.; Henry Hart Milman, *History of Christianity*, 2 vols. (New York: A. C. Armstrong and Son, 1881); Joseph Milner, *The History of the Church of Christ*, 4 vols. (London: T. Cadell, 1834); and many others.

See Rt. Rev. John Milner, *The End of Religious Controversy*, 2nd ed. (London: Keating, Brown, and Co., 1819), (Roman Catholic), and John H. Hopkins, D.D., LL.D., Bishop of Vermont, *"The End of Controversy," Controverted* (New York: Pudney and Russell, 1854), a (Protestant) "Refutation." Attention is especially drawn to chap. 5 of vol. 1 of Dr. Hopkins' work.

Our own writers have been prolific on this theme. See Dr. James E. Talmage, *The Great Apostasy* (Salt Lake City: The Deseret News, 1909); also Orson Pratt's works. For the present writer's works on this theme, see note 37 <14>, this chapter.

CHAPTER XLVI

Departure from "The Way"

BREAKING OF THE COVENANT; CHANGING OF THE ORDINANCES

In part we have already shown how men who had accepted the revelations of God—the Jew and the Christian—left the Christ as the revelation of God and went after the vain philosophies of the Greek and Roman and the Egyptian Gentiles, denying even the Lord that bought them. Now that a surer knowledge is given of the whole Christian plan of things, it becomes necessary to point out how there was a departure, not only from a true conception of God, from the right idea of creation, from the knowledge of the origin of man, and right apprehension of the purpose of God in the earth-life of man—but they have departed from the WAY of life as revealed in and through the everlasting gospel of Jesus Christ. Things became, as Isaiah predicted they would, viz., that it would be the same with master and servant, the buyer and seller, the priest and the people; the earth would mourn and fade away as to spiritual knowledge and spiritual power, until the earth itself would become defiled under the inhabitants thereof:

> Because they have transgressed the laws, changed the ordinances, and broken the everlasting covenant. Therefore hath the curse devoured the earth, and they that dwell therein are desolate; therefore, the inhabitants of the earth are burned and few men left (cf. Isa. 24:5-6).

It should be observed that this prophecy of the great Isaiah could have no reference to the law of Moses that had been given to Israel. It is an "everlasting covenant" that the prophet refers to as being broken and the ordinances thereof changed. The blood of the Christ is spoken of as "the blood of the everlasting covenant" (Heb. 13:20). Hence, it is the "covenant" sealed by the blood of the Christ that men would break. It is the ordinances of the "everlasting covenant"—or the "everlasting gospel"—that they would change; and this the Christians, even in apostolic times, began to do.

DISAGREEMENT AMONG THE OFFICERS OF THE PRIMITIVE CHURCH

It is a mistake to suppose that the primitive Christian[1] church was removed from such a possibility as this by reason of any sanctity that obtained in its membership. On the contrary, they supplied the elements for such a departure from the faith of the "everlasting covenant" predicted by Isaiah. Even the apostles were early engaged in controversies. The question which arose as to the relationship of the gospel to the Jews, who regarded themselves still under obligations to keep the law of Moses, received authoritative and amicable settlement to the effect that observance of the law of Moses should not be required of the new converts from among the Gentiles, and such was the drawing together under the spirit of that council's decision that St. Peter went down to Antioch and at first mingled unreservedly with both Gentiles and Jewish converts without distinction; but when certain ones came down from James, who resided in Jerusalem, then Peter suddenly withdrew his social fellowship from the Gentile converts; other Jewish brethren did the same–Barnabas, a friend of Paul was among the number. Whereupon Paul withstood Peter to the face directly charging him before all the brethren with "dissimulation," saying, "If thou, being a Jew, and livest after the manner of the Gentiles, and not as do the Jews, why compellest thou the Gentiles to live as do the Jews" (Gal. 2:13-14). Yet this same Paul, notwithstanding his loyalty to the Gentile converts on that occasion, his zeal for the decision which had been rendered by the council at the church at Jerusalem, and notwithstanding his usually strong moral courage, subsequently showed by his conduct that he, too, was not beyond the weakness of "becoming all things to all men" (cf. 1 Cor. 9:22). For a short time after the incident with Peter at Antioch, when in the province of Galatia, and desiring Timothy to be his companion in the ministry, Paul took him and circumcised him; for it was well known that while his mother was a Jewess his father was a Greek; and all this for fear of the Jews (Acts 16:1-3).

LAW AND GOSPEL CONTROVERSY

This question continued to be a cause of contention even after this sharp disputation at Antioch, for though the discussion of the council at Jerusalem was against the contention of the Judaizing party, yet they continued to agitate the question, and in Galatia at least, succeeded in turning the saints of that province from "the grace of Christ unto another gospel, . . . perverting the gospel of Christ" (Gal. 1:6-7). This question in fact continued to agitate the church throughout the apostolic age and was finally settled through overwhelming numbers of Gentiles

---

1. <Ms III^{c} adds "Christian"–*Ed.*>

being converted and taking possession of the church, rather than from any respect for the decision of the council at Jerusalem.

The withdrawal of John Mark from the ministry while accompanying Paul and Barnabas on their first mission in Asia Minor, and which withdrawal grew out of a faltering of his zeal or a misunderstanding with his companions,[2] will be well remembered (Acts 13:13). Subsequently, when Paul proposed to Barnabas that they go again and "visit the brethren in every city where they had preached" while on their first mission, a sharp contention arose between them about this same John Mark. Barnabas desired to take him again into the ministry, but Paul seriously objected; and so pronounced was the quarrel between them that these two friends and fellow yokemen in the ministry parted company. It is just possible also that in addition to this misunderstanding about John Mark, the severe reproof which Paul administered to Barnabas in the affair of dissimulation at Antioch had somewhat strained their friendship.

CHARACTER OF CHURCH MEMBERSHIP[3] IN APOSTOLIC TIMES

Turning from these misunderstandings and criminations among the leading officers of the church, let us inquire how it stood with the members. The epistles of Paul to the church at Corinth discloses the fact that there were serious schisms among them; some boasting that they were of Paul, others that they were of Apollos, others of Cephas, and still others of Christ; which led Paul to ask sharply, "Is Christ divided? Was Paul crucified for you?" (1 Cor. 1:13). There were endless strifes as well as divisions among them, which caused Paul to denounce them as carnally minded (1 Cor. 3:3-4). Among them also was such fornication as was not named among the Gentiles, "that one should have his father's wife!" (1 Cor. 5:1). And this shameful sin had not humbled the church at Corinth, for Paul denounced them for being puffed up in the presence of such a crime, rather than have mourned over it. They were in the habit of going to law one with another, and that before the world, in violation of the teachings of Jesus Christ (1 Cor. 6:1-8). They desecrated the ordinance of the Lord's Supper by their drunkenness, for which they were sharply reproved by the apostle (1 Cor. 11:20-22, 29-30). They ate and drank unworthily, "not discerning the Lord's body; for which cause many were

---

2. <The review committee objected to Roberts's suggestion as to the reason for John Mark's departure: "The cause of John Mark leaving the ministry, questioned" ("Doctrinal Points Questioned by the Committee Which Read the Manuscript of Elder B. H. Roberts, Entitled The Truth, The Way, The Life," attached to Rudger Clawson, Letter to Heber J. Grant, [15 May 1930], in David J. Buerger Collection, Manuscript 622, Bx 10, Fd 8, Manuscripts Division, Marriott Library, University of Utah, Salt Lake City)–*Ed.*>

3. <Ms III[*] "Status of Church Membership"–*Ed.*>

sickly among them, and many slept," that is, died (cf. 1 Cor. 11:29-30). There were heresies also among them (1 Cor. 11:18-19), some denying the resurrection of the dead, while others possessed not the knowledge of God, which the apostle declared was to[4] their shame (1 Cor. 15:12-34).

It is true, this sharp letter of reproof made the Corinthian saints sorry, and sorry, too, after a godly fashion, in that it brought them to a partial repentance; but even in the second epistle, from which we learn of their partial repentance, the apostle could still charge that there were many in the church who had not "repented of the uncleanness and fornication and lasciviousness which they had committed" (2 Cor. 12:21). From this second letter, also, we learn that there were many in the church at large who "corrupted the word of God" (2 Cor. 2:17); that there were those, even in the ministry, who were "false prophets, deceitful workers, transforming themselves into the apostles of Christ" (2 Cor. 11:13).

Of the churches throughout the province of Galatia it is scarcely necessary to say more than we have already said concerning the invasion of that province by Judaizing Christian ministers, who were turning away the saints from the grace of Christ back to the beggarly elements of the law of carnal commandments; a circumstance which led Paul to exclaim:

> I marvel that ye are so soon removed from Him that had called you into the grace of Christ, unto another gospel; which is not another; but there be some that trouble you, and would pervert the gospel of Christ (Gal. 1:6-7).

TWO PARTIES IN THE CHURCH OF THE FIRST CENTURY[5]

That there were two distinct parties in the church at this time (apostolic age) between whom bitter contentions arose, from thirty A.D. to the close of the first Christian century, is further evidenced by the letter of Paul to the Philippians. Paul says:

> Some preached Christ even of envy and strife, and some of good will. The one preach Christ of contention, not sincerely, supposing to add affliction to my bonds; but the other of love, knowing that I am set for the defence of the gospel (cf. Philip. 1:15-17).

He said again to the same people:

> Beware of dogs, beware of evil workers, beware of the concision (Philip. 3:2).

He admonished them:

---

4. <Ms III^{c} adds "to"—*Ed.*>
5. <Ms III^{c} adds "Two Parties In The Church Of The First Century"—*Ed.*>

> Brethren, be followers . . . of me, and mark them which walk so as ye have us for an example. For many walk, of whom I have told you often, and now tell you even weeping, that they are the enemies of the cross of Christ: whose end is destruction, whose God is their belly and whose glory is their shame, who mind earthly things (Philip. 3:17-19).

To the Colossians Paul found it necessary to say:

> Beware lest any man spoil you through philosophy and vain deceit, after the traditions of men, after the rudiments of the world, and not after Christ. . . . Let no man beguile you of your reward in a voluntary humility and worshipping of angels, intruding into those things which he hath not seen, vainly puffed up by his fleshly mind (Col. 2:8, 18).

EVIDENCE OF EARLY DISSENSION AMONG PRIMITIVE CHRISTIANS

But it is in Paul's pastoral letters that we get a deeper insight into corruptions threatening the early church, and even beginning to lay the foundation for the subsequent apostasy which overwhelmed it. The apostle sent Timothy to the saints at Ephesus to represent him, that he might charge some to teach no other doctrines than those which he had delivered unto them; "neither give heed to fables and endless genealogies, which minister questions, rather than godly edifying which is in faith," for some had turned aside from the commandment of "charity, out of a pure heart, and a good conscience, and faith unfeigned, . . . unto vile jangling,[6] desiring to be teachers of the law, understanding neither what they say, nor whereof they affirm" (1 Tim. 1:3-7). Others concerning faith had made shipwreck, of whom were Hymenaeus and Alexander, whom Paul had "delivered unto Satan that they might learn not to blaspheme" (1 Tim. 1:19-20). Others had "erred concerning the faith" and had "given heed to babbling and opposition of science falsely so called" (cf. 1 Tim. 6:20-21). In his second letter to Timothy, Paul informs him that all the saints in Asia had turned away from him, of whom were Phygellus and Hermogenes (2 Tim. 1:15). He admonished Timothy again to:

> Shun profain and vain babblings, for they will increase unto more ungodliness and their word will eat as doeth a canker; of whom is Hymenaeus and Philetus, who, concerning the truth, have erred, saying that the resurrection is past already,[7] and overthrow the faith of some (2 Tim. 2:16-18).

Demas, once a fellow-laborer with Paul, had forsaken him, "having loved this

---

6. <The King James Version text has "vain jangling"—*Ed.*>

7. <Ms III "is passed already," but the King James Version text has "is past already"—*Ed.*>

present world" (2 Tim. 4:10). At Paul's first answer, that is, when arraigned before the court at Rome, no man stood with him, but all men forsook him; he prays that God will not lay this to their charge (2 Tim. 4:16). Paul admonished Titus to hold fast to the faith, for there were "many unruly and vain talkers and deceivers," especially those of the circumcision, who subverted "whole houses, teaching things which they ought not, for filthy lucre's sake"; and were "giving heed to Jewish fables and commandments of men" and turning from the truth (Titus 1:9-11, 14).

ST. PETER'S PROPHECIES ON APOSTASY

Peter also had something to say with reference to the danger of heresies and false teachers, which menaced the church. He declared that there would be false teachers among the saints, "who privily would bring upon themselves swift destruction.[8] And many," said he, "shall follow their pernicious ways; by reason of whom the way of [9] truth shall be evil spoken of. And through covetousness shall they with feigned words make merchandise of you; whose judgment now for a long time lingereth not, and their damnation slumbereth not. For if God spared not the angels that sinned, but cast them down to hell and delivered them unto chains of darkness to be reserved unto judgment," he argued that the Lord would not spare these corrupters of the gospel of Christ, who, like the dog had turned again to his own vomit, and the sow who was washed to her wallowing in the mire (2 Pet. 2:1-4, 22). He charged also that some were wresting the epistles of Paul, as they were some of the "other scriptures," unto their own destruction (2 Pet. 3:16).

TESTIMONY OF ST. JOHN ON APOSTASY

John, the disciple whom Jesus loved, also bears testimony to the existence of anti-Christs, false prophets, and the depravity of many in the early church. He said:

> It is the last time, and as ye have heard that anti-Christ shall come, even now there are many anti-Christs; whereby we know that it is the last time. They went out from us . . . that they might be manifest that they were not all of us (1 Jn. 2:18-19).

He said in the same epistle:

> Try the spirits, whether they are of God; because many false prophets are gone out into the world (1 Jn. 4:1).

---

8. <Since 2 Peter 2:1 reads "who privily shall *bring* in damnable heresies, even denying the Lord that bought them, and *bring* upon themselves swift destruction," it appears that either Roberts or his secretary skipped from the first to the second occurrence of "bring"—*Ed.*>

9. <Ms III^{c} adds "way of"—*Ed.*>

Again:

> Many deceivers are entered into the world, who confess not that Jesus Christ is come in the flesh. This is a deceiver, <and> an anti-Christ (2 Jn. 1:7).

Jude also is a witness against this class of deceivers. He admonished the saints to:

> Contend earnestly for the faith which was once delivered unto the saints; for there are certain men crept in unawares, . . . ungodly men, turning the grace of our God into lasciviousness and denying the only Lord God and our Lord Jesus Christ (Jude 1:3-4).

The rest of the epistle he devotes to a description of their wickedness, comparing it with the conduct of Satan, and the vileness of the inhabitants of Sodom and Gomorrah.

PURPOSE OF THE REVIEW

We have given this review of the condition of the Church of Christ in the apostolic age not with the intention of establishing the idea that the church at that time was in a complete state of apostasy; nor have we dwelt upon the weaknesses and sins of the early saints for the purpose of holding them up for contempt. Our only purpose has been to dispel, first of all, the extravagant ideas that obtain in many minds concerning the absolute sanctity of the early Christians; and secondly, and mainly, to show that there were elements and tendencies existing in the early church, even in the days of the apostles, that would, when unrestrained by apostolic authority and power, lead to its entire overthrow.

We have no good reason to believe that there occurred any change for the better in the affairs of the church after the demise of the apostles, no reason to believe that there were fewer heresies or fewer false teachers or false prophets to lead away the people with their vain philosophies, their foolish babblings, and opposition of science falsely so-called. On the contrary, one is forced to believe the prediction of Paul, viz., that "evil men and seducers would wax worse and worse, deceiving and being deceived" (2 Tim. 3:13). For who, after the apostles were fallen asleep, would stand up and correct the heresies that were brought into the church, rebuke the schismatics, the false teachers and false prophets that arose to draw away disciples after them? If false teachers insinuated themselves into the church, brought in damnable heresies "by reason of which the way of truth was evil spoken of" (cf. 2 Pet. 2:2), and the pure religion of Jesus Christ corrupted even while inspired apostles were still in the church, it is not unreasonable to conclude that all these evils would increase and revel unchecked after the death of the apostles.

THE EFFECT OF EARLY PERSECUTIONS ON THE CHURCH[10]

Running parallel with this rise of false teachers and multiplication of heresies was running the effects of persecution of the church during the first three centuries of its existence. Let no one attempt to minimize the effect of successive persecutions upon the Christians. True, they endured much and many died faithful in their devotions to what they regarded as the true religion of Jesus Christ, but heretics as well as true Christians suffered in these persecutions and some of the heretics with equal heroism to those who were true martyrs to the Christian faith. Suffering martyrdom in a cause does not always mean that the cause itself is true; a fact of which the history of all persecutions abundantly attests. Meantime, the effect of these early persecutions of the Christians by the Jews, and later by the Roman emperors, had the result of breaking down the faith and constancy of many, until it can be truly said that the saints were worn out (Dan. 7:25), or so nearly so that only weak and timorous men were left to ineffectually resist the paganization of Christianity and the destruction of the real Church of Christ. That the Roman emperors considered the destruction of the Christian church[11] completed by the Diocletian persecution (beginning 303 A.D. and lasting through ten years) is witnessed by the inscriptions upon monuments and medals. Two pillars in Spain erected to commemorate the reign of Diocletian bore the following inscriptions:

> DIOCLETIAN JOVIAN, MAXIMIAN HERCULEUS, CAESARES AUGUSTI, FOR HAVING EXTENDED THE ROMAN EMPIRE IN THE EAST AND WEST, AND FOR HAVING EXTINGUISHED THE NAME OF CHRISTIANS, WHO BROUGHT THE REPUBLIC TO RUIN.
>
> DIOCLETIAN, ETC., FOR HAVING ADOPTED GALERIUS IN THE EAST, FOR HAVING EVERY WHERE ABOLISHED THE SUPERSTITION OF CHRIST, FOR HAVING EXTENDED THE WORSHIP OF THE GODS.

And on the medal of Diocletian this:

> THE NAME OF CHRISTIAN<S> BEING EXTINGUISHED.[12]

We know it will be said that this supposed triumph over Christianity announced on these monuments was almost immediately followed by the triumph of Christianity under Constantine, called "the Great," and then the Christian religion became practically the state religion of the empire; but was it the Christian

---

10. <Ms III^{c} adds "On The Church"—*Ed.*>

11. <Ms III^{c} adds "church"—*Ed.*>

12. Joseph Milner, *The History of the Church of Christ*, 3rd ed. (London: T. Cadell, 1834), century 4, chap. 1, 2:22.

religion that thus triumphed, or a merely paganized form of religion bearing that name? We are sure that prophetic history and the truth of history will sustain the view that the Christianity of the early decades of the fourth century and through all the centuries following the fourth was no longer the gospel of Jesus Christ; nor the churches that survived–Roman Catholic, Greek Catholic, and the Protestant sections[13] of Christendom, with all its subdivisions, were not, and are not, the Church of Jesus Christ. A sweeping declaration we know, but an extensive inquiry into the subject, running through many years of study and writing upon that branch of history has led to the conclusion so positively drawn,[14] namely: that there was a universal turning away or apostasy from the religion of Jesus Christ as established in the Dispensation of the Meridian of Times. It has also been noted in this writing that a dispensation posterior to the Meridian Dispensation–"The Dispensation of the Fullness of Times"–would follow the age of the Christ and his apostles.

PAUL'S GREAT PROPHECY ON UNIVERSAL APOSTASY[15]

We shall only pause here to introduce one great testimony concerning this universal[16] apostasy which, however, while brief, is complete and conclusive on the subject. It is found in the second epistle of Paul to the Thessalonians and consists of a prophecy which, if the apostasy of so-called Christendom has not been complete and universal, proves beyond all question that the great apostle of the Gentiles was a false prophet. On the other hand, if fulfilled, then it proves that the Church of Christ, so far as its existence in the earth is concerned, was to be destroyed; that another church, one founded by men, was to usurp the place of the Church of Christ; a worldly church, dominated by the very spirit of Lucifer, who under its rule would oppose and exalt himself above all that is called God; and sit in the temple of God, showing himself–so far as this world is concerned–that he is God. Moreover, Paul declared in this very prophecy we are about to quote, that the forces which would ultimately bring to pass this universal apostasy from the

---

13. <Ms III[c] adds an "s" to make the plural "sections"–*Ed.*>

14. See the writer's account of the "Apostasy" from the gospel and also the "Destruction of the Christian Church" in his *Outlines of Ecclesiastical History*, that is in its fourth edition (1924) <Ms III[*] "that is now (1924) in its fourth edition"–*Ed.*>; also his introduction to the *History of the Church of Jesus Christ of Latter-day Saints, Period I: History of Joseph Smith, the Prophet by Himself* (Salt Lake City: Deseret News, 1902), 1:xxiii-xciv. Also a treatise on the same theme in his *New Witnesses for God* (Salt Lake City: Deseret News Press, 1911), vol. 1, thesis ii, 45-136. <A note very similar to this footnote appeared in Ms III[*] on a separate sheet between chapters 46 and 47–*Ed.*>

15. <Ms III[c] adds "Paul's Great Prophecy On Universal Apostasy"–*Ed.*>

16. <Ms III[c] adds "universal"–*Ed.*>

Christian religion—"the mystery of iniquity" (2 Thes. 2:7)—was already at work even in his day.

With this introduction, which is also to be considered as our comment upon, and interpretation of, the prophecy, we quote Paul's great prediction on the universal apostasy from the true Christian religion:

Paul's Prophecy of Universal Apostasy

> Now we beseech you, brethren, by the coming of our Lord Jesus Christ and by our gathering together unto him, that ye be not soon shaken in mind, or be troubled, neither by spirit, nor by word, nor by letter as from us, as that the day of Christ is at hand.
>
> Let no man deceive you by any means: for that day shall not come, except there come a falling away first, and that man of sin be revealed, the son of perdition, who opposeth and exalteth himself above all that is called God, or that is worshipped; so that he as God sitteth in the temple of God, shewing himself that he is God.
>
> Remember ye not, that when I was yet with you, I told you these things? And now ye know what withholdeth that he might be revealed in his time. For the mystery of iniquity doth already work: only he who now letteth [hindereth] will let [hinder], until he be taken out of the way [i.e., the true servants of God, the apostles of the church—the true priesthood of God resisting the encroachments of the evil power—until they should be taken out of its way by persecution and death]. And then shall that Wicked be revealed, whom the Lord shall consume with the spirit of his mouth, and shall destroy with the brightness of his coming: even him, whose coming is after the working of Satan with all power and signs and lying wonders, and with all deceivableness of unrighteousness in them that perish; because they received not the love of the truth, that they might be saved.
>
> And for this cause God shall send them strong delusion, that they should believe a lie: that they all might be damned who believed not the truth, but had pleasure in unrighteousness (2 Thes. 2:1-12).

If prophecy be regarded as history reversed, then here is an important historical as well as prophetic document, all which tends to prove what is contended for in this chapter.

THE SUM OF THE MATTER CONTENDED FOR

The sum of the matter stands thus: when the appointed time was come, Jesus of Nazareth, the Son of God, came and made the appointed atonement for the transgression of Adam and the sins of the world, and brought men under the dominion of love and its consequent his mercy. He taught the gospel; he brought life and immortality to light; he brought into existence a church, and then ascended on high to his Father.

For a time the gospel in its simplicity was preached in the world by the chosen apostles, though even in their day men began to mar it with their vain philosophies, their doctrines of science falsely so-called; and when the apostles passed away in death—then corruptions ran riot in the church; doctrines of men were taught for the commandments of God; a church made by men was substituted for the Church of Christ; a church full of pride and worldliness; a church which, while it clung to the forms of godliness, ran riot in excesses and abominations—until spiritual darkness fell like a pall over the nations; and thus they lay for ages—called the "Dark Ages."

In vain men sought to bring about "Reformations," and through them bring back the religion of Jesus Christ and the Church of Christ. To do that, however, was beyond the power of these men, however good their intentions. The gospel taken from the earth, divine authority lost, the Church of Christ destroyed, there was but one way in which all this could be restored, namely, by reopening the heavens and dispensing again a knowledge of the gospel; by once more conferring divine authority upon men, together with a commission to teach all the world, and reestablish the Church of Christ on earth. In a word, to bring in the promised "Dispensation of the Fullness of Times," which shall unite into one all former dispensations and "gather together in one all things in Christ, . . . even in him" (Eph. 1:10).[17]

17. <Ms III* "'gather together in one all things in Christ, even in him.' The account of bringing in such a dispensation is to be the subject of our next chapter"—*Ed.*>

CHAPTER XLVII

Renewal of "The Way"

SCRIPTURE READING LESSON

Analysis

I. Testimony of Prophecy on the "Renewal of The Way."
   (a) St. Peter: "Time of the Restitution of All Things."
   (b) St. Paul: Coming of the "Dispensation of the Fullness of Times."
   (c) St. John's Vision of the Restoration of the Gospel.
II. The Opening of the New Dispensation.
III. The First Vision of the New Dispensation.
IV. The Second Vision of the New Dispensation—The Book of Mormon Revealed.
   (a) The Jaredites.
   (b) The Nephites.
   (c) Summary of the Book and Translation.
V. Third Vision: Restoration of the Aaronic Priesthood.
VI. Fourth Vision: Restoration of the Melchizedek Priesthood.*
VII. Development of the New Dispensation.
VIII. Organization of the Church.
IX. Enlargement of the New Dispensation over Others. Visions in the Kirtland Temple:
   (a) Vision of the Savior.
   (b) Of Moses.
   (c) Of Elias.
   (d) Of Elijah.
X. The Message of Elijah—Salvation for the Dead.

References

Orson Pratt, "Remarkable Visions," in *Orson Pratt's Works* <*A Series of Pamphlets* (Liverpool: Franklin D. Richards, 1851>.

Osborne J. P. Widtsoe, *The Restoration of the Gospel.*

B. H. Roberts, *Outlines of Ecclesiastical History,* part iv, 303-460.

Joseph Smith, *History of the Church,* 6 vols.

D&C 1, 20, and all other sections, *passim.*

Lucy Smith, *History of the Prophet Joseph Smith,* rev. by George A. Smith and Elias Smith (Salt Lake City: Improvement Era, 1902), *passim.*

For "Message of Elijah—Salvation for the Dead," see D&C 110, 127, 128. Also article in *Improvement Era* for September 1928, "The Epistle of Kallikrates," <purportedly translated by James M. Witherow>. An article, "A New Witness to a Great Truth—Early Christian Baptism for the Dead," on this strangely discovered letter appeared in the *Deseret News* of April 21, 1928, by B. H. Roberts.

Frederic Huidekoper, *The Belief of the First Three Centuries concerning Christ's Mission to the Underworld,* 4th ed., *passim,* but especially p. 49.

*For the time and place of the restoration of the Melchizedek Priesthood, see D&C 128:20; and *History of the Church,* 1:40-42 and footnotes.

CHAPTER XLVII

Renewal of "The Way"

THE TESTIMONY OF PROPHECY ON RENEWAL OF THE WAY

(a) St. Peter–The Time of Restitution of All Things[1]

St. Peter to a multitude of Jews in Jerusalem excited by the healing of the impotent man at the gate of the city, testified that the healing was a manifestation of the power of God through Jesus Christ, and then went on to say that the God of their fathers had glorified Jesus, whom they had delivered up to a false judgment and denied the Holy One, and the Just, and had killed the Prince of Life, whom God had now raised from the dead, whereof he and his brethren were witnesses.

His words to the multitude were:

> Repent ye therefore, and be ye converted, that your sins may be blotted out, when the times of refreshing shall come from the presence of the Lord; and He shall send Jesus Christ, which before was preached unto you, whom the heaven must receive until the times of restitution of all things, which God hath spoken by the mouth of all His holy prophets since the world began (Acts 3:19-21).

We emphasize by repeating in substance, namely, there is to be, subsequent to the days of Peter and his associate apostles, a "time for the restitution of all things, which God hath spoken by the mouths of the holy prophets since the world began." A "time of refreshing from the presence of the Lord," when there may be hope for Judah's eyes to be opened to the fact that their Messiah was Jesus of Nazareth, whom they and their rulers had crucified. A time when God would "again send Jesus Christ, who before had been preached unto them," but whom, meanwhile, the heaven must retain until this time of "the restitution of all things."

(b) St. Paul–The Coming of the Dispensation of the Fullness of Times[2]

And so St. Paul, evidently on the same subject, says:

---

1. <Ms III[c] adds "(A) St. Peter–The Time of Restitution Of All Things"–*Ed.*>

2. <Ms III[c] adds "(B) St. Paul–The Coming Of The Dispensation Of The Fullness Of Times"–*Ed.*>

> He [God] hath abounded toward us in all wisdom and prudence; having made known unto us the mysteries of His will, according to His good pleasure which He hath purposed in Himself; that in the dispensation of the fullness of times, He might gather together in one all things in Christ, both which are in heaven and . . . in earth, even in him (Eph. 1:8-10).

It has already been set forth in these pages that a dispensation pertaining to the gospel is a giving out by revelation of the things of God; giving out knowledge concerning this plan of salvation; bestowing divine authority upon man to act in the name of the Lord, both in teaching and administering the ordinances of the gospel; and it has also been shown that there have been many such dispensations from the days of Adam until the days of the Christ. And now in this prophecy we have a promise that there shall be a "Dispensation of the Fullness of Times," which can only mean a dispensation of which all others we have considered so far are but parts. And now comes this "Dispensation of the Fullness of Times," which shall include them all in one, and that dispensation is undoubtedly the "time of the restitution of all things spoken of by the prophets"; a dispensation in which God will again send Jesus Christ to the earth, fulfilling the predictions concerning him; fulfilling the words of the angels who appeared to that group of friends watching the receding form of the risen Christ from the earth, and who put the question to that group: "Ye men of Galilee, why stand ye gazing up into heaven? This same Jesus which is taken up from you into heaven, shall so come in like manner" (Acts 1:11).

And again St. Paul:

> The Lord Jesus shall be revealed from heaven with his mighty angels, in flaming fire taking vengeance on them that know not God and that obey not the gospel of our Lord Jesus Christ, who shall be punished with everlasting destruction from the presence of the Lord and from the glory of his power; when he shall come to be glorified in his saints, and to be admired in all them that believe (2 Thes. 1:7-10).

Surely the voice of prophecy requires us to believe in the incoming of this dispensation subsequent to the Meridian Dispensation.

(c) St. John—Vision of a Restoration of the Gospel in the Hour of God's Judgment[3]

Among many visions given to St. John on Patmos was this masterful one:

> I saw another angel flying in the midst of heaven, having the everlasting gospel to preach unto them that dwell on the earth, and to every nation, and kindred, and tongue, and people. Saying with a loud voice, "Fear God and give glory to Him; for

3. <Ms III^{c} adds "In The Hour Of God's Judgment"—*Ed.*>

the hour of His judgment is come; and worship Him that made heaven, and earth, and the sea, and the fountains of waters" (Rev. 14:6-7).

This vision is to be realized in the hour of God's judgment. A period that connotes with St. Peter's "times of the restitution of all things," when Jesus Christ, whom the heavens are retaining now, will be sent again to the earth and in judgment; also it connotes with St. Paul's "dispensation of the fullness of times," in the which all things shall be gathered together in one in Christ, things both in heaven and in earth. And let it be observed that the emphasis in this message given to St. John on Patmos comes on the part where the men of all nations, kindred, tongues, and people are called back to the worship of the true God, He "that made heaven and earth and the sea and the fountains of water," implying most strongly that the whole world in the hour of God's judgment would not be worshipping the true and the living God, creator of heaven and earth. Also, since this gospel restored to the earth by the ministering of an angel in the hour of God's judgment is to be preached to every nation, kindred, tongue, and people, it[4] strongly implies that all nations, kindred, tongues, and people would be without the gospel; hence, it is restored to the earth to be universally proclaimed.

None are to escape the warning voice of it. It shall be preached as the Christ himself declared:

> For a witness unto all nations; and then shall the end come. . . . And he shall send his angels with the great sound of a trumpet and they shall gather together his elect from the four winds, from one end of heaven to the other. . . . Heaven and earth shall pass away, but my word<s> shall not pass away. But of that day and hour knoweth no man, no, not the angels of heaven, but my Father only. But as the days of Noah were, so shall also the coming of the Son of Man be (Matt. 24:14, 31, 35-37).

What a unity there is in all this voice of prophecy upon the incoming of this "time of refreshing from the presence of the Lord"; this "times of the restitution of all things"; the incoming of a "dispensation of the fullness of times"; the restoration by angelic ministration of "the everlasting gospel" to be universally preached as a witness and then the end to come with the glorious appearing of the Lord Jesus Christ unto judgment!

THE OPENING OF THE NEW DISPENSATION

The opening of this "dispensation of the fullness of times" came by the opening of the heavens to the prophet appointed of God, to stand at the head of it. This prophet was Joseph Smith.[5] He was born in Sharon, Windsor County,

---

4. <Ms III[c] adds "it"–*Ed.*>

5. <For recent biographies of Joseph Smith, see Richard L. Bushman, *Joseph Smith*

state of Vermont, U.S.A., in the year of our Lord 1805, on the 23d of December. His childhood and early youth knew but poverty and hardship. At the age of ten his family moved and settled in Palmyra, in what is now known as Wayne County, state of New York. When about fourteen years of age a religious excitement arose in the vicinity of his home and his mind became intensely engaged upon the question of religion. A neighborhood revival participated in by several churches disclosed how much at variance the different sects were in relation to questions of religion; and these dissensions, together with manifest jealousy and ill will towards each other, excited the wonderment of the youth, Joseph Smith, and led him in the midst of the war of words and tumult of opinions to frequently ask himself the question: "What is to be done? Who of all these parties are right?" At this juncture his attention was called to the golden text in the Epistle of St. James:

> If any of you lack wisdom, let him ask of God, who giveth to all men liberally and upbraideth not; and it shall be given him. But let him ask in faith, nothing wavering. For he that wavereth is like the wave of the sea, driven by the wind and tossed. Let not that man think that he shall receive any thing of the Lord (James 1:5-7).

THE FIRST VISION OF THE NEW DISPENSATION

Upon this scripture he pondered frequently until it became[6] as the voice of God in his soul, and at last he resolved on putting this inspired message from St. James to the test. Having selected a place in a grove upon his father's farm, he retired to it and endeavored to pray for the wisdom that he felt of all persons he most needed. It was while engaged in this prayer that the heavens were opened to him, a glorious light, surpassing the brightness of the sun at noonday surrounded him, and in the midst of that intense light appeared two glorious personages, glorious beyond any power he possessed to describe them.[7] They were alike, for although Father and Son, age writes no wrinkles upon the ever-youthful face of immortals. They were alike, but one said to the other: "JOSEPH, THIS IS MY BELOVED SON, HEAR HIM."

---

and the Beginnings of Mormonism (Urbana: University of Illinois Press, 1984), and Donna Hill, *Joseph Smith: The First Mormon* (Garden City, NY: Doubleday and Co., 1977–*Ed.*>

6. <Ms III[*] "until at last it became"–*Ed.*>

7. <The earliest known account of the first vision, discovered and published thirty-two years after Roberts died, mentions only one personage, Jesus Christ. See Paul R. Cheesman, "An Analysis of the Accounts Relating Joseph Smith's Early Visions," M.R.E. thesis, Brigham Young University, 1965; James B. Allen, "Eight Contemporary Accounts of Joseph Smith's First Vision–What Do We Learn from Them?" *The Improvement Era* 73 (Apr. 1970): 4-13; and Milton V. Backman, *Joseph Smith's First Vision: Confirming Evidences and Contemporary Accounts*, 2d ed. (Salt Lake City: Bookcraft, 1980)–*Ed.*>

And then to this second person the youth addressed in substance his question: "Which of all these contending sects is true, which is Thy church; and which shall I join?" It speaks well for the steadiness of the temperament of this youth that in such a presence he could clearly hold in mind the object that had brought him to his first verbal prayer. He gives the message he received from this second personage, the Son of God, to whom he was directed by the Father, in the following language:

> I WAS ANSWERED THAT I MUST JOIN NONE OF THEM, FOR THEY WERE ALL WRONG, AND THE PERSONAGE WHO ADDRESSED ME SAID THAT ALL THEIR CREEDS WERE AN ABOMINATION IN HIS SIGHT: THAT THOSE PROFESSORS WERE ALL CORRUPT; THAT "THEY DRAW NEAR TO ME WITH THEIR LIPS, BUT THEIR HEARTS ARE FAR FROM ME; THEY TEACH FOR DOCTRINES THE COMMANDMENTS OF MEN: HAVING A FORM OF GODLINESS, BUT THEY DENY THE POWER THEREOF" (cf. Matt. 15:8-9; 2 Tim. 3:5). HE AGAIN FORBADE ME TO JOIN WITH ANY OF THEM, AND MANY OTHER THINGS DID HE SAY UNTO ME, WHICH I CANNOT WRITE AT THIS TIME.[8]

In a subsequent statement the Prophet added the following as part of what had been said to him in addition to the direct message above:[9]

> I was informed that I was chosen to be an instrument in the hands of God to bring about some of His purposes in this glorious dispensation.[10]

THE SECOND VISION:[11] THE BOOK OF MORMON REVEALED

Three years after this first[12] revelation an angel of God named Moroni[13] was sent to the prophet to reveal the existence of an ancient volume of scripture known as the Book of Mormon, a book which gives an account of the hand-dealings of

---

8. Joseph Smith, *History of the Church of Jesus Christ of Latter-day Saints, Period I: History of Joseph Smith, the Prophet by Himself*, ed. B. H. Roberts (Salt Lake City: Deseret News, 1902), 1:6; also Writings of Joseph Smith, "Extracts from the History of Joseph Smith, the Prophet," in the Pearl of Great Price, p. 48. <JS-H 2:19-20—*Ed.*>

9. <Ms III^{c} adds "in addition to the direct message above"—*Ed.*>

10. Joseph Smith, *History of the Church*, 4:537, from a letter to John Wentworth.

11. <Ms III^{c} adds "The Second Vision"—*Ed.*>

12. <Ms III^{c} adds "first"—*Ed.*>

13. <An important event during Roberts's tenure as mission president of the Eastern States Mission was the celebration on 21-22 September 1923 of the centennial of the Angel Moroni's visitation to Joseph Smith and the uncovering of the golden plates of the Book of Mormon at the Hill Cumorah. See the circular letter "The Conference at Cumorah; Identical Letter to the Missionaries of the Eastern States Mission," 10 Aug. 1923, and the program at the Hill Cumorah, located in Elsie Ross Whitaker Collection, Accession 1324, Fds 5 and 8, in Manuscripts Division, Marriott Library, University of Utah, Salt Lake City—*Ed.*>

God with the people whom he brought to the continents of America from what we now call the "Old World."

(a) The Jaredites

The first colony came from the tower of Babel at the time of the dispersion of the people from the Euphrates Valley; they were called Jaredites, after their leader, named Jared. They occupied the land locating in the southern part of Central America[14] and founded a nation which existed for about sixteen centuries, and then were overwhelmed at last in a series of wars, which ended in their complete destruction on account of their great wickedness. This <was> about 600 B.C.

(b) The Nephite Colony

It was about the time of the destruction of the Jaredites that a small colony was led from Jerusalem, under divine guidance, to the western continents, where they too developed into a great people and into national life. This colony was made up of Israelites of the tribes of Ephraim and Manasseh, and later augmented by a second small colony made up[15] of Jews. They continued in occupancy of the land—chiefly in North America—until about 400 A.D. Then came their destruction because of their rebellion and wickedness against God. They lost touch with faith and righteousness until their civilization was overthrown, and they survived only in the tribal relations such as existed at the advent of the Europeans.[16]

(c) Summary of the Book and Its Translation[17]

This record discloses the hand-dealings of God with these ancient people through the prophets and teachers God sent unto them, and also gives the account of the visits of the risen Christ to them, the introduction of the fullness of the gospel by his ministry, which established a true Church of Christ in the western world, with all the principles and ordinances of the gospel necessary to salvation. Therefore, it contains the fullness of the gospel.

In this record God has brought forth a New Witness to the truth of the things whereof the Hebrew scriptures, the Old Testament and the New, also bear witness. Thus, an angel came bringing the everlasting gospel, which is to be preached to every nation, kindred, tongue, and people. This American volume of scripture—God's New Witness to the old truths of the everlasting gospel—Joseph Smith was

---

14. <For the great variation in the theories of Book of Mormon geography, see John L. Sorenson, *The Geography of Book of Mormon Events: A Source Book* (Provo, UT: Foundation for Ancient Research and Mormon Studies, 1990), 59-222—*Ed.*>

15. <Ms III^c adds "made up"—*Ed.*>

16. <Ms III* "at the event of the Europeans"—*Ed.*>

17. <Ms III^c adds "(C) Summary of the Book and Its Translation"—*Ed.*>

commanded to translate, and was given the power and means by which he could translate the unknown language of these ancient American peoples. The "means" provided was a "Urim and Thummim."[18] This consisted of two transparent stones set in the rim of a bow, a divine instrument used in ancient times for obtaining knowledge from God. This instrument for translation was found with the gold plates, on which the above record was engraven. Joseph Smith translated the Book of Mormon, and through a century now, it has been published to the world. It is translated into fifteen of the world's languages.[19]

THIRD VISION:[20] THE RESTORATION OF THE AARONIC PRIESTHOOD

While engaged in the work of translating the Book of Mormon, and in answer to earnest prayer for light—and this time upon the subject of baptism—Joseph Smith and Oliver Cowdery were visited by a messenger of God, no other than John the Baptist, now raised from the dead, who in addition to giving them the needed instruction on baptism laid his hands upon their heads and said unto them:

> Upon you, my fellow servants, in the name of Messiah, I confer the Priesthood of Aaron, which holds the keys of the ministering of angels, and of the gospel of repentance, and of baptism by immersion for the remission of sins; and this shall never be taken again from the earth, until the sons of Levi do offer again an offering unto the Lord in righteousness (D&C 13:1).[21]

This occurred on the 15th of May, 1829.

Having given to these men the authority from God to baptize, they at once baptized each other in the clear water of the beautiful Susquehanna River at the point where the visitation had taken place, the angel—John the Baptist—standing upon the banks supervising it. Surely the manner of it and the purpose of it would be correct when introduced under such supervision.

FOURTH VISION:[22] THE RESTORATION OF THE MELCHIZEDEK PRIESTHOOD

Later, most likely in the month of June following, and in fulfillment of a

18. <Ms III "Thumin"—*Ed.*>

19. <Ms III[*] "published to the world in fifteen of the World's languages." As of April 1994 the Book of Mormon has been translated and published in forty-two languages—*Ed.*>

20. <Ms III[c] adds "Third Vision"—*Ed.*>

21. Cf. Joseph Smith, *History of the Church,* 1:39-43, and footnote.

22. <Ms III[c] adds "Fourth Vision"—*Ed.*>

promise made by John the Baptist, when conferring upon these young men the Aaronic Priesthood, viz., that a higher authority than he conferred would later be given to them—in fulfillment of this promise, Peter, James, and John, three apostles of the Meridian Dispensation, came to Joseph Smith and Oliver Cowdery and conferred upon them the Melchizedek Priesthood, a priesthood after the order of the Son of God—even the apostleship;[23] and bestowed upon them the keys of the kingdom under which plenary power they were authorized to proceed with the preaching of the gospel, organizing the church, and doing whatsoever might be necessary to bring in and establish the New Dispensation of the gospel, and prepare the world for the glorious coming of the Lord Jesus, and the founding of his kingdom on earth as it is in heaven.

THE DEVELOPMENT OF THE NEW DISPENSATION[24]

This fullness of priesthood restored, Joseph Smith guided by further and almost continuous revelation organized the Church of Christ to be known finally as the Church of Jesus Christ and to distinguish it from the Church of Christ in more ancient times, the phrase was added "of Latter-day Saints"—"The Church of Jesus Christ of Latter-day Saints." The Church of God and the Church of the people. A compound title representing a most beautiful possession of this institution, the Church of God and the Church of the people.

Under the direction[25] of revelations from God, bishops were chosen, with priests, teachers, and deacons, grouped into quorums bearing these names, and constituting a complete organization of what is known as the "Lesser" or "Aaronic Priesthood" of God's church. This division of the organization is charged chiefly with administering in the temporal things of the church—the outward ordinances of the gospel and the administration of the details of the financial affairs of the church, in gathering tithes, and accounting for them and distributing the charities

23. The exact date of the restoration of this order of the priesthood is not definitely known; but the approximate date can be fixed as of this time named in the text. The matter is considered at length in the *History of the Church*, 1:40-42 and footnotes. <The reason that the restoration of the Melchizedek Priesthood cannot be dated is because the name "Melchizedek" was not associated with the priesthood until 1831 and early references in 1829 and 1830 refer only to "authority" (not "priesthood") being received from an unnamed angel. For an historical discussion of the developing concept of priesthood, see Gregory A. Prince, *Having Authority: The Origins and Development of Priesthood during the Ministry of Joseph Smith* (Independence, MO: Independence Press, Herald Publishing House, 1993), 17-42—*Ed.*>

24. <Ms III[c] adds "The Development Of The New Dispensation"—*Ed.*>

25. <Ms III[*] "Gradually, Under the direction"—*Ed.*>

of the church. All this, however, under the supervision of the presidency of the other division of the priesthood, namely, the Melchizedek Priesthood, which presidency presides over the whole church and all its affairs.

The higher or Melchizedek Priesthood consists of high priests,[26] apostles, seventies, and elders, clothed with authority to act for God, more especially in the spiritual activities of the church: preaching the gospel and administering in all its ordinances, including the ordinances in the holy temples,[27] in teaching and expounding its truths; warning the nations of judgments to come, and of the approaching time when the Son of Man shall again appear on the earth and open up the promised reign of righteousness and peace.

THE SPIRIT OF PRIESTHOOD GOVERNMENT[28]

All this administrative work, both in the Aaronic and Melchizedek Priesthoods, is to be in the spirit of unfeigned love for, and interest in, the people of the world. It is part of the law given unto this Church of Jesus Christ of Latter-day Saints that "no power or influence can or ought to be maintained by virtue of the priesthood"—authority derived from God—"only by persuasion, long-suffering, gentleness, by meekness, and by love unfeigned; by kindness, and pure knowledge, which shall greatly enlarge the soul, without hypocrisy and without guile—reproving betimes with sharpness, when moved upon by the Holy Ghost" to do so, and "then showing forth afterwards an increase of love" towards those who have been reproved that they might know that the faithfulness of God's priesthood is "stronger than the cords of death" (D&C 121:41-44). In this spirit the church government, which is purely moral government, is to be administered.

The church so organized brings back the same organization, though somewhat amplified, as that which was established by the ministry of the Christ and his apostles in the great Meridian Dispensation. It has two great functions to perform, this church: viz., to teach God's revealed truth to all the people—to every nation, and kindred, and tongue,[29] and people; and second, to perfect the lives of those who accept this proclamation of God's message, the everlasting gospel of our Lord Jesus Christ—the Truth.

26. <Ms III[*] "consists of the High Priests"—*Ed.*>

27. <Ms III[c] adds "including the ordinances in the holy Temples"—*Ed.*>

28. <Ms III[c] adds "The Spirit of Priesthood Government"—*Ed.*>

29. <Ms III "tongues," but the partial underlining and a question mark in the margin are taken to mean that the word should be in the singular—*Ed.*>

THE ORGANIZATION OF THE CHURCH[30]

This organization in its humble first forms,[31] began its existence on the sixth day of April, 1830, in Fayette township,[32] Seneca County in the state of New York, and thence has passed through its century of existence until now knowledge of it has spread over all the earth, and through it is restored to the world the WAY, meaning by that a full and complete restoration of the everlasting gospel, uniting in one all the previous dispensations of it, and expanding toward that fullness of knowledge through the revelations of God yet future until it shall indeed gather together all things in Christ, both things which are in heaven and in earth, "even in Him."

ENLARGEMENT OF THE NEW DISPENSATION OVER OTHERS: VISIONS IN THE KIRTLAND TEMPLE[33]

As showing the enlargement of the New Dispensation over all other dispensations that have preceded it, attention is called to several important administrations that took place in the Kirtland Temple in 1836.

(a) Vision of the Savior[34]

First, following the solemn dedication of the temple on the third of April, the Savior appeared to Joseph Smith and Oliver Cowdery in the temple proclaiming the acceptance of the house, and of the people who had erected it; the latter as his church, then struggling into existence, and blessed them. The description of our Lord's appearance was worth of the occasion:

---

30. <Ms III[c] adds "The Organization of the Church"—*Ed.*>

31. <The review committee objected to Roberts's referring to the "humble first forms" of the church: "We think that this expression may be misunderstood and that the thought may be conveyed that the forms of the Church have been changed, rather than developed." Roberts wrote in the margin that this objection was "nonsense!" ("Doctrinal Points Questioned by the Committee Which Read the Manuscript of Elder B. H. Roberts, Entitled The Truth, The Way, The Life," attached to Rudger Clawson, Letter to Heber J. Grant, [15 May 1930], in David J. Buerger Collection, Manuscript 622, Bx 10, Fd 8, Manuscripts Division, Marriott Library, University of Utah, Salt Lake City)—*Ed.*>

32. <Recent historical research indicates that the organization of the church more probably occurred in Manchester, New York. See H. Michael Marquardt, "An Appraisal of Manchester as Location for the Organization of the Church," *Sunstone* 16 (Feb. 1992): 49-57—*Ed.*>

33. <Ms III[c] adds "Visions in The Kirtland Temple"—*Ed.*>

34. <Ms III[*] has the heading, "Vision of The Savior," located before the quotation from D&C 110:2-7, 10—*Ed.*>

> We saw the Lord standing upon the breastwork of the pulpit, before us; and under his feet was a paved work of pure gold, in color like amber. His eyes were as a flame of fire; the hair of his head was white like the pure snow; his countenance shone above the brightness of the sun; and his voice was as the sound of the rushing of great waters,[35] even the voice of the Jehovah, saying:
>
> "I am the first and the last; I am he who liveth, I am he who was slain; I am your advocate with the Father. Behold, your sins are forgiven you; you are clean before me; therefore, lift up your heads and rejoice. Let the hearts of your brethren rejoice, and let the hearts of all my people rejoice, who have, with their might, built this house to my name. For behold, I have accepted this house, and my name shall be here; and I will manifest myself to my people in mercy in this house. . . .
>
> "And the fame of this house shall spread to foreign lands; and this is the beginning of the blessing which shall be poured out upon the heads of my people. Even so. Amen" (D&C 110:2-7, 10; cf. Rev. 1:12-18).

(b) Of Moses[36]

After this vision closed, the heavens were again opened and Moses appeared before them and committed unto them the keys of the gathering of Israel from the four parts of the earth, and of the leading of the ten tribes from the land of the north. Thus, the way was opened for the restoration of Israel to his proper place in God's plan of things. For the restoration of Israel to their lands and to the favor of God are among the things to be achieved in the New Dispensation.

(c) Of Elias[37]

This vision closed, one Elias appeared, and "committed the dispensation of the gospel of Abraham," saying that in these brethren and their seed all the generations after them should be blessed (D&C 110:12). This personage was one, it appears, who had been associated with Abraham, and he came to deliver the keys of the dispensation held in the earth in the days of Abraham, and since he was the one chosen to deliver such keys, he undoubtedly stood at the head of that dispensation; and most probably was Melchizedek, the great High Priest of Abraham's time, who even blessed Abraham, and to whom Abraham paid his tithes; and as St. Paul suggests, undoubtedly the lesser "is blessed of the greater" (Heb. 7:7). Also, it is to be noted that he restored something of patriarchal power and blessing, since he said unto the brethren that in them and in their seed all generations after them should be blessed and this is of patriarchal character, that

---

35. <Ms III* "the rushing of many waters"—*Ed.*>

36. <Ms III^c adds "(B) Of Moses"—*Ed.*>

37. <Ms III^c adds "(C) Of Elias"—*Ed.*>

would be fittingly delivered by a patriarch, whom we have already identified tentatively with the Patriarch Shem, the son of Noah.

(d) Of Elijah[38]

Following this vision of Elias[39] came one which is characterized by those who received it as "great and glorious." For Elijah, the prophet, who was taken to heaven without tasting death, stood before them and said:

> Behold, the time has fully come which is spoken of by the mouth of Malachi, testifying that he [Elijah] should be sent, before the great and dreadful day of the Lord come—"To turn the hearts of the fathers to the children, and the children to the fathers, lest the whole earth be smitten with curse." Therefore, the keys of this dispensation are committed into your hands, and by this you may know that the great and dreadful day of the Lord is near, even at the doors (D&C 110:14-16).

From the keys of knowledge which Elijah restored great light is thrown upon the plan of salvation, showing it to be of more extensive application to the human race than was ever dreamed of in the conceptions of men previous to this visitation of Elijah.

Brief allusion to this extension of the application of the atonement, and of the whole plan of the gospel, to those who had not had opportunity to learn of it in this life, or who, having heard it, failed to avail themselves of its sovereign grace—as in the case of those who lived in the days of Noah (see 1 Pet. 3:18-20; 4:6)—has already been made in chapter 40; but the importance of the subject requires that further details be added here.

It is learned from the keys of knowledge which Elijah restored that the hundreds of millions who have died without a knowledge of Christ or of his gospel, including all the so-called heathen races, together with those who have been misled by the teachings of pseudo-ministers of Christ, are not eternally lost, but that, since the spirit of man when separated from the body retains all the faculties of mind, the gospel is preached in the spirit world to the disembodied spirits, and that on condition of their accepting the gospel, and living according to the laws of God in the spirit, they may be saved on condition of the outward ordinances of the gospel being administered vicariously for them upon the earth by their agents—their relatives or chosen friends.

THE MESSAGE OF ELIJAH—SALVATION FOR THE DEAD

That the gospel is preached to departed spirits is evident from the scriptures:

38. <Ms III[c] adds "(D) Of Elijah"—*Ed.*>
39. <Ms III[c] adds "of Elias"—*Ed.*>

> For Christ also hath once suffered for sins, the just for the unjust, that he might bring us to God, being put to death in the flesh, but quickened by the Spirit: by which also he went and preached unto the spirits in prison: which sometime were disobedient, when once the longsuffering of God waited in the days of Noah, while the ark was a preparing, wherein few, that is, eight souls, were saved by water (1 Pet. 3:18-20).

The plain, simple statement here is that the spirit of Christ, while his body lay in the tomb, went and preached to the spirits which were disobedient in the days of Noah. Turning again to the subject in the chapter following the one just quoted, the apostle says:

> For this cause was the gospel preached also to them that are dead, that they might be judged according to men in the flesh, but live according to God in the spirit (1 Pet. 4:6).

That the ancient saints also knew something abut performing ordinances vicariously for the dead is evident from this remark of the apostle Paul:

> Else what shall they do which are baptized for the dead, if the dead rise not at all? Why are they then baptized for the dead? (1 Cor. 15:29).

And we ask—if there was no such thing among the ancient saints as baptism for the dead, why then does Paul refer to it in such positive terms?[40]

---

40. <In the synopsis to this chapter Roberts refers to his article on baptism for the dead published in the *Deseret News* and to the translation of "The Epistle of Kallikrates" published in the *Improvement Era*. This document has a convoluted history. In March 1928 the *Atlantic Monthly* announced the recent discovery of the Epistle of Kallikrates, the son of Euphorbus, written to the Apostle Paul about 64 A.D., preserved on a papyrus using Greek uncial letters of the second century, and translated by James M. Witherow. Its interest to an LDS audience consists mainly in a reference to Kallikrates' praise to Kephas, i.e., the apostle Peter, for arranging the proxy baptisms of his pagan parents, who had died twenty years earlier (cf. 1 Cor. 15:29). In his article Roberts refers to "this convincing testimony" of Kallikrates and concludes by saying that the LDS church rejoices "in the discovery of such supplemental testimony of the truth as this Epistle of Kallikrates found by man 'in desert sands' to confirm his [God's] revealed word, confound his adversaries, and to magnify above all his name" (see B. H. Roberts, "A New Witness to a Great Truth—Early Christian Baptism for the Dead," *The Deseret News*, 21 Apr. 1928). Later that year the entire text of Kallikrates' letter was reprinted in the church's *Improvement Era*, then edited by Heber J. Grant (see J. M. Witherow, trans., "The Epistle of Kallikrates," *Improvement Era* 31 [Sept. 1928]: 899-909). Unfortunately, the Epistle of Kallikrates is a modern forgery. Edgar J. Goodspeed, a New Testament scholar, said in 1931 that the point of view seen in the Epistle of Kallikrates was "a modern, not an ancient one, and so obvious was this that the antiquity and authenticity of the 'Epistle' were hardly anywhere even broached" (Edgar J. Goodspeed, *Strange New Gospels* [Chicago: University of Chicago Press, 1931], 99-100). It was simply

OTHER ORDINANCES FOR THE DEAD[41]

If baptism may be performed vicariously for the dead, it stands to reason also that other ordinances associated with securing salvation for man may also be vicariously administered in behalf of the dead: confirmation into the Church of Christ, and to baptism of the Spirit; ordination to the priesthood; marriage, eternal marriage—by which the parties to the marriage covenant are married as men and women are married who are in the flesh, who are alive: married in the bonds of an eternal covenant of marriage, not merely "until death do us part," but married for always, "for time and for eternity"! For such is the nature of the marriage covenant under the authority of the holy priesthood, the power which binds on earth and it is bound in heaven; which looses on earth, and it is loosed in heaven. This <is> the power Jesus bestowed upon St. Peter when he gave unto him "the keys of the Kingdom of Heaven," saying:

> And whatsoever thou shalt bind on earth shall be bound in heaven; and whatsoever thou shalt loose on earth shall be loosed in heaven (Matt. 16:19).

So that while it may be true, as saith the Christ it is, that in the resurrection they "neither marry, nor are given in marriage" (Luke 20:35); that means no more than that earth-life and the earth are the time and place of marriage, as it is also the place and time of baptisms, and confirmations, and ordinations, and all ordinances and ceremonies pertaining to the earth-life of man and his salvation; and not that the marriage status does not obtain in the eternal worlds—in our world when it shall become a sanctified and glorified sphere—a celestial world—a heaven, inhabited by the redeemed of this world and shall be their heaven.[42]

The gospel of Christ is not limited, then, in its power to save to this earth-life or this world alone. Its powers enter into the spirit world. And by its proclamation in the world of spirits the fathers will learn that they are dependent upon their posterity still in this world for the performance of the outward ordinances of the gospel; hence, their hearts will be turned to the children. The children on the earth will learn that it is within their power to attend to ordinances of the gospel for their

---

Witherow's concoction to explain the difficulty of applying Paul's teachings to twentieth-century life—*Ed.*>

41. <This heading and the following two paragraphs (which fill one typed manuscript page with the number "XLVII - 17 1/2") are inserted into chapter 47. At the top of the page the handwritten Ms III^c adds the instruction "add ch. 47 following p. 17." This page was probably inserted into this chapter at the same time that chapter 55 on eternal marriage was added—*Ed.*>

42. See chapter 55 of this work for further treatment of marriage in the New Dispensation.

progenitors; hence, the children will be turned to the fathers and the two worlds will be linked together in sympathetic relations. It is because of this—because of the knowledge restored by Elijah, that the Latter-day Saints, wherever they have planted their feet, have sought, even in the days of their greatest poverty, to build a temple, the proper place in which to attend to these ordinances of the dead; and they thus witness to the world that the hearts of the children are turned to the fathers, and "that the great and dreadful day of the Lord is near, even at the doors!" (D&C 110:16).

Thus has been brought to pass the renewal of THE WAY—the restoration to earth of the everlasting gospel in a New Dispensation of it—the Dispensation of the Fullness of Times—in which all things will be gathered together in one—even[43] in Christ—and consummated; completed by the coming, at last, of the kingdom of God on earth, and the doing of the will of God on earth even as it is done in heaven.[44]

If the successive events stated in this chapter be considered, the volume of them, and the glory of them, they will of their own force carry a weight of conviction to the open mind that will go far in establishing their truth. This method of considering them will be a fine illustration of a mind-principle much relied upon by the prophet of the dispensation who brought them forth. "Every word that proceedeth forth from the mouth of [God], Jehovah," he said, "has such an influence over the human mind—the logical mind—[45]that it is convincing without other testimony. Faith cometh by hearing." His trust in the absoluteness of truth is further illustrated by his continuing remarks on the above occasion: "If ten thousand men testify to a truth you know, would it add [anything] to your faith? No. Or will ten thousand testimonies destroy your knowledge of a fact? No." Then concluding his remarks he said: "I do not want any one to tell I am a prophet, or attempt to prove my word."[46] Which is to say that he relied upon the innate power of the truth in that word he spoke—that message he delivered—to be the convincing power of it. He had been taught of God to regard the mind of man as native to the truth and possessed of power to cognize it. "Man was in the beginning with God" is his doctrine, revealed to him of God.

> Intelligence, or the light of truth, was not created or made, neither indeed can be. . . . Behold, here is the agency of man, and here is the condemnation of man; because

43. <Ms III[c] adds "Even"—*Ed.*>

44. <Ms III[*] "in heaven. Even so, God, the Eternal Father, may it come, and come quickly!"—*Ed.*>

45. <Ms III[c] adds "—the logical mind—"—*Ed.*>

46. Joseph Smith, "Remarks at Nauvoo, August 6th, 1843," *History of the Church*, 5:526.

> that which was from the beginning is plainly manifest unto them, and they receive not the light. And every man who<se spirit> receiveth not the light is under condemnation. For man is spirit (D&C 93:29, 31-33).

And being spirit, in the chief fact of him, he has power by reason of that fact to cognize the things of the spirit, for this spirit is native to the things of the spirit, and he is under condemnation when he does not receive them. Hence, our prophet, shortening up Paul's phrase, and making it more direct, frequently cried aloud in his discourses—"Faith cometh by hearing the word of God" (Rom. 10:17). And upon that "hearing of the word of God," the prophet of the New Dispensation relied for the convincing power of its truth. And in that same spirit and confidence of its innate power of convincing men of the truth, we submit this brief account of the restoration of THE WAY of eternal life to the children of men.

PART III
THE LIFE

"I am . . . the Life."
Jesus to his Disiples.

(JOHN 14:6)

CHAPTER XLVIII

The Life: Manifested in the Christ

SCRIPTURE READING LESSON

Analysis

I. Jesus the Life.
II. The Gospel Must Be a Life.
III. The Keynote of the Life.
IV. Type of the Life: Prodigal Son or the Christ?
V. Accessibility to the Life.
VI. The Graciousness of the Life to Friends.
VII. The Life More Than Morality.

References

All the citations of scriptures in this lesson and their context.

I can recall no other works that may be referred to with advantage; except that a more exhausting research of the four books of our scripture may be made than is represented by the citations used in the texts and footnotes of this chapter.

CHAPTER XLVIII
The Life: Manifested in the Christ

JESUS THE LIFE

> I am . . . the Life (John 14:6).
>
> In him was life and the life was the light of men (John 1:4).
>
> I am the Light and the Life of the world (3 Ne. 9:18).
>
> I am the light of the world: he that followeth me shall not walk in darkness, but shall have the light of life (John 8:12).

Just as Jesus proclaimed himself to be the TRUTH and the WAY, so also he proclaimed himself to be THE LIFE in God's plan of things for man's earth existence. But just what does that mean? We know that he is proclaimed in the revelations of God as being "the resurrection and the life," and that though men were dead, yet in him should they live. This is followed by the singular statement, "whosoever liveth and believeth . . . shall never die" (John 11:25-26). Also, in his Gethsemane prayer he said, "and this is Life Eternal, that they might know Thee, the only true God, and Jesus Christ, whom Thou hast sent" (John 17:3). It would appear, then, that "eternal life" comes through "belief," through a "knowledge of God," and that would lead us to believe that these scripture references to Jesus being "The Life" have a broader scope and meaning than the securing of physical immortality[1] through the resurrection from the dead.

From what has gone before throughout these pages, we have already learned that death has two phases; first, spiritual death; second, physical death. The Lord Jesus, the "Anointed One," came "to seek and to save" that which was lost; and as what was lost was spiritual life, dependent upon union with God; and physical life, dependent upon union of spirit and earth element, this we have already concluded, is what Jesus came "to save" by restoring the spiritual and the physical life of man. A noble mission, indeed, comprising a redemption of the world, the salvation of a race, a task worthy of Deity, whatever the sacrifice might be, and Deity's shame had it not been performed, since Deity alone could achieve such a work.

---

1. <Ms III[c] adds "im" because Ms III[*] has "physical mortality"—*Ed.*>

And yet there is something more than this in the mission of the "Anointed One." He is the TRUTH respecting the things of God. He reveals God in his own person, for he is declared to be the very image of the Father's person, and "the brightness of his glory" (Heb. 1:3). "In him dwells all the fullness of the Godhead bodily" (Col. 2:9; cf. 1:19). He is God manifested in the flesh, and in respect of being the revelation of God, and the fullness of that revelation, he is the whole TRUTH of it; and that becomes the very heart of all truth in the world, the knowledge of God, the highest knowledge, and the heart of all truth that may be learned and realized by the intellect and the heart of man. It will lead to the solving of all mysteries, to the attainment of all knowledge of that which is, or has been, or shall become; and our Lord Jesus is the complete manifestation of that Truth. He is the Truth!

Also, as we have seen, He is THE WAY. No man can come unto the Father but through him—meaning that no man can come to the knowledge of God and into fellowship with God but through him; and no man cometh unto the Christ, "except the Father . . . draw him" (John 6:44). The Father and the Son work together; they are in cooperation; and the Holy Ghost is in the union also, in the way of being the Witness to the Truth.

> And no man, speaking by the Spirit <of God>, calleth Jesus accursed, and no man can say that Jesus is the Lord, but by the Holy Ghost (1 Cor. 12:3).

And yet, magnificent as all this is, it is not the whole of the story. There is still to be accounted for "I am . . . the Life," and "the Life is more than meat, and the body is more than raiment" (cf. Matt. 6:25). We are told in the scriptures that in the Lord Jesus "was Life: and the Life was the light of men"; and though "the light shineth in darkness, the darkness comprehendeth it not";[2] • andthoughhethatwas the Light coming to his own, yet he was rejected of them. Nevertheless, we are assured, to "as many as received him"—to as many as will receive him—"to them gave he power"—and to them he will give power—"to become the sons of God; even to them that believe on his name." To those that were born of him, "not of blood, nor of the will of the flesh, nor of the will of men—but of God" (John 1:4-13). He gives his promise that whosoever will follow him, "shall not walk in darkness, but shall have the light of Life" (John 8:12).

No wonder that when contemplating his mission the Master said to his followers:

> I am the bread of Life; he that cometh unto me shall never hunger; and he that believeth on me shall never thirst (John 6:35).

---

2. <Ms III* "the darkness may not comprehend it"—*Ed.*>

THE GOSPEL MUST BE A LIFE[3]

All this means that the gospel of Jesus Christ is not only a plan, a Way, it must be a LIFE. The gospel must be a Life to be understood—to be realized. God must provide, in order to complete his plan, not only a theory of living, an outline, verbal or written, and frequently repeated, and by such repetitions reveal it from many angles—but it must be set forth by example, and the example must be perfect. Men may not be able in this our mortal life to live up to its perfections, but the perfections must be seen, the one perfect life must be lived so that men shall know what it is they are to strive for. As the Paschal Lamb, the symbol of the real sacrifice, had to be without spot or blemish—foreshadowing that the One making the real atonement would[4] be without blemish—so this "Life," which is to be the type-life under God's plan—the gospel—must be perfect; without blemish, or spot, to stand out above the horizon of the world forever present in man's vision as the perfect Life aimed at in gospel-living. Or as Jesus, the Anointed, stands in the foreground of all history, as the complete and perfect revelation of what Deity is, God completely revealed, so, too, must the perfect Life stand out revealed clearly to the consciousness of men, so that there can be no question as to either Deity revealed or the perfect Life portrayed to the consciousness of men, and there must be no possibility of doubt in either case. Two splendid words: God! Life! And these are revealed in Jesus Christ that men may know both the one and the other.

And now as to this Life. Let us go back to the starting point to find out what it is to be. God in the Council of Gods—Divine Personages, archangels, angels, and spirits of men, said:

> We will make an earth whereon these may dwell; and we will prove them herewith, to see if they will do all things whatsoever the Lord their God shall command them. They who keep their first estate [that pre-existent spirit estate in which they would accept the proposed plan of Deity for their advancement] shall be added upon [i.e., shall be put in the way of progression]; and they who keep not their first estate shall not have glory in the same kingdom with those who keep their first estate; and they who keep their second estate [the estate of their earth-life, and in that estate of earth-life will "do all things whatsoever the Lord their God shall command them"]—they shall have glory added upon their heads forever and forever (Abr. 3:24-26).

From this prelude to the opening chapter of man's earth-life we learn that said earth-life[5] is to be the trial period, the testing field for man. God "will prove them herewith, to see if they will do all things whatsoever the Lord their God shall

3. <Ms III[c] adds "The Gospel Must Be A Life"—*Ed.*>
4. <Ms III[c] adds "would"—*Ed.*>
5. <Ms III* "we learn that it"—*Ed.*>

command them." The test is to be obedience; the submission of man's will to God's will—to God's law. The will must learn to control all other qualities of mind. It must be the master quality of mind, acting upon intelligence, after intelligence has surveyed the whole field and submits report to consciousness as to what is evil, what is good, and better, and best. Then the "will" must at the last pronounce the determination as to what shall be done—that is the all-important matter—what shall be done?

Upon the right answer to that hangs the salvation of every soul of man in the world. Happy is he who, learning the Truth and finding the WAY, comes to that point where he conforms his "will" to law, to the will of God. Whatsoever God saith unto him that will he do; for that will be the highest manifestation of wisdom that men can anywhere or anyhow arrive at; for in doing that, men but submit to the highest possible wisdom—wisdom that arises from perfect knowledge. All things then will be "done in the wisdom of Him who knoweth all things" (2 Ne. 2:24), and there will be no mistake. Man's faith and action will find sure foundation at last, if he will say with Joshua: "As for me and my house, we will serve the Lord" (Josh. 24:15).

THE KEYNOTE OF THE LIFE[6]

Now again, "The Life," the keynote of it. The Life that was lived, the one perfect Life.[7] Thought of it takes us back again to the council preceding the creation of the earth. After all things had been explained and God had made His covenant with men to give to them eternal life—spiritual life and physical immortality—it became known that a sacrifice would have to be made in order to restore that which would be lost by the breaking up of the harmony of things, and the question arose, "Whom shall I send?" That is, to make the sacrifice and bring to pass the necessary redemption of man. The approved answer by the Son of God was, "Father, Thy will be done, and the glory be Thine forever" (Moses 4:1). And the keynote thus struck in that council became the keynote of the Life that the Son of God lived in the earth. This was the chief characteristic of him repeatedly expressed. In youth it was:

> Wist ye not that I must be about my Father's business? (Luke 2:49).

Later:

> I seek not to do mine own will, but the will of the Father, which sent me (cf. John 5:30).

6. <Ms III[c] adds "The Keynote Of The Life"—*Ed.*>
7. <Ms III[*] "the one perfect Life the Life of Jesus"—*Ed.*>

Again:

> I came down from heaven not to do mine own will, but the will of Him that sent me (John 6:38).

It followed him, this principle, to the very last phase of his mortal, earth-life. If it were possible, he would have been pleased to have had some other way taken to the accomplishment of God's purpose: "O Father, if it be possible, let this cup pass from me"–the cup of his bitter suffering and his approaching humiliation and[8] crucifixion–"if it be possible, let this cup pass from me"; but then and instantly, as if he feared he had asked too much; instantly–"nevertheless, not as I will, but as Thou wilt" (Matt. 26:39). No answer coming, he bowed reconciled to the inevitable. Afterwards he said to the assembled Nephites to whom he appeared on the Western Continent–and now triumphantly, since he had endured the cross and gained the crown–"I have drunk out of that bitter cup, which the Father hath given me, and have glorified the Father in taking upon me the sins of the world, in which I have suffered the will of the Father in all things from the beginning" (3 Ne. 11:11). Later still, to the prophet of the New Dispensation, in referring to his passion, he said:

> Which suffering caused myself, even God, the greatest of all, to tremble because of pain and to bleed at every pore, and to suffer both body and spirit–and would that I might not drink the bitter cup. . . . Nevertheless, glory be to the Father, <and> I partook and finished my preparations unto the children of men (D&C 19:18-19).

Here was one (the Lord Jesus) who proved beyond all human imagining that he would do whatsoever "the Lord his God would command him." And that is the ensample, the perfect ensample, of what God would have men to do: be obedient.

> If thou wilt enter into life, keep the commandments (Matt. 19:17).

TYPE OF THE LIFE: "PRODIGAL SON" OR THE CHRIST?[9]

The prodigal son, made so much of in emotional religious appeal, as exhibiting God's power in redemption, is not the type of what God would have men to be. True, since there are those–and many of them–who among the children of men will be prodigal sons, it is a glorious reality that they can repent and through repentance find their way back to their father's home and receive royal welcome and start anew in the way of keeping the commandments after the terrible

8. <Ms III^{c} adds "humiliation and"–*Ed.*>
9. <Ms III^{c} adds "Type Of The Life: 'Prodigal Son' Or The Christ?"–*Ed.*>

experiences of folly and sin; but that is not the type that God would have upheld before men as an example to follow. The Christ-type is the divine ideal, the mould and form, God would have followed by men—the perfect life. This the Christ emphasized, when he said to his Judean disciples:

> Be ye therefore perfect, even as your Father which is in heaven is perfect (Matt. 5:48).

And to the Nephite disciples the Christ made this clear by putting to them the question, "What manner of men ought ye to be?" <and then> answered, "Verily, I say unto you, even as I am" (3 Ne. 27:27).

> Though he were a Son, yet learned he obedience through the things which he suffered; and being made perfect, he became the author of eternal salvation to all those who obey him, [even as he, of course, obeyed the Father] (Heb. 5:8-9).

In all his life, as we have said, the Christ was dominated by this master conception of duty—obedience to God. He was here to do the will of the Father that sent him. And in all the events of his life and his dealings with men, this principle gave a noble graciousness to all that he did. Truly his chief apostle could well say of him:

> God anointed Jesus of Nazareth with the Holy Ghost and with power: who went about doing good and healing all that were oppressed of the devil; for God was with him (Acts 10:38).

And not only was God "with him," but "in him": to wit, that "God was in Christ, reconciling the world unto himself" (2 Cor. 5:19); and he was revealing God at work.

ACCESSIBILITY TO THE LIFE

How richly the incidents of his life unfold the principle upon which the Christ worked, we may not know, but by contemplation of it! The value of the Life will be in proportion to its accessibility to mankind; and how accessible was and is the Life of the Christ to the world! To the rich, to the poor, to the sorrowful, and to the joyous. To the unfortunate, the cripples, the sick, the lepers, the halt, dumb, and blind. To the rulers and the magistrates, the despised Samaritans, the publicans, and the sinners; the beggar by the wayside, the widows—of which she of Nain was typical. To those grateful for his administrations, and to those ungrateful; to the penitent thief on the cross; even to those who crucified him, he could say, "Father, forgive them, for they know not what they do" (Luke 23:34). To Nicodemus, who for fear of the Jews would only come to him under cover of the night—to him he could teach the mystery of being born again; to the dwarfed, waddling Zacchaeus,[10] who must needs climb a tree to behold him above the heads of the crowd—in his house he would dine! To the woman taken in adultery and dragged to his feet by her accusers—to her he could be gracious, refuse to accuse her, but bade her to "go her way but to[11] sin no more" (John 8:11). To shyster lawyers, seeking to entrap him into inconsistency of utterance, even with them he could be patient. What a heterogeneous mass had full access to him! And none who came turned he away!

All this reflects the graciousness and majesty of God the Father, who "maketh His sun to rise on the evil and on the good, and sendeth rain on the just and on the unjust" (Matt. 5:45); that scorns to love only them that love him—for the publicans do so—but the divine love for our example is extended to even those who mock and revile God.[12]

THE GRACIOUSNESS OF "THE LIFE" TO DISCIPLES[13]

To his close adherents[14] and friends, how benign and sweetly benevolent the Christ could be and was! St. Peter, the oldest man of the group of his immediate followers,[15] rough and tempestuous as he was, the Master corrected with firmness; but loved and trusted him beyond expected[16] measure. What a world of feeling there is in that soul-cry of his over this apostle when he said:

> Simon, Simon, behold, Satan hath desired to have you, that he may sift you as wheat: but I have prayed for thee, that thy faith fail not; and when thou art converted, strengthen thy brethren (Luke 22:31-32).

This man, Peter, boasted that though all men should be offended at the Christ, yet never would he be offended with him. But Jesus said to him: "Verily, I say unto thee, that this night, before the cock crow, thou shalt deny me thrice." To which Peter answered, "Though I should die with thee, yet will I not deny thee" (Matt. 26:34-35).

But Peter fulfilled the master's prediction; that night he denied him thrice and with cursing! And what was the punishment? Nay, rather the correction? The

---

10. <Ms III "Zacheus"—*Ed.*>

11. <Ms III[c] adds "to 'go her way but to"—*Ed.*>

12. <Ms III[*] "and revile God, for he knows that they know not what they do"—*Ed.*>

13. <Ms III[c] adds "The Graciousness of 'The Life' to Disciples"—*Ed.*>

14. <Ms III "his close adherence," an error of hearing—*Ed.*>

15. <Ms III[*] "To the oldest man of the group of his immediate followers, St. Peter"—*Ed.*>

16. <Ms III[c] adds "expected"—*Ed.*>

Master after the resurrection forced Peter to a three-fold declaration[17] of his love. St. John tells the story: "Simon, son of Jonas, lovest thou me more than these?" Referring to the other disciples present–lovest thou me more than these do? For Peter is already designated as the head of the church, to whom had been given in a special way the keys of the kingdom; and, therefore, more may be demanded of him than of the others. Also, both the Christ and the other disciples must know the soundness of Peter's mind and love for the Master, the supreme thing both for the disciples and the one to be entrusted with the very keys of the kingdom. Hence–"Lovest thou me more than these?" And Simon answered: "Yea, Lord; thou knowest that I love thee." And the Christ said, "Feed my lambs." Again, the second time, "Simon, son of Jonas, lovest thou me?" And the answer, "Yea, Lord; thou knowest that I love thee." And the Christ said unto him, "Feed my sheep." Then the third time, "Simon, son of Jonas, lovest thou me?" Perhaps Peter was beginning to see the drift of the Master's purpose, that three-fold denial was being replaced by a three-fold declaration of love and loyalty. Peter was grieved because he said unto him the third time, "Lovest thou me?" And doubtless in tears Peter said, "Lord, thou knowest all things; thou knowest that I love thee." Jesus saith unto him, "Feed my sheep" (John 21:15-17).

And the apostle who had denied the Christ thrice, and with cursing, was after three times affirming his love, reinstated with trust and confidence, and with commission to be the feeder of the lambs and of the sheep, to be the chief shepherd of the flock, the head of the church on earth in that dispensation, so long as he lived, holding the keys of the kingdom, having power to remit whose-soever sins he would remit, and retain whose-soever sins he would retain.

"THE LIFE" MORE THAN MORALITY

Dealing with the Gospel-Life, there are those who misapprehend it. It becomes with some a tangent that leads away from the truth, in that they would reduce the whole of the gospel to merely right moral living–a system of morality–what men call human or natural righteousness, and so they say "doctrine does not matter"; forms, ceremonies, symbols, ordinances, right conceptions of truth, right mental attitude towards existence, towards God,[18] does not matter. Practical righteousness is what counts.[19] The gospel is not a "power of God unto salvation"; has nothing to do with being born again, born of the water and of the Spirit; nothing to do with knowing the only God and Jesus Christ whom He hath sent, as being

17. <Ms III[*] "a three-time declaration"–*Ed.*>
18. <Ms III[c] adds "towards God"–*Ed.*>
19. <Ms III[c] adds "Practical righteousness is what counts"–*Ed.*>

necessary to eternal life. That which is recognized as plain, human morality will be sufficient for salvation, with the logical result that God and Christ with plans of salvation, atonements, and redemptions through love, may be ruled out of the reckoning, except as the moral life of the Christ may be taken as an ideal.

It is true also that from one point of view the gospel may be regarded chiefly[20] as a life; but to be complete and perfect, it must be a life founded on truth and on a system of truth that requires right conception of true principle and doctrine and the satisfactory gospel Life must be a lived-out[21] consequence of that truth and system of doctrine. The gospel has a history, and "The Life" required in it is based upon the facts of that history. "The Life" also must be lived with a view of conforming it to the purpose of God in the creation, and the purpose He has in making possible the earth-life of man. Religion is more than mere morality; it is a new birth, a spiritual power; it is a conformity to the purpose of God, a spiritual union with God, and a submission to His will, and a careful performance of all that He has ordained as necessary to the completion of "the Life"! Let no one, therefore, attempt to displace God's gospel plan by a substitution of humanitarianism, by which is here meant a system of morals based upon what is recognized as contributing to human welfare, the basis merely of social relations and individual well-being. Truly the gospel is expressed in a Life, but it is a Life in harmony with God's purposes; with fellowship and complete union with God, established through spiritual birth[22] and consciousness of a oneness with God's life.

20. <Ms III[c] adds "chiefly"–*Ed.*>

21. <Ms III[c] adds "lived-out"–*Ed.*>

22. <Ms III[*] "and fellowship, and complete union with him through spiritual birth"–*Ed.*>

CHAPTER XLIX

The Life: Under Commandments of God

SCRIPTURE READING LESSON

Analysis

I. The Crux of the Life—Obedience.

II. The Institution of Sacrifice—Symbol of the Life.

III. Sacrifice Expounded.

IV. Moses and the Law.

V. The Voice from the Wilderness.

VI. The Teaching of the Christ.

VII. Christ's Restatement of the Law.

VIII. From Negative to Positive Form.

IX. Love of God.

X. Love of Man.

XI. Identity of Principle in Love of God and Love for Man.

References

Careful study of all citations of scriptures of the text and the footnotes and their context.

These references to the scriptures may be greatly multiplied.

All four books of the scripture—Bible, Book of Mormon, Doctrine and Covenants, Pearl of Great Price (Book of Moses and Book of Abraham), *passim*, on the various subdivisions given in the analysis of this lesson.

CHAPTER XLIX
The Life: Under Commandments of God

THE CRUX OF "THE LIFE"—OBEDIENCE

The Life as we have seen is the Lord Jesus, and the thing emphasized in that Life is obedience; and that obedience contemplated by the gospel is obedience to the commandments of God: the keynote of which is expressed by God the Father when He said:

> We will prove them herewith, to see if they will do all things whatsoever the Lord their God shall command them (Abr. 3:25).

That declaration presents the whole case. It was restated by the inspired writer of Ecclesiastes, when he said:

> Let us hear the conclusion of the whole matter. Fear God and keep His commandments, for this is the whole duty of men (Eccl. 12:13).

All that follows can only be by way of illustration and commentary. But for the purpose of making this central truth of "the Life" impressive, let us contemplate it through illustrations.

To Adam this law made its first appearance when God said to him and his spouse, and blessed them:

> Be fruitful and multiply and replenish the earth and subdue it, and have dominion over . . . every living thing that moveth upon the earth (Gen. 1:28).

This from that time on became the commandment of God to Adam[1] and through him to the race, since only through those who were born of him, following in the same commandment and responsibility, could this commandment be carried out.

The next development of the duty of man by receiving commandments from God was the edict against eating the fruit of the tree of the Knowledge of Good and Evil. A commandment with a penalty attached, "Thou shalt not eat of it. In the day thou eatest thereof thou shalt surely die" (Gen. 2:17). The circumstance of

---

1. <Ms III* "of God to him"—*Ed.*>

man's transgression of this law, with its developments, has already been considered, and it is not necessary to reiterate or amplify what was then said.

THE INSTITUTION OF SACRIFICES—THE SYMBOL OF THE LIFE

Then came the commandment of the Lord through Adam to his posterity, that:

> They should worship the Lord their God, and should offer the firstlings of their flocks for an offering unto the Lord (Moses 5:5).

This sacrifice was to be a perfect lamb without spot or blemish—it was to be slain and offered upon an altar as a burnt offering unto the Lord:

> And Adam was obedient unto the commandment<s>. . . . And after many days an angel of the Lord appeared unto Adam, saying, "Why dost thou offer sacrifice<s> unto the Lord?" And Adam said unto him, "I know not, save the Lord commanded me" (Moses 5:5-6).

The commandment was given as an arbitrary direction, no explanation made, no reason given for such a sacrifice at that time, or the purpose of it; but Adam, having received the commandment from God, obeyed it and taught his children to make the sacrifices. From this arises a very effective and beautiful lesson in obedience. "Blind obedience," some would call it; but Adam's obedience was not blind. He doubtless perceived by reflection that to follow God's commandment would be following the highest wisdom which arose from perfect knowledge, and, therefore, his obedience was intelligent obedience, and an act of trust in the knowledge and wisdom of God.

THE SACRIFICE EXPOUNDED

The visiting angel now offered the following explanation:

> This thing is a similitude of the sacrifice of the Only Begotten of the Father, which is full of grace and truth. Wherefore, thou shalt do all that thou doest in the name of the Son, and thou shalt repent and call upon God in the name of the Son forevermore (Moses 5:7-8).

This was now the law of God unto Adam, and obedience to it became the measure of his duty. With this came also the law of baptism by water and baptism of the Holy Ghost, and continued adherence to laws of righteousness, as they were developed by continuous revelations from God, whose commandments were always in all ages the moral and spiritual law unto those who came into allegiance, through faith, with God. In this patriarchal period in which all the patriarchs wrought from Adam to Enoch and Noah and Shem, and Abraham, it was so; and this period, as we have already seen, was characterized by the continuation of the revelations of God unfolding the duties of men.

THE TESTING OF ABRAHAM

Abraham's experience with reference to offering up his son Isaac gives an important lesson[2] on this principle of obedience. He received a commandment to offer up his son Isaac as a sacrifice unto God upon an altar, and since the commandment was of God, Abraham prepared himself and his son to make such a sacrifice, notwithstanding it seemed to wreck all the hopes that the patriarch had regarded as being centered in this son of promise, and as the one through whom he and all the nations of the earth were to be blessed. But Abraham was one of those spirits who stood amid the hosts of spirits who were characterized as being "great" and "noble" and "good"; one, who before the creation of the world was to illustrate the great testing process on which loyalty to God is founded–and "we will prove them herewith, to see if they will do all things whatsoever the Lord their God shall command them" (Abr. 3:25). And so the offering was prepared and would have been consummated, but when the patriarch had demonstrated his faith and implicit trust in God, and his integrity to God, he was relieved of the burden of slaying his son as a sacrifice. A substitute was found in the ram in the thicket, which was offered instead of Isaac.

MOSES AND THE LAW

So, too, with Moses, who came to Israel first with a dispensation of the same gospel which was had among the patriarchs, both in ante-diluvian and post-diluvian times, but the people, brutalized by their bondage of four hundred years of captivity in Egypt, were not equal to fulfilling its requirements, and so a lesser law, the law of "carnal" commandments, was given to them with a labored ritual of types and symbols, which should be followed by the reality which would finally come in the atonement and sacrifice of the Son of God, with its influx of spiritual forces and powers.

Yet attending upon even this the "lesser law," made heavy with its burden of ceremonials, came also the great moral law which belongs to the gospel in every dispensation of it. This found expression at Mount Sinai in the "Ten Words" of God, or the "Ten Commandments." Those commandments now became the law to Israel. They constituted a noble outline of Israel's duty toward God and toward men.

---

2. <Ms III "an important lessons"–*Ed.*>

I. I am the Lord thy God . . . Thou shalt have no other Gods before me.
II. Thou shalt not make unto thee any graven image; . . . thou shalt not bow down thyself to them nor serve them.
III. Thou shalt not take the name of the Lord thy God in vain.
IV. Remember the sabbath day, to keep it holy.
V. Honor thy father and thy mother.
VI. Thou shalt not kill.
VII. Thou shalt not commit adultery.
VIII. Thou shalt not steal.
IX. Thou shalt not bear false witness against thy neighbor.
X. Thou shalt not covet (Ex. 20:2-5, 7-8, 12-17).

These "ten commandments," while directly given to Israel, may well be taken over by all races and nations of men as fundamentals in universal righteousness, so excellent are they; and especially as expounded and modified by the Son of God during his ministry in the Meridian Dispensation.

THE VOICE FROM THE WILDERNESS

These "ten commandments" and performance of the ceremonials of types and symbols of "the better things to come" constituted the obligations of Israel to God and to each other until the coming of the forerunner of the Christ, who to Israel (then a long time wandered from "the path direct," marked off by the great law given to Moses) came with a serious message of repentance, and a prophecy of the coming of the Messiah with the greater things of the gospel and the higher spiritual life that it had to introduce, and a somewhat new basis from which to fashion man's attitude of mind towards God. John the Baptist's shrill cry of repentance, which attracted the attention of Israel, and his baptism in water for the remission of sins, became then the law of the Life to the people of God:

> Repent ye, for the kingdom of heaven is at hand. . . . There cometh after me one that is mightier than I, whose shoes I am not worthy to bear, he shall baptize you with the Holy Ghost and with fire; whose fan is in his hand and he will thoroughly purge the floor and gather his wheat into the garner, but he shall burn up the chaff with unquenchable fire (cf. Matt. 3:2, 11-12).

THE TEACHING OF THE CHRIST

When Jesus came, he continued John's message of repentance. And throughout his ministry he not only preached the gospel but lived its Life and unfolded the law and the gospel as no other teacher or prophet in Israel ever unfolded it. Let us contemplate his doctrine of "The Life" in his teaching, as we have already considered it in his living.

THE CHRIST'S RESTATEMENT OF GOD'S LAW

Lawyer: "Master, which is the great commandment in the law?" [This the question of the lawyer who came tempting Jesus.]

Jesus: [1] "Thou shalt love the Lord thy God with all thy heart, and with all thy soul, and with all thy mind. This is the first and great commandment, and the second is like unto it– [2] Thou shalt love thy neighbor as thyself. On these two commandments hang all the law and the prophets" (Matt. 22:36-40).

FROM NEGATIVE TO POSITIVE FORM

It is to be observed that this restatement of the commandments is a statement which is all-inclusive of what is written in the law and in the prophets, and also it reinstates all the moral and spiritual law of the patriarchal dispensations, for it must be remembered that running all through the ages there is but one law of righteousness which attaches to the one gospel,[3] and this generalization, hit off by the Christ in answer to the lawyer's question, is a full restatement of the whole law of righteousness.

Two things should be noticed in respect of this restatement of the law as compared with the Ten Great Words of God to Moses: namely, (1) that the Christ changes the basis of the statement from the negative to the positive form. Except for two commandments out of the ten, the negative form is used by Moses. The two exceptions are, first, the imperative commandment, "Remember the Sabbath day to keep it holy"; and the second is like unto it in form, "Honor thy father and thy mother." Undoubtedly the affirmative form of statement as given by the Christ in his summation of the law is more impressive than the "Thou shalt not" style of the ten commandments. (2) That the Christ's generalization is based upon "love" as the motive force in God's law. That is to say, obedience to God's law properly comes, and can only properly come, from love of God, not from fear of Him.

We note the saying of the Psalmist: "The fear of the Lord is the beginning of wisdom" (Ps. 111:10); but we also remember that the scriptures teach that "the fear of the Lord is to depart from evil" (cf. Prov. 3:7) and "the fear of the Lord is to hate evil" (Prov. 8:13). Martin Luther's translation of the passage in the Psalms–"the fear of the Lord is the beginning of wisdom"–appeals as more nearly true than the translation in our Authorized Version, namely, "Reverence for God is the beginning of wisdom." "Fear of the Lord" places the approach on the lower plane. It may not be doubted that men do many things and refrain from doing many other things from "the fear of the Lord," but it adds something to human dignity to think of men as keeping the commandments of God because of "reverence" for Him,

3. <Ms III* "to one the gospel"–*Ed.*>

rather than to be moved thereto by fear. Better yet, and rising to the plane on which the Christ would have us work, that men keep the divine commandments from love of God.

LOVE OF GOD

First, however, there stands the question, how can we love God and be obedient to Him through love? There is but one way: men must learn to know Him; and if men can only learn to know God, love will follow as natural consequence. And in order that we mortal men might know God and by that means love Him, He has given the sublime manifestation of Himself through our Lord Jesus, our Elder Brother. He is God's manifestation in the flesh. St. Paul says:

> Without controversy, great is the mystery of Godliness: God was manifest ["manifested" is the suggested marginal translation, see Oxford S.S. Edition of the Bible] in the flesh, justified in the Spirit, seen of angels, preached unto the Gentiles, believed on in the world, received up into glory (1 Tim. 3:16).[4]

All this in plain allusion to the Christ. Again, the testimony of Paul:

> God, who at sundry times and in divers manners spake in times past unto the fathers by the prophets, hath in these last days spoken unto us by His Son, whom He hath appointed heir of all things, by whom also He made the worlds; who being the brightness of His glory, and the express image of His person and upholding all things by the word of His power, when he had by himself purged our sins, sat down on the right hand of the Majesty on high (Heb. 1:1-3).

"The brightness of His [God's] glory" and the "express image of His [God's] person" is an averment that Jesus Christ was the revelation of God the Eternal Father. The scriptures are replete with iteration and reiteration of the truth:

> In the beginning was the Word, and the Word was with God, and the Word was God. . . . And the Word was made flesh and dwelled among us, (and we beheld his glory, even the glory of the Only Begotten of the Father,) full of grace and truth (John 1:1, 14).

This, our Lord Jesus. This, God manifested in the flesh.

> "Lord, show us the Father, and it sufficeth us."

---

4. <Roberts's bracketed comment in the middle of the quotation refers to the fact that the translators of the King James Version provided an alternate rendition in the margin; i.e., "manifested" instead of "was manifest." The main problem with 1 Tim. 3:16 in the KJV is the ascription of deity to Jesus ("God") instead of the use of a relative pronoun ("who") as discussed in chapter 19, note 4—*Ed.*>

> Jesus: "Have I been so long with you, and yet hast thou not known me, Philip? He that hath seen me hath seen the Father; and how sayest thou then, Show us the Father? Believest thou not that I am in the Father and the Father in me? The words I speak to you I speak not of myself, but the Father that dwelleth in me, he doeth the works" (John 14:8-10).

In other words, Christ is the revelation of Deity. The revelation of all that can be called God, both in personality and in attributes and, therefore, representatively he is the Father as well as well as the Son. He is, and represents, all that can be thought upon or conceived of as God.

> For it pleased the Father that in him should all fullness dwell (Col. 1:19).

And again:

> For in him dwelleth all the fullness of the Godhead bodily (Col. 2:9).

God, then, is manifested for us men in the flesh through Jesus Christ; and with the "Spirit of God" that proceeds forth from His presence to fill the immensity of space and in our modern revelations called "the Light of Christ" (D&C 88:6-12), He becomes truly God manifested as personage in the flesh; and by His Spirit He is also immanent in the world, by which we mean, everywhere present by His Spirit, and everywhere present with all the attributes of God not only as creative force, but also as world-sustaining power, intelligence-inspiring power,[5] "the light which lighteth every man that cometh into the world"; also, the vital force–life-giving power, "in Him was life and the life was the light of men" (John 1:4, 9); and preeminently Jesus is the Love manifested power of God in the world.

We learn God, then, through the revelation He has given of Himself in Christ Jesus our Lord; and knowing him as the very Son of God, and the complete revelation of all that can be thought upon as God, who can withhold love, or refuse to obey God when God is revealed in Jesus Christ? Thus revealed it is not difficult to accept and obey the first part of the great commandment, namely, "thou shalt love the Lord thy God with all thy heart, and with all thy soul, and with all they mind" (Matt. 22:37); for it is but a question of knowing him, then, love will follow[6] as effect follows cause.

---

5. <Ms III* "not only as creative force, but intelligence-inspiring power"—*Ed.*>
6. <Ms III* "knowing him and love will follow"—*Ed.*>

LOVE OF MAN

> And the second [commandment][7] is like unto it: Thou shalt love thy neighbor as thyself (Matt. 22:39).

"Thou shalt love thy neighbor as thyself." Just how comprehensive is this? Who is my neighbor? In the incident of the man who fell among thieves[8] enroute from Jerusalem to Jericho and was stripped of all, and passed up by the priest and the Levite but helped by the Samaritan—one of the outlawed from fellowship with Israel[9]—as related by the Christ, the idea is conveyed that he who is helpful to us in our misfortunes is truly our neighbor, a friend in need. But that is only half the story, he who needs our help is also our neighbor; and if this interpretation be accepted, then it would go far towards bringing all men within the definition of "our neighbor"; and indeed, that is undoubtedly intended to be the law. It is not merely those who help us that fulfill the law numerically as neighbor;[10] the great principle is love of man, sympathetic interest in all men, so that the great generalization of the Christ as to the greatest commandment in both parts of it would be, love of God, and love of man, without limitation.

This being true, we are confronted at first glance with a law extremely difficult to comply with—love of man—love of men—love of all men! It was pointed out in our treatment of the first part of this law, that it was easy to fulfil it, in that it only required a knowledge of God, as revealed in Jesus Christ, to have love follow as a matter of course. For to know God is to love Him. But when it comes to loving men—and meaning by that love of all men—the obstacles seem insuperable. How can we love all men, when so many of them are repulsive? Repulsive both in person and in nature of them—vile many of them in every way; filthy in apparel and in their bodies; vicious by nature, thieves, drunkards, liars, deceitful, treacherous, riotous, boisterous, revengeful, stupid, hopeless in depravity, contemptible, without natural affection, lecherous, and if there is any other thing that makes for badness, some of them have it, and have it all! How shall we love these? Is it not unreasonable that the law of God should require us to love them? And if such characters be included in the commandments to "love men," how can we live the law?

Undoubtedly God loves them, but not their vileness, not their sin, for the scripture informs us that He "cannot look upon sin with the least degree of allowance" (D&C 1:31). The scriptures represent Him also as abhorring sin, and yet while condemning the sins, He may nevertheless, and does, love the soul even

---

7. <Ms III[c] adds "[commandment]"—*Ed.*>
8. <Ms III[*] "among the thieves"—*Ed.*>
9. <Ms III[c] adds "—one of the out-lawed from fellow-ship with Israel—"—*Ed.*>
10. <Ms III[c] adds "as neighbor"—*Ed.*>

of the sinner. And why? And how? Because God looks into the depths, and knows while men are sinful and vile, yet they can depart from sin, they can repent, and have created in them a new heart and a new mind; they can be born again, and change their attitude in relation to the whole of [11] life. They may be washed clean and stand upright in justice, in righteousness, in truth.

So God loves them, not because of their sin, nor in spite of their sin, but because of what they may become. He views them in the light of their possibilities. There are values within them that are hidden from their fellow men, hidden from themselves even; but clearly seen of God. The outside, aye, and most of the inside, may be utterly vile and repulsive, but within it all there is that which, if only it can be reached and awakened, may start a life that will work from within outward, sluffing off the vileness of both inside and outside, until it shall cleanse itself, even as rolling water by movement and sunshine and atmosphere, purifies itself; and out of the chrysalis of sinful man may at last evolve a regenerated man, a sinner born again and made a child of God. God all the while sees these possibilities, He sees His own image, His own divine nature under all that mass of accumulated unrighteousness and moral filth, and sees and loves His image, even there. And God's task through the gospel is to call that image forth and develop it.

The end of the argument is that man, if he would keep the second part of the great commandment and love his neighbor—he must learn to look upon his fellow man as God looks upon him; and view him in the light of his possibilities, and extend the neighborly hand that shall draw him out of his fallen state and make him realize that he is a son of God. Let those who are converted assume no pose of self-righteousness in their attitude of mind towards those who may be esteemed as fallen, and too frequently as hopeless. Rather let this be the attitude: "When thou art converted, strengthen thy brethren" (Luke 22:32). Remember, too, the case of the Pharisee and the Publican, and know that the sinner, conscious of his sins and struggling by confession to abandon them, may be more acceptable to God than the more righteous person, proudly conscious and over-conscious of his few virtues, and extolling himself into a smug self-righteousness.

IDENTITY OF PRINCIPLE IN LOVE OF GOD AND LOVE FOR MAN[12]

The same principle is at work in this second part of the Christ's summary of the law as in the first, namely: first, to love God it is necessary to know Him, and knowing Him love follows; and second, love of man—the race—will come by knowing him, and knowing him in the light of his possibilities, what he may

11. <Ms III^{c} adds "of"—*Ed.*>
12. <Ms III^{c} adds "Identity of Principle in Love of God And Love For Man"—*Ed.*>

become; love will follow, accompanied too by a determination to do the neighbor-act; namely, to assist in his redemption, work with the Christ in the salvation of men, remembering that Christ died for sinners. And "herein is love, not that we loved God,[13] but that He loved us, and sent His Son to be the propitiation of our sins" (cf. 1 Jn. 4:10). And the fullness of the law is "He who loveth God loveth his brother also" (1 Jn. 4:21). That is to say, coming to know the first part of the law and living it, will lead to knowing the second part of the one law, and living that, too. For surely it would be a solecism to affect love of God, and then not love the things God loves. And so the conclusion of the whole matter is: those who would be sons of God, saints of God, must learn to go the whole distance with the law—love of God and love of man; otherwise there would be a halting by the way. On these two commandments, united as parts of one law, hang all the law and all the prophets. Hence the scripture: "Love is the fulfilling of the law" (Rom. 13:10). As St. Paul so well puts it:

> Owe no man any thing, but to love one another: for he that loveth another hath fulfilled the law. For this, Thou shalt not commit adultery, Thou shalt not kill, Thou shalt not steal, <Thou shalt not bear false witness,> Thou shalt not covet;[14] and if there be by any other commandment, it is briefly comprehended in this saying, namely, Thou shalt love thy neighbor as thyself. Love worketh no ill to his neighbor. Therefore, love is the fulfilling of the law (Rom. 13:8-10).

---

13. <Ms III* "not that we love God"—*Ed.*>

14. <Ms III "thou shalt not steal, thou shalt not covet," but due to skipping from one "thou shalt not" to the next "thou shalt not" the words "Thou shalt not bear false witness," from the quoted scripture were accidentally omitted (though it was never added to the text as a Ms III[c])—*Ed.*>

CHAPTER L

The Life: The Sermon on the Mount I

SCRIPTURE READING LESSON

Analysis

I. The Sermon on the Mount: St. Matthew's Version.

II. The Beatitudes.

III. Discipleship—the Glory and Responsibility of It.

IV. Anger and Hatred without Cause.

V. The Sin of Adultery.

VI. Divorcement.

VII. Perform to the Lord Thine Oaths; the "Better Way."

VIII. An Eye for an Eye.

IX. Of Loving and Hating.

X. Be Ye Perfect—the Ideal.

XI. Almsgiving, The Spirit of.

XII. Prayer: "The Christian's Vital Breath."*

XIII. The Lord's Prayer.

XIV. Defect in St. Matthew's Version of the Lord's Prayer.

XV. Of Fasting.

XVI. Singleness of Service: No Serving of Two Masters.

References

Matt. 5-7; Luke 6 and 12.

Cf. 3 Ne. 12-14; cf. D&C 42, 45.

Whole of the four gospels, *passim.*

Also, D&C, *passim.*

*On prayer, see James Montgomery's hymn, "Prayer is the Soul's Sincere Desire," in LDS hymn book, *Sacred Hymns and Spiritual Songs for the Church of Jesus Christ of Latter-day Saints*, 24th ed. (Salt Lake City: The Deseret News Co., 1905), 358.

CHAPTER L

The Life: The Sermon[1] on the Mount I

"THE SERMON ON THE MOUNT"—ST. MATTHEW'S VERSION

The next great document to the Christ's summary of the gospel law is the Sermon on the Mount; and this is but an extension into detail, and a commentary on the statement and a summary of the law already considered.

I shall follow the sermon as set forth in St. Matthew, as it is there in the completest form among the New Testament writers. St. Luke is the only other writer in the gospels who gives any considerable part of this sermon, and he divides it really into two parts and gives it in two widely-separated chapters—the sixth and the twelfth. The first part—St. Luke 6:17-49—seems to be a different occasion and a different setting from that given on the mount according to St. Matthew. For Luke's setting is in a "plain" in the presence of a great multitude out of all Judea and Jerusalem and from the sea coast of Tyre and Sidon. Many came to be healed of physical infirmities. To this mixed multitude the Master delivered a discourse, which includes a large part of the principles set forth in Matthew, chapters five, six, and seven; but greatly curtailed, extending only from verse seventeen to forty-nine of Luke's chapter six. Another part of the sermon—a fragment—is found in Luke <chapter> twelve, which seems more especially directed to those whom the Master had called[2] to be his disciples—more especially the Twelve (see Luke 12:22).

THE BEATITUDES

The beatitudes with which the Sermon on the Mount opens—following from now on St. Matthew—might well be regarded[3] as statements of the results growing out of acceptance of, and living in harmony with, the Master's all-inclusive one "Great Commandment"—love of God and love of man. For love of God and love of man is the "fulfilling of the law," and reaching its complete fruition shall mellow

1. <Ms III* "THE LIFE: UNDER THE SERMON"—*Ed.*>

2. <Ms III* "whom he had called"—*Ed.*>

3. <Ms III* "the Sermon on the Mount—following from now on St. Matthew—opens, might well be regarded"—*Ed.*>

man's nature and his life to the beatitudes combined. The Christ was all the beatitudes express.

DISCIPLESHIP: THE GLORY AND RESPONSIBILITY OF IT[4]

Having closed his exordium on the beatitudes, the Savior directly addressed the disciples as to their responsibilities as disciples, destined to follow his doctrines:

> Ye are the salt of the earth (Matt. 5:13).

Salt <is> the preservative element, the symbol in man's thought of wholesomeness, that which renders tasteless things palatable. The symbol also of wisdom, but best regarded as the preservative element. How gracious the characterization: "Ye are the salt of the earth"; but what a tremendous responsibility runs parallel with that asseveration! "But, if the salt have lost his savor! wherewith shall it [the world] be salted?" The salt "is thenceforth[5] found good for nothing, but to be cast out and to be trodden under foot of man" (cf. Matt. 5:13). Discipleship means nothing unless it holds first to the doctrine and the example of the Christ, both in form and substance; unless disciples do this, they are as salt that has lost its savor and good for nothing, and become despicable!

Again, the Christ to his disciples:[6]

> Ye are the light of the world. A city that is set on a hill cannot be hid. Neither do men light a candle and put it under a bushel, but on a candlestick; and it giveth light unto all that are in the house (Matt. 5:14-15).

Again, noting the exalted place granted to his following and with that exaltation comes again an equal responsibility. Hence, the admonition:

> Let your light[s] so shine before men, that they may see your good works and glorify your Father which is in heaven (cf. Matt. 5:16).

Then comes a most important statement, linking up the true and pure system of ethics the Christ is unfolding with the righteous law of God of previous dispensations. He said:

> Think not that I come to destroy the law or the prophets: I am not come to destroy it, but to fulfill. . . . Until heaven and earth pass, one jot and one tittle[7] shall in nowise pass from the law, until all be fulfilled. Whosoever therefore shall break one of these

---

4. <Ms III[c] adds "It"–*Ed.*>

5. <Ms III "is thence found"–*Ed.*>

6. <Ms III[*] "The Disciples of Christ, 'The Light Of The World': And again to his disciples"–*Ed.*>

7. <Ms III "title"–*Ed.*>

> least commandments [referring to the previous law of God's system of righteousness], and shall teach men so, he shall be called the least in the kingdom of heaven; but whosoever shall do and teach them, the same shall be called great in the kingdom of heaven (cf. Matt. 5:17-19).

Solidarity of the righteousness of God's law through all dispensations is here affirmed, and the duty of his disciples is to adhere unto that law of righteousness, both ancient and in his own times, which were the modern times then; and it shall be true of all times and dispensations, this solidarity of God's law of righteousness.

In illustration of the relationship of his teaching to the law the Master proceeds to intensify the law of the ancients and reveals the spirit of the law, which the teachers of Israel were reducing to the mere letter of the law and losing sight of its spirit. Hence, a series of apparent changes in the law, but really an amplification to set forth their spirit and intensify their power. So the Christ proceeds:[8]

ANGER AND HATRED WITHOUT CAUSE

It was said by them of old,

> Thou shalt not kill, and whosoever shall kill shall be in danger of the judgment. But I say unto thee, Whosoever is angry with his brother without a cause shall be in danger of the judgment, and whosoever shall say to his brother, "Raca," shall be in danger of the council, and whosoever shall say, "Thou fool," shall be in danger of hell fire (cf. Matt. 5:21-22).

This treatise has to do with the beginning of those emotions of anger and hatred, in which murderous thoughts have their inception. The Christ's teaching would stop this murderous spirit at its source, and, therefore, eliminate hatred and anger[9] and the expression of them which may lead in the ultimate development to murder. As he would have men avoid the appearance of evil, so would he have them eliminate the possibility of anger and hateful thoughts. And if these be eliminated, there will be no possibility of murder. So important did the Christ esteem this lesson that he bade his disciples that, if men bringing a gift to God's altar, they there remembered that a brother had ought against them, they should leave their gift and go their way and become reconciled to their brother, "then come and offer thy gift" (Matt. 5:24).

As in a way supplementing this instruction the Master counseled sapience[10] in dealing with adversaries. "Agree with thine adversary quickly, whilst thou art in

8. <Ms III* "So he proceeds"—*Ed.*>

9. <Ms III* "eliminate the development of hatred and anger"—*Ed.*>

10. <Ms III "councilled sapiency"—*Ed.*>

the way with him," lest at any time the adversary getting advantage should deliver thee to the judge, and the judge to the officer, and thence to prison, whence there may be no release until the utmost farthing is paid (cf. Matt. 5:25-26). Reconciliation, conciliation with adversaries, is the path of wisdom to follow, which the Christ gave the foregoing as his advice.

THE SIN OF ADULTERY

Again, to the law and its intensification:

> Thou shalt not commit adultery (Matt. 5:27).

We have already in an incidental way (see ante chapter <blank>) pointed out the Master's intensification of this part of the law, which demanded the elimination even of lustful desires,[11] and we need not repeat that here, but include this addition with it, that the Master pointing out the importance of eliminating lustful contemplation and desires remarked in his striking manner in way of illustration:

> If thy right eye offend thee, pluck it out and cast it from thee, for it is profitable for thee that one of thy members perish and not that thy whole body should be cast into hell (cf. Matt. 5:29-30).

And the same as to the right hand, if it offend thee, cut it off, and cast it away, with the same end in view, viz., entering heaven. In the Book of Mormon version of this same sermon, this particular matter is put in this form:[12]

> Behold, I say unto you, that whosoever looketh on a woman, to lust after her, hath committed adultery already in his heart. Behold, I give unto you a commandment, that you suffer none of these things to enter into your heart, for it is better that ye should deny yourselves of these things, wherein ye will take up your cross, than that ye should be cast into hell (cf. 3 Ne. 12:28-30).

If this be taken as the commentary of the Christ on his principle, how beautifully clear this principle of purity in thought is set forth, and surely relieves the principle of that implication that has been read into it by fanatics, which lead in some cases to self-mutilation in order to comply, as was supposed, with the admonition, "If thy right eye offend thee, pluck it out and cast it from thee."

---

11. <Ms III[*] "desire"–*Ed.*>

12. <For a study of the Book of Mormon account of this sermon, see John W. Welch, *The Sermon at the Temple and the Sermon on the Mount: A Latter-day Saint Approach* (Salt Lake City: Deseret Book Co., 1990; Provo, UT: Foundation for Ancient Research and Mormon Studies, 1990)–*Ed.*>

DIVORCEMENT

Closely connected with the matter of the above paragraph is the law of divorcement:

> It hath been said, whosoever shall put away his wife, let him give her a writing of divorcement (Matt. 5:31).

Such was the law of Moses. The Master said:

> But I say unto you, that whosoever shall put away his wife, save for the cause of fornication, causes her to commit adultery, and whosoever shall marry her that is divorced, committeth adultery (cf. Matt. 5:32).

Observe in passing that under the Christ's exposition of the law, so far from being destroyed it is intensified at each touch. It is quite clear that "God hateth putting away," as was said by Malachi:

> Let none deal treacherously against the wife of his youth, for the Lord, the God of Israel, saith that he hateth putting away (Mal. 2:15-16).

But one sin may justify the "putting away," the sin of breaking the marriage covenant; the sin of high treason on the part of man or wife, the sin of adultery, that is the law of Christ. It is doubtful, however, if this statement of the law is to be understood as applying to the innocent parties to divorcement. For example, here is the case of a young wife, not guilty of the offense that would justify her husband in putting her away, but blameless. Her husband, however, has become weary of her; she no longer pleases his fancy; he may already have found some one more desirable to him, and so puts away his wife that he may marry the creature of his lust. Of course, in effect he commits adultery, and the woman he marries, having guilty knowledge of his course, might well be thought to participate in his guilt of adultery. But in the case of the innocent, cast-off wife, where does she appear in blame or guilt? Not at all, if she remain unmarried, of course. But is the law in her case to be so interpreted that, though innocent, she must be condemned to this sort of widowhood, perhaps, through a long period of[13] life, or if she marry be adjudged guilty of adultery, together with him who marries her? Here would be manifest injustice; and it may be followed as a safe rule of interpretation of our Lord's precepts, that that interpretation which would result in manifest injustice is not the law, nor the right interpretation of it. For God's law must be held to be in harmony with God's attributes, of which justice is equal to the others; and that which is not justice is not law.

The statement of this divorce law as found in St. Mark may be nearest the

13. <Ms III^c adds "of"–*Ed.*>

truth, being the Christ's statement and his interpretation of what he had said to the Pharisees on the subject. For when the disciples were entered into a friend's house, they questioned him as to what he had said to the Pharisees outside.

> And he saith unto them, "Whosoever shall put away his wife and marry another, committeth adultery against her. And if a woman shall put away her husband and be married to another, she committeth adultery" (Mark 10:11-12).

This limits the sin of adultery to those who are the guilty parties to the "putting away" and of course to the putting away[14] for other causes than that which the Master recognized as a justification for divorce. They are the parties to "adultery,"[15] under this divorce doctrine of Messiah, not the innocent parties—those who were sinned against in the transaction.[16]

PERFORM TO THE LORD THINE OATHS: THE BETTER WAY

Again to the law:

> Thou shalt not forswear thyself, but shalt perform unto the Lord thine oaths (Matt. 5:33).

So strictly was this law regarded in Israel, that Israel's chieftain Jephthah, having vowed that if God would give him a victory over the Ammonites, he would offer as a burnt offering whosoever should come forth from his house to meet him. And when his only daughter came forth with timbrels and dancing to meet him, she became the sacrifice for the oath's sake (Judg. 11:29-40)! This matter of keeping oaths crystallized for Israel in this formula: "Lord, who shall abide in Thy tabernacle? Who shall dwell in Thy holy hill?" and the answer is, "He that sweareth to his own hurt, and changeth not" (Ps. 15:1, 4). But the Master pointed out a more excellent way than all this:

> Swear not at all; neither by heaven, for it is God's throne; nor by the earth, for it is His footstool; neither by Jerusalem, for it is the city of the great King. Neither shalt thou swear by thy head, because thou canst not make one hair white or black. Let your

---

14. <Ms III[c] adds "and of course to the putting away"—*Ed.*>

15. <Ms III[*] "the parties of 'adultery'"—*Ed.*>

16. <The review committee objected to Roberts's three-page discussion about divorce: "The question of divorce does not seem clear to us as here stated, and in harmony with the words of the Savior." Roberts wrote in the margin that there is "nothing more to be said" ("Doctrinal Points Questioned by the Committee Which Read the Manuscript of Elder B. H. Roberts, Entitled The Truth, The Way, The Life," attached to Rudger Clawson, Letter to Heber J. Grant, [15 May 1930], in David J. Buerger Collection, Manuscript 622, Bx 10, Fd 8, Manuscripts Division, Marriott Library, University of Utah, Salt Lake City)—*Ed.*>

communication be, yea, yea; nay, nay: for whatsoever is more than these cometh of evil (cf. Matt. 5:34-37).

How excellent the teacher that moveth stumbling blocks from our path! "Thou shalt not forswear thyself . . . perform unto the Lord thine oaths!" "Swear not at all."

"AN EYE FOR AN EYE"

Ye have heard that it hath been said, An eye for an eye, and a tooth for a tooth (Matt. 5:38).

The law of vengeance, supposed to be of exact, stern, inexorable justice. Pay me what you owe me to the last farthing; there shall be no mitigation; there shall no circumstances be considered. The pound of flesh is due; the pound of flesh exactly shall be paid. Now on this law of exaction of an "eye for an eye," and a "tooth for a tooth," the Christ said:

I say unto you, that ye resist not evil; but whosoever shall smite thee on thy right cheek, turn to him the other also. And if a man will sue thee at the law and take away thy coat, let him have thy cloak also. And whosoever shall compel thee to go a mile, go with him twain. Give to him that asketh thee, and from him that would borrow of thee turn thou not away (Matt. 5:39-42).

"Utterly impracticable!" would cry out your man of affairs, and especially your modern man of affairs. "Utterly out of the question, this course of procedure, unfair; it would produce a race of mollycoddles, of non-resisting, unaggressive simpletons." But let us not be too quick in judgment on these sayings of the sermon. Let us regard them as setting forth, not so much the precise things that shall be done in the respectively given cases, but as setting forth in these few bold strokes, the spirit in which men should live; holding in mind that the letter killeth, but the spirit giveth life.[17] And here may be shown the spirit of the Life in which men should live; not stressing the "eye for an eye" and "tooth for a tooth" doctrine so far as not to admit into our personal economy of life the willingness, so far as possible to live in peace with all men; but living in the spirit that "a mild answer turneth away wrath" (cf. Prov. 15:1); and so a willingness to mitigate the stern demands that justice alone might warrant as to bring forth a spirit of conciliation and reconciliation into the affairs of life, by living in the unaggressive and unexacting spirit that the Master here enjoins.

---

17. <Ms III* "but it is the spirit that giveth life"—*Ed.*>

OF LOVING AND HATING

> Ye have heard that it hath been said, Thou shalt love thy neighbor and hate thine enemy, but I say unto you, Love your enemies, bless them that curse you, do good to them that hate you, and pray for them that despitefully use you and persecute you (cf. Matt. 5:43-44).

A difficult undertaking, possible only when the mind is capable of immense vision, conscious of the truth respecting God and man, especially conscious of one's own soul—having knowledge also of man's mission in this earth-life, with right apprehension as to immortality and eternal life. Only then can one hope for a man to attain to this nobility of soul which shall put aside the things of evil and live only in the spirit of the things that are great, and noble, and good. Also being able to view men, not as they are, but in the light of their possibilities, as eternal intelligences on their way to progress—men in the making! Fortunately the Christ in his commentary on the principle here stated, cites God in his graciousness towards things wicked and ungodly, and points out with what liberal hand He bestows blessings, not only upon the obedient, but upon the disobedient, admonishing his disciples to pursue the course indicated that:

> Ye may be the children of your Father which is in heaven; for He maketh His sun to rise on the evil and on the good, and sendeth rain on the just and on the unjust (Matt. 5:45).

He would have the children to be even as the Father. He would have the disciple to be as his master, and then the argument:

> For if ye love them which love you, what reward have ye? Do not even the publicans the same? And if ye salute your brethren only, what do ye more than others? Do not even the publicans so? (Matt. 5:46-47).

Already he had served notice upon his disciples in a previous paragraph (see Matt. 5:20) that unless their righteousness should exceed the righteousness of the scribes and the Pharisees, they should in no case enter the kingdom of heaven. It is equally true of the Master's discipleship today.

"BE YE PERFECT"—THE IDEAL

And now the climax, the setting forth of the ideal, and sternly demanding its achievement:

> Be ye therefore perfect, even as your Father which is in heaven is perfect (Matt. 5:48).

And our Book of Mormon version of the same discourse, delivered to the Nephites on the continent of America, makes this variation:

> I would that ye should be perfect, even as I, or your Father who is in heaven, is perfect (3 Ne. 12:48).

At this point in the Book of Mormon version of the discourse, and closing out the references to the things which had been said in former times, the Christ adds:[18]

> Therefore, those things which were of old time, which were under the law, in me are fulfilled. Old things are done away and all things have become new (cf. 3 Ne. 12:47).

ALMSGIVING, THE SPIRIT OF

The next instruction has to do with almsgiving and the spirit in which helpfulness shall be imparted to needy.

> Do not your alms before men to be seen of them; otherwise you have no reward of your Father which is in heaven. Therefore, when thou doest thine alms, do not sound a trumpet before thee, as the hypocrites do in the synagogues and in the streets that they may have glory of men. Verily I say unto thee, they have their reward. But when thou doest alms, let not thy left hand know what thy right hand doeth, that thine alms may be in secret and thy Father which seeth in secret Himself shall reward thee openly (cf. Matt. 6:1-4).

Nothing can be added by way of amplification that will add to the beauty of the spirit of this injunction.

PRAYER: "THE CHRISTIAN'S VITAL BREATH"

Now the instructions on prayer, opening with a warning that the disciples must not pray as the hypocrites do, who prayed standing in the synagogue and in the corner of the streets that they might be seen of men. In that they had their reward in the praises of men. The Master said:

> But thou, when thou prayest, enter into thy closet, and when thou hast shut thy door, pray to thy Father which is in secret, and thy Father which seeth in secret shall reward thee openly (Matt. 6:6).

Then the warning against vain repetition, as was the custom of the heathen, who thought they would be heard for their much speaking.

> But be not ye therefore like unto them, for your Father knoweth what things ye have need of before ye ask Him. After this manner therefore pray ye (cf. Matt. 6:8-9).

---

18. <Ms III[*] "he adds"—*Ed.*>

THE LORD'S PRAYER

> Our Father which art in heaven, hallowed be Thy name. Thy kingdom come. Thy will be done in earth, as it is in heaven. Give us this day our daily bread and forgive us our debts, as we forgive our debtors, and lead us not into temptation, but deliver us from evil; for Thine is the kingdom, and the power, and the glory, forever. Amen (Matt. 6:9-13).[19]

Such <is> the prayer the Master outlined for the disciples,[20] and this his commentary on the more salient point of forgiveness:

> For if ye forgive men their trespasses, your heavenly Father will also forgive you. But if ye forgive not men their trespasses, neither will your Father forgive you (cf. Matt. 6:14-15).

This prayer was not given as a set form to be always followed, and used on every occasion, but rather as an illustration of the spirit in which prayer should be offered and also as illustrating the admonitions preceding it as to simplicity and directness in which one should pray, and in these respects how excellent it is! It has been much praised by writers, who love it for its literary merit and its pure spirituality; its sweet spirit of trust and faith; and for its appropriateness as an address of the soul to the heavenly Father. Dean Paley in his *Christian Evidences* says of it:

> For a succession of solemn thoughts, for fixing the attention upon a few great points, for suitableness, . . . for sufficiency, for conciseness without obscurity, for the weight and real[21] importance of its petitions, it is without equal or a rival.[22]

A DEFECT IN ST. MATTHEW'S VERSION OF THE "LORD'S PRAYER"

All this in the main may be allowed; but as the prayer stands in St. Matthew, it may not be said to be quite without fault. The phrase, for instance, "Lead us not into temptation" (Matt. 6:13). Is it conceivable, quite, that a God of infinite goodness and wisdom would lead men into temptation? Knowing man's proneness to evil, and his weakness under temptation, and knowing that in nine hundred

---

19. <The evidence is strong that the doxology—"for thine is the kingdom, and the power, and the glory, forever"—was not originally part of the text of Matthew; see Herman Hendrickx, *The Sermon on the Mount* (London: Geoffrey Chapman, 1984)—*Ed.*>

20. <Ms III* "outlined for them"—*Ed.*>

21. <Ms III^{c} adds "weight and real" in order to agree with Paley's text—*Ed.*>

22. <William Paley, *A View of the Evidences of Christianity*, ed. E. A. Litton (London: Society for Promoting Christian Knowledge, 1871), 360; in the ellipsis Roberts deleted Paley's words "to every condition"—*Ed.*>

and ninety-nine cases[23] in a thousand men yield to temptation? Would it be like God to do a thing of that kind? There is in this petition also—"lead us not into temptation"—the contradiction of another scripture. St. James says:

> Let no man say when he is tempted, I am tempted of God: for God cannot be tempted with evil, neither tempteth He any man, but every man is tempted when he is drawn away of his own lust, and enticed. Then when lust hath conceived, it bringeth forth sin; and sin, when it is finished, bringeth forth death (James 1:13-15).

There is named the source of temptation, and the death it brings. "God tempteth no man"! Then why pray, "Lead us not into temptation," since that is something God will not do? The inconsistency of that sentence in the beautiful prayer as it stands in Matthew is evident; and so our Prophet of the New Dispensation, in correcting many things that are erroneous in the imperfect reporting or translation of the Master's words, corrected this utterance, and makes it to[24] read in his version, "Suffer us not to be led into temptation, but deliver us from evil." With that correction made on it, the praise and admiration expressed by Dean Paley can be accepted.

OF FASTING

In fasting the Master again warns his disciples against the practices of the hypocrites, who in their fasting went about with sad countenances and disfigured faces, that they might appear unto men to fast. The Master's comment was:

> Verily I say unto you, they have their reward. But thou, when thou fastest, anoint thy head and wash thy face, that thou appear not unto men to fast, but unto thy Father which seeth in secret; and thy Father which seeth in secret shall reward thee openly (cf. Matt. 6:16-18).

This presents the thought of cheerfulness in fasting, light-heartedness and joy, for the keynote in which these several duties of almsgiving, prayer, and fasting shall be done; not as if they were burdens hard to bear, but pleasant duties, sweet responses of the soul to God, and not for worldly fame or glory or a reputation for piety, but as so many dear and unseen approaches into the fellowship and communion with God. Let men's sacrifices—if sacrifices they be considered at all—be held dear, as showing a willingness to give an offering of the soul for the reaction

---

23. <Ms III[*] "Knowing that in nine-hundred and ninety-nine cases," but due to skipping from "knowing" to "knowing" the words "man's pronness [*sic*] to evil, and his weakness under temptation and knowing" from the earlier draft were accidentally omitted and these are reinserted above the line—*Ed.*>

24. <Ms III[c] adds "to"—*Ed.*>

of fellowship with God: laying up of treasure in heaven, "where neither moth nor rust doth corrupt, and where thieves cannot break through and steal" (cf. Matt. 6:20); and with the confidence that where our treasure is, there will our heart be also. Continuing this sermon, the Christ said:

> The light of the body is the eye; if, therefore, thine eye be single, thine whole body shall be full of light. But if the eye be evil, thy whole body shall be full of darkness. If, therefore, the light that is in thee be darkness, how great is that darkness! (cf. Matt. 6:22-23).

SINGLENESS OF SERVICE:[25] NO SERVING OF TWO MASTERS

There must be singleness of purpose also in the service of God. For on this the Master said:

> No man can serve two masters, for either he will hate the one and love the other, or else he will hold to the one and despise the other. Ye cannot serve God and mammon (Matt. 6:24).

Herein we may see the so-called "jealousy" of God. Those who would serve Him, must serve Him wholly, with singleness of purpose. Acceptance of God as God Almighty admits of no divided allegiance. Loyalty must be wholly given else service is not acceptable. Through this Sermon on the Mount comes up the consciousness, the truth of the whole law:

> Thou shalt have no other Gods before me (Ex. 20:3).

All images of God are "verboten." Men can not serve two masters. There must be singleness of mind and purpose in this.

> Men cannot serve God and mammon (cf. Matt. 6:24).

They may not worship the "golden calf" and Jehovah; neither worship the gold of the calf and the Christ. There must be no divided allegiance in the services of God.

---

25. <Ms III[c] adds "Singleness of Service"—*Ed.*>

CHAPTER LI

The Life: The Sermon on the Mount II

SCRIPTURE READING LESSON

Analysis

I. Division of the Sermon on the Mount.
II. The Book of Mormon Version of "Take No Thought."
III. Judge Not.
IV. Sacredness of Holy Things.
V. Of Asking.
VI. The Golden Rule.
VII. Admonitions.
VIII. Exordium.

References

See all the citations given in Lesson 50.

Especially compare version of Matthew and Luke with 3 Ne. 12-14. See also B. H. Roberts, *New Witnesses for God* (Salt Lake City: The Deseret News, 1909), 3:432-40, where these comparisons are worked out in parallel columns from King James' translation (Protestant Bible), the Douay Bible (the Catholic version), and the Book of Mormon version of the sermon.

CHAPTER LI

The Life: The Sermon[1] on the Mount II

DIVISION OF THE SERMON ON THE MOUNT

And now we come to a part of the great sermon which lays it open to criticism, and that has been criticized perhaps more severely than any other part of it. The Christ is represented as saying: "Take no thought for your life, what ye shall eat or what ye shall drink, nor yet for your bodies, what ye shall put on. Is not the life more than meat and the body more than raiment?" The fowls of the air are represented as not sowing or reaping, nor storing, yet the heavenly Father feedeth them. "Are ye not much better than they?" And why take thought of raiment? "Consider the lilies of the field, how they grow; they toil not neither do they spin," yet in raiment they outshine Solomon in all his glory. If God will so clothe the grass of the field, shall he not much more clothe you? "O ye of little faith." And hence, as is generally thought, men are admonished to take no thought of what they shall eat or what they shall drink or wherewithal they shall be clothed. After these things the Gentiles seek, but the followers of the Master are admonished to "seek first the kingdom of God and his righteousness," to take no thought for the morrow, for the morrow shall take thought for the things of itself. "Sufficient unto the day is the evil thereof" (cf. Matt. 6:25-34).

"An impossible manner of life," men cry out; and they cry out thus from practical, human experience. Men may not live as the birds live, nor expect to be clothed as the lilies of the field in beauty and in glory. Civilization can not be established and perpetuated by taking no thought of tomorrow. Civilization has its beginning by man taking thought for tomorrow; by planning for the future. The sacrifices of today, which shall provide for the future day, is the beginning of the creation of capital, the means through which great things are achieved, and is the process by which civilization advances. So this admonition as it stands in Matthew, advising men to live as the birds live, and to trust for clothing as the lilies do for beauty and glory, and to take no thought for tomorrow as to what they shall eat or drink or wherewithal they shall be clothed, seems like folly, and wholly at variance with true economic principles and the stern requirements of common sense.

---

1. <Ms III* "THE LIFE: UNDER THE SERMON"–*Ed.*>

THE BOOK OF MORMON VERSION OF "TAKE NO THOUGHT"[2]

Here, however, by what has come to light in the New Dispensation of the gospel through the Book of Mormon version of this matchless sermon, there comes a sidelight which removes every objection to this part of the discourse of the Christ, and destroys all the force of infidel argument against it in this: that this part of the sermon on "take no thought," etc., is not addressed to the multitude before the Savior, but having delivered the admonitions concerning almsgiving, prayer, and fasting, and emphasizing the importance of singleness of purpose in the worship of God to the multitude, then:

> And now it came to pass that when Jesus had spoken these words he looked upon the Twelve whom he had chosen and said unto them: "Remember the words which I have spoken. For behold, ye are they whom I have chosen to minister unto this people. Therefore I say unto you, take no thought for your life, what ye shall eat, or what ye shall drink, or yet for your body, what ye shall put on" (cf. 3 Ne. 13:25).

And then follows consecutively the admonitions that they go forth in their ministry wholly consecrated to the service of God, and He will provide for their temporal needs. Closing this portion of his discourse with these words:

> Take therefore no thought for tomorrow, for the morrow shall take thought for the things of itself. Sufficient is the day unto the evil thereof (3 Ne. 13:34).[3]

This admonition, then, of taking no thought for food, or raiment, or any of the material things of life, can be safely addressed to twelve men, who have been chosen to make an absolute consecration of their lives to the accomplishment of the special spiritual things of God's kingdom; but not expanded to cover the general economic principles of a whole community, or nation, or the world.

The thought struggling for expression here is that, if this part of the sermon was especially addressed to the Twelve when the sermon was delivered in America, may it not be that it was likewise limited when delivered in Palestine?

JUDGE NOT

I resume now my quotation from St. Matthew: "Judge not, that ye be not judged" (Matt. 7:1), said the Christ, pointing out how inadequate men are to judge each other, because of their inability to see clearly the mote in their brother's eye,

---

2. <Ms III* "The Book of Mormon Version Of This Part Of The Sermon"—*Ed.*>

3. Note the difference in the closing of this division of the Christ's sermon as given in Matthew and as given in the Book of Mormon. In Matthew it stands: "Sufficient unto the day is the evil thereof" (Matt. 6:34), but in the Book of Mormon more logically it reads: "Sufficient is the day unto the evil thereof."

while perhaps a beam is in their own. How shall such an one judge righteously? It is reserved to God alone to so judge. To judge righteously one must know all; not only what is done, but has been resisted; the hungering and thirsting and striving for righteousness will enter into just judgment, as well as the lapses in the midst of those strivings. The sum of the matter is, then, to leave judgment to one who knows all and sees the whole and not part only. And this warning is given with the admonition:

> For with what judgment ye judge, ye shall be judged; and with what measure ye mete, it shall be measured to you again (Matt. 7:2).

Sufficient <is> the warning surely to lead one to abstain from judgment of his fellow men. For us men, the heart and mind of our fellows is something of a sealed book, and we are incompetent to judge with righteous judgment: hence, judge not!

SACREDNESS OF HOLY THINGS

Then comes the admonition in the sermon to hold sacred the holy things:

> Give not that which is holy unto the dogs, neither cast you<r> pearls before swine (Matt. 7:6).

These sacred things will not be appreciated by the "dogs" and the "swine," and they may trample precious things under their feet and turn and rend you.

OF ASKING

> Ask, and it shall be given you; seek, and ye shall find; . . . every one that asketh, receiveth; and he that seeketh, findeth (Matt. 7:7-8).

Again appears the truth, men shall have according to their desires, inasmuch as that interferes not with the general purposes of God, both in particular cases and in the general scheme of things; for we must remember that we live in a world of broken harmonies from which men are to learn certain great and important things; and some of these can only be realized through disappointments and suffering. So our asking must be in wisdom, and not in petulant selfishness, but always in the spirit of the Master, who, let us remember, when he asked that the bitter cup of his suffering might pass, if that were possible, or be consistent with the will and purposes of God; yet, though asking for the passing of the cup, that petition was quickly followed with "not my will, but Thy will be done" (cf. Luke 22:42). So he would have his disciples pray, for his own actions are to be taken as the illustration of his doctrine.

But the Master gave encouragement on this point of asking by trying to convince those who heard him that the heavenly Father would be as reasonable in giving, surely, as earthly fathers would. So:

> What man is there of you, whom if his son ask for bread, will he give him a stone? Or if he ask a fish, will he give him a serpent? If ye then, being evil, know how to give good gifts to your children, how much more will your Father, which is in heaven, give good gifts to him that ask Him? (cf. Matt. 7:9-11).

And here I might add: if the wisdom of parents sometimes prompts them to withhold the gift that would be injurious to their children, considering their age, and their circumstances, and the effect upon their lives of granting an unwholesome wish that might be mischievous, shall not our Father in heaven do likewise?

THE GOLDEN RULE

Now comes a new summary of all the truths the Master is teaching:

> All things whatsoever ye would that men should do to you, do ye even so to them: for this is the law and the prophets (Matt. 7:12).

This is called, and worthily called, the "Golden Rule." Its essence will be found in love of God and love of man; it is the Master's generalization of all law and of all prophets. A generalization in fact even of the Christ's generalization when he said:

> Thou shalt love the Lord thy God with all thy heart, and with all thy soul, and with all thy mind. . . . Thou shalt love thy neighbor as thyself (Matt. 22:37, 39).

This is the great commandment, and he made it inclusive of all the law and all the prophets. And now all this is again condensed into this "Golden Rule," the rule which bursts into an act of doing. Doing to others as you would have them do unto you.

It detracts nothing from this great rule of supreme Christian conduct, because others catching a glint of the same glory have said something akin to it. Confucius, for instance, long before Christ (551-478 B.C.), is credited with saying: "Do not to others what you would not wish done to yourself." But this is negative in form and only half the truth of the Golden Rule, the Chinese chief teacher only went so far as to say, do not those things to others that you would not have them do to you. But the Golden Rule admonishes not only to refrain from doing evil that you would not have done to yourself; but by putting it into the positive form it bids you to do unto others what you would wish might be done unto and for you, under like circumstances.

So with the saying accredited to the good Rabbi Hillel, when a would-be proselyte demanded to be taught the whole law while he stood upon one leg, the Rabbi answered, and won a proselyte by saying: "What is hateful to thyself, that do not thou to another. This is the whole law; the rest is commentary."[4] But this saying, excellent as it is, has the same defect that the negative statement of Confucius carries.

Aristotle, the subtle Greek philosopher, approached the summary of the Golden Rule most nearly of all the ancients, when he said in answer to the question: "What should be one's conduct towards one's friends?" He replied: "As we would that they should act towards us." Here again is a defect, for his statement of the principle is limited to "our friends." Not so the Golden Rule of the Christ. There it stands in all its perfection:

> ALL THINGS WHATSOEVER YE WOULD THAT MEN SHOULD DO TO YOU, DO YE EVEN SO TO THEM (Matt. 7:12).[5]

ADMONITIONS[6]

We are hastening to the close of the sermon, and hence we find admonition predominant, and warning:

> Enter ye into the strait[7] gate; for wide is the gate and broad is the way that leadeth to destruction, and many there be which go in thereat. Because strait[8] is the gate and narrow is the way, which leadeth unto life, and few there be that find it (cf. Matt. 7:13-14).

Let those who cry there are many ways leading to the one place, the kingdom of heaven, and it matters not by what route we may elect to make the journey—let them know that[9] their theory is contradicted by this teaching of the Divine Master. There is a unity in truth; there is a oneness of way; there is oneness of the gospel life. "Strait[10] is the gate, narrow the way, that leadeth unto life,[11] and but few find it," because wide is the gate, devious and many the paths that lead to destruction and many find them, since both gate and ways[12] lead along lines of least resistance.

"Beware of false prophets" rings out the warning of the Christ; they may come

---

4. John R. Dummelow, ed., *A Commentary on the Holy Bible by Various Writers, Complete in One Volume* (New York: The Macmillan Co., 1922), at Matt. 7:12.

5. <To the left of the quotation Ms III has "(caps)," which appears to be Roberts's instruction to print this quote in full capitals—*Ed.*>

6. <Ms III[*] "Closing Admonitions"—*Ed.*>

7. <Ms III "straight"—*Ed.*>

8. <Ms III "straight"—*Ed.*>

9. <Ms III[c] adds "let them know that"—*Ed.*>

10. <Ms III "straight"—*Ed.*>

11. <Ms III[c] adds "that leadeth unto life"—*Ed.*>

12. <Ms III[*] "gates and ways"—*Ed.*>

in sheep's clothing, but inwardly they are ravening wolves. He gives as an invariable sign for their detection—"Ye shall know them by their fruits"; and then the pertinent inquiry, "Do men gather grapes of thorns, or figs of thistles?" (Matt. 7:15-16). A tree is known by its fruit. A good tree bringeth forth good fruit; a corrupt tree bringeth forth evil fruit; and the reverse can not be true. And the end of evil trees and false prophets, of course, will be destruction.

And now against mere pretensions of sanctity and pretensions of following the Master:

> Not every one that saith unto me, Lord, Lord, shall enter into the kingdom of heaven, but he that doeth the will of my Father which is in heaven (Matt. 7:21).

The utterances of prophecies in the name of the Christ, casting out of devils, and doing many wonderful works in the name of the Christ may not sanctify those who are influenced by mere pretensions, by show of sanctity, and religious fervor. To such he represents himself as saying in finality:

> Depart from me, ye workers of iniquity; I never knew you (cf. Matt. 7:21-23).

And now the Master's peroration to the master sermon of all ages. Referring to all subdivisions of the discourse, the closing it up in one splendid utterance:

EXORDIUM

> Therefore, whosoever heareth these sayings of mine, and doeth them, I will liken him unto a wise man, which built his house upon a rock: and the rain descended, and the floods came, and the winds blew, and beat upon that house; and it fell not: for it was founded upon a rock.
>
> And every one that heareth these sayings of mine, and doeth them not, shall be likened unto a foolish man, which built his house upon the sand: and the rain descended, and the floods came, and the winds blew, and beat upon that house; and it fell, and great was the fall of it.
>
> And it came to pass, when Jesus had ended these sayings, the people were astonished at his doctrine: for he taught them as one having authority, and not as the scribes (Matt. 7:24-29).

THE LIVING SERMON ON THE MOUNT

The best part of this sermon is not expressed in the words of it, however gracious, or apt, or profound, or splendidly placed, or true. The best part of the sermon consists in the fact that he who delivered it, LIVED IT! The Christ's Sermon on the Mount is but the blueprint of the Christ's earth-life; and he lived his life according to the blueprint—the plan.

Thus, the Christ meets us at every point of THE WAY. Considered directly as the ensample of what God would have revealed as the one perfect Life–the ideal of all ages–behold the CHRIST-LIFE!

Considered as fulfilling the law given to Moses–behold the Christ!

Considered as the founder of the church in the Meridian Dispensation, revealing God in his own person, and the love of God in the atonement, and in expounding the ethic of the gospel, shifted from the negative to the positive form, and basing it on the love of God and love of man, reinforcing it by living it–behold the Christ!

Considered as setting forth a universal ethic without limitations of age or place–timeless–eternal!–and exemplifying every precept of it in his life–again, behold the Christ!

CHAPTER LII

The Christian Character: The Teachings of the Apostles I

SCRIPTURE READING LESSON

Analysis

I. Apostolic Literature:
   (a) The Gospels;
   (b) The Epistles.
II. The Primacy of St. Peter.
III. The Doctrine of St. Peter:
   (a) The Deity of the Christ;
   (b) The Life of the Christ To Be Reflected in the Disciples;
   (c) Spirit of the Christian Ministry.
   (d) Summary of Christian Virtues.
IV. St. Paul: The Deity of the Christ Proven by His Resurrection.
V. St. Paul's Doctrine of Obedience.
VI. The Ethic of St. Paul.
VII. Final Admonition: "Be Ye Followers of God."

References

A careful study of the Acts and the epistles of the New Testament, *passim*, of which the nineteen <scriptural> citations in the text of this lesson will be a guide.

For supplemental reading: the Book of Mormon, *passim*; but especially 1 and 2 Ne., Mosiah 4-5, and 3 Ne.

D&C 42, 45.

CHAPTER LII

The Christian Character: The Teachings of the Apostles I

APOSTOLIC LITERATURE

(a) The Gospels

The four gospels of the New Testament may be said to represent a Life, and the teachings exclusively, of the Christ. They contain the facts of the development both of his doctrine and of his Life, and may be said to be exclusively his. The Book of Acts of the Apostles, and the epistles contain the doctrine of the apostles, which doctrines are but reflections of the teachings of the Christ through their minds. They represent the efforts of inspired men to put into practical application the doctrines of the Christ, and make them doctrines woven into character.

It is surprising to find how few of the apostles attempted this work of writing. The Acts of the Apostles may properly be regarded as an historical document, the extension of the gospel according to St. Luke, for it is quite generally conceded that he wrote both books. The Acts, being historical, deal with Christian character-development of the several active agents in the work of founding the church. Mentioning briefly the early action of the apostles and some few associates as a body cooperating together; then of Stephen, and Philip, and Barnabas, James, brother of St. John, and also John Mark, cousin of Barnabas, and author of the gospel which bears his name. After the sixteenth chapter the book resolves itself into a narrative of the missionary activities of St. Paul, and others pass out of the picture.

All the epistles together with the Apocalypse or Revelation may be referred to St. Paul, St. Peter, St. John, and St. James. The authorship of St. Jude is somewhat doubtful.[1]

---

1. <For the pseudonymous authorship of the epistle of Jude, see Edwin D. Freed, *The New Testament: A Critical Introduction* (Belmont, CA: Wadsworth Publishing Co, 1986), 387-88–*Ed.*>

(b) The Epistles[2]

One other thing may help to a right understanding of the New Testament and to its interpretation; namely, the fact that the epistles and not the four gospels are the earliest Christian documents; and that the gospels, coming later, may be regarded as the more seasoned statements concerning both the facts of the Life of the Christ and his doctrines. To show what is here meant, we may take for example the facts about the resurrection as set forth by St. Paul in his fifteenth chapter of First Corinthians. If when writing that chapter St. Paul had had the four-fold account given in the four gospels on the subject of the resurrection, and Christ's very definite appearances not only to the apostles, but to the women among the disciples, Paul would have been able to have given a much fuller account of that great central Christian event than he did in the aforesaid chapter of the epistle to the Corinthians. And so in respect of many other things. But even so, the doctrine of the apostles in their epistles very admirably bring forth those doctrines and give admonitions concerning ethical principles of the gospel as to plainly set forth the Christian character to be striven for, and which alone will both represent and vindicate the doctrines of the gospel of Christ as applied to human lives; and underneath all doctrinal exposition, and admonitions to right living, we shall find at work that great primary principle, which from the beginning has ever been present in God's plan for the mortal life of man, namely:

> We will prove them herewith, to see if they will do all things whatsoever the Lord their God shall command them (Abr. 3:25).

THE PRIMACY OF ST. PETER

Emphasis upon obedience was manifested in the opening of the mission of the apostles to the world. In obedience to the injunction of the Master, the apostles remained in Jerusalem until endowed by power from on high—the outpouring of the Holy Ghost upon them. This in the visible manifestation as tongues of flaming fire, when the multitude at Pentecost, overwhelmed by the visible presence of God's power, cried out in great anxiety, "Men and brethren, what shall we do?" In answer to that question they were required first of all to give evidence of the first great law of the gospel—they must render an act of obedience to the message sent to them. Hence, St. Peter, as chief of the apostles, said to them: "Repent and be baptized every one of you in the name of Jesus Christ, for the remission of sins"; and then he gave the promise to them of a baptism also of the Holy Ghost (Acts 2:37-38).

---

2. <Ms III[c] adds "(B) The Epistles"—*Ed.*>

We must regard St. Peter as the head of the church after the departure of the Christ, and in close association with him, St. James and St. John; for to them throughout the New Testament is accorded a certain primacy, which admits of no doubt as to their being the selected presidency[3] of the church on earth. To St. Peter the Lord himself had said:

> I give unto you the keys of the kingdom of heaven, and whatsoever you bind on earth shall be bound in heaven, and whatsoever thou shalt loose on earth shall be loosed in heaven (cf. Matt. 16:19).

This primacy follows him throughout the Christian documents, and in connection with him is the special association of James and John, observable even during the public ministry of the Master.

THE DOCTRINES OF ST. PETER

(a) The Deity of Christ[4]

Because of the primacy of St. Peter, we follow him first in the development of those doctrines and admonitions, in which he gives practical instructions to be woven into character and life.

In this part of his ministry described in the Acts of the Apostles, we note him as the chief witness of the divinity of our Lord, saying to the multitudes assembled in Jerusalem on the day of Pentecost:

> Let all the house of Israel know, that God hath made that same Jesus, whom ye have crucified, both Lord and Christ (cf. Acts 2:36).

He taught repentance and baptism for remission of sin as preparation for reception or baptism of the Holy Ghost. He severely reproved[5] those who thought the Holy Ghost and its spiritual gifts could be purchased with money (Acts 2:38-39; cf. Acts 8:14-23). He rebuked those who dealt deceitfully in matters of consecrations of moneys to the common interests of the church, and charged them with lying unto God when they lied unto the Holy Ghost. The instant death of the offenders emphasized his reproofs.[6] He taught that men ought to obey God rather than man, when human and divine jurisdiction were in conflict (Acts 5:29). St. Peter also introduced the gospel to the Gentiles, through the household of Cornelius as

---

3. <Ms III* "selected head presidency," with the deletion of "head" probably occurring immediately before the typing of "presidency"—*Ed.*>

4. <Ms III^c adds "(A) The Deity of Christ"—*Ed.*>

5. <Ms III* "He scorned and severely reproved"—*Ed.*>

6. Acts 5, the case of Ananias and Sapphira.

detailed in the tenth chapter of the Acts. He sat in council with "the apostles and elders" afterwards held in Jerusalem to determine the question of including the Gentiles within the gospel covenant,[7] and was the chief witness to the grace of God being extended to the Gentiles; his testimony with that of St. Paul and Barnabas, being the determining factors that induced the favorable decision of the council in the behalf of the Gentiles (Acts 15).

After that St. Peter's activities are no further recorded in the Acts of the Apostles, and we may know him as an expounder only through his epistles. In these St. Peter is true to himself and his own experience, in laying the foundation of his knowledge of the TRUTH and the WAY and the LIFE, on the complete acceptance of Jesus Christ as the Son of the living God, true deity in himself, as well as in what he derived from the Father.

(b) The Life of the Christ To Be Reflected in His Disciples[8]

This is the foundation of his doctrine and admonition not only in the first epistle, but in the second also. From this ground he urges the striving of the saints for the end of their faith, "even the salvation of their souls," and hence this admonition to them:

> Wherefore, gird up the loins of your mind, be sober, and hope to the end for the grace that is to be brought unto you at the revelation of Jesus Christ; as obedient children, not fashioning yourselves according to the former lusts in your ignorance; but as he which hath called you is holy, so be ye holy in all manner of conversation; because it is written, Be ye holy; for I am holy. . . . Ye know that ye were not redeemed with corruptible things, as silver and gold, from your vain conversation received by tradition from your fathers; but with the precious blood of Christ, as of a lamb without blemish and without spot: . . . Seeing ye have purified your souls in obeying the truth through the Spirit unto unfeigned love of the brethren, see that ye love one another with a pure heart fervently; being born again, not of corruptible seed, but of incorruptible, by the word of God, which liveth and abideth forever (1 Pet. 1:13-16, 18-19, 22-23).
>
> Wherefore, laying aside all malice and guile and hypocrisies and envies and all evil speakings, as newborn babes desire the sincere milk of the word, that ye may grow thereby[9] (cf. 1 Pet. 2:1-2).

---

7. <Ms III[*] "to determine the question of extending the gospel to the Gentiles"—*Ed.*>

8. <Ms III[c] adds "(B) The Life Of The Christ To Be Reflected In His Disciples"—*Ed.*>

9. <The King James Version translates a late Greek text that omits two significant words *eis sōtērian*, adding the concept that Christians should grow up "into salvation." See the editor's "Omissions in the King James New Testament," *Dialogue: A Journal of Mormon Thought* 11 (Autumn 1978): 129—*Ed.*>

Again he said to them:

> Ye are a chosen generation, a royal priesthood, an holy nation, a peculiar people; that ye should show forth the praises of Him who hath called you out of darkness into His marvelous light. . . . Dearly beloved, I beseech you as strangers and pilgrims, abstain from fleshly lusts, which war against the soul; having your conversation honest among the Gentiles: that, whereas they speak against you as evildoers, they may by your good works,[10] which they shall behold, glorify God in the day of visitation (cf. 1 Pet. 2:9, 11-12).

He admonishes them to be subject to the civil authorities and announces it to be:

> The will of God, that with well doing ye may put to silence the ignorance of foolish men; as free, and not using your liberty for a cloak of maliciousness. . . . Honor all men. Love the brotherhood. Fear God. Honor the king (1 Pet. 2:15-17).

He also gave instruction on the domestic relations, urging that husband and wife so live "as being heirs together of the grace of life" (1 Pet. 3:7) and urged the community to be:

> All of one mind, having compassion one of another, loving as brethren, being pitiful and courteous, not rending evil for evil, or railing for railing; but contrariwise blessing, knowing that ye are thereunto called, that ye should inherit a blessing. For he that will love life, and see good days, let him refrain his tongue from evil, and his lips that they speak no guile; let him eschew evil and do good; let him seek peace and ensue it (cf. 1 Pet. 3:8-11).

(c) Spirit of the Christian Ministry[11]

And so on practically through all the virtues; and towards the close of the first epistle, he gives out the following as the spirit in which the church government is to be exercised. To the elders among the churches:

> Feed the flock of God which is among you, taking the oversight thereof, not by constraint, but willingly; not for filthy lucre, but of a ready mind; neither as being lords over God's heritage, but being ensamples to the flock (1 Pet. 5:2-3).

He advised the younger to submit unto the elder; that they be clothed with humility, "for God resisteth the proud and giveth grace to the humble" (1 Pet. 5:5).

---

10. <Ms III* "they may be your good works," the "be" being a typographical error for the "by" in the King James Version wording (which is being quoted) "they may by your good works"; the Ms III^{c}, responding to the incorrect Ms III*, changes the text to "they may see your good works"—*Ed.*>

11. <Ms III^{c} adds "(C) Spirit Of The Christian Ministry"—*Ed.*>

He gives them assurance that God careth for them—even for the humble. "Be sober, be diligent"[12] he admonishes them (1 Pet. 5:8).

(d) Summary of Christian Virtues[13]

In the second epistle, addressed, it is generally conceded, to the same people, he points out the unerring way, by which those who have undertaken the Christian life may be "partakers of the divine nature" (2 Pet. 1:4), and who have escaped the corruption that is in the world through lust; and now:

> Beside this, giving all diligence, add to your faith virtue; and to virtue knowledge; and to knowledge temperance; and to temperance patience; and to patience godliness; and to godliness brotherly kindness; and to brotherly kindness charity. For if these things be in you and abound, they make you that ye shall neither be barren nor unfruitful in the knowledge of our Lord Jesus Christ. But he that lacketh these things is blind, and cannot see afar off, and hath forgotten that he was purged from his old sins. . . . If ye do these things, ye shall never fail (cf. 2 Pet. 1:5-10).

Building with these foundation stones here enumerated, together with the other admonitions of this apostle—living[14] in strict harmony with all this—what a desirable character a true Christian[15] would be! What a Life, coming in sequence of a knowledge of the Truth, and a knowledge of the Way, both through the doctrine of the Christ, the example of his Life and the harmonious instruction in the doctrines of this, the chief apostle!

ST. PAUL: THE DEITY OF CHRIST WITNESSED BY HIS RESURRECTION[16]

Following St. Peter in setting forth the Christian Life and character, and second only to him in that work, is St. Paul. We may not follow even in outline the personal history of this remarkable man, nor relate the adventures of his missionary journeys, nor seek to point out in detail the doctrinal development to be found in his epistles. It will be enough to say that like St. Peter, St. Paul founded his conception of the gospel upon the reality of Deity being revealed in Jesus Christ, as the very Son of God. For Paul the truth of this is upheld by the fact of the Christ's resurrection

12. <The King James Version correctly translates *grēgorēsate* at 1 Pet. 5:8 as "be vigilant," and it appears that Roberts misremembers or misquotes the biblical text here—*Ed.*>

13. <Ms III* "The Second Epistle: Christian Virtues"—*Ed.*>

14. <Ms III^{c} adds "living"—*Ed.*>

15. <Ms III* "a true Christian character"—*Ed.*>

16. <Ms III^{c} adds "The Deity of Christ Witnessed By His Resurrection"—*Ed.*>

from the dead. He closes his great testimony on the Deity of the Christ in Mars Hill by saying:

> Whereof He [God] hath given assurance unto all men [that Jesus will judge the world—hence Deity], in that He [God] had raised Him from the dead (cf. Acts 17:31).

Throughout his work we[17] may say that St. Paul is as much the apostle of the resurrection as he is of the Gentiles.

What is here stated briefly as to Paul's acceptance of the Deity of the Christ is clearly and more emphatically stated in a number of other places in his writings, but in none clearer perhaps than in the letter to Timothy, wherein he says:

> Without controversy great is the mystery of godliness: God was manifest in the flesh [marginal rendering "manifested"], justified in the Spirit, seen of angels, preached unto the Gentiles, believed on in the world, received up into glory (1 Tim. 3:16).

All this in reference to the Christ whom Paul accepted as God and the very revelation of God.

In Hebrews (and I make no question but Paul is the author of the Epistle to the Hebrews)[18] Paul reaffirms the doctrine of the Deity of the Christ:

> God, who at sundry times and in divers manner spake in times past unto the fathers through the prophets, hath in these last days spoken unto us by His Son, whom He hath appointed heir to all things, by whom also He made the worlds; who being the brightness of His glory and the express image of His [the Father's] person, and upholding all things by the word of His power, when he had by himself purged our sins, sat down on the right hand of the Majesty on high, being made so much better than the angels, as he hath by inheritance obtained a more excellent name than they (cf. Heb. 1:1-4).

And through the rest of this first chapter of Hebrews he reaffirms in a number of forms the Deity of the Christ.

ST PAUL'S DOCTRINE OF OBEDIENCE

This <is> the foundation of Paul's doctrines, as well as of St. Peter's, and he recognizes the gospel as God's plan and covenant of granting eternal life to man, declaring in his letter to Titus that he himself lived in "hope of that eternal life, which God, that cannot lie, promised before the world began" (cf. Titus 1:2).

---

17. <Ms III[c] adds "we"—*Ed.*>

18. <For a discussion of the various proposed authors of Hebrews and the tentative conclusion of anonymous authorship, see Harold W. Attridge, *The Epistle to the Hebrews: A Commentary on the Epistle to the Hebrews* (Philadelphia: Fortress Press, 1989), 1-6—*Ed.*>

While Paul greatly stressed faith as the means of approach to that form of doctrine which would bring salvation, and producing righteousness as an effect, he stressed, nevertheless, that principle which underlies the whole gospel plan and which received its impetus in that pre-earth council with the spirits designed to live upon the earth, announced by the Father:

> We will prove them herewith, to see if they will do all things whatsoever the Lord their God shall command them (Abr. 3:25).

And this finds echo in Paul's teaching in the following passage, introducing it with reference to the Christ as the Son of God:

> Though he were a Son, yet learned he obedience by the things which he suffered; and being made perfect, he became the author of eternal salvation to all them that obey him (Heb. 5:8-9).

THE ETHIC OF ST. PAUL

The teachings of St. Paul as affecting and building up the Christian character—doctrine which would mold[19] a Christian life—may really be summarized from his letter to the Ephesians. In this letter he reminds the Ephesians that as Gentiles, now brought into the faith of the gospel, they have received the gospel as a peculiar gift of grace from God, and most earnestly he prayed that God would grant unto them:

> According to the riches of His glory, to be strengthened with might by His Spirit in the inner man; that Christ may dwell in your hearts by faith; that ye, being rooted and grounded in love, may be able to comprehend with all saints what is the breadth and length and depth and height; and to know the love of Christ, which passes knowledge, that they might be filled with all the fullness of God (cf. Eph. 3:16-19).

Later on he admonishes them that henceforth they:

> Walk not as other Gentiles walk, in the vanity of their mind, having the understanding darkened, being alienated from the life of God through the ignorance that is in them, because of the blindness of their heart: who being past feeling have given themselves over unto lasciviousness, to work all uncleanness and greediness.
>
> But ye [he triumphantly exclaims] have not so learned Christ; if so be that ye have heard him and have been taught by him, as the truth is in Jesus: that ye put off concerning the former conversation the old man, which is corrupt according to the deceitful lusts; and be renewed in the spirit of your mind; and that ye put on the new man, which after God is created in righteousness and true holiness. Wherefore, putting

19. <Ms III* "for doctrine which would mould"—*Ed.*>

away lying, speak every man the truth with his neighbor, for we are members one of another.

Be ye angry and sin not; let not the sun go down upon your wrath; neither give place to the devil. Let him that stole, steal no more; but rather let him labor, working with his hands the thing which is good, that he may have to give to him that needeth. Let no corrupt communication proceed from your mouth, but that which is good to the use of edifying, that it may minister grace unto the hearers. And grieve not the Holy Spirit of God, whereby ye are sealed unto the day of redemption. Let all bitterness, and wrath, and anger, and clamor, and evil speaking, be put away from you with all malice; and be ye kind one to another, tenderhearted, forgiving one another, even as God for Christ's sake hath forgiven you (Eph. 4:17-32).

FINAL ADMONITION: BE YE FOLLOWERS OF GOD

Be ye therefore followers of God, as dear children; and walk in love, as Christ also hath loved us, and hath given himself for us an offering and a sacrifice to God for a sweet-smelling savor. But fornication, and all uncleanness, or covetousness, let it not be once named among you, as becometh saints. Neither filthiness, nor foolish talking, nor jesting, which are not convenient: but rather giving of thanks. For this ye know, that no whoremonger, nor unclean person, nor covetous man, who is an idolater, has any inheritance in the kingdom of Christ and of God. Let no man deceive you with vain words; for because of these things cometh the wrath of God upon the children of disobedience. Be not ye therefore partakers with them. For ye were sometimes in darkness, but now are ye light in the Lord. Walk as children of light, for the effect of the Spirit is in all goodness and righteousness and truth (cf. Eph. 5:1-9).

Much more might be gleaned from Paul's writings and admonitions, tending to outline and establish Christian character, but what more can be needed than this? And how excellent it all is! Think of a life founded in this faith and sanctified by these admonitions[20] until the life becomes realized in the character! What could be desired more? It is merely filling in the detail of the admonition of the Christ:

Be ye perfect, even as I, or your Father which is in heaven, is perfect (3 Ne. 12:48; cf. Matt. 5:48).

Surely the Christian character molded under Paul's instruction would be all that could be desired and represents truly the LIFE founded upon the gospel.

---

20. <Ms III[c] adds an "s" to make the plural "admonitions"—*Ed.*>

CHAPTER LIII

The Christian Character: The Teachings of the Apostles II

SCRIPTURE READING LESSON

Analysis

I. St. James: The Apostle of Works.

II. Things of Special Value:

(a) Men Not Tempted of God;

(b) The Golden Text—the Key to Wisdom.

III. St. Jude: Warning and Promise.

IV. St. John: His Place in the Apostolate and in the Church.

V. The Distinctiveness of St. John's Doctrines.

VI. The Doctrine of St. John's Gospel and Epistles.

VII. Exposition of St. John's Chief Ethic.

VIII. Men as the Sons of God.

References

In a general way all the citations in this column in Lesson 52. The Epistles of St. James, St. Jude; the Gospel and Epistles of St. John, and the Book of Revelation, especially the "Messages to the Seven Churches," chaps. 1-3 inclusive.

Careful study of the thirteen <scriptural> citations of the text and footnotes in this chapter. They may be greatly multiplied from the books referred to.

CHAPTER LIII

The Christian Character: The Teachings of the Apostles II

ST. JAMES: THE APOSTLE OF "WORKS"[1]

St. James somewhat stands in antithesis to St. Paul in his conception of the gospel, in that whereas Paul stresses faith as an approach to the Christian life, St. James emphasizes works as the essential thing to the forming of a Christian character. His epistle urges the things to be done, and the excellence to be attained by doing. "Be ye doers of the word, and not hearers only, deceiving your own selves" (James 1:22) is the keynote of his message.

> If any man be a hearer of the word and not a doer, he is like unto a man beholding his natural face in the glass, for he beholdeth himself and goeth his way, and straightway forgetteth what manner of man he was; but whosoever looketh into the perfect law of liberty, and continueth therein, he being not a forgetful hearer, but a doer of the work, this man shall be blessed in his deed. . . . Pure religion and undefiled before God and the Father is this, to visit the fatherless and widows in their affliction, and to keep himself unspotted from the world (cf. James 1:23-25, 27).

And so he argues it out to the end of his message. It amounts to the same thing all the way through.

> If ye fulfill the royal law, according to the scripture, Thou shalt love thy neighbor as thyself, ye do well (James 2:8).

This <is> an echo from the generalization of the "law and the prophets," given by the Christ.

> Thou believest that there is one God; thou doest well: the devils also believe and tremble. But wilt thou know, O vain man, that faith without works is dead? (James 2:19-20).

Let it be understood, however, that while St. James stresses works, he would have faith combined with works.

---

1. <Ms III^{c} adds "The Apostle of 'Works'"—*Ed.*>

> What doth it profit, my brethren, though a man say he hath faith and have not works? Can faith save him? (James 2:14).

And now he puts his principle to a practical illustration:

> If a brother or sister be naked and destitute of daily food, and one of you say unto them, Depart in peace, be ye warmed and filled;[2] notwithstanding ye give them not those things which are needful to the body; what doth it profit? Even so faith, if it hath not works, is dead, being alone. Yea, a man may say, Thou hast faith and I have works: show me thy faith without thy works, and I will show thee my faith by my works (James 2:15-18).

The epistle sets out in bold form the richest of the Christian doctrinal standards that characterize the epistles of St. Peter and St. Paul; and the gospel and epistles and Revelation of St. John. It is the practical application of the principles of the Christian faith that constitutes the uniqueness and gives value to the epistle of St. James as a contribution to Christianity.

THINGS OF SPECIAL VALUE

(a) Men Not Tempted of God[3]

Two things above all others make the epistle of value. One is the admonition which forbids men saying, when they fall into divers temptation, that they are tempted of God; for "God cannot be tempted of evil," says St. James, "neither tempteth He any man" (James 1:13). Then with a master stroke he points to the source of man's temptation:

> Every man is tempted, when he is drawn away of his own lust and enticed. Then when lust hath conceived, it bringeth forth sin; and sin, when it is finished, bringeth forth death (James 1:14-15).

Then in antithesis to this the solemn averment:

> Do not err, my beloved brethren. Every good gift and every perfect gift is from above, and cometh down from the Father of lights, with whom is no variableness, neither shadow of turning (cf. James 1:16-17).

Solid ground, this. God <is> not the source or cause of evil, neither is God the cause of men's temptations.

---

2. <Ms III[*] "be ye warmed and fed," but the King James Version has "be ye warmed and filled"—*Ed.*>

3. <Ms III[c] adds "Things of Special Value (A) Men Not Tempted of God"—*Ed.*>

The other thing of high value in the Epistle of St.[4] James is the counsel which places men, so to speak, next to God, immediately in contact with Him, as the source of wisdom and guidance.

(b) The Golden Text: The Key to Wisdom[5]

> If any of you lack wisdom, let him ask of God, that giveth to all men liberally and upbraideth not; and it shall be given him. But let him ask in faith, nothing wavering. For he that wavereth is like a wave of the sea, driven by the wind and tossed. Let not that man think that he shall receive any thing of the Lord (cf. James 1:5-7).[6]

If this principle be applied in the practical spirit of[7] the Epistle of St. James, then we have for the molding of the Christian character and life the guiding hand[8] of the Lord himself; and what could be better than that for fashioning the Christian character and life?[9]

ST. JUDE'S WARNING AND PROMISE

Of St. Jude, the minor writer in the New Testament, it need only be said that his epistle contains a warning and a promise. A warning against false teachers, who are always evil, that had crept into the church to work mischief: "Spots" in the Christian feast of charity are they:

> Clouds that are without water, carried about of winds, trees whose fruit withereth, without fruit, twice dead, plucked up by the roots (cf. Jude 1:12).

There let them lay!

The promise of St. Jude is concerning the glorious coming of the Lord, of whom Enoch, the seventh from Adam, prophecied, saying:

> Behold, the Lord cometh with ten thousands of His saints, to execute judgment upon all, and to convince all that are ungodly among them of all their ungodly deeds, which they have ungodly committed, and of all their hard speeches, which ungodly sinners have spoken against Him (Jude 1:14-15).

---

4. <Ms III[c] adds "St."–*Ed.*>

5. <Ms III[c] adds "The Key To Wisdom"–*Ed.*>

6. It was this text, be it remembered, that led Joseph Smith, the Prophet, to seek for wisdom by asking God for it, that led to the open vision of God, with which the work of the Lord in these last days began.

7. <Ms III[*] "in the practical spirit which characterizes"–*Ed.*>

8. <Ms III[*] "then we have for the fashioning and moulding of the Christian character and the Christian life the very counsel and guiding hand"–*Ed.*>

9. <Ms III[*] "for the fashioning of the Christian character and the Christian life?"–*Ed.*>

The ethical value of St. Jude's epistle consists of his denunciation of evils, gross self-indulgences of certain church members, by which it is to be understood that the attainment of the opposite virtues to the vices denounced by Jude is the Christian objective. This, and his solemn admonition that those whom he addresses "earnestly contend for the faith once delivered unto the saints" (cf. Jude 1:3).

ST. JOHN: HIS PLACE IN THE APOSTOLATE AND IN THE CHURCH[10]

St. John was one of the earliest of the apostles to come into contact with the person of the Christ, and to enter into the spirit of his mission. It is generally thought that he was of a family in rather better worldly circumstances than the families of the other apostles. He was the son of Zebedee[11] and Salome,[12] and had some connection with members of the Sanhedrin, though the father, Zebedee, and his two sons, James and John, followed the vocation of fishermen. It was while engaged in this pursuit that the two brothers were called by the Master to become his followers. St. John, who was of a deeply pious mind, had previously come in contact with John the Baptist, forerunner of the Christ; and had already given evidence through his association with the Baptist of the profoundly religious nature, which so characterized him in his associations with the Christ, and afterwards through long years with the church.

His great influence in the church is to be traced to his association with the Christ, all which is set forth in his marvelously spiritual gospel, in his epistles, and in the rather mysterious, yet wonderful, book, known as the Apocalypse, or the Revelation of St. John. His gospel, which stands fourth in the series of the accounts of the life of the Christ, is supposed to be the last written of the New Testament documents. It is generally thought that in writing his gospel he had before him the writings of the three other evangelists, and therefore his own account of events took on its supplementary character, mentioning many things omitted by the earlier writers, and probably omitted many things which he perhaps thought sufficiently stated by them. It is quite clear that the object of his writing the gospel was to emphasize clearly (1) the Deity of Christ, and (2) the power of love, as the means by which men are[13] to be brought to acceptance of the truth and obedience to its laws. We shall find the emphasis placed upon these two things in the written contributions made by this apostle to the literature of Christian origins are distinctively characteristic.

---

10. <Ms III^{c} adds "His Place In The Apostolate And In The Church"–*Ed.*>
11. <Ms III "Zebadee" in both instances–*Ed.*>
12. <Ms III "Solome"–*Ed.*>
13. <Ms III* "by which men were"–*Ed.*>

DISTINCTIVENESS OF ST. JOHN'S DOCTRINE

The Deity of the Christ, his relation of oneness with the Father, the new birth into fellowship by union with these–the Father and the Son–and the indwelling of God in the human soul–these with love of God and man as the solvent of all duties, constitute the ground plan of the ethic of St. John–"The Life." "Except a man be born again," he records the Christ as saying, "he cannot see the kingdom of God" (John 3:3). But so born? Then what?

> Truly our fellowship is with the Father, and with his Son, Jesus Christ. . . . If we say that we have fellowship with Him [God–the Christ] and walk in darkness, we lie, and do not the truth. But if we walk in the light, as He is in the light, we have fellowship one with another, and the blood of Jesus Christ His Son cleanseth us from all sin. If we say that we have no sin, we deceive ourselves, and the truth is not in us. If we confess our sins, He is faithful and just to forgive us our sins, and to cleanse us from all unrighteousness. If we say that we have not sinned, we make Him a liar, and His word is not in us (1 Jn. 1:3, 6-10).

THE DOCTRINE OF ST. JOHN'S GOSPEL AND EPISTLES

This is the doctrine of St. John's gospel:

> That they might know Thee, the only true God, and Jesus Christ, whom Thou hast sent (John 17:3).

And this is the doctrine of the First Epistle:

> Hereby we know that we know him, if we keep his commandments. He that saith, I know him, and keepeth not his commandments, is a liar, and the truth is not in him (cf. 1 Jn. 2:3-4).

Again:

> Whoso keepeth His [God's] word [i.e., lives in harmony with God's law], in him verily is the love of God perfected; hereby know we that we are in him (1 Jn. 2:5).

And now the test:

> He that saith he abideth in him ought himself also so to walk, even as he [the Christ] walked (1 Jn. 2:6).

And again:

> The darkness is past, and the true light [the Christ] now shineth (1 Jn. 2:8).

And again the test:

> He that saith he is in the light, and hateth his brother, is in the darkness even

> until now. He that loveth his brother abideth in the light, and there is none occasion of stumbling in him (cf. 1 Jn. 2:9-10).
>
> Love not the world, neither the things that are in the world. If any man love the world, the love of the Father is not in him (1 Jn. 2:15).

And should one ask what is "the world" that one must not love, save at the sacrifice of his fellowship of the Father, the answer is immediate:

> For all that is in the world, the lust of the flesh, and the lust of the eyes, and the pride of life, is not of the Father, but is of the world. And the world passeth away and the lust <thereof>; but he that doeth the will of God abideth for ever (1 Jn. 2:16-17).

Again, and harking back to the premise of St. John's ethic—the birth into fellowship with God:

> Whosoever is born of God doth not commit sin; for his seed remaineth in him; and he cannot sin, because he is born of God. In this the children of God are manifest, and the children of the devil: who doeth not righteousness is not of God, neither he that loveth not his brother. For this is the message that we have heard from the beginning, that we should love one another (1 Jn. 3:9-11).

Further he saith:

> He that keepeth God's commandments dwelleth in God, and God in him. And hereby we know that He abideth in us, by the Spirit which He hath given us (cf. 1 Jn. 3:24).

EXPOSITION OF ST. JOHN'S CHIEF ETHIC

There is much iteration to the same effect, but this is sufficient to make "The Life" apparent according to St. John. The true disciple of the Christ is born of God, and by that birth men participate in the divine nature, and that nature abiding in men (and so long as that relationship obtains) men will not sin, but will be righteous. Here, of course, must be recognized the fact that the full attainment of righteousness is a matter of growth as well as of birth. In this our mortal life, even disciples of Christ are but men and women in the making; and perfection in righteousness is an attainment reached by slow degrees and by painful striving. It is a matter of character building under God's guidance and helpfulness, in which there may be lapses, many failures, and much discouragement; but the Spirit into which one has been born, according to St. John's ethic, will impel the renewal of the struggle. There will be no permanent yielding to evil so long as that Spirit remains alive in the soul. There will be no silencing his demand for the renewal of striving for righteousness until a complete victory has been achieved.

I adjudge this to be the attitude of St. John himself, for he says:

> These things write I unto you [the church], that ye sin not (1 Jn. 2:1).

And yet:

> If any man sin, we have an advocate with the Father, Jesus Christ, the righteous, and he is the propitiation for our sin<s> (1 Jn. 2:1-2).

And again:

> If any man see his brother sin a sin which is not unto death, he shall ask, and He shall give him life for them that sin not unto death. There is a sin unto death; I do not say that he shall pray for it. All unrighteousness is sin: and there is a sin unto death (1 Jn. 5:16-17).

In the light of St. John's view of the Life, that "whosoever is born of God doth not commit sin; for His [God's] seed remaineth in him; and he cannot sin, because he is born of God" (1 Jn. 3:9), the doctrine must be understood within such relative lines as those defined above, and in no absolute sense. But how noble the conception of St. John (and of all the apostles whose testimony is of record–only he has stressed it more than the others) that the disciples of Jesus have been born of God, and hence have partaken of the "divine nature" (2 Pet. 1:4), and as that is righteous they, too, must ultimately become righteous. There has been planted in them a spiritual Life by the "rebirth" contemplated in the gospel, and that Spirit born in them must develop according to the great law of life–each[14] "after its kind." It must and will develop according to type–after the type of the God Life, and with this we may bring to its climax and glory the ethic of St. John:

MEN AS THE SONS OF GOD

> Behold, what manner of love the Father hath bestowed upon us, that we should be called the sons of God: wherefore, the world knoweth us not, because it knew Him not. Beloved, now are we the sons of God, and it doth not yet appear what we shall be: but we know that, when He shall appear, we shall be like Him; for we shall see Him as He is. And every man that hath this hope in him purifieth himself, even as He is pure (1 Jn. 3:1-3).

And here St. John's ethic joins the Christ's:

> Be ye, therefore, perfect, even as your Father which is in heaven is perfect (Matt. 5:48).

---

14. <Ms III^{c} adds "each"–*Ed.*>

CHAPTER LIV

The Ethic of the Dispensation of the Fullness of Times

SCRIPTURE READING LESSON

Analysis

I. "THE LIFE" under the New Dispensation.
II. The Treatment of the Sick.
III. The Law for Physical Salvation—"The Word of Wisdom."
IV. "The Word" as Warning.
V. The Negative Phase of the "Word of Wisdom."
VI. The Positive Phase of "The Word."
VII. The Psychological Phase of "The Word."
VIII. Provision Made for the Poor.
IX. The Law of Consecration and Stewardship.
X. Concluding Reflections: The One Law of Righteousness.

References

See all the scripture citations of this lesson—they may be increased from the context.

See John Taylor's *The Kingdom <Government> of God* (Liverpool: S. W. Richards, 1852).

Recent discourses by President Heber J. Grant, *passim*; and other leading elders of the Church.

See "Pure Food Law," Statutes of the United States, 1908; also *The World Almanac and Encyclopedia for 1908* (New York: Press Publishing Co., 1908), 187-88 (synopsis).

B. H. Roberts, *New Witnesses for God* (Salt Lake City: Deseret Book Co., 1911), vol. 1, chap. 27.

A paper prepared for Columbia University Library, Economic Section, on "The Economic Aspects of the Career of the Mormons."

CHAPTER LIV

The Ethic of the Dispensation of the Fullness of Times

"THE LIFE" UNDER THE NEW DISPENSATION

As the New Dispensation is but a renewal of THE WAY after the world's departure from it, and is the "Everlasting Gospel" restored in a final dispensation, it can not be otherwise than that its ethic—what we call its "LIFE"—must be the same as "THE LIFE" or ethic of the other dispensations of the same gospel. The only change to be looked for would be in the direction of clarification, and perhaps of emphasis; and in this there is no disappointment. For instance, increased emphasis in the New Dispensation is placed upon the law of chastity, by saying that those who persist in unchaste looking upon women to lust after them not only commit adultery in their heart, as the Savior taught, but they "shall deny the faith," and "shall not have the Spirit" (i.e., of God), and if they repent not, "shall be cast out"—disfellowshipped from the church (D&C 42:23).

The same fate is to befall those who kill, steal, or lie; and the murderer is to die (of course, under the law of the land, and when condemned under due process of law). And also it is written of the murderer that he "shall not have forgiveness in this world nor in the world to come" (D&C 42:18).

Evil speaking is condemned:

> Thou shalt not speak evil of thy neighbor, nor do him any harm; . . . he that sinneth and repenteth not shall be cast out (D&C 42:27-28).

"All things" are to be done in "cleanliness" before the Lord (D&C 42:41). Idleness is condemned. The word of God in the New Dispensation says:

> Thou shalt not be idle, for he that is idle shall not eat the bread nor wear the garment<s> of the laborer (D&C 42:42).

And "the idler is to be had in remembrance before the Lord" (D&C 68:30); that is, idleness is just cause of complaint against the idlers before the church and its tribunals. For, as it is written:

> The idler shall not have place in the church, unless he repent and mend his ways (D&C 75:29).

Also if "any man"—or person—rob, lie, or steal, or commit murder, he is to be delivered up unto the law of the land for punishment, when proven guilty according to the laws of the land.[1] The church may not shield those who become criminals under the law of the land.

TREATMENT OF THE SICK

Special sympathy is enjoined in behalf of the sick. The ordinance of administration for the sick, as given in the Epistle of St. James, is revived in the New Dispensation. The elders of the church are to be sent for, who shall anoint the sick with oil, and pray over them:

> And the prayer of faith shall save the sick and the Lord shall raise them up; and if they have sinned, they shall be forgiven[2] (James 5:15).

As given in the modern revelation, it also says, that if the sick have not faith to be healed, but believe, they "shall be nourished with all tenderness, with herbs and mild foods, . . . and if they die, they shall die unto me," saith the Lord, "and if they live, they shall live unto me. . . . And it shall come to pass that those that die in me shall not taste of death, for it shall be sweet unto them" (D&C 42:43-44, 46). Referring again to the sick, who are to be administered to as above set forth, he that hath faith in the Christ "to be healed, and is not appointed unto death, shall be healed" (D&C 42:48). The blind "who hath faith to see shall see" (D&C 42:49); and so following with the deaf and the lame.

> And they who have not faith to do these things, but believe in me [saith the Lord] shall have power to become my sons; and inasmuch as they break not my commandments, thou [the church] shalt bear their infirmities (cf. D&C 42:52).

How excellent and merciful, O Lord, are all thy ways!

THE LAW FOR PHYSICAL SALVATION—THE WORD OF WISDOM

Better yet than provisions made for healing the sick is the revelation of the Lord on the preservation of health—God's law of health and physical well-being, known as the "Word of Wisdom," showing forth:

> The order and will of God in the temporal salvation of all saints in the last days—given for a principle with promise, adapted to the capacity of the weak and the weakest of all saints (D&C 89:2-3).

---

1. The great body of all that is here set down as the moral law of the New Dispensation is found in D&C 42, given to the church as revelation February 1831.

2. <Ms III "if they have sinned (St. James) they shall be forgiven"—*Ed.*>

This revelation to be sent <by> "greeting," not, however, by commandment or constraint, but by revelation, and "the word of wisdom" (D&C 89:2).[3]

It was given also:

> In consequence of evils[4] and designs which do and will exist in the hearts of conspiring men in the last days, I have warned you, and forewarn you, [said the Lord,] by giving unto you this word of wisdom by revelation (D&C 89:4).

"THE WORD" AS WARNING[5]

The date of this revelation was February 1833. It was about three quarters of a century before a national pure food law was enacted in the United States;[6] and during the interim of three quarters of a century, adulteration of, and misbranding of poisonous and deleterious foods, drugs, medicines, wines, malt products, and liquors, and the transportation and sale of these adulterated and mislabeled products to the people ran riot in America to the disgrace of our country and to its civilization. The long list of adulterations at which the national law is leveled is a terrible indictment against the manufacturers of the country and its commercial integrity.

That period of three quarters of a century of food, medicine, drug, and liquor adulteration, clearly vindicated the prophetic spirit of the "Word of Wisdom."[7] For it was given:

> In consequence of evils and designs which do and will exist in the hearts of

---

3. <Examination of the 1835 edition of the Doctrine and Covenants shows that the first three verses of D&C 89 (where it is numbered as section LXXX) were originally an italicized prefatory statement (similar to that preceding D&C 22), and the revelation proper began with what we now call verse 4—*Ed.*>

4. <Ms III[c] adds an "s" to make the plural "evils"—*Ed.*>

5. <Ms III[c] adds "'The Word' As Warning"—*Ed.*>

6. The first national pure food law went into effect on the first of January 1907. It was declared to be an act for "preventing the manufacture, sale, or transportation of adulterated or misbranded or poisonous or deleterious foods, drugs, medicines, and liquors, and for regulating traffic therein." Then throughout its many sections it enumerates the various articles and classes of them that have been subject to adulteration, also of misbranding and sale under these false brands, endangering the health and life of the people. A fine synopsis of the National Pure Food Law will be found in the *The World Almanac and Encyclopedia for 1908* (New York: Press Publishing Co., 1908), 187-88. Also U.S. status <i.e., statutes> for same year (1908).

7. <For a study on the possible environment factors contributing to the Word of Wisdom, see Lester E. Bush, Jr., "The Word of Wisdom in Early Nineteenth-Century Perspective," *Dialogue: A Journal of Mormon Thought* 14 (Autumn 1981): 47-65—*Ed.*>

> designing men in the last days, I have warned you, [saith the Lord,] and forewarn[ed] you, by giving you this word of wisdom by revelation (D&C 89:4).

How valuable the warning was can be appreciated when the "Word of Wisdom" itself is considered:

THE NEGATIVE PHASE OF "THE WORD OF WISDOM"

> Inasmuch as any man drinketh wine or strong drink among you, behold it is not good, neither meet in the sight of your Father, only in assembling yourselves together to offer up your sacraments before Him. And behold, this should be wine, yea, pure wine of the grape of the vine, of your own make.
>
> And again, strong drinks are not for the belly, but for the washing of your bodies. And again, tobacco is not for the body, neither for the belly, and is not good for man, but is an herb for bruises and all sick cattle, to be used with judgment and skill.
>
> And again, hot drinks [having in mind, those say who have interpreted the law from the beginning, tea and coffee as the hot drinks] are not for the body or belly (D&C 89:5-9).

This is the prohibitive part of the law; and when considered with reference to that riot of adulteration through which our country passed shortly before the date of the revelation[8] to the passage of the first pure food law–three quarters of a century–the value of God's "warning" appears; for it was upon the articles whose use is forbidden to the saints, that the heaviest adulteration fell. But apart from adulteration these forbidden things in themselves are quite generally recognized as evil in their effects upon the constitution and health of man.

THE POSITIVE PHASE OF "THE WORD"[9]

On the positive side of the "Word of Wisdom," that which recommends things for the use of man, rather than dealing with prohibition of things, the "wisdom" of God is also manifest:

> And again, verily I say unto you, all wholesome herbs God hath ordained for the constitution, nature, and use of man–every herb in the season thereof, and every fruit in the season thereof; all these to be used with prudence and thanksgiving.
>
> Yea, flesh also of beasts and of the fowls of the air, I, the Lord, have ordained for the use of man with thanksgiving; nevertheless, they are to be used sparingly; and it is pleasing unto me that they should not be used, only in times of winter, or of cold, or famine.

---

8. <Ms III[*] "our country passed from the date of the revelation"–*Ed.*>
9. <Ms III[c] adds "Of 'The Word'"–*Ed.*>

> All grain is ordained for the use of man and of beasts, to be the staff of life, not only for man but for the beasts of the field, and the fowls of heaven, and all wild animals that run or creep on the earth; and these hath God made for the use of man only in times of famine and excess of hunger. All grain is good for the food of man; as also the fruit of the vine; that which yieldeth fruit, whether in the ground or above the ground—
>
> Nevertheless, wheat for man, and corn for the ox, and oats for the horse, and rye for the fowls and for swine, and for all beasts of the field, and barley for all useful animals, and for mild drinks, as also other grain (D&C 89:10-17).

A whole chapter in commentary would be insufficient to point out the dietetical value, and health-promoting wisdom of these suggestions. Such commentary we may not indulge here, nor is it imperatively necessary, since the reasonableness of it all, and the simple phraseology, in which it is couched in the revelation,[10] leaves nothing to be desired in the way of clearness, and makes its high value as a hygienic law obvious. From it may easily be arranged the dietetical program for the invalid, the athlete, or the student. All modern science of dietetics and hygiene will approve and applaud its soundness.

PSYCHOLOGICAL PHASE OF "THE WORD"[11]

And now to its psychological value—its spiritual reaction—how great it is!

> And all saints who remember to keep <and do> these sayings, walking in obedience to the commandments [that is, honoring all the law of God by obeying it, and not confining one's self to just obedience to these Word of Wisdom precepts, but in addition thereto "walking in obedience to the commandments," then—] shall receive health in their navel and marrow to their bones; and shall find wisdom and great treasures of knowledge, even hidden treasures; and shall run and not be weary, and shall walk and not faint. And I, the Lord, give unto them a promise, that the destroying angel shall pass by them, as the children of Israel, and not slay them (D&C 89:18-21).

What an encouragement for striving for attaining perfection in observing the whole law of God!

PROVISION MADE FOR THE POOR

As a sympathetic attitude toward the sick and the afflicted is enjoined in the New Dispensation, so too is there sympathy and a policy of helpfulness enjoined towards the poor. For in this New Dispensation, as in former ones, it is the poor

---

10. <Ms III^c adds "in the revelation"—*Ed.*>
11. <Ms III^c adds "Of 'The Word'"—*Ed.*>

that have had the gospel preached unto them; it has been the common people who, so far, have heard the message of the Lord gladly; and as the meek—who are also usually the poor—since the meek are to "inherit the earth" (Matt. 5:5) the Lord's plans in the New Dispensation contemplate provisions for the achievement of their welfare. Hence, the words of the Lord to the church:

> Thou shalt remember the poor and consecrate of thy properties for their support . . . and inasmuch as ye do impart of your substance unto the poor, ye do it unto me (D&C 42:30-31).

For this and other church uses for revenue the law of tithing is instituted, the payment of the Lord's tenth, or tithing, one-tenth of one's interest annually; for general church expense purposes, which includes "care of the poor."

This is the present arrangement for meeting the church's need of revenue. The revelations of God in the New Dispensation, however, contemplate a broader provision for the betterment of the material welfare of the membership of the church than this, and especially for the humble and poor, and those who lack initiative in the creation of wealth by developing the world's resources, or directing the application of capital to industries, commerce, and trade. In outline the plan contemplates men regarding the earth and all that is in it as belonging to the Over-Lord who created it—land, and sea, and air, and all that comprises it; all wealth of life, and all its wealth of resources in soil fruitfulness, in forests, in grass-covered plains, in mountains underlaid with coal beds—the stored-up sunshine of past geological ages; the mountains seamed with silver lodes, and honey-combed with gold-bearing quartz; plains, again, underlaid with oil lakes; deeper reaches of the ancient gravel beds where lie the precious gems for adornment; the power of the waterfall—all the force and power of gravitation—all animal power, all chemical forces—everything that is wealth or can be transmuted into wealth—all these things are God's. His by right of proprietorship unquestioned and unquestionable; for He created them, man did not.

In the larger provision of the law, then, yet to be accepted by those who recognize God, not only as creator of all that is in the world, and of the world, but as sustaining and perpetuating Power of the world, proprietor, and rightful Over-Lord of it—these will desire to give outward manifestation of this inward faith by confessing themselves stewards merely of that portion of God's wealth that comes into their hands, and will hold themselves responsible to Him for the administration of that stewardship committed to them by the providences of God. Hence, the contemplated fuller development of the law of God, governing material economic relations, among those who accept the New Dispensation, will yet lead them to accept the principle and live the Law of Consecration and Stewardship. This means:

THE LAW OF CONSECRATION AND STEWARDSHIP[12]

I. An acknowledgement of the proprietorship of God in the world and to all that is in it; an acknowledgement of Him as its creator and the sustaining power of it; and its Over-Lord. This acknowledgement on the part of man being made by a solemn consecration of all he possesses of wealth or wealth-creating powers; this consecration will include all lands and their equipment; all mines and their output; all industries, trades, professions; all special gifts to develop natural resources, or to direct labor to develop resources—all which are wealth-creating powers—of all this men in their respective places, and possessions, and callings, and natural gifts for the creation of wealth and its distribution, not for selfish, personal ends, but for the common good and welfare of all. Men, I say, will consecrate all this and themselves with it as stewards unto the Over-Lord of the created world.

II. The second part of this Law of Consecration and Stewardship contemplates that after such a whole and complete consecration on the part of the believer and disciple of the New Dispensation, the disciple shall receive as permanent steward, his allotment in the economic scheme of things. That which shall be his to have and to hold and develop according to his own initiative and judgment, and in perfect freedom, but under consciousness of responsibility to God for the faithful management of the stewardship received as from God.

III. And then, as perpetuating the remembrance of both the consecration and the stewardship, the steward will deliver into a common fund or "storehouse," not as now, "the Lord's tenth," or tithing, but all his surplus—perhaps annually—arising from the management of his stewardship; and in turn having claims upon the common storehouse (known in the New Dispensation parlance as the "Lord's Store House") for capital, with which to enlarge his stewardship; better stock the farm, enlarge or re-equip the factory, improve the shipping facilities, drain the mines or explore for new ore bodies, improve efficiency in professions by making possible extension work at institutions of technology; and to inventors and explorers in pursuit of new knowledge, grant opportunity for research work. All this, but of course much more, is contemplated in the New Dispensation economics for its membership. What is here set down is in barest outline and at present in the church no formative steps are taken to realize the ideals of the Law of Consecration and Stewardship contemplated by the revelations given in the first decades of the existence of the church.[13]

---

12. <Ms III[c] adds "The Law Of Consecration & Stewardship"—*Ed.*>

13. These revelations begin with a commandment respecting the consecration of property for the poor "with a deed and covenant that cannot be broken," also that every man shall be made accountable unto the Lord, "a steward over his own property," etc. (D&C 42:30-32). Revelation given in February 1831, Ohio. Also, D&C 51 (all of it relates to this

An effort was made by the church to put into practice the Law of Consecration and Stewardship in both Jackson County, Missouri, and in Kirtland, Ohio, in the first decade of the existence of the church; but such were the disturbed conditions in which the church existed in those years, so frequent and violent the persecutions which followed the saints, that it was impossible in these disturbed conditions to carry out the new economic scheme and God-given principles for the betterment of the conditions of the people in their temporal affairs; and in July 1838, the present law of tithing was given under which the church, then assembled in Missouri, were required to place all their surplus property in the hands of the bishop of the church[14] in Zion (Missouri), for the building of a "house of the Lord"—then under contemplation—and the settling of the indebtedness of the church; and after that they were required to pay one-tenth of all their interest annually; and this has been the law under which the church has lived since that time, and which is now the law of the church under which her membership live.[15]

---

subject), given in May 1831. D&C 58, given in August 1831, gives direction for the allotment of several stewardships of lands in Jackson County, Missouri, to certain elders who had gathered there to that land. Instructions on stewardships in D&C 70; also, D&C 82, and D&C 104; and other revelations, *passim*. A brief treatise on this whole subject will be found in the author's *New Witnesses for God* (Salt Lake City: The Deseret News, 1911), chapter 27 on "The Evidence of Inspiration" of the Prophet Joseph Smith, 1:372-91, derived from the wisdom in the plan proposed for the betterment of the temporal condition of mankind.

Also, a later treatise prepared for the section of Columbia University's (N.Y.) economic library, which received the following acknowledgement:

Columbia University
in the City of New York
Department of History

December 22, 1924.

> My Dear Mr. Roberts:
> This is a long-delayed note to express to you my thanks for your article entitled "Economic Aspects of the Career of the Mormons," which you so kindly prepared for our library more than a year ago. I have just completed a chapter of a projected work entitled "Pioneers and the Transmississippi," in which, among other things, I especially stressed the economic system of the Mormons and their influence as colonizers of the West. Your manuscript, which was very helpful to me, I have had catalogued and placed on the shelves of our college study.
> With all good wishes, I am,
>
> Very cordially yours,
>
> (signed) Harry J. Carman.

14. <Ms III* "Church"—*Ed.*>

15. See D&C 119. Undoubtedly the requirement as to all "surplus property" being

CONCLUDING REFLECTIONS: THE ONE LAW OF RIGHTEOUSNESS

The foregoing items brought forth in chapter 54[16] are some of the respects in which THE LIFE in the New Dispensation of the gospel is deepened, a little enlarged, and emphasized over and above what is to be found in other dispensations. But the thing which most of all affects the life in the New Dispensation and makes it to abound most with influence for the founding of God's one and only universal law of eternal righteousness, the same through all ages and in all places, and making the duty of man under the gospel comprehensive—consists in bringing over into modern knowledge the passage from the pronouncement of God in the great council, held before the world was:

> We will prove them herewith, to see if they will do all things whatsoever the Lord their God shall command them (Abr. 3:25).

This makes the commandments of God the law of man's moral life, the law of his progress, the measure of his duty, and the manifestation of his love for God:

> For this is the love of God, that we keep his commandments (1 Jn. 5:3; cf. John 14:15).
>
> Whosoever committeth sin transgresseth also the law; for sin is transgression of the law, . . . [and] all unrighteousness is sin (1 Jn. 3:4; 5:17).

"put into the hands of the bishop of Zion" for the building of the house of the Lord (the temple at Far West), etc., "as the beginning of the tithing of my people" was a commandment especially directed to the saints then assembled and assembling in Missouri, to alleviate the immediate distresses then existing, both as to the church as an organization and many of the saints sorely in need. It was a temporary commandment and not designed as a perpetual requirement for all time to come upon the saints as the payment of one-tenth of their income annually was. I judge this to be the case, because at no time since the Missouri days have the saints, or converts on entering the church, been required to put all their surplus property into the hands of the bishop of the church. It has been considered all sufficient, apparently, if members from their entrance into the church have paid their tithing, which is one-tenth of their interest annually. In the later years of President Brigham Young's life an effort was made in various settlements in Utah and Idaho to institute what was called "The United Order," involving some of the principles of consecration and stewardship—but not all of them. After a few uncertain years of precarious life, the experiments were abandoned (see "The Economic Aspects of the Career of the Mormons," Columbia (N.Y.) University Library, manuscript, Economic Section). <For a modern study on the economics of the United Order, see L. Dwight Israelsen, "An Economic Analysis of the United Order," *Brigham Young University Studies* 18 (Summer 1978): 536-62—*Ed.*>

16. <Ms III[*] "in chapters LIV and LV," which was altered to Ms III[c] "in chapters LIV." These "Concluding Reflections" were originally the conclusion to chapter 55, but Roberts later moved them to their current postition at the end of chapter 54—*Ed.*>

The law of God, then, made up, of course, of the commandments of God, is the universal gospel ethic, common to all its dispensations. And hence, when the final dispensation—the Dispensation of the Fullness of Times—was ushered in, there came with it the whole law of eternal righteousness, based upon the commandments of God.

Hence, all the law of righteousness of the patriarchal dispensations, of the Mosaic Dispensation, and the law under the prophets of Israel—all this enters into the new and final dispensation of the gospel. The Ten Commandments, and especially as generalized by the Christ into the two all-inclusive commandments—love of God and love of man; all the precepts of the Christ in the Sermon on the Mount—these are reinstated as the law of God. The Sermon on the Mount taught in the precepts of the Master and exemplified in his life, is the law of God in the New Dispensation. That dispensation is characterized by a fullness of the law of the righteousness; as it is by a fullness of ordinances; of authority from God, or priesthood; of a fullness of events that will restore all things to the order that God has decreed for them, completing both the salvation of men and the redemption of the earth itself, to the status of a celestial world, the habitat of immortal and glorified Intelligences.

CHAPTER LV

The Marriage Institution of the New Dispensation

SCRIPTURE READING LESSON

Analysis

I. The Unit of Society—the Family.

II. What Is Achieved through Marriage?

III. Its Purposes: Companionship and Offspring; The Family, Society, Civilization.

IV. The Modern World's Departure from the Marriage Institution.

V. Recent Discussions on Marriage:

(a) Book Treatment;

(b) Church Treatment.

VI. New Grouping of Society's Units.

VII. Effects of Science on Morals.

VIII. Church Unity on Marriage Lacking.

IX. Companionate Marriage.

X. Effects of Easy Divorce.

XI. Existing Sex and Social Relations.

XII. Other Phases of the Social Evil.

XIII. Moral Standards and Changes.

XIV. Position of the Church in the New Dispensation on Marriage.

XV. The Law of Chastity.

XVI. Per Contra: Facing the Real Modern Problems.

XVII. Hopes—Faith.

XVIII. Appendage to Chapter 55 <on Polygamy>.

References

Gen. 1 and 2; also all the scriptures quoted and referred to in this chapter; also books and magazine articles and discussions cited.

Article, "Solemnization of Marriage," Church of England Book of Common Prayer.

D&C 132, on marriage of the Church of the New Dispensation.

B. H. Roberts, "History of the 'Mormon' Church," *Americana* 6 (March 1911): 287-303, chap. 40 and notes to chapter; ibid., 9 (June 1914): 511-41, chap. 107 and footnotes; ibid., 10 (June 1915): 480-537, chap. 121.

Doctrine and Covenants, Edition of 1922, Official Declaration of Wilford Woodruff, following section 136 <now, following D&C 138>.

Also B. H. Roberts, *Outlines of Ecclesiastical History*, 4th ed. (Salt Lake City: Church of Jesus Christ of Latter-day Saints, 1924), part iv, section ix, and note 5.

For the appendage of Chapter 55, see Martin Madan, *Thelyphthora; or, A Treatise on Female Ruin*, 3 vols. (London: J. Dodsley, 1781).

On Bible marriage, <Orson> Pratt—<John P.> Newman Debate <i.e, *The Bible and Polygamy. Does the Bible Sanction Polygamy?*>, 1877, and three sermons attached to the debate.

CHAPTER LV

The Marriage Institution of the New Dispensation[1]

THE UNIT OF SOCIETY—THE FAMILY[2]

Hitherto we have considered "The Life" mainly with reference to the individual only. "The Life" would be incomplete, however, if it were not considered with reference to the unit of society—the family; man and woman united and offspring as the result of their union. In a word, marriage and what comes of it; the relations it creates, the duties it imposes, the things it designs to achieve, the society it brings into existence, the civilization it creates.

It is evidenced as much in the nature of man as it is clearly written in the revelations of God, that "it is not good for man to be alone" (cf. Gen. 2:18); the nature of both man and woman cries out aloud—each needs the other for completion. Completed man is man-woman. Each is but half of a necessary whole; both—and together—are needed for perpetuation of human life—of race. Hence, in this story of the creation, when it is proposed that man be made, God said: "Let us make man in our image, after our likeness" (Gen. 1:26); and then:

> So God created man in His own image, in the image of God created He him, male and female created He them. And God blessed them, and God said unto them, "Be fruitful, and multiply, and replenish the earth and subdue it" (Gen. 1:27-28).

In the second story of the creation, where the mystery of procreation is veiled under the story of the "rib" (Gen. 2:21-22), woman is derived from man (and also, though it is not written, man is derived from woman), the mutual need of man and woman and their union is further emphasized. In all the animal creation brought to the lone Adam to be named by him, according to this story, there was not found an helpmeet for Adam. God had observed before that it was not good

1. <Early in 1928 B. H. Roberts published "Complete Marriage—Righteousness; Mutilated Marriage—Sin," *Improvement Era* 31 (Jan. 1928): 181-92; in 1929 Roberts added chapter 55 to TWL, which is based upon this article—*Ed.*>

2. <Ms III^{c} adds "The Family"—*Ed.*>

for man to be alone, and hence, He declared the creation of an helpmeet for him; and so brought one forth, not from the animal creation to which Adam had given names, but one derived from the same nature and race as Adam himself, from man, and brought her to Adam, who recognized in her "bone of my bones and flesh of my flesh; she shall be called woman, because she is taken out of man" (that is, derived from the same race and is of the same nature); and "therefore shall a man leave his father and his mother, and shall cleave unto his wife, and they shall be one flesh" (Gen. 2:23-24).

Thus was "man" completed; the family–the community[3] unit–the unit of civilization–was made possible; two great, necessary things provided for; true companionship for man and woman; and the lawful perpetuation of the race.

WHAT IS ACHIEVED THROUGH MARRIAGE

Much has been written upon this institution of marriage as above set forth in Genesis, much in high praise of it, and worthily. An old English writer says of it:

> Marriage is the mother of the world and preserves kingdoms and fills cities and churches and heaven itself. . . . Like the fruitful bee,[4] it builds a house, gathers sweetness from every flower and labors and unites into societies and republics and sends out colonies and feeds the world with delicacies and obeys . . . and keeps order and exercises many virtues and promotes the interest of mankind, and is that state of good <things> to which God hath designed the present constitution of the world.[5]

And I might say, for those who accept the New Dispensation of the gospel as set fourth in this work, the constitution of all worlds. Marriage does all that is described above, and more. It constitutes the true community unit–the family–which is the source of national life and civilization; both depend upon the maintenance and perfection of this institution.

ITS PURPOSES:[6] COMPANIONSHIP AND OFFSPRING

It will be observed that two major things are provided for in the Bible account of the marriage institution. These are (a) companionship–"it is not good for man to be alone" (cf. Gen. 2:18)–nor for woman either; and (b) man and woman in

---

3. <Ms III^c adds "community"–*Ed.*>

4. <Taylor's text is "like the useful bee"–*Ed.*>

5. <Jeremy Taylor, *Selected Works*, ed. Thomas K. Carroll (New York: Paulist Press, 1990), 266–*Ed.*>

6. <Ms III^c adds "Its Purposes"–*Ed.*>

the marriage relation must perpetuate the race–God's commandment: "Multiply and replenish the earth" (Gen. 1:28); and together subdue it.

The marriage relation is associated with the tenderest sentiments, the strongest passions (I use the word in its best sense), and the deepest interests of human life. It has to do with human love, and sex, and offspring–the perpetuation of life, the family, the home, and the race. It is the chief cornerstone in the temple of human existence. From the family comes the home, and it has become something of a fixed conviction with thoughtful statesmen, and others who give serious attention to the welfare of society and of nations, that no state can rise higher than its homes; and no church can be more righteous or influential than the firesides from which its members come. It follows that the stability of the home and its perpetuation become, nay, are, major factors in the concerns of society, of church, of state, and of humanity itself. The importance of marriage demands that every solemnity and stability that can be fused into it shall be claimed and secured for it. The great strength of marriage consists in the fact that it is an institution founded of God; that is a religious institution–sacrament would be the better term–a relationship established by the law of God, and its purposes and obligations are determined by that law.

It is to be observed, in passing, that when instituted in Eden, marriage was a relationship that was established before death appeared in the Adamic race; and had not death been thrust into the scene, the relation of marriage between the first pair would have been perpetual–eternal. The question suggests itself–why, in view of the assured resurrection from the dead–the renewal of individual life in immortality–why should the passing incident of a temporary death break the eternity of the marriage covenant? More on this later.

THE MODERN WORLD'S DEPARTURE FROM THE MARRIAGE INSTITUTION

All the foregoing in relation to marriage, however, its solemnity, its sacredness, its perpetuity, the probability of the eternity of the relationship it establishes–all this is widely being departed from in modern life, until the whole fabric of the institution as it has hitherto been known, is menaced by the so-called march of recent progress–the trend in modern thought and action to divide the marriage purpose–companionship and offspring–and make it chiefly and in many cases entirely "companionate" with satisfaction of sex desire, without offspring as a result of sex relation;[7] thus canceling one of the two major features of the marriage

7. <Ms III[*] "with offspring, as a result of sex relation, eliminated," while Ms III[c] has "without offspring," but fails to cross-out the word "eliminated"–*Ed.*>

institution. Perhaps in nothing in our modern life has there been such a wide departure from established moral standards, both of the recent past and more ancient times, than in the Christian, modern view of marriage.

RECENT DISCUSSIONS ON MARRIAGE[8]

The subject has been discussed of late (1928-29) in some rather pretentious books; also in both the monthly and weekly magazines. It has been discussed from the lecture platform, also from the pulpit, in the daily press, and has been made the theme—*pro et con*—of movie picture films. It has been the subject of discussion in very important church conferences, conventions, and congresses.[9]

(a) Book Treatment

The books that have treated of this subject are quite numerous. I shall refer only to two of these, and this because they are quite typical of the spirit in large part of the others.

The first is under the title *Our Changing Morality*. It is edited by Freda Kirchwey, and is in the nature of symposium. This book has fifteen writers of considerable prominence, both in our own country and also in England; each contributes a chapter. Some of the subtitles in this book are: "Styles in Ethics," "Modern Marriage," "Changes in Sex Relations," "Women—Free for What?" "Can Men and Women Be Friends?" Under such subtitles, sex relations, love, and marriage are discussed with extreme frankness. The trend of thought throughout the symposium may be judged from a few typical quotations.

First, it is held that:

---

8. <Ms III[c] adds "On Marriage"—*Ed.*>

9. As an indication of how far-flung the discussion is, attention is called to the fact that Italy's dictator, his Excellency Benito Mussolini, has contributed a pretentious article to one of the popular American magazines on "Marriage," dealing with some of the modern problems arising in connection therewith (see "Mussolini on Marriage," *Hearst's International Combined with Cosmopolitan* 85 [September 1928]: 45, 175). One paragraph is of first-rate importance and worthy of consideration as it fittingly rebukes a too-common evil of levity in relation to the marriage state: "The marriage contract should be engaged in with due care for its importance and due regard for the high purpose of its function. Marriage is not a travesty of life. It cannot be made the subject for pleasantries in the columns of the daily newspapers, or the target for farcical thrusts on the stage. Actors and actresses blessed with simple mediocrity in the drama often find humor to be exploited in references to the married state or to the man with a family. The social conscience must be made stern against any influence which effects a travesty on the sacred purposes of a married existence. Marriage and family life are hallowed institutions, fitting into the fabric of the state in harmony with its function and growth."

> All sexual intercourse should spring from the free impulse[s] of both parties, based upon mutual inclination and nothing else. . . . The cramping of love by institutions [the family and churches, for instance] is one of the larger evils[10] of the world.[11]

Again:

> Every person who allows himself to think that an adulterer must be wicked, adds his stone to the prison in which the source of poetry and purity and love[12] is incarcerated by priests in black gowns.[13]

From these excerpts may be judged somewhat the spirit in which sex questions, love, marriage, and divorce in that symposium are discussed.

Second: another typical book on this line is *The Right To Be Happy* by Mrs. Bertrand Russell. Her chapter on "Sex and Parenthood" is the chapter that represents the very heart of her book, and it should be entitled, "A Plea for Unbridled License in Sex Relations." Perhaps I ought to forewarn the reader that this theme of necessity requires great frankness in the use of terms that are generally regarded as better unused for the general reader. To secure a right understanding of the subject must be my excuse for repeating some of these plain terms.

In the opening paragraph of the chapter referred to in Mrs. Russell's book, a statement is made that "starvation or thwarting of the instinct of sex-love"—which would include, of course, sex self-restraint—"causes more acute unhappiness than poverty, disease, or ignorance."[14] In the regime[15] proposed under this scheme set forth in *The Right To Be Happy*, this question is asked:

> What hinders us from establishing a social system, in which young men and women who are out in the world earning may enter into open temporary sex partnerships,[16] without harm to the work and legitimate ambitions of either?[17]

A rather bold question, and this question is answered by the author as follows:

> Nothing whatever, excepting our false picture of woman and our ingrained ascetic

---

10. <Russell's text has "the major evils"—*Ed.*>

11. <Bertrand Russell, "Styles in Ethics," in *Our Changing Morality: A Symposium*, ed. Freda Kirchwey (New York: Albert and Charles Boni, 1924), 14—*Ed.*>

12. <Russell's text has "the source of poetry and beauty and life"—*Ed.*>

13. <Russell, "Ethics," in *Changing Morality*, 15—*Ed.*>

14. <Countess Dora Winifred Black Russell, *The Right to Be Happy* (New York: Harper and Brothers, 1927), 128—*Ed.*>

15. <Ms III[*] "under the regime"—*Ed.*>

16. <Roberts adds a "not" to Russell's text, making Ms III read "may not enter into open temporary sex partnerships"—*Ed.*>

17. <Russell, *Right To Be Happy*, 153-54—*Ed.*>

> belief that sex is wicked if enjoyed and not immediately succeeded by the pains and anxieties and penalties of parenthood. Yet such companionships, not despised and concealed, would work great changes in the character of individuals.[18]

Undoubtedly it would! Again:

> The idea of sin must be banished, as must any demand for special service or sacrifice by women. . . . There would be passionate griefs, disappointments, and broken ideals, but none of this is so damaging to <human> personality as atrophy. . . . Men frequently regret what the moralist calls pre-marital indiscretions, and pre-marital experience for women is definitely still thought a crime. . . .
>
> It is not impossible that a time may come when pre-marital experience will no longer be regarded as a crime, or even as an indiscretion [!][19] . . . The superstition of chastity[20] is a part of that same false psychology, which makes moral virtue consist in emptiness and abstention.[21]

Such is the spirit of the discussion throughout the book.[22]

(b) Church Treatment

With equal frankness in magazines and the daily press, this question is debated. I think, however, I shall get the points of the debate before the reader best if I call attention to a very noted paper presented at the American Episcopal Church Congress held in San Francisco, in July 1927.

This paper has resulted in very much criticism of its author, the Rev. Henry H. Lewis, of Ann Arbor, Michigan. His paper carried this title: "Moral Standards in an Age of Change." The intent of the topic so introduced was to bring out first, what changes are taking place in moral standards; second, how these changes are related to Christian standards, which the church proclaims; and third, the message of the church in relation to "the existing facts." Of necessity I give a few excerpts from this paper, especially on that division of the topic that deals with "the existing facts":

NEW GROUPING OF SOCIETY'S UNITS[23]

"The first thing, I believe," said the author, "which strikes us all is what we have largely substituted for the family groups other and larger groups." And then:

---

18. <Ibid., 154–*Ed.*>
19. <Ms III[c] adds the exclamation mark "!"–*Ed.*>
20. <Ms III "jealousy" is clearly an error, since Russell's text has "chastity"–*Ed.*>
21. <Russell, *Right To Be Happy*, 155-56, 158-59–*Ed.*>
22. <Ms III[*] "throughout the book to which attention is called"–*Ed.*>
23. <Ms III[c] adds "Of Society's Units"–*Ed.*>

> A generation ago, the home, the children, the cousins, the neighbors made the all-important nucleus around which life was built and maintained. There was a sound honor, a simple goodness, a charm about it all. Today that scene is seldom repeated.

Yet that picture he draws for us was only a generation ago, and he now declares that it is seldom repeated! "The emphasis has shifted." Continuing, he says:

> We have other groups which form the centers around which life revolves; for older brother and sister in college—the fraternity and sorority; for mother, her reading or social clubs or health culture group; for father, the Rotary or Kiwanis or lodge—clubs of all kinds—not to mention hotels for men, and hotels for women. In any discussion of the present moral situation, such new groupings—which often have usurped the central place of family life—should be recognized. . . . The philosophy of many is to live for the moment, and to get the most out of life. . . . Is it any wonder that we have a behavioristic psychology, which tells us that the main thing in life is to express ourselves, or get the greatest thrill we can? That is held up to be the modern goal to which life is moving; and it is not difficult to see under it the old formula "eat, drink, and be merry, for tomorrow we die" (1 Cor. 15:32).

Again he says:

> With such a philosophy it is hard to find a definite purpose toward which one is going.

In other words, modern life is losing its sense of direction, and seems not to appreciate or understand or even believe that there is a great objective in this earth-life of man. A little further on the author says:

> The result is that many an individual has an independence which amounts to complete disregard of anyone else.

Then he cites the fact that science is playing an important part with reference to moral standards.[24]

EFFECT OF SCIENCE ON MORALS

> The introduction of science is the outstanding fact of our time, and in morals science has created an entirely new moral situation. You have done away with that old but very effective weapon, which has deterred many a person from going beyond the accepted moral code—fear of consequences. That fear no longer rests in the breast of any scientifically educated man or woman, and along with the passing of that fear is also going a vast amount of ignorance and misinformation upon the whole sexual relationship. The results are only partially manifest. To many young people what used to be considered lapses from the moral code are now considered to be acts which are

---

24. <Ms III* "to moral standards. He says:"—*Ed.*>

as natural as eating and drinking. Indeed, youth often decides on the basis of expediency or "worthwhileness," whether sexual intercourse should be indulged in, never thinking of any after-effects, because they believe there will be none.

They see no harm in it–science will protect them, and science generally does. Even with those who do not go so far, the idea that many of us had, that such things as petting or overfamiliarity with the opposite sex, should be saved at least until the time of engagement, if not until marriage, on the basis that married life would be happier if one did–this had disappeared.

The youth of the day we know are not appealed to by any such idea. . . . Whatever we may think of such conduct, the thing for us to notice is that it does exist, and that largely because of scientific knowledge many people are finding reasonable justification for doing things they never would have thought of a generation ago.

CHURCH UNITY ON MARRIAGE[25] LACKING

The foregoing was the presentation of "the facts" in that aforesaid[26] church congress! Further on the discussion shows how these modern changes as to the marriage institution are related to Christian standards, which the church proclaims. Of course, there can be but one answer to that, and that is that the conduct of modern life, represented by these "facts," is[27] revolutionary of all moral ideas of the churches. They must have credit for that, though they answer with varying voices, and there is a lack of unity in proclamation from the various divisions of Christendom. The churches are supposed to voice the law of God with reference to such matters. Those in controversy with them say–"That would be all right, if we only knew what the law of God was." And indeed here "the church"–having reference to all Christendom–all divisions and sub-divisions of it–is at a disadvantage in meeting that flippant, rather than profound, remark. This[28] because of a lack of unity in their ideas with reference to what the law of God is.

The other point to be considered, and which was considered in the discussion at the Episcopal Church Congress on the occasion referred to is–"What is to be the message of the church in relation to the existing facts?"

COMPANIONATE MARRIAGE

Just at present the church seems not to have clearly answered this question; but within the churches there are those who would make the answer in such form as not only to condone these conditions that are here pointed out, but would make

25. <Ms III[c] adds "on Marriage"–*Ed.*>
26. <Ms III[c] adds "aforesaid"–*Ed.*>
27. <Ms III[*] "by these 'facts' are"–*Ed.*>
28. <Ms III[c] adds "This"–*Ed.*>

them respectable by legalizing them. Hence arises the suggestion of "companionate marriage," accompanied by birth control and by easy divorces; which means when considered in its effects, free love legalized. That is the meaning of the movement, when stripped of all its pretenses and its disguises.

It is merely a form of marriage which is to continue as long as the parties to it desire the relationship to continue, but which may be dissolved mutually or at the pleasure of either party: divorce is to be easy. The object is not offspring and family and permanence of the home, but companionship, and pleasure, and sex liberties without the consequence or responsibility of children. These may be limited or eliminated according to desire.

It would not be difficult to forecast what the effect would be, if such a scheme should be carried into effect. It would greatly weaken the marriage institution, and tend to the destruction of family life. "Home" would be a word without meaning! The "contract" of the "companionate marriage," held lightly from the first and designed to be easily dissolved would stand little or no strain; would leave the parties to it free to contemplate other possible associations, free to seek them, constituting mate-hunting a continuous performance, wrecking all continence, and inevitably resulting in the destruction of chastity both of mind and conduct; and instituting practically a free-love regime to the confusion of stable marriage and family life.

THE EFFECT OF EASY DIVORCE

What would be the effect of breaking down the moral restraints in sex relations may well be judged by the new laws governing divorce in England. England has long been renowned for the stability of her family life. She in the past has made divorce as difficult as possible by her laws. A few years ago, however, England began granting what since have been called "secret divorces," that is, divorces without publicity, limiting the press to publication of the facts in barest outline, and without the scandal that usually attaches to such trials. The result has been a great multiplication of divorce cases; in London alone rising from about five hundred in 1901, to more than two thousand four hundred cases in 1927. Showing that if you make divorce easy by making its processes secret even, it results in greatly increasing divorces—a conceded evil because of the disruption of family life. One thoughtful observer says:

> It would be difficult to guess how far the ease and popularity of divorce may be making inroads into that constancy and tolerance which used to be considered the great glory of English family life.

EXISTING SEX AND SOCIAL CONDITIONS

That conditions are now bad in relation to sex life and social life, admits of no doubt. It was reported in 1927 that there were six millions of young men in our country (United States) of marriageable age who refused to take upon themselves the responsibility of marriage and family, largely because of the economic difficulties involved. As it would be unreasonable to suppose that this large body of the youthful manhood of the country abstained from sexual pleasures, such a condition proves, even of itself, how widespread promiscuous and unlawful intercourse must be, and what the extent of prostitution. In the school and college life, as well as in the industrial life of our country, so many are already said to be involved in "companionate marriage," and are living in defiance of the law in relation to such matters, that it is urged that their method of life should be legalized! Granting that this deplorable condition may exist,[29] yet take away the restraints that now exist, and there would be evoked the spirit of absolute recklessness which will mean the destruction of family life and home,[30] and basic unit of civilization. How may the spendthrift be cured? By filling his pockets with money? Is that the cure for reckless spending? Granting that the social evils that exist are appalling, will they be made less appalling by declaring them respectable, by legalizing such relations as "companionate marriages," with its birth control, its easy and inexpensive divorce system?

OTHER PHASES OF THE SOCIAL EVIL

This effort to meet the conditions presented by "flaming," modern youth, as yet unmarried, but involved in sex relations without legal sanctions, is but one phase of the social evil; there are others, and these evils are to be found[31] among those who have already entered into the marriage status. Among these evils are, notably, the increasing love of pleasure, by indulgence in the sensual delights[32] of sex without incurring the risks, the pains, and the responsibilities of parenthood. Or, if a concession must be made to the convention of family under marriage, then offspring among such people, it is thought, must be limited to one or at most two children. This among the wealthier and educated classes, where wealth creates opportunity for leisure and artificially stimulates desire for greater variety of entertainment with diminishing effort, and an increasing sense of luxury and freedom from responsibility. As large families would be a hindrance to all this

---

29. <Ms III* "that all this deplorable condition may be true"–*Ed.*>
30. <Ms III* "the destruction of all idea of family life and home"–*Ed.*>
31. <Ms III^{c} adds "evils are to be found"–*Ed.*>
32. <Ms III^{c} adds "s" to make the plural "delights"–*Ed.*>

self-indulgence, large families are canceled out of the reckoning by that class of the population best qualified, in a material way, to meet the obligations of large families.

This practice of limiting families by so-called "birth control" leads to many evils, physical and moral and spiritual. It endangers and wrecks the health of women, since it involves them in methods for prevention of conception and *foetus* destruction, leading frequently to abortions and to infanticide—which is murder. Prevention, both by mechanical and chemical means, endangers the health of women who indulge it, impairs vitality, shatters nervous energy, and deteriorates the race. The moral effect of such methods of living is nothing less than disastrous. It brutalizes and makes a shame of sexual pleasure itself, and kills the sentiment of love, which alone refines the act to endearment. It ministers to the gross desire for sexual promiscuity; for with a felt security, through knowledge of a preventative nature from consequences that would expose infidelities to the marriage covenant, temptations to fornications and adulteries are greatly multiplied and the moral tone of a community greatly lowered, if not destroyed.

The baneful effects of all this frequently appear in the divorce courts. It is the divorce record of England in the year 1927[33] that in forty percent of the divorce cases the couples seeking separation were childless, and in thirty percent of the cases they had but one child! These facts tell their own story. A thoughtful writer commenting upon the above state of facts declares:

> Children create a bond which influences parents to think many times before they give way to divorce, and this may develop the tolerance of each other's faults and characteristics, without which no marriage can be happy. But the bond being absent, there is no incentive to overcome the obstacles to a satisfactory union of a man and a woman, and divorce results.[34]

It will be said perhaps that in all this there is nothing new; that these several recognized evils constituting menaces to the marriage institution, to the family, to the integrity of community life, to national life, and to civilization itself have of a long time now been trumpeted by prophets of evil, and yet the marriage institution persists, the family survives, children are regularly born in constantly increasing numbers in most nations; and while it is recognized that many evils and dangers abound, they always have existed more or less, yet there seems to be no real cause of alarm, for[35] human nature is essentially sound and it seems likely that our cherished institutions will somehow be preserved. A comforting line of comment, doubtless; but shallow and inadequate to the world's present needs, and not at all

33. <Ms III^c adds "in the year 1927"—*Ed.*>

34. *The New Age*, December 1927.

35. <Ms III^c adds "for"—*Ed.*>

reassuring in face of the conditions that now obtain and the changing mental attitude of the present generation toward the aforesaid cherished institutions. In that changed mental attitude lies the immediate danger to marriage and all that it concerns.

MORAL STANDARDS

A word in relation to this phrase "Moral Standards" as used above. In commerce and trade we have standard weights and standard measures. It will have to be conceded, I think, that in the world of trade and commerce, there is more or less fraud and trickery, of theft even; of false values fraudulently imposed upon the unsuspecting. How shall these evils be corrected? By tampering with standards of weights and measures? Or by demanding that the thing sold shall be honestly sold and shall be of proper weight, of proper measure, of the agreed number of feet or yards or pounds? Make commercial trade and industrial transactions conform to standards of weights, lengths, measures, and values. And so with marriage and its obligations. Let it be completed marriage, which is righteousness; and not mutilated marriage, which is sin.

POSITION OF THE CHURCH IN THE NEW DISPENSATION ON MARRIAGE[36]

I have gone into the consideration of all these things so far because I want to consider the position of the Church of Christ in the New Dispensation in relation to these very important subjects.

What is the message of the Church of the Latter-day Saints to its own people about these vital questions of sex, morality, and of marriage? What message on these subjects has she for the world? Or has she no word to give? I think the Church of the New Dispensation has a message both for her own people and for the world.[37] Moreover, that message[38] comes without uncertainty and under such sanctions of divine authority that heed should be given to it.[39]

The message of the church starts[40] with the great principle of Christ's Sermon on the Mount:

---

36. <Ms III* "The Church of Jesus Christ In The New Dispensation On Marriage"—*Ed.*>

37. <Ms III* "What message on these subjects has it for the world? Or has it no word to give. I think it has a message both for its own people and for the world"—*Ed.*>

38. <Ms III* "that word"—*Ed.*>

39. See note at end of chapter <i.e., the references to Matt. 5:27-28; D&C 42:22-23, cited at the end of the main text of chapter 55, before the "appendage">.

40. <Ms III* "It starts"—*Ed.*>

> Seek ye first the Kingdom of God and His righteousness and all these[41] things shall be added unto you (Matt. 6:33).

"Seek"—not one's own conceptions of righteousness, not one's neighbor's conception of righteousness,[42] not human standards at all; for "there is a way which seemeth right unto a man, but the end thereof are the ways of death" (Prov. 14:12). Then, with reference to righteousness, men may easily be mistaken about it. Apart from the law of God's righteousness, men are likely to place wrong emphasis upon this or that part of righteousness, distorting it and perhaps making it of no avail. Men are subject to misconceptions on generalizations about righteousness; but there can be no doubt with reference to the righteousness of God, and the righteousness of His law. And when men make the law of God their standard of righteousness, and the measure of their duty, they occupy sure ground. That is where the Church of Jesus Christ of Latter-day Saints stands. The membership of that church accept their moral duties as growing out of the commandments of God. They hark back in their conception of things in relation to the law of God's righteousness, back to the beginning, when it was said by the divine Creator:

> We will prove them herewith [pre-existent spirits that were to become men in earth-life], to see if they will do all things whatsoever the Lord their God shall command them (Abr. 3:25).

This makes the commandments of God, in the sum of them, the revealed righteousness of God;[43] and the obedience of man to that righteousness is the full measure of his duty, and the acme of human morality.

THE LAW OF CHASTITY

In the Sermon on the Mount—as we have already seen—the Christ gave the supreme law of chastity that is still of binding force to those who make any pretention of following the Master, or of following[44] effectual purity; namely:

> Ye have heard that it was said by them of old time, Thou shalt not commit adultery; but I say unto you, That whosoever looketh upon a woman to lust after her hath committed adultery <with her> already in his heart (Matt. 5:27-28).

That, I say, holds not only as to those who are in the marriage relation, but

---

41. <Ms III^c adds "these" in order to agree with Matt. 6:33—*Ed.*>

42. <Ms III^c adds "conception of righteousness"—*Ed.*>

43. <Ms III* "the commandments of God the sum of the revealed righteousness of God"—*Ed.*>

44. <Ms III^c adds "of following"—*Ed.*>

to those who have not yet entered into the marriage relation. Purity of mind, chastity of thought, as well as chastity of conduct is God's great law upon this subject. And when the Lord repeated that law of chastity in the New Dispensation of the gospel, He made these important additions to it, by saying, that whosoever "looketh upon a woman to lust after her shall deny the faith, and shall not have the Spirit, and if he repents not, he shall be cast out" (D&C 42:23); that is, cast out of the church.

That is the message and the warning which the Church of the Latter-day Saints has for her membership.[45] To the world the church declares that she regards as her moral standards the law of God. That law requires and demands purity of thought as well as chastity in conduct; and this as well before marriage as afterwards. The church takes no part in striking down the restraints that a wholesome public opinion and the surviving fragments of God's law among the Christian sects of the world projects about these problems of sex morality and marriage. The correct way of meeting these problems is by preaching repentance to those who violate the laws governing such relations. The Church of the New Dispensation stands for sanctity of the family and its permanency. In proof of this I call attention to our marriage ceremony as performed in the holy temples. The ceremony which ends not with a covenant "till death us do part,"[46] but with a covenant which extends into eternity—"for time and all eternity!"[47] That is the guarantee of the church to all the world that the Latter-day Saints believe in the permanency of marriage and of the home. Marriage, family, and the home have contributed so much to the happiness, peace, and progress of mankind, and built up and maintained such civilization as exists in the world today, that it may be trusted to achieve still greater things throughout the eternities in which men will live. The family founded upon true and complete marriage—marriage for companionship and marriage for family—becomes not only a sacred unit in our mortal life, but it will continue to be a sacred unit also in the eternal life toward which men are moving.

---

45. <Ms III[*] "the message and the warning the Church of the Latter-day Saints has for its membership"—*Ed.*>

46. Church of England, The Book of Common Prayer, Title, "The Form of Solemnization of Marriage."

47. *The Appropriateness of the Wedding Ring in the Marriage Ceremony of the Latter-day Saints:* In view of the eternity of the marriage covenant by the Church of the Latter-day Saints no people more appropriately may use the wedding ring in the marriage ceremony as a symbol of its nature. The circle is the most perfect of geometrical figures; the symbol of completeness and of eternity. Therefore, by them, the wedding ring may most fittingly be used as the symbol of the marriage covenant.

PER CONTRA–FACING THE REAL MODERN PROBLEMS[48]

Meantime, however, is nothing to be said of the real difficulties attendant upon the economic and industrial changes that have come over the world in recent years, making for many the ideal family marriage more difficult of realization? Nothing of the childless marriages, or the very, very limited offspring in the marriage life of the highly educated and wealthy classes on the one hand; and of the over-prolific poor and ignorant and even criminal classes on the other hand? Undoubtedly something needs to be said upon all these problems; but surely nothing like what is being presented by the ultra, would-be "reformers" should be said. Their scheme is no panacea for these recognized ills of modern social life.

Briefly, for the really criminal classes, of both sexes, marriage and family should be prohibited–they should be barred the propagation of their kind!

What should be said to the highly educated and wealthy classes who are shirking their responsibilities, and duties to life and to society, should be in the way of admonition to repentance; and to acceptance of the law of God as the measure of their moral obligations in the married state, an appeal to sound reason and to conscience, that they become lovers of God and duty more than "lovers of pleasure" and of ease and of luxury. Would such an appeal only be met with quiet smiles of contempt, or perhaps with shouts of derision from their gilded, childless palaces–mis-called homes? Or by shouts of derision from their pillowed divans, or the banquet-laden tables of their club houses? Then be it so. Nothing more may be done than to make this appeal to plain duty. That failing,[49] let them perish with their luxury and love of it, as they will so perish, if they repent not, and will die[50] unloved, unhonored, and unsung–leaving naught but a wrack behind!

Of the over-prolific poor and ignorant, multiplying beyond all reason of hope to provide for bare necessities, to say nothing of opportunities for good prospects in life, wholesome nourishment, decent clothing, and education–for these, enlightenment and patient instruction, education; and such improvement in economic policies as will lead to betterment of industrial conditions. Mere generalities these, I know, but I may not go beyond generalities on this head in this writing. In the instruction to this class would fall proper sex information, by competent and conscientious teachers; not for the introduction of knowledge of mechanical and chemical means for prevention of conception, *foetus* destruction, or abortions, much less infanticide; but instructions in sex-cleanliness and health; in prudential self-restraint, that shall not be onanism either, but based upon such regard for the

48. <Ms III^c adds "Facing the Real Modern Problems"–*Ed.*>
49. <Ms III^c adds "That failing"–*Ed.*>
50. <Ms III^c adds "and will die"–*Ed.*>

health of mothers and welfare of offspring that there shall be periods of continence self-imposed—out of loving consideration for the wife and mother that shall make for respect of wifehood and motherhood, and keep the family within hailing distance of rugged well-being. This too much to expect of the classes to which such an appeal is to be made? Again, be it so; but this is the only appeal which in safety to the marriage institution may be made; adjustment by slow but persistent and patient methods of instruction against merely brutal self-indulgence. What is it Paul says of the mutual duties of man and wife in their intimate relations?

> Defraud ye not one the other, except it be with consent for a time, that ye may give yourselves to fasting and prayer; and come together again, that Satan tempt you not for your incontinency (1 Cor. 7:5).

If such admonition can hopefully be given in the interests of religious observances—fasting and prayer—why not invoke it in the interests of the well-being of wifehood and motherhood, and in the interests of the family, and the home, and the church and the state? And why not hope for its achievement in the one case as in the other? In any event the processes of permanent reform will necessarily be by the slow processes[51] of enlightenment, and not by the race-destructive methods proposed by the ultra "reformers."

Already it is deplored that the highly-educated and wealthy classes are so limiting their offspring that they are not perpetuating their class. What may be hoped for from a method likely to result in producing the same status in what we consent to call, for convenience, the great "middle class"—the rank and file of the people?

HOPES—FAITH!

Meantime, and fortunately, one may believe sufficiently in the soundness of human nature as to be confident that the program of the ultra "reformers" will not be projected into our modern life to any great extent; for humanity's sake let us hope not; out of respect for the wisdom and the striving of our ancestors who sought for better things, and wrought into the fabric of church and state better things than these proposed by the ultra "reformers" of our times—for their sake, and their honor, let us hope the ultra[52] "reformers" will not get far with their program to legalize vice; and especially for the sake of posterity, let us hope not.

If one may hope for the failure of this evil program on the score of belief in the essential soundness of human nature generally, one may feel an increase of

51. <Ms III^c adds "es" to make the plural "processes"—*Ed.*>

52. <Ms III^c adds "ultra"—*Ed.*>

confidence in its failure when thinking of what influence the appeal will have upon the membership of the Church of the Latter-day Saints. For while I know this church membership is not immune from the invasion of this pestiferous program, and there may be those among them who would give welcome to such canonization of vice as is proposed—yet that number can never be large nor influential. No; the program of the ultra-modern "reformers" will never be an attractive marriage system, or rather anti-marriage system, among people of the New Dispensation. As a church they stand committed to quite an opposite program from this. Their religion and their church stand for the purity and the permanence of the home. For full and complete marriage, celebrated in their temples, open to all the membership in good standing, celebrated by a covenant not only "until death do them part," but for "time and all eternity," extending into and holding good in the immortal life brought to pass by the resurrection from the dead, of which the Christ was the first fruits.

Marriage to the Latter-day Saints means completed or perfect marriage—companionship, and offspring, family. "Multiply and replenish the earth" (Gen. 1:28) is God's commandment to them; and this, under the law of God, may be legitimately carried out only in wedlock. As for all the rest, their ideal is pure minds and clean lives, for only such can "see," that is "realize," God.

> Blessed are the pure in heart, for they shall see God (Matt. 5:8).

Lust of the eyes, and of the mind, and of the heart, is forbidden by the law of God to them, either inside or outside of the marriage status (Matt. 5:27-28; D&C 42:22-23). And this ethic of sex relations and marriage, they hope to see become—by the grace of God—the sex and marriage[53] ethic of the world.

NOTE: APPENDAGE TO CHAPTER 55

Anything which a Latter-day Saint writer may have to say upon the subject of marriage will be regarded distrustfully by many readers because of the relationship of his church to a unique sort of plural marriage doctrine and practice, which was inaugurated and upheld for a time by the church; by reason of which circumstance great prejudice was aroused against that church and especially with reference to any message it might have on the subject of marriage. Since candor, however, requires that something should be said in relation to the subject in such a work as this, I prefer to say it here at the close of this chapter.[54]

In 1831 in Hirum Township, Portage County, Ohio, Joseph Smith and Sidney

53. <Ms III^{c} adds "sex and marriage"—*Ed.*>

54. <Ms III^{c} adds the marginal instruction "Print sm. case"—*Ed.*>

Rigdon were engaged in a revision (sometimes, and generally, referred to as a "translation") of the Old Testament. In the course of that work Joseph Smith was much impressed with the apparent approval and sanction which the Lord gave to those patriarchs and prophets of the Old Testament period in the matter of their having "many wives." He was told in answer to his questions that a plurality of wives as practiced by the worthy prophets and patriarchs, under the sanctions of God, was righteous and approved; and the time would come when plural marriages would be introduced into the New Dispensation. This time came some years later, and on July 12, 1843, the knowledge previously received was committed to writing as a revelation (see D&C 132).[55]

Joseph Smith introduced the plural wife feature of marriage into the Church of the Latter-day Saints both by taking plural wives himself, and giving them to others.[56] Not so much because there was evidence of Bible sanction for the righteousness of such unions among the worthy and approved patriarchs and prophets of God, as from the fact that revelation to himself sanctioned that order of marriage and authorized it. The revelation said:

> If any man espouse a virgin, and desire to espouse another, and the first give her consent . . . then is he justified . . . for they are given unto him to multiply and replenish the earth, according to [the Lord's] commandment; and to fulfill the promise which was given by [the] Father, before the foundation of the world; and for their exaltation in the eternal worlds, that they might bear the souls of men; for herein is the work of [the] Father continued, that he may be glorified (D&C 132:61, 63).

There is nothing here or elsewhere in the revelation promising ease or happiness or pleasure; there is nothing but an exalted motive presented for this marriage system—the "bearing of the souls of men," "replenishing the earth" with the race of men. Procreation of the race is emphasized as the highest purpose of this phase of the marriage institution, all else incidental; and procreation under conditions the most favorable to the welfare of the offspring, and hence to the race. First in giving in larger measure progenitors of high character—men who have given evidence of upright, temperate, virtuous lives; women chaste, and willing to consecrate their lives to the duty of motherhood; to this end sacrificing earthly

55. <For a discussion of how D&C 132 was written down in an effort by Joseph Smith to get Emma's permission for him to enter into plural marriage, see Linda King Newell and Valeen Tippetts Avery, *Mormon Enigma: Emma Hale Smith, Prophet's Wife, "Elect Lady," Polygamy's Foe, 1804-1879* (Garden City, NY: Doubleday and Co., 1984), 151-53—*Ed.*>

56. <According to Richard S. Van Wagoner, *Mormon Polygamy: A History*, 2d ed. (Salt Lake City: Signature Books, 1989), 5-6, 9-11, Joseph Smith's relationship with Fanny Alger, which occurred in 1835, may have been as a first plural wife, a concubine, or a common-law wife—*Ed.*>

pleasure, including the exclusive companionship of the husband—expected in monogamous marriage. As some women, against the promptings of natural inclinations of the social instincts, of the cravings for wedlock companionship, and the desire for offspring will renounce the world and the noble office of motherhood itself, and retire into dismal retreats and spend their lives in prayer and meditation, only emerging into the world to render service of teaching the youth, visiting the needy, or nursing the sick; so plural wives among the Latter-day Saints, and first wives who consented to their husbands entering into these relations, accepted the institution from the highest moral and religious motives. First as being a commandment of God instituted "for their exaltation in the eternal worlds, that they may bear the souls of men"; and second, that they might bear the souls of men under conditions that gave largest promise of improving the race and bringing forth superior men and women, who shall lead the way to that higher state of things for which the world is waiting; and which the first condition precedent to obtaining, is a consecrated fatherhood and motherhood, such as is contemplated in the plural marriage system of the Latter-day Saints.[57]

The saints did not accept into their faith and practice the plural wife system with the idea that it increased the comfort, or added to the ease of any one. From the first it was known to involve sacrifice, to make a large demand upon the faith, patience, hope, and charity of all who should attempt to carry out its requirements. Its introduction was not a call to ease or pleasure, but to religious duty; it was not an invitation to self-indulgence, but to self-conquest; its purpose was not earth-hap-

---

57. On this phase of the subject, the Right Rev. D. S. Tuttle, D.D., LL.D., formerly Bishop of Montana, Idaho, and Utah; and for seventeen years a resident of Utah and, therefore, in personal contact with "Mormonism," and later Bishop of Missouri, has an enlightening passage. He says in a chapter on "Mormonism": "I pause to remark that if some strength accrues to Mormonism from its adjustment to the nature of man, some unsuspected strength also is won to it by its appeal to the nature of woman. The self-sacrifice in woman, the appeal is made to that. One knows not much of human life, if he is ignorant that one of the dominating characteristics of woman is the power of self-sacrifice. If self-sacrifice in woman is continually in evidence in mothers, in wives of worthless husbands, in sisters in religious communities, and in women giving up all in devotion to love, or duty, or religion, who wonders that the appeal to it, as in the matter of polygamy, strange as it seems, must be accounted an element of strength to Mormonism. As matter of fact, there were no more strenuous and determined upholders of polygamy than most of the Mormon women who were personally sufferers by it. To their nature it was calamity and hateful. To their spirit it was religious duty and a call for self-sacrifice. Therefore, they were loyal to it, determined to live in it, and if need be, to die for it. Spirit, roused and active, evermore predominates over nature" (Daniel S. Tuttle, *Reminiscences of a Missionary Bishop*, 2d ed. [New York: Thomas Whittaker, 1906], 307-308).

piness, but earth-life discipline, undertaken in the interest of special advantages for succeeding generations of men. That purpose was to give to succeeding generations a superior fatherhood and motherhood, by enlarging the opportunities of men of high character, moral integrity, and spiritual development to become progenitors of the race. To give to women of like character and development a special opportunity to consecrate themselves to the high mission of motherhood. Race culture, then, was the inspiring motive of the plural wife feature of this revelation on marriage. It was in the name of a divinely-ordered species of eugenics that the Latter-day Saints accepted plurality of wives.

It should be observed also, in passing, that the Church of the Latter-day Saints never advocated the indiscriminate, or the general practice of a plural wife system, under merely human, legal sanctions. Such a general practice would doubtless be mischievous and lead to the disasters which opponents have from time to time charged to the more limited and specifically guarded practice of the principle under what the Latter-day Saints held to be divine sanctions, restraints, and regulations. It was indeed a principle of religion to them, a holy sacrament, and not at all designed to become a general practice under merely human laws. It is unfortunate that the world outside of the church was not impressed with this phase of the subject; for then it would have been apparent that the thing the world argued against and fought against—a general plural marriage system free for all to adopt, considered to be destructive of the monogamous system and a menace to the home itself—was not the thing upheld and contended for by the Latter-day Saints, who believed that the privilege of plural marriage is to be limited to persons of high character, approved lives, and living under the most sacred obligations to chastity, and granted this privilege of the marriage system only under the most carefully-guarded permission amounting to divine sanction. Such were the limitations put upon the practice of the plural feature of the marriage system of the Latter-day Saints.

Against this plural feature of marriage a series of federal enactments were passed by the Congress of the United States, under the assumption that congress held plenary power to legislate for the territories. This series of enactments began in 1862 and continued intermittently until 1887, when what was known as the Edmunds-Tucker Law was passed, which, in addition to increasing the penalties for violations of the law against plural marriage and its relations, also confiscated the church property and dissolved the church as a corporation. Even after this, still more drastic enactments were pending; but finally in September 1890, President <Wilford> Woodruff, and after every effort that could be made had been made before the courts to test the constitutionality of the law, moved thereto by an impression of the Spirit of the Lord, announced the discontinuance of the system of plural marriage, and called upon the Latter-day Saints "to refrain from contracting any marriage forbidden by the law of the land" (Official Declaration—1) This

"Manifesto," as it came by usage to be called, was afterwards adopted by the church in general conference assembled, and is now the rule of the church.[58]

In this matter of plural marriage the Latter-day Saints are neither responsible for its introduction nor for its discontinuance. The Lord commanded its practice, and in the face of the sentiment of ages and in opposition to the teachings of their own traditions, many of the saints obeyed the commandment, and in the midst of weakness, of great difficulties, and dangers, sought to carry out the law as revealed to them. For about half a century they maintained its practice in the face of opposition sufficient to appall the stoutest hearts. They defended it in the public press, proclaimed it from the pulpit, debated it on the platform with many of those who chose to assail it, and practiced it in their lives, notwithstanding fines and imprisonments and exile followed as consequences.[59] A whole generation was born and had grown to manhood and womanhood in this marriage system, and the affections of family ties were entwined with it. Then, under the pressure of suffering brought upon the people through the laws of the United States, the Lord inspired the president of the Church of Christ to proclaim its discontinuance, and the people with sorrowful hearts submitted to the will of God thus expressed and there the matter rests. If the labors and sufferings of the Church of Christ for this principle have done nothing more, this much at least has been accomplished—the saints have borne testimony to the truth connected with marriage, sanctioned and approved of God in ancient times, and revealed anew in this present age.

It should be remembered that in the Dispensation of the Fullness of Times, all things are to be gathered together in one—"all things in Christ, both which are in heaven and which are on earth; even in him" (Eph. 1:9-10). This "Dispensation of the Fullness of Times" is identical with that "Times of the Restitution of all things, which God hath spoken by the mouth of all the holy prophets since the world began" (cf. Acts 3:21). This prediction was made by St. Peter as something future from his day; and, therefore, this principle and practice of plurality of wives

58. <For the approval and practice of post-Manifesto polygamy, see D. Michael Quinn, "LDS Church Authority and New Plural Marriages, 1890-1904," *Dialogue: A Journal of Mormon Thought* 18 (Spring 1985): 9-105. For Roberts's own involvement in post-Manifesto polygamy in marrying Margaret Curtis Shipp about 1894, see B. Carmon Hardy, *Solemn Covenant: The Mormon Polygamous Passage* (Urbana: University of Illinois Press, 1992), 247-48, 271, 416—*Ed.*>

59. <For a first-hand account of prison-life in the 1880s for a Mormon convicted of unlawful cohabitation and polygamy, see Rudger Clawson, *Prisoner for Polygamy: The Memoirs and Letters of Rudger Clawson at the Utah Territorial Penitentiary, 1884-87* (Urbana: University of Illinois Press, 1993). For Roberts's own imprisonment for unlawful cohabitation from May to September 1889, see Gary James Bergera, ed., *The Autobiography of B. H. Roberts* (Salt Lake City: Signature Books, 1990), 174-81—*Ed.*>

by men and women of God in old Bible times, and with the approval of God, must at least be restored, as to the knowledge of it, together with other ancient truths; and witnessed to the world by the saints and the Church of the New Dispensation, whatever else may become of it. And this was done as stated above; and it is left for God to vindicate His own truth, of which His people have borne record by suffering, in His own time and in His own way.

It is to be understood, of course, that the foregoing statements are but an academic setting forth of the plural marriage feature of the marriage system of the Church of the New Dispensation, and is not intended as propaganda of that feature.

APPENDIX

Correspondence Related to "The Truth, The Way, The Life"

1. B. H. ROBERTS TO RUDGER CLAWSON

September 17, 1928

President Rudger Clawson
of the Council of the Twelve.

Dear Brother:

I note that in a letter signed by you under date of November 11, 1927, that the statement was made with reference to courses of study for the quorums of the Melchizedek Priesthood, that "The Council of the Twelve, the First Council of Seventy, and the Presiding Bishopric will give consideration of the texts and courses projected from time to time for these quorums." For the course of study for the quorums during 1928-29 the First Council have heard nothing concerning any plans for courses of study for this year and naturally we feel anxious as to what course of study you will propose for these quorums. In the meantime many inquiries come to the office of the First Council concerning courses of study for this year and we can make no answer as to what is intended for them as outlines for study. Of course, we are deeply interested in our 185 quorums of Seventy throughout the Church and would like to see them provided with a suitable course to prepare them for their work in the ministry. In view of the fact that we have heard nothing from the Council of the Twelve on what their plans are, I beg leave, with the approval of the members of the First Council who are within reach, to submit to you and to your Council a book upon which I have been working definitely for now over one year, and I might say for many years, and which I designed at the commencement of it as a course of study for our Seventies quorums, and of course if suitable for them it may be equally suitable for the High Priests and Elders. The book in volume of matter it contains—between five and six hundred pages, more nearly six hundred than five hundred—therefore would be ample in quantity of matter for more than one year, perhaps even two or three years as a text book.

The title of the work is to be: *The Truth, The Way, The Life; An Elementary*

Treatise on Theology. I hope to incorporate within its pages a full harvest of all that I have thought, and felt, and written through the nearly fifty years of my ministry, that is, on the theme of the title. The present status of the work is that I have the whole subject covered, taking in all 53 chapters, 43 chapters of which could now be placed in the hands of the printer and the remaining chapters will be re-written and completed for the printer by the 10th or 15th of October, and I am informed by the Deseret News Book Printing Department that they could produce such a work once the manuscript is in their hands in the course of four or five weeks, so that it will be possible to issue this book from the press by the middle of November, if it is thought desirable to have it printed for the use herein proposed.

I spent the six months vacation accorded to me last summer by the First Presidency in dictating the rough draft of this book, and the last few months have been revising and directing the rewriting of it for use by the printer, until it is now brought to the status of preparation described above.

About one-half of the book is taken up with the first division of the subject, THE TRUTH, and occupies 28 chapters of the 53. This part of the work deals with great fundamentals of the existence of things, what we know about the universe, the solar system, our own earth, with a treatise on creation, with man's advent to the earth, the preparation for man's life upon the earth, with the institution of the gospel in the council of God, the possibility and probability and the absolute assurance, at the last, of revelation and what revelation has brought forth as the Gospel.

The second part, THE WAY, is the development of the everlasting Gospel, in which a brief resume of the different dispensations of it are treated, and in this part the atonement of Jesus Christ is worked out under the scriptures and philosophy, as far as philosophy can be made to apply to it. Six chapters are devoted to that one theme alone. Then comes a chapter on the departure from THE WÅY and another chapter closing this middle section on the Restoration of THE WAY.

The third part, THE LIFE, is a development of about six chapters of the perfect life of the Christ as the ideal of the Gospel.

This in headlines is a description of the treatment of the subject. Each chapter has been written with a design that it would make one lesson and a lesson analysis has been given of each chapter, two samples of which I am enclosing, being the analysis of each chapter of two divisions: Chapter 1 on THE TRUTH; Chapter 29 on the introductory part, THE WAY. This analysis will afford those who are going to use it as a textbook the outlines of a lesson, and will constitute an easy division for assigning parts of the lesson to the respective students.

The experience of the First Council in conducting courses in theology for the five years through which our Seventy's course of theology ran, some twenty years ago, lead us to believe that this method of providing lesson analysis will be again as successful as in our former experience.

All this, President Clawson, is submitted to your council as an offering on the part of the First Council of Seventy for a course of study—more especially for our seventies quorums, but it may be equally available for the quorums of the High Priests and Elders, and we feel that in this book we are following a line of subject matter that will give to them the proper comprehensive outline upon the Gospel as a whole and prepare them for presenting more intelligently the simple, specific message that we have to offer to the world.

Trusting that it may appeal to you and your Council, and that we shall have a prompt consideration of it in time to make it available to our quorums of seventy during the present year.

All of which is

Respectfully submitted,

BHR

P.S. I enclose <for> you herewith the sample lesson analysis as referred to in the body of the letter.

<B. H. Roberts to Rudger Clawson, 17 Sept. 1928, in B. H. Roberts Correspondence, Manuscript SC 1922, Special Collections and Manuscripts, Lee Library, Brigham Young University, Provo, Utah; hereafter abbreviated to Roberts Correspondence at BYU—*Ed.*>

2. RUDGER CLAWSON TO THE READING COMMITTEE

October 3, 1928

Elders George Albert Smith,
David O. McKay,
Joseph Fielding Smith,
Stephen L. Richards, and
Melvin J. Ballard

Dear Brethren:

The correspondence herewith enclosed was returned to the Council of the Twelve by the First Presidency, with verbal instructions that a committee be appointed (preferably the Committee of Courses of Study for the Melchizedek Priesthood) to examine the manuscript of Brother Roberts's work, and make a recommendation as to its suitability for the study of the High Priesthood.

You are now appointed to act as said committee and to make report to the Council of the Twelve.

Sincerely your brother

<signed> Rudger Clawson

<Rudger Clawson to Elders George Albert Smith, David O. McKay, Joseph Fielding Smith, Stephen L. Richards, and Melvin J. Ballard, 3 Oct. 1928, in the Ernest Strack Collection, Ms A 296, Library, Utah State Historical Society, Salt Lake City; hereafter abbreviated to Strack–*Ed.*>

3. B. H. ROBERTS TO THE READING COMMITTEE

October 20, 1928

TO THE COMMITTEE:

I am assured by the Deseret News Publishers that this book can be printed and bound thirty days after the manuscript (which is now perfected) can be placed in their hands.

Respectfully,

<signed> B. H. Roberts

<B. H. Roberts to the Committee, 20 Oct. 1928, in the Edwin B. Firmage Collection, Accession 1074, Bx 45, Fd 17, Manuscripts Division, Marriott Library, University of Utah, Salt Lake City; hereafter abbreviated to Firmage–*Ed.*>

4. GEORGE ALBERT SMITH TO RUDGER CLAWSON

October 10, 1929

President Rudger Clawson and
Members of the Council of Apostles

Dear Brethren:

The subcommittee of the Council of the Apostles appointed to read the manuscript written by Elder B. H. Roberts entitled, THE TRUTH, THE WAY, THE LIFE, make the following report.

The committee secured the manuscript and very carefully and systematically read it through, sitting two sessions each week, until the work was finished.

In the main the manuscript is very worthy treating subjects dealing with the mission of Jesus Christ and gospel principles, which it would be well for all members of the Church to understand. These subjects are faith promoting and would prove to be helpful to the young people of the Church. However, the manuscript could be greatly reduced without injury to the thoughts expressed.

The members of the committee regret to say that there are some objectionable doctrines advanced which are of a speculative nature and appear to be out of harmony with the revelations of the Lord and the fundamental teachings of the Church. Among the outstanding doctrines to which objection is made are: The doctrine that there were races on the earth before Adam; That Adam was a translated being who came to this earth subject to death, and, therefore, did not bring death upon himself and his posterity through the fall; That Adam was placed on the earth when the earth was in a desolate condition and before any other life, belonging to the "dispensation of Adam" was on the earth; That all life preceding Adam was swept off, even to the fishes of the sea, by some great cataclysm so that a new start had to be made; That God the Father is still discovering hidden laws and truth which he does not know, but which are eternal.

The members of the committee met with Brother Roberts on two or three occasions and discussed these matters with him, making the request that he eliminate from his work these objectionable features, but this Brother Roberts has refused to do. At the last interview with him, he informed the committee that if he could not adjust matters and therefore did not obtain the approval of the committee, he would, perhaps, at some future time publish the work on his own responsibility.

The committee, therefore, recommends to the Council of the Twelve that a report of its findings be laid before the First Presidency, with the recommendation that in its present form, the manuscript be not published.

Very respectfully submitted,
<signed> Geo. Albert Smith
Chairman of subcommittee

P.S. A list of objections is here attached.

<On a separate page>

List of Points on Doctrine
in Question by the Committee
in Relation to B. H. Robert<s>'s Ms

Ch.	Page	Subject
1	8	The superiority of the Prophet's definition questioned.

4	1	Size of the sun—figures do not agree with other figures.
4	2	The number of sidereal days of Mars should be checked; also of Jupiter and Saturn.
7	8	The wisdom in referring to Haeckel's theory, which is disputed by many scientists, is questioned.
16	7	Tree had seeds of life and death? The Scriptures do not say so.
18	2	When does the spirit unite with the body? Statement questioned.
27	5	Intelligence and Spirit—confusing terms.
27	12	Spirit-body of Christ—the Word?
27	12	Mind, spirit, and soul? Questioned.
29	5	Baptisms for remision of sins—plural incorrect.
30	6	Place of man in creation. This is not in harmony with the revelations.
31	1	Races on the earth before Adam. This is not a doctrine of the Church.
32	1	Reference to destruction of pre-Adamites. Objected to.
32	3	Adam in a desolate earth. Not accepted by the brethren.
32	3	Adam a translated being. This must be corrected.
34	2	Tree not evil?
34	4	Like God in every respect?
34	5	To know must experience—after "fall" sacrifice?
35	3	Translation development.
35	1	Tree of Life?
35	6	Abel, Adam's "second son," questioned.
35	9	Cain's sacrifice "not what the Lord appointed"?
35	–	When did Adam receive law of sacrifice—in or out of the Garden of Eden?
36	8	Cain's offering? Conflict with Temple account.
38	13	Esaias and Melchizedek the same? Conflict with D&C 84.
38	14	Salem and Samaria the same? Not so.
39	7	Comment on keeping "Commandments"?
41	1	Law of Moses not an eternal law? Inference that it is.
41	4	Evolution and Devolution of worlds?
41	8	Majesty of law—the law vindicated?
41	9	Experimentation and righteousness.
41	10	Vindication of law—4th sentence.

42	9	Progression of God in Knowledge? (Limiting God, questioned.)
46	4	The cause of John Mark leaving the ministry?
47	13	Humble first form<s> of the Church?
50	6-8	Information on divorce? Questioned.

<George Albert Smith to Rudger Clawson, 10 Oct. 1929, with attached "List of Points on Doctrine in Question by the Committee in Relation to B. H. Robert<s>'s Ms," in Roberts Correspondence at BYU—*Ed.*>

5. REPORT OF COMMITTEE TO THE COUNCIL OF THE TWELVE

<early May 1930>

The committee of the Council of the Apostles appointed by the First <P>residency to read the manuscript of Elder B. H. Roberts' "THE TRUTH, THE WAY, THE LIFE" have the following suggestions to make in relation to the points of doctrine considered.

In the main, the committee passed favorably on the manuscript and the members are unanimously of the belief that the work is very timely and will be the means of accomplishing much good among the Latter-day Saints, if some of the teachings can be eliminated. In the judgment of the committee the questioned statements and chapters can be eliminated without violence to the main theme of the book.

It is the duty of the general authorities of the Church to safeguard and protect the membership of the Church from the introduction of controversial subjects and false doctrines, which tend to create factions and otherwise disturb the faith of the Latter-day Saints. There is so much of vital importance revealed and which we can present with clear and convincing presentation and which the world does not possess, that we, the committee, see no reason for the introduction of questions which are speculative, to say the least. More especially so when such teachings appear to be in conflict with the revelations of the Lord.

If the following subjects can be modified, or eliminated where modification will not answer, we would like to recommend that the work be published and used as a text for the Priesthood of the Church in the Gospel Doctrine department.

Chapter 16, page 7, lines 19-21.

"The commandment was given concerning a certain fruit, which seemed to have in it in some way the element<s> of life and death." Since the tree had in it the seeds of death, and no reference is made to seeds of life, cannot this word be eliminated?

Chapter 18:2.

This is a wrong reference, but the statement is in regard to the time the spirit and the body unite. The First Presidency have refused to give a definite answer to this question at any time. Therefore, we feel that a definite statement should not be given.

Chapter 27:5, par. 1.

In this paragraph the thought is not made clear and may lead one to conclude that unorganized, or unbegotten, intelligences may rebel against God. In the opinion of the committee the intention is that these intelligences, after they become *spirits* may rebel, as Lucifer did. Can this be clarified to say this. We do not have any revelation stating that intelligences have power to rebel.

Chapter 29: 5, line 10.

"Baptisms" should be in the singular. We have but one baptism.

Chapter 30.

This entire chapter is questioned by the brethren. It pertains to man's place in the creation. It is not in harmony with the revelations, especially the ceremonies of the Temple, which were given by the Prophet by revelation.

Chapter 31.

This entire chapter is out of harmony with the teachings of the authorities of the Church. The doctrine of pre-Adamites has never been accepted by the Church and is viewed by the brethren as being in conflict with the revelations of the Lord. This is so with the Temple ceremonies.

References in other chapters to these two thoughts–the place of man in creation and pre-Adamites–should be eliminated.

Chapter 32.

Reference to the destruction of pre-Adamites is objected to on the grounds previously stated.

Chapter 32:2.

The expression that Adam was placed in a "desolate earth" is contrary to the views of the authorities, and in our opinion contradicts the revelations of the Lord. It does not harmonize with the Temple ceremonies.

Chapter 32:3.

The statement that Adam and Eve were "translated" beings, who came here from some other world, is not accepted by the brethren. This doctrine does not clear up, but complicates, the question of the Fall.

Chapter 34:5.
The statement that one must "experience evil" may convey the thought that one must commit sin in order to know righteousness. Christ did not sin, yet he "experienced" evil. Can this be changed to avoid this ambiguity?

Chapter 35 to 41—missing.

Chapter 35:6.
The Pearl of Great Price teaches that Cain and Abel were not the first children of Adam and Eve. This reference speaks of Abel as Adam's second son.

Chapter 35:9.
The statement that Cain's sacrifice was not accepted because it was not what the Lord appointed is in conflict with the Temple ceremony. His rejection was because he hearkened to Satan.

Chapter 36:8.
Cain's offering, here mentioned again, is in conflict with Temple teaching.

Chapter 38:13.
Section 84 of the Doctrine and Covenants does not hold with the thought that Melchizedek and Esaias were the same.

Chapter 38:14.
Salem and Samaria were not the same.

Chapter 39:7.
There is here a question on keeping the commandments, but the chapter is missing.

Chapter 41:1.
We feel that, inadvertantly, the statement is made that the law of Moses was an eternal law. It was a temporary one.

Chapter 41:10.
Vindication of law, fourth sentence?

Chapter 42:9, par. 2.
What is the need of stating that God is progressing in knowledge? In other words, that there are laws and eternal truths, which he does not know? This will only lead to controversy and needless discussion and argument, and no purpose accomplished. In the judgment of the committee the state-

ment should not be made. There are scriptures which contradict this thought.

Chapter 46:4.

The statement as to why John Mark left the ministry is questioned. This statement, also, is not necessary to the argument.

Chapter 47:13.

The expression in this chapter, page 1, line 1, may give a false impression. It may appear that the forms of the Church were changed. Some other word could be used.

Chapter 50.

Some things in the argument on divorce were questioned, as appearing in conflict with the revelations.

<Report of Committee to the Council of the Twelve, early May 1930, including a listing of objections, in the David J. Buerger Collection, Manuscript 622, Bx 10, Fd 8, Manuscripts Division, Marriott Library, University of Utah, Salt Lake City; hereafter abbreviated to Buerger—*Ed.*>

6. COUNCIL OF THE TWELVE TO HEBER J. GRANT

May 15, 1930

President Heber J. Grant and Counselors
Building

Dear Brethren:

The Council of the Twelve, to whom was referred the work of Elder B. H. Roberts, "The Truth, the Way, the Life," for consideration, beg to report that they do not regard said work in its present form as a suitable study for the Priesthood quorums of the Church.

Their objections to Elder Roberts's work are clearly set forth in the exceptions taken by their subcommittee, who with Brother Roberts read the manuscript carefuly and discussed the doctrinal points in question. Elder Roberts declined to make the changes or modifications suggested by the Twelve.

The Twelve now submit herewith a copy of the exceptions referred to and also a letter addressed by Elder Roberts to the subcommittee, dated April 28, in which he defines his attitude in regard to his work covered by the manuscript.

Sincerely your brethren,

THE COUNCIL OF THE TWELVE

____

President

<Council of the Twelve to Heber J. Grant, 15 May 1930, in Buerger, Bx 29, Fd 4–*Ed.*>

7. DOCTRINAL POINTS QUESTIONED BY THE COMMITTEE WHICH READ THE MANUSCRIPT OF ELDER B. H. ROBERTS, ENTITLED THE TRUTH, THE WAY, THE LIFE <15 MAY 1930>

Ch.	Page	Subject
<16>	7	That the Tree of the Knowledge of Good and Evil had in it the seeds of life and death, is questioned by the committee.
<21>	9	The committee questions the advisability of stating any given time when the spirit unites with the body. This question has never been definitely settled, although it has been asked of the First Presidency from time to time. The record in the Book of Mormon where Nephi received the word that the Savior was to come into the world is not looked upon as a criterion by which we are to be governed.
27	5-7	Intelligence and Spirit as used in this chapter are confusing terms. The thought may be gathered that "Intelligence"–that eternal entity which was not created, may, and sometimes does, rebel against truth and God. We do not so understand it. Those who rebelled in the world of spirits were *begotten* spirits, who, if they had remained faithful, were prepared to come into this mortal world. The revelation which speaks of intelligence says: "Man was in the beginning with God." (When was this beginning?) Then this thought follows: "Intelligence, or the *light of truth*, was not created or made, neither indeed can be." Again we are taught that "Light and truth"–intelligence–"forsaketh that evil one." This being true, and treating intelligence as an entity, then that entity cannot rebel against light and truth, for it would rebel against itself. <Roberts' handwritten responses were "*clarify*" and that this objection was "*of no substance or importance*" and that there

was a "*misapprehension here,*" since Intelligence was "*that which perceives truth.*">

27 12 The use of the expression "spirit-body of Christ," and "the Word," is not made clear to use, and we are left to wonder if these terms apply to the "Intelligence" or to the begotten spirit of Jesus Christ.

<Roberts' handwritten response was: "clarify.">

27 12 The use of "Mind, spirit, and soul" appears confusing to us.

29 5 "Baptisms for the remision of sins." We question the plural.

30 6 The place of man in the order of creation is questioned, as it is taught in this chapter. The expression, "the first flesh upon the earth also," is not interpreted by members of the committee as you have expressed it here. We feel that the arguments as given contradict the accounts given in all our scriptures, and more especially in the temple ceremonies. As we understand it the term, "first flesh also," does not have reference to Adam as being the first living creature of the creation on the earth, but that he, through the "fall" became the first "flesh," or mortal soul. The term "flesh" in reference to mortal existence is of common usage. We find it so used in the scriptures. Adam, having partaken of the fruit, became mortal and subject to death, which was not the condition until that time. We are taught in the Temple, as well as in the scriptures, that man was the last creation placed upon the earth, before death was introduced. Adam was the first to partake of the change and to become subject to the *flesh*. This is the view expressed by President Joseph F. Smith and President Anthon H. Lund. Following are example<s> bearing out this thought:

"They shall wander in the flesh, and perish" (1 Ne. 19:14).

"And now, if I do err, even did they err of old; not that I would excuse myself because of other men, but because of the weakness which is in me, according to the flesh, I would excuse myself" (1 Ne. 19:6).

"And it is a rare thing that the king requireth, and there is none other than can shew it before the king, except the gods, whose dwelling is not with flesh" (Dan. 2:11).

"That he no longer should live the rest of his time in the flesh to the lust<s> of men, but to the will of God" (1 Pet. 4:2).

"No man hath seen God at any time in the flesh, except quickened by the Spirit of God" (D&C 67:11).

31 1 This entire chapter deals with the question of "pre-Adamites." This doctrine is not taught by the Church; it is not sustained in the scriptures. It can only be treated as an hypothesis, and the result will be uncertain, confusing, for after all is said it is speculation leading to endless controversy. We are aware that one of the brethren (Orson Hyde) in an early day advocated this teaching. However, we feel that the brethren of the general authorities cannot be too careful, and should not present as doctrine that which is not sustained in the standards of the Church. It appears to us that all which has been revealed is contrary to this teaching, especially that given in the Temple.

<Roberts' handwritten responses were that he had *"not so presented"* this teaching and that Orson Hyde's teaching *"was approved also by Pres. Young."*>

32 3 "They came to plant their race in a desolate earth."
This is questioned by the committee. According to the revelations bearing on the question, the earth was fully prepared for Adam and pronounced "good," before he was placed upon it, and was full of life and beauty.

32 3 The doctrine that Adam came here a "translated" being from some other world is not accepted as a doctrine of the Church. The theory that he came here from some other world a "translated" being does not take care of the element of "death" as that condition came into the world, for translated beings are subject to death according to the teaching in the Book of Mormon (3 Ne. 28:36-40). The scriptures teach us that Adam was not subject to death before the "fall," and would have lived for ever in that innocent state, if he had not "transgressed" the law. His "fall" changed the condition and brought death into the world, which could not have happened if death was already here. It is true that Adam had not passed through the resurrection (2 Ne. 2:22, Alma 12:26, and other passages).

34 5 "To know any one of these you must experience its opposite."
This thought raises some questions. While it is necessary that there be opposition in all things, yet a man does not have to sin, or come in contact with wickedness by partaking

		of it, to know it. We may have failed in grasping the meaning here.
35	3	The question of "translation" comes in here, and is questioned, as in 32.
35 [34]	1	"Temporal physical life." This we question in the light of the Book of Mormon revelation (2 Ne. 2:22).
35	6	"Abel, Adam's second son." We question this in the light of the writings of Moses. Adam may have had many sons and daughters before Cain was born; so it appears.
35	9	Cain's sacrifice, not what the Lord appointed. Also
36	8	the statement in regard to Cain's offering, because he offered fruits. It was not because he offered fruits, but because he hearkened unto Satan rather than unto God (P. of G.P., Moses 5:18-23).
35	–	There is a question as to the time the law of sacrifice was given, whether it was in or out of the Garden.
38	13	We question the statement that Esaias and Melchizedek are the same, based on what is written in D&C 84. <Roberts' handwritten response was *"obj[ection] not valid."*
38	14	We also question the statement that Salem and Samaria are the same. <Roberts' handwritten responses were *"obj[ection] not valid"* and *"not mine quote Ency. Jewish."*
39	7	The law of Moses not an eternal law. In the chapter it is so stated with other law.
41	4	Evolution and devolution of worlds, as stated here, is questioned. Worlds pass away, just as this earth shall, but go on through the resurrection, or renewing, to continue their existence in permanent or immortal form (D&C 29 and 88).
41	8	The Majesty of law—vindicated?
41	9	Experimentation and righteousness, last two lines, par. 1?
41	10	Vindication of law, fourth sentence?
42	9	Progression of God in knowledge. This thought is not accepted by members of the committee. We do not feel that it is wise to express a thought limiting God in this manner, which will cause needless controversy. While we believe in eternal progression and that God is progressing, it is not in quest of hidden truth or laws yet undiscovered to Deity. We prefer to believe with Nephi: "O how great the holiness of our God! For he knoweth all things, and there is not anything save he

		knows it" (2 Ne. 9:20). Moreover, we believe that His progress is because of his knowledge and that he is the author of law (D&C 88:42). <Roberts' handwritten response was "*meaningless.*">
46	4	The cause of John Mark leaving the ministry, questioned.
47	13	"Humble first forms of the Church." We think that this expression may be misunderstood and that the thought may be conveyed that the forms of the Church have been changed, rather than developed. <Roberts' handwritten response was "*nonsense!*">
50	6-8	The question of divorce does not seem clear to us as here stated, and in harmony with the words of the Savior. <Roberts' handwritten response was "*nothing more to be said.*">

<This list, entitled "Doctrinal Points Questioned by the Committee Which Read Manuscript of Elder B. H. Roberts, Entitled The Truth, The Way, The Life," appears to have been attached to the Council of the Twelve, Committee Report to Heber J. Grant, 15 May 1930. The list is located in Buerger, Bx 29, Fd 4; the italicized comments that follow several of the committee statements give the marginal handwritten responses of B. H. Roberts, which are more legible in the copy located in Firmage–*Ed.*>

8. B. H. ROBERTS TO HEBER J. GRANT

December 15, 1930

President Heber J. Grant
And Counselors
Building

Dear Brethren:

I am writing you to ask if the article published in the *Utah Genealogical and Historical Magazine* of October 1930, under the title "Faith Leads to a Fulness of Truth and Righteousness," dealing mainly with the antiquity of the life and death upon the earth and treated as a discourse by Elder Joseph Fielding Smith on the 5th of April, 1930, is a treatise on that subject that was submitted to and approved by the Council of the First Presidency and perhaps the Quorum of the Twelve? And is it put forth as the official declaration of the Church on the subject treated? Or is it the unofficial and personal declaration of the opinion only of Elder Smith?

In the latter event then I feel that that fact should have been expressed in the discourse; or if it is an official pronouncement of the Church, then that fact should have been avowed; for the strictly dogmatical and the pronounced finality of the discourse demand the suggested explanation in either case.

If the discourse of Elder Smith is merely his personal opinion, while not questioning his right to such opinions, and also the right to express them, when so avowed as his personal opinions, yet I object to the dogmatic and finality spirit of the pronouncement and the apparent official announcement of them, as if speaking with final authority.

If Elder Smith is merely putting forth his own opinions, I call in question his competency to utter such dogmatism either as a scholar or as an Apostle. I am sure he is not competent to speak in such manner from general learning or special research work on the subject; nor as an Apostle, as in that case he would be in conflict with the plain implication at least of the scriptures, both ancient and modern, and with the teaching of a more experienced and learned and earlier Apostle <Orson Hyde> than himself, and a contemporary of the Prophet Joseph Smith–whose public discourse on the subject appears in the *Journal of Discourses* and was publicly endorsed by President Brigham Young, all which would have more weight in setting forth doctrine than this last dictum of Elder Smith.

My question is important as affecting, finally, the faith and status of a very large portion of the Priesthood and educated membership of the Church, I am sure; and I trust the matter will receive early consideration. All which is respectfully submitted.

Very truly your brother,

<signed B. H. Roberts>

BHR/c

<B. H. Roberts to President Heber J. Grant and Counselors, 15 Dec. 1930, in the Scott G. Kenney Collection, Ms 587, Bx 4, Fd 19, Manuscripts Division, Marriott Library, University of Utah, Salt Lake City–*Ed.*>

9. B. H. ROBERTS TO RUDGER CLAWSON

December 31, 1930

President Rudger Clawson
Building

Dear Brother:

Referring to our telephone conversation of yesterday, I think very likely I misapprehended the purpose of your request for a more definite statement of my objections to the discourse of Elder Joseph Fielding Smith, published in the *Utah Genealogical Magazine* of October 1930, that <than> what was found in my letter to the First Presidency of December 15, 1930. At first I thought you had in mind the preparation and submission of a paper presenting the whole volume of statement of facts together with such argument as I might wish to make in presenting the whole subject to the council of the twelve, who are asked to consider the matter presented in Elder Smith's discourse and my letter.

Thinking of the matter afterwards, however, has convinced me that I was mistaken in that view, and desiring to facilitate progress in developing consideration of the subject before your memorable body, I herewith submit the following explanation of my letter.

First. The purpose of my letter meant to secure from the First Presidency a simple statement whether or not the discourse of Elder Smith had been submitted to them, and perhaps to the Twelve, and had been approved by them as representing what was to be considered the attitude of the Church upon that subject. If that were the case, I tried to express the thought that that fact ought to have been mentioned in the discourse, because of the apparent air of finality and authority of the pronouncement. It occurred to me that if the discourse was to be regarded as the authoritative attitude of the Church it ought to have been made by someone else than Elder Smith, or else the announcement made that he was authorized to speak for the Presidency and other authorities of the church, since hitherto the Church has made no authoritative statement on the subject.

Second. If the dogmatic and apparently final utterance on the subject treated was after all but the expression of Elder Smith's personal views, then such fact ought somewhere to appear in the discourse that the hearers and readers might know what weight to accord the pronouncement made.

Third. I meant to imply by what was said in my letter that if the discourse of Elder Smith was but the expression of his personal views, then I questioned his competency to speak with such dogmatic finality as he does in the discourse on the subject, (a) either by reason of his general learning or any known special research on the subject involved, and (b) that as an apostle Elder Smith was not competent to make such a positive and apparently not-to-be questioned pronouncement, because an earlier and a more experienced and learned apostle had made a directly opposite statement on the subject, which statement Brigham Young, President of the Church, publically approved, both which statement and approval, were published in the *Journal of Discourses*.

Fourth. I meant to imply in my letter that in view of all this, Elder Smith was not warranted in making such a positive and dogmatic statement, and that I had the right to know if he spoke by the authority of an agreed upon attitude of the present administration of the church or not–hence the questions of my letter to the First Presidency.

Fifth. To all this I add the following: I call in question the accuracy of Elder

Smith's position in reference to the whole doctrine of his discourse, as being contrary to a great volume of well developed and ascertained truth, established by the researches of scientists of highest character, of profoundest learning, and world-wide research. I hold his doctrine contrary at least to the plain implications of the scriptures; as tending also to reduce the church of the New Dispensation to the character of a narrow, bigoted sect, forsaking the God-given world movement idea of it; and as injurious to the continued faith in, and adherence to, the teachings of the Church not by a "scattered few," but by a very great number of its membership.

Of course, I stand ready to maintain the truth of these statements, if given the opportunity, and I respectfully ask for permission to do so.

Very respectfully,

BHR

<B. H. Roberts to Rudger Clawson, 31 Dec. 1930, in Strack–*Ed.*>

10. B. H. ROBERTS TO HEBER J. GRANT

<9 February 1931>

President Heber J. Grant and Counselors
Building

Dear Brethren:

I feel almost as if I ought to apologize in addressing this letter to you lest you think that I am over-persistent in the representation of things referred to herein.

You will recall that the letter I wrote to you asking the questions in relation to the status of Elder Joseph Fielding Smith's discourse published in the *Genealogical Magazine* for October last, was referred to the Twelve for consideration. Agreeably to a request of theirs I submitted a paper (fifty typewritten pages) setting forth precisely some of the objections I had to the discourse. Two weeks later, bringing us to January 21, Elder Smith submitted a paper of about the same length to the Apostles, myself being present. Since which time I have understood that a report was made to the First Presidency of which I have no copy. That is now three weeks ago and just what the status of the discussion or action upon it is I have not, up to the present, learned.

The questions involved are of very great importance from my standpoint. As for instance, I would not like the matter to go to judgment as matters now stand until I have an opportunity to point out what to me are the weakness and inconsistency of Elder Smith's paper. There was really no discussion on the subject before the Twelve, except the presentation of these two papers, and they represent solely the basis of discussion, not the discussion itself. And I have much more to present after hearing Elder Smith's reply to my paper, which should be said before any decision is rendered.

To me both the discourse on the points questioned and the paper in defense of them is slighter than a house of cards. Yet it was on such pabulum as this that suspended the publication of my book—now in manuscript—"The Truth, The Way, The Life"! This book from my judgment of it is the most important work that I have yet contributed to the Church, the six-volumed *Comprehensive History of the Church* not omitted.

Life at my years and with an incurable ailment is very precarious, and I should dislike very much to pass on without completing and publishing this work. I therefore ask that in any arrangement that may be made for a further hearing, I may be permitted to present my views on Elder Smith's paper in reply to mine, and if the position he has taken can be met successfully, then I think the principal cause of suspending the publication of my work, "The Truth, The Way, The Life" will be removed.

All which is respectfully submitted,

Very truly your brother,

(signed) B. H. Roberts.

<B. H. Roberts to Heber J. Grant and Counselors, 9 Feb. 1931, quoted in 5 Apr. 1931 letter of the First Presidency to the General Authorities, in Roberts Correspondence at BYU—*Ed.*>

11. FIRST PRESIDENCY TO THE GENERAL AUTHORITIES

April 5, 1931

TO THE COUNCIL OF THE TWELVE,
THE FIRST COUNCIL F SEVENTY,
AND THE PRESIDING BISHOPRIC.

Dear Brethren:

On the 5th of April, 1930, at a conference of the Genealogical Society of Utah, Elder Joseph Fielding Smith delivered a sermon under the title "Faith Leads to a Fulness of Truth and Righteousness."

This sermon was published in the *Utah Genealogical and Historical Magazine*, and copies of it in pamphlet form were distributed, which gave it wide circulation.

In the sermon referred to, Elder Smith devotes the greater portion of his remarks to the subject of the creation of the earth and the relationship of our Father Adam to it and its inhabitants. He refers to the conflict which exists between geologists and the scripture dates which are given, in regard to the period of time that has elapsed since the creation to the present, and definitely states that there was no death upon the earth, either vegetable, insect, or animal, prior to the fall of man, and that human life did not exist upon the earth prior to Adam.

On the 15th of December, 1930, Elder B. H. Roberts submitted the following letter to the First Presidency:

> President Heber J. Grant, and Counselors
> Building.
>
> Dear Brethren:
>
> I am writing you to ask if the article published in the *Utah Genealogical and Historical Magazine* of October 1930, under the title "Faith Leads to a Fulness of Truth and Righteousness," dealing mainly with the antiquity of life and death upon the earth and treated as a discourse by Elder Joseph Fielding Smith on the 5th of April, 1930, is a treatise on that subject that was submitted to and approved by the Council of the First Presidency and perhaps the Quorum of the Twelve? And is it put forth as the official declaration of the Church on the subject treated? Or is it the unofficial and personal declaration of the opinion only of Elder Smith?
>
> In the latter event then I feel that that fact should have been expressed in the discourse; or if it is an official pronouncement of the Church then that fact should have been avowed; for the strictly dogmatical and the pronounced finality of the discourse demand the suggested explanation in either case.
>
> If the discourse of Elder Smith is merely his personal opinion, while not questioning his right to such opinions, and also the right to express them, when avowed as his personal opinions, yet I object to the dogmatic and finality spirit of the pronouncement and the apparent official announcement of them, as if speaking with final authority.
>
> If Elder Smith is merely putting forth his own opinions, I call in question his competency to utter such dogmatism, either as a scholar or as an Apostle. I am sure he is not competent to speak in such manner from general learning or special research work on the subject; nor as an Apostle, as in that case he would be in conflict with the plain implication at least of the scriptures, both ancient and modern, and with the teaching of a more experienced and learned and earlier Apostle <Orson Hyde> than himself, and a contemporary of the Prophet Joseph Smith—whose public discourse on the subject appears in the *Journal of Discourses* and was publicly endorsed by President Brigham Young, all which would have more weight in setting forth doctrine than this last dictum of Elder Smith.
>
> My question is important as affecting, finally, the faith and status of a very large portion of the Priesthood and educated membership of the Church, I am sure;

and I trust the matter will receive early consideration. All which is respectfully submitted.

Very truly your brother,
(signed) B. H. Roberts.

The sermon referred to, with this letter, was handed by the Presidency to the Council of Twelve with the request that the matter be taken up, and the difference of opinion which existed between the two brethren be composed.

At a meeting of the Council of Twelve, Elder Roberts was invited to be present and submit his findings upon the question at issue, the principal point involved being: Is the age of the earth greater than that set forth in the scripture, as it is given in the Bible, and was Adam the first human life upon it, or does he represent the first of the human race that now occupy it, and may human life have existed prior to his advent.

Elder Roberts appeared before the Council of Twelve and submitted a paper of fifty pages, in which he quotes copiously from the sermon of Elder Smith, and then proceeds to discuss the following statements made in the sermon:

> All life in the sea, on the earth, in the air, was without death. Things were not changing, as we find them changing in this mortal existence, for mortality had not come. I denounce as absolutely false the opinion of some that this earth was peopled by a race before Adam. I do not care what scientists say in regard to dinosaurs and other creatures upon the earth millions of years ago, that lived and died, and fought and struggled for existence.

Elder Roberts quotes from the scripture and extensively from the conclusions reached by the leading scientists of the world, to show that the earth is older than the time given to its creation in Genesis indicates. He places much stress upon the command of the Lord to Adam in which he says: "Be fruitful, and multiply, and replenish the earth" <Genesis 1:28>. The word replenish he defines to mean to do a thing which has been done before, or refill that which has been made empty.

He quotes a statement made by Apostle Orson Hyde who, at a general conference of the Church, held October 1854, declared that there were people upon the earth prior to the advent of Adam. Brigham Young and other of the presiding officers were present, and after the remarks made by Elder Hyde, President Young arose and said:

> I do not wish to eradicate any items from the lecture Elder Hyde has given us this evening, but simply to give you my views in a few words on the portion touching Bishops and Deacons. We have had a splendid address from Brother Hyde, for which I am grateful. I say to the congregation, Treasure up in your hearts what you have heard tonight, and at all other times.

Two weeks after Elder Roberts had submitted his paper Elder Smith appeared before the Council of Twelve and submitted a paper consisting of fifty-eight pages, in which he answers the arguments advanced by Elder Roberts, his contention being that Adam was the first man to come to this earth, and that consequently it could not have been previously inhabited by man; that there was no death upon the earth prior to the fall, neither vegetable, insect, or animal, which of course includes man.

In support of his argument he quotes extensively from the scripture, and from sermons of presiding men of the Church, particularly from the sermons of Orson Pratt, who refers to Adam as the first man, the first of all men, the Ancient of Days, etc. To meet the argument of Elder Roberts in the application of the word replenish he shows that the word may be used, and signifies, to fill as well as to fill again.

To meet the statement of Orson Hyde, Elder Smith says that Orson Hyde was not discussing the subject of Pre-Adamites, but was preaching upon marriage, and referred to Pre-Adamites incidentally. He admits that President Young was present, and that he endorsed the remarks made.

While there are many quotations cited by Elder Smith which refer to Adam as the first man, the following is the only one in which a pre-Adamic race is referred to. It is quoted under the heading, "Testimony of Charles W. Penrose":

> It is held by some that Adam was not the first man upon this earth, and that the original human being was a development from lower orders of the animal creation. These, however, are the theories of men. The word of the Lord declares that Adam was the first of all men (Moses 1:34), and we are, therefore, in duty bound to regard him as the primal parent of our race.
>
> (signed) Joseph F. Smith
> John R. Winder
> Anthon H. Lund.

While this quotation is signed by the Presidency of the Church, it is given under the heading of "Testimony of President Charles W. Penrose."

After hearing granted to Elder Smith the following communication was received by the Presidency:

January 21, 1931

President Heber J. Grant & Counselors,

Dear Brethren:

We, the Council of the Twelve, to whom was referred the letter of Elder B. H. Roberts addressed to the First Presidency, a criticism of a certain discourse delivered by Elder Joseph Fielding Smith and published in the *Genealogical Magazine*, October 1930, beg leave to report that we have given the time of three rather lengthy meetings to this matter.

At the first meeting Elder Roberts read and submitted a paper embodying his views at some length on the theory of pre-Adamic races, based on scientific investigation—a theory, we understand, which Elder Roberts has promulgated in some of his public utterances among the Latter-day Saints.

At the third meeting Elder Joseph Fielding Smith read and submitted a paper in which he defended the claim he made in the sermon published in the *Genealogical Magazine* above referred to, viz.; that pre-Adamic races on the earth is simply a theory and not a Church doctrine, and is not true. This he sought to prove by quoting Joseph Smith, the Prophet, Brigham Young, Parley P. Pratt, Orson Pratt, John Taylor, and other high Church Authorities, particularly the late First Presidency, Joseph F. Smith, John R. Winder, and Anthon H. Lund.

He also quoted a number of passages from the Bible, Book of Mormon, Doctrine & Covenants, and Pearl of Great Price, pointing to the facts, as he construed them, that there were no pre-Adamic races of man on the earth, neither was there death upon the earth prior to the time of Adam.

We quote a sentence from Elder Roberts' letter: "If Elder Smith is merely putting forth his own opinions, I call in question his competency to utter such dogmatism, either as a scholar or as an Apostle. I am sure he is not competent to speak in such manner from general learning or special research work on the plain implication at least of the scriptures, both ancient and modern, and with the teaching of a more experienced and learned and earlier Apostle than himself, and a contemporary of the Prophet Joseph Smith."

This reference and language we regard as very offensive on the part of Elder Roberts, who fails to show the deference due from one brother to another brother of higher rank in the Priesthood. However, it may be said that these brethren affirmed at the close of the meeting that they entertained no ill feeling, one toward the other.

Elder Roberts' letter is herewith returned, and the two papers alluded to are now submitted to the Presidency. The Twelve await your further instructions relative to this matter, if you have any to give.

Sincerely your brethren,
The Council of the Twelve
By (signed) Elder Clawson, Pres.

It will be observed that no suggestion is made in this communication regarding the attitude of the Council of Twelve in respect to the question involved in the controversy under consideration.

On February 9th the following communication was received from Elder Roberts:

President Heber J. Grant and Counselors
Building

Dear Brethren:

I feel almost as if I ought to apologize in addressing this letter to you lest you think that I am over-persistent in the representation of things referred to herein.

You will recall that the letter I wrote to you asking the questions in relation to the status of Elder Joseph Fielding Smith's discourse published in the *Genealogical Magazine* for October last, was referred to the Twelve for consideration. Agreeably to a request of theirs I submitted a paper (fifty typewritten pages) setting forth precisely some of the objections I had to the discourse. Two weeks later, bringing us to January 21, Elder Smith submitted a paper of about the same length to the Apostles, myself being present. Since which time I have understood that a report was made to the First Presidency of which I have no copy. That is now three weeks ago and just what the status of the discussion or action upon it is I have not, up to the present, learned.

The questions involved are of very great importance from my standpoint. As for instance, I would not like the matter to go to judgment as matters now stand until I have an opportunity to point out what to me are the weakness and inconsistency of Elder Smith's paper. There was really no discussion on the subject before the Twelve, except the presentation of these two papers, and they represent solely the basis of discussion, not the discussion itself. And I have much more to present after hearing Elder Smith's reply to my paper, which should be said before any decision is rendered.

To me both the discourse on the points questioned and the paper in defense of them is slighter than a house of cards. Yet it was on such pabulum as this that suspended the publication of my book—now in manuscript—"The Truth, The Way, The Life"! This book from my judgment of it is the most important work that I have yet contributed to the Church, the six-volumed *Comprehensive History of the Church* not omitted.

Life at my years and with an incurable ailment is very precarious, and I should dislike very much to pass on without completing and publishing this work. I therefore ask that in any arrangement that may be made for a further hearing, I may be permitted to present my views on Elder Smith's paper in reply to mine, and if the position he has taken can be met successfully, then I think the principal cause of suspending the publication of my work, "The Truth, The Way, The Life," will be removed.

All which is respectfully submitted,
Very truly your brother,
(signed) B. H. Roberts.

After receipt of this latter communication the Presidency carefully reviewed the papers which had been submitted to the Council of Twelve, and after prayerful consideration decided that nothing would be gained by a continuation of the discussion of the subject under consideration.

The statement made by Elder Smith that the existence of pre-Adamites is not a doctrine of the Church is true. It is just as true that the statement: "There were not pre-Adamites upon the earth" is not a doctrine of the Church. Neither side of the controversy has been accepted as a doctrine at all.

Both parties make the scripture and the statements of men who have been prominent in the affairs of the Church the basis of their contention; neither has produced definite proof in support of his views.

We quote the following from the *Millennial Star*, February 19, 1931:

> The sun is giving out energy daily. In a few million (or billion) years its energy will be gone. The other heavenly bodies are radiating and losing their heat; and in time they will be no better off than the age-bitten sun. The universe will run down. Then, on earth, there will be no summer and winter, perhaps no light and day, but just eternal twilight of middle-African temperature, in the monotony of which all life will perish. So warns Sir James Jeans, famous British scientist and brilliant writer and lecturer. Well for us that <the> day is distant—a billion years or so—but think of the grandchildren!
>
> There is a ray of hope!
>
> Dr. Robert A. Millikan, famous American scientist and brilliant writer and lecturer, has discovered cosmic rays, sources of energy, that come from the uttermost confines of the universe to replenish the energy we lose by radiation. Out in the depths of space, by means unknown to us, the lost energy is assembled, converted, concentrated, and sent back to delay the evil day. In short, Dr. Millikan says that this is a self-winding, self-repairing, deathless universe. Day and night, summer and winter, may follow one another endlessly. That is more cheerful.
>
> Whom are we to believe? These men are both world famous, both experimenters of the first rank, both honest men. Perhaps Dr. Millikan gives us a clue in his address as retiring president of the American Association for the Advancement of Science, delivered last Christmas week. He says: "If Sir James Jeans prefers to hold one view and I another on this question, no one can say us nay. The one thing of which you may all be quite sure is that neither of us *knows* anything about it" <John A. Widtsoe, "When Doctors Disagree," *The Latter-day Saints' Millennial Star* 93 (19 February 1931): 120>.

This is the frank and truthful admission of one of the foremost scientists of the world, an honest man, earnestly searching after truth, which he admits has not been definitely discovered.

The Prophet Joseph Smith said:

> Oh, Ye Elders of Israel, hearken to my voice; and when you are sent into the world to preach, tell those things you are sent to tell; preach, and cry aloud, repent ye, for the kingdom of heaven is at hand; repent and believe the gospel; declare the first principles, and let mysteries alone, lest ye be overthrown. Elder <Pelatiah> Brown, when you go to Palmyra say nothing about the four beasts, but preach those things the Lord has told you to preach about—repentance and baptism for the remission of sins <*History of the Church of Jesus Christ of Latter-day Saints, Period I* (Salt Lake City: Deseret News, 1909), 5:344>.

We call attention to the fact that when one of the general authorities of the Church makes a definite statement in regard to any doctrine, particularly when the statement is made in a dogmatic declaration of finality, whether he express it as his opinion or not, he is regarded as voicing the Church, and his statements are accepted as the approved doctrines of the Church, which they should be.

Upon the fundamental doctrines of the Church we are all agreed. Our mission is to bear the message of the restored gospel to the people of the world. Leave Geology, Biology, Archaeology, and Anthropology, no one of which has to do with the salvation of the souls of mankind, to scientific research, while we magnify our calling in the realm of the Church.

We can see no advantage to be gained by a continuation of the discussion to which reference is here made, but on the contrary are certain that it would lead to confusion, division, and misunderstanding if carried further. Upon one thing should all be able to agree, namely, that Presidents Joseph F. Smith, John R. Winder, and Anthon H. Lund were right when they said: "Adam is the primal parent of our race."

Heber J. Grant,
Anthony W. Ivins,
Charles W. Nibley,
First Presidency.

<First Presidency to the Council of the Twelve, the First Council of Seventy, and the Presiding Bishopric, 5 Apr. 1931, in Roberts Correspondence at BYU; a copy of pp. 5-7 of the seven-page letter is in Strack—*Ed.*>

12. RUDGER CLAWSON TO GEORGE ALBERT SMITH

April 10, 1931

George Albert Smith, Chairman

David O. McKay,
Joseph Fielding Smith,
Stephen L. Richards,
Melvin J. Ballard,
Members of Committee

Dear Brethren:

Under the reference made by the First Presidency to the Twelve on Thursday, I appoint you as the committee to call in Brother Roberts and to make an earnest effort to compose matters and induce him, if possible, to consent to the elimination from his manuscript of any illusion <allusion> to the theory of a pre-Adamic race or races on the earth, and also other minor objections already reported by your committee.

If Brother Roberts refuses to eliminate from the manuscript the objectionable features referred to, he should be given to understand that his manuscript cannot be published and could not be used as a textbook by the quorums of the Priesthood of the Church.

Trusting that Brother Roberts will see the wisdom of making the concessions desired, that an excellent work may not go unpublished and be lost to the Church, I am,

Sincerely your brother,

(signed) Rudger Clawson

H.

<Rudger Clawson to George Albert Smith and Committee, 10 Apr. 1931, in Strack–*Ed.*>

13. B. H. ROBERTS TO JAMES E. TALMAGE

March 18, 1932

My Dear Dr. Talmage:

I am sending you the chapter from "The Truth, The Way, and The Life" agreed upon in our conversation. I am sending it to you in the same form it passed into the hands of the Committee of the Twelve, but since its return I have added a few pages more of evidence in relation to the Antiquity of Man than was contained in the chapter as they read it. The spirit and facts of the chapter, however, are in no way changed, but the evidence has been a little increased.

I shall appreciate it, if after you have read it you will return same. I do not wish to have it copied by anyone.

Truly yours,

<signed B. H. Roberts>

Dr. James E. Talmage,
Building.

<B. H. Roberts to James E. Talmage, 18 Mar. 1932, in the B. H. Roberts Collection, Manuscript 106, Bx 18, Fd 1, Manuscripts Division, Marriott Library, University of Utah, Salt Lake City–*Ed.*>

14. JAMES E. TALMAGE TO B. H. ROBERTS

March 21, 1932

President B. H. Roberts
Building

My dear Brother Roberts:

Herewith I return with thanks the chapter from "The Truth, The Way, and The Life," which you so kindly sent to me, at my request, on the 18th.

I have read the chapter with much interest and profit, and am glad to have now a personal knowledge of its contents. Sometime, perhaps, I may have the privilege of a personal chat with you on the subject so comprehensively treated in this chapter. The paper has not left my hands since I received it, and no copy of any part thereof has been made.

With best wishes for your welfare, now and forever.

Sincerely, your brother,

<signed> James E. Talmage

S

<James E. Talmage to B. H. Roberts, 21 Mar. 1932, in the B. H. Roberts Collection, Manuscript 106, Bx 18, Fd 1, Manuscripts Division, Marriott Library, University of Utah, Salt Lake City–*Ed.*>

SELECTED BIBLIOGRAPHY OF B. H. ROBERTS'S WRITINGS

(in chronological order)

Roberts, B. H. "Self Government." *The Contributor* 1 (Jan. 1880): 93-94.

____________. "The Warfare Then and Now." *The Contributor* 1 (Sep. 1880): 285-86.

____________. "Justice and Mercy." *The Contributor* 2 (Sept. 1881): 373-75.

____________. "Social Evils." *The Contributor* 3 (July 1882): 309-11.

____________. "Does the Bible Contain All the Scriptures?" *The Contributor* 5 (Nov. 1883): 69-72.

____________. "Slander." *The Contributor* 5 (Feb. 1884): 181-84.

____________. "Perfect Law of Liberty." *The Contributor* 5 (Mar. 1884): 222-24.

____________. "An Inspired Prayer." *The Juvenile Instructor* 19 (1 May 1884): 130-31.

____________. "A Fair Infidel." *The Juvenile Instructor* 19 (15 May 1884): 148-49.

____________. "Tying up a 'Mormon' Elder." *The Juvenile Instructor* 19 (1 June 1884): 171-72.

____________. "Fruits of Disobedience." *The Juvenile Instructor* 19 (15 June 1884): 178-79.

____________. "The Tennessee Massacre." *The Latter-day Saints' Millennial Star* 46 (15 Sept. 1884): 577-80.

____________. "Advantages of the Youth of Zion." *The Juvenile Instructor* 19 (15 Sept. 1884): 283-84.

____________. "Celestial Marriage and Acts of Congress." *The Contributor* 6 (Nov. 1884-Apr. 1885): 50-54, 107-11, 134-39, 168-72, 205-10, 252-56.

____________. "Joseph Smith's Mission." *Journal of Discourses* 25 (1884): 130-43.

____________. "The Gospel." *The Juvenile Instructor* 20 (Jan.-Feb. 1885): 4-5, 28-29, 43, 52-53.

____________. "To the Youth of Israel." *The Contributor* 6 (May-Sept. 1885): 294-99, 336-40, 377-81, 410-13, 456-59.

____________. "Celestial Marriage." *The Latter-day Saints' Millennial Star* 49 (28 Mar. 1887): 193-97.

____________. "A Prophecy and Its Fulfillment." *The Contributor* 9 (Nov. 1887): 27-29.

____________. "Mormonism." *The Latter-day Saints' Millennial Star* 50 (30 Jan. 1888): 65-67.

____________. "The Gods and Their Government." *The Contributor* 9 (Jan. 1888): 115-18.

____________. "Mormonism and Education." *The Contributor* 9 (Feb. 1888): 157-60.

____________. "The Growth and Stability of Mormonism." *The Latter-day Saints' Millennial Star* 50 (12 Mar. 1888): 163-66.

____________. "David Whitmer." *The Contributor* 9 (Mar. 1888): 169-72.

____________. "Missionaries and Their Treatment." *The Contributor* 9 (Apr. 1888): 226-28.

____________. "False and True Notions of a God." *The Contributor* 9 (May 1888): 251-53.

____________. *The Gospel: An Exposition of Its First Principles.* Salt Lake City: The Contributor Company, 1888; the rev. and enlarged 2d ed. of 1893 has "Man's Relationship to Deity" as a supplement; the 3d ed. of 1901 has title as *The Gospel: An Exposition of Its First Principles; and Man's Relationship to Deity.*

____________, using penname "Horatio." "Legitimate Fiction." *The Contributor* 10 (Feb. 1889): 133-36.

____________. "Man's Relationship to Deity." *The Contributor* 10 (Mar.-May, Oct. 1889): 177-83, 212-16, 263-68, 451-55.

____________. "Moroni: A Sketch of the Nephite Republic." *The Contributor* 11 (Nov. 1889-Oct. 1890): 15-18, 54-58, 81-85, 131-36, 164-68, 227-31, 262-66, 293-96, 335-40, 385-88, 445-50.

____________. "Joseph the Prophet." *The Contributor* 12 (Dec. 1890): 57-60.

____________. "Public Speaking." *The Contributor* 12 (Oct. 1891): 457-59.

____________. "Comprehensiveness of the Gospel." *The Contributor* 13 (July 1892): 393-98.

____________. *Life of John Taylor, Third President of the Church of Jesus Christ of Latter-day Saints.* Salt Lake City: George Q. Cannon and Sons Co., 1892.

____________. *Outlines of Ecclesiastical History.* Salt Lake City: George Q. Cannon and Sons, 1893.

____________. *Succession in the Presidency of the Church of Jesus Christ of Latter-day Saints.* Salt Lake City: The Deseret News Publishing Co., 1894.

____________. *A New Witness for God.* Salt Lake City: George Q. Cannon and Sons, 1895; *New Witness for God,* listed as vol. 2, and used as the Young Men's Mutual Improvement Association manual for the years 1903-1904 and 1904-1905; published in 3 vols. in 1909-1911 with title, *New Witnesses for God.*

____________. "A Sufficient Answer to Josephites." *Improvement Era* 1 (Feb. 1898): 272-81.

____________. "The Claims, Doctrines, and Organization of the Church of Jesus Christ

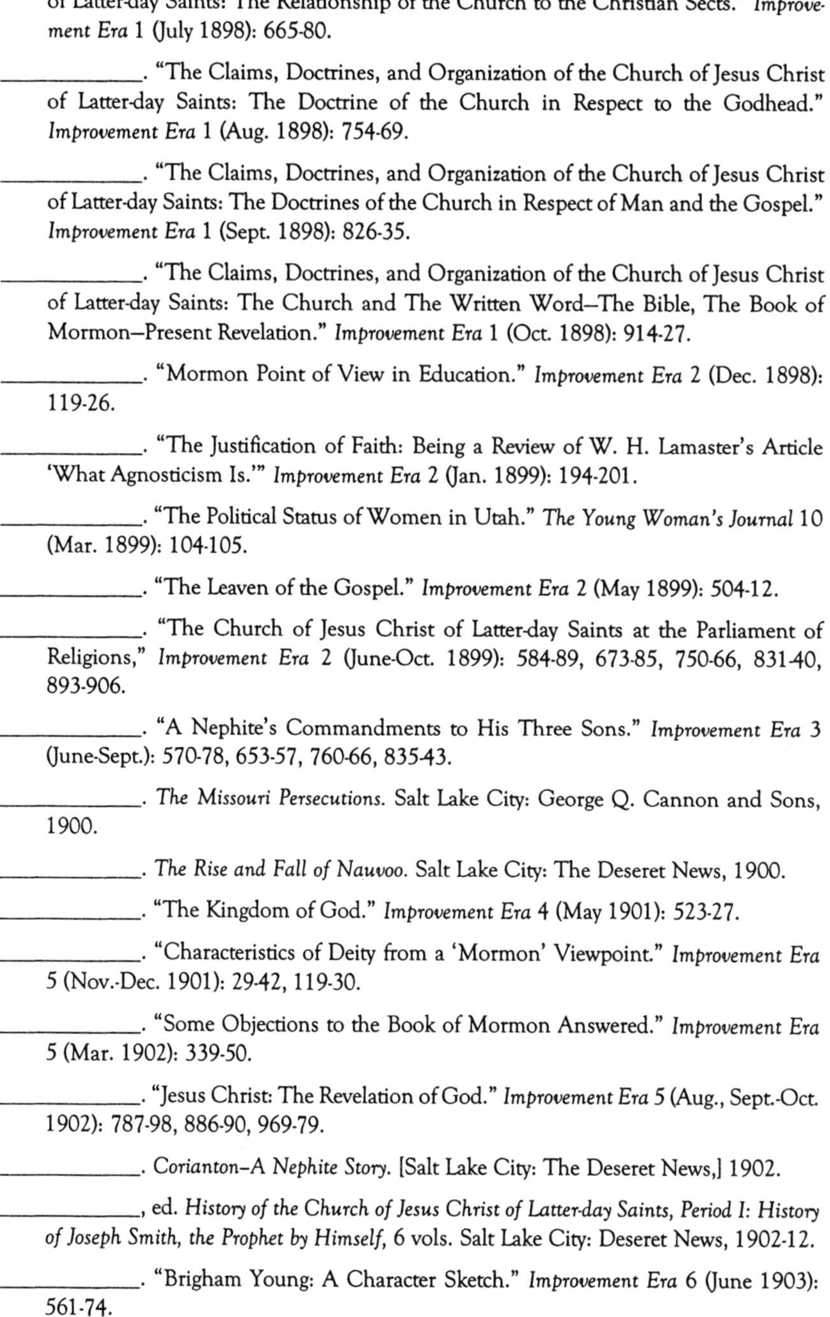

of Latter-day Saints: The Relationship of the Church to the Christian Sects." *Improvement Era* 1 (July 1898): 665-80.

____________. "The Claims, Doctrines, and Organization of the Church of Jesus Christ of Latter-day Saints: The Doctrine of the Church in Respect to the Godhead." *Improvement Era* 1 (Aug. 1898): 754-69.

____________. "The Claims, Doctrines, and Organization of the Church of Jesus Christ of Latter-day Saints: The Doctrines of the Church in Respect of Man and the Gospel." *Improvement Era* 1 (Sept. 1898): 826-35.

____________. "The Claims, Doctrines, and Organization of the Church of Jesus Christ of Latter-day Saints: The Church and The Written Word–The Bible, The Book of Mormon–Present Revelation." *Improvement Era* 1 (Oct. 1898): 914-27.

____________. "Mormon Point of View in Education." *Improvement Era* 2 (Dec. 1898): 119-26.

____________. "The Justification of Faith: Being a Review of W. H. Lamaster's Article 'What Agnosticism Is.'" *Improvement Era* 2 (Jan. 1899): 194-201.

____________. "The Political Status of Women in Utah." *The Young Woman's Journal* 10 (Mar. 1899): 104-105.

____________. "The Leaven of the Gospel." *Improvement Era* 2 (May 1899): 504-12.

____________. "The Church of Jesus Christ of Latter-day Saints at the Parliament of Religions," *Improvement Era* 2 (June-Oct. 1899): 584-89, 673-85, 750-66, 831-40, 893-906.

____________. "A Nephite's Commandments to His Three Sons." *Improvement Era* 3 (June-Sept.): 570-78, 653-57, 760-66, 835-43.

____________. *The Missouri Persecutions.* Salt Lake City: George Q. Cannon and Sons, 1900.

____________. *The Rise and Fall of Nauvoo.* Salt Lake City: The Deseret News, 1900.

____________. "The Kingdom of God." *Improvement Era* 4 (May 1901): 523-27.

____________. "Characteristics of Deity from a 'Mormon' Viewpoint." *Improvement Era* 5 (Nov.-Dec. 1901): 29-42, 119-30.

____________. "Some Objections to the Book of Mormon Answered." *Improvement Era* 5 (Mar. 1902): 339-50.

____________. "Jesus Christ: The Revelation of God." *Improvement Era* 5 (Aug., Sept.-Oct. 1902): 787-98, 886-90, 969-79.

____________. *Corianton–A Nephite Story.* [Salt Lake City: The Deseret News,] 1902.

____________, ed. *History of the Church of Jesus Christ of Latter-day Saints, Period I: History of Joseph Smith, the Prophet by Himself,* 6 vols. Salt Lake City: Deseret News, 1902-12.

____________. "Brigham Young: A Character Sketch." *Improvement Era* 6 (June 1903): 561-74.

____________. "How?" *Improvement Era* 6 (July 1903): 658-72.

____________. "The Fulfillment of a Prophecy: The Testimony of Floods." *Improvement Era* 6 (Sept. 1903): 801-809.

____________. *The Mormon Doctrine of Deity; The Roberts-[Cyrill] Van Der Donckt Discussion, to Which Is Added a Discourse, Jesus Christ, The Revelation of God.* Salt Lake City: The Deseret News, 1903.

____________. *Mormonism: The Realtion of the Church to Christian Sects, Origin and History of Mormonism, Doctrines of the Church, Church Organization, Present Status.* Salt Lake City: Deseret News Print, [c. 1903].

____________. "Bible Quotations in the Book of Mormon; and Reasonableness of Nephi's Prophecies." *Improvement Era* 7 (Jan. 1904): 179-96.

____________. "The Probability of Joseph Smith's Story." *Improvement Era* 7 (Mar.-Apr. 1904): 321-31, 417-32.

____________. "Relation of Inspiration and Revelation to Church Government." *Improvement Era* 8 (Mar. 1905): 358-70.

____________. "Originality of the Book of Mormon." *Improvement Era* 8 (Sept.-Oct. 1905): 801-15, 881-902.

____________. "Translation of the Book of Mormon." *Improvement Era* 9 (Apr.-May, July 1906): 425-36, 544-53, 706-713.

____________. "The Creation of Enthusiasm and Loyalty." *Improvement Era* 9 (Sept. 1906): 833-45.

____________. "Immortality of Man." *Improvement Era* 10 (Apr. 1907): 401-23.

____________. "Answer to Ministerial Association Review." *Improvement Era* 10 (July 1907): 689-744.

____________. *The Seventy's Course in Theology: First Year, Outline History of the Seventy and A Survey of the Books of Holy Scripture.* Salt Lake City: The Deseret News, 1907; reprint, Dallas: S. K. Taylor Publishing Company, 1976.

____________. *Defense of the Faith and the Saints,* 2 vols. Salt Lake City: The Deseret News, 1907-12.

____________. "The Western Gateway of Civilization." *Improvement Era* 11 (Feb. 1908): 241-51.

____________. "Patrick Henry's Forum." *Improvement Era* 11 (July 1908): 655-67.

____________. "The Origin of the Book of Mormon: A Reply to Mr. Theodore Schroeder." *American Historical Magazine* 3 (Sept., Nov. 1908): 441-68, 551-80; 4 (Jan., Mar. 1909): 22-44, 168-96.

____________. *The Seventy's Course in Theology: Second Year, Outline History of the Dispensations of the Gospel.* Salt Lake City: Skelton Publishing Co., 1908; reprint, Dallas: S. K. Taylor Publishing Company, 1976.

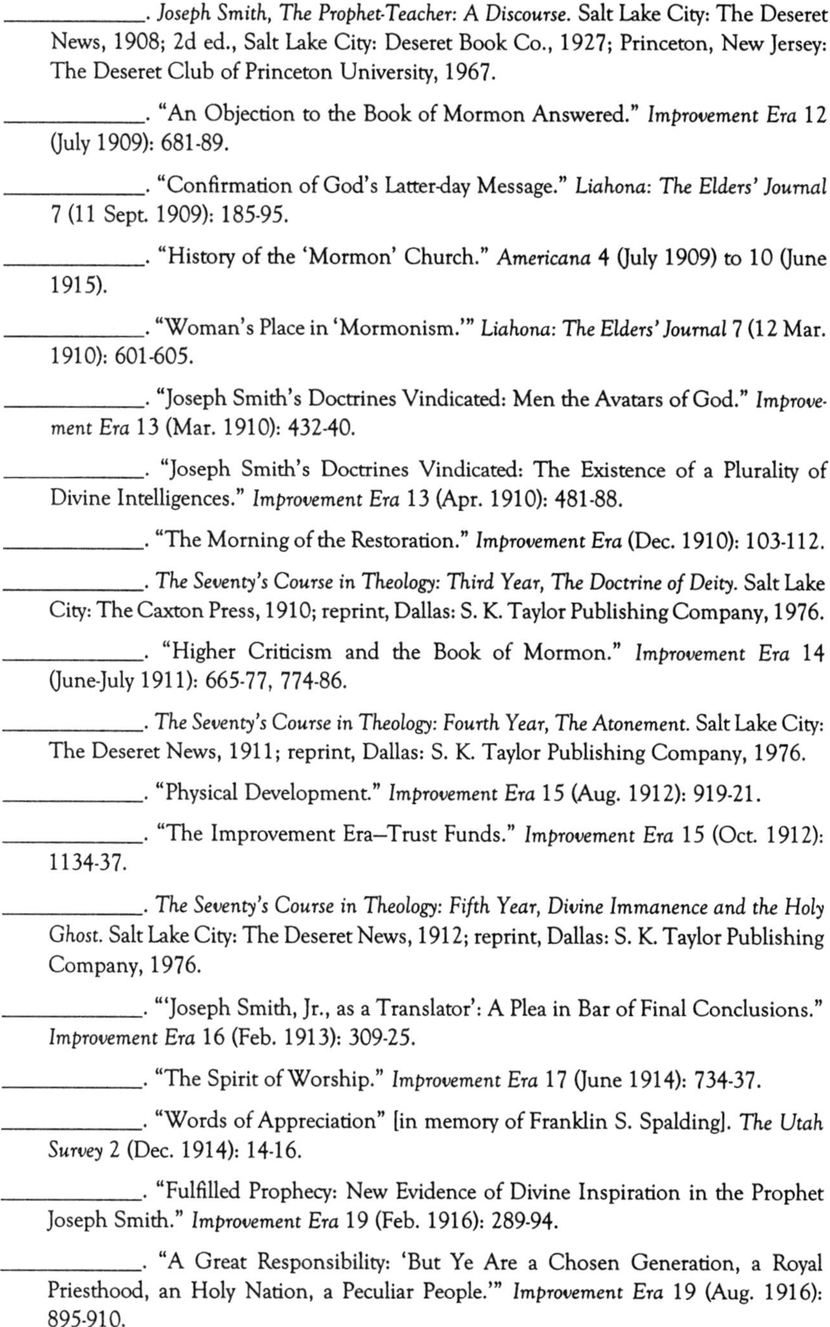

____________. *Joseph Smith, The Prophet-Teacher: A Discourse.* Salt Lake City: The Deseret News, 1908; 2d ed., Salt Lake City: Deseret Book Co., 1927; Princeton, New Jersey: The Deseret Club of Princeton University, 1967.

____________. "An Objection to the Book of Mormon Answered." *Improvement Era* 12 (July 1909): 681-89.

____________. "Confirmation of God's Latter-day Message." *Liahona: The Elders' Journal* 7 (11 Sept. 1909): 185-95.

____________. "History of the 'Mormon' Church." *Americana* 4 (July 1909) to 10 (June 1915).

____________. "Woman's Place in 'Mormonism.'" *Liahona: The Elders' Journal* 7 (12 Mar. 1910): 601-605.

____________. "Joseph Smith's Doctrines Vindicated: Men the Avatars of God." *Improvement Era* 13 (Mar. 1910): 432-40.

____________. "Joseph Smith's Doctrines Vindicated: The Existence of a Plurality of Divine Intelligences." *Improvement Era* 13 (Apr. 1910): 481-88.

____________. "The Morning of the Restoration." *Improvement Era* (Dec. 1910): 103-112.

____________. *The Seventy's Course in Theology: Third Year, The Doctrine of Deity.* Salt Lake City: The Caxton Press, 1910; reprint, Dallas: S. K. Taylor Publishing Company, 1976.

____________. "Higher Criticism and the Book of Mormon." *Improvement Era* 14 (June-July 1911): 665-77, 774-86.

____________. *The Seventy's Course in Theology: Fourth Year, The Atonement.* Salt Lake City: The Deseret News, 1911; reprint, Dallas: S. K. Taylor Publishing Company, 1976.

____________. "Physical Development." *Improvement Era* 15 (Aug. 1912): 919-21.

____________. "The Improvement Era–Trust Funds." *Improvement Era* 15 (Oct. 1912): 1134-37.

____________. *The Seventy's Course in Theology: Fifth Year, Divine Immanence and the Holy Ghost.* Salt Lake City: The Deseret News, 1912; reprint, Dallas: S. K. Taylor Publishing Company, 1976.

____________. "'Joseph Smith, Jr., as a Translator': A Plea in Bar of Final Conclusions." *Improvement Era* 16 (Feb. 1913): 309-25.

____________. "The Spirit of Worship." *Improvement Era* 17 (June 1914): 734-37.

____________. "Words of Appreciation" [in memory of Franklin S. Spalding]. *The Utah Survey* 2 (Dec. 1914): 14-16.

____________. "Fulfilled Prophecy: New Evidence of Divine Inspiration in the Prophet Joseph Smith." *Improvement Era* 19 (Feb. 1916): 289-94.

____________. "A Great Responsibility: 'But Ye Are a Chosen Generation, a Royal Priesthood, an Holy Nation, a Peculiar People.'" *Improvement Era* 19 (Aug. 1916): 895-910.

____________. "Flag of the United States of America–Our Country." *Improvement Era* 19 (Sept. 1916): 973-79.

____________. "The Personality and Omnipresence of God." *Liahona: The Elders' Journal* 14 (28 Nov. 1916): 341-42.

____________. "Man Is That He May Have Joy." *Liahona: The Elders' Journal* 14 (6 Feb. 1917): 512.

____________. "Christ's Personal Appearance in the Western Hemisphere: The Supreme Message of the Book of Mormon." *Improvement Era* 20 (Apr. 1917): 477-99.

____________. "Christ in the Traditions of American Native Races." *Improvement Era* 20 (May 1917): 571-97.

____________. "After World's Sorrow and Sacrifice Will Come Peace and Blessing." *Liahona: The Elders' Journal* 15 (16 Apr. 1918): 657-61.

____________. "A League of Nations to Enforce Peace." *Improvement Era* 22 (Apr. 1919): 474-81.

____________. *The Mormon Battalion, Its History and Achievements.* Salt Lake City: The Deseret News, 1919.

____________. "Brigadier-General Richard W. Young: An Appreciation." *Improvement Era* 23 (Feb. 1920): 321-26.

____________. "Joseph Smith, the Modern American Prophet." *Improvement Era* 23 (Apr. 1920): 526-32.

____________. "Our Duty to Tested Truths of the Past: Government by Class Consciousness Must Be Resisted and One Hundred Per Cent Americanism Is Expected of All." *Improvement Era* 23 (Aug. 1920): 903-908.

____________. "The Bible and the Book of Mormon." *Liahona: The Elders' Journal* 19 (19 July 1921): 48.

____________. "Man's Need of God." *Improvement Era* 24 (July 1921): 811-17.

____________. "God's Need of Man." *Improvement Era* 24 (Aug. 1921): 907-11.

____________. "Monument at Pioneer View." *Improvement Era* 24 (Sept. 1921): 959-68.

____________. "Qualifications in Leadership." *Improvement Era* 24 (October 1921): 1059-64.

____________. "The 'Mormons' and the United States Flag." *Improvement Era* 25 (Nov. 1921): 4-7.

____________. "A Call to Repentance." *Improvement Era* 26 (Dec. 1922): 159-65.

____________. "Christ in the Book of Mormon: His Appearance on the American Continent." *Improvement Era* 27 (Jan. 1924): 188-92.

____________. "Destruction of Ancient Nations in America." *Improvement Era* 27 (Feb. 1924): 288-92.

____________. "The Book of Mormon a Witness for the Christ." *Liahona: The Elders' Journal* 22 (21 Oct. 1924): 176.

____________. "The Beginning of the 'Improvement Era.'" *Improvement Era* 28 (July 1925): 869-72.

____________. "God the Father's Purposes in Creation." *Improvement Era* 29 (Jan. 1926): 230-37.

____________. "What Is the Divine Purpose in Man's Creation?" *Liahona: The Elders' Journal* 23 (9 Feb. 1926): 326-29.

____________. "The Testimony of the Holy Ghost Promised." *Liahona: The Elders' Journal* 24 (5 Oct. 1926): 192.

____________. "Notes on [Charles] Lindbergh." *Improvement Era* 30 (July 1927): 820-23.

____________. "Complete Marriage–Righteousness; Mutilated Marriage–Sin." *Improvement Era* 31 (Jan. 1928): 181-92.

____________. "Sir, We Would See Jesus–Ecce Homo! 'Behold the Man!' Ecce Deus! 'Behold God!'" *Liahona: The Elders' Journal* 25 (7 Feb. 1928): 385-90.

____________. "A New Witness to a Great Truth–Early Christian Baptism for the Dead." *The Deseret News*, 21 Apr. 1928.

____________. "The 'Mormon' Missionary." *Improvement Era* 31 (May 1928): 547-51.

____________. "'Mormonism' Survives Liberty Jail." *Improvement Era* 31 (July 1928): 740-43.

____________. "Book of Mormon's Contribution to the Sacred Literature of the World–Another Witness for the Christ." *Liahona: The Elders' Journal* 26 (18 Sept. 1928): 145-50.

____________. "Additional Light upon the Plan of Salvation Contained in the Scriptures Brought Forth in Modern Times." *Liahona: The Elders' Journal* 27 (1 Oct. 1929): 169-72.

____________. *A Comprehensive History of the Church of Jesus Christ of Latter-day Saints, Century I*, 6 vols. Salt Lake City: The Church of Jesus Christ of Latter-day Saints, 1930.

____________. *The "Falling Away" or the World's Loss of the Christian Religion and Church.* Salt Lake City: Deseret Book Co., 1931.

____________. "The Latter-day Dispensation of the Gospel–Glorious Privilege of Being Witnesses for God and Christ." *Liahona: The Elders' Journal* 30 (27 Sept. 1932): 169-74.

____________. "Joseph Smith: An Appreciation." *The Improvement Era* 36 (Dec. 1932): 81.

____________. *Rasha, the Jew: A Message to All Jews.* Salt Lake City: Deseret News Press, 1932.

____________, ed. *History of the Church of Jesus Christ of Latter-day Saints, Period II: From the Manuscript History of Brigham Young and Other Original Documents*, volume 7. Salt Lake City: Deseret News, 1932.

____________. "What College Did to My Religion." *The Improvement Era* 36 (Mar. 1933): 259-62.

____________. "The Revolt against God." *The Improvement Era* 36 (July 1933): 530-32, 568.

____________. *The Seventies Correspondence School Directed by the First Council of Seventy.* [Salt Lake City], Sept. 1933-May 1934.

Posthumous Publications

____________. "The Standard of Peace." In *World Fellowship: Addresses and Messages by Leading Spokesmen of All Faiths, Races, and Countries*, ed. Charles F. Weller, 870-75. New York: Liveright Publishing Corp., 1935.

____________. "Economics of the New Age." In *World Fellowship: Addresses and Messages by Leading Spokesmen of All Faiths, Races, and Countries*, ed. Charles F. Weller, 875-82. New York: Liveright Publishing Corp., 1935.

____________. *Discourses of B. H. Roberts*, [ed. Elsie Cook]. Salt Lake City: Deseret Book Company, 1948.

____________. "The Disciples of Mormonism," ed. Joseph Jeppson. *Dialogue: A Journal of Mormon Thought* 1 (Winter 1966): 133-34.

____________. "B. H. Roberts on the Intellectual and Spiritual Quest." *Dialogue: A Journal of Mormon Thought* 13 (Summer 1980): 123-28.

____________. "The Truth, The Way, The Life: An Elementary Treatise on Theology [chapter 26]," ed. Gary James Bergera. *The Seventh East Press* 1 (1 Dec. 1981): 6-7, 12.

____________. *Excerpts from The Truth, The Way, The Life: An Elementary Treatise on Theology*, [ed. Brian H. Stuy]. Provo, UT: B. H. S[tuy], [1984].

____________. *B. H. Roberts, His Final Decade: Statements about the Book of Mormon.* Compiled by Truman G. Madsen. Provo, UT: Foundation for Ancient Research and Mormon Studies, 1985.

____________. *Studies of the Book of Mormon*, ed. Brigham D. Madsen. Urbana: University of Illinois Press, 1985; reprint, Salt Lake City: Signature Books, 1992.

____________. *A New Witness for God*, ed. Lynn Pulsipher. [Provo, UT:] L. Pulsipher, 1986.

____________. "God Must and Will Be Glorified." In Brian H. Stuy, comp., *Collected Discourses* 1 (1987): 17-19.

____________. "Remarks." In Brian H. Stuy, comp., *Collected Discourses* 2 (1988): 105-106.

____________. "The Need for a Peculiar People." In Brian H. Stuy, comp., *Collected Discourses* 2 (1988): 255-56.

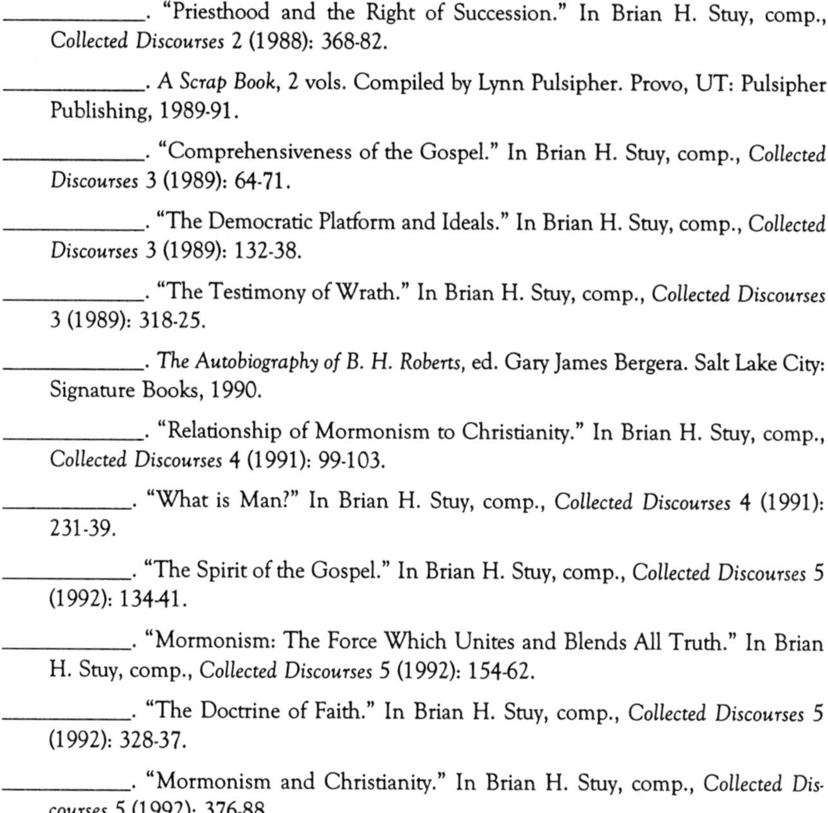

____________. "Priesthood and the Right of Succession." In Brian H. Stuy, comp., *Collected Discourses* 2 (1988): 368-82.

____________. *A Scrap Book*, 2 vols. Compiled by Lynn Pulsipher. Provo, UT: Pulsipher Publishing, 1989-91.

____________. "Comprehensiveness of the Gospel." In Brian H. Stuy, comp., *Collected Discourses* 3 (1989): 64-71.

____________. "The Democratic Platform and Ideals." In Brian H. Stuy, comp., *Collected Discourses* 3 (1989): 132-38.

____________. "The Testimony of Wrath." In Brian H. Stuy, comp., *Collected Discourses* 3 (1989): 318-25.

____________. *The Autobiography of B. H. Roberts*, ed. Gary James Bergera. Salt Lake City: Signature Books, 1990.

____________. "Relationship of Mormonism to Christianity." In Brian H. Stuy, comp., *Collected Discourses* 4 (1991): 99-103.

____________. "What is Man?" In Brian H. Stuy, comp., *Collected Discourses* 4 (1991): 231-39.

____________. "The Spirit of the Gospel." In Brian H. Stuy, comp., *Collected Discourses* 5 (1992): 134-41.

____________. "Mormonism: The Force Which Unites and Blends All Truth." In Brian H. Stuy, comp., *Collected Discourses* 5 (1992): 154-62.

____________. "The Doctrine of Faith." In Brian H. Stuy, comp., *Collected Discourses* 5 (1992): 328-37.

____________. "Mormonism and Christianity." In Brian H. Stuy, comp., *Collected Discourses* 5 (1992): 376-88.

BIBLIOGRAPHY OF WORKS REFERRED TO

Unpublished Material

Bitton, Davis. "The Truth, The Way, The Life: B. H. Roberts' Unpublished Masterwork." Typed manuscript, located in David J. Buerger Collection, Manuscript 622, Bx 10, Fd 7, Marriott Library, University of Utah, Salt Lake City.

Buerger, David J. Collection. Manuscript 622, Manuscripts Division, Marriott Library, University of Utah, Salt Lake City.

Cheesman, Paul R. "An Analysis of the Accounts Relating Joseph Smith's Early Visions." M.R.E. thesis, Brigham Young University, 1965.

Cook, Melvin A. Collection. Accession 1148, Manuscripts Division, Marriott Library, University of Utah, Salt Lake City.

Cooley, Everett L. Collection. Accession 73, Manuscripts Division, Marriott Library, University of Utah, Salt Lake City.

Eyring, Henry. Collection. Manuscript 477, Manuscripts Division, Marriott Library, University of Utah, Salt Lake City.

Firmage, Edwin B. Collection. Accession 1074, Manuscripts Division, Marriott Library, University of Utah, Salt Lake City.

Jeffery, Duane E. Collection. Accession 1372, Manuscripts Division, Marriott Library, University of Utah, Salt Lake City.

Kenney, Scott G. Collection. Manuscript 587, Manuscripts Division, Marriott Library, University of Utah, Salt Lake City.

Lloyd, Wesley P. Collection. Accession 1338, Manuscripts Division, Marriott Library, University of Utah, Salt Lake City.

Mauss, Armand L. "Mormonism and Minorities." Ph.D. diss., University of California, Berkeley, 1970.

Quinn, D. Michael. "The Mormon Hierarchy, 1832-1932: An American Elite." Ph.D. dissertation, Yale University, 1976.

Roberts, B. H. Collection. Manuscript 106, Manuscripts Division, Marriott Library, University of Utah, Salt Lake City.

____________. Correspondence. Manuscript SC 1922, Special Collections and Manuscripts, Lee Library, Brigham Young University, Provo, Utah.

Smith, George A. Collection. Manuscript 36, Manuscripts Division, Marriott Library, University of Utah, Salt Lake City.

Strack, Ernest. Collection. Manuscript A 296, Library, Utah State Historical Society, Salt Lake City.

Talmage, James E. Collection. Manuscript 229, Special Collections and Manuscripts, Lee Library, Brigham Young University, Provo, Utah.

Talmage, Sterling B. Collection. Accession 724, Manuscripts Division, Marriott Library, University of Utah, Salt Lake City.

Whipple, Walter L. "An Analysis of Textual Changes in 'The Book of Abraham' and in the 'Writings of Joseph Smith, the Prophet' in the Pearl of Great Price." M.A. thesis, Brigham Young University, 1959.

Whittaker, Elsie Ross. Collection. Accession 1345, Manuscripts Division, Marriott Library, University of Utah, Salt Lake City.

Published Works

Alexander, Thomas G. "The Reconstruction of Mormon Doctrine: From Joseph Smith to Progressive Theology." *Sunstone* 5 (July-August 1980): 24-33. Reprinted in *Line upon Line: Essays on Mormon Doctrine,* ed. Gary James Bergera, 53-66. Salt Lake City: Signature Books, 1989.

____________. "'To Maintain Harmony': Adjusting to External and Internal Stress, 1890-1930." *Dialogue: A Journal of Mormon Thought* 15 (Winter 1982): 44-58.

____________. *Mormonism in Transition: A History of the Latter-day Saints, 1890-1930.* Urbana: University of Illinois Press, 1986.

Allen, James B. "Eight Contemporary Accounts of Joseph Smith's First Vision–What Do We Learn from Them?" *The Improvement Era* 73 (Apr. 1970): 4-13.

Arnold, Edwin, Sir. *Light of Asia.* London: John Lane the Bodley Head Ltd., 1926.

Arrington, Leonard J. "The Intellectual Tradition of the Latter-day Saints." *Dialogue: A Journal of Mormon Thought* 4 (Spring 1969): 13-26.

Attridge, Harold W. *The Epistle to the Hebrews: A Commentary on the Epistle to the Hebrews.* Edited by Helmut Koester. Hermeneia: A Critical and Historical Commentary on the Bible. Philadelphia: Fortress Press, 1989.

Backman, Milton V. *Joseph Smith's First Vision: Confirming Evidences and Contemporary Accounts,* 2d ed. Salt Lake City: Bookcraft, 1980.

Baitsell, George Alfred, ed. *The Evolution of Man.* New Haven: Yale University Press, 1923.

Baldi, Philip. *An Introduction to the Indo-European Languages.* Carbondale, IL: Southern Illinois University Press, 1983.

Ball, Robert S. "Possibility of Life on Other Worlds: Recent Discoveries Bear Out Old Arguments That Other Planets May Be Inhabited." *McClure's Magazine* 5 (July 1895): 147-56.

Baring-Gould, Sabine. *The Origin and Development of Religious Belief*, 2 vols. London: Rivingtons, 1869-70.

Barrett, Clive. *The Egyptian Gods and Goddesses: The Mythology and Beliefs of Ancient Egypt*. London: Aquarian Press, 1992.

Beatty, J. Kelly, and Andrew Chaikin. *The New Solar System*, 3d ed. Cambridge, Eng.: Cambridge University Press, 1990; Cambridge, MA: Sky Publishing Corp., 1990.

Berendzen, Richard, Richard Hart, and Daniel Seeley. *Man Discovers the Galaxies*. New York: Science History Publictions, 1976.

Bergera, Gary James. "The Orson Pratt-Brigham Young Controversies: Conflict within the Quorums, 1853 to 1868." *Dialogue: A Journal of Mormon Thought* 13 (Summer 1980): 7-49.

Bergson, Henri. *Creative Evolution*. Translated by Arthur Mitchell. New York: Henry Holt and Co., 1911.

The Bible and Polygamy. Does the Bible Sanction Polygamy? A Discussion between Prof. Orson Pratt, One of the Twelve Apostles of the Church of Jesus Christ of Latter-day Saints, and Rev. Dr. J. P. Newman, Caplain of the U.S. Senate, in the New Tabernacle, Salt Lake City, August 12, 13, and 14, 1870, 2d ed. rev. and enl. Salt Lake City: Deseret News, 1877.

Bitton, Davis. "B. H. Roberts at the World Parliament of Religion, 1893, Chicago." *Sunstone* 7 (Jan.-Feb. 1982): 46-51.

Bitton, Davis, and Leonard J. Arrington. *Mormons and Their Historians*. Publications in Mormon Studies. Salt Lake City: University of Utah Press, 1988.

Blackstone, William. *Commentaries on the Laws of England*, 2 vols. Edited by William Carey Jones. San Francisco: Bancroft-Whitney Co., 1916.

Blinderman, Charles. *The Piltdown Inquest*. Buffalo, NY: Prometheus Books, 1986.

Brady, James E., and John R. Holum. *Chemistry: The Study of Matter and Its Changes*. New York: John Wiley and Sons, 1993.

Bringhurst, Newell G. *Saints, Slaves, and Blacks: The Changing Place of Black People within Mormonism*. Contributions to the Study of Religion, no. 4. Westport, CT: Greenwood Press, 1981.

Brown, Francis, and Samuel R. Driver, and Charles A. Briggs. *A Hebrew and English Lexicon of the Old Testament*. Oxford: Clarendon Press, 1907.

Brown, Hugh B. *An Abundant Life: The Memoirs of Hugh B. Brown*. Edited by Edwin B. Firmage. Salt Lake City: Signature Books, 1988.

Brown, Shelby. *Late Carthaginian Child Sacrifice and Sacrificial Monuments in Their Mediterranean Context*. JSOT/ASOR Monograph Series, no. 3. Sheffield, Eng.: Sheffield Academic Press, 1991.

Browne, Lewis. *This Believing World: A Simple Account of the Great Religions of Mankind*. New York: The MacMillan Co., 1926.

Browning, Robert. *Browning: Poetical Works, Complete from 1833 to 1868 and the Shorter Poems Thereafter*. London: Oxford University Press, 1967.

Brück, Heinrich. *History of the Catholic Church for Use in Seminaries and Colleges*, 2 vols. Translated by E. Pruente. New York: Benziger Brothers, 1884-1885.

Bruce, Frederick F. *The Canon of Scripture*. Downers Grove, Illinois: InterVarsity Press, 1988.

Brush, Stephen G. "A Geologist among Astronomers: The Rise and Fall of the Chamberlin-Moulton Cosmology." *Journal for the History of Astronomy* 9 (Feb.-June 1978): 1-41, 77-104.

Buck, Charles. *A Theological Dictionary, Containing Definitions of All Religious Terms*. Philadelphia: Woodward, 1844.

Buerger, David J. "The Adam-God Doctrine." *Dialogue: A Journal of Mormon Thought* 15 (Spring 1982): 14-58.

Burder, William A. *A History of All Religions, with Accounts of the Ceremonies and Customs, or the Forms of Worship, Practised by the Several Nations of the Known World, from the Earliest Records to the year 1872*. Philadelphia: William W. Harding, 1872.

Burkert, Walter. *Greek Religion*. Cambridge, MA: Harvard University Press, 1985.

Bush, Lester E., Jr. "The Word of Wisdom in Early Nineteenth-Century Perspective." *Dialogue: A Journal of Mormon Thought* 14 (Autumn 1981): 47-65.

Bush, Lester E., Jr., and Armand L. Mauss, eds. *Neither White nor Black: Mormon Scholars Confront the Race Issue in a Universal Church*. Midvale, UT: Signature Books, 1984.

Bushman, Richard L. *Joseph Smith and the Beginnings of Mormonism*. Urbana: University of Illinois Press, 1984.

Cannon, Donald Q. "The King Follett Discourse: Joseph Smith's Greatest Sermon in Historical Perspective." *Brigham Young University Studies* 18 (Winter 1978): 179-92.

Carlyle, Thomas. *On Heroes, Hero-Worship, and the Heroic in History*. Chicago: A. C. McClurg and Co., 1892.

Cassuto, Umberto. *A Commentary on the Book of Genesis*, 2 vols. Jerusalem: The Magnes Press, The Hebrew University, 1961-64.

The Catholic Encyclopedia: An International Work of Reference on the Constitution, Doctrine, Discipline, and History of the Catholic Church, 15 vols. Edited by Charles G. Herbermann et alia. New York: Robert Appleton Co., 1907-1912.

Cicero, Marcus Tullius. *Cicero's Tusculan Disputations; also Treatises on the Nature of the Gods and on the Commonwealth*. Translated by Charles D. Yonge. Harper's New Classical Library. New York: Harper, 1894.

Clark, J. Reuben, Jr. "When Are Church Leader's [*sic*] Words Entitled to Claim of Scripture." *Deseret News*, Church News Section, 31 July 1954, 2, 9-11.

Clarke, James Freeman. *Ten Great Religions*, 2 vols. Boston: Houghton, Mifflin and Co., 1899.

Clawson, Rudger. *Prisoner for Polygamy: The Memoirs and Letters of Rudger Clawson at the Utah Territorial Penitentiary, 1884-87*. Edited by Stan Larson. Urbana: University of Illinois Press, 1993.

____________. *A Ministry of Meetings: The Apostolic Diaries of Rudger Clawson*. Edited by Stan Larson. Salt Lake City: Signature Books in association with Smith Research Associates, 1993.

Crabb, George. *New Pantheon; or, Mythology of All Nations*. London: James Blackwood and Co., 1878.

Cruden, Alexander. *A Complete Concordance to the Holy Scriptures of the Old and New Testaments*. Hartford, CT: S. S. Scranton and Co., 1899.

Crowe, Michael J. *The Extraterrestrial Life Debate, 1750-1900: The Idea of a Plurality of Worlds from Kant to Lowell*. Cambridge: Cambridge University Press, 1986.

Darwin, Charles. *On Origin of Species by Means of Natural Selection*. London: J. Murray, 1859.

____________. *Descent of Man and Selection in Relation to Sex*. London: J. Murray, 1871.

Davidson, H. R. Ellis. *Scandinavian Mythology*, rev. ed. Library of the World's Myths and Legends. New York: Peter Bedrick Books, 1986.

____________. *Myths and Symbols in Pagan Europe: Early Scandinavian and Celtic Religions*. Syracuse, NY: Syracuse University Press, 1988.

Dew, Thomas. *A Digest of the Laws, Customs, Manners, and Institutions of the Ancient and Modern Nations*. New York: D. Appleton and Co., 1893.

Dobbins, Frank S. *Story of the World's Worship: A Complete, Graphic, and Comparative History of the Many Strange Beliefs, Superstitious Practices, Domestic Peculiarities, Sacred Writings, Systems of Philosophy, Legends and Traditions, Customs and Habits of Mankind throughout the World, Ancient and Modern*. Chicago: The Dominion Co., 1901.

Draper, John William. *History of the Conflict between Religion and Science*, 6th ed. New York: D. Appleton and Co., 1875.

____________. *History of the Intellectual Development of Europe*, rev. ed., 2 vols. New York: Harper and Brothers, 1876.

Driver, Samuel R. *An Introduction to the Literature of the Old Testament*, new ed., rev. New York: Scribner, 1910.

Drummond, Henry. *Natural Law in the Spiritual World*. New York: James Pott and Co., 1893.

Dummelow, John R., ed. *A Commentary on the Holy Bible by Various Writers, Complete in One Volume*. New York: The Macmillan Co., 1922.

Duncan, Robert K. *The New Knowledge: A Popular Account of the New Physics and the New*

Chemistry in Their Relation to the New Theory of Matter. New York: A. S. Barnes and Co., 1905.

Durant, Will. *The Story of Philosophy: The Lives and Opinions of the Greater Philosophers.* New York: Simon and Schuster, 1926.

Earhart, H. Byron, ed. *Religious Traditions of the World: A Journey through Africa, Mesoamerica, North America, Judaism, Christianity, Islam, Hinduism, Buddhism, China, and Japan.* San Francisco: HarperSanFrancisco, 1993.

Eastman, Roger, ed. *The Ways of Religion: An Introduction to the Major Traditions,* 2d ed. New York and Oxford: Oxford University Press, 1993.

Edersheim, Alfred. *The Life and Times of Jesus the Messiah,* 2 vols., 8th ed. New York: Longmans, Green, and Co., 1898.

Ehat, Andrew F., and Lyndon W. Cook, eds. *The Words of Joseph Smith: The Contemporary Accounts of the Nauvoo Discourses of the Prophet Joseph.* Religious Studies Monograph Series, no. 6. Provo, UT: Religious Studies Center, Brigham Young University, 1980.

Elliott, Charles. *A Vindication of Mosaic Authorship of Pentateuch.* Cincinnati, Ohio: Walden and Stowe, 1884.

Emerson, Ralph Waldo. *Essays: First and Second Series.* Boston and New York: Houghton Mifflin Co., 1921.

The Encyclopædia Britannica: A Dictionary of Arts, Sciences, and General Literature, 30 vols., with new American supplement, 9th ed. New York: The Werner Co., 1900.

The Encyclopædia Britannica: A Dictionary of Arts, Sciences, Literature and General Information, 28 vols., 11th ed. Cambridge: Cambridge University Press, 1910-11.

Endress, Gerhard. *An Introduction to Islam.* Translated by Carole Hillenbrand. New York: Columbia University Press, 1988.

England, Eugene, ed. "George Laub's Nauvoo Journal." *Brigham Young University Studies* 18 (Winter 1978): 151-78.

Faà di Bruno, Joseph. *Catholic Belief; or, A Short and Simple Exposition of Catholic Doctrine.* Edited by Louis A. Lambert. New York: Benziger Brothers, 1884.

Fiske, John. *Outlines of Cosmic Philosophy.* Vols. 1-4 in *The Miscellaneous Writings of John Fiske, with Many Portraits of Illustrious Philosophers, Scientists, and Other Men of Note,* 12 vols. Standard Library Edition. Boston: Houghton, Mifflin and Co., 1902.

____________. *Studies in Religion, Being The Destiny of Man, The Idea of God, Through Nature to God, Life Everlasting.* In *The Miscellaneous Writings of John Fiske,* vol. 9.

FitzGerald, Edward, trans. *Rubáiyát of Omar Khayyám,* ed. Louis Untermeyer. New York: Random House, 1947.

Fleming, Donald. *John William Draper and the Religion of Science.* New York: Octagon Press, 1972.

Freed, Edwin D. *The New Testament: A Critical Introduction.* Belmont, CA: Wadsworth Publishing Co, 1986.

Gibbon, Edward. *The History of the Decline and Fall of the Roman Empire,* 7 vols. Edited by John B. Bury. London: Methuen and Co., 1909-1914.

Gillet, Joseph A., and William J. Rolfe. *Astronomy for the Use of Schools and Academies.* New York: American Book Co. 1882.

Good, Edwin M. *In Turns of Tempest: A Reading of Job with a Translation.* Stanford, CA: Stanford University Press, 1990.

Goodspeed, Edgar J. *Strange New Gospels.* Chicago: The University of Chicago Press, 1931.

Gray, Thomas. *The Complete Poems of Thomas Gray: English, Latin and Greek,* ed. Herbert W. Starr and John R. Hendrickson. Oxford: Clarendon Press, 1966.

Guizot, François P. G. *The History of Civilization, from the Fall of the Roman Empire to the French Revolution,* 4 vols. Translated by William Hazlitt. New York: D. Appleton and Co., 1867.

Hackett, Horatio B., and Ezra Abbot, eds. *Dr. William Smith's Dictionary of the Bible, Comprising Its Antiquities, Biography, Geography, and Natural History,* 4 vols. Boston: Houghton, Mifflin and Co., 1894.

Haeckel, Ernst. *The Evolution of Man; A Popular Exposition of the Principal Points of Human Ontogeny and Phylogeny.* Translated from 5th ed. of *Anthropogenie* by Joseph McCabe. New York: G. P. Putnam's Sons, 1905

___________. *The Riddle of the Universe at the Close of the Nineteenth Century.* Translated by Joseph McCabe. New York: Harper and Bros., 1900.

Halbfass, Wilhelm. *Tradition and Reflection: Explorations in Indian Thought.* Albany: State University of New York Press, 1991.

Hale, Van. "Mormons and Moonmen: A Look at Nineteenth Century Beliefs about the Moon—Its Flora, Its Fauna, Its Folks." *Sunstone* 7 (Sept.-Oct. 1982): 12-17.

___________. "Defining the Mormon Doctrine of Deity: What can theological terminology tell us about our own beliefs?" *Sunstone* 10 (Jan. 1985): 23-27.

___________. "The Origin of the Human Spirit in Early Mormon Thought." In *Line upon Line: Essays on Mormon Doctrine,* ed. Gary James Bergera, 115-26. Salt Lake City: Signature Books, 1989.

Hardy, B. Carmon. *Solemn Covenant: The Mormon Polygamous Passage.* Urbana: University of Illinois Press, 1992.

Harrison, H. S. "Is Man an Accident? A Startling View." *The New York Times,* Magazine section, 30 Nov. 1930, 4-5.

Headley, Frederick W. *The Problems of Evolution.* New York: T. Y. Crowell and Co., 1901.

Hendrickx, Herman. *The Sermon on the Mount.* Studies in the Synoptic Gospels. London: Geoffrey Chapman, 1984.

Hibler, Richard W. *Happiness through Tranquility: The School of Epicurus*. Lanham, MD: University Press of America, 1984.

Highton, H. "God a Unity and Plurality." *The Voice of Israel* (Feb. 1844).

Hill, Donna. *Joseph Smith: The First Mormon*. Garden City, NY: Doubleday and Co., 1977.

Hodge, Archibald A. *A Commentary on the Confession of Faith, with Questions for Theological Students and Bible Classes*. Philadelphia: Presbyterian Board of Publication, 1869.

Holmes, Michael W., ed. *The Apostolic Fathers*, 2d ed. Translated by Joseph B. Lightfoot and John R. Harmer. Grand Rapids, MI: Baker Book House, 1989.

Hopkins, John H. *"The End of Controversy," Controverted: A Refutation of Milner's "End of Controversy"*. New York: Pudney and Russell, 1854.

Howison, George H. *The Limits of Evolution and Other Essays Illustrating the Metaphysical Theory of Personal Idealism*, 2d ed., rev. and enl. New York: The Macmillan Co., 1904.

Hoyt, William Graves. *Planets X and Pluto*. Tucson, AZ: The University of Arizona Press, 1980.

Huidekoper, Frederic. *The Belief of the First Three Centuries concerning Christ's Mission to the Underworld*, 4th ed. New York: Miller, 1882.

Hyde, Orson. "The Marriage Relations." *Journal of Discourses* 2 (1855): 75-87.

Hyde, Paul Nolan. "Intelligences." In *Encyclopedia of Mormonism*, 5 vols., ed. Daniel H. Ludlow, 2:692-93. New York: Macmillan Publishing Co., 1992.

Hymns of the Church of Jesus Christ of Latter-day Saints. Salt Lake City: The Church of Jesus Christ of Latter-day Saints, 1985.

Illingworth, Valerie, ed. *The Facts on File Dictionary of Astronomy*, 2d ed. New York: Facts On File Publications, 1985.

Ingersoll, Robert G. *The Works of Robert G. Ingersoll*, 12 vols. New York: The Dresden Publishing Co., C. P. Farrell, 1901.

The Interpreter's Dictionary of the Bible, 4 vols. Edited by George A. Buttrick. New York: Abingdon Press, 1962.

Israelsen, L. Dwight. "An Economic Analysis of the United Order." *Brigham Young University Studies* 18 (Summer 1978): 536-62.

James, William. *Psychology*. American Science Series, Briefer Course. New York: Henry Holt and Co., 1892.

____________. *Pragmatism: A New Name for Some Old Ways of Thinking: Popular Lectures on Philosophy*. New York: Longmans, Green, and Co., 1908.

____________. *A Pluralistic Universe: Hibbert Lectures at Manchester College on the Present Situation in Philosophy*. New York: Longmans, Green and Co., 1909.

____________. "A Pluralistic Mystic," *The Hibbert Journal* 8 (July 1910): 739-59.

Jamieson, Robert, Andrew R. Fausset, and David Brown. *A Commentary: Critical, Practical, and Explanatory of the Old and New Testaments*, 4 vols. New York: Funk and Wagnalls, 1888.

Jamison, Stephanie W. *The Ravenous Hyenas and the Wounded Sun: Myth and Ritual in Ancient India*. Ithaca, New York: Cornell University Press, 1991.

Jastrow, Robert. *God and the Astronomers*. New York: Warner Books, 1978.

Jeans, James, Sir. *The Universe around Us*. New York: The Macmillan Co.; Cambridge, Eng.: The University Press, 1929.

Jeffery, Duane E. "Seers, Savants, and Evolution: The Uncomfortable Interface." *Dialogue: A Journal of Mormon Thought* 8, nos. 3-4 (1973): 41-75. Reprinted in *The Search for Harmony: Essays on Science and Mormonism*, ed. Gene A. Sessions and Craig J. Oberg, 155-87. Salt Lake City: Signature Books, 1993.

____________. "'We Don't Know': A Survey of Mormon Responses to Evolutionary Biology." In *Science and Religion: Toward a More Useful Dialogue*, ed. Wilford M. Hess, Raymond T. Matheny, and Donlu D. Thayer, 2:23-37. Geneva, IL: Paladin House, 1979.

The Jewish Encyclopedia: A Descriptive Record of the History, Religion, Literature, and Customs of the Jewish People from the Earliest Times to the Present Day, 12 vols. Edited by Isidore Singer. New York: Funk and Wagnalls Co., 1901-1906.

Jones, Steve, Robert Martin, and David Pilbeam, ed. *The Cambridge Encyclopedia of Human Evolution*. Cambridge, Eng.: Cambridge University Press, 1992.

Josephus, Flavius. *The Works of Flavius Josephus, The Learned and Authentic Jewish Historian and Celebrated Warrior*. Translated by William Whiston. Baltimore: Armstrong and Berry, 1837.

Kaempffert, Waldemar. *Astronomy*. Vol. 1, *Science-History of the Universe*, ed. Francis W. Rolt-Wheeler. New York: The Current Literature Publishing Co., 1909.

Keith, Arthur, Sir. "Whence Came the White Race?" *The New York Times*, Magazine section, 12 Oct. 1930, 1-2, 22.

____________. "Supermen—of the Dim Past and Future." *The New York Times*, Magazine section, 23 Nov. 1930, 4-5, 15.

Keller, Jeffrey E. "Discussion Continued: The Sequel to the Roberts/Smith/Talmage Affair." *Dialogue: A Journal of Mormon Thought* 15 (Spring 1982): 79-98. Reprinted in Richard Sherlock and Jeffrey E. Keller, "The B. H. Roberts/Joseph Fielding Smith/James E. Talmage Affair," *The Search for Harmony: Essays on Science and Mormonism*, ed. Gene A. Sessions and Craig J. Oberg, 93-115. Salt Lake City: Signature Books, 1993.

____________. "When Does the Spirit Enter the Body?" *Sunstone* 10 (Mar. 1985): 42-44.

Kenney, Scott G., ed. *Wilford Woodruff's Journal: 1833-1898 Typescript*, 9 vols. Midvale, UT: Signature Books, 1983.

Kinns, Samuel. *Moses and Geology; or, The Harmony of the Bible with Science*, 2d ed. London: Cassell and Co., 1895.

Kirchwey, Freda, ed. *Our Changing Morality: A Symposium*. New York: Albert and Charles Boni, 1924.

Kitto, John, ed. *A Cyclopædia of Biblical Literature*, 2 vols. New York: Mark H. Newman, 1845.

Klein, Ernest. *A Comprehensive Etymological Dictionary of the Hebrew Language for Readers of English*. New York: Macmillan Publishing Co., 1987.

Kohn, Livia. *Taoist Mystical Philosophy: The Scripture of Western Ascension*. Albany: State University of New York Press, 1991.

Kowal, Charles T. *Asteroids: Their Nature and Utilization*. Chichester, Eng.: Ellis Horwood Limited, 1988.

Laing, Samuel. *Human Origins*. London: Chapman and Hall, 1892.

Kargon, Robert. *The Rise of Robert Millikan: Portrait of a Life in American Science*. Ithaca: Cornell University Press, 1982.

Larsen, Clark Spencer, Robert M. Matter, and Daniel L. Gebo. *Human Origins: The Fossil Record*, 2d ed. Prospect Heights, IL: Waveland Press, 1991.

Larson, Stan. "Textual Variants in Book of Mormon Manuscripts." *Dialogue: A Journal of Mormon Thought* 10 (Autumn 1977): 8-30.

____________. "Omissions in the King James New Testament." *Dialogue: A Journal of Mormon Thought* 11 (Autumn 1978): 125-32.

____________. "The King Follett Discourse: A Newly Amalgamated Text." *Brigham Young University Studies* 18 (Winter 1978): 193-208.

____________. "The Controversy concerning B. H. Roberts' Unpublished Manuscript 'The Truth, The Way, The Life.'" Sunstone Symposium, Salt Lake Hilton, 13 Aug. 1993.

____________. "Intellectuals in Mormonism: An Update," *Dialogue: A Journal of Mormon Thought* 26 (Fall 1993): 187-89.

"The Latest News from Pluto." *The Literary Digest* 106 (6 Sept. 1930): 18.

Lewis, Jack P. *The English Bible/From KJV to NIV: A History and Evaluation*. Grand Rapids, MI: Baker Book House, 1981.

Lindberg, David C., and Ronald L. Numbers. "Beyond War and Peace: A Reappraisal of the Encounter between Christianity and Science." *Church History* 55 (1986): 338-54

Livingstone, David N. *The Preadamite Theory and the Marriage of Science and Religion*. Transactions of the American Philosophical Society, vol. 82, pt. 3. Philadelphia: American Philosophical Society, 1992.

Lodge, Oliver, Sir. "Christianity and Science: The Divine Element in Christianity." *The Hibbert Journal* 4 (Apr. 1906): 642-59.

____________. *Science and Immortality*. New York: Moffat, Yard, and Co., 1908.

Long, Anthony A. *Hellenistic Philosophy: Stoics, Epicureans, Sceptics*, 2d ed. Berkeley: University of California Press, 1986.

Lyell, Charles. *The Geological Evidences of the Antiquity of Man, with Remarks on Theories of the Origin of Species by Variation*. London: J. Murray, 1863.

Lyon, T. Edgar. "Doctrinal Development of the Church During the Nauvoo Sojourn, 1839-1846." *Brigham Young University Studies* 15 (Summer 1975): 435-46.

Lyttelton, Margaret. *The Romans: Their Gods and Their Beliefs*. London: Orbis, 1984.

Madan, Martin. *Thelyphthora; or, A Treatise on Female Ruin*, 3 vols. London: J. Dodsley, 1781.

Madsen, Truman G. *Eternal Man*. Salt Lake City: Deseret Book Company, 1966.

____________. "The Meaning of Christ–The Truth, The Way, The Life: An Analysis of B. H. Roberts' Unpublished Masterwork." *Brigham Young University Studies* 15 (Spring 1975): 259-92.

____________. *Defender of the Faith: The B. H. Roberts Story*. Salt Lake City: Bookcraft, 1980.

____________. "B. H. Roberts: The Book of Mormon and the Atonement." In *The Book of Mormon: First Nephi, The Doctrinal Foundation*, ed. Monte S. Nyman and Charles D. Tate, Jr., 297-314. Provo, UT: Religious Studies Center, Brigham Young University, 1988.

Malan, Robert H. *B. H. Roberts: A Biography*. Salt Lake City: Deseret Book Company, 1966.

Mallock, William H. *The Reconstruction of Religious Belief*. New York and London: Harper and Bros., 1905.

Mansel, Henry L. *The Limits of Religious Thought, Examined in Eight Lectures Delivered before the University of Oxford, in the Year MDCCCLVIII, on the Bampton Foundation*. Boston: Gould and Lincoln, 1875.

Marquardt, H. Michael. "An Appraisal of Manchester as Location for the Organization of the Church." *Sunstone* 16 (Feb. 1992): 49-57.

M'Clintock, John, and James Strong. *Cyclopædia of Biblical, Theological, and Ecclesiastical Literature*, 12 vols. New York: Harper and Bros., 1891.

McConkie, Bruce R. *Mormon Doctrine*, 2d ed. Salt Lake City: Bookcraft, 1966.

McGraw-Hill Encyclopedia of Science and Technology, 7th ed., 20 vols. Edited by Sybil P. Parker. New York: McGraw-Hill, Inc., 1992.

McMurrin, Sterling M. *The Theological Foundations of the Mormon Religion*. Salt Lake City: University of Utah Press, 1965.

McNeile, Alan Hugh. *The Gospel according to St. Matthew: The Greek Text with Introduction, Notes, and Indices*. London: Macmillan and Co., 1915.

Metzger, Bruce M. *The Text of the New Testament: Its Transmission, Corruption, and Restoration*, 2d ed. New York: Oxford University Press, 1968.

Mill, John Stuart. *Three Essays on Religion.* New York: H. Holt, 1884.

Millikan, Robert Andrews. *Evolution in Science and Religion.* The Terry Lectures. New Haven, CT: Yale University Press, 1927.

Milman, Henry Hart. *The History of Christianity from the Birth of Christ to the Abolition of Paganism in the Roman Empire*, 2 vols. New York: A. C. Armstrong and Son, 1881.

Milner, John. *The End of Religious Controversy in a Friendly Correspondence between a Religious Society of Protestants and a Catholic Divine*, 2d ed., rev. and corr. London: Keating, Brown, and Co., 1819.

Milner, Joseph. *The History of the Church of Christ*, 4 vols. London: T. Cadell, 1834.

Milton, John. *Paradise Lost.* Edited by Roy Flannagan. New York: Macmillan Publishing Co., 1993.

Morrison, David, and Sidney C. Wolff. *Frontiers of Astronomy.* Philadelphia: Saunders College Publishing, 1990.

Müller, F. Max. *India: What Can It Teach Us?* New York: Longmans, Green, 1910.

____________. *Chips from a German Workshop*, 5 vols. New York: Charles Scribner's Sons, 1891.

____________. *Lectures on the Science of Religion; with a Paper on Buddhist Nihilism, and a Translation of the Dhammapada or "Path of Virtue"* New York: Charles Scribner's Sons, [1893].

Mosheim, John Lawrence von. *Institutes of Ecclesiastical History, Ancient and Modern, in Four Books*, 3 vols., 2d ed. Translated by James Murdock. New York: Harper and Brothers, 1839.

Mussolini, Benito. "Mussolini on Marriage." *Hearst's International Combined with Cosmopolitan* 85 (Sept. 1928): 44-45, 175.

Myers, Philip Van Ness. *General History for Colleges and High Schools*, rev. ed. Boston: Ginn and Co., 1904.

Neander, Augustus. *General History of the Christian Religion and Church*, 5 vols. Translated by Joseph Torrey. New York: Hurd and Houghton, 1871.

Nelson, Nels L. *Scientific Aspects of Mormonism.* New York: Dutton, 1904.

Newcomb, Simon. *Popular Astronomy: School Edition.* New York: Harper and Brothers, 1883.

Newell, Linda King, and Valeen Tippetts Avery. *Mormon Enigma: Emma Hale Smith, Prophet's Wife, "Elect Lady," Polygamy's Foe, 1804-1879.* Garden City, NY: Doubleday and Co., 1984.

Nibley, Hugh. "Before Adam." In *Old Testament and Related Studies: The Collected Works of Hugh Nibley*, ed. John W. Welch, Gary P. Gillum, and Don E. Norton, 1:82-83. Salt Lake City: Deseret Book Co., 1986.

Norman, Keith E. "Mormon Cosmology: Can It Survive the Big Bang?" *Sunstone* 10, no. 9 (1986):19-23.

Numbers, Ronald L. *Creation by Natural Law: Laplace's Nebular Hypothesis in American Thought*. Seattle: University of Washington Press, 1977.

____________. *The Creationists*. New York: Alfred A. Knopf, 1992.

Ostler, Blake T. "The Idea of the Pre-existence in the Development of Mormon Thought." *Dialogue: A Journal of Mormon Thought* 15 (Spring 1982): 59-78.

Oxenham, Henry N. *The Catholic Doctrine of the Atonement*, 2nd ed. London: W. H. Allen, 1869.

Pack, Frederick J. *Science and Belief in God*. Salt Lake City: Deseret News Press, 1924.

Packard, Dennis J. "Intelligence." In *Encyclopedia of Mormonism*, 5 vols., ed. Daniel H. Ludlow, 2:692. New York: Macmillan Publishing Co., 1992.

Paine, Thomas. *The Age of Reason: Being an Investigation of True and Fabulous Theology*. Chicago: Belfords, Clarke and Co., 1879.

Paley, William. *Natural Theology; or, Evidences of the Existence and Attributes of the Deity, Collected from the Appearances of Nature*. New York: Sheldon and Co., 1854.

____________. *A View of the Evidences of Christianity*, ed. E. A. Litton. London: Society for Promoting Christian Knowledge, 1871.

Parker, Barry. *The Vindication of the Big Bang: Breakthroughs and Barriers*. New York: Plenum Press, 1993.

Paul, Erich Robert. *Science, Religion, and Mormon Cosmology*. Urbana: University of Illinois Press, 1992.

____________. *The Milky Way Galaxy and Statistical Cosmology, 1890-1924*. Cambridge, Eng.: Cambridge: Cambridge University Press, 1993.

Paulsen, David L. "Omnipotent God; Omnipresence of God; Omniscience of God." In *Encyclopedia of Mormonism*, 5 vols., ed. Daniel H. Ludlow, 3:1030. New York: Macmillan Publishing Co., 1992.

Phillips, Theodore E. R., and William H. Steavenson. *Splendour of the Heavens: A Popular Authoritative Astronomy*, 2 vols. New York: Robert M. McBride and Co., 1925.

Poland, William. *The Truth of Thought or Material Logic: A Short Treatise on the Initial Philosophy, the Groundwork Necessary for the Consistent Pursuit of Knowledge*. New York: Silver, Burdett and Co., 1896.

Pratt, Orson. "Remarkable Visions." In *A Series of Pamphlets*. Liverpool: Franklin D. Richards, 1851.

____________. "Divine Authenticity of the Book of Mormon." In *A Series of Pamphlets on the Doctrines of the Gospel*. Cover title, *Orson Pratt's Works*. Salt Lake City: Juvenile Instructor Office, 1899.

Pratt, Parley P. *Key to the Science of Theology: Designed as an Introduction to the First Principles of Spiritual Philosophy, Religion, Law, and Government, as Delivered by the Ancients, and as Restored in This Age, for the Final Development of Universal Peace, Truth, and Knowledge*, 5th ed. Liverpool: John Henry Smith, 1883.

Priestley, Joseph. *An History of the Corruptions of Christianity*, 2 vols. London: J. Johnson, 1782.

Prince, Gregory A. *Having Authority: The Origins and Development of Priesthood during the Ministry of Joseph Smith*. John Whitmer Historical Association monograph series. Independence, MO: Independence Press, Herald Publishing House, 1993.

Proctor, Richard A. *Other Worlds Than Ours: The Plurality of Worlds Studied under the Light of Recent Scientific Researches*. The New Science Library. New York: J. A. Hill and Co., 1904.

Quatrefages de Bréau, Armand de. *Histoire Générale des Races Humaines*. Bibliothèque Ethnologique. Paris: A. Hennuyer, 1887.

Quinn, D. Michael. "The Mormon Hierarchy, 1832-1932: An American Elite." Ph.D. diss., Yale University, 1976.

____________. "LDS Church Authority and New Plural Marriages, 1890-1904." *Dialogue: A Journal of Mormon Thought* 18 (Spring 1985): 9-105.

Rawlinson, George. *History of Ancient Egypt*, 2 vols. London: Longmans, Green, and Co., 1881.

Redepenning, Ernst R. *Origenes: eine Darstellung seines Lebens und seiner Lehre*, 2 vols. Bonn: E. Weber, 1841-46.

Reidy, David, and Ken Wallace. *The Solar System: A Practical Guide*. North Sydney, Australia: Allen and Unwin, 1991.

Renan, Ernest. *The Life of Jesus*. Translated by Charles E. Wilbour. New York: G. W. Dillingham, 1888.

Rhodes, Michael D. "A Translation and Commentary of the Joseph Smith Hypocephalus." *Brigham Young University Studies* 17 (Spring 1977): 259-74.

Richards, Franklin D., and James A. Little. *A Compendium of the Doctrines of the Gospel*, rev. ed. Salt Lake City: Deseret Book Co., 1925.

Richards, Stephen L. "Bringing Humanity to the Gospel." *Sunstone* 4 (May-June 1979), 43-46.

Rist, John M. *Stoic Philosophy*. Cambridge: Cambridge University Press, 1969.

____________. *Epicurus: An Introduction*. Cambridge: Cambridge University Press, 1972.

Robinson, Richard H. *The Buddhist Religion: A Historical Introduction*, 3d ed. Belmont, CA: Wadsworth Publishing Co., 1982.

Robson, Kent E. "Time & Omniscience in Mormon Theology." *Sunstone* 5 (May-June 1980): 17-23.

____________. "Omnis on the Horizon [Omniscience, Omnipotence, Omnipresence]." *Sunstone* 8 (July-Aug. 1983): 21-23.

Rogers, Pat., ed. *Alexander Pope*. The Oxford Authors. Oxford and New York: Oxford University Press, 1993.

Rolt-Wheeler, Francis W., ed. *Science-History of the Universe*, 10 vols. New York: The Current Literature Publishing Co., 1909.

Russell, Dora Winifred Black, Countess. *The Right to Be Happy*. New York: Harper and Brothers, 1927.

Ryan, Abram J. *Poems: Patriotic, Religious, Miscellaneous*, 18th ed. New York: P. J. Kennedy, 1899.

Sacred Hymns and Spiritual Songs for the Church of Jesus Christ of Latter-day Saints, 24th ed. Salt Lake City: The Deseret News Co., 1905.

Sale, George, trans. *The Koran; or, Alcoran of Mohammed*. London: William Tegg, 1850.

Sandberg, Karl C. "Modes of Belief: David Whitmer, B. H. Roberts, Werner Heisenberg." *Sunstone* 12 (Sept. 1988): 10-18.

Sellers, Jane B. *The Death of Gods in Ancient Egypt: An Essay on Egyptian Religion and the Frame of Time*. London: Penguin Books, 1992.

Serviss, Garrett P. *Astronomy with the Naked Eye: A New Geography of the Heavens, with Descriptions and Charts of Constellations, Stars, and Planets*. New York: Harper and Bros., 1908.

Sessions, Gene A., and Craig J. Oberg, eds. *The Search for Harmony: Essays on Science and Mormonism*. Salt Lake City: Signature Books, 1993.

Shedd, William G. T. *A History of Christian Doctrine*, 2 vols., 10th ed. New York: Charles Scribner's Sons, 1891.

Sherlock, Richard. "A Turbulent Spectrum: Mormon Reactions to the Darwinist Legacy." *Journal of Mormon History* 5 (1978): 33-59. Reprinted in *The Search for Harmony: Essays on Science and Mormonism*, ed. Gene A. Sessions and Craig J. Oberg, 67-91. Salt Lake City: Signature Books, 1993.

____________. "'We Can See No Advantage to a Continuation of the Discussion': The Roberts/Smith/Talmage Affair." *Dialogue: A Journal of Mormon Thought* 13 (Fall 1980): 63-78. Reprinted in Richard Sherlock and Jeffrey E. Keller. "The B. H. Roberts/Joseph Fielding Smith/James E. Talmage Affair," *The Search for Harmony: Essays on Science and Mormonism*, ed. Gene A. Sessions and Craig J. Oberg, 93-115. Salt Lake City: Signature Books, 1993.

Smith, George D., ed. *An Intimate Chronicle: The Journals of William Clayton*. Salt Lake City: Signature Books, 1991.

Smith, John Clark. *The Ancient Wisdom of Origen*. Lewisburg, Pennsylvania: Bucknell University Press, 1992.

Smith, Joseph, Jr. "'The King Follett Discourse': The Being and Kind of Being God Is; The Immortality of the Intelligence of Man." Annotated by B. H. Roberts. *Improvement Era* 12 (Jan. 1909): 169-91.

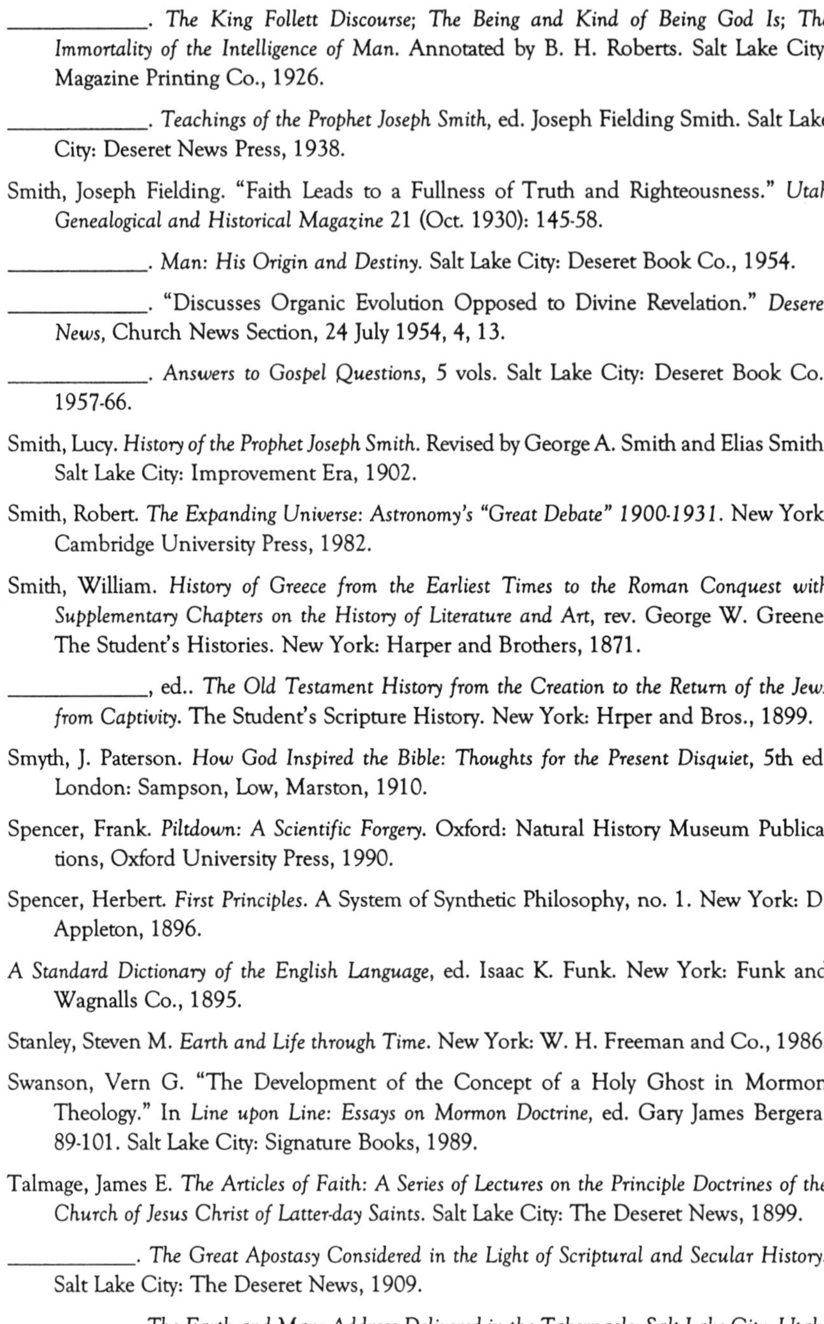

____________. *The King Follett Discourse; The Being and Kind of Being God Is; The Immortality of the Intelligence of Man.* Annotated by B. H. Roberts. Salt Lake City: Magazine Printing Co., 1926.

____________. *Teachings of the Prophet Joseph Smith,* ed. Joseph Fielding Smith. Salt Lake City: Deseret News Press, 1938.

Smith, Joseph Fielding. "Faith Leads to a Fullness of Truth and Righteousness." *Utah Genealogical and Historical Magazine* 21 (Oct. 1930): 145-58.

____________. *Man: His Origin and Destiny.* Salt Lake City: Deseret Book Co., 1954.

____________. "Discusses Organic Evolution Opposed to Divine Revelation." *Deseret News,* Church News Section, 24 July 1954, 4, 13.

____________. *Answers to Gospel Questions,* 5 vols. Salt Lake City: Deseret Book Co., 1957-66.

Smith, Lucy. *History of the Prophet Joseph Smith.* Revised by George A. Smith and Elias Smith. Salt Lake City: Improvement Era, 1902.

Smith, Robert. *The Expanding Universe: Astronomy's "Great Debate" 1900-1931.* New York: Cambridge University Press, 1982.

Smith, William. *History of Greece from the Earliest Times to the Roman Conquest with Supplementary Chapters on the History of Literature and Art,* rev. George W. Greene. The Student's Histories. New York: Harper and Brothers, 1871.

____________, ed.. *The Old Testament History from the Creation to the Return of the Jews from Captivity.* The Student's Scripture History. New York: Hrper and Bros., 1899.

Smyth, J. Paterson. *How God Inspired the Bible: Thoughts for the Present Disquiet,* 5th ed. London: Sampson, Low, Marston, 1910.

Spencer, Frank. *Piltdown: A Scientific Forgery.* Oxford: Natural History Museum Publications, Oxford University Press, 1990.

Spencer, Herbert. *First Principles.* A System of Synthetic Philosophy, no. 1. New York: D. Appleton, 1896.

A Standard Dictionary of the English Language, ed. Isaac K. Funk. New York: Funk and Wagnalls Co., 1895.

Stanley, Steven M. *Earth and Life through Time.* New York: W. H. Freeman and Co., 1986.

Swanson, Vern G. "The Development of the Concept of a Holy Ghost in Mormon Theology." In *Line upon Line: Essays on Mormon Doctrine,* ed. Gary James Bergera, 89-101. Salt Lake City: Signature Books, 1989.

Talmage, James E. *The Articles of Faith: A Series of Lectures on the Principle Doctrines of the Church of Jesus Christ of Latter-day Saints.* Salt Lake City: The Deseret News, 1899.

____________. *The Great Apostasy Considered in the Light of Scriptural and Secular History.* Salt Lake City: The Deseret News, 1909.

____________. *The Earth and Man: Address Delivered in the Tabernacle, Salt Lake City, Utah,*

Sunday, August 9, 1931. Salt Lake City: The Church of Jesus Christ of Latter-day Saints, 1931.

Tattersall, Ian. *The Human Odyssey: Four Million Years of Human Evolution*. New York: Prentice Hall, 1993.

Taylor, Henry D. *Autobiography of Henry Dixon Taylor*. [Provo, Utah:] Printed by Brigham Young University Press, 1980.

____________. *B. H. Roberts, My Mission President*. [Salt Lake City,] 1985.

Taylor, John, ed. "Ancient Ruins." *Times and Seasons* 5 (15 Dec. 1844): 744-48.

____________. *The Government of God*. Liverpool: S. W. Richards, 1852.

Taylor, Jeremy. *Selected Works*, ed. Thomas K. Carroll. The Classics of Western Spirituality. New York: Paulist Press, 1990.

Taylor, Rodney L. *The Way of Heaven: An Introduction to the Confucian Religious Life*. Leiden: E. J. Brill, 1986.

Tennyson, Alfred Lord. *In Memoriam*. Edited by Susan Shatto and Marion Shaw. Oxford: Clarendon Press, 1982.

Thomson, J. Arthur, ed. *The Outline of Science: A Plain Story Simply Told*, 4 vols. New York: G. P. Putnam's Sons, 1922.

Todd, David P. *A New Astronomy*. New York: American Book Co., 1926.

Topinard, Paul. *Anthropology*, 2d ed. Translated by Robert T. H. Bartley. London: Chapman and Hall, 1890.

Tuttle, Daniel S. *Reminiscences of a Missionary Bishop*, 2d ed. New York: Thomas Whittaker, 1906.

Van Wagoner, Richard S. *Mormon Polygamy: A History*, 2d ed. Salt Lake City: Signature Books, 1989.

Van Wagoner, Richard S., and Steven C. Walker. *A Book of Mormons*. Salt Lake City: Signature Books, 1982.

Virtanen, Leea. *"That must have been ESP!": An Examination of Psychic Experiences*. Translated by John Atkinson and Thomas DuBois. Folklore Today. Bloomington: Indiana University, 1990.

Vogt, Karl C. *Lectures on Man: His Place in Creation and in the History of the Earth*. London: Longmans, Green, and Roberts, 1864.

Warren, Samuel M. "The Soul and Its Future Life." In *The World's Parliament of Religions: An Illustrated and Popular Story of the World's First Parliament of Religions, Held in Chicago in Connection with the Columbian Exposition of 1893*, 2 vols., ed. John H. Barrows, 1:480-84. Chicago: The Parliament Publishing Co., 1893.

Webster, Noah. *A Compendious Dictionary of the English Language*. [N.p.:] Sidney's Press, 1806.

____________. *An American Dictionary of the English Language*, 2 vols. New York: S. Converse, 1828.

Webster's New International Dictionary of the English Language, eds. W. T. Harris and F. Sturges Allen. Springfield, Massachusetts: G. and C. Merriam Co., 1927.

Welch, John W. *The Sermon at the Temple and the Sermon on the Mount: A Latter-day Saint Approach*. Salt Lake City: Deseret Book Co., 1990; Provo, UT: Foundation for Ancient Research and Mormon Studies, 1990.

____________. "B. H. Roberts Affirms Book of Mormon Antiquity in Newly Released Manuscript." *Insights: An Ancient Window*, no. 6 (Nov. 1993): 2.

White, Andrew D. *A History of the Warfare of Science with Theology in Christendom*, 2 vols. New York: D. Appleton and Co., 1896.

Whittaker, Edmund T. *A History of the Theories of Aether and Electricity*, 2 vols. The History of Modern Physics, no. 7. [Los Angeles:] Tomash Publishers, 1987; [New York:] American Institute of Physics, 1987.

Whyte, Anthony J. *The Planet Pluto*. Oxford, Eng.: Pergamon Press, 1980.

Widtsoe, John A. *Rational Theology As Taught by the Church of Jesus Christ of Latter-day Saints*. [Salt Lake City:] Published for the Use of the Melchizedek Priesthood by the General Priesthood Committee, [The Church of Jesus Christ of Latter-day Saints,] 1915.

____________. "When Doctors Disagree." *The Latter-day Saints' Millennial Star* 93 (19 Feb. 1931): 120-21.

Widtsoe, Osborne J. P. *The Restoration of the Gospel*. Salt Lake City: The Deseret News, 1912.

Winsor, Justin, ed. *Narrative and Critical History of America*, 8 vols. Boston and New York: Houghton, Mifflin, and Co., 1884-1889.

Witherow, James M., trans. [*sic*]. "The Epistle of Kallikrates." *Improvement Era* 31 (Sept. 1928): 899-909.

Wright, William, ed. *The Illustrated Bible Treasury*. New York: Thomas Nelson and Sons, 1896.

Young, Brigham. "Self-Government–Mysteries–Recreation and Amusements Not in Themselves Sinful–Tithing–Adam, Our Father and Our God." *Journal of Discourses* 1 (1854): 46-53.

____________. "President B. Young's Journey South" *Journal of Discourses* 1 (1854): 103-11.

____________. "Marriage Relations of Bishops and Deacons." *Journal of Discourses* 2 (1855): 88-90.

SCRIPTURAL REFERENCES

BIBLE

DOCTRINE AND COVENANTS

INDEX

C

H

Q

R

S

T